THE GREAT WAR

VOLUME 2

Frontispiece to "THE GREAT WAR." Vol. 2.

Specially painted by C. M. Padday

The British Battle Squadron at Full Speed in "the Narrow Seas."

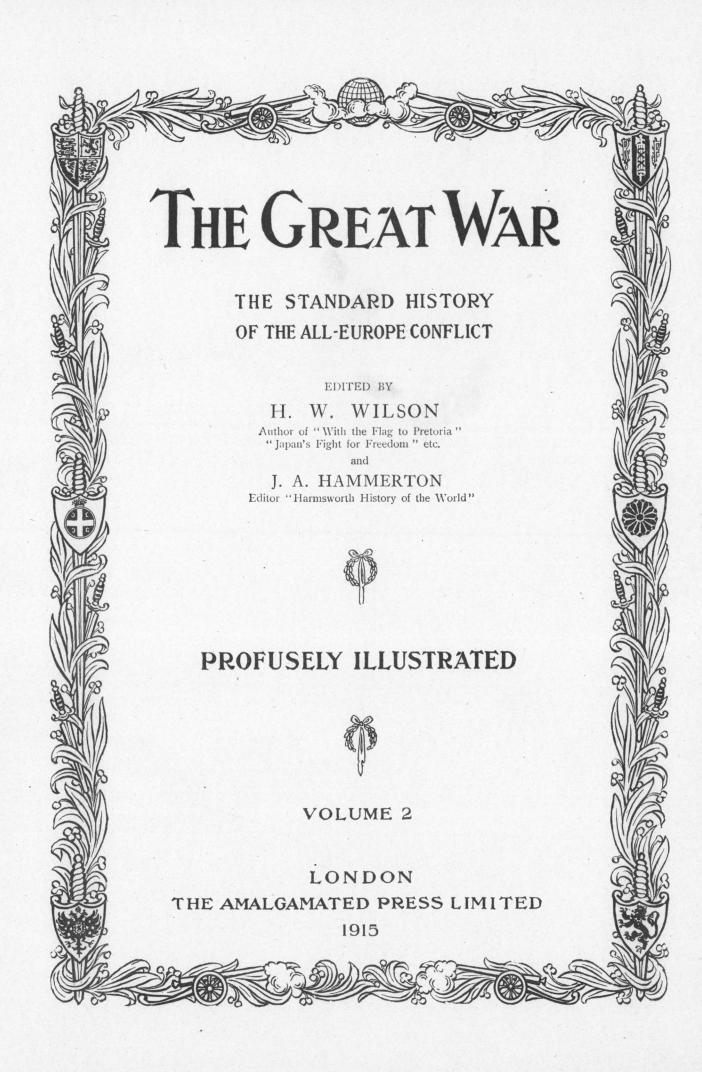

THE GREAT WAR

THE STANDARD HISTORY OF THE ALL-EUROPE CONFLICT

EDITED BY

H. W. WILSON
Author of "With the Flag to Pretoria"
"Japan's Fight for Freedom" etc.

and

J. A. HAMMERTON
Editor "Harmsworth History of the World"

PROFUSELY ILLUSTRATED

VOLUME 2

LONDON
THE AMALGAMATED PRESS LIMITED
1915

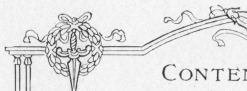

Contents of Volume 2

PHOTOGRAVURE PLATES

JOSEPH JACQUES CESAIRE JOFFRE, CHIEF OF THE GENERAL STAFF OF THE FRENCH ARMY.

General Joffre was born in the same year—1852—as Sir John French. A Bachelor of Science at seventeen, he so distinguished himself in 1870 that MacMahon made him a captain when only twenty-two. He gained the Legion of Honour in the Far East, and his lieutenant-colonelcy in the French Soudan, being appointed Chief of the French General Staff in 1911. An artilleryman, he made a close study of fortifications, and his strategy had won world-wide recognition. His headquarters were once compared to a monastery, and his methods to those of Fabius and General Grant. [*Photo by Manuel.*

THE GREAT WAR

THE STANDARD HISTORY OF THE ALL-EUROPE CONFLICT

VOLUME 2

CHAPTER XXV.

GENERAL PROGRESS OF THE WAR TO THE EVE OF MONS.

How France took up the Gauntlet of Liberty, Justice, and Reason—Rhetorical Utterances of Kaiser and Chancellor—British Answer to German Philippics—King Albert and His Gallant Little Army—Attitude of the Churches—Philanthropic Activity—Problems of Ways and Means—Gifts from Overseas—Austrian Aid for Germany in the Old French Provinces—Successes and Retirements in Alsace and the Vosges—Mr. F. E. Smith and the Press Bureau—Austria, Russia, and Serbia—The Eve of Mons.

THE position in France generally and in the capital particularly on the eve of the declaration of war was fully described by an "Eye-Witness" in Chapter VII. On August 1st President Poincaré issued his eloquent appeal to the people of France with the order for mobilisation of the troops, concluding with the noble sentence: "At this moment there are no more parties, there is eternal France—France peace-loving and resolute, the birthplace of Right and Justice, wholly united in calm and vigilant dignity." The mobilisation proceeded with an earnest, an eager promptitude at every military centre, from the English Channel to the Mediterranean and the Pyrenees, from the Bay of Biscay to the frontiers of Belgium, Alsace, and Lorraine.

On August 3rd, 1914, Germany declared war against France, and the dignity and calm with which the situation had been met generally were slightly marred in the capital by excitable roughs among the Parisian crowds attacking and looting several shops and cafés belonging to Germans and Austrians. These regrettable incidents were speedily stopped by the municipal authorities. On the same day King Albert made an appeal to his Majesty King George for diplomatic intervention on behalf of Belgium in the following terms: "Remembering the numerous proofs of your Majesty's friendship and that of your predecessor, and the friendly attitude of Great Britain in 1870, and the proof of friendship you have just given us again, I make a supreme appeal to the diplomatic intervention of your Majesty's Government to safeguard the integrity of Belgium." The result is already on record.

GENERAL FRENCH IN PARIS.
After landing at Boulogne in August, 1914, and before proceeding to the front, Sir John French visited Paris, being received by President Poincaré, and having a conference with M. Messimy, Minister of War. In the photograph he is seen arriving at the French War Office.

August 4th will always remain a red-letter date in the history of Continental Europe. President Poincaré addressed to the outside world his memorable justification of France for promptly taking up the gauntlet so outrageously thrown down by Germany. "In the war upon which she is entering," he said, "France will have on her side that right which no people, any more than individuals, may despise with impunity—the eternal moral power. She will be heroically defended by all her sons, whose sacred union in face of the enemy nothing can destroy, and who to-day are fraternally bound together by the same indignation against the aggressor, and by the same patriotic faith. She represents once more to-day before the world Liberty, Justice, and Reason. *Haut les Cœurs, et Vive la France!*"

When the Chamber of Deputies met that day an impressive scene ensued. In solemn silence, M. Viviani, the French Premier, read the declaration of the Government policy, and paid a striking tribute to the loyalty shown in the crisis by Great Britain.

which was afterwards tersely summarised by the War Minister, M. Messimy: "Valorously to face the struggle, out of which we shall come either victorious or dead—and we intend to be victorious!" On that same day Herr von Bethmann-Hollweg, the German Chancellor, in a speech to the Reichstag, made his astounding defence of the new ethic that might is right; that political and military necessities know no law. "We" (the German Government), said he, "were compelled to override the just protest of the Luxemburg and Belgian Governments. The wrong—I speak openly—that we are committing we will endeavour to make good as soon as our military goal has been reached. Anybody who is threatened, as we are threatened, and is fighting for his highest possessions, can have only one thought—how he is to hack his way through (*wie er sich durchhaut*)!" The Chancellor concluded by asking and receiving from the Reichstag authorisation for an extraordinary expenditure of £265,000,000 for the war, and that was followed by a German army of 100,000 men opening the attack on Liège.

COUNTRY BETWEEN THE VOSGES AND ALSACE.
The rocky Schlucht Pass between the French Department of the Vosges and Alsace. After their retirement from Mulhausen the French seized this and other German positions in the Passes of the Vosges.

BRIDGE DESTROYED AT DENNEMARIE, NEAR MULHAUSEN.
This bridge was destroyed by French engineers to obstruct the progress of the Germans. The centre photograph shows houses in one of the streets of Mulhausen riddled with shot after a street battle.

The answer to this philippic and that overt act of war was that Great Britain declared war on Germany, that the Government took control of the railways of the United Kingdom to facilitate the mobilisation of the Reserves and Special Reserves who had been recalled to the colours, and the Territorials; and that Admiral Sir John Jellicoe was appointed to the supreme command of the Home Fleets.

The position of affairs and the public feeling in Great Britain and Ireland up to this point, the initial remedial measures taken by the Government and Parliament to meet the financial crisis that occurred, to control internal as well as over-sea trade, to assuage the acute anxiety felt as to employment and the pressure of the times on the poorer classes of the population, the diplomatic proceedings in the different Chancelleries of Europe, the action of the Government inspired by the Foreign Secretary, Sir Edward Grey, who Mr. Asquith declared had deservedly earned the title of "Peacemaker of Europe," immediately preceding the declaration of war between Germany and Great Britain, as revealed in the famous British White Paper—penny editions of which were issued by our Government and eagerly bought up by the million in every corner of H.M.'s dominions, and in almost every civilised country except Germany and Austria, where it was taboo—all these matters have been dealt with broadly, if briefly, in our Chapters III. and IV.

The French Army began on August 5th its movement into Belgium to the help of King Albert and his gallant little Army; and his Majesty, in assuming the command, issued to it the following rousing proclamation:

"Soldiers! Without the slightest provocation from us, a neighbour, haughty in its strength, has torn up the Treaty bearing its signature. It has violated the territory of our fathers. Because we have been worthy of ourselves, because we have refused to forfeit our honour, it has attacked us. But the whole world marvels at our loyal attitude, respects and esteems our strength in these supreme moments. Seeing its independence threatened, the nation trembled, and its children sprang to the frontier. Valiant soldiers of a sacred cause, I have confidence in your tenacious courage. I greet you in the name of Belgium. Your fellow-citizens are proud of you, and you will triumph, for you are the forces serving in the interests of Right. Cæsar said of your ancestors: 'Of all the peoples of Gaul, the Belgians are the most brave.'

BRITISH TROOPS AT A FRENCH BASE ON THE EVE OF THEIR DEPARTURE FOR MONS.
In the hurry of the various railway movements it happened that some of the men were parted from their horses, and the officers had much to do to pacify their disappointment. In the foreground of the photograph is seen a section of the R.A.M.C., who rendered such splendid service to their wounded comrades in the combative lines later.

"Glory to you, Army of the Belgian people! Remember in the face of the enemy that you are fighting for the Fatherland and for your menaced homes! Remember, men of Flanders, the Battle of the Golden Spurs [when, at Courtrai, the Flemings defeated and slew Robert Count of Artois and so many of his knights that the battle came to be known by that name]. And you, Walloons of Liège, who are at the place of honour at present, remember the six hundred of Franshimont! Soldiers! I am leaving for Brussels to place myself at your head."

On the same day, Lord Kitchener, without doubt the greatest British military organiser for at least a century, who had been recalled from Dover on August 3rd, when en route to return to his duties as British Administrator—or, technically, Consul-General—in Egypt in succession to Lord Cromer, was appointed Secretary of State for War. The reason given by the Prime Minister to Parliament was that the pressure of other duties had compelled him to give up that position, which he had temporarily taken on the resignation of Colonel Seely. Lord Kitchener's first act was to issue an appeal in the King's name for 500,000 men to join the regular Army under the novel conditions "of three years' service, or until the war is over." The call was responded to with enthusiasm, like that which marked the immediate rush of Reservists and Special Reservists to rejoin the ranks.

From this date, in St. Paul's Cathedral and in almost every church, Protestant and Catholic, of the United Kingdom, intercessory services were held for the King, his people, and his Army and Navy, asking God for help as in ages past, and that He would be pleased to grant victory over all our enemies. Enthusiasm was not exhausted—either in prayers or in enlistments—of thousands of men anxious to discharge the patriot's duty of swinging the arm of the flesh. Practical philanthropy burned brightly. H.R.H. the Prince of Wales established his National Fund for the relief of distress, and he was supported by his gracious mother, Queen Mary, who appealed to the women of the country to give their services and assist in the local administration of the fund, which in the course of a few days exceeded a million pounds. Queen Alexandra pleaded for the Soldiers' and Sailors' Families' Association, which provided assistance to the wives and children of our fighting men by land and sea. Steps were taken for the organisation of military aid for the care

Aid for sufferers through the War

BRITISH 6 IN. GUNS ON THE WAY TO MONS.

The heavy battery of 6 in. guns of the 48th Battery in the advance to Belgium on August 21st, 1914. Inset: British troops taking shelter in the streets of Mons during German cannonade, awaiting orders to line the barricades at Frameries.

of the sick and wounded, for the development of the Red Cross Society's work, for hospital provision in London and throughout the country, supplemented by the offer of private mansions by noblemen and gentlemen.

The House of Commons, on August 6th, agreed *nem. con.* to the motion proposed by the Prime Minister: "That a sum, not exceeding £100,000,000, be granted to his Majesty, beyond the ordinary grants of Parliament, towards defraying expenses that may be incurred during the year ending March 31st, 1915, for all measures which may be taken for the security of the country, for the conduct of naval and military operations, for assisting the food supply, for promoting the continuance of trade, industry, and business communications, whether by means of insurance or indemnity against risk, or otherwise for the relief of distress, and generally for all expenses arising out of the existence of a state of war." Mr. Asquith, in asking the Committee of Ways and Means to agree to the resolution, said that the House and country had read the most pathetic appeal addressed by the King of Belgium to H.M. King George, and he did not envy the man who could read that appeal with an unmoved heart. "Belgians," he continued, "are fighting and losing their lives. What would have been the position of Great Britain to-day in the face of that spectacle if we had assented to the infamous proposal made by the German Chancellor? Yes, and what are we to get in return for the betrayal of our friends and the dishonour of our obligations? A promise—nothing more—a promise as to what Germany would do in certain eventualities; a promise, be it observed—I am sorry to have to say it, but it must be put upon record—given by a Power which was at that very moment announcing its intention to violate its own Treaty and inviting us to do the same! I can only say, if we had dallied or temporised, we, as a Government, should have covered ourselves with dishonour, and we should have betrayed the interests of this country, of which we are trustees."

Support from India and Overseas Dominions

The Prime Minister, on behalf of the new Secretary for War, also asked the House to grant power to increase the number of men in the Army of all ranks, in addition to the number already voted, by no less than 500,000. He was certain, continued Mr. Asquith, that "the House would not refuse its sanction, for the Government were encouraged to ask for it, not only by their own sense of the gravity and the necessities of the case, but by the knowledge that India was prepared to send certainly two divisions, and that everyone of our self-governing Dominions, spontaneously, unasked, had already tendered to the utmost limits of their possibilities, both in men and in money, every help they could afford to the Empire in a moment of need. The Mother Country must set the example, while she responded with gratitude and affection to those filial overtures from the outlying members of her family." The power asked for was granted amid the most enthusiastic cheers from all parts of the House.

As illustrative of this practical sympathy of the daughter nations of the Empire of which the Prime Minister spoke, it may here be stated that the Duke of Connaught, Governor-General of Canada, on August 6th, wired to Mr. Lewis Harcourt, Colonial Secretary, that the Government of

BRITISH SOLDIERS PREPARING FOR THE GERMAN ONSLAUGHT AT MONS.
To obstruct the advance of the Germans, the streets of Mons were hurriedly barred by barricades constructed largely of bricks and cobble-stones, dug up from the roadway, behind which the men took up their positions to cover the retreat. Shrapnel burst overhead and bullets were flying everywhere. Hence the shelter taken when possible by men and horses under the lee of the houses.

TO BREAK THE GERMAN "WAVE": CONSTRUCTING BARRICADES BETWEEN QUESNEY AND MONS.
British troops hurriedly throwing up barricades across the roadway between Mons and Quesney on the afternoon of Sunday, August 23rd, 1914.

NORTHUMBERLAND FUSILIERS AT BARRICADE WORK BETWEEN MONS AND JEMAPPES.
The formidable barricades erected in the streets between Mons and Jemappes were held by the Northumberland Fusiliers.

Canada desired to offer 1,000,000 bags of flour, of 98 lb. each, as a gift to the people of the United Kingdom, to be placed at the disposal of his Majesty's Government, and to be used for such purposes as they might deem expedient. Mr. Harcourt replied that the Government accepted with deep gratitude the splendid and welcome gift of flour, which would be of the greatest use in this country for the steadying of prices and relief of distress. Something more will have to be said at a later date of similar generous gifts from the other self-governing Dominions.

That same day (August 6th) the Kaiser, with his characteristic policy of playing the mischievous game of tit-for-tat, issued a proclamation to the German people in which he made the following audacious statements:

"Since the foundation of the Empire it has been for forty-three years the object of the efforts of myself and my ancestors to preserve the peace of the world, and to advance by peaceful means our vigorous development. But our adversaries were jealous of the success of our work. There has been latent hostility in the east and in the west, and beyond the sea. In the midst of perfect peace the enemy surprised us. Therefore, to arms! Any dallying or temporising would be to betray the Fatherland. 'To be, or not to be' is the question for the Empire which our fathers founded—to be or not to be German power and German existence. We shall resist to the last breath of man and horse, and shall fight out the struggle even against a world of enemies. Never has Germany been subdued when it was united. Forward with God, Who will be with us as He was with our ancestors."

By a curious coincidence on that very day the German cruisers Goeben and Breslau made their sinister escape from Messina, where they had taken refuge from the Anglo-French Mediterranean Fleet, in Italian territorial waters, and a few days afterwards, after a scrimmage with a British squadron, reached the safe haven of the Dardanelles. It was later officially announced from Constantinople that the two vessels had been purchased by the Turkish Government, which promised to send back their crews to Germany, but they never did. From this date Berlin, if not also other great German cities, was inflamed with a still greater fury of hatred against Great Britain and the British than that narrated in Chapter VIII.

In the meantime, according to General Joffre's original plan of campaign, the French central army, during the first and second weeks of August, advanced across the Vosges; and all France thrilled with delight on August 9th when the news arrived of a victory at Altkirch, in Alsace. A French corps captured the

ANOTHER EXAMPLE OF THE BARRICADES BEHIND WHICH THE BRITISH FOUGHT NEAR MONS.

The barricades shown in the above photograph were between Mons and Quesney, and were constructed on Sunday, August 23rd, 1914. Inset is a snapshot of General Shaw and his Staff of the 9th Brigade, 3rd Division, under the lee of houses at Frameries during the Battle of Mons. A barricade is seen at the end of the street. A few minutes after the photograph was taken two high-explosive shells burst overhead, and the street was littered with debris. General Shaw's brigade-major (Captain Stevens) was severely wounded at Le Cateau, and his Staff captain (Lieut. Harter, Royal Fusiliers) was slightly wounded.

GERMAN COLUMN MOWED DOWN BY BRITISH MACHINE-GUNS AT LANDRECIES.

In the bald language of the Press Bureau the achievement illustrated above was thus authoritatively described: "A German infantry brigade advanced in the closest order into the narrow street, which they completely filled. Our machine-guns were brought to bear on this target from the end of the town. The head of the column was swept away, a frightful panic ensued, and it is estimated that no fewer than 800 or 900 dead and wounded Germans were lying in this street alone." The affair thus summarily dismissed took place at Landrecies on August 26th, 1914.

Staff, alarmed by the French invasion of Alsace, the Austrian Government despatched two army corps to the assistance of the Germans in that province, whereupon the diplomatic relations between France and Austria were broken off. In the face of the overpowering numbers of the enemy, the French troops, on August 10th, fell back from Mulhausen to positions in the Vosges. To complete this section, there was a see-saw of successes and retirements in the Vosges and in Alsace, although at one time (August 16th) the French cavalry scouts were only twenty miles from Strasburg. It was only the German advance into Northern France, with Paris as their objective, that compelled the retirement of the French troops from Alsace and Lorraine, to hold fast to their positions in the Vosges, and fall back on the line of fortresses from the southward bend of the long line which extends from Verdun to the Swiss frontier.

trenches prepared for the protection of that fortified place, which were defended by a German brigade, and drove the enemy back in the direction of the Rhine. The victors then marched to and occupied the large town of Mulhausen. The enthusiasm was deepened by a proclamation issued by General Joffre, which rings with passionate patriotism: "Children of Alsace, after forty-four years of sorrowful waiting, French soldiers once more tread the ground of your noble country. They are the first workmen in the great task of reconquest. What a feeling of emotion and pride is theirs! To carry through their task they are ready to sacrifice their lives. The whole French nation spurs them on, and on the folds of their flag are inscribed the majestic words of 'Right and Liberty.' *Vive l'Alsace! Vive la France!*"

M. Messimy, War Minister, in a message of congratulation to the successful troops, said: "At the start of the war the energetic and brilliant offensive, which you have taken in Alsace, puts us in a position of great moral encouragement." Two days later General Joffre addressed the following inspiring words to the brave defenders of Liège and other parts within the Belgian frontier: "Having been called upon by the most odious aggression to fight against the same adversary, your admirable soldiers and those of France will bear themselves in all circumstances as true brothers under arms. Confident of the triumph of their just cause, they will march together to victory."

Under pressure of the German

To return to Paris. After the Battle of Haelen, between Liège and Brussels, which was all to the advantage of the Belgian forces, the French Chamber of Deputies, on August 14th, granted a war credit of £40,000,000 to the Government. On the same date the French were moving in aid of the Belgians in considerable force from Charleroi to Gembloux. The Belgian Government removed on August 17th from Brussels to Antwerp, and three days later the former city was formally entered by the

THE DAY BEFORE THE BATTLE OF MONS.

In the top photograph are shown two officers of the Royal Scots Fusiliers walking through the square at Quesney on the day before the Battle of Mons. The smaller view gives a good idea of the leafy luxuriance of the country through which the British transport was advancing on the eve of battle. The third shows British soldiers pulling down trees in the promenade of the town for barricades on August 23rd, 1914. These barricades were held by the Lincolns (10th Regiment).

Germans, as already described. Then followed the fall of the last fort of Liège, the beginning of the Battle of Charleroi, and the partial investment of Namur on August 22nd—two days before the Battle of Mons.

To sum up the position in Great Britain during these eventful days, on August 10th the Press Bureau was established with the Right Hon. F. E. Smith, K.C., as president. Its subsequent erratic methods were the subject of much Press and Parliamentary controversy. On the 10th Parliament adjourned till August 25th. On the same date 30,000 special constables for the London area were sworn in for the protection of public buildings, power stations, waterworks, etc.; and these were added to considerably later on. A day later the first proposal was made to arm the Irish Nationalist Volunteers for the defence of Ireland, and that was afterwards regularised, as well as the acceptance of the Ulster Volunteers, already armed, under the direction of Lord Kitchener. On the 12th, following the despatch by Austria of two army corps to the assistance of the Germans on the Alsatian frontier, war was declared for the first time between Britain and that empire. The organisation and despatch of the British Expeditionary Force to France has already been described. Its final concentration took place on August 21st, and it received its baptism of fire on August 23rd, at the never-to-be-forgotten engagement at Mons.

The first battles in East Prussia have been fully described in Chapter XXIII. These were only meant as a diversion to relieve the pressure against the Allies in the western spheres of operations in Belgium and Northern France, an object which was admirably served. After Rennenkampf's retreat to the Niemen and successful resistance to the German counter-invasion of Russian territory at Suwalki and Augustowo, preparations were made by the Russian generalissimo, the Grand Duke Nicholas, for the great struggle on the Austrian and German frontiers. He had two million of the finest

FRENCH CAVALRY ON THE WAY TO THE FIRST GREAT FRONTIER BATTLE.

In the above photograph is seen a group of French cavalrymen receiving orders during the advance into Belgium. The smaller illustration above shows them on their way to the front, advancing along the typical Belgian cobbled highway.

troops at his disposal, and in a great part of the theatre of the coming campaign he had the advantage of the support of the Polish and Ruthenian population. The Grand Duke issued a proclamation to the people of Russian origin inhabiting the Austrian dominions calling upon them to unite with the Mother Country in reviving the century-old tradition of the Russian Grand Duke Ivan Kalita, whose sympathies had always been with them. A series of engagements with detachments of Austrians on the eastern frontier of Galicia took place during the early weeks of August; but neither in that region nor in the direction of Kielce, in South-West Poland, were the efforts of the Austrians successful in taking the offensive. By August 17th the Russian advanced guard, consisting of several divisions, had penetrated into the northern part of Bukovina, and marched on Czernowitz, which is the capital of that province.

ON THE FIELD OF MALPLAQUET.
British artillery passing the monument on the field of Malplaquet, where Marlborough won his last battle in 1709.

IN THE TRENCHES AT QUESNEY.
British troops in the trenches in the picturesque surroundings of Quesney, between Mons and Le Cateau.

Germany broke off relations with Serbia on August 10th. Six days later the Austrians bombarded Belgrade, and did considerable damage; but, on the other hand, the Serbians shelled the island of Ada Kaleh, and set fire to two Austrian ships and Orsova railway-station, on the north bank of the Danube. Serbian troops also crossed the Drina, and engaged and defeated the right wing of the Austrian army. Following these operations came the Battle of Shabatz, fully dealt with in Chapter XIX.

Turning for a moment to the Far East, on August 9th the Japanese troops put to sea from Tokio under the command of Admiral Dewa, it being shrewdly understood that the objective was Kiao-chau, which, under the "mailed fist" of the Kaiser's brother Prince Henry, had been "leased" from the then impotent Chinese Government. On August 15th Japan formally joined the European Allies against the common enemy, and called upon Germany to remove her warships from Japanese and Chinese waters, and to evacuate Kiao-chau by August 23rd.

The threads of the story leading up to the momentous Battle of Mons, which signalised the beginning of the renowned retreat of the Allies in the direction of Paris, have now been gathered up, and in subsequent chapters the narrative will be a continuous presentation of the contemporaneous happenings in all the theatres of the war.

BRITISH SUPPLY COLUMN ON THE LINE OF MARCH BEFORE THE BATTLE OF MONS.
The above photograph shows a British supply column drawn up on the line of march near Mons, on August 22nd, 1914.

FRENCH'S INDOMITABLE LITTLE ARMY ON THE EVE OF THE BATTLE OF MONS.

A splendid panoramic view of the British Expeditionary Force in camp. "French's contemptible little army"—as the Kaiser described it in a famous order to his own troops—very soon after the ate of that order, showed the Germans the kind of mettle of which it was made, and won the grudging admiration of the foe. The top view is of British troops resting in a street at ——, a place the censor would not allow the photographer to name. Inset: British cavalry, on the march through a Belgian town, and soon to add new laurels to their fame.

CHAPTER XXVI.

9TH LANCERS CHARGING THE GERMAN GUNS AT LE CATEAU.

THE FRENCH FRONTIER BATTLE AND THE BRITISH STAND AT MONS.

Britain's Classic Battlefields—Moltke's Strategy—Siege-Guns *versus* Forts—Slaughter by Machinery—Charleroi—General French's Dispositions—The Kaiser's Contemptible Order—An Unexpected Stroke—Zulu Precedent for German Method—The Price we Paid—The English Way—British Hawk against German Heron—Why the British had to Retire—300,000 Men against 80,000.

MONS, the historic capital of the ancient Duchy of Hainault, is a handsome, pleasant Belgian town, with a Gothic town-hall, splendid cathedral, and a picturesque belfry, set in a black-country coal-mining region near the French frontier. To British visitors the most interesting thing about Mons is the ridge of Malplaquet, about three miles to the south, in a region of ravines and woods and hills. Here the Duke of Marlborough, in 1709, won the last, the most difficult, and the most terrible of all his battles, at a cost of 20,000 men. It was one of the most costly victories in our history, but it put an end to the ambition of Louis XIV. to become master of Europe.

Many British officers have spent a delightful and instructive holiday in carefully studying the ground about Mons where Marlborough fought. Among these officers, some years ago, was a young cavalry commander, now the famous Field-Marshal Sir John French. Keen must have been his pleasure when he learned, about the middle of August, 1914, that General Joffre, the Commander-in-Chief of the Allied Armies, had decided to assign to the British Expeditionary Force the task of holding Mons. Here was ground that Sir John knew almost as well as he knew the land about his birthplace in Kent—ground famed and hallowed by many heroic achievements of British arms. For all around Mons were the old classic battlefields of our race—Waterloo to the north-west, on the Brussels road; Namur due west, where the Irish Guards in the seventeenth century distinguished themselves; Cambrai to the east, where Marlborough, by threatening King Louis, brought about that balance of power in Europe which the Prussian was trying to overthrow; and Agincourt was not far away.

VIEW OF THE TOWN OF MONS.

Not only Sir John French, but many of his officers had studied the lay of the land, from pure interest in Marlborough's campaigns. Now suddenly, unexpectedly, their knowledge became of vital value. Once more, in the old cockpit of Europe, the old question was to be again fought out by the last argument of kings—cannon. Was Europe to be a balance of independent nations, or the silenced, oppressed appanage of a single, tyrannical war lord? Once again the British soldier, carried overseas on the back of the British sailor, stood forth to challenge the power of the military despot.

Things had changed for the worse for Britain since Marlborough and his allies and Wellington and his allies fought for the principle of freedom in civilisation on the same battleground. For in the old days our country usually put into the field a considerable army, which,

THE "STIRRUP-CHARGE" OF THE SCOTS GREYS AND HIGHLANDERS AT ST. QUENTIN.

The British Army, covering itself with new glory in the storied battlefields of Flanders, reviving memories of gallant deeds done in old Elizabethan days, performed a series of exploits at St. Quentin which recalled vividly to the public imagination the never-dying magnificent charge of the Scots Greys and Highlanders at Waterloo—a deed commemorated in Lady Butler's famous painting "Scotland for Ever!" On August 30th, 1914, the Scots Greys and the Highlanders together took part, not in one charge, but in a series of charges "as at Waterloo," bursting into the thick of the enemy, the Highlanders holding on to the stirrup-leathers of the Greys as the horsemen galloped, and attacking hand to hand. The Germans had the surprise of their lives, and broke and fled before the sudden and unexpected onslaught, suffering severe losses alike from the swords of the cavalry and the bayonets of the Highland infantrymen.

WOUNDED HELPING THE WOUNDED—PATHETIC EPISODE BETWEEN

During the progress of the war in both Belgium and France churches were used as temporary hospitals. The above picture, which is one of the most notable of the many called forth by the war, was drawn from particulars supplied by some of those who figured in the episode it depicts so graphically. A party of wounded British soldiers had been accommodated on the floor of a church situate between Le Cateau and Landrecies. Over the building a Red Cross flag had been hoisted, but

LE CATEAU AND LANDRECIES DURING THE RETREAT FROM MONS.

ere as elsewhere the sign of the Red Cross was used as a target by the German rtillerymen. A German shell burst open the door of the church, destroying its Gothic archway, and further shells continued to explode upon the building. As best they could, the wounded men, the stronger in the little party bearing the more severely injured of their comrades along with them, made their way from the doomed shelter of the church to a spot out of the range of the deadly German guns.

BRITISH VALOUR NEAR COMPIEGNE: HOW THREE GUNNERS OF THE R.H.A. WON A PLACE IN HISTORY.

In the early hours of the morning of September 1st, 1914, L Battery of the Royal Horse Artillery were suddenly subjected to a terrific enfilade fire from a ridge they had supposed to be still occupied by the French. Their positions prevented them from bringing more than three of their guns against the enemy. As the day wore on but one gun remained serviceable. It was then that three men, all of whom were wounded—Sergeant-Major Darrell, Gunner Darbyshire, and Driver Osborne—won their place in history. They kept up such a deadly fire that all but one of the remaining German guns were silenced, and, as one of the survivors remarked, "We'd both had enough of it." Both sides ceased fire, and the three heroes, all of whom were recommended for the V.C., were rescued by our cavalry and infantry.

linked to the forces of friendly nations, was little, if at all, inferior in numbers to the opposing host. But now, when other people counted their trained warriors in millions, Britain could only place 80,000 men in the firing-line, with another 20,000 men as supports. France, our ally, was also fighting at a disadvantage. She had barely more than 80,000 troops of the first line, with 36,000 reserves, to hold Charleroi, to the right of the British position, and she was greatly outnumbered along the rest of the northern front of war.

In the first great battle, that raged from Mons and Lille in the east to the Moselle and the Vosges in the west, France had to pay a heavy price for the dreams of some of her peace-loving ministers who, bent on social reforms, had grudged the cost of highly efficient preparations for a vast war. It was a generous mistake. Our own Government had not escaped from it. So the hard-headed, hard-hearted German military caste, that had skilfully forged the entire resources of two great empires into a tremendous weapon of attack, had practically every material advantage on their side.

It must also be admitted that the German commander-in-chief, General von Moltke, had managed his mighty forces with remarkable ability. Before the great battle opened he had General Joffre outmanœuvred and running into disaster.

For, by various expedients, he had got into Belgium a far larger number of troops than the French commander expected to meet, and he had then allowed the French to take the offensive in various difficult directions in which success was, in the circumstances, practically impossible. And if all this were not sufficient to give the Germans, after the first clash, a decided superiority in attacking power, there was the last surprise—the new mobile Krupp siege-guns.

BRITISH ARTILLERY OFFICER'S HEROISM AT TOURNAI.

At dawn on August 26th, 1914, 300,000 German troops were thrown on the British lines in an attempt to "wipe them out." Sir John French stated without hesitation that the saving of the left wing could never have been accomplished but for the rare and unusual coolness and intrepidity and determination of Sir H. Smith-Dorrien. The spirit of all ranks is well exemplified by the above illustration of how a British artillery officer sold his life dearly when his battery was attacked by 3,000 Uhlans on this critical day.

It was these siege-guns which brought about the total defeat of the French forward movement, and compelled the British force also to retreat from Belgium and Northern France. The Allied front, running from Mons and Charleroi, was based on the resisting power of the Belgian ring fortress of Namur. It was expected that Namur would delay the German advance as long as Liège had done. Then the French line of frontier fortresses—Lille, with its half-finished defences; Maubeuge, with good forts and a large garrison; and other strong places—would form a still more useful system of fortified points for the Allied armies.

The Germans, however, did not intend that things should fall out in this manner. They were in the extraordinary position of having committed a grave mistake at Liège, for which they were now able to make their opponents pay. They had rashly endeavoured to storm the Belgian border fortress by an infantry attack. That attack, as all the world knew, had disastrously failed. But—this was not so widely known—as soon as the new siege-guns had been brought up, the Liège forts had quickly been blown to pieces. The big, movable howitzer was master of all costly, fixed fortifications; but the Germans were not anxious to advertise this fact. It was their supreme secret. They intended to let the Allied armies repose on fortress towns, then envelop them, and smash the fortresses with surprising rapidity.

They began with Namur. Here a ring of detached forts, built of concrete, and armed with 6 in. guns and smaller howitzers placed in armour-plated turrets, was further strengthened by trenches, wire entanglements, and mines. The Germans wasted no more troops in storming operations. Instead, they brought up thirty-two enormous howitzers with 11 in. muzzles, and, from a distance of five to seven miles, pitched about 3,500 shells, each weighing 750 lb., on a single fort. The whole structure of concrete and armour-plate was smashed and rent. The small Belgian guns could not reach the assailing howitzers, and the forts, the trenches, troops, and cannon were swept quickly from the earth by the terrible big shells. It was not a battle, though 200,000 Germans were massed against 25,000 Belgians. It was merely slaughter by machinery—Krupp's engines of wholesale death against flesh and blood.

The shell fire began furiously on Friday, August 21st, and by noon the next day Namur was partly invested and doomed suddenly to fall. In the meantime the Fifth French Army, holding the passage of the Sambre, by the Belgian mining town of Charleroi, was launching its Algerian and Senegal troops at the Prussian Guard. Fierce and deadly was the hand-to-hand bayonet fight between the Arabs and negroes of French Africa and the flower of the German Army. The Arabs, who had a dash of the Berber strain and some of the blood of the old European vandals who conquered Northern Africa, advanced across the bridge of Charleroi into the factory quarter of the Belgian mining town. Such was their impetuosity that no German troops could stay them; but, unfortunately, they were at last caught by machine-guns, concealed in one of the factories, and mowed down. Superb as was their courage, they were unable to withstand the terrific fire, and as the survivors reeled back the bridge was taken.

The French infantry then sprang forward, and retook the bridge, lost it, and captured it again. The French machine-guns, left too often, it is said, in the hands of a

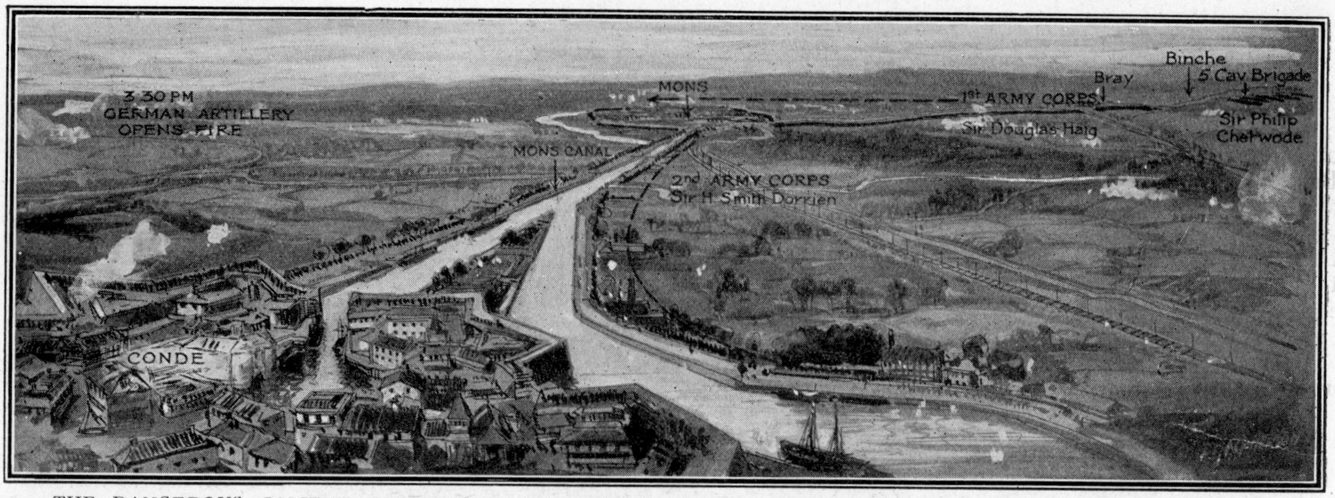

THE DANGEROUS SALIENT FORMED BY THE ANGLE OF THE CANAL AND THE RIVER SAMBRE AT MONS.

"The right of the Third Division, under General Hamilton, was at Mons, which," Sir John French pointed out in his despatch, "formed a somewhat dangerous salient, and I directed the Commander of the Second Corps....if threatened seriously, to draw back to the centre behind Mons."

few men, do not appear to have given as much support in the wild bayonet charges as the Germans received from their machine-guns. On the other hand, the light French field artillery, especially the 3 in. gun, worked tremendous havoc in the solid German ranks, as these swept on to the attack, or withdrew to gather in their supports for a fresh charge.

Then heavy German artillery was brought up, and the French, having no guns or howitzers of the same range and power, were placed in a position of disadvantage, while shell and shrapnel from unassailable hostile batteries, wrecked and searched the colliery town. At the same time the German commander, with columns of reinforcements marching south to his aid, deployed fresh troops, and hurled them in close formation, under cover of overpowering artillery fire, against the tired French soldiers. By the evening of Saturday, August 22nd, the passage of the River Sambre, near Charleroi, had been forced, and the Fifth French Army, with its reserves, was preparing to retreat.

Fifth French Army prepares to retreat

Meanwhile, things were going very well, to all appearances, with the British Expeditionary Force round Mons. Our men formed the extreme left wing of the Allied line that stretched for some two hundred miles close to the French frontier. Our task seemed a fairly easy one, for our cavalry scouts and airmen reported that only 100,000 Germans, at the most, were advancing against us. General Joffre confirmed this information from the results of his aerial reconnaissances. Our scouting horsemen, on Saturday, August 22nd, pushed out northward till they reached a point within cannon-shot of the field of Waterloo. There, in fierce, sharp little skirmishes with the enemy's cavalry screen, they tested the fighting power of the Uhlans and the Death's Head Hussars, and found that in both swordsmanship and horsemanship the Germans were, man to man, little more than food for worms. As Sir Philip Chetwode, the leader of our Fifth Cavalry Brigade, remarked, our men went through them like a knife through brown paper.

While the British cavalryman was enjoying himself in the preliminary skirmish, and avenging on Uhlan patrols the dreadful wrongs he had seen Belgian women suffering from, Sir John French put his two army corps—about 80,000 men altogether—into battle array. He had about thirty miles of front to defend, with Mons roughly in the centre of it. On the east was the little town of Condé, connecting by a canal with Mons. On the west were the smaller towns of Bray and Binche, the last about half-way to Charleroi.

The Second Army Corps, under General Sir Horace Smith-Dorrien, was lined out along the canal from Condé to Mons. The First Army Corps, under General Sir Douglas Haig, was deployed from Mons towards Bray. The Fifth Cavalry Brigade guarded Binche, while a cavalry division, under General Allenby, was kept as a reserve, ready to move to any part of the line that was endangered.

Making ready for the day of battle

This work of taking up positions was carried out on Saturday, August 22nd, and on the following day the troops went on digging themselves in along the canal and among the hills, while the gunners got their guns into good places commanding the northern banks of the canal and the country to the north-west towards Brussels. All Sunday

POSITION HELD BY THE BRITISH UNDER SHELL FIRE ON THE NIGHT OF AUGUST 23RD, 1914.

When the news of the retirement of the French forces and the serious German threatening on his front was confirmed, Sir John French determined to effect a retirement to the Maubeuge position at daybreak on August 24th 1914.

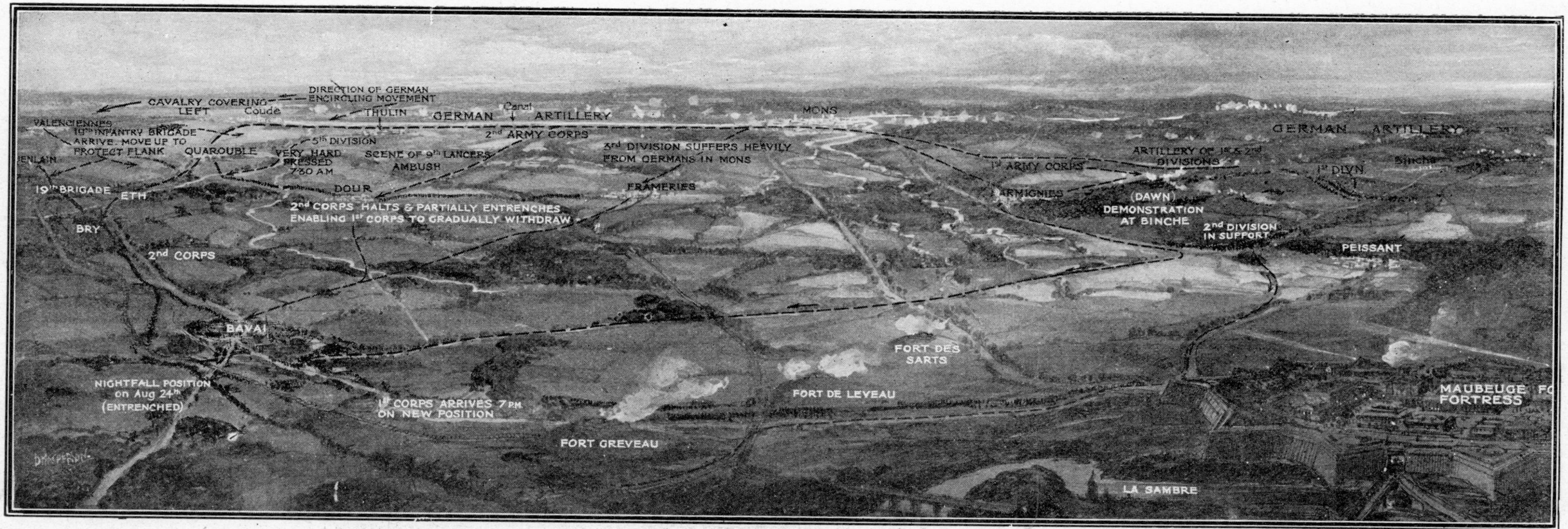

SCENE OF THE RETREAT FROM MONS ON AUGUST 24TH, 1914, WHEN DAWN BROKE OVER THE CONDÉ-BINCHE LINE, TO NIGHTFALL, ON THE LEFT OF MAUBEUGE FORTRESS.

BRITISH TROOPS LEFT MAUBEUGE IN THE EARLY MORNING OF AUGUST 25TH, 1914, FIGHTING THEIR WAY THROUGH THE FOREST OF MORMAL TO LANDRECIES.

troops continued to arrive at Mons, many of them going at once into action after their march.

The Belgian population in the neighbouring colliery villages and large industrial centres was wild with joy at the coming of the soldiers of the Great Empire to which these people had looked for help all through their tragic sufferings. There was scarcely any need for using our food stores, for the happy Belgian women pressed forward in multitudes with all kinds of eatables, and their husbands —miners, mechanics, factory hands—aided in the trench-digging with great vigour. Though the Prussian—like a buck nigger doing a cakewalk—was performing the goose-step in Brussels, and the Belgian Army, with its king, had been driven into Antwerp, all was not for ever lost, the people of Mons felt, now that a British army stood once more in battle order on Belgian soil.

DESPERATE HAND-TO-HAND FIGHTING IN AN OLD BARN.

Our drawing illustrates one of the desperate hand-to-hand encounters which took place between French and German troops on the Franco-Belgian frontier during the house-to-house search for stragglers. A small party of Germans, trapped in a quaint old village barn, resisted to the end.

From the beginning our men went about their business with remarkable coolness. There was none of the nervous, strained expectancy with which a highly-civilised conscript army prepares for its sudden, terrific ordeal. Many of our men had a bath to refresh themselves after their march; others, with a taste for angling and for a supper of fresh-water fish, tied a hooked line to the top of their bayonets and placidly fished the canal. The sappers had a hard time of it. Along the canal, in places, they had to break up the road to make defences, and many dummy trenches had to be dug to attract the enemy's shrapnel fire to spots where it would be harmless. Then the bridges had to be mined and wrecked ready for a German onset, and the country over which the Germans would attack had to be cleared and ranges fixed for the gunners. Entire forests were set on fire to prevent the enemy taking cover in the trees and brushwood.

Treacherous calm before the storm

Saturday was a day of peaceful hard work, and Sunday morning generally passed in calm, pleasant fashion. Some dove-shaped German flying machines appeared on the sky-line, and our cavalry drew back to the main army, finding the pressure suddenly grow dangerously strong against them. There was infantry fighting even on Saturday on the line towards Charleroi, and the sound of the big German guns, directed against the French position, floated down to our First Army Corps.

It was at three o'clock on Sunday afternoon that the enemy came out in force against our men. Sir Douglas Haig's front was attacked heavily; he withdrew his flank to the hills south of Bray, and the cavalry brigade holding Binche, half-way to the fallen town of Charleroi, gave up their position and also moved southward. Victorious all along the rest of the Allied line, the Germans swung out westward against our troops, reckoning them an easy prey. Something like eight hundred thousand Frenchmen were almost everywhere in retreat along the frontier, with a million and a half Germans, flushed with success, following them. What could eighty thousand British troops do to stay the sledge-hammer stroke that was falling upon them?

All that had happened to the Belgians at Namur and to the French at Charleroi was only a preliminary to an overwhelming, annihilating blow on the British force. Three days before the battle of the frontier opened Kaiser Wilhelm II. had addressed a most extraordinary order to the generals of his northern armies—to the Duke of Würtemberg, General von Hausen, General von Buelow, and General von Kluck. Notorious throughout the world as this order has now become, we must print it once more in this record of the Great War:

"It is my Royal and Imperial command that you concentrate your energies, for the immediate present, upon one single purpose, and that is that you address all your skill and all the valour of my soldiers to exterminate first the treacherous English, and walk over General French's contemptible little army."

The intense, ungoverned spirit of furious hate that breathes in this order, given by the grandson of Queen Victoria, was, at least, testimony to his fear of the outcome of the vast struggle now that the British Empire was taking part in it. A commander, certain of the justice of the cause for which he was fighting, and sure of the eventual victory of his arms, would not have indulged his soul in so unseemly a frenzy of spite and passion and slander. As soon as the position occupied by the British Expeditionary Force was known to the German War Staff, General von Moltke was able to arrange to fulfil the murderous request of his Imperial master, and at the same time to carry out a magnificent enveloping movement round Mons, which would endanger the entire French Army along a front of one hundred and fifty miles, from Lille to Verdun.

Neither Sir John French nor General Joffre expected the stroke that was being prepared against both British and French. At Mons the battle went on to our advantage. The Germans at first put scarcely more men into the fighting-line than the British did, and victory seemed within our reach, for the Germans fought at a terrible disadvantage. The infantrymen did not know how to shoot, how to take cover, how to use the bayonet. They were only harmless servants of the well-handled German machine-guns and the numerous and effective light and heavy Krupp artillery.

The German gunners—good men, but not so good as ours—fought the battle. Greatly helped at first by German airmen in Taube and other machines, who skimmed over the British trenches, found where our men were, and signalled the range to the gunners, the enemy's batteries poured a continuous storm of bursting shrapnel over our defences. To protect our defenceless infantry, our artillerymen bombarded the German guns with shells. The shells sufficiently reached their mark to induce the German gunners to adopt another way of fighting.

Leaving their shrapnel ammunition cases untouched for a while, the hostile artillery loaders brought up shell, and began a furious bombardment of our batteries, hidden among the hills to the south. Here, again, in the great artillery duel with which every modern battle opens, the Germans at first had the best of it. We had arranged a massed-fire effect by grouping our guns close together in the old-fashioned way. This made it easy for the enemy to do damage to some of the batteries as soon as he had found the position. The German guns, on the other hand, were placed in batteries at a great distance apart, each gun being well screened from aerial observation.

The massed-fire effect was obtained by means of field telephones, connecting every gun to a central fire-control station. By this method any wholesale destruction of the batteries was prevented. Each gun had singly to be found and destroyed by shell fire by the enemy. Yet all the guns—and there were over six hundred of them—could be brought to bear, by telephone control, on one spot to blow a sudden path through the hostile front. Altogether, it was a brilliant piece of organisation, and as soon as our gunners grasped the significance of it they also scattered their batteries, and used field telephones and flag signals for directing the fire. Our flag signalling was admirable. The Germans had laughed at its old-fashionedness at our manœuvres; but, as we knew from other wars, even a message sent by a fluttering

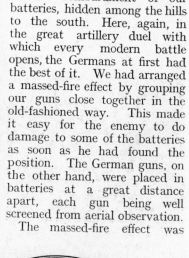

MAJOR-GENERAL SIR WILLIAM ROBERTSON. *(Maull & Fox.)*

Major-General Sir William Robertson, K.C.B., who served with distinction in India and South Africa, as Quartermaster-General with the Expeditionary Force overcame "almost insuperable difficulties with his characteristic energy, skill, and determination." Major-General Sir Nevil Macready, the Adjutant-General, performed onerous and difficult tasks in connection with disciplinary arrangements. General Snow held a difficult position with success south of Solesmes. General E. H. H. Allenby, C.B., greatly distinguished himself with the cavalry at Mons.

MAJOR-GENERAL SIR CECIL F. N. MACREADY. *(Elliott & Fry.)*

GENERAL T. D'OYLEY SNOW. *(Elliott & Fry.)*

GENERAL ALLENBY.

GUN IN ACTION AND BRINGING UP AMMUNITION.
The large photograph is of a British 60-pounder gun in action, while the smaller illustrates the rough-and-ready, though efficient, way in which ammunition, conveyed in industrial motor-waggons, commandeered in England, was brought up to the firing-line.

handkerchief can save a battalion or a battery, or help to a victory.

On the whole, our artillery, though inferior in number and weight of guns to that of the Germans, put up an equal fight in the opening gun duel. For what our men lacked in howitzer fire and heavy, mobile, motor-drawn guns, they made up in courage, experience, and ingenuity. The old game of "dead dog," for instance, was played round Mons with dreadful effectiveness.

When it was clear that our guns were clean outmatched in number by the enemy's gigantic armament, our artillerymen carefully allowed the Germans to see that their overpowering fire was having its designed result. Through their field-glasses the Teutonic artillery officers could trace the effect of their concentrated fire of big shells, and watch battery after battery along the British front grow silent. Here and there one gun, or a couple of guns, would go on valiantly ringing defiance from the hills, until the hurricane of shells put every piece out of action.

In places the German airmen may even have seen overturned and shattered things looking like wrecked guns. For such things can easily be provided for the delectation of inquisitive hostile aerial scouts, especially if there are any trees handy with trunks about the size of the barrel of a British gun.

Round Mons the German gunners apparently had their greatest triumph. The artillerymen of the "contemptible little army" seemed to have been beaten in the gun duel as completely as were the Belgians at Namur, with their old, feeble Krupp 6 in. pieces. So the grand infantry attack was launched towards the canal in order to storm the British trenches. To make their task easy, the German shrapnel cases were again opened, and a tornado of bursting bullets poured over the river valley. All the bright, warm, sunny Sabbath sky was suddenly filled with innumerable little puffs of cloud. Loud above the distant thunder of the Krupp batteries rang the screaming song of the shrapnel, which made a little puff of cloud as it exploded horribly and showered its charge of bullets down on the British trenches.

Spion Kop and the Modder nothing to Mons

This was the critical period in the ordeal of modern battle. Would our men, protected no longer by their own guns and exposed to the full power of the latest and most destructive death-machine, stand the test in patient, passive, all-enduring fortitude? Our veteran fighting men, many of them risen to the position of non-commissioned officers, admitted that the worst moments in the South African War—at Spion Kop and Modder River—were nothing to the punishment our troops had to stand at Mons.

The mere noise of the German gun-fire was nerve-racking, terrifying. It was a sort of typhoon with firework effects, mixed up with many incessant thunderstorms, and further diversified by local earthquakes where the shells hit.

A French officer, deafened by the explosions, and yet with his national curiosity still alert, resolved to go into the trenches and see how the British soldier was taking it all. In ancient days the new allies of France had been famous for their coolness under fire. But never had their fathers to endure what they were now under-

HOLDING A BRITISH POSITION ON THE MONS—CONDÉ CANAL AGAINST REPEATED ONSLAUGHTS OF THE ENEMY.
In their efforts to overwhelm the position of the British on the south bank of the Mons to Condé Canal, the Germans attacked again and again. Dragoons and Uhlans who came within reach of our guns were swept down by them or made prisoners. Then the Germans, advancing in great strength and in close formation, managed to reach the north bank, where they attempted to throw pontoon bridges across the water. Their losses were terrible. They succeeded ten times in building pontoon bridges over the canal, but each time their work was destroyed by the British gunners.

going. Was the old British stubbornness of spirit still equal to the new occasion?

He settled in the trenches, shell and shrapnel screaming and exploding above and around, and found the private British soldiers engaged in a great discussion. To the Frenchman's surprise, they were oblivious to all that was happening at Mons. What troubled them was the failure of the heavy-weight prize-fighting match between the young Englishman Ahearn and the American Gunboat Smith, whom Georges Carpentier had beaten on a foul. The American had withdrawn from the match, and our soldiers wanted to know if it was from the fear of being beaten that he had done so.

The French officer afterwards admitted that he was staggered. At best he had expected to find stern, tight-lipped, silent courage. Instead he encountered the smiling, eager, blithe faces of young athletes, who had apparently forgotten they were being hammered to death by the Germans, and were solely anxious about the pluck or want of pluck of a certain American pugilist. The men were not even interested—as many French troops would have been—in the technical problems of the battle in which they were so vitally concerned. That side of the matter they left to their leaders, confident that all would be done that man could do.

What was talked of in the trenches

Suddenly, an order passed down the line. The Gunboat Smith discussion was interrupted. The men looked to their rifles and their ammunition, sighted as their officers gave the word, and waited. The German gunners had come to the conclusion that most of the British infantry in the trenches was either dead or wounded. So the German infantrymen were coming to take possession of the stricken field, and prepare the way for the advance of the guns into France down the roads to Paris.

Out of the distant woods they deployed in vast, dim, grey-green masses, barely distinguishable from the grass and the leafage around them. They formed in lines, shoulder to shoulder and four or five deep, with machine-gun supports at fairly close intervals. Some of the light, quick-firing artillery advanced behind them, horses at the gallop, to clear any obstacle in front of their wide path. The German sappers, with pontoon sections, moved towards the canal to bridge the water for the infantry attack. Seeing that practically all the British guns had been discovered and silenced in this part of the battlefield, the grand, routing advance was to be pushed home at this breaking point.

At first all the heavy German batteries within range of the fated British trenches massed and redoubled their fire—shell as well as shrapnel now being used to complete the demoralisation of the remaining British troops. As a matter of fact, most of the British troops remained quite unhurt, owing to the skilful manner in which the trenches had been furnished with shrapnel-proof cover. Our men had not fought the Boers without profiting by what they saw, and what they learned by experience, when the big guns played on the trenches. They were safer in the earthworks they had hastily but skilfully made than they would have been in a concrete, armour-plated fort.

Useful lessons learned in the Boer War

But the Germans, accustomed only to sham battles, were unaware of the safety in which our men were waiting for them. At last the immense grey-green masses drew so near to the British lines that their own artillery had to cease firing for fear of hitting them. The sappers came with the pontoons to the water. The German infantry rose for the charge, and then the "dead dog" came again to life.

Every British gun on the heights commanding the country where the German infantry was collected spoke

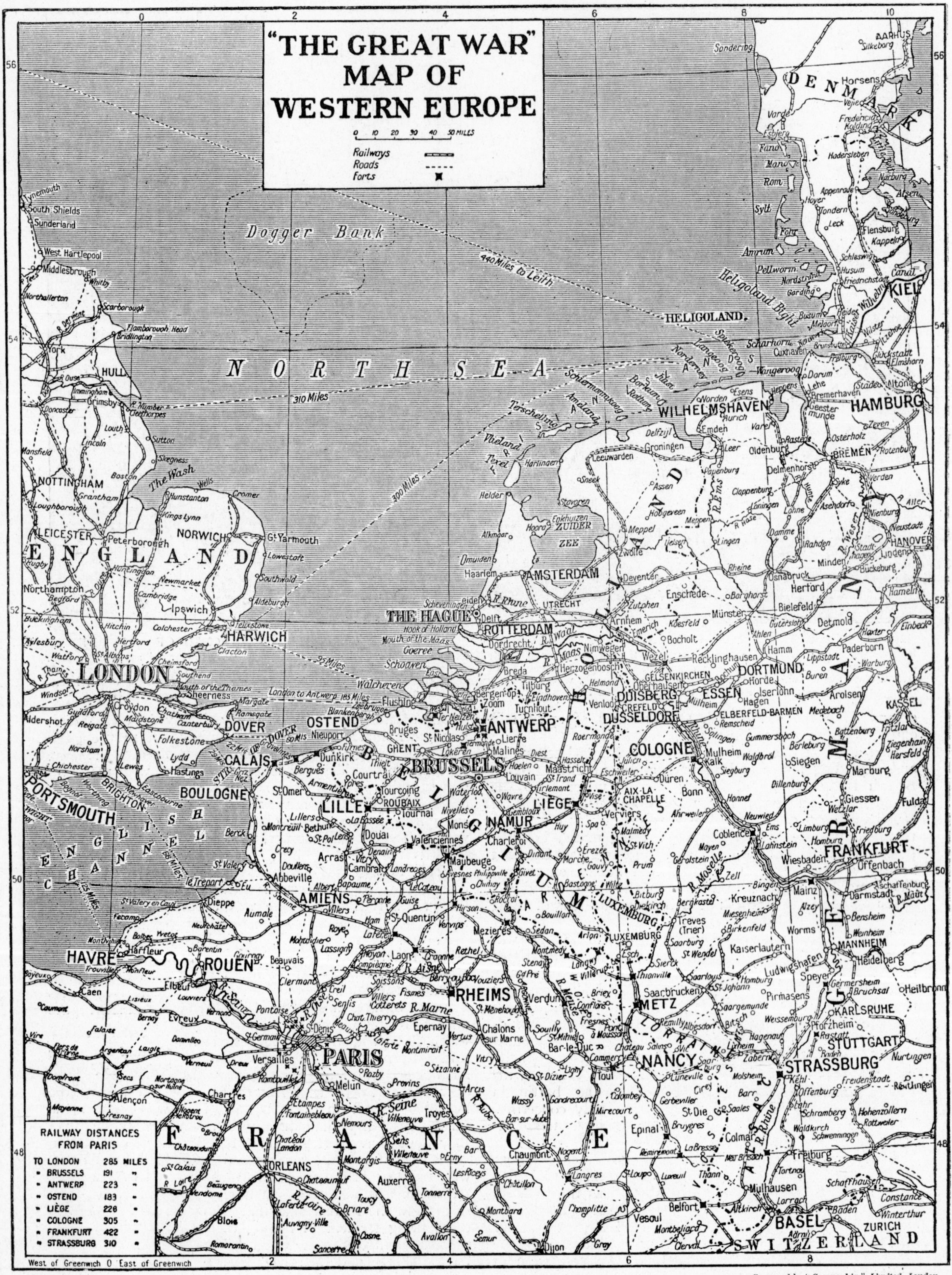

Prepared by "Geographia." Limited, London.

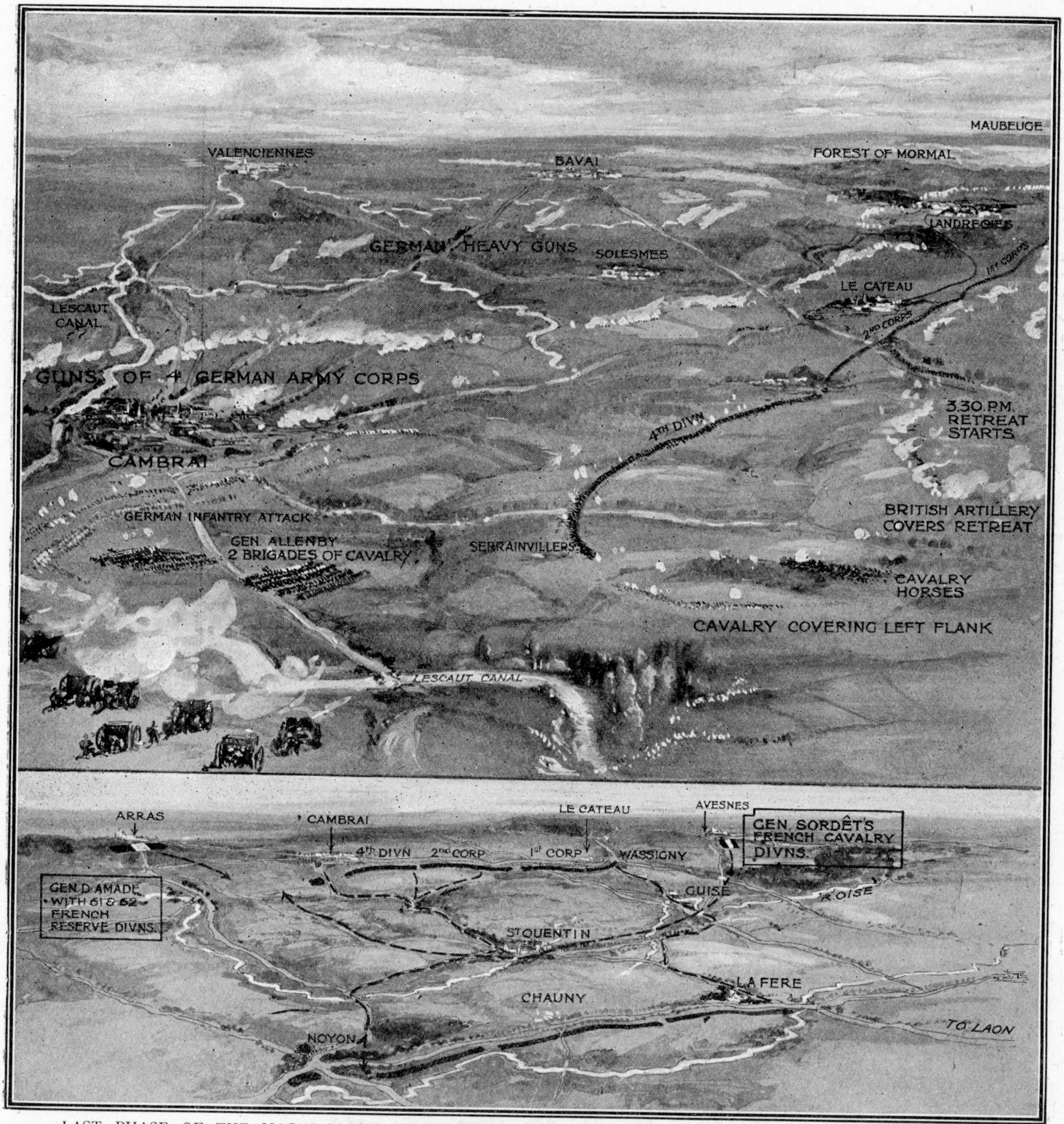

LAST PHASE OF THE MAGNIFICENT RETREAT OF GENERAL FRENCH'S LITTLE ARMY FROM LE CATEAU.
These diagrammatic maps illustrate very graphically how General Allenby's cavalry screened the retreat from Le Cateau on August 26th, and French cavalry came up to their support on August 27th and 28th, 1914.

with a voice that shattered the German dream of an easy victory. Clouds of well-timed shrapnel, firing at broad targets impossible to miss, burst over the tricked and trapped foot soldiers. But the splendid discipline of the Prussian war-machine held good. Sternly controlled by their non-commissioned officers, pushed and beaten onward by their lieutenants and captains, the grey battalions broke into a steady-running charge, though the British gunners breached their lines and shattered their formations. Our guns could not kill them quickly enough to stop them.

They came on like a human tidal wave, with too much mass and momentum for any obstacle to stop them. The gaps in their deep, locked, yelling ranks closed almost as soon as they were made. It was like the overwhelming charge of a Zulu impi, choking with its piles of dead the guns of the position it meant to capture.

In the meantime the surprised, discomfited German artillerymen resumed the bombardment of our batteries in order to draw the fire of our guns away from the advancing German infantry. But our gunners naturally refused the artillery duel, and, letting the hostile batteries fire at them without replying, kept our guns pounding away at the grey-green masses close by in the valley.

The German sappers reached the canal and flung a pontoon bridge across it. A well-placed, timely shell smashed the pontoon sections. The sappers tried again, and the infantry masses behind them approached within a few hundred yards of our trenches. By this time the British gunners were well-nigh beaten. They continued to shell the work of the pontoon-builders, but they could not destroy the German infantry masses quickly enough to break the charge. Apparently, German tactics had won. At an enormous cost of life a point had been reached from which the charge could be driven to a victorious conclusion.

It was the Zulu method, carried out with powerful modern artillery support, and improved by the use of the long-range, bayoneted rifle, instead of the assegai, and the employment of reserve detachments following the foremost troops and reinforcing every wavering point of the onward, rushing line. It was Chaka, a Zulu chief of high military genius contemporary with Napoleon, who had first devised this terrible rush method of attack—terrible to the attackers as well as to the defenders. But the Boers had discovered how the furious, inhuman onslaught could be stayed. Their discovery they had revealed to us, asking a heavy price for it.

This price we paid with the lives of eight thousand men at Tugela River, Modder River, and other places. Now, we were prepared to teach the Germans that good marksmanship, a magazine rifle, and a cool, steady eye could break any Zulu-like charge, even when guns had failed to stay it. "Sight to four hundred yards!" cried our officers. Then, after the order to fire: "Mark your man!" Our soldiers marked him, in tens, in hundreds, and when the range was three hundred yards they marked him in thousands, in tens of thousands.

Nothing living could stand against the deadly, scientific, rapid fire poured out from the British trenches. The Germans who remained upright looked about them like men dazed; then, screaming with terror, turned and fled, and again our guns on the heights caught them.

The one weak place in the British battle-line

This slaughter occurred only at intervals along the front of thirty miles—at Bray in the west around Mons itself, and at points on the canal to Condé. For so long as the Germans were only 100,000 strong, with about the same number of infantryman as Sir John French commanded, they could not deliver a general attack in mass all down the line. They had to concentrate in the distant northern woods, and then sweep out towards some spot under cover of their artillery fire.

ONE GERMAN COMMANDER'S CONSPICUOUS CHIVALRY.

"On September 10th, 1914"—we quote from Sir John French's despatch of the 11th of that month—"a small party of French under a non-commissioned officer was cut off and surrounded. After a desperate resistance it was decided to go on fighting to the end. Finally, the N.C.O. and one man only were left, both being wounded. The Germans came up and shouted to them to lay down their arms. The German commander, however, signed to them to keep their arms, and then asked for permission to shake hands with the wounded N.C.O., who was carried off on his stretcher with his rifle by his side."

In fact, it was often easy to foresee on what point the German attack would fall by studying the increasing fury of the massed gun fire that was vainly employed to clear the British trenches preparatory to the infantry onset. There was only one weak place in our battle-line. This weak place was Mons itself. After Sir Douglas Haig drew the First Army Corps back to the hilly country south of Bray, and withdrew the Fifth Cavalry Brigade from Binche, Mons formed a wedge jutting out into the enemy's lines. Held by the 3rd Division under General Hamilton, it was subject to a cross fire on both sides of the wedge, and to a double attack from either side.

Sir John French had directed that this salient—as a wedge position running into the hostile country is called—should not be held if it were seriously threatened. So, as twilight was beginning to fall on the wild Sunday afternoon, General Hamilton drew his centre back behind Mons. Some of his heavy guns then occupied the lower slopes of the historic ridge of Malplaquet, and in the woods through which Marlborough had worked British soldiers were again encamped.

When this movement had been carried out, the British lines from Condé to Bray were stronger than before. There was no weak point against which an equal number of Germans had anything like a fair chance of success. The first historic battle against the Prussian, whom we had helped to empire in the days of the elder Pitt and Frederick the Great, was going the way that Crecy and Agincourt had gone. Our riflemen, as famed for marksmanship as our bowmen had been, stood on the defensive, and prepared for their victorious charge by first shattering, in rapid, deadly, imperturbable fire, the fighting power of the enemy.

WITH THE BRITISH FORCES FIGHTING ALONG THE FRANCO-BELGIAN FRONTIER.

The first of these scenes from the battlefields of Southern Belgium shows British infantry waiting under cover for the Germans. A British field gun covered with wheat for the purpose of concealing its presence from aeroplanes is seen in the second. The third gives us a glimpse of some of the Staffordshire Regiment in a trench on the Franco-Belgian frontier.

Other nations win by the fury of their assault. The British do not as a rule. They have always had a peculiar, disconcerting way of lining up on the defensive to invite attack, letting the enemy approach perilously near, then shooting at short range with murderous precision. It is a method of warfare that supposes for its success a solid strength of character and a kind of cold-blooded intrepidity. To watch, with steady eye and hand and unquaking bowels, a great host of enemies sweeping up against one's position, the steel gleaming in their hands and the deadly lust of battle gathering in their eyes as the speed of their advance increases, requires an unusual sort of temperament. Our race has this temperament. With it we have won most of our land battles.

Temperament in the firing-line

Nearly all the apparent advantages are against the defender. For the assailant can choose his point for attack, and often concentrate against it in superior numbers, before the defender can in turn strengthen himself. Therefore all Continental experts on warlike operations agree in advocating attacking at every opportunity. But it is not the English way—at least in land warfare—and the more impetuous Scot and Irishman and Welshman now adopt the English way, though when it comes to the charge against the foe that has broken down in his attack, the Celt excels often his brother-in-arms in fury of onset.

GENERAL VON KLUCK AND HIS STAFF.

General Alexander von Kluck, here sitting in his motor-car, was born in 1846, twice wounded at Metz in 1870, and appointed commander of the 1st German Army Corps in 1907. In the fighting at Mons and Charleroi he outmanœuvred the French Generalissimo, and was only beaten at the former place by the indomitable valour of the British troops and the courage and resourcefulness of their commanders.

Had the Battle of Mons ended as it began, with the British and Germans in about equal numbers, the Germans, it is beyond a doubt, would have broken against our trenches, and then been pursued and routed. For the German infantry was helpless. It could not fire straight; it could not take cover; it could not operate in extended order and thus escape largely from gun fire and musketry fire. The foot soldiers of the two German army corps first brought up against us were knocked down like ninepins; only their brilliant machine-gun sections saved them, time after time, from rout. The German cavalry was in no better position. Our horsemen, in anything like a fight with equal numbers, had them at their mercy. Even when our light cavalry met the German dragoons, with more powerful mounts, the British won.

Germans saved by their machine-guns

In the new field of warfare—the sky—the same personal ascendancy of the Briton over the Teuton was quickly gained. Our airmen protected our infantry from gun-fire by the most daring and skilful method. Their proper rôle was to make aerial reconnaissances for the information of the Commander-in-Chief and his Staff, and then to help the gunners in finding the range and position of hostile troops and batteries. But when German flying machines came soaring over our trenches and making signals directing the German guns against our men, the British airmen attacked.

Far below, along the canal and among the hills, our army watched with wondering eyes the first great duels in the air. It was always a case of British hawk against German heron; for the Teutons, though skilful aviators, had not much stomach for the new kind of fighting. But each of the British officers, working with a pilot, was a practised revolver shot, who had thought out the best way to conduct a sky duel. Helped by his pilot, he got the vantage position and fired, and German machine after machine fell with its dead passengers to earth. Later in the campaign, when a new kind of machine-gun was mounted on many British flying machines, the German airmen became still more averse from a combat; but right from the beginning, at Mons, the Teutonic aerial scouts learned by tragic experience that their Emperor's boast of Germany having won the dominion of the air was somewhat premature.

Unfortunately the battle at Mons was not allowed to end as it began. First of all, the want of success of the immediate neighbours of the First British Army Corps—the Fifth French Army and its two reserve divisions, which failed to hold the Sambre between Charlerio and Namur—told against the British Expeditionary Force. For as the Germans had forced the passage of the Sambre the day before—that is, on Saturday—the French army was obliged to retreat south. In so doing, it exposed the right flank of the British force to a turning attack by General von Buelow's army. To prevent this the British had to retire over the French frontier, and thus keep in line with the withdrawing French front.

And this was only the preliminary difficulty that faced the British commander. Even if the French had managed to hold Charleroi, his position would have been extremely perilous. For in accordance with the Kaiser's command that the English should be exterminated, a great enveloping movement was going on around Mons. General Joffre telegraphed to Sir John French the news that at least three German army corps were, at five o'clock on Sunday afternoon, August 23rd, moving against the British front, while at the same time another corps was making a turning movement from the direction of Tournai. As it afterwards appeared, five army corps, with reserves, numbering over 300,000 men, were being launched by the German General Staff against the British force of 80,000 men. In artillery the British were outnumbered by four to one, in men by three to one, when 20,000 British reserves arrived. Such were the circumstances in which the most glorious retreat in British history had suddenly to be conducted.

SCENE OF THE HEROIC STAND OF L BATTERY, R.H.A., NEAR COMPIEGNE.

The battery horses were being watered when suddenly, from a distant range, the German guns opened a murderous fire. All the horses were soon killed, and most of the men wounded or killed. Of the three guns which got into action two were quickly silenced.

The remaining gun was fought by three men, as described on page 18, till both sides had "had enough of it," and our brave fellows were able to creep behind the haystacks seen on the left of the picture, where they were eventually rescued. The picture is from a sketch by Sergeant-Major Darrell, V.C.

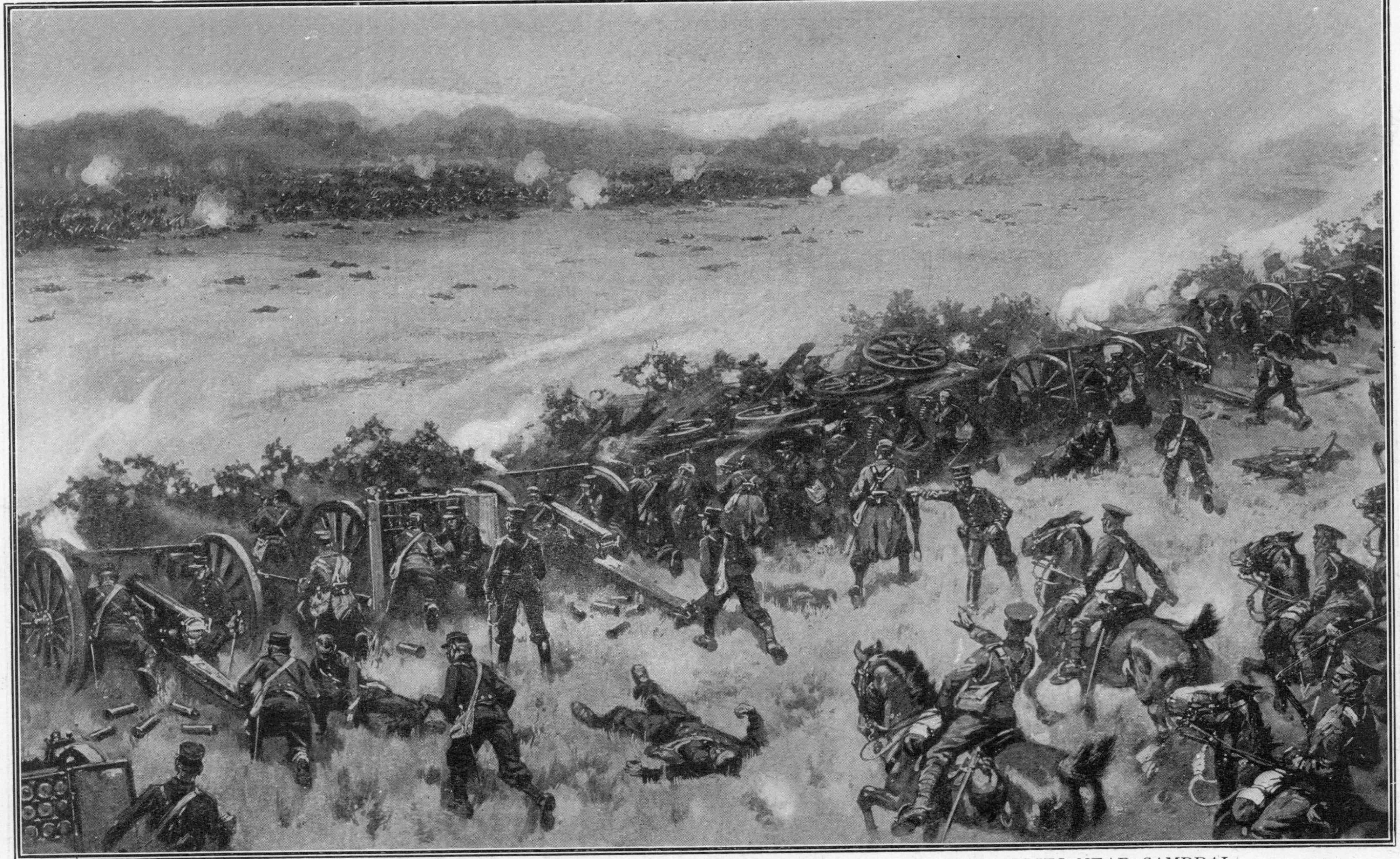

GERMAN TROOPS, FLUSHED WITH EXPECTATIONS OF VICTORY, TRAPPED BY THE ALLIES NEAR CAMBRAI.

A deadly trap was laid for the advancing German infantry near Cambrai in the shape of a masked battery of French artillery and machine guns, supported by entrenched infantry and British cavalry, during the retreat from Mons. A desultory fire from the French infantry stationed at intervals between the masked guns, drew the Germans across an intervening field. At first they advanced in broken lines. Then, their boldness increasing as the French infantry fire diminished, a massed brigade proceeded to cross the fatal ground. When they were within a range of about 250 yards, the French artillery pieces suddenly sent a hurricane of shrapnel through the German ranks, while the ambuscaded machine guns also opened fire. Some of the British cavalry who were posted in support of the French troops may be seen on the right-hand side in the foreground of the drawing, which was made from sketches by one who was present during the action.

NAMUR AND ITS FORTS WHERE THE MEUSE AND SAMBRE JOIN.

CHAPTER XXVII.

THE ANGLO-FRENCH RETREAT FROM MONS AND CHARLEROI.

The Greatest Retreat in British History—Preparing for a German Sedan—Élan of the French—The Passage of the Meuse—German Spies in Namur—The British Stand at Tournai—The German Surprise—The Wreck of Mons—Perils of the Retreat—Tactics of the Peninsular War—Sir Charles Fergusson's Division—How the Cavalry Fought—Maubeuge—Sir John French and General Sordet —Timely Reinforcements—Escape from the Iron Ring.

WHILE the British Expeditionary Force was gallantly beating back one hundred thousand German troops at Mons, on the afternoon of Sunday, August 23rd, 1914, things were going badly everywhere else on the northern front of the Allies. There was a general retreat from the coast to the Meuse below Sedan, following on an unsuccessful attempt to destroy the German armies in Belgium. General Joffre had intended merely to hold back the German advance from Brussels, while striking in its rear. With this design the front, running from Arras through Mons and Charleroi to Namur, was defended by General D'Amade at Arras with about 40,000 reserve troops of the Territorial class, by Sir John French with 80,000 British regular soldiers at Mons, by the Fifth French Army of 200,000 first-line troops at Charleroi, and by a force of some 25,000 Belgian troops at Namur. The total allied troops in this field of battle were thus about 345,000 men. Opposed to them were something like 700,000 German troops.

The French commander-in-chief was not apparently aware of this condition of things. He did not suspect that the German army below Brussels outnumbered his own northern forces by two to one. And, thinking that the line from Arras to Namur would be safely held, he launched two other French armies on a too-daring offensive movement. One of these French armies, operating on the Meuse between Namur and Givet, advanced into the difficult, wooded, broken country of the Ardennes. Still farther south along the Meuse, near Sedan, another French army marched northward to the wild, beautiful valley of the little Semois River, and continued northward to the little old Luxemburg town of Neufchateau. The idea seems to have been for the two attacking French armies to clear the Ardennes of German troops and then strike at Liège, and there cut the communications of the great German host in Central Belgium. With this host severed from its base of supplies and held from Mons to Namur, there might have been a Sedan for the Germans on a vast scale, with a million of them encircled, with no ammunition and little food.

The French fought well at all points; they fought fiercely, terribly, madly. The French gunners, with their light, handy, quick-firing field artillery, were superb in both cool courage and steady skill. They had the best gun of its kind in the world, and they fought with it in an heroic way. The French infantry was also splendid, gallant in bayonet attack and desperately stubborn in defence, and the swordsmanship of the cavalry was a revelation to the Uhlans. But all this availed nothing. The two attacking armies were not in sufficient number to make headway against the German forces collected in the Ardennes under the Duke of Würtemberg. Germany had thrown her sword into France and was using only the scabbard to keep back Russia on her eastern frontier. There were twenty-five army corps of first-line troops over the western German frontier—the entire regular army of more than a million men; and mingled with these were numerous reserve army corps amounting to another half a million or more. At all points of the fighting-line there were two Germans against one Frenchman, two Krupp guns against one French gun, and in regard to machine-guns the odds were still heavier against our allies.

In spite of the delay to part of the German forces at Liège, France had not been able to carry out her

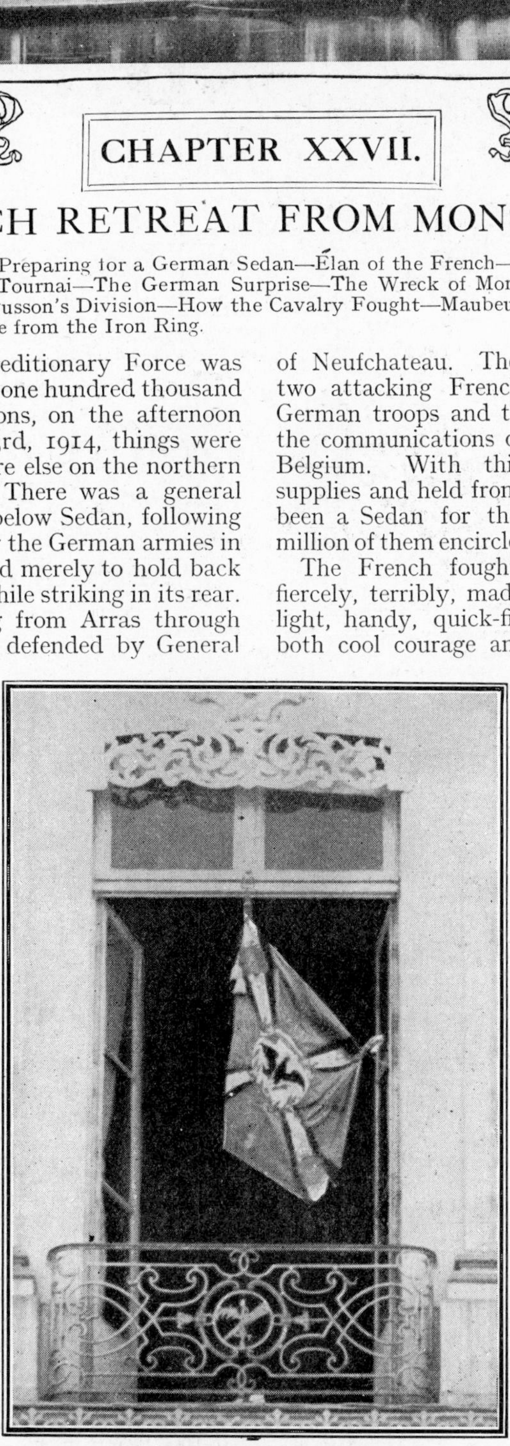

FIRST GERMAN FLAG CAPTURED BY THE FRENCH.

A trophy at the Ministry of War in Paris. The trooper who captured it was awarded £200 by a Parisian patriot.

mobilisation with the effectiveness and completeness that marked the aggressive Teutonic effort. The enemy had reached her northern border in overpowering numbers. The German forces in the Ardennes and Luxemburg, screened from aerial observation by the forests, were certainly stronger than the French Military Staff expected. The result was that the French army operating on the Semois was so violently repulsed that all the French territory to the south, from Mezières to the Argonne Forest, was won by the Germans.

Still more unhappy was the French army that was working more northward along the Meuse between Dinant and Mezières. It was thrown back to the river, and at Givet the passage of the Meuse was forced by the victorious Germans. It was mainly this disaster at Givet which determined the retreat of the rest of the allied line from Namur to Charleroi and Mons. For at Givet the Germans had won a position of tremendous advantage. They were at least twenty-five miles in the rear of the allied line at Namur. By marching directly westward they would have occupied Philippeville, Rance, Avesnes, Landrecies, Le Cateau, and Cambrai — right across the lines of retreat of the Belgian force, the Fifth French Army, and the British Expeditionary Force. As these three allied armies were already held in front by a much more powerful host, their position obviously became one of extreme peril. At Namur the commander tried to get the garrisons of each battered fort to gather together and retire quickly. But, with the

A charming view of Avesnes. And in the circle we have a glimpse of the little old Luxemburg town of Neufchateau.

In the wild, beautiful valley of the Semois. The view on the right is in the Ardennes, which the French hoped to clear of the enemy.

WHERE THE FRENCH PREPARED FOR A GERMAN SEDAN.
The lower picture is of storied Mezières, all French territory south of which, to the Argonne, was occupied by the Germans.

thoroughness that characterised all their military preparations, the Germans had ordered their spies in Namur to cut the underground telephonic communications between the forts. At the same time the enemy opened the Meuse lock-gates at Namur and lowered the water defences of the city so that their troops could enter it. Then each Belgian regiment had to fight its way out of Namur separately, against tremendous odds, and then strike into the country, with the Germans in hot pursuit, and struggle on till it met the retreating French army.

In the meantime the large French force of 200,000 men at Charleroi had already lost the command of the Sambre between Charleroi and Namur. For the Germans crossed at the village of Tamines in the afternoon of Friday, August 21st, and the French army began to withdraw on Saturday, August 22nd. Their line, however, might only have bent back somewhat, if their commander had had simply to continue to resist the pressure of the army of General von Buelow and part of the army of General von Hausen. But when the passage of the Meuse was forced by the enemy at Givet, two days' march in their rear, the French at Charleroi were compelled to withdraw for a long distance with all possible speed.

In fact, it was a question if they could save themselves from annihilation or surrender. With two German armies of 400,000 men pressing them behind or marching ahead to get on their flanks, while another hostile force threatened their line of retreat from a spot two days' march in front of them, the men of the Fifth French Army were in no position to help their British friends on their left at Mons. They could not even attempt any combined action. Hurriedly, desperately, they had to fight their way back, in rearguard action after rearguard action. Their cavalry was soon tired out by charging continually to save guns or infantry, till at last the horses could not move. Happily, General Joffre had arranged behind them a second line of reserves, on which they were falling back, and some

FRENCH PATROL TAKING COVER ALONG A RIVER-BED IN THE VOSGES.

When the French, after their early dash on Altkirch and Mulhausen, retired to the Vosges, they took up strong positions in the passes of that wildly picturesque mountainous district. Here they took advantage of all the cover they could find, moving their patrols along the bosky banks of the river-beds or other wooded shelter, which provided much natural protection from the aerial scouts of the enemy.

MEN OF DESTINY—THE LEADERS OF THE ALLIES AT THE FRONT.

General French and General Joffre directing operations at the front. The artist, M. Thiriat, to whose gifted pencil we are indebted for the above picture, wrote: "At night, somewhere near the front, inside an abandoned farmhouse in the midst of fields, the two men are together there—those on whom we are setting all our hopes, and who are giving all their knowledge, their lives, for the freedom of the world." Very often only a single sentry betrayed their temporary shelter. And automobiles waited, panting, to carry them as quickly as possible wherever their presence was needed.

of these reserves, besides helping the soldiers of their own nation, were able to come later to the aid of a hard-pressed British army corps.

Such was the disastrous condition of things on the right of the British force that was holding Mons on the tragic Sunday afternoon in the hot, stifling August weather. On the left of our troops matters were growing even worse. We seem to have had an advance guard of a few hundred men posted at Tournai, a lovely old Flemish town, a hard day's march to the north-west of our line at Mons. Though Sir John French had no reason to suspect a turning movement by the Germans at the time when he made his dispositions, he yet threw out these men to guard against the possibility of a surprise attack on his flank.

But in such force did the Germans come through Tournai on this surprise attack that the British outpost was overwhelmed. Some fifty thousand Germans, with an enormous number of guns, were sweeping from Brussels to Tournai, and from Tournai to Cambrai, to get in the rear of our army. In advance of them rode, clearing their path, a force of 5,000 German cavalrymen, with machine-guns, and light horse artillery. It was this cavalry force that came upon the British outpost.

Outnumbered by ten to one in men, and still more overpowered in artillery, our troops fought like heroes. They occupied some high ground a little way behind Tournai, and they had two guns of the garrison artillery. The British gunners quickly got the range, while the enemy was some miles away, and shelled them, but the galloping Germans soon covered the ground and the range was lost.

But our infantry and gunners held on, instead of preparing to retire, for they expected reinforcements to arrive. But none came—for our main army was then too busy fighting for life against heavy odds to do anything.

Uhlans to the number of 3,000 tried to storm our outpost position at Tournai. Riding through the town, they came to the muzzles of our field-guns, but were beaten back with terrible loss, the bayonet of the British infantryman getting under the sword of the German light cavalryman.

It was the arrival of some machine-guns in German Red Cross waggons that broke up the defence, and, after a fight of two and a half hours, 300 British soldiers—all that remained of 700—collected their wounded, saved their convoy, and fell back, reaching Cambrai by nightfall. So terribly had the German horsemen been handled that they could not pursue. The heroes of Tournai undoubtedly helped to save the British flank.

After a rest the German cavalrymen rode on to Lille, and then came on to Cambrai; but they were too late for a surprise attack. The main German army that followed them in the turning movement from Tournai was also delayed.

The French Territorials

Twenty-four hours before Sir John French learned from General Joffre that the Germans were moving towards his left flank, General D'Amade became aware that a hostile army was advancing on Tournai. To General D'Amade had been entrusted the defence of Northern France from Lille to the sea-coast. He was a brilliant French soldier, who had been military attaché with the British forces in the South African War, and afterwards directed the French operations in Morocco. He was now at Arras, with only some French Territorials within call. The French Territorial is not a young, active volunteer like the British Territorial; but an oldish man, who has passed out of the first-line troops into the militia class. General D'Amade, under-estimating the strength of the advancing Germans, sent a thousand of his Territorials from Orchies, the depot of troops nearest to Tournai.

Under Brigadier-General the Marquis de Villaret, the French battalion left Orchies before dawn on Monday morning, and completed the march of eleven miles to Tournai by seven o'clock in the morning. Many of them were fathers of families, suddenly called from office, shop, and workshop to the colours. Their march tired them; but, as they halted for a rest, a German column was discovered only a mile ahead. The Marquis de Villaret had neither Maxims nor guns, only the rifles of a thousand oldish men, who had half forgotten their drill. He was opposed by 50,000 young, picked men—a regular corps of the German first-line army, with innumerable guns and machine-guns. But the French commander did not give ground. Posting his men at street corners and railway arches, he offered battle, and at eight o'clock the Germans began to shell and shrapnel the little defending force. After an hour's cannonade the German infantry advanced on the town from all sides, the Frenchmen stubbornly resisting them round the railway.

In half an hour, grey shadows were gliding through the streets, taking cover behind posts, statues, and bushes, and shooting as they glided onward. They cleared the streets with machine-guns, driving the gallant Territorials to the bridges of the Scheldt, where all that was left of the brave battalion made their last stand. It was all over by noon, the Frenchmen being surrounded and captured. But they greatly helped to delay the turning movement against the British force, and the good work they did was continued by other troops under the command of General D'Amade.

VILLAGERS CHEERING FRENCH SOLDIERS ON THEIR WAY TO THE FRONTIER.

A scene typical of many in North-Eastern France in the early days of the war. The men marched along in solid column, some smoking cigarettes, others gratefully receiving proffered refreshments from the women and old folk of the hamlet. Everywhere the troops were welcomed with enthusiasm as they pursued their way through roads and lanes guarded so carefully that in a walk of ten miles the traveller found himself stopped a couple of dozen times, and there was trouble ahead if his papers were not in absolute order.

The German cavalry force, increased to 10,000 men, with machine-guns and artillery, began to operate below Tournai. General D'Amade at first could still only send men of the militia class to delay it. His Territorials were defeated to the south of Lille, and the victorious German horsemen then captured Cambrai—getting on the flank of the retiring British army.

By this time, however, General D'Amade had gathered 36,000 troops of the reserve class. Marching up from Arras, he arrived in time in the country around Cambrai to hang on to the German army corps and cavalry division which was trying to deliver the fatal stroke at the British rearguard. All these incidents told on the great result—the British outpost stand at Tournai, the delaying action by the French Territorials, the arrival of General D'Amade with his reserves on the right of the attacking German force. For, as we shall see, at the moment of peril at Cambrai, matters were in a critical state, and small things helped to grand issues.

The moment of peril at Cambrai

Since Sir John Moore marched through Spain with 30,000 men in 1809, pursued by Marshal Soult with 60,000 troops, no British commander had had to conduct a retreat in such difficulties as faced Sir John French on the Franco-Belgian frontier in the last week of August, 1914. Indeed, the later achievement of British arms is even more glorious than the early feat at Corunna. Sir John Moore had the odds of two to one against him, and fought but one battle, and this was against an enemy whose supply of ammunition was running out. Sir John French had the odds of three to one against him, and five to one at last, and he had to march and battle day and night for a hundred and twenty hours against a well-furnished, vigorous, and agile foe. Moreover, this foe was animated with an intense passion of hatred for the British soldier, whom he had been commanded by his Emperor to "exterminate." The German was not bent on an ordinary triumph of war, but on an act of racial, fanatic slaughter.

It was at five o'clock on Sunday afternoon that Sir John French had the supreme surprise of his life, when he learnt from General Joffre that there were at least 150,000 Germans moving against his front, with another army engaged in encircling him on the left. In the end matters appear to have been even more perilous. For in all there seem to have been more than 300,000 troops under General von Kluck, an able, energetic commander, marching, riding, or coming in motor vehicles, against 80,000 British soldiers. A hundred thousand of the Germans were then attacking the British lines, and were being beaten off. A few regiments had suffered badly early in the fight, the Middlesex

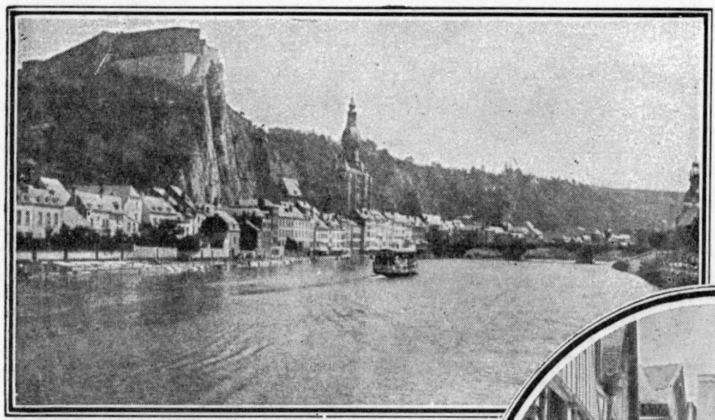

Lovely Dinant before its bombardment, showing the river-boat arriving from Namur. To the right, the main street of Landrecies, where British machine-guns mowed down masses of Germans.

and the Royal Irish Regiments in particular, but, in general, things had gone in our favour. Our infantry had to endure a severe gun fire, but they were well entrenched, and when the German foot soldiers advanced in solid masses, standing out on the sky-line, it was just rifle practice for our army of marksmen to bring them down. Our cavalry had little to do, except on the right flank, where the Scots Greys were reported to have lured ten thousand of the enemy on to a terrible machine-gun fire.

The desperate fighting began on Sunday evening, when the British commander, having planned the retreat, withdrew the Third Division from Mons to a position behind the town and called in the advanced troops along the line.

There was a British officer with sixty men guarding a railway bridge by the canal. It was part of an advanced force round the bridge that had fought the Germans off all day. But when the order to retire was given, at five in the afternoon, it never reached the sixty men and their lieutenant, and the bridge was suddenly blown up, leaving them alone against an advancing host of Germans. They met their foes with rapid fire, and then charged with the bayonet. The officer fell with most of his men, scarcely any escaping. But the next day some Belgians picked up ten of our men who were still living and took them to a convent. They said they had found 5,000 Germans dead or wounded by the bridge, and only sixty British! There had been a Scottish regiment as well as some hundreds of English troops guarding the bridge, but even so the very large number of Germans put out of action was extraordinary. It showed what a weapon the improved Lee-Enfield is in the hands of troops that had learnt to kill each ten to fifteen men in a minute.

It was this incomparable marksmanship of the British infantryman that saved the situation. Before Sir John Moore took his troops to Spain, he kept them at Hythe at rifle practice, and won Corunna by it. In the same way Sir John French and his corps commanders, Sir Douglas Haig and Sir Horace Smith-Dorrien, had devoted themselves after the Boer War to the vital task of turning every regular soldier in the British Army into a crack shot. The thing was done by very simple means. Each man who qualified was given a few pence more a week. The prize was nothing, but the spirit of emulation it excited in all the regiments proved a grand factor in the history of Europe. Instead of going out at night, many men would sit in barracks, working the trigger of their rifle to get the rapid-fire action into that condition of instinctive control that makes a man's instrument a natural part of himself. Their weapon took ten cartridges in the magazine and one in the breech—eleven shots without reloading. The German rifle took five in the magazine and one in the breech—only six shots, and they were usually wasted. Right from the beginning the British infantryman dominated the battlefield. Rifle and bayonet were useless against him; only shell and shrapnel and machine-gun fire brought him down. His wounds were mainly shrapnel wounds, which does not say much for the 200,000 German foot soldiers who opposed him.

General view of Tournai, near which town 700 British soldiers made a splendid stand against 5,000 Uhlans.

The Place de Sépulcre, Cambrai.

All Sunday night the British were under the fire of the German guns. The enemy's searchlights swung in swords of fire through the summer darkness, and whenever the light revealed a trench with figures a burst of shrapnel followed. Having four branch railway lines behind them to feed their thousand guns, the German artillerymen were not

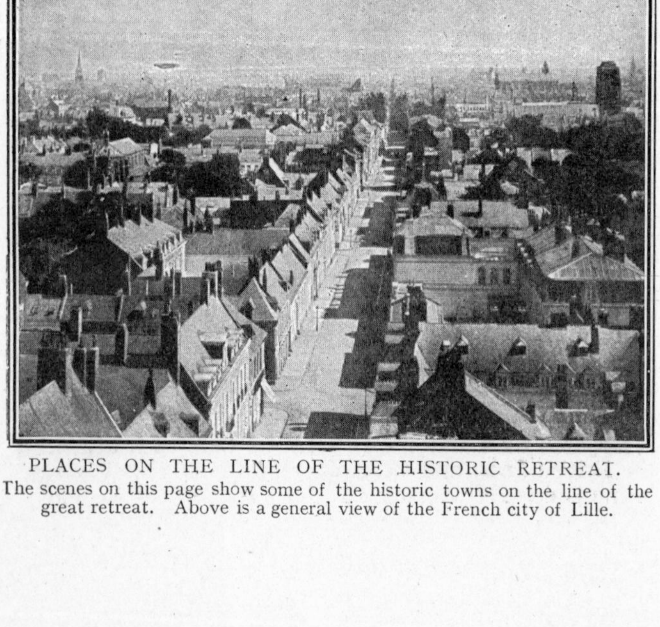

PLACES ON THE LINE OF THE HISTORIC RETREAT.
The scenes on this page show some of the historic towns on the line of the great retreat. Above is a general view of the French city of Lille.

INCIDENTS OF THE GREAT RETREAT FROM MONS.

A busy scene on the hurried but masterly retreat across the Franco-Belgian frontier. A Red Cross officer was snapped while consulting with a colleague in the combatant ranks, and, on the left, another officer will be noticed giving orders respecting the removal of the camp. The lower picture is of three Scottish officers surveying the movements of the forces across the wooded country below them.

sparing of ammunition. They designed, by a terrific, continual bombardment, to shake the nerve of our men, keep them sleepless, and wear them out for the next massed infantry attack. In any case our troops had little sleep, for the whole army was busy preparing for its retirement. It was close on midnight before all the outposts withdrew over the canal, where many of them had been firing through loopholes made in the walls of factories.

By the morning Mons was wrecked by German shells and flaming in places, and the German cavalry advanced through the streets, driving Belgian women before them to protect them from our fire. When the enemy's horse had thus cleared the path, a German army swept through Mons at daybreak, and, with its guns pushing forward and roofing the sky with shrapnel over our position at Malplaquet, the infantry attacked our Third Division under General Hamilton. There were the 3rd Worcesters, 2nd South Lancashires, the 1st Wiltshires, and the 2nd Royal Irish Rifles, under Brigadier-General McCracken. Brigadier-General Doran handled the 2nd Royal Scots, the 2nd Royal Irish, the 4th Middlesex, and 1st Gordon Highlanders. Then there was the Ninth Infantry Brigade —the 1st Northumberland Fusiliers, the 4th Royal Fusiliers, the 1st Lincolns, and the 1st Royal Scots Fusiliers—under Brigadier-General Shaw. With these three brigades were one battery of 60-pounders, the 48th, the 23rd, 40th, and 42nd Brigades Royal Field Artillery, with 18-pounder guns, and the 30th Brigade Howitzers—all under Brigadier-General Wing. The 56th and 57th Field Companies of Engineers, the 3rd Signal Company, and a regiment of cavalry completed the division, that numbered about 18,000 men.

On Marlborough's old battlefield

Desperately did the Third Division have to fight amid the woods and hills of Marlborough's old battlefield, for on it fell the first violent thrust of the advancing German host. Some of the regiments, thrown out as rearguards, got into very tight corners, but fought their way out—hundreds against thousands. While they were holding the grey masses back and, what was worse, drawing the fire of the German guns, the main body of troops marched southward. The division, however, was suffering so badly that the commander-in-chief had to assist it.

This was where Sir John French's experience in getting out of difficulties in the South African War told. Instead of hurrying up supports to his overtaxed men, and thus playing into the hands of the Germans by delaying his retreat, he struck out at the foe. On the right of the British line of retirement was the huge force of General von Buelow. If this hostile force had the Fifth French Army so well in hand that it could spare an army corps or two for operating on our right flank, our case would have been desperate. To discover the position of affairs on this side, and relieve the pressure on the Third Division, Sir John collected all the artillery of his First Army Corps, and sent it out towards Binche, on the road to Charleroi, with the Guards' Brigade, the 5th Infantry Brigade, and the 6th Infantry Brigade—some 12,000 infantrymen.

Apparently no opposition was met from General von Buelow's force, which had all it could do, with the assistance of General von Hausen's army, to fight back the Fifth French Army. Our movement, therefore, threatened to turn the right flank of General von Kluck's multitudes of moving men. For the noise of our artillery was that of an army corps working up to encircle Kluck on one side, while he was working to encircle our men on the other side. Our operation was more immediate, so the hostile commander had to counter it by concentrating troops

GLEANING OF THE REAPER WHOSE NAME IS DEATH—THE GERMAN DEAD ON THE MORNING AFTER A BATTLE.

Fair was the summer in which the Great War broke out, and as some of the most desperate of the fighting took place at night time, it was left for the roseate dawn of another day to discover strewn across the fields that had but just been cleared of their harvest the dead bodies of the slain. The above photograph was taken in the early morning in a French stubble field, the haystacks showing up on the sky-line indicating the vicinity of a farm where, but a few days before, the farmer and his hands had been employed in the peaceful pursuit of garnering in the corn, happily unconscious of the horrors to come.

far to the east of his own main position in the west. Naturally, he did not guess there were only three brigades of British infantry behind our one hundred and fifty guns. He made overwhelming preparations.

General French's counter-stroke

The position of affairs can easily be explained in pugilistic terms. Instead of trying to parry the blow coming through Mons by bringing more troops to the threatened spot, Sir John French struck out at the enemy still more quickly in another direction, and made him do the parrying. As soon as he knew, on Sunday afternoon, that Kluck was bent on enveloping his left, he planned at once the counter-stroke on his right, and collected the guns and troops in the darkness at Harmignies, a village some four miles south-west of Mons. And from there, as dawn was breaking on Monday, August 24th, the feint British attack was made.

But there was no appearance of feinting about the troops that took part in it. The men only knew that, instead of retreating against an enemy in superior force, they had to advance and attack him. This suited them very well, for they had some of the best men with a bayonet to be found in the world. There were the 2nd Grenadier Guards, the 2nd and 3rd Coldstream Guards, and the Irish Guards. With them were the 2nd Worcesters, the 2nd Oxford and Bucks, the 2nd Highland Light Infantry, and the 2nd Connaught Rangers, under Brigadier-General Haking. Then, brigaded under Brigadier-General R. H. Davies, were the 1st Liverpools, the 2nd South Staffordshires, the 1st Berkshires, and the 1st King's Royal Rifle Corps. All these composed the infantry of the Second Division of Sir Douglas Haig's First Army Corps. They had their own artillery and that of the First Division, with a cavalry regiment reconnoitring ahead.

A FARRIER IN THE THICK OF THE CONFLICT AT COMPIÈGNE.

When the 6th Dragoon Guards charged the Germans at Compiègne, on September 1st, 1914, the regimental shoeing-smith would not be left out. "Armed only with a hammer," it is recorded, "he took part in the frenzied gallop, and wielded his weapon with deadly effect."

Thus, equipped with a double armament of guns, they marched towards the little Belgian town of Binche, nearly half-way to Charleroi. Binche had been taken by the Germans on Sunday, when our cavalry withdrew there. The German troops, however, were not now in sufficient number to resist our attack, so they asked for help, and General von Kluck moved his men out of Mons and weakened his line in order to meet the surprise advance against his unprotected flank. But it takes some time to shift a couple of army corps and some hundreds of guns. So, for the greater part of Monday, the Second Division was able to draw off some of the pressure on our retiring front.

Its comrades of the First Division, withdrawn to the south-west out of range of the German artillery, acted as a reserve, but, having no guns, for the time did not come into action.

Under cover of this demonstration on the right wing, the Second Army Corps, directed by General Smith-Dorrien, began the retreat in the darkness of the early hours of Monday, August 24th. But the operation was still very difficult. For the two divisions of the Second Corps—General Hamilton's division behind Mons and Sir Charles Fergusson's division along the canal on the left wing—had each a German army of 50,000 men pressing on its front, while another 50,000 or 70,000 Germans attacked on the left flank.

General Hamilton's men—the Third Division—were now in an easier position, though they still had the odds of two to one against them, and their guns were badly knocked about. In one part of the field a strong force of German cavalry got round our infantry and charged right up to our batteries. Very few of the adventurous horsemen, however, escaped. Platoons of infantry ran to the rescue, and emptied their magazines into the hostile squadrons, and what the bullets did not finish the bayonet completed. But the heavy German ordnance, directed by airmen throwing smoke bombs, got the range of our batteries at times, and laid out entire gun detachments with shrapnel.

The German shrapnel was not well timed; it was used in such rapid profusion that most of it burst wrongly. But when it exploded properly the shields of our guns were useless against it. For it burst backwards, going just over the gun, and fanning out the charge of bullets in its rear. Now and then a German shell smashed one of our pieces, but it was largely the destruction of the horses that put the British guns out of action. There was no team left to draw them along with the retreating army; they had to be rendered useless and abandoned.

Old Peninsular tactics

As the guns retired the German infantry came up against our rearguard trenches. By this time we had fallen back, half unconsciously, half expertly, on the ancient tactics of the days of the Peninsular War. Our men seldom held a hill—though Continental troops have done so through the ages, and like to do so still. We trenched or found rough cover in the folds of the ground, where only an aerial scout could descry us. The enemy took the difficult incline of the hill without meeting with any opposition; but as soon

BRINGING GERMAN "KULTUR" TO DINANT.

Here, as elsewhere, the Germans when they entered decided they would make a permanent stay. The furthest figure is the German commandant of Dinant (Oberst-Lieutenant Beeger). Next to him is a German professor charged with the reorganisation of the schools in Dinant. Inset is a photograph which illustrates the meticulous care with which the Germans carried out their advance movements, both cavalry and infantry being sent in small parties ahead of all their main armies.

as their breasts rose above the top, a rapid fire at a few hundred yards smote them down. On came another mass some minutes later, only to meet the same fate.

The Germans then brought machine-guns up, but the deadly clarity with which every figure showed up against the sky over the ridge enabled our troops to defend themselves in their peculiar way. It was just like Corunna, where Soult's men held the hills above the bay, commanding everything, and yet meeting with defeat. The method of leaving treeless heights to the enemy, with a fine slope for him to charge down to the low British position, is not orthodox tactics. Ordinary troops cannot fight in this defensive way, in which everything depends on a quick eye, rapid, straight firing, and an imperturbable spirit. It is wonderful how our men, when they were in great difficulties, threw back at once to the unusual tricks of war of their ancestors.

When bullets could no longer keep back the German attackers, our men used the bayonet. As they charged they fired independently, dropping many a man before the steel reached him. Only a few tried to cross bayonets with the British. The rest fled, and were shot in the back as they went.

The South Lancashires in the Third Division took one of the colliery villages south of Mons with the bayonet, but the street fighting in this part of the retreat was mostly firing. Then came an Uhlan charge. Happily, the pack animals had arrived in the meantime with ammunition, and the troops had been served with sixty rounds each. They formed groups, and fired into the Uhlans at three hundred yards, throwing them into confusion. Our machine-guns were also turned on the hostile horsemen, while some crack shots knocked over the men with the German horse artillery. In the end, riderless horses came on and passed the British line, but not a lance. Half of the attacking cavalry was down, and the rest scattered without any formation. Soon the order came for the fighting British rearguard to retire. They buried their dead, took up their wounded, and tramped southward towards Maubeuge, the fortress town over the French frontier.

Uhlans thrown into confusion

Maubeuge, with its iron foundries and potteries and ring of great forts, was the place Sir John French first fixed on for his retreat. As soon as he arrived at Mons he had had the country on his rear reconnoitred in view of a possibility of being driven over the frontier. So he now resolved to rest the right wing of his army against Maubeuge, extending his line thence to the south-east of Valenciennes. His principal difficulty was to bring his left wing—the Fifth Division under Sir Charles Fergusson—down from the Mons to Condé line. The Fifth Division, forming the second half of Sir Horace Smith-Dorrien's Second Army Corps, was to win the highest honours of the retreat. It was composed of the 2nd Scottish Borderers, the 2nd West Riding Regiment, the 1st West Kents, the 2nd Yorkshire Light Infantry, brigaded under Brigadier-General Cuthbert.

The heroic Fifth Division

Under Brigadier-General Rolt were the 2nd Suffolks, the 1st East Surreys, the 1st Duke of Cornwall's Light Infantry, and the 2nd Manchester Regiment. Another brigade—the 1st Norfolks, the 1st Bedfords, the 1st Cheshires, and the 1st Dorsets—was commanded by Count Gleichen. Brigadier-General Headlam controlled the artillery, consisting of the 15th, 17th, and 18th Batteries Royal Field Artillery, with 18-pounder guns, the 8th Howitzer Battery, and the 108th Heavy Battery with 60-pounders. In all, 12,000 infantrymen, with fifty-four light guns, eighteen howitzers, and four heavy guns. There were two companies—the 7th and 59th—of Field Engineers, a regiment of cavalry, and five signal companies.

Driving on two sides against this heroic Fifth Division were at least 100,000 Germans—50,000 on their rear as they began their retreat on Monday morning, and another 50,000 on their flank. Some observers, however, estimated the German flanking force at 75,000, and it probably amounted to 100,000 men when the army corps from Tournai got into the fighting-line. In the end this hammer-head of the German host, fashioned to deliver the blow shattering the British army and ruining the entire French defensive, was able, by uniting with the German corps coming through Mons, to mass the tremendous fire of a thousand guns against the British left wing.

Right from the beginning of the retreat General Sir Charles Fergusson's division had to battle against fearful odds. Any series of rearguard actions to keep off the advance of one German army corps enabled the other German army corps to get on its line of retreat and threaten to surround it. All the weight and edge of the grand German enveloping movement, designed to exterminate the British force, and then roll up the Fifth French Army and the Fourth, pressed upon Sir Charles Fergusson's men.

GENERAL SORDET.

General Sordet, who commanded the French Cavalry Corps, consisting of three divisions, materially assisted the British retirement on August 27th and 28th, and successfully drove back some of the enemy on Cambrai.

GENERAL D'AMADE.

General D'Amade, the hero of the French Moroccan campaign, led the 61st and 62nd French Reserve Divisions in the retreat from Mons and Charleroi, and moved down from the neighbourhood of Arras on the enemy's right flank, thus taking much pressure off the rear of the British forces.

To add to the misfortunes of the sorely-pressed troops, there was on Monday a thunderstorm, with heavy rain that soaked through their summer clothing. In spite of the encircling movement on their flank, continual rearguard actions had to be strongly maintained to keep off the Germans in the rear. The overpowered British gunners were magnificent—careful in timing their fuses, yet quick and deadly on the mark. There were times when a German machine-gun began to enfilade the infantry, only to be smashed by a single shot from a distant field-piece by the artillery brigade.

Fergusson asks for help

The German gunners kept mainly to shrapnel, aiming at the British gun teams and detachments, with a view to enabling the Uhlans to make an easy capture of the horseless, manless batteries. Our men used shell in the artillery duels, wishing to smash their opponents' weapon rapidly by one well-placed shot. By half-past seven on Monday morning the division was in such grave difficulties that General Sir Charles Fergusson asked for help.

Sir John French had 4,000 men—the 19th Infantry Brigade—on his line of communications. These he brought up by railway to Valenciennes, and on Monday morning he ordered them to move north to the village of

Quarouble, some six miles south of Condé. Here they acted as defenders of the line of retreat of the struggling Fifth Division, which was trying to retire on Quarouble and entrench there. At the same time Sir John French's single cavalry division, under General Allenby, rode down to the help of Sir Charles Fergusson's infantrymen and gunners.

A strenuous time for the cavalry

Both the 19th Infantry Brigade and the cavalry division had a fierce, violent time of it, while beating off the attacks on the gallant, desperate, overwhelmed left wing. Some of the infantry brigade went into action as supports to the guns of the left wing, and were shelled by the Germans. Then they had to cover the retirement of the cavalry against a German flanking movement. But this movement was going on too fast for them. They entrenched—some 1,300 of them—and the German cavalry, 9,000 strong, swooped down on their trench. They kept them back with rapid magazine fire and Maxims, but could not beat them all off, till the small but vigilant British artillerymen poured over their heads a strong fire, under which the infantry retired.

THE CHEERING SKIRL OF THE PIPES IN THE TRENCHES.

"The Highlanders," wrote a correspondent at the front, "pipe all the time! At Mons they played while the rest shot, and the pipers can play with one hand and shoot with the other." One of our artists has illustrated such an incident noted in a trench occupied by a party of Scotsmen, who were holding a position of importance during the retreat from Mons, when a piper set the pipes askirling, meanwhile with his disengaged hand he emptied his magazine against the oncoming foe.

Then, as this retirement was proceeding, the entire German flank attack developed against the brigade. An army corps and a half—say, 60,000 men in the fighting-line—came up against the brigade, which was blocking their envelopment movement round the Fifth Division. It was a matter of 4,000 Britons against 60,000 Germans. Fighting for life, the Britons drew back and reached the cover of their artillery fire, drawing on the German right wing in extended line, until the cavalry division could attack it.

How the cavalry fought! They charged everything—even barbed-wire entanglements. They had to save the guns from hostile charging horsemen, ride at infantry, and once, when a large body of British soldiers was in extreme peril of being annihilated by shrapnel, some of our light cavalry drew the fire of the German guns and saved their comrades. This was one of the noblest achievements in our military history. It was undoubtedly the cavalry division that saved the Fifth Division.

The cavalry, under the command of General Allenby, was in four brigades. The first brigade consisted of the 2nd and 5th Dragoon Guards and 11th Hussars, under Brigadier-General Briggs. The second brigade was formed of the 4th Dragoon Guards, 9th Lancers, and 18th Hussars, commanded by Brigadier-General De Lisle. Under Brigadier-General Gough were the 4th Hussars, 5th Lancers, and 16th Lancers of the third brigade. The fourth brigade, under Brigadier-General Bingham, was made up of Household Cavalry, the 6th Dragoon Guards, and 3rd Hussars. The entire division had two Royal Horse Artillery brigades, a field company of Engineers, and a signal squadron. Never were horsemanship, swordsmanship, and general fighting ability more effectively displayed than by these 9,250 men.

General de Lisle's brigade was the most unfortunate and the most heroic. It got into tragic difficulties, and won high distinction. As the squadrons rode to the help of Sir Charles Fergusson's troops, their leader saw an opening for a charge against the flank of the hostile infantry. So he formed up and galloped at the German lines, but when five hundred yards from the enemy, our horsemen were held up by barbed-wire entanglements. The men of the 9th Lancers and the 18th Hussars suffered severely while the brigade was retiring under the enemy's fire.

The 9th Lancers, however, were not daunted, and to them fell some of the chief honours of the campaign. One of their captains, Captain Francis O. Grenfell, renowned for his dash and skill in polo, showed how British sportsmanship tells in warfare. First he led one of the charges against the unbroken masses of German infantry at Andregnies, a Belgian hamlet near Mons. Then at Doubon he achieved the gallant feat for which he was awarded the Victoria Cross. The 119th Battery of Royal Field Artillery was struck by shrapnel, and all the men but one were hit. The team was not injured, but there was no one to harness the horses, and some Germans had started to capture the battery. Captain Grenfell saw the British guns lying undefended in reach of the enemy. He rode out.

"We've got to get those guns back!" he said. "Who's going to volunteer for the job?"

Before he finished speaking, a couple of dozen of his lancers were at his side.

How Captain Grenfell won the V.C.

Since his men had seen him in the firing-line they were ready to go anywhere with him. They set out. Shrapnel and bullets whistled over them, but the captain was as cool as if he were riding to the polo field. "It's all right," he said. "They can't hit us."

The lancers got to the battery, hitched up the horses, and brought the guns back. Only three of them were struck. Captain Grenfell went on fighting till he was hit in the thigh by a bullet and had two of his fingers shot off. The 9th Lancers were tirelessly heroic. At another point on the Belgian border they outrivalled the charge of the Light Brigade at Balaclava.

VICTORIA CROSS HEROES OF MONS AND LE CATEAU.

CAPTAIN FRANCIS OCTAVUS GRENFELL, 9th Lancers, displayed gallantry in action against unbroken infantry at Andregnies, Belgium, on August 24th, 1914, and in assisting to save the guns of the 119th Battery, R.F.A.

MAJOR CHARLES A. LAVINGTON YATE, 2nd Batt. the King's Own (Yorkshire Light Infantry), at Le Cateau, on August 26th, led nineteen survivors against the enemy. He died as a prisoner of war.

CAPTAIN THEODORE WRIGHT, Royal Engineers, at Mons, on August 23rd, attempted to connect up the lead to demolish a bridge under heavy fire, and, although wounded in the head, made a second attempt.

CAPTAIN DOUGLAS REYNOLDS, 37th Battery, R.F.A., at Le Cateau, on August 26th, took up two teams and limbered up two guns under heavy artillery and infantry fire, and got one gun away safely.

LIEUT. MAURICE JAMES DEACE, 4th Batt. the Royal Fusiliers, though two or three times badly wounded, continued to control the fire of his machine-guns at Mons, on August 23rd. He died of his wounds.

CORPL. CHARLES ERNEST GARFORTH (Regtl. No. 7368), 15th Hussars, at Harmignies, on August 23rd, volunteered to cut wire under fire, his gallant action enabling his squadron to escape.

LANCE-CORPL. FREDK. WILLIAM HOLMES (Regtl. No. 9376), 2nd. Batt. the King's Own (Yorkshire Light Infantry), at Le Cateau, on August 26th, carried a wounded man out of the trenches under heavy fire.

LANCE-CORPL. CHARLES ALFRED JARVIS, (Regtl. No. 3976), 57th Field Company, Royal Engineers, displayed great gallantry at Jemappes, on August 23rd, firing charges for the demolition of a bridge.

DRIVER JOB HENRY CHARLES DRAIN (Regtl. No. 69960), with Driver Frederick Luke (Regtl. No. 71787), 37th Battery, R.F.A., at Le Cateau, on August 26th, volunteered to help to save guns under fire from hostile infantry.

For services rendered at Mons and during the retreat to Le Cateau eleven V.C.'s were awarded. We are unable to give photographs of Private Sidney Frank Godley, 4th Batt. the Royal Fusiliers, who fought his machine-gun with great gallantry at Mons on August 23rd; or of Driver Frederick Luke, mentioned above. Several of the recipients distinguished themselves in the fighting subsequent to Le Cateau.

HOW LANCE-CORPORAL JARVIS WON THE V.C. AT JEMAPPES.

Lance-Corporal Charles Alfred Jarvis, of the 57th Field Company, Royal Engineers, was among the first recipients of the Victoria Cross in the Great War. The distinction was awarded to him "for great gallantry at Jemappes on August 23rd, in working for one and a half hours under heavy fire in full view of the enemy, and in successfully firing charges for the demolition of a bridge." From unofficial sources we learn that Lance-Corporal Jarvis at first worked with his comrades. After a time, however, he sent them to the rear, finishing the perilous work alone. Wounded, he had to be invalided home, and he heard the news of the award while he was lying in the London Hospital.

ON BRITAIN'S ROLL OF HONOUR: THE RETURN FROM THE CHARGE.

Mr. R. Caton Woodville here pictures a scene following one of the many brilliant cavalry charges in which our splendid troopers, under the command of General Allenby, won new laurels for their colours, and in "going through the enemy like a knife through brown paper," displayed their indomitable courage and the results of their training in the school of General French. The "hell-for-leather" excitement, the hoarse cries, the thud-thud of the horses' hoofs over the turf, the jingle of bit and harness over, there were yet many opportunities for courage and resourcefulness, and these were signally evident in the painful and often hazardous task of helping back wounded comrades to the British lines.

RAIDING THE ENEMY'S "PRIVATE WIRE"—A GERMAN "NEST" IN A HAYSTACK.

"A favourite hiding-place of the German wire-tapper," wrote an officer at the front, "was a hole burrowed out of the side of a corn or haystack, which 'nest' was concealed by placing stooks against the opening." The illustration is of the discovery of the "private wire," but when the "nest" was entered the bird was found to have flown.

Terrible havoc had been caused in our ranks by great shells from a German battery of eleven guns posted inside a wood. Hidden in heaps of forage, that made them look like small haystacks, they kept up a continuous fire for some time, and none of our artillery was at hand to silence them. Just as they were being turned on our infantry the 9th Lancers drew their fire by a furious charge. The regiment rode straight at the guns, debouching into the open field and galloping under a heavy cannonade. But nothing could stop them. Men and horses were infuriated. They reached the guns, cut down the gunners, and put the battery out of action. Then, under fire from other hostile batteries, they rode back.

The First Army Corps at Maubeuge

By many spirited achievements such as this the cavalry division under General Allenby relieved the terrible pressure on Sir Charles Fergusson's troops and guns. Fiercely fighting, the Fifth Division fell back on the southern Belgian coal-mining towns of Dour and Quarouble, and the Third Division lined up with them near Frameries, south-west of Mons. Here the two divisions, forming the Second Army Corps, entrenched under the direction of their commander, Sir Horace Smith-Dorrien. Their shallow and hasty trenches enabled them to withstand the attacks of the enemy. For they now had the 19th Infantry Brigade at Quarouble to help them, and the cavalry division to defend their flank. By fiercely engaging the Germans they acted as a general rearguard, and while they were hotly fighting Sir Douglas Haig was able to withdraw his First Army Corps on the right wing to Maubeuge by seven o'clock in the evening.

Then, helped by the cavalry, Sir Horace Smith-Dorrien also retreated from Dour and Frameries southward to the Maubeuge road. In places there were ten miles of country to cross, with three German armies hanging on the flank and rear of the British troops. The continuous rearguard fighting was terrible; the Second Army Corps suffered heavily, but they always gave more punishment than they received. By nightfall on Monday Sir John French had completed his operation as originally planned.

He was stationed with his Staff in the centre of the British force. On his right the First Army Corps rested under the guns of the French ring fortress of Maubeuge; on his left the Second Army Corps stretched out towards Valenciennes, its flank defended, as before, by General Allenby's cavalry and the 19th Infantry Brigade. This was the position Sir John French had first designed to make a stand against the enemy. But, as he thought things over in the August twilight, he did not feel sure that his force was strongly placed for another defensive action against a vastly more numerous enemy.

The country round Maubeuge proved to be hard to hold. The crops were not yet gathered, and, with the many buildings, made the digging of trenches difficult, and greatly limited the field of fire. In the standing corn the advantages of the superior marksmanship and rapidity of fire of our infantry were greatly diminished. If the troops made trenches, they could not see the approach of the enemy. But there were a few good artillery positions, and for some considerable distance the guns of the Maubeuge forts could help against a German attack. Moreover, there was a large French garrison in the town.

The cupola forts of Maubeuge were regarded as strong, but Sir John was suspicious of all places designed to be besieged. His instinct was for a long, battling retreat farther to the south, during which he could tire and beat off the enemy, without being fettered to any fort. He rightly divined, from the severe, continual pressure on his left flank, that General von Kluck was trying to hem him against Maubeuge and there surround him.

Sir John French's vital decision

And as it is always a good plan to do what your enemy does not want you to do, Sir John French ordered his weary men to set out southward early next morning. The rearguards had to be clear of the Maubeuge road by 5.30 a.m. This meant little or no sleep for the main bodies, for not a moment could be lost in retiring to the new position. There was good reason to believe that the enemy's forces, which had suffered heavy losses, were quite as exhausted as our troops. So, by rapidly continuing the retreat, Sir John hoped to evade a vigorous pursuit.

His headquarters were at Bavai, a French village with ironworks and quarries, between Maubeuge and

SURVEYING THE LINE OF ADVANCE UNDER COVER OF THE SHELTERING HAYSTACKS.

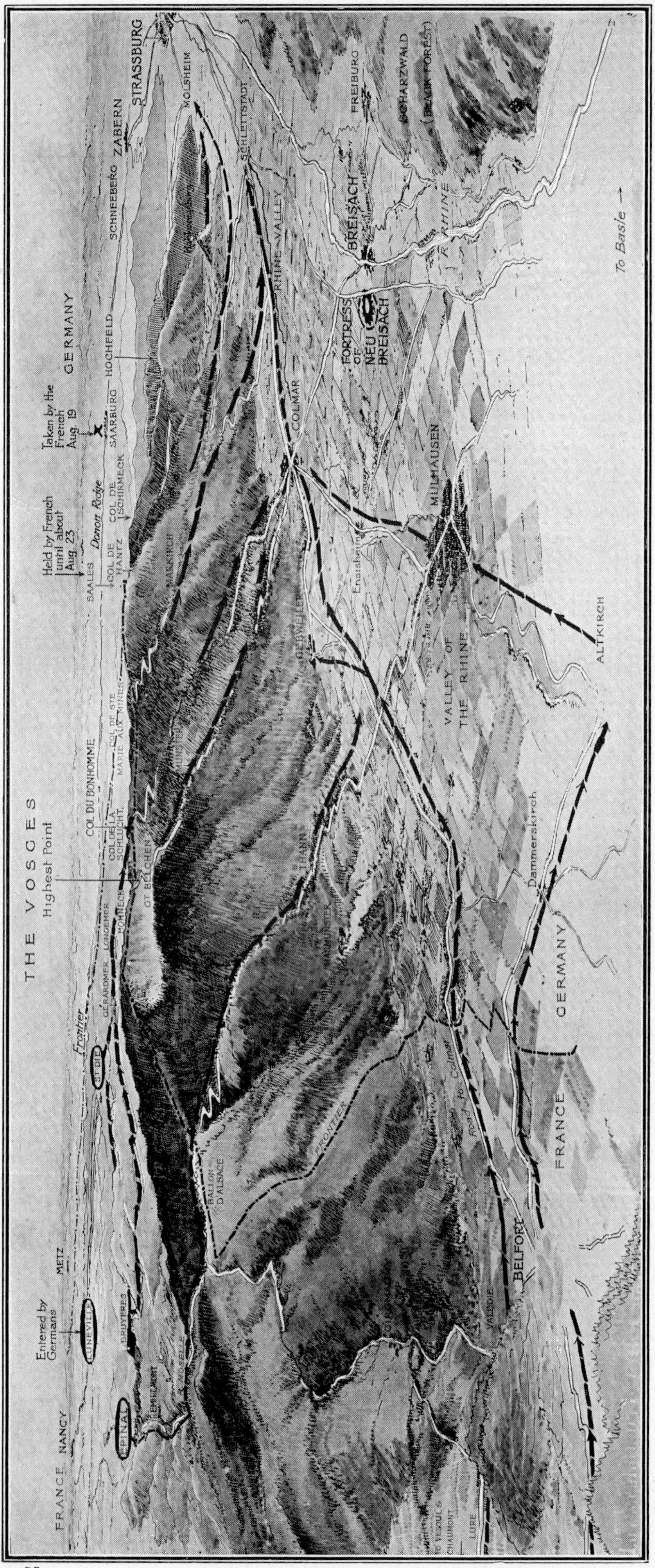

DIRECTION OF THE FRENCH ADVANCE INTO ALSACE THROUGH THE PASSES OF THE VOSGES, AUGUST 7TH-25TH, 1914.

The French advance through the Gap of Belfort is indicated on the left, where the Vosges mountains drop away. The frontier runs up the heights, along the Hohneck, to the great humpy mass, known as the Ballon d'Alsace, and then turns at right angles towards Metz and Nancy.

Valenciennes. A day's march to the south-west was the town of Avesnes, where three divisions of French cavalry were billeted. Sir John French motored to Avesnes, and earnestly asked the cavalry commander, General Sordet, for his support. But General Sordet's men had been fighting hard on the flank of the Fifth French Army against General von Buelow's host. The horses were too tired to move; so the French cavalry was unable to come to the help of the British force in the critical period of the struggle. Greatly must Sir John have regretted the absence of his own Third Army Corps, with the co-operation of which he could have beaten the Germans to a standstill, and perhaps defeated them, though the odds would still have been two to one. But this corps had been retained in England as a garrison. Now the odds were more than three to one in men, and much more than that in artillery power.

Happily, some reinforcements were available. The Fourth Division of 11,000 men, with a brigade of guns, had begun to arrive at the town of Le Cateau, to the south, on Sunday. By the morning of Tuesday, August 25th, the new force, under General Snow, was ready for service. Sir John had fixed on Le Cateau as his next stopping-place. He despatched sappers to prepare trenches there, on the Cambrai road, and ordered General Snow to deploy from the Cambrai-Le Cateau line towards the town of Solesnes northward. On this being done, General Snow's division formed a defensive line against an enveloping attack on the left wing of the Second Army Corps. It was this wise, foreseeing preparation against future difficulties that enabled our great field-marsbal to pull his little army of heroes safely through the gravest perils. When the time of extreme danger came, there was a body of 11,000 fresh British troops, with seventy-six more guns, to join in striking against an immense but tired and battered host of Germans.

Meanwhile, General von Kluck, having, as he thought, shepherded the British Expeditionary Force against Maubeuge and fixed it there, misled the German and Austrian peoples into a premature explosion of gratified hate. He informed his General Military Staff of his supposed success, and Berlin announced to the world, by a wireless message, that the British army had been driven on to Maubeuge, where a ring of iron was being fastened round it. But when Kluck's reconnoitring cavalry advanced on Tuesday morning to direct the final encircling movement, the process of extermination had to be postponed. The British army had escaped from the iron ring.

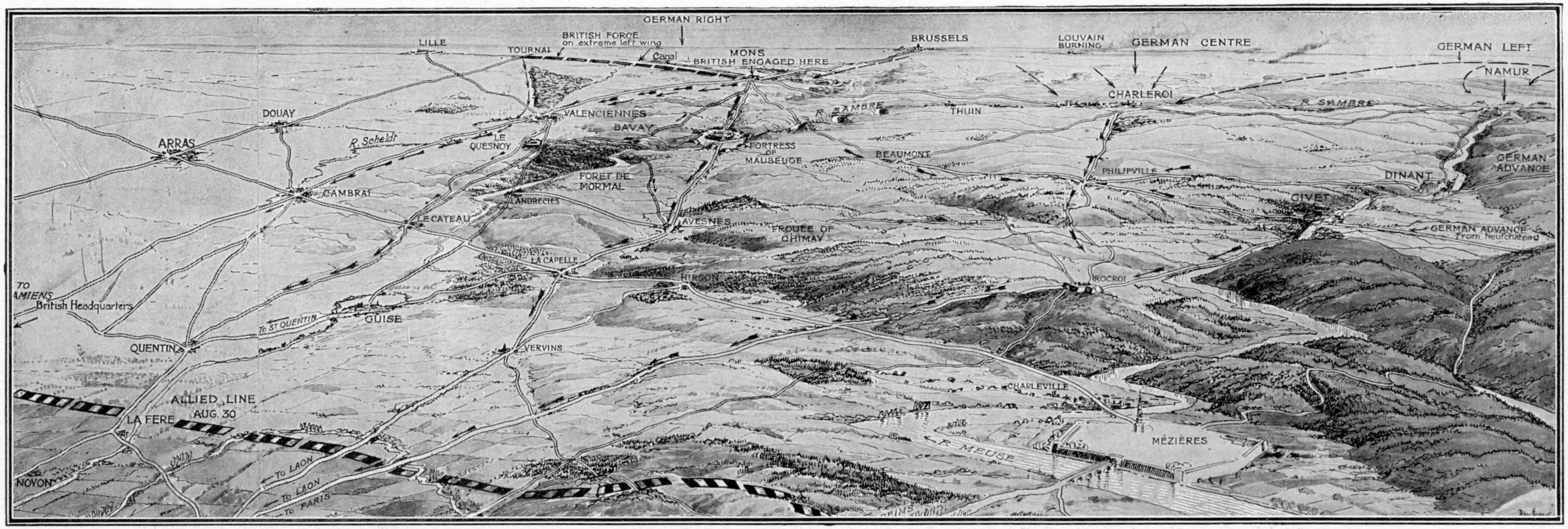

THE BRITISH FORCE HELD THE LEFT WING AS THE FRENCH ARMY FELL BACK FROM THE SAMBRE TO THE AMIENS-LAON LINE.

In the background the arrows indicate the attack by the German left, centre, and right; the other arrows show the British and French lines of retreat. The area is hilly and wooded. At Charleville the French mitrailleuse section made an heroic stand. The two main bridges at Mezières were blown up by the French when they had passed over them. At Landrecies German troops, confidently marching through a street in solid formation, were mown down by British machine-guns. From the Cambrai–Le Cateau–Hirson–Mezières line the retreat was continued into the more open country towards Laon.

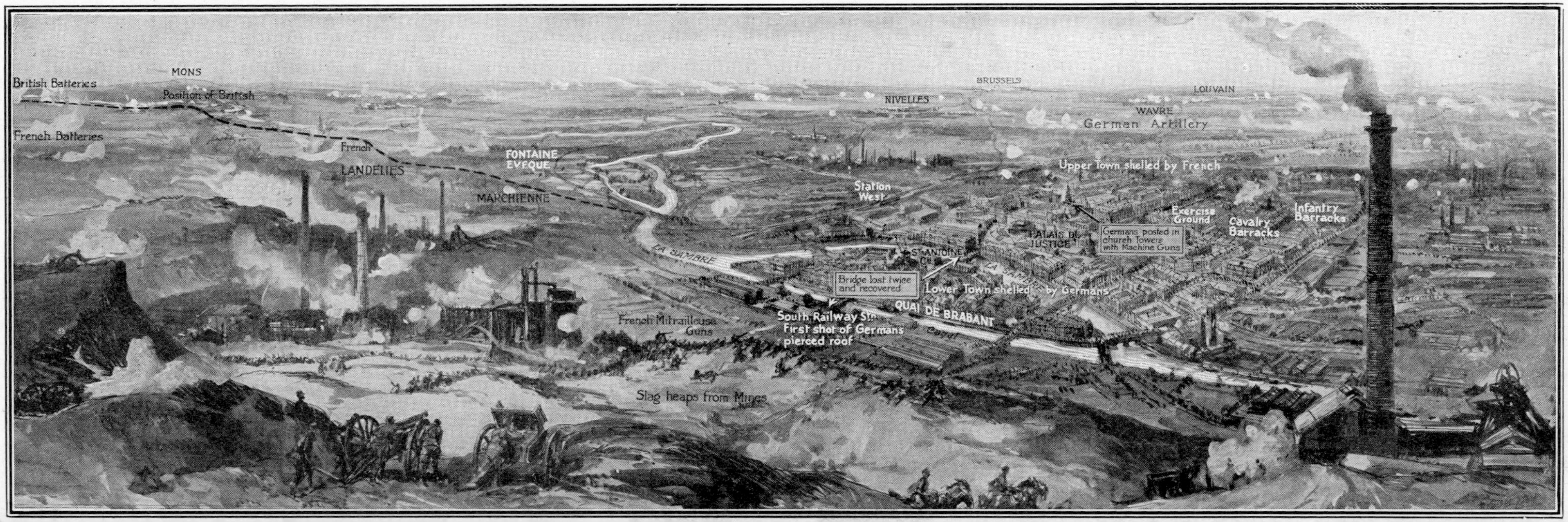

ALLIES GREET EACH OTHER ON THE WAY TO THE FRANCO-BELGIAN BATTLE-LINE.

Picturesque scene, one of many such in the wooded country in Northern France, photographed as a party of French dragoons were passing a British outpost on their way to take up a position in the firing-line on the Franco-Belgian frontier. The troops greeted each other in that spirit of camaraderie which animated the armies of France and Great Britain from the outset of the war, and effectively set the seal on the good relations initiated between the peoples of the two countries at the inception of the Entente Cordiale.

BRITISH INFANTRY AWAITING ORDERS BEHIND A SCREEN OF TREES.

CHAPTER XXVIII.

LATER PHASES OF THE GREAT RETREAT: THE BATTLES BETWEEN LANDRECIES AND CAMBRAI.

Outmarching the Germans—Early Morning Withdrawal from Maubeuge—The Guards at Landrecies—A Trap for the Germans—Terrific Rearguard Action at Maroilles—Sir Douglas Haig's Masterly Handling of his Troops—Heroism of the Munsters—The Part played by General Snow's Division—Excellent Work of the Army Service Corps—The British Soldier and his Tea—The Battle of Cambrai-Le Cateau—An Awe-inspiring Story.

IN the darkness of early morning on Tuesday, August 25th, the British Expeditionary Force began to withdraw from the Maubeuge position towards Le Cateau, a French town some twenty miles southward, by a winding road. The army had had little sleep since Saturday; some regiments, that had gone directly into action at Mons after a hard, long march, had been seventy-two hours without much rest.

But all the men had to be up and moving as soon as their meal was over. Only by outmarching the Germans could they defeat the enveloping movement intended to pin them against Maubeuge. The Germans were already getting some of their big 11 in. howitzers into position on the Belgian frontier to shatter the Maubeuge forts and shell the British army reposing on the fortress while Kluck's three hundred thousand ringed it in.

But, in the vast operations of modern warfare, it is one thing to shepherd your opponent into a trap and another thing to shut the trap door on him. Between midnight on Monday and dawn on Tuesday Sir John French's men entered the Maubeuge trap from the north side and came out of it from the south side. There were no Germans at hand in sufficient force to keep them in. The older Moltke boasted that in 1870 his troops defeated the French by outmarching them. To superior endurance and speed he chiefly attributed his victories.

BRITISH TROOPS OUTMARCHED THE GERMANS.

In spite of the partial aid received by them from motor vehicles, the German conscripts attacking the retreating British were outmatched repeatedly by the marching qualities of our troops, especially in the escape of our men from Maubeuge.

However this may have been, the Germans in 1914 did not outmarch the French. Still less did they wear down by the swiftness of their movements the athletic British regular soldiers. Everything had been done for the Germans to promote their mobility and keep them fresh and unwearied for their work in the fighting-line. In some cases the foot soldiers were conveyed in squads of fifties in motor vehicles along the roads, and dropped near the battle-front, with only a mile or two to tramp to the scene of the conflict. This ingenious method of transporting troops from the railway base to the firing-line was not used, of course, on a general scale. There were not enough motor vehicles and enough parallel or converging roads to concentrate even half of General von Kluck's infantry in this way. But it seems likely that the foot soldiers of one German army corps could, at times, be moved by mechanical means, and though the traction of the heavy artillery probably slackened the whole movement—for the guns must go with the infantry to afford mutual support—the great thing was that the troops came into action unwearied by long marches.

This method was used at Mons and later at Cambrai, when the army corps from Tournai arrived for the decisive stroke. But it could not be employed to any large extent against Sir John French in the early part of his retreat. The Germans had to tramp, from Mons to Le Cateau and

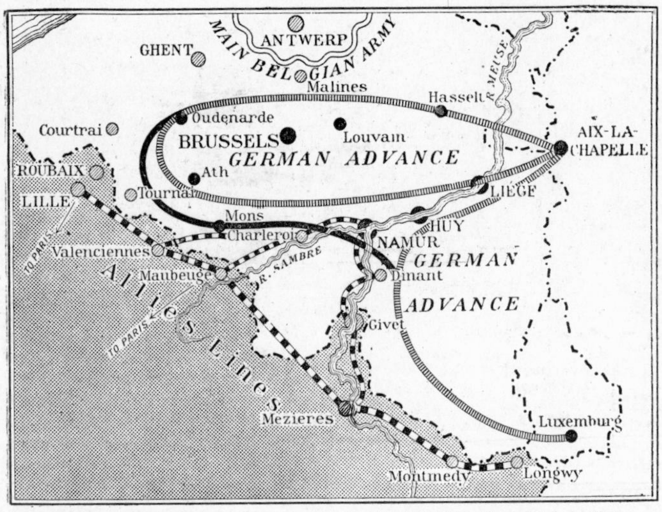

THE COLLAPSE OF NAMUR, AUGUST 25TH–26TH, 1914.
The curved elliptical lines indicate the scope of the German forces north and east of Namur, the chequered line showing how the Allies held a triangular area between Mezières, Namur, and Valenciennes.

Landrecies, over rough, hilly country, fighting hard and continually against our rearguards. Being at the best young conscript troops picked mainly from agricultural districts, they had a good deal of natural vigour, but they lacked the superb strength and hardness of body of our magnificently trained troops. The consequence was that by Monday night they were as much worn out as our men were. They had attacked in shifts, some resting while others advanced. Our men, being outnumbered, were kept incessantly fighting, marching, trenching. Yet by Tuesday morning the British soldier had for the time got the young German conscript worn down, partly by physical exhaustion and partly by heavy losses.

So the preliminary retirement from Maubeuge of the British force was not opposed. The Second Army Corps

MARCHOVELETTE FORT, NAMUR, AFTER THE GERMAN BOMBARDMENT.
Armed with old-fashioned guns of inferior calibre, the forts of Namur were unable to offer more than a feeble resistance to the weight and power of the German 42 cm. howitzers.

moved southward from Bavai towards the road running from Cambrai to Le Cateau. The First Army Corps retired with its guns along the road running by the River Sambre, from Maubeuge to Maroilles and Landrecies. On its right was a stretch of black country, with smoking factories and flaming ironworks, rising into low hills that ran into a tract of woodland—the Forest of Mormal. Through this some of the infantry had to move in an extended line to guard against a flanking surprise attack by the Germans.

Towards the evening the Guards' Brigade and other regiments of the Second Division began to arrive at the little market town of Landrecies, nestling in the sunset by the Forest of Mormal. Some years ago Robert Louis Stevenson, canoeing down the Sambre, stayed the night at Landrecies and heard the garrison guard going the round in the darkness to the beat of the dream. "It reminded you," he says in his "Inland Voyage," "that even this place was a point in the great warfaring system of Europe, and might on some future day be ringed about with smoke and thunder, and make itself a name among strong towns."

How Stevenson would have rejoiced to learn, had he but lived to full age, the manner in which the name of

PICTURESQUE SCENE AT MAUBEUGE,
showing the locks on the Sambre Canal, one of the busiest centres in the industrial district of Northern France.

Landrecies resounded to the ends of the earth! For it was his countrymen that made the little, sleepy canal town famous. After a hard day's fighting march the Guards' Brigade arrived wet and well-nigh done up, and hoping to have a good rest. They were billeted in the various houses, and were just stretching their legs, about ten o'clock at night, when the alarm was given.

A German army corps had stolen down from the Forest of Mormal and surrounded the place. Some twenty thousand of them had captured a bridge and beaten one of our regiments off. The King's Royal Rifles—1,300 strong—tried to retake it. They kept up a fight till four

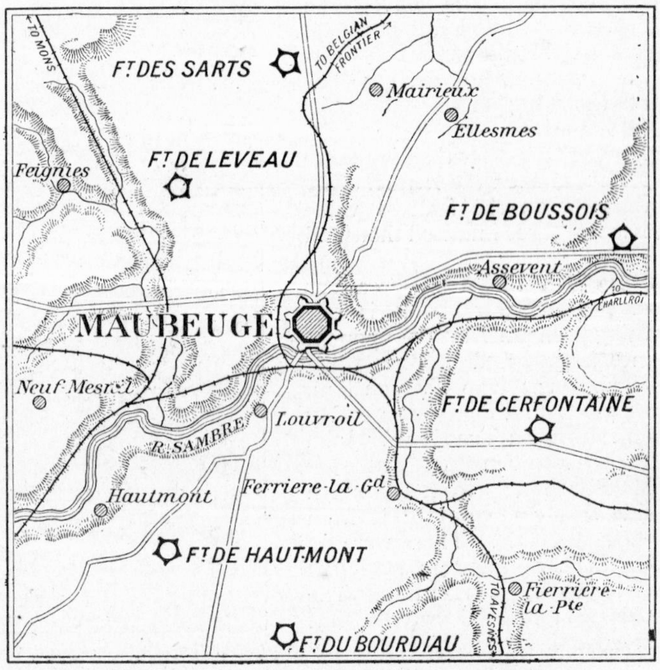

MAUBEUGE AND ITS RING OF FORTS.
Sir John French's men entered the Maubeuge trap from the north side and came safely out of it from the south side, there being an insufficient force of the enemy to keep them in.

ABANDONED BRITISH GUNS AT MAUBEUGE.
While the British escaped from the trap at Maubeuge in which the Germans expected to envelop them, they had to abandon some of their guns, but these were rendered useless before they were left.

SHELLED CUPOLA OF A MAUBEUGE FORT.
Here is another view of the effect of a German 42 cm. projectile on the cupola of a fort. Inset: One of the abandoned British guns.

FORESTALLING THE ENEMY—POWDER MAGAZINE BLOWN UP BY THE FRENCH AT MAUBEUGE.
When the French left Maubeuge before the entry of the Germans they blew up the powder magazine. In this and in other ways both the British and their Allies endeavoured to make the progress of the German attack as difficult and as unprofitable as possible.

FRENCH INFANTRY ON THEIR WAY TO CHARLEROI.
A regiment of French foot soldiers, with full equipment, marching with their traditional swing through one of the towns of Northern France on the way to Charleroi. Inset: A French gun section in action.

o'clock on Wednesday morning, lining a long hedge at intervals of two yards, and firing into the enemy at a range of three hundred yards. They rolled the Germans over by dozens, but at last had to retreat at a run. As they tore away, throwing off their packs and keeping only their weapons, the affair must have struck the riflemen as a defeat. But, while they had been gallantly retaining the infantry by the bridge, great things had been happening in the town.

Here the other division of the German corps had worked down from the forest to the other side of Landrecies and got their artillery into position. Their infantry reached the houses, and the tired British soldiers tumbled out into the streets to fight them. It was a dark night and the lamps were dim. The Coldstream Guards were out first. They fixed bayonets and doubled up the road, and some of our field artillery trundled along to support them. The British commander, in matter of fact, had not been surprised. Knowing that the forest above the town was full of enemies, he had placed outposts to give warning of their coming, while he allowed most of the tired troops to try to get a little rest. But the Germans were resolute to keep all the British force awake and active. So the Battle of Landrecies began.

How the Battle of Landrecies began

In the evening the townspeople had left in crowds, carrying away as much of their light property as they could. While the Coldstreams went out to delay the

FRENCH INFANTRY ADVANCING TO MEET THE GERMAN ATTACK IN THE NEIGHBOURHOOD OF CHARLEROI.
In general alertness in the field and in the power of bearing the strain of long and dusty marches at high pressure the French infantry proved themselves capable of holding their own against any in the world. The spring and lightness of their step in marching was the object of general and ungrudging admiration.

GERMAN ARTILLERY ON THE MARCH.

Germans were greatly indebted to the superior power of their big siege-guns at Liège and Namur. But their ordinary field artillery proved very efficient. Our smaller photograph shows a fleet of motor-cars captured and commandeered by the Germans and drawn up in the barrack square at Mons.

enemy's advance, the rest of the Guards' Brigade tore up paving stones and overturned carts to form barricades for the defence of the heads of the streets. Shell and shrapnel fire began to burst around them, while the sappers were loopholing the houses. Meanwhile the Coldstreams reached the German advanced companies and drove through them with the bayonet in one of the most terrible bayonet charges in the war, after giving them several rounds of fire at almost point-blank range. Not a German got through in the direction the Coldstreams fought. About two hundred of these Guards drove a battalion down a street, their foes squealing when the steel flashed in the light of burning houses and bursting shells. The Germans were bayoneted in scores, and the Coldstreams had to leap over barriers of the men they had slain to get more of their living enemies.

Coldstreams' great bayonet charge

Then, having cleared this thoroughfare that led to the High Street, they came upon a larger mass of them. But, being now reinforced, they pressed on, still climbing over heaps of dead and wounded to get at the others. Afterwards, the Coldstreams raced away to a newly-menaced position, where they once more ran the steel into another dim, surging multitude.

The High Street, however, refilled with a grey sea of spiked helmets, and attempts were made to get round the Coldstreams and cut them off. But each corner house, commanding two ways, had become a rifle fort, manned by squads of Grenadiers and Irish Guards, and there they worked away from ten o'clock on Tuesday night to half-past one the next morning. They all had wonderful escapes, with shrapnel bursting continuously, and high-explosive shells making a deafening racket; houses burning and falling down from the gun fire; rifles always cracking and rising into a furious rattle as the Germans attacked. The enemy's guns were brought in the darkness within fifty yards of our firing-lines. But our gunners brought up a gun

Houses as rifle forts

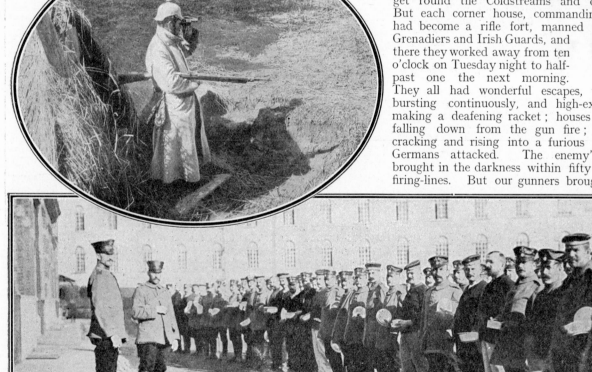

GLIMPSES OF GERMAN TROOPS DURING THE ANGLO-FRENCH RETREAT FROM MONS AND CHARLEROI.

Dinner parade by German soldiers mustered in the barrack square at Mons, and awaiting the call for their midday meal to be served to them in the basin which each was carrying. Inset: A German outpost. Note that the ground had been dug out in front of the shelter in the haystack, and that a board had been provided for the soldier to stand upon.

by hand—no horses could have lived through the stream of bullets and shells—and knocked out one German gun first shot, at sixty yards! For the gun was only a few paces behind our infantry. It was very close fighting for all arms.

The end suddenly came at daybreak, when the Germans were apparently on the point of capturing the town. Many of the Guards had been ordered from the loopholed houses and allowed—to their delight—to join in the bayonet work in the open. A street was left undefended, and an entire brigade of German infantry—some 5,000 men—advanced down the narrow thoroughfare, which they completely packed. It was a trap—a patent trap. A prudent commander would have only thrown a few companies down the street in open order, to search the houses and clear the way, after planting machine-guns at the head of the street. But the German brigadier-general commanding the brigade had not yet had the overweening fatuity of his race knocked out of him. He believed in employing force, as much force as possible, and he did not trouble about the skill necessary in leading troops in the most difficult of all jobs—street-fighting.

When his five thousand men were wedged into the street, our machine-guns, from the other end of the town, smote them. They formed a target no British Maxim lieutenant could miss. The head of the German column was swept away; the men immediately behind were seized with panic, and turned and fought their way back through their hesitating companions. But these did not hesitate when the rain of bullets reached them. The entire brigade broke and fled, leaving some 900 of their fellows lying in the street. There were also many bayoneted in other streets, and a doctor who went out to look after the wounded is said to have found 2,000 Germans dead or injured outside the town.

The total losses of the enemy were literally staggering. They certainly staggered the attacking army in the Forest of Mormal. After our men sent their wounded on by train to Guise, and then withdrew southward towards Wassigny, the German gunners went on shelling Landrecies for hours. The Germans were afraid to enter. The nerve of their infantry was broken. This was extremely fortunate for every man in the First Army Corps of the British Expeditionary Force.

For while its Second Division—or, rather, a part of it—was fighting for life in Landrecies, the First Division and the rest of the Second was in a position of even greater peril at Maroilles, a village of cheesemakers some five miles northward on the road from Maubeuge. Here a terrific rearguard action was fought from dusk to dawn against a new German army that came eastward and almost surrounded our troops in the darkness. Apparently it was not a part of the large force that advanced through the Forest of Mormal. For it came from the other side—from the direction of General von Buelow's field of operations—and encircled Sir Douglas Haig eastward and southward. The First Army Corps, divided between Maroilles and Landrecies, was for a time practically cut in two. While the Guards' Brigade were hewing their way through Landrecies streets, their comrades in Maroilles were almost ringed by a new German host. Sir Douglas Haig found that two French reserve divisions, acting on the flank of the retiring Fifth French Army, were within call. Numbering about 36,000 men, they came gallantly to his help. But it was, as Sir John French reports, mainly due to the skilful manner in which Sir Douglas handled his troops that they fought their way out of a most perilous position. All through the night the battle went on in darkness, lighted only by the flame of bursting shrapnel and shell from the enemy's batteries and the flare of the cottages of the villages. When the conflict opened, many of our troops were so dog-tired they felt they could not stand up and use their rifles. They had already marched and fought and worked for nearly three days, till the last ounce of energy seemed to be used up.

Some of the Munster Fusiliers, for instance, had seen some German lancers swoop down on one of our batteries and kill the detachment and capture the guns. With fixed bayonets the Munsters, in a wild Irish charge, put

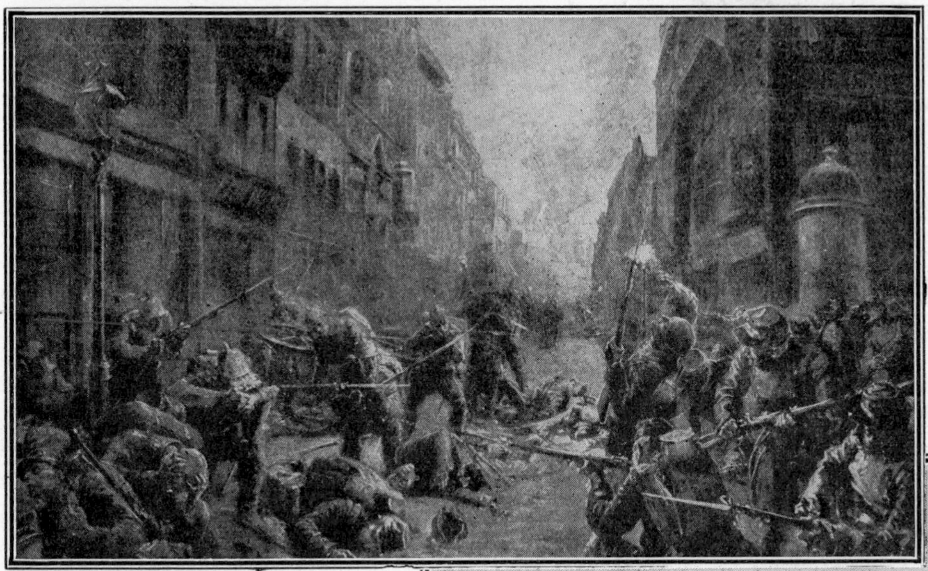

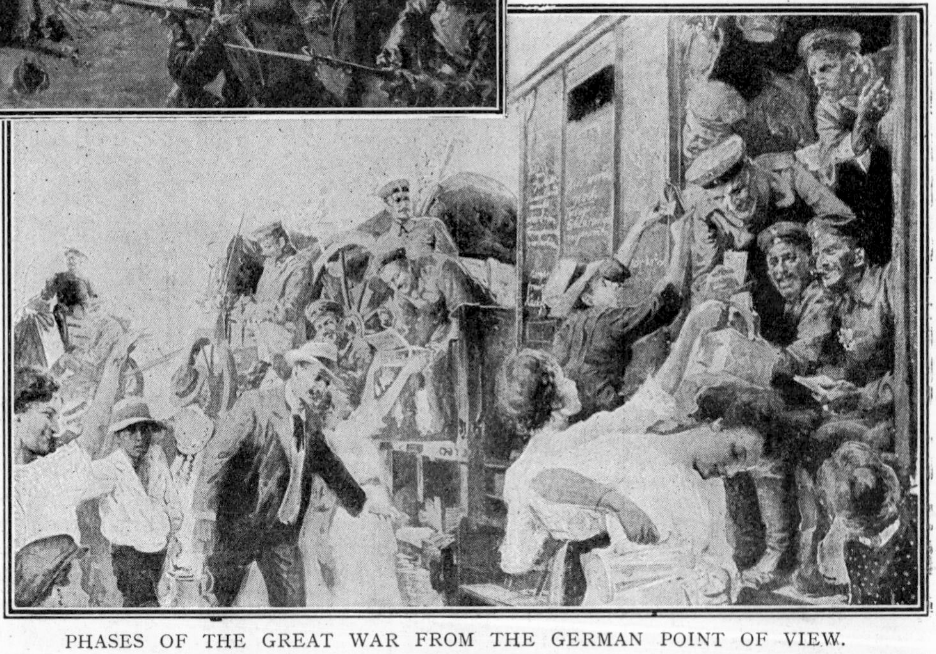

PHASES OF THE GREAT WAR FROM THE GERMAN POINT OF VIEW.

The upper picture, the work of a German artist, represents a fight by night in the streets of Mulhausen. In the lower, also from a Teuton source, is shown the departure of German troops from Leipzig. On the panel of the railway carriage were scrawled in chalk: "Down with Servia!" "Death to Russia!" "Destruction to France!"

the lancers to flight. Then they stood by the recovered guns while the German artillerymen shrapnelled them. The difficulty was that there were no horses available to get the guns along, and the Munsters—only two companies strong with some thousands of Germans in the neighbourhood—were told to abandon the battery and save themselves. It was then our infantryman showed how he loved the great weapons that protected his trenches with their fire, and cleared a path for him when he attacked. The Irishmen harnessed the guns and man-handled them to a place of safety. They captured some of the horses of the German lancers they had killed, and at last got something of a battery team together.

This, no doubt, was an exceptional piece of back-breaking work; but all the men were dull-eyed for weariness and want of sleep. They thought they had come to the end of their powers. But when the German shells began to explode with the sound of a thousand motor-tyres bursting, and the bullets began to sing around them, some hidden store of energy was released in their tired bodies. They went into the sombre, dim night battle with the old fury.

With bullet and bayonet they broke through and swept aside the host that barred their southern road, and their gunners cleared the way in front of them with fanning-out salvos of shrapnel fire. One eye-witness remarks that the Germans in turn might have been ringed with flame and steel if the French reserves had been able to arrive sooner. But, whatever the cause of their initial delay, the French came up in time to help our troops to beat the Germans back so strongly that they did not come on again.

GENERAL C. J. BRIGGS, C.B.
This able officer commanded the First Cavalry Brigade.

Had either German force in the Mormal Forest or on the eastern flank of the First Army Corps been able to continue their attack, they might have had, in the early morning of Wednesday, August 26th, an easy victory. For both British divisions were then dead beat. They just had enough strength to withdraw towards Wassigny, then they dropped down and snatched some sleep.

Sir John French had arranged for Sir Douglas Haig's corps to turn at Landrecies, and line up with the Second Army Corps at Le Cateau. But the men were so utterly spent that they could not move. Some of them dropped out of the march to sleep by the wayside; all of them, after their last fierce battles, had to stop or drop. Since their demonstration towards Binche on Monday morning they had marched farther than the Second Corps. They had had to fight without support on their flank, and they had battled by day and retreated by night until they could do no more. Happily, they had so tired out and shattered the two armies opposed to them, that they could rest for a few hours in safety.

But this exhaustion of an entire army corps—nearly half the total British force—in the critical period of the great rearguard battle, on which depended the safety of both the British soldiers and the northern French armies, desperately increased the difficulties of Sir John French's position. He was now left with his cavalry, General Snow's division, the 19th Infantry Brigade, and the two divisions of Sir Horace Smith-Dorrien's Second Army Corps. In all, at full strength, these may have amounted to some 68,000 men. But deducting the killed, wounded, and missing, and the much

BRITISH WOUNDED AT MONS CARED FOR IN A BELGIAN CONVENT.
A group of British soldiers, who were wounded at the Battle of Mons, photographed with Belgian priests and Sisters of Mercy in the Convent of Villerat, where they received the most careful and kindly treatment.

larger number of men temporarily put out of action by severe marching, there may have been less than 30,000 bayonets in the firing-line, and less than 10,000 sabres and gunners to support them.

In the darkness of Tuesday morning, August 25th, the 19th Infantry Brigade, who had at midnight reached their billets on the flank of the Second Army Corps, moved out eastward to a line of low hills below Valenciennes. There they entrenched with their artillery, which was admirably placed for effective action. The German outflanking force soon attacked them.

German airmen in action

Helped by reconnaissance officers in Taube machines, the German gunners no longer took their usual blundering sighting shots, but got the range at once, and plumped their shrapnel right on to our lines. Their flying men were clever in their work of fire-controlling. They flew low enough to sight our positions, but kept out of range. Our men tried to wing them, but failed. Later, however, they brought one down.

At eleven o'clock in the morning, when the bombardment was reckoned to have done its work fully on our trenches, the routine enveloping movement was attempted. A large force of cavalry, strengthened by horse artillery, circled round, with masses of infantry and guns tailing behind it. But our cavalry division, under General Allenby, forming the extreme left wing of the British force, appeared on the scene. There was a yelling charge at the leading German horsemen, a splatter of fire at those behind, and the curving horn of the German army drew in to its main body. The infantry of part of our Second Army Corps then came into action. Their long lines ran forward between the hills in an eastward attacking movement. They were soon hidden in the folds of the ground, but they caught the German infantry, which was still trying to outflank the 19th Brigade, and inflicted heavy loss on it. The men of the 19th Brigade seem, indeed, to have been moved out in order to entice General von Kluck to practise his daily envelopment system of military tactics.

The severe punishment he received led him to think it would be better to wait and collect a larger force before hemming the British army against Maubeuge, according to programme. Towards twilight the 19th Brigade was able to withdraw south and find comfortable quarters for the night. This freshened them for the great battle the next morning.

General Snow's division

In the meantime General Snow moved up to a position south of the little French weavers' town of Solesmes, with his division extended to the south of Cambrai. Thus placed, his men shielded the retreating Second Army Corps and its supports from an encircling frontal attack by the German army coming from Tournai. General Snow's division played an important part in the concluding battle. It consisted of three infantry brigades. There was the 18th Brigade of the 1st Warwicks, 2nd Seaforth Highlanders, 1st Irish Fusiliers, and 2nd Dublin Fusiliers, commanded by Brigadier-General J. H. L. Haldane. Then the 11th Brigade, made up of the 1st Somerset Light Infantry, 1st East Lancashires, 1st Hampshires, and 1st Rifle Brigade, under Brigadier-General Hunter-Weston. The 12th Brigade —great in the fight—was formed of the 1st Royal Lancashires, the 1st Lancashire Fusiliers, the 2nd Inniskilling Fusiliers, and the 2nd Essex, commanded by Brigadier-General H. F. M. Wilson. The field artillery, under Brigadier-General Milne, consisted of the 14th, 29th, and 32nd Brigades with 18-pounders, the 37th Howitzer Brigade and the 31st Battery of 60-pounders. A cavalry regiment, a bridging train, and the 54th Field Company of Engineers completed the division.

The 12th Infantry Brigade started on Tuesday with a hot engagement. An outpost reported that all was clear, and some of the regiments went up a hill with a large flat top. They ranged up in close formation, and the commanding officer told them to take their packs off. This was the last order he gave. From a wood only four hundred yards in front the Germans opened with machine-gun fire. The Lancashire men were mowed down, for they could get no cover. They rolled off the hill into a long straight road, only to catch it worse. For the Germans had two shrapnel guns at the top of the road that did terrible work.

All this occurred before six o'clock in the morning. The men retired in excellent order for three hundred yards, and then lined up behind a ridge. Till then they had scarcely fired a shot. But their turn came when the German infantry advanced. The British soldiers gave them lead as fast as they could pull the trigger, till they had some nine thousand Germans on the grass

ARRIVAL IN LONDON OF THE FIRST CONTINGENT OF WOUNDED FROM MONS.

Scene at a London railway-station on the arrival of the first contingent of British wounded from the battlefield of Mons. Above is a photograph of women passengers distributing little luxuries among the men on board the Folkestone boat.

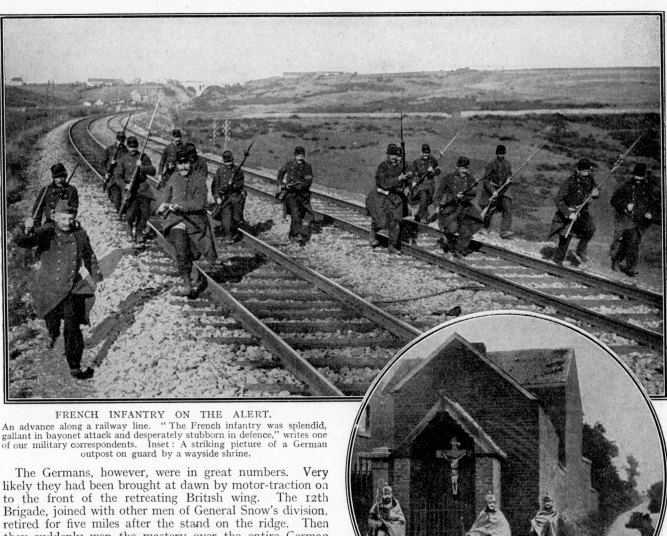

FRENCH INFANTRY ON THE ALERT.

An advance along a railway line. "The French infantry was splendid, gallant in bayonet attack and desperately stubborn in defence," writes one of our military correspondents. Inset: A striking picture of a German outpost on guard by a wayside shrine.

The Germans, however, were in great numbers. Very likely they had been brought at dawn by motor-traction on to the front of the retreating British wing. The 12th Brigade, joined with other men of General Snow's division, retired for five miles after the stand on the ridge. Then they suddenly won the mastery over the entire German force. For the British guns came up and shelled them, and with bayonets fixed our infantry got them on the run and drove them eight miles—three miles beyond the hill where the battle began.

The success of the two actions by the Fourth Division, under General Snow, and the 19th Infantry Brigade on Tuesday morning staved off the enveloping movement round Maubeuge designed by General von Kluck. At the very moment when Berlin was rejoicing over the news that the British army was ringed with steel, flame, and thunder, the British soldier had fought his way out with comparative ease. This was mainly due to the insight and foresight shown by the British commander-in-chief. Sir John French seems to have divined every detail of the German outflanking movement on his eastern wing.

Preparing for the hammer-stroke

He did this on Monday night, before General von Kluck had made his dispositions for the attack. No doubt, the British aerial scouts were able to bring their chief much useful information by Monday evening. But no one could say what movements of the German forces would go on in the darkness. Yet Sir John foresaw what the German commander would do, and had everything prepared at dawn on Tuesday to counter the great hammer-stroke when it fell.

The British cavalrymen were divided into two forces. The larger force acted with the 19th Infantry Brigade, and covered the west flank of the Second Army Corps, both the sabres and the bayonets being under the command of General Allenby. The smaller force, consisting of two cavalry brigades, operated with the two cavalry regiments attached to the Second Army Corps, and covered the movements of the retreating infantry and guns.

There were 100,000 Germans on Tuesday attempting to get round in the front of Sir Horace Smith-Dorrien's weary men. Another hostile host pressed against their rearguards from the Belgian border. Both the British infantrymen and the British cavalrymen had to strike swiftly and often to keep the enemy off. Their gunners worked like demons, and their airmen like guardian angels—with revolvers and passion for aerial duels. The cavalry was especially hard-worked. All their horsemanship was needed to keep their fagged-out mounts going, and in the continual fighting they scattered and found it difficult at times to collect again together for a new concerted movement.

General Hamilton's Third Division does not seem to have been so hard pressed on Tuesday as was Sir Charles Fergusson's Fifth Division on the west flank. The infantry of the Third Division had an easier task in the matter of actual fighting than when they held the salient at Mons. They worked in shifts, covering the retreat by steady rifle fire from hastily-prepared trenches. Thrown out along an extended front, they were instructed to hold their ground until the retiring troops were signalled safe in the next position allotted to them. When this was done, the rearguard retired past this new position and began to dig themselves in farther south. In the meantime the trenches they left were covered by the light cavalry, who kept the Germans in check as long as they could, and then fell back in turn. The next shift then took on the rearguard work till they received the signal to continue the retreat.

The Germans made some tricky moves at times with a view to cutting the rearguards off, but the British flanks were protected by cavalry, and the enemy never got very far ahead without having to fight. They usually withdrew

CORNER HOUSES AS RIFLE FORTS.
In the High Street at Landrecies each corner house, commanding two ways, became a rifle fort, manned by Grenadiers and Irish Guards, who fought from 10 p.m. on the night of Tuesday, August 25th, 1914, until 1.30 the next morning, the unhappy families hiding within in terror.

at critical periods. The British Expeditionary Force did not crawl on its stomach. Innumerable motor-vehicles—lorries, vans bearing the names of great London commercial firms, and motor-omnibuses with their familiar stopping-places painted on them—provided the hundred thousand soldiers fighting in strange lands with food, cartridges, and, at times, happy memories. To a Londoner in a moment of peril, for instance, up came a Hendon 'bus with ammunition that turned the threat of a defeat into a little shattering local victory. Well-engined or well-horsed, the speedy and excellently handled transport kept the British soldier fed, and thus enabled him to bear up against the ordeal of the long retreat. Many a man, worn out for want of sleep, had muscle and nerve whipped up for a new effort by a cup of tea. The eager preparation for tea made by the British soldier amid the fury of the terrible conflict struck some of our observing allies as the quaintest piece of insular phlegm imaginable. To them it was like interrupting the Day of Judgment to have a garden-party. There was an Irish battalion in a most sorrowful mood. They waited in the trenches for hours in the rain for the enemy. At last they came out to get a kettle boiling for tea. And just as the water boiled the Germans attacked. The Irishmen, furious at this intrusion, used their bayonets. The Germans howled for mercy and held up their hands, but the Irishmen tossed them on the steel like hay. But they lost their tea—hence their sorrowfulness.

By six o'clock most of the men of the Second Army Corps were able to have their tea, for the two divisions reached the line that had been partly trenched for them in advance by the sappers. It extended from Le Cateau, an historic French town of some 10,000 townspeople, to the neighbourhood of the village of Caudry, near to Cambrai. From Caudry the British line was continued to Leranv lliers, still closer to Cambrai, by the troops of General Snow's division and two brigades of cavalry, all that General Allenby could concentrate of his scattered squadrons, formed in the early morning south of the famous cathedral city of Cambrai.

Sir John French intended only to let the men rest for a few hours to recover from their exhaustion. Then he wished to continue the retreat until he had put the substantial obstacle of the Rivers Somme and Oise between his troops and the enemy, for they most urgently needed an opportunity for rest and reorganisation. Sir Horace Smith-Dorrien, therefore, was ordered to continue the retirement at dawn towards St. Quentin. The cavalry, under General Allenby, was directed to cover the retirement.

But General von Kluck was at last in a position to force at least the Second British Army to make a stand. He had concentrated near Cambrai the enormous host of five army corps. The German army corps in the early part of the war was larger than the British. It contained about 50,000 men while ours had about 36,000 troops. "In the German attack not less than five corps were engaged," said Lord Kitchener in his statement of the affair. This means that General von Kluck brought up at least 250,000 men against three worn, tired British divisions that cannot have put more than 30,000 rifles, at the very most, into the firing-line.

at any show of resistance, and tried to find a less costly way of impeding the well-planned retreat. But with the British troops at the top of their fighting form, all ways of interfering with them were expensive of life.

Some of the men of Sir Charles Fergusson's Fifth Division arrived on Monday midnight on the Maubeuge-Valenciennes line, and were up again at two on Tuesday morning for a thirty-mile march in wet clothes. What with shifts at rearguard actions and turns at flank defence operations, it took them eighteen hours to cover the thirty miles. They reached their position at 8 p.m., had, happily, a good meal, and next day were up and digging trenches before daybreak. The arrangements for feeding the retreating army appear to have been remarkably good, considering the extraordinary difficulties of the situation.

Work of the Army Service Corps

Here and there a regiment had its transport surrounded, and had to do the march on biscuits, or chance food given by kindly French peasants. But generally the work of feeding the army and bringing up continual supplies of ammunition was admirably carried out. In Wellington's wars in Spain French generals wrote to Napoleon in high praise of the British commander's large, abundant transport. Sir John French's Army Service Corps far excelled Wellington's. It surpassed all similar organisations. The Germans, with all their fame for thoroughness in detailed preparation, often let many of their troops famish

Gale & Polden.]
Brig.-Gen. J. E. GOUGH, C.M.G.,
Third Cavalry Brigade.

Elliott & Fry.]
Brig.-Gen. F. W. N. McCRACKEN,
C.B., D.S.O.

Gale & Polden.]
Brig.-Gen. F. C. SHAW, C.B.,
Ninth Infantry Brigade.

It looks as though either General von Buelow co-operated in the easterly flank attack on Sir Charles Fergusson's Second Division at Maroilles on Tuesday night, or that General von Kluck disposed of a much greater total force than has been estimated. Even with as large an infantry motor-transport service as all available roads made practicable, General von Kluck could not have concentrated in two or three hours almost all his army against Sir Horace Smith-Dorrien. He had a large force at Landrecies, another at Maroilles, yet he attacked on the western flank with at least 250,000 men.

Allow for German losses at Mons and in rearguard actions against Sir Horace Smith-Dorrien's troops, and against General Snow's division and the 19th Infantry Brigade, then add to these losses the number of conscript soldiers fallen out on the march. There would be reinforcements from the direction of Tournai to set against the result. There must have been at least, when everything was deducted from the 250,000 men originally available for all purposes, some 150,000 German bayonets at the Battle of Cambrai-Le Cateau. And there were at least 1,000 German guns against some 250 British guns. So the odds against the three British divisions seem to have been something like five to one in infantrymen and four to one in guns. What the odds were against the two brigades of British cavalry is impossible to calculate—something gigantic.

Such were the material circumstances in which German and Briton clashed in a battle of tremendous importance. At daybreak on the fateful Wednesday, August 26th, our infantry began to dig or deepen their trenches, but they were surprised by the enemy's fire. So strong was the attack that Sir Horace Smith-Dorrien could not safely retire against it. He sent a message to this effect to his commander-in-chief.

"I sent him orders to use his utmost endeavours to break off the action and retire at the earliest possible moment," says Sir John French, "as it was impossible for me to send him any support, the First Corps being at the moment incapable of movement."

So on the generalship of Sir Horace and the fighting ability of each man in his little force everything depended. The battle began with the sound of heavy guns, the Germans bombarding our lines to shatter the resistance of the infantry. Many of our artillerymen masked their guns in corn-sheaves to hide them from the hostile aerial scouts, and reserved their fire as long as possible. But in face of the immense artillery onslaught of the Germans finesse was vain. Shrapnel and high-explosive shell flew like giant hail about our trenches. It was a thunderstorm, mixed up with an earthquake where the heavy howitzer shells struck, and diversified with a hurricane of lead, as the shrieking shrapnel suddenly showed blue wisps of cloud and showered down their bullets.

But our guns came into action, handled by men heroic of mould and finely trained. They had to beat down the fire of the German guns in order to save the British infantry. Despite the odds against them they did it. Our 60-pounders, throwing their big shells with wonderful precision and deadly effect, were a match for two German guns of the same weight. We had not sufficient of these heavy pieces, but what we had were handled so rapidly and with such marksmanship that they smashed double the amount of their metal on the German side.

Our light artillery, with a shorter range and much less powerful shell, was terribly hard put to it to maintain any part in the duel. The story of these batteries is one of the most moving and inspiring in the war. The losses among both men and horses were appalling, yet the sections fought their guns till they dropped. In one battery only

[Gale & Polden.
Brig.-Gen. F. D V. WING, C.B.,
Royal Artillery.

[Bassano.
Lt.-Col. G. P. T. FIELDING, D.S.O.,
3rd Coldstream Guards.

[Gale & Polden.
Brig.-Gen. R. HAKING, C.B.,
General Headquarters Staff.

OFFICERS MENTIONED IN SIR JOHN FRENCH'S DESPATCHES FOR SERVICES IN THE GREAT RETREAT.

HOW THREE THOUSAND BRITISH INFANTRY AT LE CATEAU WITHSTOOD NINE THOUSAND OF THE CRACK PRUSSIAN CAVALRY.

At Le Cateau on August 26th, 1914, the men of the 12th Infantry Brigade performed a noteworthy piece of work. They included the 1st Royal Lancashire Regiment, the 1st Lancashire Fusiliers, the 2nd Royal Inniskilling Fusiliers, and the 2nd Essex Regiment. They stood against the German Cavalry Division of the Guards—the crack mounted division of the German Army. There were some nine thousand superb Prussian horsemen against, perhaps, three thousand British foot soldiers. It was a terrible charge. There was a desperate bout of hand-to-hand fighting—one bayonet against three sabres. Men and horses were mixed together in a swirling yet compact mass. But at last the pride of the German cavalry was thrown back with great loss, and many of them felt the keen edge of the bayonet as they turned and fled.

a junior officer and one man were left, but they contrived to keep a gun in action.

The German airmen searched for our guns, and dropped their smoke bombs to indicate the range. Then the shells fell thick on the British battery, and in some instances the gunners saw, across the battle-line, the German guns coming closer to them.

Undoubtedly the Germans were now courageous to the point of daring. For they were certain the most hated of their opponents were in their grasp. But in the case in question the British battery, with the smoke-bomb shell smouldering near it, turned its two centre guns on the venturous German artillerymen, caught them and hurled flesh and metal up in the air with the force of the exploding lyddite shells.

German gun fire merely deafening

In raking our trenches the hostile batteries fired in modern battleship fashion—no sighting shot, but salvos of bursting cases, filled with bullets and a high-explosive charge to propel them just as the case was bursting. If five shrapnel shells missed, the sixth, it was hoped, would hit. There was at least one German gun against every three hundred British bayonets. With aerial reconnaissance and fire-control, good marksmanship, and well-timed fuses against this number of troops without proper trenches, the German gun fire should have been annihilating. All things considered, it was merely deafening. Some damage it did do—say a fourth of the total flesh injuries of the retreat—a thousand men killed or wounded. This in a bombardment by a thousand cannon for twelve hours, against troops that had no time to entrench their position properly. What incompetence! These gunners were the best-trained troops of an empire of militarism, that had organised for generations for this very battle. By continual war experience the German artilleryman improved, no doubt, as the weeks wore on—any man with a glimmer of intelligence would do that. But it was then too late. He never had a British army at his mercy again, with the fate of France almost depending on his ability. At the Battle of Le Cateau, moreover, his guns were unworn; the rifling was true, and almost every shot should have told—or one in ten—or one in a hundred. They did not.

It is true that nearly all the wounds of our men were caused by shrapnel. But, in the circumstances, this is no testimony to the skill of the German gunner. It is merely evidence against the German infantryman. When the nerve-racking bombardment was presumed to have blown the three British divisions away, the German infantryman advanced to collect the remaining fragments. Very confidently he advanced. For, despite some staggering experiences in the last four days, the deafening thunder of his overpowering guns and the consciousness of his own overwhelming numbers revived his national conceit of superiority in war.

Like the sea at flood-tide racing over a tract of sand, the grey-green billows of the German infantry attack swept on. Wave after wave of them, in companies in close formation, surged towards the British trenches. They fired as they came, bayonets fixed, but they fired just as savages do when they first get muskets. When some African negro tribes, accustomed to charging with long spears, bought a consignment of rifles and bayonets with a view to exterminating another tribe, they were very keen on practising firing. At practice they sighted the rifle from the shoulder, in the proper way, and shot fairly well. But when they went to war with their neighbours and met them, it was the steel they relied on and not the leaden bullets. They came on with bayonets fixed, holding their weapon near the right hip, ready to stab. When they fired they still kept the rifle at the hip in the bayonet-attack position.

So did many of the German infantrymen. They fired from the hip when hundreds of yards from our trenches. Unspeakable was the scorn of the British soldier when he saw it. It was the most disgraceful thing an infantryman in a charge could do. Falling out with a feigned injury was scarcely so bad. For this showed at least that a man's conscious brain was still working. Hip-firing at long distances in a bayonet attack meant blind funk. Held up by the mass and momentum of the charge, and kept going by the stern, alert discipline of the non-commissioned officers, the conscript first-line troops of the greatest modern military nation in the world were yet cowards in a way. They had a sort of mob bravery that kept them surging towards their opponents. But their individual self-control was gone. They could not lift their rifle to their shoulder and sight it, but, with only a primitive instinct remaining for the spear kind of attack, they kept their weapon at the hip, and blindly fired it so.

Without their artillery and machine-guns, half a million troops of this kind would have achieved the same result. It was merely a question of getting up sufficient ammunition to our infantry to enable them to do their deadly work.

IRISH GUARDS AT PRAYER BEFORE GOING INTO ACTION.
Ordered to take an exposed German position, it is recorded that before going into action the Irish Guards knelt for a moment in silent prayer. Then, springing to their feet, they fixed bayonets and charged across the plateau. Many fell, but the German position was carried.

IRISH FUSILIERS AT WORK WITH THE BAYONET.

In the fighting between Landrecies and Cambrai an Irish battalion waited in the trenches for hours in the rain for the enemy At last they came out to get a kettle boiling for tea. Just as the water boiled the Germans attacked. The Irishmen, furious at the intrusion, used their bayonets, and "tossed the Germans on the steel like hay." Inset: A happy, if brief, interval between the fighting.

For some years they had been practising in sport "the mad minute." In sixty seconds most of them could fire fifteen rounds, and hit ten or eleven times out of the fifteen. Some of them could aim and fire one in three seconds—twenty rounds in "the mad minute," and fifteen hits out of them.

Now, when an enemy advances five deep in close formation, the modern bullet, driven by the new smokeless powder, will often go through several men ranged behind each other. This was what happened, and with such speed and precision that it seemed as though every British soldier was working a Maxim gun, instead of a magazine rifle. There was a time when the three divisions were practically ringed by enemy guns on one side and hostile infantry on all sides. There may have been a narrow gap, with a field hospital and some transport, all under gun-fire. But a member of the German General Staff, talking over the matter afterwards with a Dane, maintained that Sir Horace Smith-Dorrien's men were at last "literally surrounded."

Ordeal of "the mad minute"

But when the order came for the British lines to be stormed, it was the Germans, in their strategical position of victory, who were defeated. The nearer they advanced to our trenches the more they were slaughtered. When they were so numerous that even "the mad minute" left them standing in considerable numbers, the bayonet routed them. They came on like waves of a tide running to the flood, but broke, as waves often do on the British coast, against a wall of rock.

The picked marksmen of the German Army were then sent forward to attack us in Boer fashion. We, however, had a remarkable number of first-rate shots, in spite of the comparative smallness of our force. They beat the snipers at their own game. So all the German artillery resumed its thunderous work of pulverisation. When the firing ceased the German Staff officers expected to find that their foes had fled. But beyond the shell-swept zone they saw, through their field-glasses, the caps of the British troops. In sheer desperation at obtaining any decision the infantry masses were launched again and again to the assault, the cavalry trying to ride down our outer trenches.

A noteworthy piece of work was done by the 12th Infantry Brigade. This, it will be remembered, was composed of the 1st Royal Lancashire Regiment, the 1st Lancashire Fusiliers, the 2nd Royal Inniskilling Fusiliers, and the 2nd Essex Regiment. They had already suffered heavily on the hill-top on Tuesday. At Le Cateau on Wednesday they stood against the German Cavalry Division of the Guards—the crack mounted division of the German Emperor. It was some nine thousand superb horsemen against, perhaps, three thousand foot soldiers. It was a terrible charge. There was a desperate bout of hand-to-hand fighting, one bayonet against three sabres. Men and horses were mixed together in a swirling and yet compact mass. At last the German cavalry was thrown back with great loss and in complete disorder, and some of them got the bayonet in the spine as they turned to flee.

The end came about half-past three on this memorable Wednesday afternoon. The enemy was then so worn and shattered by continual repulses that his attacks weakened. The weary but exulting British infantrymen began to withdraw to the south, covered by their heroic gunners, standing up and answering the final violent massed-fire of the unavailing German artillery.

The retreat was continued far into the night of August 26th by the order of Sir John French, anxious over the movements of the enemy. All the next day and through Friday, August 28th, the southward march went on, till the outworn troops rested round the lovely old cathedral town of Noyon by the placid Oise. But there was no danger of any energetic pursuit by General von Kluck. All risk of disaster to the retiring yet invincible Britons was averted. The supreme test had come, and the men of our race had risen to the heights of heroism of our forefathers. They had saved us from disaster, and shielded France.

FRENCH INFANTRY IN ACTION DURING THE GREAT RETREAT.

CHAPTER XXIX.

WITH THE NORTHERN FRENCH ARMIES DURING THE GREAT RETREAT.

Fifth French Army Hard Pressed at Charleroi—The Deadly 3 in. Gun—General Pau's Arrival from Alsace—A Transformation—German Self-confidence Played On—The Red River by Dinant—Sedan Avenged at Charleville—Fighting at Longwy and Toul—General Joffre's Napoleonic Way—The Flight of the Citizens from the Sagging Battle-line.

WHILE the British Expeditionary Force was holding back the great enveloping movement of the main German army, and then saving itself and the Fifth and Fourth French Armies from an overwhelming, outflanking attack, the northern forces of France were fighting their way southward. The British troops seem to have escaped more lightly than their immediate comrades-in-arms at Charleroi. For the gallant Fifth French Army, after the passage of the Sambre was forced on its right, was placed in a difficult position by the failure of the Fourth Army to hold Givet, close to the point where the Meuse flows from France into Belgium.

Pressed in the rear by the army of General von Buelow, with General von Hausen, commanding the Saxon Army and the Prussian Guard, operating near their right wing, the men of the Fifth Army of France had to retire with all possible speed. For in front of them a body of Germans was advancing on Rocroi, near their distant path of retreat. To protect the retiring infantry and guns, the horsemen of the two divisions of French cavalry on the western flank rode their mounts to a standstill. As we have seen, their commander, General Sordet, was unable to get the horses to move afterwards to help our men in their hour of difficulty.

The light, deadly 3 in. French gun proved superb in the rearguard actions. It was so handy, so mobile, and yet so terribly effective. With a little support from its own troops it could break the force of an attack, and then rapidly withdraw to a new position from which to continue its work. Two divisions of the Fifth French Army, however, are said to have suffered somewhat heavily in the retreat. But at least it held the Germans who were pursuing it.

Then General Joffre showed what kind of man he was. Just where he had been struck he struck back. General Pau arrived from Alsace with large reinforcements, and the Fifth Army, that seemed so weak, suddenly became the strongest in France. Increased by a masterly use of railway transportation to four army corps, it unexpectedly turned on its pursuer at Guise. The German Guard, its reserve corps, and the Tenth German Army Corps were thoroughly defeated, the Guard and the Tenth Corps being driven over the Oise. The French commander-in-chief had, with characteristic subtlety, played on the overweening self-confidence of the German general, who regarded himself as advancing from victory to victory. He was tripped up and thrown back across the river by a retreating army.

The struggles of the Fourth Army, operating from the Meuse, were heroic. Round the picturesque old riverside town of Dinant, where they had triumphed a little while before, the French were heavily outnumbered. They fell back, and their artillery, from the distant wooded heights above the river, swept the advancing German invaders with melinite shell, while the infantry left their trenches for fresh positions southward. The

THE MULE AS AN AID IN TRANSPORT.

With the motor-lorry and the horse the mule took its place in the French supply column and proved of excellent service, as it has done in the British Indian frontier wars.

WHERE THE FRENCH ARMY TURNED ON THE PURSUERS.
At Guise the Fifth French Army, reinforced, turned and routed the Germans. The above view shows a group of Uhlans entering Guise after the bombardment. Inset: A view in the old quarter of the town.

Germans in their hour of victory were prodigal of life. At any cost to themselves they bore back the Frenchmen in the mass attacks that German commanders regarded as the only effective use of infantry.

The wide, beautiful river was strewn with floating bodies of men and horses, and in some hotly-contested places the water took for a time a red tinge. The ravines with their flashing tributary rills, forming natural lines of defence along the side of the main river course, were choked with broken cannon fodder. The most furious fighting was for the possession of the bridges. But the French engineers blew them up as the army withdrew to the French frontier. Terrible as was the German chief's sacrifice of his men, it produced at last the desired result.

Just near the threshold of France, at the little Belgian river town of Givet, the German troops got across the Meuse. Some of them advanced on Rocroi, and thence to Rethel; others ascended the Meuse against a magnificent resistance by the French. At one point a French brigade of some 5,000 troops beat back a German division of some 20,000 in a fight lasting twelve hours. In all, ninety-five German guns were said to have been taken in the river battles.

The mined bridges at Charleville

The steadily increasing power of resistance in our Allies culminated at Charleville, a town lying on the French Meuse opposite to Mezières. It is near Sedan and the great hollow in the hills in which the main French army and its leader were trapped in 1870 by Germans occupying the encircling heights. The modern French general was determined to avenge Sedan in his own way, and enable his tired troops to withdraw safely.

On Monday, August 24th, the town of Charleville was evacuated. The civilians were sent away to join the hundreds of thousands of homeless wanderers. The French army also retired, leaving a few machine-guns behind, and the French gunners concealed themselves in positions commanding the town and the three bridges that connected it with Mezières. The following day the German advanced guards came towards the two towns. They rode across the bridges into the deserted streets, and after they crossed three tremendous explosions took place behind them. The bridges, mined in preparation, had been fired. The German cavalrymen were smitten by machine-gun fire; but having Maxims with them, and, finding their foes were not numerous, they made a stand. Every French machine-gun firer was at last brought down, but at a dreadful price.

THE CASTLE AND FORTIFIED ROCK OF BELFORT.
The scene of the famous siege in 1870. It was here, in the Place des Armes, that General Pau decorated Capt. Langlois, of the French Aviation Corps, for his daring flight from Verdun to Metz.

When the main invading army advanced along the river valley, the French artillery high on the hills raked the column with shrapnel. The head of it was blown away; but, under a continual gun fire, the sappers threw their pontoon bridges across the Meuse, while the German artillerymen had to engage in a duel with the French. But the Frenchmen went on firing at the river bank until the signal was given to retire. Afterwards, between Charleville and Rethel, there was another stubborn battle, with the Germans pushing on, in reckless bravery against gun fire, and winning a victory that was also a grave.

Eastward, between Charleville and the great fortress of Verdun, the sag of the French forces went on. An army from Charleville—or rather, from its sister town of Mezières—was repulsed from the Semois region of the Ardennes by Duke Albrecht of Würtemberg with a large force. Then at Longwy, an antiquated fortress town near Verdun, the army of the Crown Prince succeeded in bursting into France, after a long siege operation, and advanced towards the Forest of Argonne on August 27th.

German Crown Prince at Longwy

On that day, the day after the Le Cateau battle, things looked very black for France. The British army did not know yet if it had saved itself. Everywhere else, from the coast almost to Verdun, there was a Franco-British retreat. At Nancy, on August 25th, there had been a fierce encounter between the Crown Prince of Bavaria and the garrison of Toul.

WAR BENEATH THE EARTH.
Unable on one occasion to silence a German gun, the French drove a gallery fifty yards through the ground to a spot immediately under the gun, with the result shown in our illustration.

LAND-MINE EXPLOSION.
The terrific displacement of earth on the explosion of one of the land-mines laid during war is shown very graphically in the above remarkable photograph.

But General Joffre was working to improve the splendid fighting forces of his great nation. Under his direction General D'Amade, on the left of the British force, organised a new Sixth Army, out of four reserve army divisions, a regular army corps, and General Sordet's cavalry. On the right of our troops came the famous victorious General Pau. Then, between General Pau's Fifth Army and the Fourth Army, General Foch interposed with a new Ninth Army, formed of three corps from the south. What is still more important, General Joffre, while leaving his re-formed battle-front to test the enemy's strength again in such battles as that at Guise, continued the general retreat on France. For he found that the new Sixth French Army, being mainly reserve troops, was not strong enough for his secret purpose. It was so unsuccessful in resisting the attack of General von Kluck's great army that all Northern France had to be left open to the enemy. But General Joffre was not perturbed. His single aim was to defeat the enemy. He was fighting in the Napoleonic way. He had a strong general reserve near Paris. It could be used to reinforce the allied line at any point where the enemy could be pierced or turned. General Joffre waited for his opportunity. The nearer Kluck came to Paris the greater danger he would run.

Meanwhile, throughout Northern France was the unexpected, sublimely pathetic spectacle of French women and children fleeing again from the old foe. First came the vast, stricken multitudes of Flemings from over the border. Scarcely had they crossed the frontier southward when French figures began to mingle with them. The flight from the neighbourhood of the sagging battle-line was heartbreaking at times to see—the broken men coming from the lost trenches, the death-carts rumbling along the roads, and the stream of hundreds of thousands of families. It was the menace of the Uhlans and the terror born in Belgium that made them homeless. In the same districts in 1870 there was not such sickening fear of the German. He had become worse since the age of Bismarck.

THE BATTLE OF CAMBRAI—WHERE THE GORDONS WERE TRAPPED BY THE ENEMY.

During the Battle of Cambrai the Gordons were in the trenches at seven o'clock on the morning of August 26th, 1914. The Germans were holding the village and wood beyond the railway. In the course of the afternoon an officer galloped up to the trenches with an order for their retirement. He had time to give the order only to one battalion when he was killed. The result was that only part of the Gordons effected a retirement. The others were cut off, and the majority of them had to be reported as missing. A few, however, hewed their way back to the British lines. Most of the company which got the order to retire were wounded as they made their way across the open country under the enemy's fire. "Though," wrote one of the men, "there was a rumour next day that Colonel Gordon was all right, we never saw him again."

WHERE PEACE TRAINING TELLS. BRITISH INFANTRY AT THE DOUBLE.

CHAPTER XXX.

THE COURSE OF EVENTS FROM MONS TO LEMBERG.

British Marines at Ostend—Lord Kitchener's First Speech as War Minister—The Rally from Overseas—Mr. Asquith's Appeal—Chancellor and War Finance—Japanese Ultimatum to Germany—Mines on the High Seas—The Balkan Imbroglio—Crown Prince and Kaiser—Parliament and King Albert—French Successes in Lunéville and Nancy—Surrender of Togoland and Apia—Operations in Poland and Galicia—Mr. Churchill and the American Interviewer.

SIMULTANEOUSLY with the retreat of the Allies from Mons, the advance guard of Uhlans of the German right wing, which was forging its way to the Belgian coast and that of North-East France, began on August 23rd a raid through Thielt, Thourout, and Leffinge, towards Ostend. The mail boat Marie Henriette was there commandeered for the conveyance of all the regular troops still left in the town to Antwerp—the main garrison having been transferred thence on the 21st. In order to avoid German reprisals, the town-guard was disarmed. A large part of the civil population had already departed—the majority for England. The British admiral, who was lying outside with his fleet, and was aware from his aviators of the presence in the immediate neighbourhood of marauding Uhlans, offered to land a force sufficient to defend the town, but the offer was declined. The City Fathers, however, altered their minds when they heard of an engagement between Germans and a sortie party of Belgian troops from Antwerp towards Malines; and in response to a request to the British Government through the Belgian Minister in London, Count de Lalaing, the First Lord of the Admiralty commissioned the admiral to land a force of Marines, with quick-firing machine-guns, at Ostend. In these operations round Malines a German detachment drove captured civilians, women, and children before them in order to prevent the Belgian soldiers, defending their own homeland, from firing at the invaders.

And what of the situation in England? On August 25th Lord Kitchener made his first speech as War Minister in the House of Lords. The passages in which he referred to the behaviour of our troops at Mons, to the response made by the young manhood of the country to his call to arms, were cheered with a vehemence rarely heard in that august assembly. He began by saying that he belonged to no party, for as a soldier he had no politics, and that the terms of his service were like those of the new Army, "Only for the war, or, if it lasts longer, then for three years, when there would be others fresh and fully prepared to take their places and see this matter through." The conflict, he continued, was none of Britain's seeking; it would strain the resources of the Empire and entail considerable sacrifices on the people. But these would be willingly borne for our honour and the preservation of our position in the world, and would be shared by our Dominions beyond the seas, who were sending contingents and assistance of every kind to help the Mother Country in this struggle. He quoted Sir John French's despatch on Mons: "Our troops have already been for thirty-six hours in contact with the superior German invaders, and during that time they have maintained the traditions of British soldiers, and have behaved with the utmost gallantry. The movements which they have been called upon to execute have been those which demand the greatest steadiness in the soldiers and skill in their commanders. In spite of hard marching and fighting, the British force was in the best of spirits." To this despatch his lordship said he replied: "Congratulate troops on their splendid work. We are all proud of them."

SOME OF THE MEN WHO OUTFOUGHT THE GERMANS.

British soldiers who took part in the desperate fighting between Mons and Cambrai on their way to a new position in Northern France.

Lord Kitchener added: "We know how deeply the French people appreciate and value the prompt assistance we have been able to afford them at the very outset of the war, and it is obvious that not only the moral but the material support our troops are now rendering must prove to be a factor of high military significance in restricting the sphere and determining the duration of hostilities. Had the conditions of strategy permitted, everyone in this country would have rejoiced to see us ranged in that superb struggle against desperate odds which has just been witnessed. But although this privilege was perforce denied to us, Belgium knows of our sympathy with her in her sufferings, and our indignation at the blows which have been inflicted upon her, and also of our resolution to make sure that in the end her sacrifices will not have been unavailing. While other countries engaged in this war have, under a system of compulsory service, brought their full resources of men into the field, we, under our national system, have not done so, and can therefore still point to the vast reserve drawn from the resources both of the Mother Country and of the British Dominions across the seas. The response which has already been made by the great Dominions abundantly proves that we do not look in vain to these sources of military strength, and while India, Canada, Australia, and New Zealand are all sending us powerful contingents, in this country the Territorials are replying with loyalty to the stern call of duty which has come to them with such exceptional force. Over seventy battalions have, with fine patriotism, already volunteered for service abroad, and when trained and organised in the larger formations, will be able to take their place in the line. The 100,000 recruits for which in the first place it has been thought necessary to call have been already practically secured, and this force will be trained and organised in divisions similar to those which are now serving on the Continent. But behind these we have our Reserves.

British sympathy for Belgium

THE HISTORIC MEETING AT THE GUILDHALL ON SEPTEMBER 4TH, 1914.

The Prime Minister, the Leader of the Opposition, Mr. Balfour, and other prominent politicians spoke on a combined platform, and made eloquent appeals for recruits. Mr. Asquith's speech was reproduced throughout the world with the best effect, especially in neutral countries.

"The special Reserves have each their own part to play in the organisation of our national defence. The empires with whom we are at war have called to the colours almost their entire male population. A principle we, on our part, shall observe is this: that while their maximum forces undergo a constant diminution, the reinforcements we prepare shall steadily and increasingly flow out until we have an army in the field which, in numbers not less than in quality, will not be unworthy of the power and responsibilities of the British Empire."

Mr. Asquith followed up this appeal for "more and still more men" in the House of Commons. Following these splendid speeches there was a rush of recruits all over the country. Everywhere throughout France in political, military, and Press circles, Lord Kitchener's "vibrating and resolute deliverance," as the "Liberté" called it, was gracefully appreciated.

The measures taken by the Chancellor of the Exchequer, of course with the approval of the Cabinet, to increase banking facilities and so maintain the trade of the country at the normal, met with general approval—Mr. Austen Chamberlain, a former Unionist Chancellor of the Exchequer, declaring in the House of Commons that Mr. Lloyd George had "dealt with all these questions with great tact, great skill, and great judgment." That Minister also introduced, and succeeded in getting Bills unanimously passed, to check the harsh exercise of legal powers by creditors, and to prevent the summary selling up of homes. These enabled the Government to bring the moratorium to an end. One result was that when the Government placed on the market Treasury Bills for £15,000,000, a total of not less than £40,000,000 was offered.

The Minister for Belgium in London communicated on August 25th to the British Government and the Press the report of the Committee of Inquiry appointed, on command of King Albert, by the Belgian Minister of Justice, and presided over by him, to investigate the charges of acts of savagery, degenerate, abysmal, committed by German troops in various parts of rural and urban districts of Belgium wherever the Teuton hordes had penetrated. The committee comprised the highest judicial and university authorities of Belgium, such as Chief Justice Van Iseghem, Judge Nys, Professors Cottier, Wodon, and others, and their report more than bore out the details of outrages given in Chapter XXIV. of our history.

Hitherto the operations of war had been confined to Europe, but now these were suddenly, though not altogether unexpectedly, extended to the Far East, and the great conflict became in fact as well as metaphor world-wide.

Japan declared war against Germany on August 23rd, on the refusal of the latter to concede demands made by the former in an ultimatum presented the previous day. These demands were that Germany should (1) immediately withdraw or disarm her warships in Chinese and Japanese waters; (2) hand over the German Protectorate of Kiao-Chau in China to Japan for restoration to China. The rescript formally declaring war set forth: "We, by the Grace of Heaven, Emperor of Japan, on the throne occupied by the same Dynasty from time immemorial, do hereby make the following Proclamation to our loyal and brave subjects. We hereby declare war against Germany, and we command our Army and Navy to carry on hostilities against that Empire with all their strength. The action of Germany has compelled Great Britain, our Ally, to

Japan declares war

THE GRAND DUKE NICHOLAS—GENERALISSIMO OF THE RUSSIAN ARMIES.

The Grand Duke Nicholas, the regenerator of the Russian Army, was fifty-eight years of age when the war broke out, and had been for some time general of cavalry and military commander of Petrograd. A former President of the Council of National Defence, he had laboured ever since the war with Japan to reorganise the military forces of the Tsar. A soldier from his youth, he gathered around him the best generals, many of whom proved the value of his judgment by their prowess in Galicia and in the fighting on the Prussian frontier.

"KAMERAD . . . PARDON!" HANDS-UP METHOD OF GERMAN SURRENDER.

German stragglers, caught by the British or French, frequently surrendered by throwing down their arms, holding up their hands, and calling out the two words "Kamerad . . . Pardon!" Many incidents of the kind have been recorded in soldiers' letters home. The hands-up method had the advantage that it put it out of a prisoner's power to attempt any individual act of treachery. At the same time it showed a consciousness of what had been done previously by Germans who, pretending to surrender, took the first opportunity of abusing the confidence of their captors.

FLASHING THE SIGNAL TO CHARGE BY SEARCHLIGHT.

A remarkable picture of a remarkable incident during the fighting in France. The enemy at an early stage of the war showed a constant desire to surprise the British by night attacks. On many occasions they found the British more than equal to them in this form of warfare. Our searchlights having found the position of the enemy, gave the signal to the British troops to advance by flashing the sign of the cross in the sky, whereupon soldiers who had been anxiously waiting for the order, leaping from the trenches, successfully charged and discomfited the foe.

French army corps taking up a position under cover of its artillery. At the outset the guns of the Allies were mainly occupied in the task of replying to the enemy's gun-fire, but later the balance was adjusted so that the Anglo-French artillery was able to render effective protection to infantry movements.

French infantry and cavalry with transport waggon passing through a village in Northern France. The frequent passage of troops on active service through the French hamlets made it impossible to keep the rural population in ignorance of the great events that were toward.

French dragoons with mitrailleuses going into action. The uses to which these handy but deadly weapons were put by cavalry and infantry alike had a great deal to do with the difference between reverse and victory; and the French handled their light artillery with remarkable skill and judgment.

WITH OUR FRENCH ALLIES—HORSE, FOOT, AND ARTILLERY—IN THE FIELD.

open hostilities against that country, and Germany is at Kiao-Chau, its leased territory in China, busy with warlike preparations, while her armed vessels cruising the seas of Eastern Asia are threatening our commerce and that of our Allies. Peace in the Far East is thus in jeopardy. Accordingly, our Government and that of his Britannic Majesty, after a full and frank communication with each other, agreed to take such measures as may be necessary for the protection of the general interests contemplated in the Agreement of Alliance; and we, on our part, being desirous to attain that object by peaceful means, commanded our Government to offer with sincerity an Advice to the Imperial German Government. By the last day appointed for the purpose, however, our Government failed to receive an answer accepting their Advice."

On August 24th the Austrian Government issued orders to the cruiser Kaiserin Elizabeth, then lying in Kiao-Chau Harbour, to disarm, and that her crew should proceed to Tientsin.

Maritime proceedings and the ordinary course of trade by vessels even of neutral Powers began to be compassed with new dangers. Up to August 23rd the British Admiralty had not laid any mines, floating or stationary, in any part of the high seas, but reserved to themselves the utmost liberty of taking action in the future against this new form of warfare. On that date two Danish vessels, the Maryland and Broberg, when taking the ordinary trade routes in the North Sea, away from the British coast, were destroyed by mines laid by the Germans; and two Dutch steamers, clearing from Swedish ports, were blown up in a similar manner by mines laid in the Baltic.

"IT IS NOTHING, MESSIEURS—IT IS FOR FRANCE!"

The intrepid valour of the men of the French ambulance corps is well illustrated in the above picture. One of these—said to be a wealthy merchant of Paris who volunteered for medical service—a gentleman who had never been under fire in his life before, greatly distinguished himself in picking up fallen men under heavy fire and conveying them on his back to safety. When congratulated by military officers for his conspicuous bravery, he answered: "It is nothing, messieurs—it is for France." Of such was the spirit nerving all ranks in the French Army.

An aftermath of the Balkan imbroglio two years before, when the effort was made by the various kingdoms and principalities to finally throw off Turkish domination, and politically reconstruct the peninsula according to the principles of nationality, was the condition of Albania. This mountainous area, inhabited by warlike tribes of various races—Albanians, Slavs in the north-west, and of Greeks in the south, whose aspiration was to be joined to their fellows in Epirus—formed a cockpit in which there were ever recurrent vendettas and religious feuds. The Powers most interested—Russia, Turkey, Austria, which had a longing eye for the Albanian ports on the Adriatic, and Great Britain—diplomatically attempted to solve the difficult problem of a settlement by creating Albania into an independent principality, and this was eventually accomplished by an International Conference held in London on May 30th, 1913. The ruler selected was Prince William Frederick Henry of Wied, who was duly installed as "Mpret," or ruler, with some considerable ceremony and apparent goodwill on the part of his diverse subjects. But peace lasted only a few weeks. Different camarillas made violent efforts to get possession of the Mpret, and invaded his palace at Durazzo, which had been created the capital, and for his protection Austrian and British troops were landed. Throughout these troublesome events Prince Wilhelm did not show himself either very wise or heroic. In the last week of August Albania was in a state of complete anarchy, a reflection of the big war in the west and east of Europe, and on the 23rd the Prince, accompanied by his wife, Princess Sophie of Schönburg-Waldenburg, and children, fled from Durazzo on the way back to Germany, viâ Brindisi.

Heroic defence of Longwy

An official announcement was made in Berlin on August 24th that the German Crown Prince had victoriously repulsed the enemy at Longwy. That place is a very old fortress of Eastern France, situated a short distance from the Luxemburg frontier. Its garrison consisted of only one battalion, and it had been bombarded since August 3rd by the German Crown Prince's army, which had been trying to break through the French lines, in order to conform with the advance of the German right in north-east France and Belgium. After holding out for twenty-one days, when more than half of the garrison had been killed or wounded, it was surrendered to the enemy. The governor, Lieut.-Colonel Baroche, had conferred upon him by the French President the Legion of Honour for his heroic defence. It was this "glorious victory" over less than half a battalion which set Berlin delirious with joy.

The Kaiser sent the following telegram to the Crown Princess, evidently in answer to one of congratulation from her Royal Highness: "My most sincere thanks, my dear child. I rejoice with you on Wilhelm's"—the Crown Prince—"first victory. How magnificently God has supported him! Thanks and honour be to Him! I bestow upon Wilhelm the Iron Cross of the first and second class. Oscar"—the Kaiser's fifth son—"is also said to have fought brilliantly with his Grenadiers. He has received the Iron Cross of the second class. Inform Ina Marie"—the Countess Ina von Bassewitz, whom Prince Oscar married on the eve of the war. "May God protect and continue to help the boys, and be with you and all the women."

GENERAL DE CASTLENAU.
This brilliant French commander was made a Grand Officer of the Legion of Honour for his fine defence of Nancy.

The unctuous self-conceit of this message is only equalled by the prayer which his Imperial Majesty, early in August, ordered to be included in the Liturgy at all public services in the churches: "Almighty and Merciful God, lead us to victory, and give us grace that we may show ourselves to be Christians towards our enemies as well." These eminently pious sentiments may be contrasted with another message—that, for instance, which he despatched to the German troops with the expedition for the relief of Peking, China, then invested by the rebels, on July 27th, 1900: "When you meet the foe you will defeat him. No quarter will be given; no prisoners will be taken. Let all who fall into your hands be at your mercy. Gain a reputation like the Huns under Attila."

The impious prayer of the Huns

When the news of the Longwy victory became known in Berlin on August 24th, as already stated, huge crowds collected opposite the Royal palace. The Empress and Crown Princess had to appear several times in response to cheers for "the fresh message of victory," and both the Royal ladies embraced on the balcony and cried with joy! Universal indignation was felt, not only in western Europe, but in England, her Dominions beyond the seas, and in America at the completion of the ruthless destruction, on August 25th, of Louvain by the Germans. This quaint city of 45,000 inhabitants was the joy of its own people, and the lovers of art and learning everywhere. The cathedral of St. Pierre, a stately monument of world interest, is now a heap of fire-blackened bricks and masonry. The exquisite town-hall and other public buildings of unrivalled architecture of the fifteenth century were shattered and levelled to the ground by German shells. Worst of all, the fine group of pavilions which housed the ancient university, known for hundreds of years as the Oxford of Belgium, was shattered to fragments, and the priceless library of 70,000 volumes and MS. were burned—a loss to letters greater than ever happened since the destruction of the Library of Alexandria by the Saracen invaders of Egypt. The excuse made by the Germans was that the civil inhabitants of Louvain had fired upon their troops; but the real fact was that a body of Germans, making for the town in disorder after a scrimmage with Belgian forces outside, were fired upon by their friends in occupation of the city, and the Kaiser's commander, in a moment of passion, to cover the blunder of his own men, ordered the city to be fired and the ashes to be scattered to the winds.

Unparalleled loss to Letters

GENERAL FOCH.
He was in command of the 20th French Army Corps at Nancy, greatly distinguishing himself there and in later operations.

The heroic defence of Liège, which has been dealt with in Chapter XXIV., came to an end on August 24th, when Major Nameche, commandant, blew up Fort Chaudfontaine, which covered the railway line between Aix-la-Chapelle and Liège by way of Verviers and the tunnel of Chaudfontaine. It was therefore of enormous importance to the Germans, and had been under continual fire since the enemy appeared before Liège. When resistance was no longer possible, Major Nameche barred up the tunnel by colliding a number of locomotive engines, and afterwards set fire to the mass. His mission was at an end, and he determined that the Germans should not take possession of his little stronghold. He lighted a fuse at the powder magazine, and blew up the fort, and himself with it. Can such an act of heroism ever be forgotten?

It was felt throughout Great Britain that some recognition should be made of these ever-memorable events by Parliament on behalf of the nation. Accordingly, on August 27th, the following resolution was carried by acclamation in both Houses: "That a humble Address be presented to his Majesty praying him to convey to his Majesty the King of the Belgians the sympathy and admiration with which this House regards the heroic resistance offered by his Army and his people to the wanton invasion of his territory, and an assurance of the determination of this country to support in every way the efforts of Belgium to vindicate her own independence and the public law of Europe."

Parliament and suffering Belgium

Mr. Asquith moved the resolution in the House of Commons in a speech loftily phrased and perfectly delivered, which moved the House to generous enthusiasm and stirred its finest emotions. How was it, he asked, that we interfered in this tremendous conflict? It was because "we were bound by our obligations, plain and paramount, to assert and maintain the threatened independence of a small and neutral State. Belgium had no interest of her own to serve, save and except the one supreme and overriding interest of every State, great or little, which is worthy of the name—the preservation of her integrity and of her national life. History tells us that the duty of asserting and maintaining that great principle, which is, after all, the well-spring of civilisation and of progress, has fallen once and again at the most critical moments in the past to States relatively small in area and in population, but great in courage and in resolve—to Athens and Sparta, the Swiss Cantons, and, not least gloriously three centuries ago, to the Netherlands. Never, I venture to assert, has the duty been more clearly and bravely acknowledged, and never has it been more strenuously and heroically discharged, than during the last weeks by the Belgian king and the Belgian people. They have faced without flinching, and against almost insuperable odds, the horrors of irruption, devastation, of spoliation, and of outrage. They have stubbornly withstood and successfully arrested the inrush, wave after wave, of a gigantic and overwhelming force. The defence of Liège will always be the theme of one of the most inspiring chapters in the annals of Liberty. The Belgians have won for themselves the immortal glory which belongs to a people who prefer freedom to ease, to security, even to life itself. We are proud of their alliance and their friendship. We salute them with respect and with honour. We are with them heart and soul, because by their side and in their company we are defending at the same time two great causes—the independence of small States and the sanctity of international covenants; and we assure them—as I ask the House in this address to do—we assure them to-day, in the name of this United Kingdom and of the whole Empire, that they may count to the end on our wholehearted and unfailing support."

DUKE ALBRECHT OF WÜRTEMBURG.

GENERAL VON HAUSEN.

GENERAL VON BUELOW.

THE CROWN PRINCE OF BAVARIA.

Mr. Bonar Law, Leader of the Opposition, in seconding the resolution, described in a fine passage the war as a struggle of the moral influences of civilisation against brute force. Declaring that Belgium deserved well of the world, he insisted that the best way in which we could pay our debt to her was by realising that this was for us, as much as for Belgium, a struggle of life and death, and by employing without haste, but without rest, all our resources for bringing it to a successful end.

Mr. John Redmond, Leader of the Irish Party, advocated the substitution of a gift of £10,000,000 to Belgium, instead of a proposed loan to that amount.

Belgium's place in history

The Marquis of Crewe moved the resolution in the House of Lords in an oration of polished, sometimes picturesque eloquence. "By her action," his lordship said, "Belgium has ranged herself by the side of the small nations famous in history who have received the crown of glory and credit for their resistance to overwhelming forces. Belgium has ranged herself by the side of Athens and Sparta against Persia, with Switzerland against the Roman Empire, and with her forebears of Flanders and the Netherlands against the might of Spain." His lordship proceeded to review the events culminating in the great European conflict, with special reference to the action of Germany in violating the neutrality of Belgium and Luxemburg, which he described as an outrage against the public law of Europe. The bid by Germany for Belgian acquiescence in the violation of her neutrality was an offer at the end of the war to respect the independence and integrity of Belgium. That might be

BRITISH ARMY SERVICE CORPS IN FRANCE.

In Wellington's wars in Spain French generals wrote to Napoleon in praise of the British commander's transport. Sir John French's Army Service Corps far excelled Wellington's. Inset: French womenfolk interested in a roadside kitchen and the British soldiers' cookery.

taken to mean that Belgium, acquiescing now, at the end of the war would become a German protectorate. We could not, therefore, be surprised that the offer received no attention. After narrating the events of the siege of Liège, followed by the occupation of Brussels by the Germans, the noble marquis said that that was not the whole story. It was not only a story of a military invasion encountered with courageous resistance by an inferior military force. For it was impossible to disregard the official and authentic reports by the Committee of the Belgian Foreign Office of the infamous conduct of the invading army contrary to all laws and usages of war. In conclusion he said: "This is not the time for us who, as a nation, are engaged in this struggle to give utterance to any sort of threat, or to engage in any kind of prophecies as to what may be the outcome of this tremendous war. But this I do say, that history will tell us that no nation has ever outraged public law, or has systematically conducted war by inhuman and brutal methods, without sooner or later paying for it. The time or the form of punishment or reparation that may be exacted, it is, of course, impossible to say; but I do venture to declare that any nation that so conducts itself pays for it soon or late, and pays to the uttermost farthing. It is our part to see that the sword is not sheathed until the fullest assurance is obtained that these great wrongs will be redressed to the full. I am certain that in saying this, and also expressing in the terms of the motion our cordial sympathy with the Belgian nation, and our determination to do everything we can as a nation to vindicate the independence of that country and the public law of Europe, I shall have the full concurrence of your lordships' House."

Lord Lansdowne, Leader of the Opposition, in the course of his speech, dwelt on the fact that all who were lovers of liberty, all who could appreciate the virtue of self-sacrifice, all who were able to admire patriotism, and to entertain respect for Treaty obligations, must feel that Belgium had rendered to the civilised world a signal service by what she had done.

The French in Alsace-Lorraine

In an earlier chapter mention was made of the French invasion of German Alsace and Lorraine. General Castelnau, who was in command of the French Expeditionary Force in Upper Alsace, began on August 23rd to fall back, pressed by overwhelming German and Austrian forces, into French territory as far as Champenoux, beyond which line, which practically coincides with the Grand Couronne of Nancy, the Germans, try as they would, never set foot. General Pau, in command of the raid into Lorraine, also fell back on the line of fortresses within the French frontier stretching from Verdun to the Swiss frontier, while a portion of his army was directed westward for the defence of the Meuse. He himself had his head-quarters at Belfort before he was recalled to Paris to organise the divisional army which was to play an important part at "the turning of the tide." During the general's operations in Lorraine Captain Langlois, an officer in the Aviation Corps, made a daring flight from Verdun to Metz. At Frascati he dropped bombs on the Zeppelin station, captured at Bouillar a German aeroplane, and, though wounded, succeeded in bringing his own machine back to the French lines. For this brilliant deed the French President conferred upon him the cross of the Legion of Honour, and for "the encouragement of the others," as the French saying goes, General Pau bestowed the decoration in the Place des Armes, Belfort, in the presence of the whole garrison and a vast concourse of the general public. In pinning the cross to Captain Langlois's uniform the general said: "In the name of the Government I declare you a Chevalier of the Legion of Honour before these trophies taken from the enemy"—pointing to the guns taken at Altkirch and Thann—"and I give you an accolade with a sabre taken from a German officer." This instant recognition of brave deeds was received by the troops with the greatest enthusiasm. In their retirement Generals Castelnau and Pau always had the game well in hand until they made their final stand. Eleven thousand dead Germans lay in the fields and forests round Lunéville, which was bombarded by the French and partly burned by the Germans, and twenty thousand between Nancy and Champenoux.

The German colony of Togoland, in West Africa, surrendered to an Anglo-French expedition on August 26th, and an expeditionary naval and military force, despatched by the Government of the Dominion of New Zealand, landed on August 29th at Apia, the chief town of the Samoan group of islands in the Western Pacific, and took possession of it from the German authorities without firing a shot. The commander of the expeditionary force announced that he had annexed to the Dominion, on behalf of Great Britain, the whole of the islands in the group which had been occupied by and allotted to Germany under an international treaty.

Among the earliest aspirations for "a place in the sun" of the German bureaucrat expansionists was the possession of tropical colonies and a naval base in the Western Pacific. Accordingly, a German man-of-war was despatched thither in 1879, and she took possession, in the name of the Teutonic Empire, of the harbour of Salnafata. Great Britain and the United

BY A RIVERSIDE DURING THE HOT WEATHER IN FRANCE.
British cavalrymen watering their horses after a forced and dusty march in the blazing sun of August. They were the leaders of the column, part of which is seen crossing the bridge in the background. Inset. Officers' roadside luncheon.

GERMAN METHODS IN FRANCE.

In most of the French villages occupied by Germans all suspected persons were kept under guard. The above photograph is of French peasants compounded in a village church. The smaller view was taken behind the German lines, after the arrival of gifts from Berlin for the troops The event was accompanied by much popping of corks.

States protested—the former at the instigation of the Australian Colonies—and a sort of international arrangement was come to, by which none of the three Powers was actually to appropriate any of the islands.

In 1887 a civil war broke out over the succession to the native kingship, and the European and American settlers who had bought up land from the heads of the local tribes to exploit them for copra, the product of the coconut palm, or for sugar-growing, took sides. The Germans supported one kingly claimant and the British and Americans another. Some fighting ensued, a number of German sailors being killed and wounded. At the suggestion of Germany, a conference of the three Powers chiefly interested was held in 1889 in Berlin, which elaborated a treaty, under which the independence and autonomy of the Samoan Island group were guaranteed under King Malietoa, but imposing a virtual protectorate over them. The arrangement worked with considerable friction from the first, and Robert Louis Stevenson, in "A Footnote to History" (the result of his careful investigation of the causes of the native trouble, made in 1889, on his first visit to the island, where from 1890 until his death in 1894 he made his home), referred to the malicious trickery of the Germans against poor distracted Malietoa. On the kinglet's death there were again rival aspirants to the unstable throne—Matuafa being supported by the Germans and Malietoa Tanu by the British and Americans. Fighting took place, but this time it was the American and British sailors who were killed. An international commission made inquiry on the spot, and in the result the Treaty of Berlin was abrogated, and Great Britain withdrew, much to the chagrin of the Australian and New Zealand Governments, her claims to any portions of the beautiful island group—receiving compensation from Germany in another direction, while the United States withdrew from all the islands west of Tutuila. Germany then stood possessed of the two largest islands of the group—Savaii and Upolu, in which latter is the fine port of Apia, and a naval base which constituted, in Australian and New Zealand eyes, a dangerous sea watchdog against the Commonwealth and the Dominion The resident German population in the islands in 1913 was 329.

On August 26th and 27th two Danish and Norwegian traders and three British trawlers, two of them engaged in mine-sweeping, were blown up by mines in the North Sea off the Tyne, with a total loss of seventeen killed and eleven injured. About the same date the German fast cruiser Magdeburg ran ashore in a fog on the island of Odensholm, in the Gulf of Finland. As a Russian squadron was preparing to attack, the commander of the cruiser sacrificed her by partially blowing her up, and her destruction was completed by shell-fire from the Russian ships. A majority of the crew were rescued by a German torpedo-boat. The naval Battle of Heligoland Bight on August 28th has already been described in a separate chapter.

Fate of the Magdeburg

Meantime, important events were taking place in the eastern theatre of operations. At the close of Chapter XXIII. it was stated that General von Hindenburg had

New movable French battery which travels along a specially-laid railway line. Note the observation tower, the howitzers on their turntable, and the ammunition waggon.

British soldiers handing out English 6 in. howitzer shells for inspection by their French comrades, who took a very deep interest in everything connected with British artillery.

Specimen of the British 6 in. howitzer which was sent to oppose the German 8 in. howitzer, and outfought it. It throws a shell of 100 lb., and has a muzzle velocity of 1,285 lb. per second.

One of the French howitzer guns. This formidable piece of ordnance is supported on steel arms, which give to it a great stability when it is fired. As will be seen, it is brought up to the field of action on a railway, and provided with shield, turntable, and mechanism for adjustment to the required elevation.

BIG GUNS EMPLOYED BY THE ALLIES AGAINST HEAVY ARTILLERY OF THE GERMANS.

Givet, a picturesquely placed little village in the Ardennes, where the Germans crossed the Meuse against a magnificent resistance by the French. Inset: A road in the Forest of Mormal.

pushed across the Russian frontier, but was met on the Niemen by General Rennenkampf, who took his revenge for the disaster of Tannenberg, described in a previous chapter, and drove the Germans once more back, between August 23rd and 25th, to Gumbinnen, where he gained a complete victory against three Teuton army corps, part of which had attempted to turn the Russian right flank, and captured fifty-five guns. Rennenkampf practically was then in possession of East Prussia, and from Gumbinnen he pushed forward to Allenstein, and invested Königsberg, while his Cossacks pushed on to the neighbourhood of Dantzic. So serious was this position for the Germans that on August 29th and 30th they drew troops from the French frontier to

Longwy, where the army of the German Crown Prince succeeded in bursting into France, a small town W.S.W. of Luxemburg. Inset: Verdun, the great French fortress town west of Metz.

reinforce their eastern front, which was being so hard pressed.

A battle, extending over a front of thirty miles between Neigenburg and Gilgenburg, took place on August 28th and 29th, when two German army corps were reported to have been cut up by the Russians. Continuing their pursuit of the enemy, the Russians occupied Soldau, whence they had the command of the railway to Dantzic—the retreating Germans firing the towns they vacated, while the innocent inhabitants fled from their fury. The position taken up by Hindenburg, with his peculiarly intimate knowledge of the geography of East Prussia and Poland, barred the further advance of Rennenkampf.

In mid-August the Grand Duke Nicholas began his preparations for the serious advance of his armies into Poland and Galicia—on a line extending from the Niemen down almost to the borders of Rumania. West Poland had been invaded by a German army under the Crown Prince, who had been transferred thither from the Argonne in the western sphere of operations, and who hoped to make a swoop on Warsaw from the eastern German border, by way of the Vistula. Like a wise diplomat, as well as an excellent soldier, the Grand Duke Nicholas followed up the Tsar's Rescript, promising, in the event of a successful war, to make Poland an autonomous State under the Crown of Russia (see page 304, Vol. I.) by an Army Order, making it known to the active Army and the whole population of the Empire that Russia was waging war in consequence of a challenge thrown down by the common enemy of all Slavs. "The Poles in Russia," the order proceeded, "and those of Germany and Austria, who show their loyalty to the Slav cause, will have the special protection of the Russian Army and Government, in so far as their personal and material security is concerned. Any attempt to interfere with the personal rights of Poles who

Charleville, opposite Mezières, another centre of the fierce fighting between the French and Germans during the retreat from Charleroi.

have not been guilty of acts hostile to Russia will be punished with all the severity of martial law." The Russian Generalissimo was himself in command of the army opposing the main German army under the German Crown Prince, and preliminary engagements took place along the long line. In one of these a Russian squadron charged a battery and captured all the guns from a detachment of the enemy, when the German soldiers discarded their rifles and the officers threw away their swords and helmets and fled. The incident had a personal interest for the Tsar, as will be seen from a special telegram which the Grand Duke sent to his Imperial Majesty.

SCENES ALONG THE EASTERN FRONTIER OF FRANCE.
Panoramic view of Nancy, the capital of Meurthe-et-Moselle.

"I would not have dared," said the telegram, "to disturb your Majesty with a report of this little affair, but I have decided to make it to you as the commander of the Nijni Novgorod Regiment of Dragoons. A party of seventy picked German scouts came into collision with a squadron of the Nijni Novgorod Regiment. All the enemy were sabred, except six who were taken prisoners. Our losses were four wounded, two seriously."

Operations in Galicia

After a couple of weeks' manœuvring, two Russian armies, one under the command of General Russky, and the other under General Brussiloff, made a concentrated thrust into the Austrian position in Eastern Galicia, and completely routed five of the enemy's army corps, capturing 70,000 prisoners and an immense number of guns and much war material.

The battle-front in the Galician theatre was narrowed on August 30th, and the enemy forces in the province of Kielce crossed the Vistula in order to join hands with the armies engaged in the province of Lublin, their main efforts being chiefly concentrated on the roads leading to Lublin, where desperate fighting went on for nearly a week. South of Lublin the Russian troops drove back the enemy's forces, helpless and bewildered, and advanced amid heaps of slain Austrians, left unburied by the flying and demoralised army. On August 31st and September 1st the Austrian lines round Lemberg were broken, and the capital of Galicia was captured, with an unheard-of number of guns and other machinery of war. General Russky with his division then swept onward and, in conjunction with Brussiloff's army, pulverised the Austrian main army, shattering, at any rate at that date, the military strength and prestige of the Dual Monarchy.

As giving some insight into the Russian soldier's mentality, a correspondent transcribed literally some parts of a dialogue which took place between a gigantic trooper who had returned from the front wounded and was interviewed by the Tsar in the hospital at Petrograd. The trooper, carrying his left arm in a sling, stood at attention before his Majesty. His breast was decorated with three Crosses of St. George, of which one had the distinctive badge conferred only when the recipient had been wounded in carrying out some gallant exploit.

"And you," said his Majesty, "have again been wounded?"

"Yes, sire. Last time in Manchuria. This time near Gumbinnen."

"I hear you captured five Germans?"

A PATHETIC INCIDENT—FOR THE GERMAN HORSES.

Street scene in Northern France. Two German cavalry scouts halted in the market-place to give their tired steeds a refreshing drink at the fountain—to find that the water supply had been cut off. The smaller view is of a German prisoner being interrogated by his French captors.

BRITISH REINFORCEMENTS BROUGHT UP BY MOTOR-'BUS.

The London motor-'bus, whatever its future may be, will have an honoured place in the history of the Great War. It was used for the rapid conveyance of troops from one spot to another, for the bringing up of ammunition and other supplies, and very often with its body replaced by a lorry body. Motor-'buses were used in a similar fashion by both French and Germans.

"Yes, your Majesty, we stormed a village. They were hiding in the houses. I pulled them out one by one and drove them along. Just then somebody put a bullet into my arm from behind, but I brought them in all the same."

"But how did you storm the village?"

"Well, your Majesty, we dismounted, threw out skirmishers, and then we rushed them. But the Germans aren't good fighters. They turned and ran."

"Is there anything you wish for?" asked the Emperor laughingly.

"Oh, yes, your Majesty; let me go back. My arm will be all right in a few days. It is all very dull here, and so interesting there. We see new towns, and every day there's plenty of interesting work."

To return to Northern France. From Guise—the operations around which have been dealt with in a separate chapter—the Allies retired to a line drawn between Amiens and Verdun, the British covering and delaying troops being frequently engaged; while on September 1st the British Cavalry Brigade and the 4th Guards Brigade were sharply engaged with the enemy near Compiègne, the 9th Lancers in a brilliant charge capturing ten German guns.

In Paris itself during these eventful days the citizens were at intervals alarmed by the dropping of bombs from German aeroplanes.

It may be well here to refer to the unparalleled, overt, and underground attempts that were made at this period by Germany—at a cost, so it was alleged at the time, of over a million sterling—to influence opinion in the United States in favour of the Germans as against the case of the Allies. Writing from Washington, on August 30th, "The Times" correspondent said that the leaders of the Teutonic element there, headed by the German Ambassador, were indulging in a campaign which was in direct contravention of the President's fine appeal for neutrality of comment by the native and alien Americans alike. Not only was the Ambassador using his official position for all it was worth, but the German Consular corps were also mobilised to bring financial and other pressure to bear on behalf of German interests. Astounding letters were sent to editors for publication, and a covert campaign was organised to frighten the proprietors of newspapers by letters threatening loss of subscribers if they continued to be pro-British.

Mr. W. G. Shepherd, representative of the United Press Association of America, sought an interview with the First Lord of the Admiralty, for the purpose of obtaining his view of the immediate cause of the war, as a checkmate to the extraordinary statements thereanent circulated in the States by German officials and sympathisers. This interview was of historic importance, and may be referred to in a little detail. Mr. Churchill handed his interviewer the celebrated White Paper containing all Sir Edward Grey's negotiations with the Chancelleries of Europe, saying: "There is our case, and all we ask of the American people is that they should study it with severe and impartial attention." Mr. Shepherd then asked what was the underlying cause, apart from the actual steps which led to the war; and Mr. Churchill replied that the war was started and was being maintained by the Prussian military aristocracy, which set no limits to its ambition of world-wide predominance. In a word, it was the old struggle of a hundred years ago against Napoleon. The grouping of forces was different; the circumstances were different; the occasion was different; the man, above all, was different—happily. But the issue was the same. Great Britain stood right in the path of Prussian militarism. Our military force was perhaps small, but it was good, and would grow, our naval and financial resources were considerable; and with these we stood between a mighty Army and a dominion which would certainly not be content with European limits.

Mr. Churchill discusses the origin of the war

In answer to a question as to whether the end of the war would see some abatement of the struggle of armaments, Mr. Churchill replied: "That depends on the result. If we succeed, and if, as the result of our victory, Europe is re-arranged, as far as possible with regard to the principle of nationality and in accordance with the wishes of the peoples who dwell in the various disputed areas, we may look forward with hope to a great relaxation and easement. But if Germany wins it will not be the victory of the quiet, sober, commercial elements in Germany, nor of the common people of Germany with all their virtues, but the victory of the blood and iron military school, whose doctrines and principles will then have received a supreme and terrible vindication.

"Now that the great collision has come," continued Mr. Churchill, "it is well that the democratic nations of the world—the nations where the peoples own the Government, and not the Government the people—should realise what is at stake. The French, British, and American systems of government by popular election and Parliamentary debate, with the kind of civilisation which flows from such institutions, are brought into direct conflict with the highly efficient Imperialist bureaucracy and military organisation of Prussia. That is the issue. No partisanship is required to make it plain. No sophistry can obscure it."

American interest in the war

As to the question whether the democracy of the United States, apart from the moral issues involved, had any direct interest in the result of the war, the First Lord said: "If Great Britain were reduced in this war—or another, which would be sure to follow from it if this war were inconclusive—to the position of a small country like Holland, then, however far across the salt water the United States might lie, the burden which we in Great Britain are bearing now would fall on American shoulders. He did not mean by that that Germany would attack the States, or that if they were attacked that they would need to fear the results, so far as the States are concerned. The Monroe Doctrine, however, carried them very far in South as well as North America; and was it likely that victorious German militarism, which would then have shattered France irretrievably, have conquered Belgium, and have broken for ever the power of Great Britain, would allow itself to be permanently cut off from all hopes of that oversea expansion and development with which South America alone could supply it?" In conclusion, Mr. Churchill said: "Now the impact is upon us. Our blood, which flows in your veins, should lead you to expect that we shall be stubborn enough to bear that impact. But if we go down and are swept in ruin into the past, you are next in the line. This war is for us a war of honour, of respect for obligations into which we have entered, and of loyalty towards friends in desperate need. But now that it has begun it has become a war of self-preservation. The British democracy, with its limited monarchy, its ancient Parliament, its ardent social and philanthropic dreams, is engaged for good or for ill in deadly grapple with the formidable might of Prussian autocratic rule. It is our system of civilisation and government against theirs. It is our life or theirs. We are conscious of the greatness of the times. We recognise the consequence and proportion of events. We feel that, however inadequate we may be, however unexpected the ordeal may be, we are under the eye of history, and, the issue being joined, Great Britain must go forward to the very end."

"Under the eye of history"

Towards the close of the interview a telegram came to the First Lord from Belgium, announcing the total destruction of Louvain as an act of military execution. Handing it to his interviewer, he said: "What further proof is needed of the cause at issue? Tell that to your fellow American countrymen. You know," he added, "I'm half American myself."

THE UBIQUITOUS AND ADAPTABLE MOTOR-'BUS IN FRANCE.

Bringing up supplies for the troops at the front. Paris motor-'buses passing through the Forest of Compiègne. The smaller photograph shows how the London motor-'buses were converted into lorries.

WITH THE SOLDIERS OF AUSTRIA: DIFFICULTIES OF ARTILLERY TRANSPORT.

During the autumn campaign in Galicia the roads became very muddy, and as a result the artillery was exceedingly difficult to handle. In the above illustration, which gives a realistic idea of the nature of the soil, an Austrian gun is seen being helped up an awkward incline by a draft of infantry.

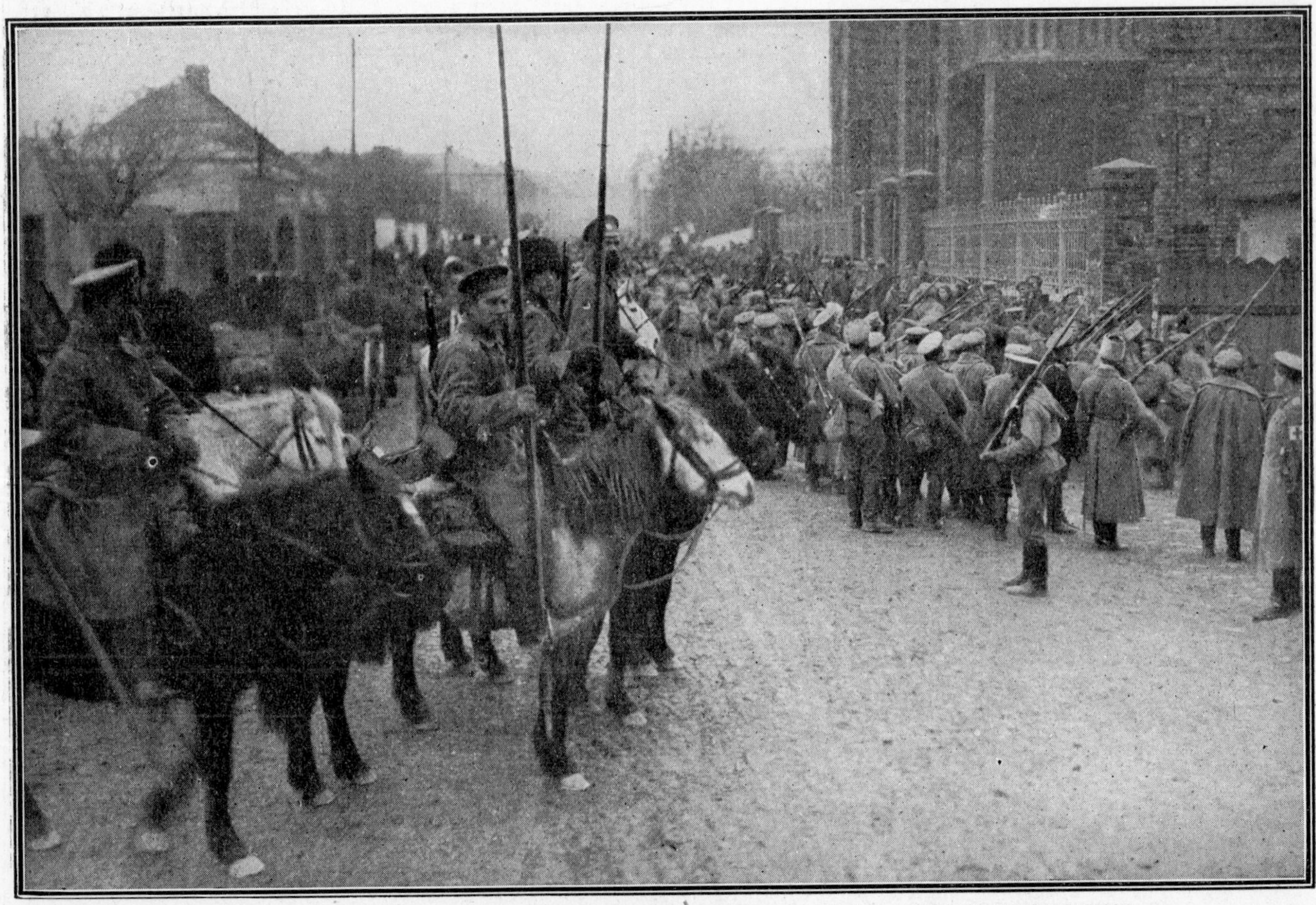

ON THE PRUSSIAN FRONTIER—RUSSIANS OCCUPY A TOWN DURING NIGHT-TIME.

The German armies having evacuated a Prussian frontier town during the night, an advance party of Cossacks, "Germany's grey nightmare," and Russian infantry occupied the position. The Prussians then attempted a night surprise, but this was provided against and defeated.

GERMANY'S "GREY NIGHTMARE": COSSACKS CROSSING A STREAM.

CHAPTER XXXI.

THE RUSSIAN VICTORIES IN GALICIA AND THE CAPTURE OF LEMBERG.

The Austro-German Plan of Campaign—How the Russians Divided the Teutonic Allies—The Austrian Invasion of Russian Poland—Russia Prepares a Napoleonic Stroke—The Russian Army Steals Along the Dniester—Another Russian Force Moves Southward to Co-operate—The Extraordinary Secrecy of the Combined Movements—The Sudden Onset at Halicz—A Great Russian Victory—The Storming of Lemberg and the Re-conquest of the Ancient Russian Duchy of Galicia.

ON both fronts of war Germany had arranged a programme of victories. But as she needed three millions of troops in France, leaving only a million men mainly of the militia class for defence against Russia, she had to depend upon Austria-Hungary for offensive operations in the eastern theatre of conflict. A plan of combined attack was prepared for the conquest of Russian Poland.

An Austrian army of a million troops of the first line was to advance from Galicia, between Cracow and Lemberg. At the same time a German force, of about equal number but inferior quality, was to strike at Warsaw from Eastern Prussia and German Poland. The defending Russian army would then be assailed on three sides, and either routed or driven back from its railway centre at Brest-Litovsk.

Like all German war plans, this was excellent on paper. Had the Russians also done the obvious thing in reply to the obvious movements of the Teutonic forces, the Grand Duke Nicholas and his Chief of Staff, General Sukhomlinoff, might have been outgeneralled. Unfortunately for the Austrians, the Russian Military Staff was well aware of the German war plan, and engineered a series of surprises that completely disarranged from the beginning the Teutonic programme. The German forces were violently wrenched from all co-operation with the Austrian armies by General Rennenkampf's sudden raid into East Prussia. His immediate menace to Königsberg, his destruction of the food resources of Berlin, and his threat at Thorn and Dantzic, played on the Germans' instinct for self-preservation. Alarmed for their own fields and cities, they withdrew from Russian Poland, where their advanced guard had reached Lodz on the way to Warsaw, and hastily, madly concentrated in Prussia against the Cossack invaders.

PART OF THE PRICE OF VICTORY—AND DEFEAT. AFTER THE BATTLE OF LEMBERG.

Russian and Austrian wounded on their way to the base hospital at Lemberg. The capture of Lemberg by the Russians removed a great obstacle to the advance of the Tsar's soldiers against the military power of Austria, and enabled them to strike at Germany from the south.

This left the Austrian armies in the west of Russian Poland at the mercy of the Russian Military Staff. The Austrian Commanders—General Dankl, General Auffenberg, and several archdukes—did not lose confidence. Possessing two thousand five hundred guns and a million young, picked men of the regular Army, with large militia supports in Galicia, they regarded Russia as a sleepy, gawky giant who could be stabbed to death before he was half awake. Speeding up their mobilisation, they launched two great armies over the frontier. One marched along the Vistula and the other along the Bug Rivers. They formed a battle-front some eighty miles long that swept everything before it as it advanced, towards the middle of August, on Lublin and Kholm, preparatory to striking at Warsaw or Brest-Litovsk.

The events of the Russo-Japanese War made both the Austrians and the Germans think that the Russian Empire could be rocked to its foundation by a swift onset. It was expected that the Russians would not have an army of any considerable size mobilised before the beginning of September at the earliest. It was in this matter that the Russian Military Staff, with General Sukhomlinoff at its head, prepared a surprise for Austria, even greater than the surprise it had arranged for the Germans in East Prussia. Lack of a network of railways and good roads prevented the Russian Staff from concentrating at once the full forces of the Empire near the Teutonic frontiers. Nevertheless, the Austrian force of a million men was held by a Russian force of smaller number with superior artillery. Admirably served by his Chief of Staff, the Russian Commander-in-Chief, the Grand Duke Nicholas, had only to decide how he would meet the Austrians.

According to the modern, orthodox Moltke method, he should have concentrated against the Austrian advance and tried to turn one of its flanks. This was the method which the Russians had employed against the Japanese, and which the Japanese had employed against them. It led, when the hostile troops were fairly balanced, to a new kind of open-air siege warfare that seldom produced a decisive result. But since the Manchurian campaign the Russians had thrown over the Moltke system and returned to the Napoleonic way of war. The way of Napoleon, with its unexpected lightning strokes and direct frontal attacks, was bound to produce decisive results—one way or the other. It meant a quick great victory, or a quick great defeat. In the first case the fighting power of the Austrian Empire would be shattered before the Germans, busy in East Prussia, could come to the help of their ally. The great defect of the Napoleonic method was that its master used it on battle-fronts a few miles long, on which troops could be rapidly manœuvred from one flank to the other. With the immense armies of the new era of general national service, the battle-fronts stretched from two to four hundred miles. Russia had no network of railways to shift her troops over this distance for sudden mass attacks. Her men had to march hundreds of miles to carry out a Napoleonic movement. They had to fight first with their feet before they used their hands—march as men had never marched before, and yet come vigorous and irresistible into the firing-line. But General Sukhomlinoff and the Grand Duke Nicholas felt certain that the wonderful physique of the young moujik would carry him successfully through the ordeal.

The Moltke system thrown over

Defect of the Napoleonic method

To the army of Bessarabia and Podolia, under General Brussiloff, was assigned the first great march that should end in the first Napoleonic surprise stroke. Composed partly of Odessa troops, this army crept round Northern

RELICS OF THE AUSTRIAN DEBACLE AT LEMBERG.
On September 2nd General Russky drew up his troops within cannon shot of the fortressed capital of Galicia, an Austrian army of 200,000 men was utterly beaten, and Lemberg captured next day, together with the entire artillery of the Austrian force.

AUSTRIAN STAFF OFFICERS WITNESSING THE RUSSIAN ATTACK ON LEMBERG.

From a drawing by the German artist W. Gause. The Archduke Frederick, the Austrian Commander-in-Chief, is seen on the extreme right of the group, behind the range-finder. Prince Charles Francis Joseph, heir to the Austrian throne, is the tall figure in the foreground.

TYPES OF HEAVY GERMAN AND AUSTRIAN GUNS BEING MOUNTED FOR BOMBARDMENT.

In the early stages of the war there appears to have been an interchange of heavy artillery between the Germans and Austrians. These great pieces of ordnance often had a decisive effect in bombardment, but they had to be sent back for renewal after a comparatively short "life."

Rumania into the eastern corner of the Austrian province of Galicia. At the same time a larger force of Little Russians from Kiev, under General Russky, moved from a point some hundreds of miles away to co-operate with the Bessarabians. Russky, however, seemed to be merely the left wing of the main Russian armies guarding Russian Poland. He rested on the River Bug, still far away from

PHASES OF THE STRUGGLE IN GALICIA.
The first view is of a Russian railroad battalion at the captured Galician town of Ravaruska. In the large photograph is seen a Russian transport column on the road from Tomashov to Lublin. In their flight from Tomashov the Austrians are reported to have used Red Cross waggons to facilitate their progress, and the illustration on the right shows some of these waggons abandoned by them.

the scene fixed for the first decisive stroke. His connection with Brussiloff's movement was veiled for a fortnight from the enemy.

General Brussiloff had also to move to the attack without exciting notice. This was done by both commanders—Russky and himself—throwing out a screen of hard-fighting Cossacks all along the frontier of Eastern Galicia. For a hundred and fifty miles the Cossacks skirmished at every border road or bridge between the Dniester and Bug Rivers. They began it as soon as war was declared, and, after a couple of weeks of this inconsequential warfare, the Austrian commander at Lemberg grew to look upon it as mere fussiness. It amused the Cossacks and it did not hurt him. But towards the third week in August he sent a force of 2,000 men to make a reconnaissance in Podolia.

Secrecy of the Russian plans

They arrived at Gorodok, a little townlet across the border, where their presence was not wanted. For General Brussiloff was then advancing with a large army through Gorodok on towards Galicia. The Austrian reconnoitring force had to be stopped, and there were only nine hundred Cossacks at Gorodok to screen their main army. These Cossacks had to repulse the enemy without calling for large reinforcements to excite the suspicions of any fugitive from the fight.

The Cossacks lined out in the woods beyond the village. Then thirty of them went forward from cover to cover, until they came suddenly upon the Austrians. Pretending to be scared by the surprise, the Cossack band turned and fled in apparent panic. Their foes entered headlong into pursuit, and were led into an ambush, where a cross-fire of rifles and machine-guns brought a thousand of them down. The rest were chased by the Cossacks over the border, and the invasion of Galicia was begun by their main force.

Cossacks lead the foe into ambush

Then came the perilous part of the enterprise. The army of Russky was moving on Lemberg from the north; the army of Brussiloff was converging on the Galician capital from the east. When united, the two Russian forces would outnumber the Austrian force guarding Lemberg. In the meantime, however, either Brussiloff or Russky alone was too weak to escape defeat. Both might have been met singly and overwhelmed. But such was the skill with which their combined operations were conducted that General Brussiloff was able to steal into Galicia and conquer a large part of the territory before battle was joined.

Extraordinary was the secrecy with which his great movement was executed. It took place in daylight, over a period of thirteen days, from August 19th to August 31st. The Austrians had a host of spies, working with

Bringing back the body of a Russian officer from Tomashov.

Abandoned Austrian Red Cross waggon on the battlefield of Biellgitz.

Railway waggons captured from the Austrians.

Trenches occupied by the Austrians before their retreat from Tomashov.

SCENES ON THE LINE OF THE DISASTROUS AUSTRIAN RETREAT IN GALICIA.
In the lower photograph may be seen a large number of shells abandoned by the Austrians in the retreat near Ravaruska.

RUSSIAN SCOUT MOUNTED ON A STURDY SIBERIAN PONY.

they thought to force the Russians to concentrate against them. It was so simple this Moltke method, as explained by Field-Marshal von der Goltz. The attackers had merely to advance strongly and conqueringly in order to compel their opponent to attempt to stop them. Nothing else mattered. Cossack activity southward in Galicia was merely a feint and a vain distraction.

Meanwhile, General Brussiloff made the very most of his opportunities. As quietly and as gently as possible he moved over the tributaries of the Dniester, in Galicia, and pushed back the Austrian cavalry screen without revealing his strength. On the versatile Cossack fell all this preliminary work. He had to do without infantry support or any considerable show of artillery power. Neither the infantryman nor the ordinary field artillery could be brought into action without revealing that which it was necessary to conceal.

Versatile Cossacks in their element

The Cossack horseman had to veil his main army and clear its path through forts, block-houses, and bridge-heads, while appearing to be merely a border raider. Excellently was he suited for this kind of work. Far in advance of the tramping foot soldiers and the labouring big-gun teams, moving at the rate of eight miles a day, the Cossack kept up a continual skirmish with every sort of hostile arm—cavalry scout, infantrymen, and gunners in Teutonic thoroughness; they had a large force of well-mounted, dashing cavalry-men, including the cavalry division of the Hungarian Guards—the best horsemen in either Austria or Germany. They had scouts in flying machines darting over the frontier. Yet the Russian turning movement in Eastern Galicia was not discovered until too late.

This was partly due to the fact that the country through which Brussiloff was working was an ancient Russian duchy that had been torn from the ancestors of the Tsar. Eastern Galicia was the Alsace-Lorraine of the Slav Empire, peopled by a Slav race, with the same language, religion, and customs as the men of Brussiloff's army. At the villages priests and people came out with banners to meet their "little brothers." In the towns flowers were thrown from the upper windows along the streets upon the armed redeemers of the ancient duchy. And all that could be done by silence or pretended ignorance to mislead the Austrians and Hungarians was done by the peasants. It is, moreover, very likely that Russian Secret Service agents had well prepared the Little Russians of Galicia for the happy invasion.

But this does not palliate the disastrous stupidity of the Austrian General Military Staff. They knew what Eastern Galicia meant to Russia. Why, then, were they not fully forearmed against the inevitable attack? The probable explanation is that they were so obsessed by the Moltke system of warfare that they were blind to everything except the "scientific" scheme of operations they were carrying out farther to the north-west, in Russian Poland. They had a strong front between the Vistula and the Bug Rivers, and by continually moving forward into Russia,

WAR DOGS ATTACHED TO THE RUSSIAN LIFEGUARD HUSSARS.

OFFICER OF COSSACK SCOUTS
giving information relative to the enemy's position to his commander who is studying a map.

RUSSIAN TROOPS AT PRAYER.
A religious service on the battlefield. Shells were falling while it was in progress.

RUSSIAN FIELD GUN.
Ready for action in a carefully prepared position.

FIRE AND SWORD IN GALICIA—WITH THE RUSSIAN FORCES IN THE WAR AGAINST AUSTRIA.
Russians entering the burning town of Mikolaiev, in Eastern Galicia, during the Muscovite invasion of the dominions of the Emperor Francis Joseph. The circular view shows Russian soldiers eating a meal in a Galician village.

AUSTRIAN REINFORCEMENTS ON THE WAY TO CRACOW.
An Austrian engineer division on the way to strengthen the garrison at Cracow. Inset: Bridge over the River Dniester blown up by Austrians in retreat.

fortified places, and even armoured trains. Helped only by his own light artillery, he fought in every manner practised by modern troops. He charged with his lance; he dismounted and took positions with the bayonet that all Russian cavalry carry; at need, he entrenched, and proved himself a marksman.

The Cossack is what the Prussian would like to be, but is not—the member of a military caste, born, bred, and trained entirely for a life of war. His ancestors, hammered into shape by continual conflict with warlike Mongol races, had built up the kingdom of Poland and then, to preserve their independence, had gone over to the Duke of Moscow and become the empire-builders of Russia.

Empire-builders of Russia

Never had the Cossack enjoyed himself as he did in Galicia against the Hungarians and Austrians. On their unfortunate heads he emptied all his box of tricks. It would be interesting to learn from some survivor of the famous cavalry division of the Magyar Guards, who met the Cossacks near Lemberg, and then—after a railway journey across Europe—encountered the British lancers and dragoons at Ypres, which of his two foes he found the more formidable. Certainly the Cossacks are more tricky fighters than our horsemen. They could beat any circus performer.

In Galicia, when hard pressed, they fell dead in heaps, their dead horses beside them. As the enemy came to search their bodies the dead men used their carbines with surprising effect. Another time, a herd of little Cossack horses would stampede, and the riderless animals would sweep towards some guarded bridge-head or block-house. Even little Cossack horses are useful to Austrian soldiers; they can be sold for good money to Galician farmers. But, just before the animals were caught, grey figures

A SHADED AUSTRIAN ENCAMPMENT.
Officers resting for a midday meal in an Austrian camp pitched in a wood in Galicia.

HALICZ, THE CAPITAL OF ANCIENT GALICIA.
The view is from the right bank of the River Dniester, and Russian officers are shown surveying the position from the Austrian observation station. The town is seen in the middle distance. Near the town are the ruins of a castle where the once powerful rulers of the ancient principality used to reside. Inset: Austrian chiefs in the field, a photograph taken at the Austrian headquarters, and showing the Archduke Frederick and General Conrad von Roetzendorf, Chief of the Austrian General Staff.

swung from beneath them, lance in hand, and charged. It was like a show in the arena, but deadly for the spectators. When it came to a straightforward cavalry fight, sabre against sabre, the Cossack still won.

All the tricks of war, however, were not practised by the Russians. The Austrians, on occasions, showed themselves masters of craft. An instance occurred on August 23rd in the frontier fight for Tarnopol, an important Galician town on the Sereth River, seventy miles east-south-east of Lemberg. Piercing the enemy's front line, a Russian division swept onward to meet the main body of their foes. They passed an Austrian officer who was sitting on the earth bandaging his leg. Naturally they did not hurt this wounded man. But their attack failed—it failed repeatedly. No matter in what way they endeavoured to get with the bayonet in the enemy's trenches, he was prepared, and brought them down with a terrible, concentrated fire.

Austrian tricks in the battlefield

Withdrawing after one of these reverses, a Russian officer noticed a wire running along the road. He found it led to a field telephone, and by this concealed instrument the supposed wounded Austrian was sitting, and giving warning to his general of all the Russian movements. When the bandage round the man's leg was removed, it was seen that his limb was quite sound. After this the telephone operator was stopped, the Russian bayonet went over the Austrian trenches, and the Cossacks rode down the fugitives.

The trick of pretending to be wounded and lying on the ground and gathering information while the opposing troops sweep by has been used by many informers in both Austrian and German armies. It is one of the reasons for the fiendish inhumanity with which the Teutons have often dealt with wounded men belonging to the armies of civilisation. The wicked are always suspicious. Having debased, for purposes of espionage, the soldier's natural feeling of pity for his injured foes, the new barbarians when they advanced killed their wounded opponents, for fear that their own dirty trick of shamming hurt and then spying would be played on themselves.

In spite of the continual skirmishings, drawing nearer and nearer to Lemberg, no alarm was felt by the Austrian commander until General Brussiloff's army, after crossing stream after stream, forced the passage of the golden Lipa. Even then the Austrian General Military Staff suspected that a blow was coming southward against the rear of their main armies. They had three army corps round Lemberg to protect from any turning movement their one hundred and fifty mile battle-front, stretching north-west through Russian territory. But this was not sufficient when General Russky's army and General Brussiloff's army were at last seen combining for attack. The Austrians hurried up two more army corps that moved against Russky, while several divisions of foot-line infantry and brigades of militia troops reinforced the position to be held against Brussiloff's force. In all there were at last about three hundred thousand Austrian troops round Lemberg.

Austrian precautions taken too late

All this, however, was done too late in the last days of August. General Russky and General Brussiloff had united, some forty miles east of the city. The combined

POLISH SOLDIERS RESTING IN THE CARPATHIANS.

The Carpathians, the second great mountain range of Central Europe, is generally clothed with wood to a height of more than 4,000 feet. The scenery all round is full of grandeur. A tragic side of the war in this part of the world was the division of the Poles in the rival forces. Inset: A typical trainload of Austrian prisoners, who offered a noticeable contrast to the carefully groomed soldiers of their Russian escort.

armies then acted under the leadership of General Russky in a concerted attack upon the capital of Galicia. In both brains and fighting power the Austrian Archduke Frederick and his Staff were outmatched. General Russky was one of the leading strategists of the new Russo-French school, a quiet, bookish, scholarly man, hardened to war in Manchuria, where he had distinguished himself by bold leading and personal courage. General Brussiloff was another brilliant and yet sound leader, with high, practical experience in modern warfare. Then, with the two Russian generals was the hero of Bulgaria, General Radko Dimitrieff, who had vanquished the German-trained Turkish army at Kirk Kilisse and other recent battles of the Balkans. He had thrown up his appointment under the Bulgarian Government in order to go as a volunteer to help the imperial Slav people in its grand struggle against the Teuton, whose intrigues had brought Bulgaria low in the hour of her victory and disrupted the Balkan Alliance.

In numbers the two opposing armies seem to have been, in the end, about equal. But the Russian artillery, made chiefly by French gun-makers, was superior to that of the Austrian. Moreover, the Austrians had lent the German host in Belgium and France their latest, greatest weapon—the famous three-piece 12 in. howitzer—invented, it was rumoured, by an American, and made by Baron von Skoda, of Pilsen. For Krupp, though loud and unceasing in self-advertisement, had not all the siege artillery wanted at Namur and Maubeuge. So the Austrians had to weaken their great frontier fortresses, such as Lemberg, in order to assist their braggart ally with howitzers and with large numbers of artillery officers and men.

In addition to this disadvantage in the machinery of warfare, the southern Austrian army was caught in a moment of disarray. Its main reinforcement of two army corps was intercepted on August 29th by General Russky at Zloczow, a town to the south-east of Lemberg. There it was shattered, and the victorious Russians moved on and occupied a height known as the Naked Hill, from which they dominated Lemberg. In the meantime General Brussiloff's army, forming the western Russian wing, swung round to encircle Lemberg from the south. In so doing it struck against the main southern Austrian army entrenched at Halicz, a fortress town on the muddy Lipa that pours its turbid waters into the Dniester.

Austria's main reinforcement shattered

The Austrians were bent on carrying out the obvious Moltke tactics of getting round Brussiloff's southern flank and then rolling up the combined Russian forces. But this manœuvre did not succeed. General Brussiloff

POLISH CHURCH CONVERTED INTO A PARCELS OFFICE.
Nothing proved sacred to either Austrians or Germans, and in the above illustration we see how a Polish church was occupied by soldiers of the two Kaisers, and converted by them into a military parcels post receiving office. Inset: Russian Army doctors and nurses at the hospital at Kovno, the principal town of the Russian province of the same name. Kovno was Napoleon's advanced base in 1812.

held up the turning movement, and his gallant Bulgarian assistant, General Radko Dimitrieff, made a terrible frontal attack on the enemy on the lower course of the muddy Lipa.

The Austrian position was naturally very strong and difficult to assail, with bluffs of volcanic rock and extinct craters; the natural defences had been improved by Austrian engineers, and thirty small forts had been built round Halicz. The river passage was, in fact, regarded as impregnable. But the Russian bayonet went over river, rifle pit, and trench, while the Russian gunners swept a path for their infantry and smashed the hostile batteries and destroyed the forts. The Russians advanced in open order at first, creeping up and firing in thin, prone lines; then, getting nearer in a spurt, and again holding the ground by rifle fire till their supports could come up. Then they rose up to prove the truth of their old saying, handed down from the days of Suvoroff: "The bullet is a fool and the bayonet a hero."

Brilliant work of the Russian bayonet

The Austrians and Hungarians fought well. They faced the bayonet courageously and used it themselves, but their rifle fire was not sufficiently well-aimed to stop the rushes. The battle opened on August 31st and went on for twenty-four hours, till the Austrian line was pierced, and twenty thousand of the defenders were killed or wounded. The hand-to-hand fighting at the Battle of Halicz was fierce and dreadful, but the drive and steadiness of the Russian troops made them at last irresistible. Seventeen days of hard marching had not tired them, and they bore the main part in the struggle for Lemberg.

After the victory they closed in on the capital from the south, driving the fragments of the broken Austrian wing before them. Meanwhile, Russian aeroplanes were flying over the doomed city, and General Russky's army, rapidly covering the forty miles between Zloczow and Lemberg, captured some fortified positions close to the city. On the north and the north-east the Russians deployed, and then the heights on the south-east were also taken. For six days the battle raged—from August 29th to September 3rd. The Russians at first fought from dawn to darkness, their big guns thundering over them as they attacked or threw back counter-attacks; finally they fought night and day.

The Austrians battled on with great energy in a good position. The progress of the Russians was impeded by the hilly nature of the ground, and especially by the great number of extinct volcano craters, that formed admirable natural forts, all held by strong bodies of the enemy. Out of these craters the Austrians had to be shrapnelled and bayoneted at heavy cost. Their artificial defences were only trifling obstacles compared with these natural fortifications. The country was stony and devoid of water, and the overworked, struggling Russian troops suffered badly from thirst in the hot, wearing summer weather.

The nearer they drew to Lemberg the fiercer the fighting became. But it had already been apparent at Zloczow that the Russian guns ruled the battlefield, and on September 1st, just as General Brussiloff was winning at Halicz, General Russky succeeded in driving the main Galician army beneath the shelter of the Lemberg forts. The Russian troops were then very tired, but, exultant at the prospect of victory, they fought more furiously than before. For two more days the battle flamed and thundered round the forts, both armies being terribly swept by shrapnel from the opposing guns.

Devastating Russian siege artillery

But the Russian howitzer batteries had also been throwing heavy shells at the steel cupolas and concrete walls of the forts. All that the Belgians had suffered in Liège and Namur, all that the French were then enduring in Maubeuge against the long-range Skoda howitzers, was avenged on the garrisons of the fortress towns in Galicia. Dearly did the Austrians pay for the help they gave in siege artillery to the Germans. For their own forts were rapidly battered in by high-angle shell fire from the concealed and mobile howitzers built by the French for the Russian armies. Having stood a six months' siege in Port Arthur, the Russians were well acquainted with the weakness of fixed fortifications in the face of heavy howitzer fire. On this matter they knew even more than the Germans.

MAP ILLUSTRATING THE RUSSIAN ADVANCE ON LEMBERG.

In a couple of days the Russians had smashed or wrecked the guns and armour-plated defence works of Lemberg — the fourth most important town in the Austro-Hungarian Empire and the chief fortress and store place of Galicia. As the answering fire weakened, the infantry was ordered to storm the first line of works. The armed moujiks leaped out and forward at a run, took the defences, and bayoneted the few men who remained by the few guns which had not been dismounted by the Russian howitzers. Then, from the second line, the Austrians tried to annihilate the attackers by shrapnel from light field artillery and by rifle and machine-gun fire. But the enemy's heavy guns on the second line were by this time also too badly damaged to counter the big Russian guns. These shelled and shrapnelled the opposing light artillery and machine-guns, and thus relieved the infantry occupying the first Austrian lines. When all the enemy's artillery had been mastered, the defending troops did not await the final bayonet attack, but retired from their works—the retreat changing into a rout as their rearguards gave way.

This rearguard action was of the most extraordinary kind—only in a German or Austrian retreat could it have occurred. To save themselves and their own countrymen the Austrian and Hungarian officers ranged on their rear the Slav regiments—Little Russians of Galicia, Poles, Serbs of Bosnia, and mutinous Bohemians. This rearguard screen was thrown out on the road to Gorodok, and, to prevent the Slavs from refusing to fight and from going over to the Russians, a line of Hungarians stood behind them, with orders to shoot them in the back the moment they showed any hesitation. Happily, this state of things became known to the Russian commander. At the critical moment he ordered a devastating artillery fire, with the guns at a high angle, to be opened on the rearguard. The shells and shrapnel were so aimed that they passed high over the heads of the Slav regiments and fell and exploded on the retreating Austrians and Hungarians. It was this surprising, terrifying hail of high-explosive shells and wrecking shrapnel bursts that changed the retreat from Lemberg into a panic flight. The columns broke and scattered along all the western paths, abandoning guns, ammunition, and supplies, and fleeing in terror towards the next fortress of Gorodok.

North and east and south the Russians closed on the town, taking the last line of forts, and then pouring into the streets at nine o'clock on Thursday, September 3rd. Some Austrian detachments tried to fight back the victors in the thoroughfares of the city, but were cut off and captured. The Slav population welcomed the Russians with shouts of joy, and the sound of their happy voices singing the Russian National Anthem mingled with the last shots fired by the routed enemy outside the capital of the ancient Russian duchy.

As the conquerors, dull-eyed and weary from a battle that had raged at last night and day without ceasing, passed down the streets they forgot their fatigue and their hunger and thirst. Flowers fell on them from the crowded, cheering windows, and men and women, speaking a language they could understand, pressed by their side and offered them food and drink and kissed their hands.

At half-past ten the Russian flag fluttered out from the staff of the town-hall, and a deputation of townspeople waited on General Russky and said that the desire of all the Slav population was to become true and loyal sons of the mighty Russian Empire. Admirable was the conduct of the victorious troops. Having a large provision train, they had no need to ask the people for any assistance, and exemplary order was at once maintained by the military authorities, with the co-operation of the municipal bodies. The only booty taken was the Austrian Army stores, with two hundred guns and much baggage. The war material was enormous, as it had been collected from all parts of Austria-Hungary and stored in Lemberg to provide the armies on the frontier with supplies for six months or more. Its capture was of much importance.

But large as were the immediate consequences of the storming of the fortressed capital of the Alsace-Lorraine of Russia, these were only the by-products of the great victories at Halicz and Lemberg. The great thing was that the Napoleonic stroke had succeeded.

300,000 troops shattered and fugitive

Three hundred thousand hostile troops, forming the powerful right wing of the greatest army that ever invaded Russia, were shattered and fugitive. They had been gathered to protect the two main Austrian-Hungarian armies operating in the country to the north. Their defeat and flight exposed the main armies to an attack from the rear as well as on the front and flank. General Russky with his men went northward at once with a large force, while General Dimitrieff and General Brussiloff acted together round Lemberg against the army they had broken, which was being reinforced by German troops and Hungarian militia.

SWEEPING ALL BEFORE THEM WITH THE BAYONET—RUSSIAN SOLDIERS STORMING THE OUTSKIRTS OF JAROSLAV.

After the rout of the Austrians at Lemberg the Russian army swept westward, driving large numbers of both Germans and Austrians into Jaroslav and Przemysl, and capturing the former fortress, which is said to have been stronger than Liège, within two days. Later Jaroslav had to be evacuated, owing to the advance of the enemy on Warsaw. The picture is from a drawing by a Russian artist, M. Vladimiroff.

THE GREAT ROUT OF THE AUSTRIANS AT LEMBERG—RUSSIAN L

In the above view the spectator is looking towards the great range of the Ca pathians, distant about eighty miles. On the extreme right are Lublin an Kholm, where the Austro-German advance was checked. The positions Cracow, Jaroslav, Tomashov, Ravaruska, and Przemysl are clearly indicate In the centre lies the important town of Lemberg, whose capture prove

The city of Lemberg is noted for its many beautiful buildings. The view above shows the principal square with Municipal Theatre.

Panoramic view of the outskirts of the old Polish capit

Przemysl, "the Gibraltar of the Austrian Empire."

Large castle with church attached in Galician fighting area.

Before it was taken by the Russians, Lemberg is believed to have bee converted into a semi-fortified place. A series of lunettes, redoubts, etc had been more or less hastily prepared. It was the headquarters of th 11th Austrian Corps, which included the famous 43rd Landwehr Infantr Division, and was divided into three brigades. The forts outside th town were said to have been armed with 10·5 cm. siege-guns, made of steel with Krupp action, and firing high-explosive shell or shrapnel. One of th forts is also said to have had a battery of three 24 cm. heavy siege-guns of quit

N THE FOREGROUND AND THE CARPATHIANS IN THE DISTANCE.

ne of the decisive events of the earlier hostilities in the eastern theatre of the ar, while on the left are Halicz and Podayce. Not since Alexander the Great verthrew the mighty empire of Darius in a battle near Nineveh has there been swift and complete a destruction of a great and ancient State as befell ustria-Hungary between August 30th and September 12th, 1914.

Kholm, where Russia's Austrian prisoners were interned.

v, showing the railway bridge over the River Vistula.

modern pattern. When they were able to assume the offensive, the Russians rove the Austrians from their trenches at the point of the bayonet. A esperate attempt at a counter-attack only resulted in the capture of 5,000 Austrian prisoners. The immediate result of the Battle of the Vistula and Oniester was to throw the most ancient of Teutonic Empires into the power of he Prussian Empire. Forged by blood-and-iron methods, of which the reigning Austrian Emperor and his people had been among the first victims at Königratz, he Empire of the Prussians at once absorbed both Austria and Hungary.

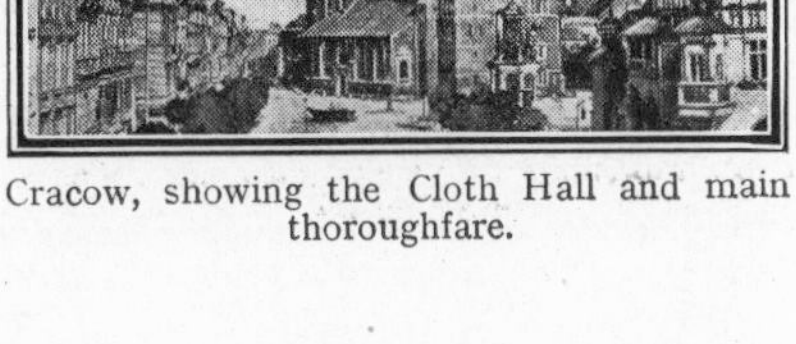

Cracow, showing the Cloth Hall and main thoroughfare.

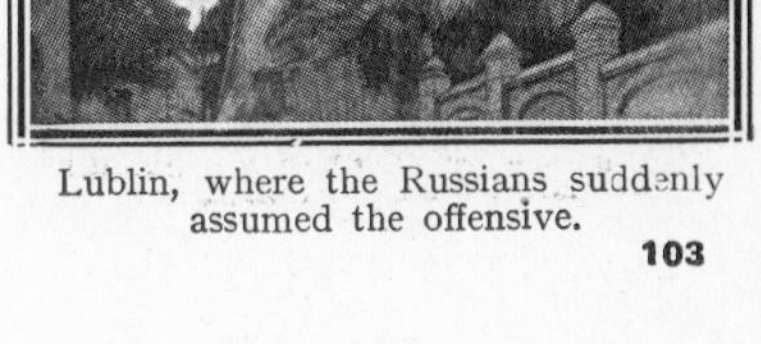

Lublin, where the Russians suddenly assumed the offensive.

POLISH CAVALRY IN THE KAISER'S SERVICE.

Group of young Polish officers awaiting orders for the front. Although the national sympathy of the Polish people was with Russia, Germany and Austria had many Poles in their armies. The headgear and the youthfulness of the men in the above group will be remarked. Inset: An aide-de-camp assisting Prince Charles Francis Joseph at Przemysl to adjust his uniform.

PRINCE CHARLES FRANCIS JOSEPH, HEIR TO THE AUSTRIAN THRONE, AND HIS STAFF.

The above photograph was taken at the Austrian Headquarters at Przemysl. Prince Charles is a son of the late Archduke Otto, and became heir to the Austrian throne after the assassination of the Archduke Francis Ferdinand at Serajevo on June 28th, 1914.

PALACE OF SCHOENBRUNN: ROYAL RESIDENCE AT VIENNA.

CHAPTER XXXII.

THE RUSSIAN VICTORIES OF THE VISTULA AND DNIESTER and the Destruction of the Main Armies of Austria-Hungary.

A Million Austro-Hungarian Troops Invade Russia—German Plan of Co-operation in Attacking Warsaw is Defeated—Austria Carries Out the Operation Herself—Russian Commander-in-Chief Lures the Invaders Far from their Railways—Advancing Towards the Russian Railway, the Austrians are Beaten Back—Their Right Wing is Broken by a Frontal Attack, their Centre is Encircled, their Left Wing Turned and Broken—Complete Disaster, Ending in a Rout in the River Marshes—Germany Saves Her Ally from Total Destruction.

FOR some centuries Austria has been the whipping-top of Europe. She has been lashed by the Turks, the Swedes, the Prussians, and the French, among others. The Polish king, John Sobieski, alone prevented the Crescent from displacing the Cross at Vienna—a debt the Austrians afterwards repaid by sharing largely in the destruction of Poland. The Russians alone prevented the Hungarians from breaking up the Empire in the middle of the nineteenth century—another debt the Austrians have now attempted to discharge, with characteristic cynical ingratitude, by the invasion of Russia.

This, however, was mere infatuation on the part of the Austrians. Even with the help of the Hungarians, still anxious for vengeance on the Russians for putting down their movement of independence, the attack on Russia was an act of madness. For nearly one half of the Austrian Army consisted of men of the Slav race, oppressed by their Germanic and Magyar lords, and looking to their fellow-Slavs in mighty Russia for redemption and liberation. Half of the Austrian Army consisted largely of troops anxious to kill the Austrians and fight for Russia.

It was this unparalleled condition of things that doomed Austria to destruction as soon as she dared to take the field against Russia. Russia was the one Power she could not attack with the shadow of a hope of success. Far easier would it have been for her to attempt to conquer her old foe Prussia. But, tricked by the Prussian, and egged on by the vengeful, ambitious Hungarian, Austria set out on the road to her final disaster as an Imperial Power. In the first three weeks of the campaign of invasion everything went well. Along the frontier, running parallel with the Russian boundary, was a strategic system of railways, including two trunk lines, with a daily capacity of seventy trains, and ten cross lines. This system, constructed on the plan of the German system of attacking railways, enabled the Austrians to assemble a mighty host between Cracow and Przemysl. Crossing the border, this host of some 500,000 men deployed on Russian territory, and advanced towards Warsaw and Brest-Litovsk.

Unser Kaiser im Gebet.
Vater im Himmel, Lenker der Sonnen,
Zeuge für mich, der in Demut Dir naht!
Ich nicht habe den Kampf begonnen,
Ich nicht streute die blutige Saat!
Doch von Feinden und Neidern umgeben
Rief ich mein Volk zu eiserner Wehr.
Laß Deinen Geist uns're Waffen umschweben,
Uns sei der Sieg — und Dir sei die Ehr'.
Harry Sheff

THE AUSTRIAN EMPEROR AT PRAYER.

From a postcard issued in the Austrian capital. Appended is a translation of his supposed "prayer":

"Father in Heaven, Ruler of the Universe,
Have pity for him who bows before Thee.
I did not start the strife nor strew the earth with blood.
Surrounded with foes and envy,
I called my people to the defence of arms.
Let Thy mercy surround our lines.
Ours will be the victory and Thine the honour."

Very slowly did the great army move forward. Spread out on both sides of the Vistula, it crept towards Radom on the left side of the river and Lublin and Kholm on the other side.

The fact was the Austrians were waiting for the Germans to co-operate with them. But German vanguards touched at Lodz and Petrokov, on a line with Kielce, and then withdrew. The Russian counter-stroke through Eastern Prussia engrossed all the forces Germany could spare from France. Austria, having been lured on to a most desperate enterprise by a solemn promise of a vigorous co-operation, was left alone at the critical period to pursue her perilous undertaking without assistance.

It is, therefore, not to be marvelled at that General Dankl, commanding the Austrian left wing, and General Auffenberg, directing the main Austrian army, should have hesitated to penetrate far into Russian

ON THEIR WAY TO LEMBERG.

Russian lancers going to the front. Inset: The City Hall and Municipal Buildings at Warsaw. The Germans reached a point about six miles from Warsaw, but were then compelled to retire.

territory. The farther they went the longer their lines of communication grew, in a country where railways were few and good roads scarce. There was Napoleon's disastrous campaign in the same country to deter them from any swift and crushing swoop, such as their allies were working up to in the western theatre of war.

While the Austrians were hesitating the Russians were acting with decision and foresight. Though the Russian mobilisation was far from complete, a very considerable force had been collected between Warsaw and Kiev, and screened by cavalry this force began to shepherd the Austrian armies to their place of doom. In the great bend that the River Vistula makes as it curves from Cracow to Thorn, the progress of the Austro-Hungarian troops was not encouraged. All attempts to move towards Warsaw and Ivangorod were fiercely opposed, and the point of junction between the German militia troops and the Austrian soldiers of the first line could only be safely fixed at the upper course of the Warta River, close to the Silesian and German Poland province.

Inflating the vanity of Vienna

On the other side of the Vistula, however, in the rolling wooded country between that river and its great eastern tributary the Bug, the Austrian armies were at first enticed to sweep onward, especially towards Kholm.

The advanced guards of the Russians were small and yielding, and the manner in which they continually gave ground enabled the hostile commanders to inflate, by daily reports of victories, the vanity of Vienna and the pride of Buda-Pesth. Rapid and tremendous victories were indeed a vital necessity to the Austrians and Hungarians. They needed them to daunt and dishearten their mutinous Slav subjects. For even in Vienna two Czech or Bohemian regiments had to be decimated in order to induce them to go to the front. Therefore every successful little outpost skirmish was magnified into an important battle, at which Russian armies had been routed.

Thus victoriously, General Dankl and General Auffenberg advanced on the towns of Lublin and Kholm, some fifty miles inside Russian territory. About August 25th they were within striking distance of these towns and of the railway that connected them and communicated with Ivangorod and Warsaw. But they were not allowed to capture either the towns or the railway. They had reached the line between the Vistula and the Bug, where the Grand Duke Nicholas had resolved to hold them. By this time the Russian armies under General Russky and General Brussiloff were moving southward through Galicia. Until they had strongly engaged the third Austrian army round Lemberg, which formed the right wing of the invading host, it would have been premature to join battle with the enemy's centre and left wing.

Austrians bogged in a swamp

So from August 22nd to August 28th the Russian commander-in-chief merely kept the invaders away from the Lublin-Kholm railway line. The first engagement of importance appears to have taken place at Krinitz, near the railway, when the Austrians attempted to advance beyond the line fixed by their opponents. Two machine-gun officers took a position on a height from which they were able to enfilade the ranks of the invaders, and the action was decided by a splendid bayonet charge from which the Austrians fled, only to get bogged in a swamp. Six thousand of them were rescued with ropes and made prisoners.

The Russian bayonet was peculiarly effective in all large engagements with the mixed troops of the Austrian Empire. Against the Germans it was just a good, shaking instrument of attack. Against the Austrians it was a rending force of quite extraordinary power. It led to the capture of a quarter of a million prisoners in the first series of battles between the Polish rivers. This was due to the dispositions made by the Austrian and Hungarian leaders to compel their Slav regiments to fight. The disaffected troops were usually placed in the front trenches, with Teutonic or Magyar supports behind them, ready to shoot them down.

The idea was to compel them, against their will, to fight for their lives against the Russians whom they wanted to help. The Russian generals, however, were well aware of the disposition of troops opposing them, and they

GENERAL MEYENDORFF.
Awarded the Order of St. George.

GENERAL RUSSKY SURROUNDED BY SOME OF HIS OFFICERS.
Note the bearded and bespectacled Orthodox chaplain in the background

GENERAL KONDRATOVITCH.
Awarded the Order of St. George.

GENERAL VON AUFFENBERG.
Leader of the Austrian forces in Galicia.

skilfully took full advantage of the circumstances. They directed their guns, after the opening artillery duel was over, to shrapnel the enemy's second line, and sent the infantry in a bayonet charge, with little artillery support, against the first trenches. At first the Russian foot soldier marvelled at the badness of the Austrian rifle fire. For, naturally, most of the bullets from the front trenches were aimed over the heads of the attacking parties. Then, when the Russian infantry closed in with bayonets at the charge, the Slav regiments opposed to them were only too glad to surrender without a struggle.

In one case, however, the bayonet charge failed, and a sergeant-major helping to lead it was taken prisoner. Finding it was a Slav officer under whose charge he was placed, the Russian began to talk to him—their languages being close enough in origin to make conversation possible. With great eloquence the sergeant-major discoursed on the kindness with which all Slav troops were received in the Russian camp, and the great work of liberation the Russians were performing for all Slav peoples. The upshot was that the Slav officer and his company crept out of the Austrian lines and surrendered to the Russians.

The Germans got out of a similar difficulty by using up many of their Polish regiments in the attack on Liège, where they fell in tens of thousands. But Austria could not rely on her Slav troops either in the Serbian battles or the Russian conflicts. She was fighting Slavs on both fronts of war, and all her subject populations were Slavs by race or by sympathy—Serbs, Croatians or Catholic Serbs, Russians, Bohemians, and Slovaks, or Rumanians.

To these men the Russian bayonet, when it came close enough to their trenches to make surrender safe, was an instrument of liberation from political and military tyranny. Hence the extraordinary number of prisoners taken in the war with Austria-Hungary.

The Austrians and Hungarians might well have stood against the Russians until Germany was able to afford vigorous help if they had relied entirely on soldiers of their own race. They would then have been able to bring up against Russia only about half a million first-line troops, instead of gathering more than a million of the regular Army for a mighty offensive movement. They would have had a small chain with no weak part in it, instead of a large chain with almost every alternate link of it near breaking point. As it was, the Grand Duke Nicholas and his Chief of Staff, General Sukhomlinoff, had the enemy at their mercy as soon as they were ready to strike. In numbers their armies were probably inferior to those of General Dankl and General Auffenberg and the Archduke Frederick. For as soon as the Austrians felt the menacing pressure on their front, stretching from Radom across the Vistula to the left bank of the River Bug, they began to hurry up reinforcements. In the

GENERAL DIMITRIEFF.
Bulgaria's "Iron General" serving with Russia.

GENERAL ROETZENDORF.
Chief of the Austrian Military Staff.

GENERAL LOBKO.
Awarded the Order of St. George.

SCENE DURING THE TEMPORARY RELIEF OF PRZEMYSL BY THE AUSTRIANS.
When the German advance on Warsaw compelled a portion of the Russian forces around Przemysl to be withdrawn, the Austrian commander sent a relief force to the assistance of the town. This force was welcomed with enthusiasm. Of this the camera affords evidence in the above photograph, which shows the Austrian commander, General F. M. L. von Kusmanek, in a balcony on the left.

end they had about 700,000 men between the Polish rivers, another 300,000 deployed in a refused right wing in Galicia, with divisions of Landwehr troops for supports and guarding the lines of communication.

The four opposing Russian armies amounted at first to little more than six hundred thousand men. Battalions were continually detraining from the railway head and marching into the firing-line, but this channel of reinforcement was not ample enough at the critical period. To supply the Grand Duke Nicholas with the men he needed, General Sukhomlinoff did a most daring thing. He drew off some of the army corps that had invaded East Prussia and railed them to Ivangorod to strengthen the Russian left wing at Lublin.

General Sukhomlinoff's daring

This was carried out when the German commander, General von Hindenburg, was massing at Thorn for his counter-attack upon the two Russian forces of invasion at Tannenberg and Königsberg. The two Russian army corps defeated under General Samsonoff at Tannenberg, in Prussia, were sacrificed to the exigencies of the position at Lublin and Kholm. General Rennenkampf at Königsberg was given the difficult task of fighting his way back to his own frontier, with a weakened force, against superior pressure of Hindenburg's army. He had yet to keep Hindenburg so fully employed as to prevent any considerable part of the German army in Prussia from being railed into Poland to help the Austrians.

Strengthened meanwhile by part of General Rennenkampf's troops, the main Russian army at Lublin and Kholm suddenly assumed the offensive. This was done on August 26th, when the Russian right wing advanced against General Dankl's army near Krasnic. As the attack was not driven home, the Austrians claimed the victory. But the action had the effect intended. General Dankl was made anxious. To increase his strength he brought across the Vistula part of the Austrian force operating round Kielce in expectation of German support in a movement towards Warsaw and Ivangorod. This weakened the subsequent outflanking attack delivered on the other side of the river at Ivangorod. Even more immediately important was the check to General Dankl's advance towards Lublin. In conjunction with the attack that afterwards followed on Ivangorod, the progress of Dankl's army along the other bank of the Vistula would have endangered the entire Russian position. It would have cut the Russian armies in Prussia, Poland, and Galicia in two. Dankl was so placed as to be extremely dangerous; he was therefore repressed. Auffenberg, as he advanced towards Kholm, was only running his neck into a noose; he was therefore encouraged to proceed.

A two-hundred-mile battle-front

Such were the circumstances in which the decisive stage of the battle opened on Friday, August 28th. Far in the south, at the extreme right wing of the two-hundred-mile battle-front, General Russky and General Brussiloff were then fiercely engaging the Lemberg armies. To prevent any troops being shifted from the Austrian left wing or centre to the support of the overwhelmed right wing, the Russian Commander-in-Chief strongly attacked all along the line. The centre, by Tomashov, close on the frontier and near the railway running to Lemberg, was

AUSTRIAN CADETS' ENTHUSIASM ON THE DECLARATION OF WAR.
After being sworn in, the Austrian "sucklings," or cadets, were drawn up in a square, where they gave loud "Hochs!" for their Kaiser as they lifted their unfleshed swords high in the air. From the vacant stand on the right of the picture a stirring harangue had just been delivered.

the point from which reinforcements could most easily have been moved. So there the Russian attack was driven with most violence, with the result that the 15th Hungarian Division was smashed and routed.

The general battle raged for a week between the Vistula and the Bug without any decision being fought out. The fact was that this period of the conflict was not important from the standpoint of the Russian commander. He only wished to hold back Dankl, and so to annoy Auffenberg as to prevent him from helping the Archduke Frederick in Galicia. There, at Zloczow, Halicz, and Lemberg, General Russky and General Brussiloff and General Radko Dimitrieff were breaking through the southern Austrian right wing, and thus turning the other Austrian positions northward between Lublin and Kholm. The main Russian army had to wait for a successful issue of its detached southern forces.

Breaking the Austrian right wing

Naturally, both Dankl and Auffenberg knew what was happening far to the south. Furious were the attempts they at once made to retrieve the defeat of their distant right wing by shattering the main Russian army in front of them. They knew now what was coming up against their rear, taking them in the back. So they tried hard to break through the enemy before them while they had time. They still had a strong force near Radom, across the Vistula. On August 31st this force made a desperate

WITH THE TROOPS OF THE EMPEROR FRANCIS JOSEPH ON THE OUTBREAK OF HOSTILITIES.
Austrian troops entraining for the front, outside the arsenal in Vienna. Inset: Austrian sentry guarding a railway line on the Galician frontier.

advance on Ivangorod, a fortress town possessing the only available bridge over the great river. Had Ivangorod been won, the main Russian army would have had the tables turned on it and been taken in the rear. But the Ivangorod garrison, with Russian forces operating round Warsaw, defeated the Austrians. These retired up the river towards Opole, where General Dankl had entrenched, threw two pontoon bridges over the water, and joined his army. Strengthened by them, Dankl again tried to reach the Lublin railway, but the Russian commander, having thrown all his reinforcements on this side, beat back the advance once more.

The Austrian attack on Ivangorod

While the attack on Ivangorod was being made by the Austrians over the river, with Dankl co-operating with them on the opposite side, General Auffenberg in the centre also violently assailed the Russian main army. Instead of the Grand Duke Nicholas having to stir him to activity to prevent him reinforcing the unhappy Archduke Frederick, the Russian Commander-in-Chief was hard put to it to resist Auffenberg's driving assault. In this part of the battlefield the Russian lines had to be drawn back, and it looked as though Kholm would be captured. For this was the weakest spot in the Russian front; it was allowed to remain weak, and a severe strain was put on the troops defending it.

But the position of the opposing forces suddenly changed about September 6th. By a wonderful feat of marching General Russky brought some of his troops up from Lemberg, and Auffenberg's army was then attacked on three fronts. All the offensive was knocked out of it by the heavy losses it suffered; it was completely reduced to a defensive rôle, and compelled at some points to retreat.

For a few hours it looked as though the Austrian front would be pierced. But both General Auffenberg and the Archduke Frederick worked with great energy to repair their centre and right wing. A magnificent reinforcement of 300,000 German troops with heavy artillery was railed to them in the nick of time, together with some excellent supports from the Tyrol and Hungary. One hundred and fifty thousand of the Germans marched with their big guns into Russian territory, and were placed on the hills round Turobin, between Dankl's and Auffenberg's forces.

Opportune German aid

The other three German army corps were used to stiffen a new right wing, formed of the fresh Austro-Hungarian troops, and the fugitives from the Battles of Halicz and Lemberg. These fugitives were mainly loyalists, the disaffected Slavs to the number of 70,000 having surrendered to the Russians. Refitted, reorganised, and emptied of mutinous troops, the broken Galician army was really more powerful than it had been before. But this was not known until the test came. It is impossible not to admire the speed and ability with which the Austrian

THE RUSSIAN RED CROSS SERVICE—ONE OF THE MOST PERFECT IN THE WORLD.

Russian Red Cross train about to leave Petrograd for the front. On the right are seen the Russian Minister for War and the Grand Duchess Anastasie Nicholaieovna. Inset: A hospital under canvas. Corner of a village that sprang up in the war area in answer to the call of the Russian Red Cross. The Russian and Japanese Red Cross organisations are among the best in the world. Only a day or two before the war the Moscow Municipal Council voted £1,000,000 for the Red Cross service.

RUSSIAN SOLDIERS AT PRAYER OUTSIDE A COTTAGE IN GALICIA.
The simple, devout faith of the Russian soldier is proverbial. This remarkable photograph shows a group outside a rural cottage in Galicia during a lull in the fierce fighting there. Among the men is an official of the Red Cross Society.

Commander-in-Chief—the Archduke Frederick—restored the greater part of his army from a condition of disaster to a state of strength.

The final position on which the Austrians posted themselves was a strong line to hold. Indeed, it might have been regarded as excellent, if it were not for the marshes behind it and its distance from the frontier railways. The troops were ranged between the Vistula and the Bug on a line running from Opole to Zamosc and Tomashov. In one place they were still within gunshot of the Lublin railway.

The country was rolling and wooded, affording good cover for infantry, and admirable positions for foliage-screened batteries. The first German force of 150,000 men, with heavy artillery, entrenched at Turobin on hills a thousand feet high, with a river running at the foot and moating their earthworks. They formed the central point in the main battle-front, and some 900,000 Austrians, Hungarians, Italians from the Trentino, and subject Slavs extended the lines for 200 miles. They had at least about 2,500 pieces of artillery, including the German guns, and Maxims in great abundance.

Central point of main battle-front

No outflanking movement by the Russian army seemed possible. The first Austrian force, under Dankl, stretched from Opole, above Krasnic, and was protected by the wide, deep, unbridged waters of the Vistula. Moreover, Austrian war-boats, with quick-firing guns, joined in the battle from the river, in somewhat the same way as the British monitors afterwards took part in the Nieuport conflict in the North Sea.

There was, as an additional measure of security, a German division operating on the other side of the broad stream. General Dankl's army appear to have included the three German army corps on the Turobin heights. Connecting with the Germans was the second Austrian army, under General Auffenberg, that held the hilly region from Turobin to Tomashov. The third army, hastily organised after the defeat of the Galician forces, guarded the rear of Auffenberg's and Dankl's troops. It extended like a defending wall from north to south, about a day's march from Lemberg. The fortress of Gorodok, westward on the Lemberg road, was its pivoting point, and the town of Ravaruska, near the Russian frontier, was the point at which it was concentrated for the protection of Auffenberg's army. The third army formed what is technically known as a refused wing. Instead of prolonging the general front, like an ordinary wing, it bent sharply downwards at Ravaruska, almost at a right angle to the main Austrian line between the rivers. A refused wing of this kind is the best posture of defence against a turning movement.

Austrian concentration at Ravaruska

From the orthodox point of view of the Teutonic and Magyar strategists of the Moltke school, they had recovered from the effects of the Galician reverses, and brought their opponents suddenly to the position of a stalemate. For their armies were as strongly posted in Russian Poland in the first week in September as the German armies were in France in the third week of that month. The Turobin heights, especially where heavy guns were being hauled into their pits, looked more difficult to storm than the plateau of Soissons in the Aisne valley. A frontal attack up long slopes and over streams and marshes, against thousands of guns, tens of thousands of Maxims, and a million rifles, entrenched with wire entanglements, seemed to the Austrian commander a thing impossible of success. And the obvious enveloping

GUNS OF THE RIVAL FORCES IN GALICIA.

Striking photograph of a battery of Austrian heavy guns, intended to repel the Russian advance into Galicia. The view on the left is of a specially constructed gun fixed in one of the Russian trenches for the purpose of bringing down hostile aircraft.

movement by the flank was prevented by the waters of the Vistula on one side, and on the other by the fortress of Gorodok and by a larger army than the Russians possessed at Lemberg.

Therefore, there remained only, from the defenders' standpoint, a slow open-air siege battle of the Mukden kind, in which the Russians would be busily occupied until General von Hindenburg could swing round from Prussia to the Lower Vistula and threaten to take the Russians in the rear. The German railways were so built as to make this operation facile and rapid of execution.

Avoiding an open-air siege battle

But since the Russians themselves had fought the first modern siege battles in Manchuria, they had thought out a way of avoiding them. They proceeded to show the Austrians how it could be done. They intended a terrific frontal attack in the old Napoleonic fashion, but against such a power of defensive machinery as Napoleon never faced even at Waterloo. Instead of throwing all his troops forward, the Russian commander collected a general reserve, which was manœuvred behind the battle-front and shifted by severe marches to the point that promised to yield and break.

To begin with, a feint thrust was made at a point far removed from the spot chosen for the real piercing attack. We have seen that for some time the Russian commander had been driving fiercely down on Auffenberg's army, that formed the centre of the Austrian battle-line. After the fall of Lemberg part of the victorious Southern Russian forces also began to drive vehemently up towards Auffenberg.

Subtle tactics of the Grand Duke Nicholas

Auffenberg thus had good reasons for supposing that on his troops the main offensive movement of his opponents would fall. So it did in the end. But all the first operations against him were a feint. The Russians desired to shift the bulk of the Austro-German reinforcements towards the centre and the right wing of their enemy.

It was on the left wing of the Austrians that the real frontal attack was to be made. So, against all expectations, General Dankl, in his apparently quite impregnable position on the Vistula and the Turobin hills, was the first to feel the full weight and edge of Russia's power. For some days the long battle continued in a close-pressed Russian offensive all along the line. Auffenberg suffered most at Tomashov, where General Russky was co-operating in the attack. When this delusive operation had taken effect, the hammer-stroke fell some forty miles eastward on Dankl's army.

The decisive tactics of the Grand Duke Nicholas had a characteristic subtlety about them. He massed a strong force with many guns on the opposite side of the Vistula. It was composed of the troops who had defeated the Austrian attack on Ivangorod. They could easily destroy the single German division that was holding the left bank of the river. This they did about September 8th. Meanwhile, General Dankl was invited to advance from his strong, entrenched position. The pressure upon his front was entirely relaxed now that the general reserve had been massed behind the troops that had been holding him. No doubt General Dankl concluded that the pressure exerted on his colleague General Auffenberg was obtained by weakening the forces opposed to him.

He resolved to take advantage of this state of things, and also to relieve the pressure at Tomashov, by another swift, forceful offensive movement towards his customary objective—Lublin and the railway line. The road was left clear for him to within eight miles of the alluring railway to Warsaw. Then, however, his men were hurled back with great violence and speed. The cavalry had to be thrown out to the Cossacks to prevent these swarming, furious horsemen from riding down the retreating infantry and getting at the guns. A few days before the Cossacks had already won in a smashing charge against the Austrian horsemen, and now they were riding to the great victory. Rearguard after rearguard had to be sacrificed to them and to their rapidly advancing infantry supports. Before the infantry went the Russian horse artillery; behind them rumbled the main ordnance—light quick-firers, heavy guns, and howitzers.

The Austrians were barely back in their trenches when the first great frontal attack of the modern era was delivered. It was no Zulu-like charge, in dense crowds that relied only on the steel, such as the German attempts to pierce the British lines at Mons and Le Cateau. The Russian infantry instructors had learnt in the Far Eastern campaign to modify charging tactics so as to lessen losses from shrapnel fire, and to make the power of the long-range rifle tell on the enemy in the trenches before the bayonets came close enough to shake his courage.

There was the preliminary artillery duel, in which the superior Russian guns were pushed forward to search and overpower the hostile batteries. This result was largely achieved. Some Austrian river gunboats tried to get an enfilading fire against the Russians, only to be smitten from the side themselves. For by this time the Russian force on the farther bank of the Vistula had routed the German division and brought up their guns to take part in the battle. The hostile gunboats had to sink or retire, and the riverside Russian batteries then began in turn to enfilade the Austrian position.

Infantry tactics learnt in the Far East

While this side conflict was proceeding, with important consequences for General Dankl's troops in their hour of retreat, the decisive infantry attack on the front opened. In grey lines the armed peasants of Russia moved onward from cover to cover, making quick rushes, and then lying prone and firing steadily at any heads showing in the trenches, while their supports were running into position behind them. In patience under heavy fire they were as good as British soldiers; they stood severe punishment without losing their nerve. But in extended order, and in situations calling for individual initiative, they were not each a born, trained non-commissioned officer of the first class, as most of our privates have proved themselves. Accustomed in their village life to act collectively, they tended to crowd together at critical moments. Yet they were magnificent troops. They retained completely all the sterling old qualities of their race, and showed themselves finer marksmen and more brilliant fighters than their fathers. They judged the ranges quickly and well, and they did not lose their head as the time neared for bayonet work. Unlike our soldiers, they saw no hip-firing among their opponents. Their only criticism of the Austrians was that they made targets of themselves by kneeling to fire, instead of lying prone and aiming.

The frontal attack revived

But excellently trained though the Russian sōldier was in modern infantry work, the bayonet remained his supreme instrument of warfare. For he had been instructed by his masters of the new Russian school, who had revived the doctrine of the frontal attack, that the steel would again win the victory. And so it did, in spite of quick-firing guns, magazine rifles, and aerial reconnaissance work, wire entanglements, and the deadly Maxim's stream of bullets.

Except for wire entanglements and sheltering trenches, all these new weapons could be used by the attackers as well as by the defenders. The storming companies, if held up by fire from the trenches, could suddenly open out and let the machine-guns, brought up behind them, rake the defending riflemen and sweep the hostile Maxims. The artillery of the offensive army had a fixed mark when the position of the defending trenches was discovered, as the range and the time-fuse could be exactly measured by the gunners supporting the infantry attack. The rival artillerymen, on the other hand, had in the advancing troops a series of rapidly shifting targets over which it was often difficult to get shrapnel to burst at the accurate place and moment.

With all this, however, the Russians had to suffer heavily to win their goal. In neither old nor new wars had a well-defended front been pierced without great sacrifice of life. Slowly, stubbornly, the quiet, enduring moujik advanced under the cover of his thundering guns. At last, when he reached the edge of possible safety, he closed in crowds and charged. He fell. His immediate supports came on at the double. They, too, fell. But a great host was

KRAVCHENKO, A DISTINGUISHED RUSSIAN WAR ARTIST, SKETCHING A SPY DISGUISED AS PEASANT.

A spy masquerading as an inoffensive peasant had been brought into the Russian lines by a Cossack patrol, and his picturesque appearance attracted the attention of the famous Russian artist, Kravchenko, who, it will be noticed, was wearing military uniform. This was compulsory for all war correspondents accompanying the Russian forces.

pressing behind them, ranged company after company, battalion after battalion. Every yard the fallen leaders gained was held by their advancing, innumerable comrades. The sun went down and the stars came out in the darkness, and in the obscurity of the night the attackers pressed their advantage and broke the enemy's front just as dawn was breaking.

It was at the village of Vysoky, eastward of Krasnic, that the lines of General Dankl's army were pierced on September 9th. There the Russian bayonet came over the Austrian trench, stabbing with dreadful skill as it passed. Behind, the machine-guns were pushed through the first broken defence, to help in the decisive work of shattering the enemy's second line. As the foremost troops were fighting in the twilight of daybreak against the re-forming Austrians, another mass of grey, tall figures crashed into the conflict—troops fresh and unblooded to human slaughter, but worked into pitiless fury by the sight of the heaps of dead or maimed comrades that cumbered the ground over which they came. The Austrians broke and fled.

Success that came with the dawn

General Dankl abandoned his position with great speed. The danger was that the Cossack cavalry, pouring through the gap, would get on his rear and break up the retreat. The Germans at Turobin bitterly complained afterwards that they had been deserted by the men who had called them up to aid them. But the fact was that the Austrians had to retire with vehement rapidity to prevent an annihilating rout. For besides being broken in front, they were enfiladed as they collected in masses by shrapnel fire from the Russian guns on the opposite side of the river. In the end they managed to get out rearguards and withdraw along the Vistula in order.

But the suddenness of their unexpected retreat exposed the German army of 150,000 on Turobin heights to a surprise flank attack. The Germans had not even got all their big guns into position when the victorious Russians attacked them sideways through the opening in the front left by the retreating Austrians. After losing 5,000 men, they had to abandon their heavy artillery—thirty-two splendid new guns engraved with the monogram of the German Emperor. But, fighting bravely, they withdrew to the south-east, in the direction taken by their allies, and reached the Vistula at Annapol.

All this Austro-German left wing could have been completely routed, and even annihilated, by the attacking army and its powerful supports on the opposite bank of the Vistula. But the Russian commander was aiming at larger results than the immediate destruction of General Dankl's forces. In pursuit of these results he detached only sufficient troops to keep the beaten wing on the move along the shore of the Vistula, and thrust it back if it tried to turn eastward and grope for a connection with its centre.

Every other Russian soldier was then marched, weary but nerved by victory to more labour and fighting, against the western flank and rear of the central Austrian armies under General Auffenberg. For the flight of the Germans from the heights of Turobin had naturally exposed their neighbours on their left to a turning movement similar to that which had made them retire.

But the Grand Duke Nicholas did not intend the Austrian centre to escape by a retreat. All through the evening and night of September 9th the Russian troops marched, some corps covering a remarkable distance by a splendid display of endurance. The result was that Auffenberg's army on September 10th was completely encircled. General Russky held it on the south-west near Tomashov. Round Zamosc and along the northern front it was retained by its old opponents; on the east and south part of the Russian left wing barred all the roads. It was a greater Sedan.

In the hope of avoiding the ghastly work of slaughtering some hundreds of thousands of men, the Russian commander sent an officer under a white flag to ask General Auffenberg to surrender. But, as usually happens in such circumstances in modern warfare, Auffenberg declined, for he was determined to attempt to break through the enveloping army. Any good general would have taken this course. For it is now generally known that even at Sedan, in spite of Moltke's strategy, the French had a fighting chance of piercing the ring around them. There was a weak point in it, which if discovered and struck would have opened a path of retreat. With fair supplies of ammunition and food, an encircled army that strikes fiercely and rapidly, as the Germans afterwards did at Lodz, can often get out with the loss of a fourth or a fifth of its numbers.

ALL THAT WAS LEFT OF A FINE BRIDGE IN POLAND BY RETREATING GERMANS.

This was what General Auffenberg essayed to achieve. But he did not entirely succeed. After a day of frightful slaughter his men began to lose their cohesion. North and east and west the Russians drove in upon them, and though the southernmost attacking force drew off, leaving an apparent path of retreat, this movement was as deadly in effect as an attack would have been. For the only line of retirement thus allowed to the broken Austrians led to the wide, disastrous swamp lands of the River San. Into this terrible trap Auffenberg's army was forced by blow after blow on flanks and rear.

At the same time Dankl's army, now separated by a two days' march from its broken centre, was more vigorously handled by the Russian commander. Vast as his battlefield was, portable wireless instruments and aerial messenger service by high-speed flying machines enabled the Grand Duke Nicholas and his Chief of Staff to control all operations over a front of two hundred miles better than Napoleon had controlled Grouchy at Waterloo.

As soon as Auffenberg's forces were scattered and bogged in the southern river swamps some of the Russian troops were again moved towards the Vistula to co-operate in drawing Dankl's army in disorder into another stretch of marshland between the Vistula and its tributary the San. The water draining from the Carpathian Mountains into Galicia turns both rivers into streams that ooze and trickle for miles into the country on either side, and turn the land, even in the month of September, into green, untraversable morasses. It was bad strategy on the part of the Austrian Commander-in-Chief to place his armies with

Austrian commander's bad strategy

AN AUSTRIAN FIELD TELEGRAPH IN OPERATION IN POLAND.

their backs on a wide, long stretch of swamp. But he had been so confident of at least holding the Russian attack that he did not trouble to arrange for the possibility of a sudden retreat. In the end this cost him half his army, almost all his war stores, and a large number of his guns—some captured in the fight, but more bogged during the murderous rout through the river swamps.

For two or three days after the victory over the enemy's left wing and centre, the two immense bodies of defeated troops were shepherded into difficulties rather than continually cut down. For most of the victors were as fatigued as the vanquished, though the Cossack managed to make himself ubiquitous and indefatigable. He swam across the Vistula—no narrow flood of water—and blew up war stores piled for the use of the retreating army; he attacked armoured trains near the German frontier and wrecked them by a trick. And, chiefly, he kept the routed forces moving and allowed them no rally places.

Meanwhile, the Russian commander was again drawing off troops from the centre for more battle work. For the Austrian right wing in Galicia, between Ravaruska and Gorodok, close to Lemberg, was putting up a magnificent fight. This stand was unexpected, for, as we have seen, many of the troops had been thoroughly defeated in the first battles around Lemberg. The conflict appears to have begun soon after the capture of Lemberg, when the Bulgarian General Dimitrieff advanced with some 40,000 men to drive in the still retreating wing and thus expose the army of General Auffenberg to a rear attack.

On this part of the battlefield, however, there were suddenly poured enormous reinforcements, including the second three German army corps sent in answer to Austria's appeal. Radko Dimitrieff's troops were then tested almost as severely as were Sir Horace Smith-Dorrien's army corps at Le Cateau a week or so before. The Austro-Germans took the offensive and made continual attacks of a most determined kind. The brunt of these assaults fell upon the 40,000 men under the heroic Bulgarian. In this place the Austrians and Germans outnumbered the Russians by four—or even five—to one. The Russians fought in a splendidly stubborn and enduring manner. For three days and nights the conflict raged unceasingly, and Dimitrieff had to use his troops to the uttermost, allowing none of them a moment's rest. Not a single detail could be given the least repose. The fatigue was so overpowering that on the last day the men fell asleep under fire.

Radko Dimitrieff's formidable task

One officer dropped off and never woke through all the tremendous bombardment, the rifle firing, and the attempt to take his trenches. When he opened his eyes he found himself lying close to a pile of dead, and on trying to move he discovered he was hurt. Two of his toes had been cut off by a shrapnel bursting while he slept. Between sleeping and waking General Radko Dimitrieff's heroes held their ground against artillery fire, varied by bayonet attacks, until reinforcements arrived and the enemy was for the time driven off.

Exhausted soldiers fall asleep under fire

It was General Brussiloff who came to the help of his former companion in victory at Halicz. But even when their forces were united they were still outnumbered by the opposing army directed by the Archduke Frederick. Good Chiefs of Staff take care when an archduke, or a Crown Prince, or any other Royal commander is given control of an army that he shall have more troops than his opponent. General Conrad von Roetzendorf, the head of the Austrian General Military Staff, had so arranged matters in this case. A large part of the Russian Galician army had marched northward, under General Russky, to help in the envelopment of Auffenberg's forces. General Brussiloff and General Dimitrieff had to struggle along with scanty forces until Russky, having thrust back Auffenberg, could again march from the north and co-operate with them.

AUSTRIAN REFUGEES IN VIENNA.

Vienna, like Berlin, as a result of the Russian advance in the early stages of the Great War, witnessed a big incursion of refugees from the east. Our picture gives ample evidence of the haste with which the fugitives—men, women, and children—fled to the Austrian capital before the rolling tide of the Russian invasion.

The Russian Commander-in-Chief certainly worked his troops tremendously hard. Both his generals and his men had to force themselves to the limit of their powers. It was only by each of them performing the work of two to three men that they outmanœuvred, outfought, and finally destroyed the fighting power of a million enemy troops of the first line. By doing treble the amount of marching and double the amount of fighting, the Russians, though inferior in numbers to their foes, exerted against them twice the amount of warlike power. This is the grand, the classic strategy—the strategy of Napoleon and Nelson, of Marlborough and Turenne. Great commanders in land warfare almost always overwork their men. They get more out of them than the men dreamt they possessed. Hence, the extraordinary force they display. Hence also, on the modern battle-fronts, a hundred or more miles in length, the need for young, athletic troops with the quick recuperative vigour of youth.

The mounted Cossack did not count for much in the decisive battles. His horsemanship told only in the preliminary reconnaissances and in the rout of the enemy. But there was one period of peril to the Russian force near Gorodok when the Cossack horsemen, like the British cavalry division at Mons, saved the situation.

A considerable power of Austrians and Germans assailed the Russian advance guard, with a view to shattering it and then breaking through the centre. The Russian infantry and guns were strongly entrenched. In reserve there were several Cossack detachments. At first the Austrian foot soldiers attacked under cover of a bombardment. But they encountered so heavy a gun fire and rifle fire that they wavered and fell back.

Where the Cossack saved the situation

Then an attempt was made to carry the trenches by a cavalry charge. The flower of the Austro-Hungarian army—the Buda-Pesth Guard Division—officered by the Magyar nobility, was hurled against the Russian front. The Hungarians, in their bright jackets, galloped furiously forward in close order. It seemed as though nothing could stay their impetuous course. Massed shrapnel fire made great gaps in their ranks; a rain of bullets from the machine-guns swept away their leading squadrons; at last the magazine rifles of the Russian infantry volleyed at them.

But the Hungarians never hesitated. Those who survived only urged their horses to cover the ground more quickly, and prepared to strike. The Russian infantry rose with their bayonets in a hopeless attempt to repel an overwhelming charge. In less than a minute, it seemed, the trenches would be taken. But behind them the infantry heard a thud of hoofs and clatter of steel, and the Hungarians were countered by a whirlwind of Cossacks. For two hours the Austrian and Russian infantry watched with excited eyes the scene of carnage, each cheering on their men, and getting in a quick helping shot on occasion. In the end not a man was left of the First Cavalry Division of the Buda-Pesth Guard. Its commander, General Frohreich, it was reported, could not bear the disgrace of the defeat and shot himself on the battlefield.

With desperate valiancy the Austro-German right wing tried to maintain its position between Ravaruska and Gorodok. When its centre and left wing gave way the need for holding out against the southern Russian army became still more urgent. For it then had to cover the retreat of Dankl's and Auffenberg's forces, and prevent General Brussiloff and General Dimitrieff from sweeping down also upon the broken fugitives. But on September 12th General Russky joined again with General Brussiloff and General Dimitrieff. The Archduke Frederick's force was turned in the north, and it, too, fled westward. More fortunate than the other two Austro-German armies, it was able to fall back towards the famous fortress of Przemysl—the Gibraltar of the Austrian Empire—which required a long siege, even with modern howitzers, to reduce it. But it was only a disorganised rabble that arrived at Przemysl. For Russky pressed so hard on it from the north, while his subordinate commanders drove at its rear as it turned, that it was rent with terrible losses and then impelled along the western road in a huddle of spiritless men.

Altogether the disaster that overtook the military forces of the Austrian Empire in their attempted invasion of Russia was the greatest catastrophe known since Napoleon's retreat from Moscow. The modern invaders, however, were not defeated by the bitter Russian winter weather, or lessened in number to the point of weakness by the necessity of guarding an extremely long line of communications. They were abruptly overthrown when they were at their full strength and posted in a position of extraordinary defensive power. The Battle of the Vistula and the Dniester—if we may name it by the rivers between which the opposing fronts extended—was one of the greatest victories in history, both from the military and the political points of view.

It suddenly brought to an end the Imperial rule of the Hapsburgs. For the immediate result of it was to throw the most ancient of Teutonic Empires, linked by its traditions of the Holy Roman Empire with the age of Charlemagne, into the power of the northern parvenu Prussian Empire. Forged by blood-and-iron methods, of which the reigning Austrian Emperor and his people had been among the first victims at Königratz, the Empire of the Prussians at once absorbed both Austria and Hungary.

Practically the entire military force of any value of the ancient Empire was, in the middle of September, reduced to half a million men struggling for their lives in morasses and besieged fortresses against the victorious troops of Russia. There followed a dreadful week of nightmare horrors for the floundering, broken Austrians and Hungarians still being pursued between the Vistula and the San Rivers. For the Germans, retreating in their turn before the conquering Franco-British forces, were in too great difficulties to afford any help to their apparently doomed ally. It looked for a time as though the Russians would kill or capture every regiment of the million troops that had invaded their territory.

A week of nightmare horrors

But, by her stand on the heights of the Aisne, Germany recovered herself in time to help her broken ally. Large bodies of fresh troops and vast supplies of new war material were quickly railed towards Cracow, and at last the pressure was taken off the beaten, driven armies of Austria. What remained of them was refitted and reorganised, and then placed under the control of the German Military Staff. For practical purposes Austria-Hungary as a military Power had ceased to exist. She had suddenly declined from an independent Empire into a contemned, subservient vassal territory, exploited for the defence of Germany. Hungary, especially, was robbed of troops necessary for the defence of the Carpathian passes and the wheatfields of the Danube, in order that her finest men should perish in tens of thousands at Ypres in a vain attempt to conquer Calais for the Prussian.

THE SLEEP OF EXHAUSTION.

A wounded Russian soldier, utterly worn out in the warfare in Galicia, fallen asleep near the trenches where he had been fighting against the Austrians.

THE WINTER PALACE AND SQUARE, PETROGRAD.

CHAPTER XXXIII.

THE MARCH OF EVENTS FROM AUSTRIA'S DEBACLE AT LEMBERG TO THE TURN OF THE TIDE IN THE WEST.

Phases of the Recruiting Problem in Great Britain—The War and the Chemical Industries—The King and the Belgian Mission—M. Clemenceau's Optimism—Paris under Martial Law—Protection for Masterpieces in the Louvre—Refugees from Northern France—Petrograd—The Enemy at Amiens—Compiègne a City of the Dead—The Fighting at Solesmes—The British Working Classes and the War—Patriotism of the Dominions—From Paris to Bordeaux: M. Poincaré's Inspiring Address—General Gallieni's Proclamation—Evacuation of Rouen—Saving of the British Exhibits at Leipzig—The United States and the War—Mr. Asquith at the Guildhall—Turkey and Germany—New Naval and Marine Brigades—The Allies and Peace—Fine Utterance by Lord Rosebery—Italian Sympathies—A Russian Governor for Galicia—The Anglo-French Retreat to the Marne—The Dykes Opened in Flanders—Controversies in Berlin—The Chancellor and the Silver Bullets.

IN the early days of September the problem of recruiting for the strengthening of the British Expeditionary Force co-operating with our allies in France and Belgium was the subject of earnest consideration throughout the United Kingdom. The spirit of patriotism and self-sacrifice was abroad. In London alone on some days as many as 5,000 offered themselves for enlistment. Some firms granted a bonus of £2 to young, single men in their employment who took, in the old phrase, the King's shilling. Others promised from five shillings a week to half their pay if the youngsters would join the colours. Some railway companies treated all single men who responded to the recruiting sergeant as on leave with full pay.

An appeal to young Nonconformists to enlist without delay was made by Sir William Robertson Nicoll, editor of the "British Weekly," the leading exponent of Nonconformity in the British Press. "That Nonconformists are neither cowardly nor incapable," he said, "when called to a righteous war, the glorious name of Oliver Cromwell sufficiently attests. That this is a most righteous and necessary war is a proposition which cannot be contested. If we were subjugated by Germany, we have no higher future before us than the life of a tributary province, harassed and humiliated at every point—a life so intolerable that death is infinitely preferred. The result may depend on a very slight preponderance of forces on either side. Every man who can fight is wanted at once. Hitherto there has been no attempt to drive the people, because it is felt that they can be led, and that when the issues are clearly set before them they will abhor as infinitely worse than death the stain of cowardice. For the Order of the White Feather there will soon be no room in our land."

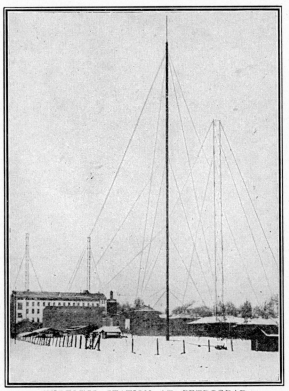

WIRELESS STATION AT PETROGRAD, by means of which communications could be carried on with London and Paris.

Other public men, like Lord Charles Beresford, had a clarion note on "the imperative duty of every man in Great Britain to back up on land by our own sacrifice and devotion the onus that we were placing on the Fleet." Dealing with the cry that went up against the young men of Britain who were still playing sports and games, the gallant admiral added: "I cast no stones. The men who play football, cricket, and other games are our finest specimens of British manhood. I put it to them to consider—they are fit, strong, healthy, and as sportsmen they are cheery; health makes vigour, cheeriness makes pluck—I put it to them, that we must now all be prepared to stand by our country, and to suffer for our country. We want a million men. Why do I say a million? Because a million men will safeguard us, and—it is a very important point—when

SIR WILLIAM HENRY PERKIN.
He made the discovery which laid the foundation of the coal-tar dye industry. The factory erected by him and his brother at Greenford Green, near Harrow, in 1857, still exists, but the industry was almost wholly monopolised by the Germans.

the war is over we shall then have power behind our policy to uphold Great Britain in the councils of Europe."

Lord Kitchener himself inquired of the leaders of the great political parties if they would jointly agree that their organisations should give full co-operation in securing the enlistment of more men. This suggestion was at once adopted, and the official party organisations, consisting of the leaders, whips in both the Commons and the Lords, and chief officials, united for the purpose, with Mr. Asquith, Mr. Bonar Law, and Mr. Arthur Henderson, leader of the Labour Party, as presidents. Associated with them were Major-General Sir H. S. Rawlinson and Major A. B. Gossett, as representing the War Office. The headquarters of the movement were fixed at 12, Downing Street, the office of Mr. Percy Illingworth, the chief Government Whip, with whom was associated Lord Edmund Talbot, the chief Unionist Whip.

In many football unions it was decided to cancel all fixtures during the war, on the ground that it "would be desecrating their playing-fields to use them for sport at such a time."

Mr. Runciman, President of the Board of Trade, appointed a committee, of which the Lord Chancellor was chairman, to consider and advise as to the best means of obtaining for the use of British industry sufficient supplies of chemical products, colours and dye-stuffs, of kinds hitherto largely imported from countries with which we were at war. A little later the Government agreed to finance to some extent a company to begin the manufacture of colours and dye-stuffs, which are so necessary in every branch of the textile trade, more especially the woollen, in order to maintain employment, and prevent these trades languishing, if not collapsing. There was a species of retributive justice in this, as it was in Great Britain that the practicability of these colours and dye-stuffs being drawn from the bye-products of coal-tar was discovered and demonstrated by British chemists. It was only the slackness in British enterprise which enabled German organisation to take up their manufacture and create almost a monopoly of supply to the textile trades.

ELIZABETH, QUEEN OF THE BELGIANS.
Queen Elizabeth, who was married to King Albert in 1900, is a fully qualified doctor of medicine. Visiting the trenches, forts, and hospitals, her people wondered at times if she was not the spirit of their dear country, wandering with them to the last.

THE BELGIAN MISSION IN LONDON.
M. Carton de Wiart (Minister of Justice) in centre, and M. Emile Vandervelde (Socialist leader) on the right. They were received in London by the King on their way to Washington to lay before the United States Government a statement of the German excesses in Belgium.

H.M. King Albert of Belgium commissioned M. Carton de Wiart, Minister of Justice, M. de Saedeleer, M. Hymans, and M. Vandervelde, Ministers of State, with Mme. Vandervelde, and Count de Lichtervelde as secretary, as a royal mission to the President of the United States, empowered to submit definite proofs of German savagery during the enemy's occupation of their beloved land. On September 1st the members of the mission visited King George at Buckingham Palace, and had the honour of being presented to his Majesty by the Belgian Minister, the Lord Stanmore (Lord-in-Waiting) and the Master of the

EAGER YOUNG RECRUITS FOR LORD KITCHENER'S NEW ARMY.
Crowds of young men besieging the recruiting offices in Whitehall, London, during the early days of Lord Kitchener's call for men.

Household being in attendance. M. Carton de Wiart, head of the mission, read an address to his Majesty on their behalf, in which he said: "We have considered it to be our duty to make a stay in the capital of the British Empire to convey to your Majesty the respectful and ardent expression of gratitude of the Belgian nation. We have never forgotten that Great Britain presided at the birth of Belgian independence. She had confidence in the wisdom and loyalty of our country. We have tried to justify this confidence by remaining strictly true to the rôle which had been assigned to us by international politics. In spite of all this suffering in Belgium, which has been made the personification of outraged right, the country is resolute in fulfilling to the utmost her duties towards Europe. Whatever may happen, she must defend her existence, her honour, and her liberty."

London's send-off to the Belgian Mission

A sympathetic meeting, held in the Hotel Cecil on September 2nd, under the auspices of the Eighty Club, and attended by a large number of Members of Parliament, gave a send-off to the Belgian Mission. M. Hymans and M. and Mme. Vandervelde made interesting speeches, in which they expressed unqualified faith in the final victory of the Allies over their ruthless German foes; and the latter read a letter written on behalf of the Queen of the Belgians, in which her Majesty "approved of the plan of putting before the public opinion in Great Britain and the United States the suffering which the German invasion had inflicted upon their peaceful population. Five of the provinces of Belgium were devastated, thousands of families driven out of their houses were at that moment without a home, and it was deserving well of one's country and of humanity to try to help them. The best wishes of the Queen accompanied the mission to these two countries which love to help those in distress."

The spirit of France was reflected in a stirring statement made to a correspondent by M. Clemenceau, the great French statesman, on September 1st. Forgetting all personal differences with the existing Ministry, he said: "If we were to be defeated again, and yet again, we should still go on. This is not my personal resolve alone. The Government is just as grimly determined. It is strange that one should come to feel like this—that the Germans could destroy all those beautiful places that I love so much." Referring to the havoc made at Louvain, and other towns and cities, he exclaimed:

Fighting for the dignity of humanity

"They may blow up all the museums, overthrow the monuments — it would leave me still determined to fight on. It would not abate by one fraction our vigour and our decision. In this terrible war we must all realise how unutterably great are the stakes. It is we in France and our friends in Belgium who are doomed to suffer the most bitterly. Great Britain will be spared much that we must endure. But we must all make sacrifices almost beyond reckoning. We are fighting for the dignity of humanity. We are fighting for the right of civilisation to continue to exist. We are fighting so that nations may continue to live in Europe without being under the heel of another nation. It is a great cause; it is worth great sacrifices. I say this to convince you of the indomitable spirit of the French nation. But the situation is not yet so grave. We knew our frontier would be invaded somewhere. We are still resisting doggedly, and have many troops in reserve for the big battle that will follow this one. The Germans cannot invest Paris. Its size is too vast, and its defences will be assisted by armies now fighting on the Oise, seventy miles away. The fortifications of Paris are by no means the feeble defence they were in 1870. From our wireless stations on the summit of the Eiffel Tower we can control

"GRAPPLING IN THE CENTRAL BLUE."
An aeroplane action over Paris. After a time the aerial visitors from Germany were met by French aviators, and more than once the populace had an opportunity of witnessing an encounter in mid-air in which the German aeroplane was destroyed.

the movements in co-operation with our armies in the provinces of France. Although the Germans have invaded France, we will fight on and on until this attempt to establish tyranny in Europe has been completely overthrown."

A correspondent of "The Times," referring to the great importance of Paris considered as a fortress, described it thus briefly: "Paris was defended in 1870-71 by a ring of detached forts, and was garrisoned mainly by National Guards and Mobiles. It was not properly victualled, but energetic measures enabled it to hold out for four months. Since 1871 there has been added to the old fortification an exterior line of forts, and on the line of these new forts the active defence of the place will rest. The old line begins in the north at St. Denis—Forts la Briche, du Nord, and de l'Est—and continues through Forts d'Aubervilliers, Romainville, Noisy, Rosny, Nogent, Vincennes, Charenton, Ivry, Bicetre, Montrouge, Vanves, d'Issy, to Mont Valérien. The perimeter of these works is about thirty-four miles.

Paris almost a fortified province

"The new line of works makes Paris almost a fortified province. It embraces in the defended area Enghien, Argenteuil, Versailles, and the Forests of Saint-Germain and Bondy. The perimeter is over eighty miles. Starting from the north there are in succession Forts Cormeilles, Montlignon, Domont, Montmorency, Ecouen, and Stains, forming the northern group. To the east there are Forts Vaujours and Chelles. Between the Marne and the Seine come Forts Villiers, Champigny, Sucy, and Villeneuve-Saint-Georges. To the south is Fort Palaiseau, while the hills from Palaiseau to Chatillon are crowned by various batteries. On the west stand Forts Villeras, Haut-Buc, St. Cyr, and Marly, with numerous batteries.

"If Paris is invested the line held by the enemy will be not less than a hundred miles in length, and if this line is held in the same relative strength as in 1870, no less than 500,000 men will be required to occupy it. Such numbers will so materially weaken the German armies that it is possible that on this occasion the Germans will select one section of the defence, the capture of which will enable them to bombard the capital, and bring up against the forts selected for attack the heavy howitzers which played such havoc with Liège and Namur."

Possible eventualities had, however, to be provided for. General Gallieni, who had been appointed Military Governor of Paris, issued a decree which ordered all the occupiers or landlords of buildings of any kind within the field of fire of the forts and defensive works of Paris, both ancient and modern, to leave them within four days, and to demolish them completely, otherwise they would be demolished by the military. The result was that in a few days houses, shops, factories, warehouses, and barns were destroyed, until each fort looked out over no more than a desert of shapeless ruins across which it could direct the fire of its heavy guns at an advancing army without hindrance. Further, the French War Minister called up the Territorial Reservists of all classes not yet summoned to the colours from the North and North-East Departments.

General Gallieni's preparations for a siege

That very evening, September 1st, a German Taube monoplane appeared over Paris. It was not observed until it was well over the centre of the city, just above the Gare St. Lazare, where it dropped a bomb. When it was over the Place de l'Opéra guns opened fire on it. Immediately after the first shot had been fired a bomb was dropped into the courtyard of a building just off the Rue du Quatre Septembre. There was ten minutes of panic. Men, women, and children rushed to cover, and the streets were emptied in the twinkling of an eye. The panic was increased by the fact that the majority of persons took the reports of the guns for explosions of German bombs. Only the first bomb, however, took any effect. The window-panes of two storeys of a building were broken by the explosion, but the persons who were sitting at the windows escaped without a scratch! The effect of the explosion on the population was transitory, but the Government organised a flotilla of armoured aeroplanes, with quick-firing guns, to chase German aeroplanes which in future flew over the capital.

The American Ambassador addressed a report to his Government on the methods of warfare adopted by the Germans of dropping bombs indiscriminately on the civil population, which were not only an outrage against humanity, but in absolute violation of The Hague Convention signed by Germany herself.

Measures were taken by the French Government to protect the chief works of art in the Louvre from this danger

BRITONS AND AMERICANS LEAVING PARIS.
Scene at the Gare du Nord, Paris, as the last train was leaving with passengers bound for England one night in the first week of September, 1914.

of bombs from the air. In 1870 the "Venus de Milo" was walled up in a subterranean niche. She was now enclosed in a steel room. "The Winged Victory" was protected behind heavy iron piles, and "La Gioconda" smiled inscrutably in obscurity. The Grecian Hall, which contains the masterpieces of Phidias, was protected by sacks filled with earth. The upper storeys of the Louvre with their glass roofs were turned into hospitals under the charge of the Red Cross.

The stream of refugees from the stricken towns of Middle France began to arrive in Paris on September 1st. The scene was thus described by a correspondent of "The Times":

"For ten miles along the long, straight road that runs to Compiègne one sees nothing unusual. You have only to turn your head, and there are the cupolas of Sacre-Cœur, the great white church on the hill of Montmartre, floating mistily in the hot air behind. And here is nothing but flat fields and golden cornstacks and green copses in the folds of the ground. Gradually one comes to notice that nearly all the people we meet along this dusty road are pushing 'mail-carts,' or barrows filled with bundles. And there are farm carts lumbering along with parties of old folks in them—not jolly old folks, who might be going to a Sunday beanfeast that way, but heavy-eyed, depressed-looking people holding bundles on their knees. There are the strangest old motor-cars, too, filled likewise with people and piled with bundles.

"There are taxicabs that seem to have come out from Paris on some special errand, and furniture vans, and milk vans, and in all these motley conveyances, or lying by the side of the road, or plodding wearily along it, are still depressed-looking people with bundles. For these are the refugees of two whole departments of France. Some have walked a hundred miles already. They have been driven out by the advance of the Germans as people flee before a forest fire, or as they came 1,600 years ago across this very same country seeking refuge from the Huns. They have left everything they could not carry and gone, thankful to bring life and limb with them."

THE EXODUS FROM PARIS TO THE SOUTH.
In view of the threatened siege, inhabitants of the Paris suburbs were compelled for military reasons to leave their houses, and the above picture shows them rushing to the Gare d'Orleans, en route for the south and south-east.

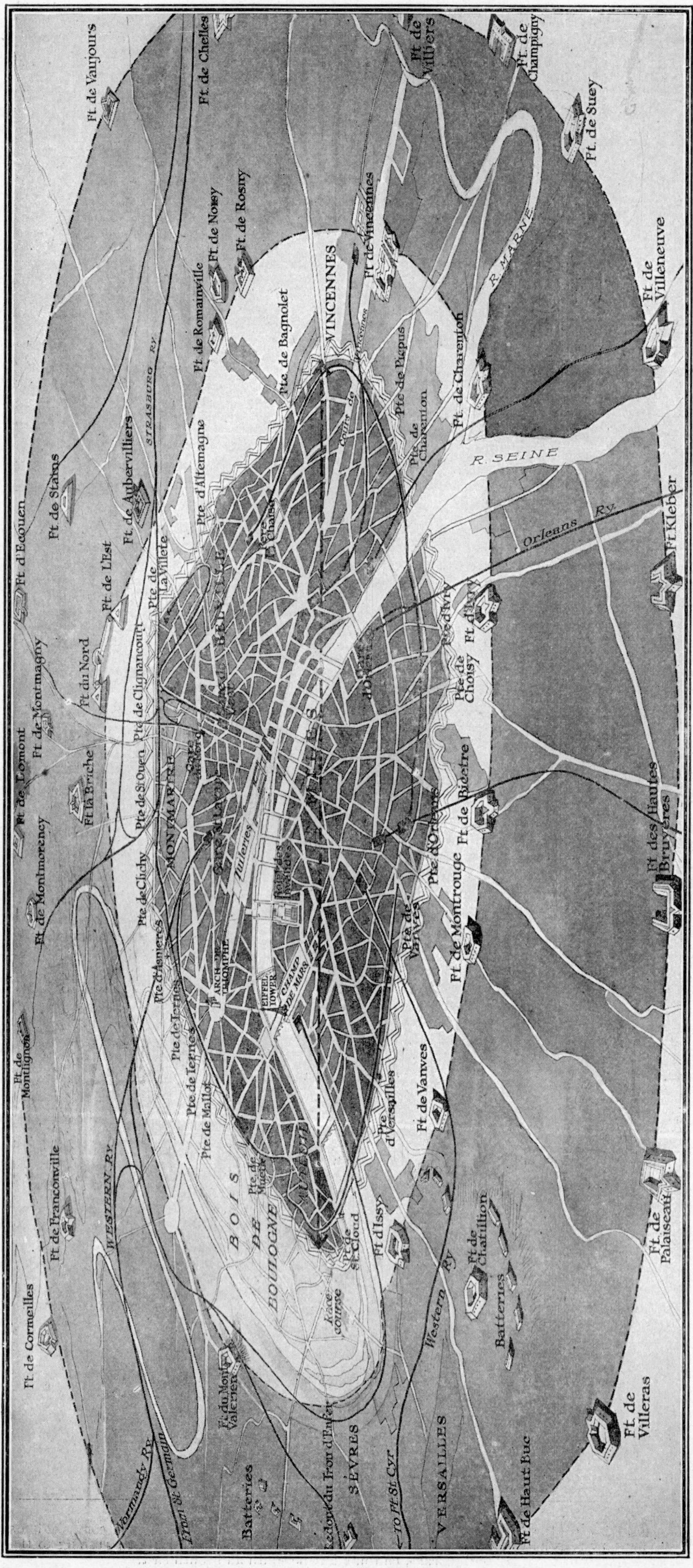

THE DEFENCES OF PARIS, WHICH, ACCORDING TO THE ORIGINAL GERMAN PLANS, SHOULD HAVE BEEN ENTERED ON SEPTEMBER 2ND, 1914.

Immediately surrounding the city are the old ramparts, twenty-one miles in length. Around is seen the circle of forts dating from 1870, but considerably strengthened since then. The third line of defence, constructed in 1878, includes forty fortresses and batteries. The network of railways in the city and suburbs could be utilised to convey troops from point to point as their presence might be needed. Assuming that the outer forts were not captured, the effective fire of a besieging force would only extend to the second line of forts, leaving the area between these forts and the city itself almost immune from gun-fire. To the north of Paris, through the gates of St. Ouen and Clignancourt, some thousands of refugees from the territory occupied by the Germans entered the capital during the first month of the Great War.

That is one description of a weary and sorrowful march. Here is another by a distinguished French artist who had been arrested by the enemy at St. Gerard, near Namur, and was being taken as a prisoner to Germany, the home of culture, by protagonists of the same: "After sleeping in a barn with Zouave prisoners, a soldier standing over us with fixed bayonet, we were called at five the next morning. The prisoners were told to peel potatoes for the field kitchen. I made my toilet while a guard followed me about.

"At six all the soldiers began to form up. Orders came from the officers like pistol-shots, the click of heels and the thud of shoulder arms coming as from one man. Woe to the man slightly out of line! The close-cropped officer spat at him a flow of expletives, showing his teeth like a tiger ready to spring. I was placed in the middle of a marching column, and as I was loaded with my knapsack and coat (a soldier near me carrying my papers), I could take part in the sensation of the men under the iron discipline of the officers. The road lay inches thick of chalky dust, which rose in clouds above our heads. Never were we allowed to open out and let the air circulate.

"We plodded on the whole day, the only rest being when there was an occasional block on the road. The march was as if on parade. Should one fall out of step, the shouts of his superior soon brought him up. Now and then men were waiting with buckets, and as the column swung by the soldiers dipped in their aluminium cups. Another man would be holding a biscuit-tin full of sweets, or it might be handfuls of prunes; but still the march went on.

"It was remarkable to see the field post-office at work. The armed, blue-coated postmen stood close by the marching column, receiving the postcards handed to them. Sometimes an officer would hand over a fowling-piece or antique with the address hanging from it. At noon I was handed over to officers, and I left the regiment. I was on the box-seat of a char-à-banc full of officers, and could observe the marvellous organisation of the column. The pace was at a walk, but continuous. Ammunition-waggons, field-pieces, carts filled with flour, whole trains of

THE FOOD SUPPLY OF PARIS IN CASE OF SIEGE.
View of one of the outer walls of Paris, which was used as a grazing ground for 30,000 head of cattle for the supply of the city in case of siege. The animals were fed and guarded by the military authorities. Inset: Wireless station on the Eiffel Tower and camp below.

enormous pontoons pulled by heavy horses, and great traction-engines pulling siege-guns, landaus and motor-cars filled with doctors and officers whose only distinguishing mark was a strip of colour at the neck—all advanced at the same pace. Should a slight block occur, the whole column would stop as one train, the drivers passing the message back by a pumping movement made with the fist on high. The warning of a declivity or bend in the road passed backwards like musketry fire. All vehicles belonged to the Army. Some had chalked on their grey sides 'Berlin—Paris.' Sometimes the column would let an enormous grey motor-omnibus dash by, and through the glass sides I saw Staff officers bending over maps. Every driver and service man carries his weapons, the great waggons simply bristling with rifles. On our way we passed crowds of peasants returning to their ruined homes. It was pitiful to see them humbly raise their hats to the invaders. We passed many villages in ruins. Locked-up houses were instantly broken open and searched. The better-class houses were pillaged for wine, every soldier marching with bottles sticking out of his knapsack."

Ruined homes of French peasants

Perhaps the most arresting outcome of the war, apart from its military issues, was the uprising spirit of nationalism manifested alike in the East as in the West. But nowhere was it more strikingly demonstrated than in Russia. It, therefore, came not altogether as a surprise when on September 1st an Imperial rescript announced that thenceforth the city of St. Petersburg should be known as Petrograd. The termination "grad" is the Slavonic equivalent of the German "burg"—town. This decision of Nicholas II. was hailed with exultation, combining hatred of everything German and intense patriotic feeling, by practically the whole Slav world. The significance of the act was immense, for it marked a deliberate breach with an old and bad tradition which brought many evils on their race. For generations there had been an unholy alliance between the reactionaries on the Neva and those on the Spree, based on their common desire to keep down the people for the honour and emolument of those classes in both countries which arrogated to themselves the exclusive privilege of bearing rule. The political comment of "The Times" was: "The step taken by the Tsar is a proclamation to the entire Slav race in all its branches

THE OUTSKIRTS OF THE "GAY CITY" UNDER MARTIAL LAW.

Guarding the main roads round Paris: A vision of the suburbs at night. Under the control of the military governor, General Gallieni, the most strict surveillance was exercised over the exits and entrances of the capital.

that this unholy alliance is no more, and that his policy henceforth is a policy of 'Russia for the Russians,' freed from the last vestige of subservience to Berlin. For all who had ears to hear he had, indeed, made this announcement already. When he issued his proclamation to the Poles of East Prussia and of Posen, as well as to their countrymen of Galicia and within his own dominions, he shattered at a blow the corner-stone of Russo-German friendship. That friendship began in the partition of Poland; it has been nourished by her oppression and her abasement; it has ended with the Imperial promise of her resurrection. . . . To end their sufferings and to give his Polish subjects a safe and honourable place within his Empire has always been the personal wish and the personal ambition of the present Tsar. Austria-Hungary's threat to destroy the independence of a small Slav kingdom by inflicting upon it humiliations from which no State could recover, and Germany's declaration of war upon him for taking measures to support his protest against this menace, have led him to give his aspirations a wider scope.

Friendship based on complicity in crime

"He has summoned all the Poles to take their place as a united nation in the great Slav family. By that summons he has bound himself to undo the work of the three Germans—Frederick of Prussia, Catherine, and Joseph II.—who consolidated the friendship of the Eastern Powers on complicity in crime. By the Russian people that friendship has always been disliked. Not all the greatness and all the conquests of Catherine herself could make them forgive her German blood. They have resented the influence of the Germans they have employed in the past, and the wisest of their rulers have respected this national sentiment. . . . The new name of St. Petersburg—the city of the Great Tsar who, however richly he rewarded foreigners, made it his rule that in Russia Russians must be first—will be welcomed by them as the most marked homage which their 'Little Father' could pay to their highest ideals and their most cherished feelings. 'Petrograd' is a pledge and a symbol to them with whom symbols count for much, that it is indeed for those ideals and those feelings he bids them draw the sword."

A pledge and a symbol to Slavdom

In this connection it may be stated that among the thousands of prisoners taken during the Lemberg affair, passing through Kieff early in September, were a vast number of Galicians, Poles, Czechs, and other Slavs, and these all admitted that Austrian Slav feeling against the Prussians was very bitter. A Polish Sokol said: "If the Russian Government would give us rifles we would go and fight against the Prussians immediately." Polish members of Parliament visiting Petrograd and political leaders from Warsaw collectively signed the following response to the Grand Duke Generalissimo's second appeal to their countrymen: "Polish public opinion regards persons participating in the various volunteer organisations co-operating with the Austrian Army as unconscious defenders of Germanism and enemies of Polish interests and of Slavdom. With still greater indignation Polish public opinion condemns the use of explosive bullets." From statements made by Austrian Polish prisoners at Kieff, it appeared that they were kept in entire ignorance of the Grand Duke's proclamation and appeal. Austrian

For purposes of defence in case of necessity, trenches were dug in many of the streets of Paris. Our view is of one in Porte Maillot.

Main line railway at Amiens which was destroyed by the French in order to hinder the progress of the German invaders.

Offices of the Gare du Nord, Paris, transformed into a refuge for the fugitives arriving from Northern France.

Example of the destructive work of a bomb dropped from a German aeroplane on the roof of Notre Dame, Paris.

Scene in the Rue Faubourg St. Antoine, Paris, where a horse was killed by a German aerial bomb. The incident took place in front of the Hospital of St. Antoine.

GLIMPSES OF PARIS UNDER THE THREAT OF ANOTHER SIEGE BY THE PRUSSIANS.

propaganda had instilled in them the idea that Russia was the aggressor.

Amiens in the last days of August was found to be untenable because the right flank of the German army was then reaching a point which appeared seriously to endanger Sir John French's line of communications with Havre ; and it was resolved that the Valley of the Somme should be abandoned. The garrison of ten thousand French troops, mainly reservists, accordingly retired westward, through Picquigny, blowing up both bridges over the Somme. One of these bridges was historically interesting as the scene of an interview in the latter half of the fifteenth century between our own King Edward IV. and Louis XI. of France, to settle matters regarding the war then raging between England and France. A party of Uhlans entered Amiens immediately afterwards with a Parliamentaire and demanded from the mayor, M. Fiquet, the surrender of the ancient capital of Picardy. This was formally given, and the burgesses were enjoined not to create the slightest disturbance, and above all to abstain from any action, overt or covert, against the soldiery. Any failure in that respect would be punished with death. This done, M. Fiquet and twelve municipal councillors were escorted in carriages to the general-officer commanding the invaders, and thereafter the tricolour was hauled down from the town-hall, and the German standard hoisted in its place. Later horse, foot, and artillery—Brandenburgers and men of the "Iron Guard"—entered the town, but not with military music as at Brussels ; only with the raucous singing of "Die Wacht am Rhein" and "Deutschland über Alles."

Entry of the Germans into Amiens

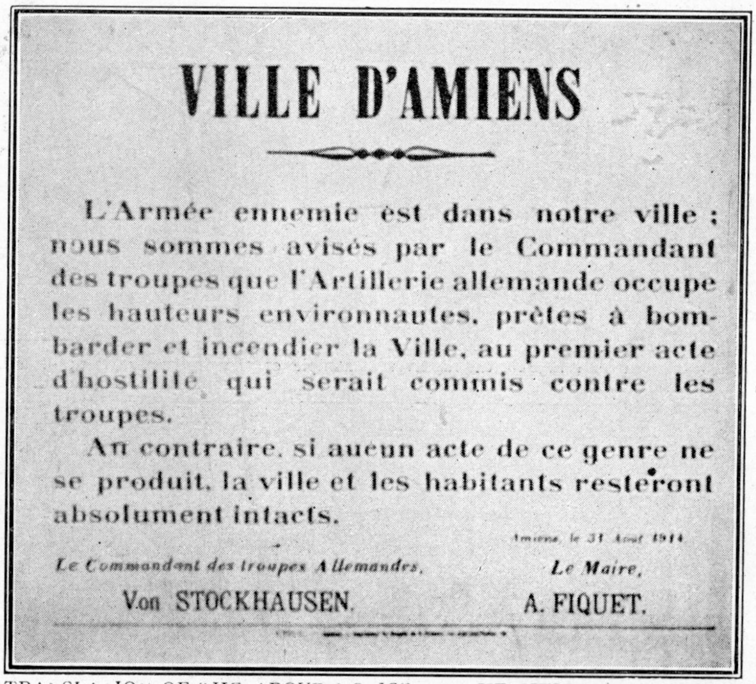

VILLE D'AMIENS

L'Armée ennemie est dans notre ville ; nous sommes avisés par le Commandant des troupes que l'Artillerie allemande occupe les hauteurs environnantes, prêtes à bombarder et incendier la Ville, au premier acte d'hostilité qui serait commis contre les troupes.

Au contraire, si aucun acte de ce genre ne se produit, la ville et les habitants resteront absolument intacts.

Amiens, le 31 Août 1914

Le Commandant des troupes Allemandes, Von STOCKHAUSEN.

Le Maire, A. FIQUET.

TRANSLATION OF THE ABOVE NOTICE TO THE CITIZENS OF AMIENS.

The army of the enemy is in our city ; we are informed by the commandant of the troops that the German artillery occupies the neighbouring heights, ready to bombard and set fire to the town on the first act of hostility that may be committed against the troops. On the contrary, if no such act takes place, the town and its inhabitants will remain quite intact.

Amiens, 31st August, 1914.

Commandant of the German Troops, Von Stockhausen.

The Mayor, A. Fiquet.

It became also necessary to withdraw from Compiègne, forty-five miles north-east from Paris and rather more than thirty miles from the outer fortifications of the capital—a very pleasant town with a great château memorable for the Tsar's visit there on the occasion of the institution of the Franco-Russian Alliance, and with something more approaching, under normal circumstances, country life and society than anywhere else in France. With the approach of the Germans in the beautiful weather of early autumn, wrote an eye-witness, Compiègne became like a city of the dead, or a city buried alive. Rows of white houses with fastened shutters, empty flower gardens, tenantless streets, no sound but the angry hum of the German aeroplane overhead. As the church clock struck noon it sounded like a toll. Inside the church many candles were burning before the altar, and nobody else but one woman kneeling behind the high altar. So it always is when the Germans are coming for rapine and for shame. Practically the whole of the inhabitants had fled, and a pitiful sight it was along miles of the highway to encounter hay-wains and carts laden with fugitives. Other poor creatures walked, burdened with household gear on their shoulders. Some pushed perambulators with children in them, the bundles lying on the children for need of space. Old women prone on straw in shaky vehicles looked about vacantly, young ones in their arms crying. Most of these wretched people were calm enough, plodding along as if they, too, were taking part in a tactical evacuation. All of them spoke with affection and respect of the British soldiers, whose behaviour at Compiègne was certainly beyond all praise. Lord Kitchener's message to his troops was being followed to the letter.

When retiring from the thickly-wooded country to the south of Compiègne on September 1st our 1st Cavalry Brigade was overtaken by some German cavalry who were marching down the Oise on the Forest of Compiègne. They momentarily lost a Horse Artillery Battery, and several officers and men were killed and wounded. With the help, however, of some detachments operating close at hand, they not only recovered their own guns but succeeded in capturing twelve of the enemy's. Similarly to the eastward the 1st Corps, retiring south, also got into some very difficult forest country, and a somewhat severe rearguard action ensued at Villers-Cotterets, in which the 4th Guards Brigade suffered considerably.

Nearer the Belgian frontier about the same date the German artillery, according to a correspondent, was the bane of our troops, and caused terrible havoc in our ranks by great shells from a battery posted inside a wood. By the disposal of large quantities of forage the guns had been given the appearance of small haystacks, and their first fire caused much loss among our men who approached them unsuspectingly. It seemed impossible to silence their fire, but the 9th Lancers, at the word of command, rode straight at the enemy's guns—debouching into the open and charging under a hail of melinite or lyddite from other German guns. Men and horses were infuriated. They reached the enemy's heavy guns, which almost approximated to siege-guns, cut down all the gunners and put the guns out of action. Then, like their prototypes in the charge of the Six Hundred at Balaclava, they rode back, and on their return they fell in greater numbers still than in that famous charge immortalised by Tennyson.

Glorious charge of the 9th Lancers

Captain F. O. Grenfell, of the 9th Lancers, was hit in both legs, and had two fingers shot off at the same time. Almost at the moment he received these wounds a couple of guns posted near were deprived of their servers, all of whom save one man had been struck by bursting shrapnel. The horses for the guns had been placed under cover. "We'll get the guns back !" cried Captain Grenfell, and with the assistance of a number of his men, in spite of his wounds, he did manage to harness the guns up and get them away. He was then taken to the hospital.

ENTRY OF GERMAN TROOPS INTO AMIENS AT THE END OF AUGUST, 1914.

At that part of the retiring front at Solesmes, east of Cambrai, a number of English infantry regiments—the East Lancashires, Middlesex, Dorsets, Rifle Brigade, Hampshires, and the Essex—held an exposed position. They were expecting support all the day from the French, but that was delayed, and the enemy crept round in strength. The British force, to avoid being encircled, charged the gradually-enclosing German ring with the bayonet. The men went at it, yelling and shouting, and they got through where there wa a gap of no more than eight hundred yards between the enveloping German ranks. On this gap the German artillery was trained with unfailing regularity, and the losses of all these regiments was great. The East Lancashires especially suffered severely, but behaved with great courage. A transport column taking rations for the East Lancashires had to do marches of twenty to thirty-six miles on successive days on two biscuits per man, "but," as one of the regiment said, "we had our revenge by taking the whole German supply column."

The Scots regiments were heavily engaged, and the Argyll and Sutherland Highlanders distinguished themselves particularly, while the Rifle Brigade and the Carabiniers fought finely in a difficult position near Ouiévrant. A splendid personal action was that of the major of the L Battery of the Royal Horse Artillery, who in a rapid retirement while hostile cavalry were threatening, and the battery horses were disabled, pushed the battery into position with his own hands, aided by his officers and

ENTRY OF THE HUNS INTO THE OLD CAPITAL OF PICARDY.

German troops marching through Amiens on their way south and, as they thought, to Paris. The smaller view shows French troops leaving Amiens just prior to the German occupation. They are wearing anti-sunstroke flaps at the back of their shakos.

men, along a road to a point of vantage. The fire which his battery was thenceforward able to open counteracted the enemy's offensive.

That the spontaneous uprising of patriotic feeling throughout the United Kingdom was not in any sense sectional was demonstrated on September 3rd by the issue of two very important manifestos from the largest representative bodies of the working classes of the country.

Trades Union leaders and conscription

In that issued by the Parliamentary Committee of the Trades Union Congress, after a two days' conference, it was stated that "the Committee was especially gratified at the manner in which the Labour Party in the House of Commons had responded to the appeal made to all political parties to give their co-operation in securing the enlistment of men to defend the interests of their country, and heartily endorse the appointment upon the Parliamentary Recruiting Committee of four members of the party, and the placing of the services of the National Agent at the disposal of that Committee to assist in carrying through its secretarial work."

The manifesto proceeded: "The Parliamentary Committee are convinced that one important factor in the present European struggle has to be borne in mind, so far as our country is concerned—namely, that in the event of the voluntary system of military service failing the country in this its time of need, the demand for a national system of compulsory military service will not only be made with redoubled vigour, but may prove to be so persistent and strong as to become irresistible. The prospect of having to face conscription, with its permanent and heavy burden upon the financial resources of the country, and its equally burdensome effect upon nearly the whole of its industries, should in itself stimulate the manhood of the nation to come forward in its defence, and thereby demonstrate to the world that a free people can rise to the supreme heights of a great sacrifice without the whip of conscription. Another factor to be remembered in this crisis of the nation's history, and most important of all, so far as Trade Unionists and Labour in general are concerned, is the fact that upon the result of the struggle in which this country is now engaged rests the preservation and maintenance of free and unfettered democratic government, which in its international relationships has in the past been recognised, and must unquestionably in the future prove to be the best guarantee of the peace of the world.

"The near contemplation of the overbearing and brutal methods to which people have to submit under a government controlled by a military autocracy—living, as it were, continuously under the threat and shadow of war—should be sufficient to arouse the enthusiasm of the nation in resisting any attempt to impose similar conditions upon countries at present free from military despotism.

"But if men have a duty to perform in the common interests of the State, equally the State owes a duty to those of its citizens who are prepared—and readily prepared—to make sacrifices in its defence and for the maintenance of honour Citizens called upon voluntarily to leave their employment and their homes for the purpose of undertaking military duties have a right to receive at the hands of the State a reasonable and assured recompense, not so much for themselves as for those who are dependent upon them, and no single member of the community would do otherwise than uphold a Government which, in such an important and vital matter, took a liberal and even generous view of its responsibilities towards those citizens who come forward to assist in the defence of their country.

"We respectfully commend this suggestion to the favourable consideration of the Government of the day.

"Long life to the free institutions of all democratically governed countries."

This manifesto was signed by Mr. J. A. Seddon, chairman, Mr. W. J. Davis, vice-chairman, the other members of the committee, and by Mr. C. W. Bowerman, M.P., secretary.

MAIN FRONT OF THE BEAUTIFUL AND HISTORIC CHATEAU AT COMPIÈGNE.

This famous royal chateau was visited by the Tsar on the occasion of the institution of the Franco-Russian Alliance. It is situated forty-five miles north-east from Paris. The beautiful and historic town of Compiègne was the centre of some severe fighting, and had to be evacuated, eventually becoming, we are told, "like a city of the dead," the chateau with its treasures, and other fine buildings, being at the mercy of the invaders.

The Dockers' Union were not less anxious to take a hand in administering the death-blow to Kaiserism. Their manifesto, signed by Mr. Ben Tillett, the secretary, said that: "Every resource at our command must be utilised for the purpose of preserving our country and nation. Every able-bodied man must either fight or be ready to defend his country. Every family of those men who go to the front must be guaranteed a competence and food.

"We first of all propose that all able-bodied men should shoulder the responsibilities this war imposes, that local units of men having worked and lived together constitute units of a thousand each, for the better purpose of training and preparation. That these units of our members or of Trade Unionists from a given area be registered.

Dockers' manifesto against Kaiserism

"Kaiserism and militarism should receive its death-blow in this Armageddon. Our traditions at least stand for the best, our limitations and inequalities are largely of our own making, and will be so long as the workers are contented slaves under a vicious wage-system.

"I want to see our men drilled daily, even if the War Office cannot help us. There are plenty of open spaces. Many of our men are ex-soldiers; they could help in the

BIBULOUS GERMAN SOLDIERS LET LOOSE IN THE WINE LAND OF FRANCE.

A party of German infantry discovered by French troops in a wine-cellar in the Champagne country. "For days," a note found on a German prisoner stated, "we could not find a single piece of bread, but we could have wine as we liked." And they did "like"—in many instances to their undoing, not only in France, but in Belgium also. Their fondness for wine had also, there is little doubt, its effect in many of the outrages committed by the Kaiser's troops in the towns and villages they entered on their march towards Paris.

FRENCH INFANTRY HURRYING FORWARD TO MEET THE H

This masterly camera picture, taken at the front, shows the advance guards of a French infantry column, with bayonets fixed and colours flying, hurrying forward to thrust back a counter-attack by the enemy in North-Eastern France. Twice before, in 1792 and in 1870, Frenchmen had this task before them. The count shown is open and rolling like that of the Argonne, where Prussians and Austrian one misty autumn day over a century ago, were driven back by the forces und

RY FOE ON THE BATTLEGROUND OF NORTHERN FRANCE.

umouriez and Kellermann, after an ineffectual but bold attempt to reach Paris rough the Passes of the Argonne. As Mr. Hilaire Belloc has recently demonrated, the treacherous chalky clay soil of the Champa gne Pouilleuse is in rainy autumn weather waterlogged and practically impassable. And this factor in 1792 was the real cause of the important defeat of the invaders at Valmy—a defeat which saved the Revolution and had a direct influence on the future.

THE NEW WORLD'S INTEREST IN THE OLD WORLD'S WAR.

Crowds of New Yorkers coming out of the down-town offices in the evening and watching the war bulletins posted up outside the offices of "The World," "The Sun," and "The Tribune." "Europe," wrote a New York correspondent, "should realise that America has been moved inexpressibly by 'German methods in war.'" These methods and the extended circulation given to the British White Paper proved effective antidotes to the propaganda of the German Ambassador at Washington, and of German Consuls all through the United States.

drilling. Municipal authorities and employers could help. Employed and unemployed could help; the War Office should help those who can enlist, subject to guarantees from the Government giving protection to the families left behind."

Orange Ulster, while still maintaining resistance to Home Rule, agreed to a political truce which put that issue for a time in the background. Sir Edward Carson, K.C., M.P., on September 3rd presided over a great meeting in Belfast of the Ulster Unionist Council as representing the anti-Home Rule Volunteer Force. The meeting was attended by, among others, the Marquis of Londonderry, Earl of Clanwilliam, Earl of Leitrim, Earl of Kilmorey, and Lord Dunleath. In proposing the resolution, "That being of opinion that the first duty at the present time of every loyal citizen is to the Empire, we not only cordially approve of the arrangement made by our leaders with the War Office for the enlistment for active service abroad of one or more Ulster divisions, but we urge all loyalists who own allegiance to our cause, and who are qualified, to enlist at once for service with such division," Sir Edward paid a glowing tribute to the gallantry of Belgium, which aroused a storm of sympathetic cheers, and then proceeded: "Great Britain has engaged not only in a just, but an inevitable war. Under these circumstances what we have to do is to assist with our last man in the destruction of the tyrant who has brought this about. . . . Our country, our Empire, is in danger. We have never yet been beaten, we never will. We have got to win, and we *will* win. Under these circumstances, knowing that the very basis of our political faith is our belief in the greatness of the United Kingdom and of the Empire, to our Volunteers I say without hesitation, 'Go and help to save your country and your Empire; go and win honour for Ulster and for Ireland.' To every man who goes, or has gone—and not to them only, but to every Irishman—you and I say from the bottom of our hearts, 'God bless you, and bring you home safe and victorious.' . . . If we get enough men to go from the Ulster Volunteer Force they will go under the War Office as a division of their own, and if we get enough they can go as two or more divisions, and will be allowed by the War Office to have their own officers, and be trained, at all events first, in Ulster camps."

The attitude of Orange Ulster

As the days passed the patriotic ardour of our Dominions beyond the seas seemed to burn with a fiercer flame. On September 3rd, so considerable had been the response to the call for an active service contingent of 25,000 men in Canada, that it was decided to form additional brigades at Valcartier and other camps, so as to furnish, if need be, as many as 100,000 fully-equipped troops to the British Expeditionary Forces in France and Belgium, together with reserves to fill up the gaps by the waste of war. A marked feature in the activity in volunteering was the eagerness of American settlers in the Canadian West, many of whom had seen active service in the American Army, to prove their loyalty to their new citizenship by joining the Canadian contingent destined for the front.

This loyal sentiment found further practical expression in the raising of a patriotic fund, which amounted to several million dollars in a few days. Nor were the newspapers of Canada backward in their support of the Government and their action, illustrative of which may be quoted the following inspiring appeal which appeared in the "Montreal Star": "'The Hun is at the gate.' Kipling's stark line presents with all his native, naked force the tragedy which overhangs us. Let there be no delusion in any man's mind as to what will be the fate of the British peoples if their effort to save Europe from worse than Napoleonic despotism proves finally a failure. Their prestige will be gone; their Empire will be marked off for dismemberment; the final volume of their history will be written, and we shall take our place among the classics.

"To avert this fate no sacrifice is too great. As in other times of stress, when other peoples were pushed to the last extreme, women have brought their jewels to the war chest, and men have marched out to die for their country. So must we be prepared to-day to strip ourselves utterly of the materials of

"Comfort, content, and delight,
The ages' slow-bought gain,"

and to devote every ounce of strength, be it contained in gold and lands or in flesh and blood, to the defence of this Empire, which is itself humanity's chief defence of liberty."

THE "WAR AGAINST GERMANY'S TRADE."
An exhibition of German and Austrian made goods, organised by the British Board of Trade for the benefit of our manufacturers. The idea was to give information which should lead to a revival of home industries, so long materially affected by German and Austrian competition, and to promote new efforts to supply goods at home which hitherto had been imported from those hostile countries.

Nor were the people of Australia less keen in their determination to help the Homeland in the war crisis. The Commonwealth Government agreed to send a second contingent of 10,000 fully-equipped men to the front, and Mr. Millen, Minister of Defence, gave very apt reasons for this action in the course of an address to his constituents in the first week of September. "Unless the Empire won," said he, "Australia would be a prize claimed by the victor, as being the only spot with wide, fertile lands and few people. We are not fighting for something distant, but for the right to continue a free, self-governing community."

Sedan Day festivities in Berlin

While the Slav world was manifesting their delight at the Tsar's rescript changing the name of the capital of the Russian Empire from St. Petersburg to Petrograd, Germany held high festivity and military parades in Berlin and the other cities of the country on the same day in celebration of the anniversary of Sedan, which saw the fall of Napoleon the Little and the birth of the Third French Republic.

In Paris the quietude of the people, as fateful event crowded upon event, was worthy of the courage of the

THE HORSE IN THE WAR: TAKING HORSES OF THE QUEEN'S BAYS—During the great retreat from Mons the 2nd Dragoon Guards (Queen's Bays) were surprised while dismounted and at breakfast in the early morning near Compiègne. A few figures on the sky-line were attracting the attention of those who had field-glasses, and a discussion as to their identity was in progress, when all doubt was scattered by the arrival of a succession of shells on the camp.

children of the Republic under arms. As was said, it was the moment for those who act, not for those who talk. Unbounded confidence was felt in the President, who had come to the momentous decision to remove the seat of Government from Paris to Bordeaux, and in General Gallieni, the Military Governor of the capital, both as organiser and as soldier. On September 3rd M. Poincaré issued the following inspiring message to the nation:

"PEOPLE OF FRANCE.

"For several weeks relentless battles have engaged our heroic troops and the army of the enemy.

"The valour of our soldiers has won for them at several points marked advantages, but in the north the pressure of the German forces has compelled us to fall back.

"This situation has forced the President of the Republic and the Government to a painful decision.

"In order to watch over the national welfare it is the duty of the public powers to remove themselves temporarily from the city of Paris. Under the command of its eminent chief, the French Army, full of courage and zeal, will defend the capital and its patriotic population against the invader.

The Allies' motto: "Endure and Fight"

"But the war must be carried on at the same time on the rest of its territory. Without peace or truce, without cessation or faltering, the struggle for the honour of the nation and the reparation of violated right must continue.

"None of our armies is impaired. If some of them have sustained too considerable losses, the gaps have immediately been filled up from the reserves, and the appeal for recruits assures us of new resources in man and energy.

"'Endure and Fight'—such must be the motto of the allied British, Russian, Belgian, and French armies. Endure and fight, while at sea the British aid is cutting the communication of our enemy with the world. Endure and fight, while the Russians continue to advance to strike the decisive blow at the heart of the German Empire.

Duty of French Government and people

"It is the duty of the Government of the Republic to direct this stubborn resistance. Everywhere Frenchmen will rise for their independence, but to ensure the utmost spirit of efficacy to the formidable fight, it is indispensable that the Government shall remain free to act.

"At the request of the military authorities the Government is therefore temporarily shifting its headquarters to a place where it can remain in constant touch with the whole of the country.

"LET US BE WORTHY.

"It calls upon members of Parliament not to remain away from it, in order that they may form with their colleagues the symbol of national unity.

"The Government only leaves Paris after having assured the defence of the city and of the entrenched camp by every means in its power. It knows that it does not need to recommend to the admirable population of Paris that calm resolution and coolness which it is showing every day, and which is equal to its highest duties.

"People of France! Let us be worthy of these tragic circumstances. We shall gain the final victory! We shall gain it by unflagging will, endurance, and tenacity.

"A nation which does not wish to perish, and which in order to live does not flinch either from suffering or sacrifice, is sure of victory."

—TO THE REAR (FIVE TO A MAN) IN AN ACTION NEAR COMPIÈGNE.
Many men and a large number of horses were killed. At once the order "Action front!" rang out, and the horses were taken to cover. The now famous L Battery of the Royal Horse Artillery, accompanying the Bays, went into action on the left. The German attack was pressed very hard, and our cavalrymen had a hot time until the 4th Cavalry Brigade, comprising squadrons of the 6th Dragoon Guards (Carabiniers) and the 3rd Hussars, with the brigade guns of the Royal Horse Artillery, came up to their support.

The President, accompanied by all the Ministers, left Paris early in the morning, and was followed at noon by the members and the Presidents of the Senate and Chamber of Deputies, the main body of the administration, and the reserves of the Banque de France, which were as necessary to the Government as ammunition was to the military Governor of Paris—all which filled two special trains. Of the major Embassies only those of Spain and the United States remained, and the neutrality of the American Republic was marked by the fact that Mr. Herrick, the United States Ambassador, took charge of the records of the British, the German, and the Austrian Ambassadors. The higher legal machinery of France was likewise transferred to Bordeaux, fifteen magistrates being selected from among the three sections of the Cour de Cassation. The Municipal Authority was constituted by the President of the City Council and the Council of the Seine Department, who were empowered to direct the city's civil affairs under the authority of the Military Governor, the Prefect of Paris, and the Prefect of Police.

The move from Paris to Bordeaux

General Gallieni issued the following proclamation: "Army of Paris! Inhabitants of Paris! The members of the Government of the Republic have left Paris in order to give new impetus to the national defence. I have received the order to defend Paris against the invader. This order I shall fulfil to the end." Guns were mounted on the old walls of the city, and even on the roofs and other buildings. The outer rings of forts have already been described, and are indicated in the diagram on page 122.

Over 10,000 Parisians left the capital for Bordeaux, Biarritz, and other southern cities. Several thousand Britons and Americans left for England by the Havre route.

That very day—September 3rd—the Germans were at Suippes, Ville-sur-Tourbe, and Château Thierry, and preparing to cross the Marne at La Ferté-sous-Jouarre.

Rouen, which from the time when the Germans first entered France was the principal hospital base of the allied forces, was evacuated in a military sense on the same day the Government changed its venue from Paris to Bordeaux. The British wounded were sent to Havre, and the French and Belgians elsewhere. Only a small detachment of French soldiers were left to keep order and perform sentry duty. Among the troops withdrawn were a Belgian contingent with a number of machine-guns drawn by the famous dogs, and the British were sent on to the front by way of Nantes, as communication by way of Amiens had been cut off.

British exhibits at Leipzig saved

From Germany it was reported that our pavilion at the International Book Exhibition at Leipzig had been destroyed by the Germans with its contents. The British Board of Trade, however, at once allayed the fears of those private owners who had generously contributed to the British loan collections by stating that all these exhibits had been safely removed by Mr. Edmund Wyldbore Smith, the British Commissioner, and his staff immediately before their hurried departure after the declaration of war. The collections thus rescued included the Shakespeariana; English books of travel and discovery during the last two hundred years; the historical collection of juvenile and illustrated books; specimens of type representative of the revival in the printing of books, which dates from the establishment of the Kelmscott Press by William Morris in 1891; examples of bookbinding in leather and cloth; the collection from the St. Bride Foundation, illustrating the main tendencies of British book printing from Caxton to Morris—including a copy of Caxton's "Boethius"; and the works exhibited by British artists in the International Section of Contemporary Graphic Art in the Kultur Hall.

Still further evidence was furnished in these early days of September of the real trend of opinion in America as to the merits of Britain's participation in the Great War, notwithstanding the undiplomatic—to say the least of it—propaganda of the German Ambassador at Washington, and the German Consuls all through the United States. "Europe should realise that America has been moved inexpressibly by 'German methods in war,'" wrote the New York correspondent of the London "Daily Telegraph." "America, North and South, English-speaking and Latin, with vehemence and unanimity, is voicing to-day the protest of outraged civilisation." "When autocracy," wrote the "New York World," "makes war, it hesitates at nothing. Who could conceive of American Army officers murdering women and mangling children by bombs hurled from an airship at night into a sleeping city? Who could imagine American soldiers raining death from the sky upon unsuspecting and helpless non-combatants, and upon wounded prisoners in hospitals flying the Red Cross flag? Who could picture American admirals ruthlessly sowing the deep sea with mines to destroy ships and sailors of neutral nations engaged in the pursuit of peaceful commerce? Who could think of American troops grimly engaged in shooting down disarmed peasants who had tried to defend their little possessions? To these pointed queries, anyone knowing this country (United States) might well reply: 'It is all unthinkable.' No American officer who did what Germans

American abhorrence of German "kultur"

THE OVERSEAS RALLY IN AID OF THE MOTHERLAND.

The upper photograph shows some of the brave and hardy fellows New Zealand sent overseas to the aid of the Mother Country on the outbreak of the Great War. The second photograph is of their brothers of the Australian contingent embarking on a transport at Melbourne for their long journey to the battlefields of Europe. They first of all landed in Egypt, there to complete their training and, incidentally, to aid in the defence of that country against the threatened incursion of the Turks.

Infantry of the First Canadian Contingent passing Stonehenge on their way from Salisbury Plain to London.

Canadian Transport and Field Artillery embarking at Quebec for England.

Parade of Canadian Highlanders on Salisbury Plain. The First Contingent of Canadians consisted of 33,000 men, who were to be increased in time to 108,000.

CANADA'S AID IN THE WAR—SUPERB RALLY OF 108,000 MEN FOR ACTIVE SERVICE.

COURT-MARTIAL ON A GERMAN POLICE-OFFICER IN EGYPT.
Robert Casimir Otto Mors, an officer in the service of the City Police of Alexandria, was tried by court-martial on four charges, the gist of which was that he had returned from Germany to act as an agent of the German Government against British authority in Egypt. He was found guilty, and sentenced to penal servitude for life. The above photograph shows the epaulettes being removed from the uniform of Mors after the reading of the sentence.

have done at Antwerp, who did what Germans have done in the North Sea, who did what Germans have done in Belgium, could withstand for a single day the avalanche of American criticism. His own people would instantly repudiate him as a barbarian, and no excuse of military advantage over the enemy would be accepted or tolerated."

German and Japanese methods contrasted

The "New York Herald," recalling the Kaiser's famous picture of "The Yellow Peril," contrasted the Japanese Baron Kato's formal notice of his intended attack on Tsing-tau (in the German leased territory of China), in order that neutrals and non-combatants might leave, with the "Christian" Teutonic method of bombarding undefended cities and villages without notice at all.

In the centre of the activities of the greatest city in the world—the old Guildhall, with the statues about him of statesmen who had moulded the traditions of the Empire—traditions which his speech shiningly carried forward—Mr. Asquith delivered what has been rightly called a monumental appeal to the nation's manhood on September 4th. In doing so, he inaugurated a campaign suggested by Lord Kitchener, as previously noted, to explain to the people why Great Britain was at war, and to urge recruits to flock to the flag in even still greater numbers than had yet rushed to enlist, so that the great principles for which we were fighting might be ultimately assured. The gathering was unique in the annals of the Guildhall, which was crammed to its utmost capacity, while many thousands were unable to obtain admission. The Lord Mayor, Sir Charles Johnstone, presided, and supporting Mr. Asquith on the platform were Mr. Bonar Law (Leader of the Opposition), Mr. Arthur Balfour, the First Lord of

HOW THE NEWS OF WAR WAS RECEIVED IN CONSTANTINOPLE.
Turks, in the neighbourhood of Constantinople, celebrating the outbreak of war with Russia. The photograph was taken during the Feast of Bairam, one of the two great movable Feasts of the Moslems. It corresponds to the Christian Easter.

the Admiralty, Mr. Birrell, Mr. Hobhouse, Lord Lucas, Mr. Masterman, Mr. McKinnon Wood, Mr. J. A. Pease, Mr. H. J. Tennant, most of the metropolitan M.P.'s and mayors, members of the L.C.C., representatives of the Port of London, the Stock Exchange, City banks, Lloyd's, the Baltic Exchange, the Chamber of Commerce, the Trade Unions and Labour Exchanges, and the Overseas Dominions.

Of his long record of oratorical triumphs, the Prime Minister's speech was by universal consent his greatest, and he never secured a bigger or more instant effect. There were moments when the silence of the infinite reigned as his voice sank and vibrated with tense passion when describing the prostration of Belgium. Again an approving, angry storm of cheers came from the vast assembly and rolled through the open rafters of the hall when, in stinging phrase, he pilloried the treachery of Germany. Even reserved statesmen like Mr. Arthur Balfour, Mr. Winston Churchill, and Mr. Bonar Law were visibly moved with the thrill of some of the passages, whose pathos or lofty patriotism reached the highest spiritual heights.

Mr. Asquith began by a reference to the meeting held in the Guildhall three and a half years before to celebrate the joint declaration of the two great English-speaking States, that, for the future, any differences between them should be settled, if not by agreement, at least by judicial inquiry and arbitration, and never in any circumstances by war. Little then did he, or they, anticipate the terrible spectacle which now confronted us—a contest which for the number and importance of the Powers engaged, the scale of their armaments and arms, the width of the theatre of conflict, the outpouring of blood, and the loss of life, the incalculable toll of suffering levied upon non-combatants, the material and moral loss accumulating day by day to the higher interests of civilised mankind—a contest which, in every one of these aspects, was without precedent in

TEMPORARY SEAT OF THE FRENCH PRESIDENCY AT BORDEAUX.
President Poincaré's official home when the Government moved from Paris to Bordeaux.

THE MILITARY GOVERNOR AND THE BOY SCOUTS OF PARIS.
General Gallieni, the Military Governor of Paris, reviewing French Scouts and Boys' Brigades at the Military School in the French capital. Inset: General Gallieni. Born in 1849, this distinguished soldier fought in the Franco-Prussian War of 1870–71, served in 1877–81 in the Upper Niger territory, and was from 1896 to 1905 Commander-in-Chief in Madagascar.

the annals of the world. After reviewing the diplomatic proceedings which led up to the war, and our efforts for peace, he traced with lucidity the ultimate responsibility of Germany for the war. "Then it was that, reluctantly and against our will, but with a clear judgment and a clean conscience, we found ourselves involved with the whole strength of the Empire in the bloody arbitrament between might and right."

Mr. Asquith and the holocaust in Belgium

He next proceeded to enlarge on "the memorable and glorious example of Belgium" when, "at the instance and by the action of Prussia and Austria, who had guaranteed with the other Powers her neutrality and independence, her neutrality was violated, her independence strangled, her territory made use of as affording the easiest and most convenient road to a war of unprovoked aggression against France." "If the British people had stood by with folded arms, and with such countenance as they could command, while this small and unprotected State, in defence of her vital liberties, made a heroic stand against overweening and overwhelming forces, what would have been our position?" The speaker went on in tones of dramatic scorn to say: "We should have been admiring as detached spectators the siege of Liège, the steady and manful resistance of the small Belgian Army, the occupation of her capital, with its splendid traditions and memories, the gradual forcing back of the patriotic defenders of their native land to the ramparts of Antwerp, countless outrages suffered by them, buccaneering levies exacted from the unoffending civil population, and, finally, the greatest crime committed against civilisation and culture since the Thirty Years' War—the sack of Louvain, with its buildings, its pictures, its unique library, its unrivalled associations, the shameless holocaust of irreparable treasures, lit up by blind barbarian vengeance. What account could we, the Government and the people of this country, have been able to render to the tribunal of our national conscience and sense of honour, if, in defiance of our plighted and solemn obligations, we had endured, and had not done our best to prevent, yes, to avenge these intolerable wrongs? For my part"—and here there was a ring of passion in the speaker's voice which echoed throughout the hall—"I say that sooner than be a silent witness—which means, in effect, a willing accomplice—to this tragic triumph of force over law, and of brutality over freedom, I would see this country of ours blotted out of the pages of history."

Outlining German ambitions, the Prime Minister went on to say that "the cynical violation of the neutrality of Belgium was not the whole, but a step, a first step, in a deliberate policy of which, if not the immediate, the ultimate and not far distant aim was to crush the independence and the autonomy of the free States of Europe. First Belgium, then Holland, then Switzerland, countries like our own, imbued and sustained with the spirit of liberty, were, one after another, to be bent to the yoke of these ambitions, which were fed and fostered by a body of new doctrines, a new philosophy, preached by professors and learned men . . . who have made force their supreme Divinity, and upon its altars are prepared to sacrifice both the gathered fruits and the potential charms of the unfettered human spirit."

The peril to the free States of Europe

He proceeded to say that we had upon the seas the strongest and most magnificent fleet that had ever been seen, and narrated what it had done to guard our shores against the possibility of invasion and to achieve for British and neutral commerce, passing backwards and forwards, from and to every part of our Empire, a security as

THOUSANDS OF GALLANT CHARGERS LAY DOWN THEIR LIVES ON THE BATTLEFIELD.

Dumbly but gloriously thousands of horses pay the dread toll of war. Special efforts were made to relieve the wounded and for the shooting of the hopelessly injured, but even so these faithful creatures suffered terribly in the awful conflict on the Continent. The above photograph was taken near Compiègne and Nery, where the Bays and the "L" Battery of the Royal Horse Artillery distinguished themselves so notably during the retreat from Mons. It shows the graves of the Bays' horses. The shed was used as a sleeping-place, and bears the marks of shrapnel and machine-gun bullets.

ITALIAN DEMONSTRATION AT THE QUEEN'S HALL, LONDON.

ITALIAN SYMPATHY FOR GREAT BRITAIN: CHEERING THE AMBASSADOR IN LONDON.

The top picture is of the great meeting in the Queen's Hall, London, on September 5th, 1914, which was attended by many who had fought for freedom under Garibaldi. On the declaration of Italian neutrality there was an enthusiastic demonstration outside the Italian Embassy in London, when patriotic airs were sung, and British, French, and Italian flags were much in evidence. Inset: The Italian Ambassador acknowledging the cheers of the crowd.

OPENING THE FLOOD-GATES IN FLANDERS.

In Flanders, early in September, 1914, the Germans, bent on the conquest of Antwerp, launched heavy attacks on Termonde and Alost, which were countered by the Belgians opening the dykes and flooding the country. The enemy were suddenly thrown into confusion, and men and horses were soon struggling in the inundated fields. Many guns had to be abandoned, and German soldiers, climbing into the trees to escape from drowning, were later made prisoners. The Belgian artillery, turning on the enemy, nearly converted the Teuton retreat into a rout.

complete as it had ever enjoyed in the days of unbroken peace. Then he insisted that the Expeditionary Force then in France and Belgium had never been surpassed, as its glorious achievements in the field had already made clear, not only in material and equipment, but in the physical and the moral quality of its constituents.

"But there was a call for a new, a continuous, a determined, and a united effort not merely to replace the wastage caused by casualties, not merely to maintain our military power at its original level, but we must, if we are to play a worthy part, enlarge its scale, increase its numbers, and multiply many times its effectiveness as a fighting instrument." After emphasising the imperious urgency of this supreme duty, Mr. Asquith continued: "Our self-governing Dominions throughout the Empire, without any solicitation on our part, have demonstrated with a spontaneousness and a unanimity unparalleled in history, their determination to affirm their brotherhood with us, and to make our cause their own.

"From Canada, Australia, New Zealand, South Africa, and Newfoundland, the children of the Empire, not as an obligation, but as a privilege, asserted their right and their willingness to contribute money and materials, and, what is better than all, the strength and sinews, the fortunes, and the lives of their best manhood. India, too, with no less alacrity has claimed her share in the common task. Every class and creed, British and natives, Princes and people, Hindus and Mohammedans, vie with one another in noble and emulous rivalry. . . . . . We welcome with appreciation and affection their offered aid. In an Empire which knows no distinction of race or cause, we are all alike, as subjects of the King-Emperor, joint and equal custodians of our common interests and fortunes."

The right hon. gentleman then made a glowing appeal for more men—men of the best fighting quality, and for officers who had experience in handling troops, not only to go to the front, but to train the new recruits.

Not the least effective part of the speech was the peroration. "Finally," said he, "let us recall the memories of the great men and the great deeds of the past, commemorated, some of them in the monuments which we see around us on these walls, not forgetting the dying message of the younger Pitt, his last public utterance, made at the table of one of your predecessors, my Lord Mayor, in this very hall: 'England has saved herself by her exertions, and will, as I trust, save Europe by her example.' The England of those days gave a noble answer to his appeal, and did not sheathe the sword until, after nearly twenty years of fighting, the freedom of Europe was secured. Let us go and do likewise."

After admirable speeches from Mr. Bonar Law, Mr. Balfour, and Mr. Churchill, the following resolution was carried by acclamation on the motion of the Lord Mayor, seconded by Mr. Cunliffe, Governor of the Bank of England: "That this meeting of the citizens of London, profoundly believing that we are fighting in a just cause, for the vindication of the rights of small States, and the public law of Europe, pledges itself unswervingly to support the Prime Minister's appeal to the nation, and all measures necessary for the prosecution of the war to a victorious conclusion, whereby alone the lasting peace of Europe can be assured." The meeting concluded with the singing of the National Anthem, and rounds of cheering for the Navy and Army.

German collision with Russian warships

A British submarine arrived at Harwich on September 4th, bringing a German naval lieutenant and a mechanic who were captured in the North Sea, where they were found clinging to a floating aeroplane. They had been two hours in the water. The aeroplane was sunk, after bombs, papers, and the engine had been taken out. On the same day seven German destroyers and torpedo-boats reached Kiel in a damaged condition, from, it was afterwards admitted, a collision with the Russian warships in the vicinity of the North Sea and Baltic Canal. The Wilson liner Runo was sunk by a mine twenty miles off the East Coast, and all the crew and passengers were saved, except twenty Russian emigrants. Next day the Admiralty announced that a German squadron, consisting of two cruisers and four destroyers, had succeeded in sinking fifteen British fishing boats in the North Sea, the crews being taken to Wilhelmshaven as prisoners of war. In view of these events the British Admiralty announced that "All aids to navigation on the East Coast of England and Scotland, both by day and night, may be removed at any time, and without any further warning than is contained in this announcement."

Efforts to embroil Turkey on behalf of Germany in the war were becoming more manifest in Constantinople at this date, September 4th. The number of Germans in the Turkish service now amounted to seventeen hundred, three hundred having arrived from Sofia, disguised as German workmen for the Bagdad railway, although they were really garrison artillerymen with their non-commissioned officers, and they were sent to Tchataldja and the Dardanelles. The German military mission was also increased British merchantmen in the Black Sea were ordered home.

September 5th was a day crowded with many important events, both in Britain and on the Continent. The Secretary of the British Admiralty announced the formation of a new force of fifteen thousand men for service on sea or land. After providing for all present needs of the fleets at sea, there remained available a large number of men belonging to the Royal Marines, Royal Naval Volunteer Reserve, Royal Fleet Reserve, and Royal Naval Reserve. These were constituted into two Royal Naval Brigades and a Royal Marine Brigade, each consisting of four battalions —each battalion being named after former British admirals. The King approved of the appointment of the following officers as Hon. Colonels of the several brigades: First Royal Naval Brigade, Admiral of the Fleet Lord Fisher of Kilverstone, G.C.B., O.M., G.C.V.O.; Second Royal Naval Brigade, Admiral of the Fleet Sir Arthur K. Wilson, G.C.B., O.M., G.C.V.O.; Royal Marine Brigade, Admiral Lord Charles Beresford, G.C.B., G.C.V.O., M.P.

No better evidence of the solidarity of the Allies in their aims and determination was ever given than the declaration which was signed at the Foreign Office, London, on September 5th, by the Ambassadors of the Triple Entente, as hereunder:

"The undersigned, duly authorised thereto by their respective Governments, hereby declare as follows:

"The British, French, and Russian Governments mutually engage not to conclude peace separately during the present war. The three Governments agree that when terms of peace come to be discussed no one of the Allies will demand terms of peace without the previous agreement of each of the other Allies. In faith whereof the undersigned have signed this declaration and have affixed thereto their seals.

"Done at London in triplicate the 5th day of September, 1914.

E. Grey,
His Britannic Majesty's Secretary of State for Foreign Affairs.

Paul Cambon,
Ambassador Extraordinary and Minister Plenipotentiary of the French Republic.

Benckendorff,
Ambassador Extraordinary and Minister Plenipotentiary of his Majesty the Emperor of Russia."

BRITISH MINE-LAYERS AT WORK IN THE NORTH SEA.

This form of warfare was forced upon us by the Germans, who strewed the open sea with mines, regardless of the safety of neutral shipping. We only extended our mine defences in the North Sea in the neighbourhood of East Coast ports on November 21st, 1914

A HAUL IN THE ENGLISH CHANNEL.

British torpedo-boat capturing a German four-masted sailing-ship in the English Channel. The "haul" of prizes by Great Britain was enormous, while the British ships captured by Germany were much fewer. On September 28th, 1914, the British Admiralty announced that 387 German ships with a tonnage of 1,140,000 had been lost, while the British losses were 86 ships, totalling 229,000 tons.

THE BATTLE OF THE MARNE. MIXED FORCE OF BRITISH AND TURCOS FIGHT THE GERMANS FOR POSSESSION OF A VILLAGE IN BRIE.

At the turn of the tide on the Marne, hand-to-hand fighting took place in almost every village in which the Germans and the allied troops came into contact. Here and there (says one account), at the foot of a ruined factory, behind haystacks, and under cover of the banks, the men rallied and rapidly formed a more or less cohesive company, improvising officers and N.C.O.'s as best they could. It was such a mixed company as this that attacked, in the manner illustrated above, a German force at a village in the district of Brie, and eventually drove the enemy into headlong flight before them.

A COMPANY OF THE FAMOUS ZOUAVES ON THE MARCH TO THE FIRING LINE IN NORTHERN FRANCE.
The Zouaves were originally Kabyle soldiers of the French Army, recruited in Algeria; but since 1840, though the picturesque semi-Moorish uniform, with its baggy trousers and jauntily-coloured jackets, had been retained, the Zouaves had been native-born Frenchmen. They were attached to what was known as the Metropolitan Army.

The crusade against the playing of football during the war took a new phase by a telegram sent to his Majesty the King by Mr. F. N. Charrington, the East End temperance worker, in which he said: "May it please your Majesty to remember that Lord Roberts recently said it would be disgraceful if football was continued during the war. The Football Association have now decided to continue their matches, despite all protest. Your Majesty has set an example to the nation in sending your two noble sons to the front. Millions of your Majesty's loyal subjects will be anxious to know if your Majesty's name will still be used as patron of the Football Association."

To this telegram Lord Stamfordham, his Majesty's Lord-in-Waiting, writing from Buckingham Palace on September 5th to Mr. Charrington, replied: "The question raised in your telegram to the King has received the careful consideration and respect which is due to anyone speaking with your great experience and authority. I gather that the Football Association are in direct communication with the War Office, and a general desire has been expressed by the Association to assist in obtaining recruits for the Army. I understand that there may be difficulties in giving up all the matches of professional football clubs in view of contracts which have been made with players. But the doings of the Association will be carefully followed, having regard to the King's position as its patron."

Lord Rosebery, as Lord-Lieutenant of Linlithgowshire, addressed a meeting on September 5th at Broxburn, the object of which was to give an impetus to recruiting in the county. His lordship said that they had met at a very solemn moment in the history of this country—more solemn than any that had occurred in the history of the world. After describing the origin of the crisis, his lordship said: "This is the greatest war the world has ever seen. The Battle of Leipzig, in which Russia, Austria, and Prussia fought against the Emperor Napoleon and crushed him, was called the 'Battle of the Nations.' But it was not the battle of the nations; it was the battle of great armies. It was reserved for this war to be the battle of the nations. Every man in the large countries of the Continent of Europe, except Italy, who can bear arms is under arms at this moment. We are not in that position. We have never gone in for conscription, we have never demanded that every man should bear arms for his country; though, remember this, that by the common law of Great Britain every man valid and capable of bearing arms is bound at the call of his country to do so. You may say, 'It is all very well, you are an elderly gentleman. You will not be called out. You will sleep in your bed

ON GUARD.
British outpost guarding a railway bridge while the Battle of the Marne was raging.

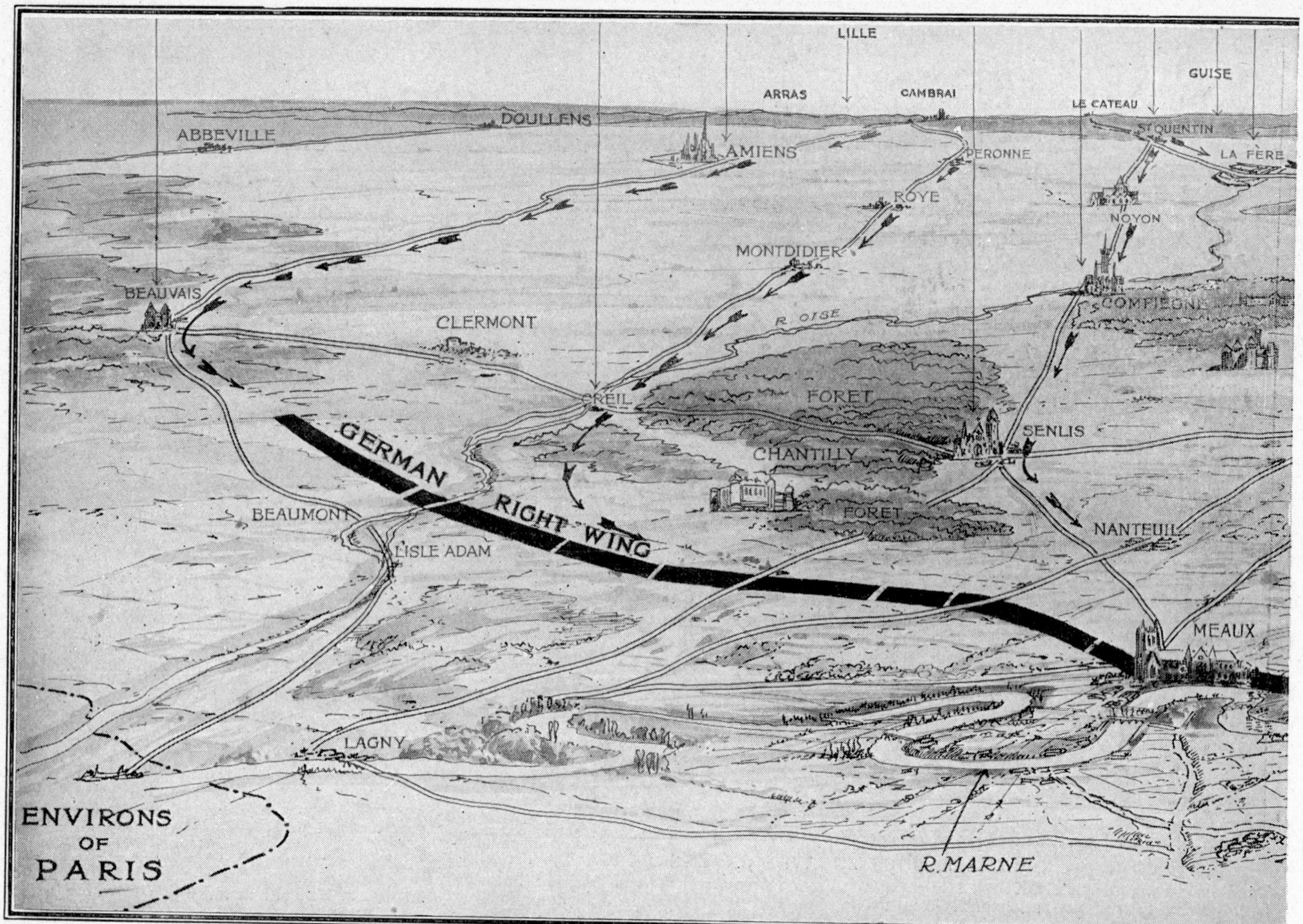

DIAGRAMMATIC BIRD'S-EYE VIEW OF THE ADVANCE OF THE GERMAN ARMIES—The Allies retired in the first week of September, 1914, before the advance of the Germans, along the main roads indicated by the black arrows. From Cambrai the Germans pushed through Amiens to Beauvais about September 2nd. From Peronne they marched on to Roye, Montdidier, Creil, and the Forest of Chantilly. From the region of Le Cateau and St. Quentin the advance was by Noyon to Compiègne, at which point they had to fight for every inch of ground. They then passed through Senlis down to Meaux

at nights. You will have your meals. It is easy for you to come and exhort us, who are younger and able to fight, to go out to the war.' But I do not think that, after all, the position of us, the elderly ones who have to dwell among the sheepfolds and listen to the bleating of the flock while you go out to war, is so much preferable to your position. It is an indication, at any rate, that we are in the decline of vigour, and in the sere and yellow leaf, and do you suppose there is not one single man of my age who would not gladly exchange with one of you and go out to the front?" He described the cause for which we were fighting as a righteous one, fighting not only for Belgium, France, and the sanctity of public law, but fighting to secure our own liberties against an oppression which would be intolerable. "Make no mistake about it," said his lordship in conclusion, "we shall win. We are fighting with our back to the wall to prevent a shame and defeat such as Britain has never sustained, and is not now prepared to endure. We are going to win because a nation and an Empire like ours cannot be extinguished by any such warfare like this. We are going to win because we have our people united as they have never been before. We are going to win because our Dominions and Empires outside these islands vie with each other in generous emulation as to which shall give us most support in supplies, and money, and men. Above all, we are going to win because we have a high, a pure, and a just cause, and we can appeal with humble but, I think, earnest confidence to Him Who, in the words of our beautiful old paraphrase, we recognise as the

Lord Rosebery on "Why we shall win"

> "God of Bethel, by Whose hand
> Our people still are led.'

That same afternoon, September 5th, a remarkable demonstration of Italian sympathy with Great Britain and her Allies took place in the Queen's Hall, London. On the platform, under the outstretched flags of Britain and Italy, were gathered quite a large number of British and Italian veterans who had fought under Garibaldi for the liberty of Italy; and in the body of the hall were massed together the Italian Foreign Legion, which had volunteered for service with the British Expeditionary Forces in France and Belgium; while in the galleries were hundreds of Italian residents in the British metropolis. The Duke of Sutherland, who had hereditary claims to sympathy with free and united Italy—his father had entertained Garibaldi, "the Liberator"—occupied the chair, and in a stirring address said that the liberty-loving nations of the world were ranged together against the German tyrant. The fate of the world was in the balance. Was it to be ruled by oppression and military dictatorship, or would the free countries of both hemispheres stamp out the evil growth of Kaiserism?

Cavaliere Ricci, the aged organiser of the Italian Foreign Legion, in an eloquent and moving speech recalled that he had fought against the Germans in 1866, and again in 1870, when he was in Paris throughout the siege. "By raising this Foreign Legion," he declared, "I am trying to fight the Germans for the third time, and I thank God I have been spared to enjoy this pleasure and this honour. The cursed Triple Alliance," he went on, "has trodden over Italy for the last thirty years; and the German Kaiser even kept a Resident (Prince von Bülow) in Rome. Germany has been the enemy of Italy for the last 1,600 years, since the fall of the Roman Empire. Have you forgotten that there is still the Trentino to unite to Italy—that Trentino where we with Garibaldi were beaten in 1866? There is Trieste, with its command of the Adriatic Sea. There is Fiume, with its arsenals. They must be ours. Away with the cowardly policy of neutrality. After the war, should Italy remain neutral, she would be ruined whoever be victorious. If the Germans

The enemy of Italy for 1,600 years

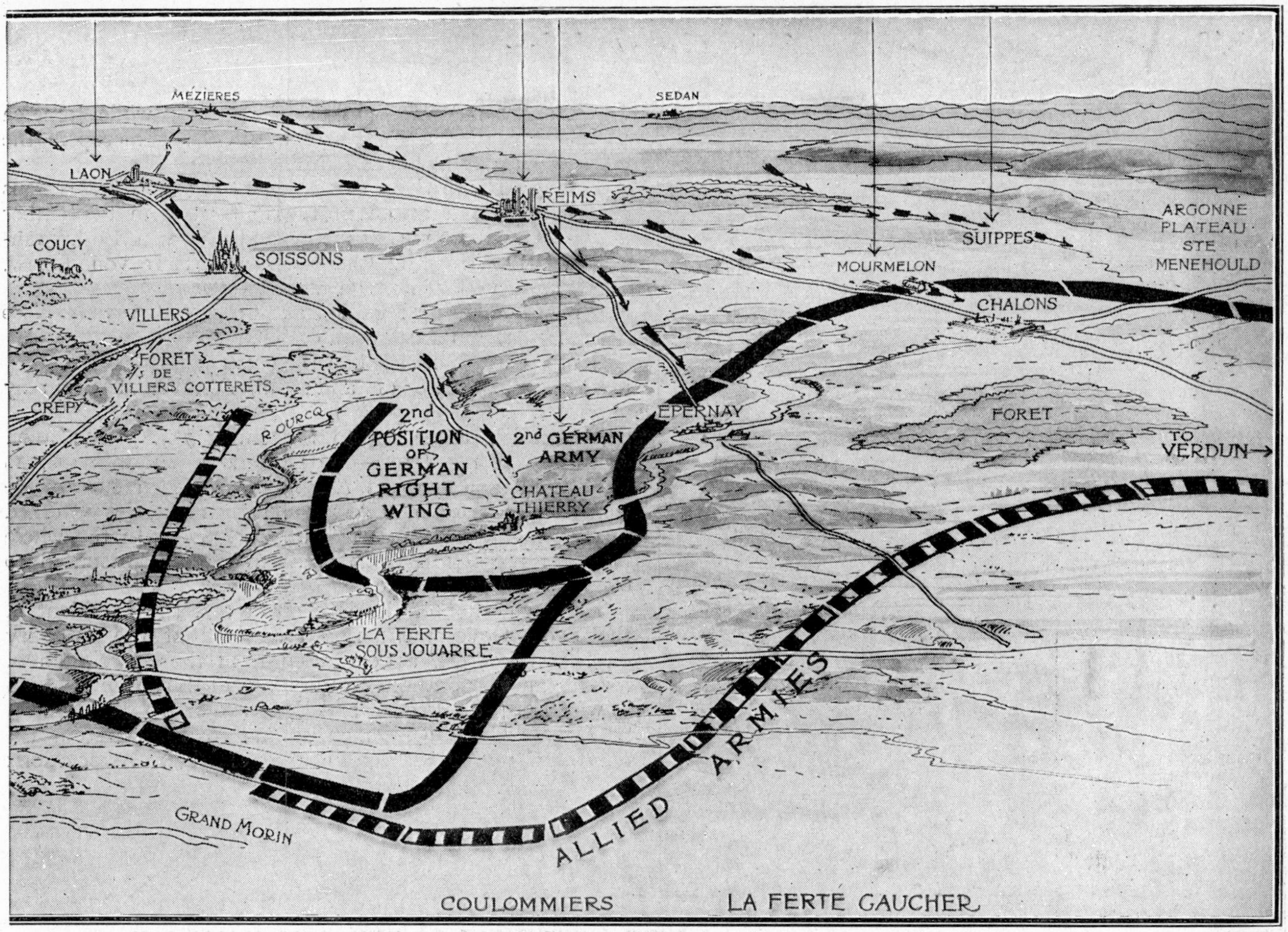

—ACROSS THE PLAINS OF FRANCE TO THE TURNING POINT ON THE MARNE.
Laon, though heavily fortified, was relinquished by the Allies during their retirement; and the enemy advanced thence to Soissons and Chateau Thierry. Farther to the east the invasion from Mézières passed by Rheims to Epernay, Mourmelon, and Chalons. Another force coming from the direction of Longwy appeared to be operating through Suippes and on the wooded Argonne plateau, with its five passes famous in the action in 1792 which preceded the dramatic Battle of Valmy. The vertical arrow-lines signalise the points of importance in the German advance.

were to win—which God forbid!—they would make Italy feel still more the iron heel of their power; and if the Allies win, as we are sure they will do, she cannot expect any reward for having remained neutral and indifferent to the glory of destroying a power which is the negation of all liberty and of God."

Lord Midleton followed with an animated speech in which he declared that Great Britain was fighting, not for anything she herself desired, but for the freedom of Europe.

Signor Bocchi moved the following resolution: "That in the great hour of destiny the sympathy of Italians in England is on the side of Great Britain, and the sword of Italy, ever consecrated to the cause of freedom, should always be ready to defend the liberties of humanity." The signor insisted that if the neutrality of Italy ceased they must take up arms in the right cause, and so help to avoid the success of a terrible despotism. Their arm could not possibly be raised against their Latin sisters, or against Great Britain, who for so many years had defended and helped to make their great poem 'Italy one,' a reality." The resolution was adopted amid great enthusiasm.

Galicia and the Russian Empire

In Russia on the same day, September 5th, General Count Brobrinsky was appointed Governor-General of Galicia, and thanksgiving services were held throughout the Empire to celebrate the reunion of that province with the Russian Empire. In virtue of a law passed by the Duma, the Zemstvos assumed the work of distribution of the State relief for the wives and families of reservists who had been called out for active service. A scheme was devised, in consultation with members of the Legislature, for increasing taxation to make good the deficit due to the prohibition of the sale of alcohol, amounting to nearly a hundred millions sterling; and it was determined to organise an extensive series of public works to be carried out by the enormous number of German and Austrian prisoners who had somehow to be provided for.

Progress was made with the campaign in France. A general action began on September 6th along the vast curving front from Senlis to Verdun, over a space of one hundred and fifty miles; and the German right was forced to retreat by the vigorous assaults of the French, powerfully assisted by the British forces. This was the first occasion on which, in the western campaign, the German armies were driven back. The Germans had previously crossed the Marne on September 3rd, and pushed forward to a point ten miles south of it. General Pau, then in command in the North of France, received on September 6th a telegram from head-quarters, stating that the German centre had been hurled back at Precy-sur-Oise, about twenty-five miles north of Paris; that General D'Amade covered the enemy's left wing compelling it to fall back on Landrecies, about eighty-six miles north of Precy; that Sir John French with his British forces was crushing the enemy's right which was falling back on Villers-Bretonneux, about forty-seven miles north of Precy; and that the Imperial Guard, called upon to surrender, was wiped out by the British. The great Battle of the Marne is dealt with in a separate chapter.

The turn of the tide in the West

In Flanders the Germans made an attack on our Allies at Termonde and Alost, towards Ghent, which was countered by our Allies opening the dykes and flooding the country.

On the other hand the Germans, by shell fire and incendiarism, destroyed on the same date Dinant-sur-Meuse and shot a hundred prominent citizens in the Place d'Armes, including the manager of a large weaving factory, M. Hummers, and the son of a former senator, M. Poncelet—the latter in the presence of his six children. German

PRISONERS OF WAR THAT WERE WORTH TAKING.

British soldiers convoying captured German artillery and transport horses through a French village after the fighting on the Marne.

troops appeared at the branch of the National Bank, where they demanded all the cash in the safe, and when the manager refused to give them the money or open the safe for them, he was immediately shot, together with his two sons.

Previous mention has been made of gifts offered by different Dominions and Colonies to the Motherland for the use of the nation at large, or to make special provision for the troops at the front, or to some institution or organisation for special charitable or patriotic work. British Columbia on September 6th intimated a gift of 1,200,000 1 lb. tins of salmon, and in doing so Sir Richard McBride, the Premier, telegraphed to the Colonial Secretary: "Canada has already given an earnest of her intention of casting all her resources into the scale with the Motherland in this struggle to uphold the banner of liberty throughout the world. The other provinces of the Dominion have responded in magnificent fashion to the need of increasing Britain's food supplies, but what they have already contributed is, I am sure, only a sample of what their generosity shall be, if put to a further test; and this, I am equally sure, is the attitude of the whole of the people of the province of Columbia. The shipment of tinned salmon will go forward to London just as soon as the despatch can be arranged for."

On the same day the Government of New Brunswick offered to, and the offer was accepted by, his Majesty's Government 100,000 bushels of potatoes; and the planters of Mauritius presented a million pounds of sugar to the Navy, and a million pounds to the Army; while Jamaica promised to send a portion of the next sugar crop in the colony as a gift to Great Britain.

Through Rome there came the intelligence that serious controversy had arisen in the first week in September between the German Emperor and Dr. von Bethmann-Hollweg, the Imperial Chancellor, and Herr von Jagow, the Secretary for Foreign Affairs—the two Ministers being regarded as responsible for the unreadiness of German diplomacy which had led to the existing unsatisfactory state of affairs in Berlin and Germany generally.

Alien enemies in the United Kingdom

In London alone, up to September 7th, 37,293 alien enemies were registered—27,944 Germans, of which 8,129 were women, and 9,349 Austrians, of which 1,687 were women. In these numbers 3,000 alien enemies interned in concentration camps were not included. In the whole kingdom the registrations of alien enemies amounted to over 100,000 up to date.

The Chancellor of the Exchequer and the President of the Local Government Board received at the Treasury on September 8th a deputation from the Association of Municipal Corporations, consisting of Sir Robert Fox, Town Clerk of Leeds, and Mr. Alderman Hobson, of Sheffield. These gentlemen submitted to Ministers the following resolutions on behalf of their Association:

"TO THE LEFT, MONSIEUR, BY THE MILL."

Member of a British cycling corps, uncertain of his way in the windmill country of France, being directed by a peasant. The fully-laden bicycle and the general fitness of both man and machine indicate the nature of the duty on which the soldier was engaged.

(1) "That the Government be requested to raise in their War Loan such an amount as they may think necessary, and from this sum to make advances to the Corporations at cost price, in order that the new capital for municipal undertakings may be secured upon the best possible terms, with power for the Corporations to repay on giving reasonable notice." (2) "That the Trustees Act be amended so as to provide that the mortgages of the Corporations mentioned in that Act shall be trustee securities, and that the stock and mortgages of all Corporations

"THE HOUSES WERE DEMOLISHED LIKE PACKS OF CARDS."

"We had a most trying time in a village," a British cavalryman wrote home from France, "and were bombarded by eight German guns. The houses were demolished like packs of cards, and after six hours of mental agony we had to retire one by one across a pontoon bridge, subjected to an awful fire. But with the loss of a few men we got clear, and the general complimented us on the absence of panic."

WRECKAGE ON THE MARNE.
The view above is of the town of Meaux. Floating baths and wash-houses were sunk to prevent their military use by the Germans.

whose boroughs have a population of over 20,000 be trustee securities."

In the course of conversation with Ministers it was elicited that by the first resolution the Association did not propose to ask the Government to advance money except for new works put in hand to provide employment during the war.

Mr. Lloyd George, in reply to the deputation, said it was obvious that it was to the interest of the municipalities and of the State that they should not be competing in the same market in what must be difficult borrowing times. He had no hesitation, therefore, in saying that it was desirable that the Government should accede to the deputation's first request, that whatever money they borrowed for the purpose of responding to the invitation of the Local Government Board to make provision for distress in their districts should be advanced out of the War Loan which the Government put on the market. The municipalities, as to terms, must be subject to the same time obligations as the Government, who were quite prepared to lend at the rate of interest they paid themselves, with an allowance for the actual expenses to the State.

Making provision for industrial distress

The right hon. gentleman went on to say: "We think it is absolutely necessary that the money should be spent for the relief of distress. This is not the time to embark in great municipal enterprises which have no reference to distress. After all, we want every penny we can raise to fight the common enemy, and our first consideration ought to be to win, to come out triumphant in this struggle. Unless we do that there will be no country for municipalities or Governments to administer. As finance is going to play a very great part we must husband our resources. . . . We raise the ten millions for you in the same market as we raise the ten millions for our armies on the Continent. Therefore, in my judgment, the last few hundred millions may win this war. The first hundred millions our enemies can stand as well as we can; but the last they cannot, thank God! . . . That is where our resources will come in, not merely of men, but of cash. We have won with 'silver bullets' before. We financed Europe in the greatest war we ever fought, and that is what won. Of course, British tenacity and British courage always came in, and they always will, but let us remember that British cash told, too. When the others were absolutely exhausted, we were getting our second breath, and our third, and our fourth, and we shall have to spend our last before we are beaten." In conclusion the Chancellor of the Exchequer said: "Speaking purely as the Treasury, we will find the money for you only where there is really actual insistent distress in the districts. It is very much better to work in things that are normal if you can. Our trade is not going. The seas are ours, and they will remain ours. We shall get not only our own trade, but we shall get a good deal of the enemy's trade as well, and, of course, there is always a business which is necessary in order to keep the war going."

"We have won with silver bullets before"

Mr. Samuel, President of the Local Government Board, spoke on the same lines as the Chancellor of the Exchequer, and the deputation withdrew.

WRECK OF A RED CROSS TRAIN NEAR LIZY.
The centre and lower photographs were taken after a train with wounded soldiers had been blown up by the Germans as it was crossing the River Ourcq, near Lizy. Forty soldiers were drowned.

FIELD TELEGRAPH EQUIPMENT CARRIED BY MOTOR-CAR.

CHAPTER XXXIV.

THE BATTLES OF THE OURCQ, MORIN, AND MARNE RIVERS.

A Conflict of Four Million Men—Joffre Outgenerals Moltke—Recoiling for a Leap, He Draws on the German Right Wing—Kluck is Trapped between Three Allied Armies—Moltke Prepares a Counter-stroke in Eastern France—Joffre Returns to the Napoleonic Method—Race for Victory Between Paris and Nancy—The Sixth French Army Held Up—The British Force Surprises Kluck—Drives in His Flank and Threatens His Rear—Brings Help to the Sixth French Army—The Great Victory that Saves France—The Pursuit to the Aisne.

OF all great historic conflicts, the most tremendous, the most exciting, the most fateful was the supreme clash, between Paris and Nancy, of the armies of France and Germany, with the comparatively small British Expeditionary Force intervening. The gigantic struggle must not be allowed to go down in our history under the name of the Battle of Meaux. The fighting round Meaux was only part of the wrestle of the two largest military Powers in Western Europe. The battle-front stretched three-quarters of the way across France. Engaging in it were more than four millions of men. On one side were six French armies, with the British force making the seventh army. On the other side were seven German armies—more than equal in number to their opponents. Each had brought every possible man into the field.

Germany emptied her great fortresses—Metz, Strassburg, Thionville—and poured the troops over the border. France hurried a number of reservists into her eastern fortifications—Verdun and Toul—turned the garrisons into field forces, and transformed the defence army of Paris into an attacking host.

The preparations for the decisive struggle began towards the end of August. General von Moltke wished it to take place on the line running by the upper course of the Somme and along the Aisne to Rethel and the Meuse. It is quite probable that the work done by German agents in preparing gun positions in the Aisne quarries, which they had been working in 1913, was performed in view of this plan. But General Joffre refused to fight, in spite of the fact that one of the most brilliant of his subordinate generals, General Pau, had checked the enemy at Guise, and the British force had turned at bay in the Forest of Compiègne and taken ten German guns there.

The position the invaders had chosen was too strong. Near its centre, on the Aisne, it had, in the plateau of Soissons, the most formidable natural line of fortification in Northern Europe. It could retain half a million French troops there, while its right and left wings curved round both French flanks. So General Joffre retired on Paris. He had, in so doing, to abandon Northern France to the invaders, but his sole object was to keep his armies concentrated, with a good railway line running all along their front, to enable him to shift the troops quickly and strengthen any weak part.

Even when he had withdrawn his forces to the line on which he intended to offer battle he had still a very grave difficulty to face. Up to that time his left wing had been his weakest point. Even when a new army was formed under General D'Amade, on the left of the British Expeditionary Force, and new forces were brought up on the right of the British soldiers by General Pau, the German club-end, directed by Kluck, continued to smash back the Franco-British left wing. D'Amade was defeated, and the old pressure on the British force was resumed. Our local success in the Forest of Compiègne was merely a delaying action. Our men had to continue their retreat at the beginning of September.

By this time, however, matters were not so bad as they seemed on the allied left wing. General Joffre, with characteristic subtlety, had quickly

GENERAL MAUNOURY.
At great personal risk he saved the lives of two private soldiers during the Battle of the Marne.

KINDNESS OF FRENCH PEASANTRY TO BRITISH SOLDIERS UNDER FIRE—During the great retreat to the Marne many acts of kindness were shown by the French people to the hardly-pressed British soldiers. In the above view we see a number of men of the Gloucester Regiment, who after an exhausting march had halted in a village to form a rearguard position. A platoon is erecting a breastwork from stones lying at the hill-side. The villagers immediately flocked out with gifts of fruit, chocolate,

transformed General D'Amade's failure to protect North-Western France into a source of strength in the future. He allowed the three retreating armies—General D'Amade's, Sir John French's, and General Pau's—to give ground to the enemy. He sent them no reinforcements. Also, as we have seen, he informed the French Government that he was not able to guarantee to save the capital from a siege. So the Germans received the gratifying news that Paris had been abandoned by the President and the legislating and administrating authorities of the country.

All this, however, was only a stratagem on the part of General Joffre. He was trying to appear weakest at the very point at which he had suddenly become strongest. He wanted to induce General Kluck to continue to advance into a gigantic ambush. Paris was not only fully garrisoned, but a new French army was waiting in it, under General Maunoury, to co-operate with the allied left wing in a surprise attack on Kluck's forces. All that afterwards happened in the conflicts round the Ourcq and Morin Rivers was prearranged to occur at any spot Kluck cared to select.

The surprise awaiting Kluck in Paris

There is no reason to suppose that the famous German commander decided on the course which he then adopted. The affair was far too important for him to manage it. He referred it, about the beginning of September, to General von Moltke and the German Military Staff. For a day, perhaps, they hesitated. For a great battle, in which three-quarters of a million men were conflicting, was taking place from Rethel to the Meuse. Here the Ninth French Army, under General Foch, and the Fourth French Army, under General de Langle Cary, were stubbornly holding up the Saxon army, under General Hausen, and the army of the Duke of Würtemberg, while the Third French Army, composed of the garrison of Verdun, checked the advance of the Crown Prince's forces.

The three French generals had received an express order from their Commander-in-Chief to fight a delaying action with the utmost fierceness. So well did they carry out this order that the German Military Staff thought for a time that the grand decisive battle was actually in progress. In fact, it was thus officially reported in Berlin on September 2nd. But General Joffre only wanted the German centre and left wing to be held firmly back until he had fully prepared his real battle-line in the south.

In the meantime General von Moltke and his Staff worked out their plan of battle. Kluck was ordered to swerve away from Paris and attempt, by a swift movement to the south-east of the French capital, to cut the French army there from the city. He was given a hard and important task, but it was not the decisive stroke. The armies of General Bülow, General Hausen, and the Duke of Würtemberg were massed in the centre of the line. They had to try to pierce the French centre. But

—DURING THE GREAT RETREAT FROM MONS TO THE MARNE.

and cigarettes, and others were soon at work making and serving out coffee. Though German gunners as quickly found the range, the villagers bravely continued their kindly ministrations. An infantry attack was warded off by our artillery, and the retreat continued. The kindness of the French was the more noteworthy as our men were not victors, but hard-pressed troops in retreat.

their work also was not expected to be decisive. For the Crown Prince, with much trouble and delay, had at last managed to get near to the main scene of conflict. His forces stretched from the north of Verdun, through the hilly Argonne Forest, to a southern point a little above the town of Bar-le-Duc. Only a weak French army, consisting of the garrison troops of Verdun, under General Sarrail, opposed him. Here, therefore, the German General Staff prepared its heaviest stroke, as a counter to the blow that General Joffre was about to deliver against Kluck's forces near Paris. A grand decisive movement by the Crown Prince would gloriously enhance the personal prestige of the Hohenzollern family, and thus have an important bearing on the domestic policy of the German Empire. From a strategical point of view, also, it was both sound and brilliant. So the garrisons of Metz and Saarbrucken marched to assail General Sarrail in his rear, along the heights of the Meuse, between Verdun and Toul. At the same time the Crown Prince's army attacked the troops of General Sarrail on the north flank and the western front.

The French army, based on the neighbouring fortress town of Toul, in the south, could not assist the Verdun garrison. For it was fighting against overwhelming German forces from Strassburg and Alsace, which were bent on taking Nancy and pouring through the Gap of Lorraine on to the rear of General Sarrail's army at Bar-le-Duc. He would then have been completely encircled, and in any case only part of his troops could have escaped by a wild flight. Their comrades from Toul were trying to prevent this crowning disaster. But so certain were the German General Staff of capturing Nancy and all the French right wing that the Kaiser came to watch the victory from a hill close to the capital of French Lorraine.

Such were the perplexing perils that the French Commander-in-Chief had to meet. He was bringing his hammer-stroke down in the west on Kluck's forces. To ward it off, General von Moltke was bringing down a still more crashing blow in the east on the field armies of Verdun and Toul. The orthodox movement would have been to rail at once the British army from Paris to Bar-le-Duc to reinforce General Sarrail. Apparently Kluck, as he continued his sweep to the south, thought this had been done.

Joffre's return to the Napoleonic method

But General Joffre had other gifts besides the extraordinary patience, tenacity, and defensive skill with which he had conducted the grand retreat. After having played the scientific, methodical German game in a way that astonished the Germans themselves, and made them admire the directing mind they were fighting against, the great Gascon surprised them by revealing another side of his character.

At heart he was a fighter of the school of Nelson and Napoleon. As an engineer and an expert in fortification,

FRENCH CAVALRY CROSSING A BRIDGE OF BOATS OVER THE RIVER MARNE.

he could be as cautious and as solid in an offensive-defensive campaign as Wellington had been. But it was in the thunderbolt attack that his full genius was shown. Patiently he forged the thunderbolt. At times he spent weeks on it; at times, months. But, when at last it was ready for launching, he struck with the swift, intense fury of his race. He had so skilfully arranged everything that he could hit quicker and harder with his left wing than General von Moltke could strike at his right wing. He had three armies round Kluck; there were only two armies immediately round Sarrail. So, shifting none of his troops, the great Frenchman offered battle.

The region in which he fought was the classic battle-ground of France. In the heath to the north, below the vineyards of Champagne, where the grapes were ripening in the scorching September sunshine, was the monument of defeat of the first of the Huns—the camp of Attila. It was an immense oval of earthworks, where Attila and his horde rested before the battle that ended in the barbarians being routed by the Gauls and Romans. The plain around was the practising ground of the French Army—their Aldershot—and the range of every visible object was known to the French artillerymen. In their retreat through this familiar scene the gunners had already given the enemy a terrible foretaste of their surprising speed and accuracy of fire.

Exciting country to fight in

Closer to Paris, amid the marshes of Saint Gond and the tributary streams of the Marne, Napoleon had fought against the Prussians in 1814, his back to the wall and his genius at its height. Every French officer knew by heart the details of this brilliant campaign by the most brilliant of all French leaders in war. They had studied every yard of the ground, and Sir John French, an ardent admirer of Napoleon's military skill, was also acquainted with the scene of the 1814 battle.

It was exciting country to fight in. There were woods, like the Forest of Crecy, a few miles south-east of Paris, where an army could shelter from aerial observation. Sir John French concealed his forces there, and they escaped the notice of scouting German airmen. There were many heights, giving good gun positions. There were streams to impede movements on both sides, and innumerable farmhouses to be loopholed for rifle and Maxim fire; and in places were bluffs, moated by a river, where a couple of well-placed machine-guns could hold up an army corps.

Meaux, the principal town of the region, was some twenty miles from the forts of Paris. A charming old cathedral town on the Marne, it had been in peaceful days the Henley of France, and a line of houseboats, rowing-boats, and canoes still floated on its placid stream. Above Meaux the waters of the Ourcq flowed into the Marne, running from some hilly eastern country, through which it had cut a ravine. On the steep eastern bank of the Ourcq General Kluck left his heavy artillery, with some 100,000 men, to protect his flank against the turning movement threatening from Paris.

Germans in sight of the promised land

Then, with about 150,000 troops, he crossed the Marne and struck south towards La Ferté Gaucher. Two streams, the Petit Morin and the Grand Morin, were traversed by his troops. All the time he was moving, the British army was watching him across the farther bank of the Grand Morin, and the Fifth French Army was waiting in trenches ahead of him by the next southern stream, the Aubelin.

The German patrols, scouting ahead of their main force, found, however, nothing to alarm them. The British commander had left a gap of a mile or so between the British and French armies. Through this gap the happy Uhlans rode southward till they were at Nogent, far below Paris, with the rich prospect of Central France opening before their delighted eyes. Such was the situation on the morning of Sunday, September 6th, 1914.

It was extraordinary. Here was an invading army, reckoned to have the most efficient organisation in the world. Its cavalry scouting system was strengthened by

AN EARLY-MORNING ENCOUNTER AT LA FERE.

At La Fère a party of French soldiers had retired to a cottage for a few hours' sleep, only to be awakened ere dawn had broken by German shells bursting above their heads. Jumping up hastily, they immediately replied to the enemy's fire, retreating from their position only when compelled to do so by the overpowering numbers of the foe.

an aerial method of reconnaissance, carried out by skilful pilots who held the record for the highest flights. It had very powerfully-engined flying machines, and every scientific aid to observation that could be devised. Besides its cavalry scouts and reconnaissance officers in flying machines, this invading army was reputed to possess the best system of espionage in the world, and to have covered its lines of advance with spies. Yet with the old-fashioned help of a forest Sir John French was able to arrange an ambush on so large a scale that, compared with it, Stellenbosch, in the days of the South African War, when aerial scouting was impossible, was merely an affair of outposts.

Sir John, it is clear from the account he afterwards gave, was astonished by the success of his manœuvre. It ranks as one of the great surprises in the Great War. It was probably undertaken first just as a simple precaution against the discovery of our dispositions and artillery sites. Then, when our advance guards drew back, more to report the enemy's movements than to conceal themselves, the news of the continual progress of the main German force diagonally across our front was received with amazed joy.

Blind to his own peril, General Kluck was trying his customary movement of envelopment against the Fifth French Army. Many explanations have been attempted, but none of them explains anything. The affair stands pre-eminent as one of the most decisive blunders in military history. Grouchy's mistake at Waterloo in wasting time and men by attacking a Prussian rearguard, and allowing Blücher to march unopposed with his main army to co-operate with Wellington, was not so gross an error as Kluck's.

Kluck was afterwards degraded for it. He suddenly fell from the glorious position of the leading German general in the western theatre of war into the obscurity of something little better than a corps commander in the dullest part of the battle trenches. But the blunder may not have been due entirely to him. In all likelihood the German Military Staff reckoned that they had forced General Joffre to weaken his left wing in order to resist the pressure on his right. This wrong preconception of the state of affairs may have made Kluck unsuspicious of the whereabouts of his most stubborn foes, while the remarkable ascendancy which the men of the British Flying Corps had won over the German airmen may have restricted the scope of his aerial reconnaissance. After the battle General Joffre sent a special message of thanks to our Flying Corps for the important work they had done.

German intelligence at fault

Of course it would have been a tremendous thing if the First German Army could have been lured right through the gap left by Sir John French. But Kluck was not quite so over-confident as to march to entire destruction. He had to attack the whole front of the Fifth French Army, that stretched from the hills near the village of Courtecon to the little town of Esternay, with a railway supplying it in its rear. This he did on Sunday, September 6th, while trying at the same time to work round the French left flank.

Battle-line of the Ourcq conflict

Meanwhile, the large force that he had entrenched in his rear along the heights of the Ourcq had become engaged with the Sixth French Army operating from Paris. The battle-line of the Ourcq conflict extended from the town of Nanteuil-le-Haudouin, some ten miles below the Forest of Compiègne, to Meaux, some twenty miles from the north-eastern Paris forts. The French took the offensive on Saturday, September 5th, and to this date we may assign the real beginning of the immense Battle of Eastern France.

THE PROBLEM FOR THE AERIAL BOMB-DROPPER.

View of the target presented by a military convoy as seen from an aeroplane. Reproduced by the courtesy of the Royal Flying Corps and the editor of "Flight," it shows how small a target is presented to a bomb-dropper who is at a height of over 1,000 feet. Some five or six military waggons were drawn up alongside the road, partly under cover of trees. They can be discerned within the white circle.

In the Ourcq section the fight went on furiously in the hilly country stretching for some ten miles westward of the river. All the French troops, vehemently excited by being able at last to take the offensive against the invader, were eager to get to work with the bayonet. Their rushes were superb displays of their old, characteristic military prowess. Skilfully helped by their fine light field artillery, they quickly cleared the western hills of Germans. When, however, they approached the river heights on September 6th, they found themselves opposed by machinery that no personal courage could overcome. One gallant Zouave battalion, for instance, lost eight hundred out of a thousand men. In two days they only gained a mile and a half. They fought like lions, but the German artillery fire shattered their advance.

The numerous heavy howitzers and big guns that formed the most formidable part of Kluck's striking power were set in position over the stream and dominated all the crossings. No temporary bridge of any kind could be thrown over the Ourcq; the terrible fire destroyed everything. The German gunners had measured the ranges of every natural object round about, and they kept off something like a quarter of a million troops, who possessed no armament of equal power. For against large howitzers—that could fire without giving any indication of their position—the small 3 in. French gun was of little use. It was, in short, an open-air siege battle—the first important affair of the kind in the western theatre of war. By it the Germans proved that the trouble they had taken to drag about an unusual number of heavy pieces of ordnance with their armies was more than repaid by the defensive powers of these cumbersome batteries.

The French, in their artillery, had sacrificed power to mobility. Their light quick-firing gun was almost as handy as a Maxim in an ordinary battle, and yet, with its melinite shells, as terrible against infantry or cavalry as

FRENCH CAVALRY ON THE MARCH ALONG A ROAD IN NORTHERN FRANCE.

FRENCH TROOPS DRIVING BACK THE INVADERS ABOVE THE MARNE.

When the enemy had been driven across the Marne, some desperate fighting took place near May-en-Multien, north-east of Meaux, where the sketches from which the above illustration was made were taken. When their resistance was broken the Germans were hotly pursued by the French with artillery, cavalry, and infantry. The artillery dislodged the last German battery in the village on the left of the picture. Then, without waiting to think about taking cover, the French infantry charged the foe, who were driven farther back with heavy loss.

ON THE HEIGHTS ABOVE LENHAREE—THE SCENE OF TER

There was no harder fighting during the German advance south than took place at Lenharée, the scene of which has been drawn from sketches made on the spot by our special war artist, Mr. Sydney Adamson. In the early days of September, 1914, after a series of sanguinary encounters, the French were forced to retreat ten kilometres. But in five days the Germa beaten in the Battle of the Marne, streamed across these same fields, purs by the victorious French. Our artist has chosen one of the earlier counters for illustration. The village of Lenharée, near Chalons, lies in a holl

he left below the church, which was the centre of some of the fiercest of the agements. To the right of the picture is to be seen the German first engaged with the French. The German second line is advancing, under er of the artillery on the extreme right, to the support of the first line, which is being hotly engaged. The smoke rising from behind the church is of the village in flames. Amidst the bursting shells French Red Cross officials are carrying their wounded to shelter across the cabbage garden in the rear of the fighting line.

THE TAXI-CAB IN WAR: EXCITING INCIDENT IN THE TOWN OF SENLIS.

After being in possession of Senlis for three days, during which they burnt the town and shot the mayor and two of the principal inhabitants, the Germans were suddenly surprised by a dash of Turcos, who whirled into the town in taxi-cabs and, after a fierce fight, drove out the invaders.

a gun twice its size. But in siege warfare, against long-range, hidden howitzers, it could make no progress. This fact afterwards decided the German Commander-in-Chief to use the heights of the Aisne valley for a siege defence on a larger scale, using the immense guns that had destroyed the Maubeuge forts to beat off the allied armies.

In the meantime there was for a time a practical defeat of the sound and brilliant French operation on the Ourcq, intended to cut the lines of communication of several German armies and turn their coming retreat into a rout. It had appeared most hazardous of Kluck to leave only two reserve army corps to guard his rear and the main line of German communications. But the event showed that the German general's faith in his heavy artillery was well founded. The German rearguard was not thrown back from the Ourcq until some heavy guns of the British army were brought up from Meaux to shell the enemy's artillery positions. By this time, however, Kluck had drawn back over the Marne, and the Sixth French Army had then no opportunity of turning his flank.

The French out-gunned on the Ourcq

So, in their chief object, the French operations on the Ourcq section of the battlefield can hardly be said to have succeeded. It was the fault neither of the general nor of his spirited, plucky men. It was the fault of the French Ministry for War of more than a decade before. They had given the French Army the finest light field artillery in the world, but they had made a mistake in neglecting the change which the progress of motor-traction had produced in the conditions of the old problem of so moving heavy guns and heavy howitzers as not to slacken the march of an army.

The French people had for long been foremost in developing the private motor-car industry. They had indeed constructed the first armoured motor-car carrying a Maxim or a small quick-firer. But in military motor-tractors and vehicles the German and Austrian armament firms had been encouraged by their Governments to make such progress as left all other nations, at the outbreak of war, at a disadvantage. General Joffre in July, 1914, was training a force of heavy field artillerymen, but the war came before they were fully prepared. One of the things that made our comparatively small Expeditionary Force so useful to our Allies was that—taught by our experience in the South African campaign, when we had to face at times big Krupp guns—we had a proportion of fairly heavy batteries in our field artillery.

In regard to the machinery of slaughter, the Teutons were probably correct in assuming that they had the best mechanical means for conquering the other land forces of the European continent. But machinery is not everything. Men and leadership are even more important. All that Kluck's big guns did was to save him from complete rout. They did not save either him or the other six German army commanders from defeat in a battle that created a new era in history.

In this battle, where millions of men rocked for ten days in unceasing conflict, a hundred thousand British soldiers played a strangely decisive part—out of all proportion to the smallness of their numbers. Victory at the point they occupied was practically certain. The French Commander-in-Chief, by his skilful disposition of forces against Kluck's depleted army, had organised in advance the success that ensued. On the southern front Kluck had only 150,000 men, worn by long marches, if not seriously diminished in number since they fought their first fight at Mons.

Until the official German account of the operations appears—if ever it appears—we shall not know if the German armies received drafts to replace losses before the great battle occurred. We know that shortly before the battle some of the German armies were reorganised. We then may take it that Kluck still disposed of about a quarter of a million men. He left 100,000 to guard his rear on the Ourcq, and marched across our front to attack the Fifth French Army under General d'Espérey. In so doing his remaining force of 150,000 became caught on two sides by 100,000 Britons and 200,000 Frenchmen. Thus, as General Joffre had arranged, a German defeat in this section of the field of battle was as certain as any human plan could be. For the quality of all the opposing troops was by this time clearly known. But what General Joffre could not arrange, against as bold and skilful a leader as Kluck had proved himself, was a rapid victory.

But a rapid victory was most urgently needed. In the critical centre of the French front the position of General Sarrail's army was growing dangerous. The Germans had brought heavy siege artillery against the line of small forts running along the heights of the Meuse from Verdun to Toul. One of these forts, Fort Troyon, was being battered in a most terrible way by great howitzer shell fire. If the fort fell, then General Sarrail's troops would be pressed on the front by the Crown Prince's army, and assailed in the rear by the Metz force advancing through the gap made in the defences of the heights of the Meuse. At best they could take shelter in Verdun, and there stand against the siege train that had quickly wrecked Maubeuge. Meanwhile, the two victorious German armies would proceed to roll up the entire French line.

Sir John French's pre-arranged triumph

It was a race between the German eastern wing and the Franco-British western wing. Both were within reach of a sectional victory, and the wing that won quicker would roll up the entire hostile line and so decide the battle. Sir John French's success in concealing his forces and getting a clear line of attack against his opponent's flank brought success very near. And the splendid fighting qualities

GERMAN GUNS THAT WOULD TROUBLE THE ALLIES NO MORE.
Limber-waggons of German guns, with piles of ammunition lying about, abandoned by the retreating troops of the Kaiser during the Battle of the Marne. The guns were captured by General French's "contemptible little army."

DRIVING THE TEUTONS BEYOND THE MARNE.
A remarkable photograph of French artillery passing through the village of Chauconier, near Meaux, on the River Marne, in pursuit of the retreating Germans, some of whose handiwork can be seen in the burning farm on the right.

THE HALL-MARK OF THE HUN.
Another view of the burning farm shown in the top photograph. The farmer is seen witnessing the destruction of his property.

FRENCH MACHINE-GUN SECTION IN THE FIELD.
In the infantry these guns, with their ammunition, were carried by pack animals, and each battalion had a complete section of two guns.

of the British soldier consummated the success. The result was that the Crown Prince and the Kaiser, while preparing for their great, immortal triumph, were suddenly transformed into fugitives. It was French's "contemptible little army," still unexterminated, which was the immediate instrument in bringing suddenly to dust and bitterness the towering, glorious hopes of the War-maker of the World. Quite likely General Joffre, with ironic humour, used our troops to deal the unexpected, sideways sledge-hammer stroke that broke the German line because of the terms in which the Kaiser had spoken of them. Quite likely, also, the position given to our men by the French Commander-in-Chief was a generous, cordial mark of appreciation of the fine work they had done between Mons and Le Cateau.

However this may be, the British force certainly had a prearranged triumph in the greatest battle in history. All it had to do, in co-operation with the magnificent fighting men of the Fifth French Army, was to go forth and win, and win quickly. But now comes an unexpected inversion of ideas. By reason of the skill with which the French Commander-in-Chief had prepared it, the victory of the allied forces between the Morin and the Marne scarcely ranks among the highest achievements of British arms. The retreat from Mons does, the storming of the Aisne heights does, the defence of Ypres does; but our affair on Kluck's flank was only a sound, solid, workmanlike job, carried out with all possible finish and despatch. It was General Sarrail's Third Army round Verdun and Bar-le-Duc, holding out heroically against overpowering odds, and the Iron Division of Toul holding out at Nancy that won the supreme honours of the immense Battle of Eastern France. And the Fourth Army, under General de Langle Cary, and the Ninth Army under General Foch, and our immediate comrades, the Fifth Army under General d'Espérey had each a harder task than the British force.

Our men had what the Kaiser, in his notorious order

CHASING THE FLYING ENEMY IN THE VICINITY OF THE MARNE.
A notable camera-record of French dragoons in pursuit of the flying German lines passing through one of the villages on the River Marne. These men did great execution in chasing the flying enemy.

of August 19th, vainly asked the commanders of his northern armies to see that General Kluck had in his attack on us—a "walk-over." The British soldier walked over what had been the Kaiser's best army; he kicked it across three rivers—the Grand Morin, the Petit Morin, and the Marne—and then chased it as it tore away in precipitate flight. The action began early in the morning of Sunday, September 6th. The British force advanced from the Forest of Crecy. It consisted of five divisions of infantry and five brigades of cavalry. It was arranged in three army corps. Sir Douglas Haig still commanded the 1st and 2nd Divisions; Sir Horace Smith-Dorrien commanded the 3rd and 5th Divisions; and the 4th Division, General Snow's, and the 19th Brigade, though lacking the number of troops proper to a corps, were termed the Third Army Corps, and placed under the direction of General W. P. Pulteney. In numbers the British Expeditionary Force had not increased since its great battles in Belgium and North-Western France, but all its losses had been made good by fresh drafts.

As a precaution, apparently, against a flank attack from Paris, Kluck had placed some 9,000 cavalrymen near the forest in which our troops were hidden; another 9,000 of his mounted men watched on the Grand Morin by the town of Coulommiers in front of our right wing. Helped by our airmen, our gunners got the range of these unsuspecting hostile forces. The two German cavalry divisions were waiting for their infantry to throw back the Fifth French Army and enable them to pursue it. But a sudden storm of shrapnel and case-shot from the quiet, sunny western woods put them to flight. Before, however, the guns spoke our cavalry had worked round as close as they could get to the enemy without alarming his patrols. They now rode out, as the German horsemen fell back towards their infantry and guns, under a storm of shrapnel. Then the hostile horse artillery tried to create a diversion, while our infantry crept forward in open order to the attack.

RUINED CHATEAU ON THE MARNE.
This once beautiful chateau was the centre of an engagement between the Germans and the British, who shelled them out of the position.

REPAIRING THE DESTRUCTIVE WORK OF THE GUNS.
Temporary bridge-work over the Marne, the stone structure of which was destroyed during the Battle of the Marne.

Sir John French, however, did not press in the advanced forces of Germans suddenly. He first moved his three army corps forward as quickly as possible, and gained a full half-day's march before General Kluck knew what had happened. Our troops began to advance at dawn, and it was not until noon that the German commander learnt what was threatening him. Instead of retreating, he tried to break through the front of the Fifth French Army. This desperate movement of his made the task of the British troops easier. We had only to clear the woods and hills and valleys of his advanced guards of infantry, which were protected by light artillery placed on the heights.

The tables turned on the German gunners

At first some British regiments tried to entrench before the German guns and creep up to them. But it was soon found to produce quicker results if our men worked round toward the rear of the German positions. The enemy then saved his artillery by retreating at top speed. The increased pace of our forward movement more than compensated us for the escape of the guns. The main thing was to shift the enemy as rapidly as possible and thus uncover the rear of his main force.

The enemy seldom stopped to fight, and when he did so, the British turning movement shook the nerve of the German gunners. Now that they were in a position similar to that which our artillerymen had occupied at Mons they did not show much heroism. Neither their shells nor their shrapnel were well-timed, and our losses were slight. Our men crossed the Aubelin brook on planks, captured hamlet after hamlet, and at evening held a line a little way from the Grand Morin River. All the German cavalry and infantry advanced guards were driven in, and Kluck sent as a reinforcement against us an army corps which entrenched by the Grand Morin near Coulommiers.

SMASHING A GERMAN PONTOON BRIDGE ACROSS THE MORIN.
To cross the Petit Morin River on September 7th, 1914, the retreating Germans tried again and again to throw a pontoon bridge over the water. But our artillery commanded the range, and, having waited until the pontoon structure was all but completed, smashed it into atoms. This went on until darkness descended. Our picture shows an officer of British infantry watching and waiting to advance.

ARTILLERY DUEL IN A THUNDERSTORM.
While the Germans were being repulsed in the valley of the Marne on September 7th, 1914, Nature's artillery vied with man's. Rain fell in torrents. But the turn of the battle rendered our men regardless of the elements, and they revelled in the work of silencing the guns of the enemy and then driving them farther back.

This pleasant little riverside town was Kluck's headquarters, and Prince Eitel, the second son of the Kaiser, seems to have visited him there the night before our attack began. M. Delsol, the mayor, and two other important citizens of Coulommiers were taken as hostages, and commanded to deliver 12,000 francs and a large quantity of bread and forage within two hours. Kluck himself declared he would shoot the three Frenchmen if this were not done. The ransom money and the bread were given to the barbaric spoilers, but no forage for their horses could be found in Coulommiers.

Dramatic episode at Coulommiers

"You are liars!" exclaimed the German commander when the mayor said there was no forage available. "All Frenchmen are liars. You know you have a large amount of forage, and you want to cheat me. All three of you shall be shot!"

Two hours later M. Delsol and his two companions were taken into the street and placed against a wall. A platoon of German infantry marched up to execute them. As they were leaving the house one of Kluck's Staff officers sat down at the piano and played Chopin's funeral march. But the mayor and his friends were suddenly left standing against the wall, and the German soldiers tore off in mad haste. The British troops had suddenly crossed the river, and began to enter Coulommiers!

Prince Eitel, General Kluck, the young officer at the

THE "HOUGOMONT" OF THE BATTLE OF THE MARNE.

The beautiful old Chateau of Mondement, about four miles east of Sezanne, was the scene of some of the fiercest fighting in the Battle of the Marne. The French troops occupied it first, but the old chateau changed hands four times before the French gained a permanent hold on it. The regiments engaged were the 32nd of the French Line and the 231st Territorials. They were opposed by the redoubtable Prussian Guards. The fine old chateau was reduced to ruins. As was the case at Hougomont in 1815, the position at Mondement was of considerable strategic importance.

piano, and other members of the Staff—all sitting in the house with bottles of champagne opened and half-emptied—had to run down to their motor-cars and fly along the road north to Rebais. It was here that the army corps sent to hold the flank had entrenched. The line of the Grand Morin River was too long for them to hold, even with the assistance of their two cavalry divisions and infantry advanced guards. The massed fire of our guns shattered all opposition, and by Monday evening, September 7th, our sappers had made crossings for the troops, and the great German retreat had definitely commenced.

The two divisions of German cavalry were thrown out to act as rearguards. This enabled our horsemen to get at last full revenge for all they had undergone between Mons and Compiègne. The numbers were still not quite equal—the German cavalrymen being about three to two. But this was equal enough for our men, especially the famous 9th Lancers, the gallant 18th Hussars, and other regiments in General de Lisle's brigade. Catching their old enemies in one of the clear spaces between the copses and woodlands, they rode at them with a yell, and, killing as they went, swept through squadron after squadron, then turned their excited horses and doubled back in another furious charge. In spite of the acclaimed efficiency of the great German Army, its cavalrymen were not good at swordsmanship. They lacked the deadly coolness which our men showed, when by furious riding they had got within sword reach of the foes. Thousands of the Germans fell in these fierce hand-to-hand combats, and when they broke off the action our guns caught them as they fled.

The position of the German infantry at Rebais was turned by Sir Douglas Haig and his men of the First Army Corps. They took the village of La Tretoire to the north-west of the German position on Tuesday, September 8th, and then advanced towards the next river, the Petit Morin. Here, on the hills by the northern bank, the Germans tried to make a stand. They had their guns on the high ground with their infantry entrenched near the river. But our troops got round them so quickly that several of their machine-guns were taken and many prisoners made. For while our 2nd Division held the enemy on the front, the 1st Division and some cavalry brigades crossed higher up the stream and swept down on the enemy's flank.

Then, to delay the further advance of our First Corps, which was now close to the Marne River, General Kluck collected his retreating troops and suddenly flung them back on our men in a furious attack.

Marvellous work of our aerial scouts

But our aerial scouts—who worked marvellously well all through the operations—prevented anything like a surprise. The Germans were received in front with rifle fire, Maxim hail bursts, and shrapnel, and again they were partly outflanked, with the result that more of their guns and a great many more of their troops were captured.

All three British corps—Sir Douglas Haig's, Sir Horace Smith-Dorrien's, and General Pulteney's—drove the enemy before them in a wide sweeping movement towards the Marne.

The next day—Wednesday, September 9th—Haig and Smith-Dorrien succeeded in forcing the passage of the Marne, between the cathedral town of Meaux and the town of La Ferté Jouarre, and with a force of some 80,000 men marched into the wooded country north of the river, pursuing the enemy.

The small Third Army Corps was less fortunate. It attacked La Ferté Jouarre, a town lying on the north of the Marne, just where the waters of the Petit Morin flow into the larger river. The bridge was destroyed, and

THE TRAIL OF WAR AMID THE PEACEFUL VINEYARDS OF NORTHERN FRANCE.

Our picture was taken in a vineyard of the Champagne district of France. Within sound and almost within sight the heavy guns of the contending armies were vomiting thunder and death. Yet as the troops were marching past to the battle-line the peasants in the vineyards seemed to pay little heed to them, many even not attempting to look up from their work. It might have been fatalism that caused this; maybe, it was their one safe course. To look up might have meant to break down. Inset: Chalons-sur-Marne, where Attila, Emperor of the Huns, was defeated in the fifth century.

SAVING AN "EYE" OF THE FRENCH ARMY.

An incident near Berry-au-Bac. Emile Dubonnet, a wealthy French sportsman, aeronaut, and racing motorist, was observing for the French guns when his balloon was attacked by two German Taubes. The French had to hold their fire for fear of hitting the balloon. Eventually a couple of armoured Maurice Farman biplanes went aloft and drove the Teuton airmen back to their own lines. Meanwhile M. Dubonnet coolly continued telephoning his observations while the balloon was being wound to the ground by its motor-lorry.

BRITISH INFANTRY DISLODGING THE GERMANS.

Many sanguinary encounters took place in the French villages along the line of the German retreat from the Grand Morin, a retreat which at one time looked like a disordered flight. During the retirement of the enemy across the Petit Morin a British force surprised a party of Germans in the small hours of the morning and compelled them to engage, the result of the encounter being disastrous to the Teutons.

a strong German rearguard with machine-guns dominated the stream. Our sappers tried to build a pontoon bridge, but in spite of their heroic attempts the enemy's fire beat them back. It was not until night fell and screened the movements of our troops from the German machine-gun officers that the passage was forced.

This completed the British victory. How important it was to the general scheme of operations, planned by the French Commander-in-Chief, may be judged from the fact that the Sixth French Army, at the time our forces crossed the Marne, was still heavily engaged to the west of the Ourcq River. The great German armament still swept all the main approaches against Kluck's lines of retreat and communication, and it was apparently only with the help of some of our heavy batteries that the passage of the Ourcq was at last forced.

How the passage of the Ourcq was forced

Kluck certainly showed himself an able commander when the tide of war turned against him. He used his men mercilessly till they dropped, in order to prevent the retreat becoming a rout. The forces that our troops defeated and flung in headlong flight northward were collected by the German general and hurled in a last desperate effort against the Sixth French Army on the Ourcq. Kluck in his hour of irretrievable disaster was magnificent. He was like a big beast of prey, so accustomed to the lordship of the jungle that no conception of defeat entered its raging brain. When he first felt the British attack on his flank he drove with savage fury against the front of the Fifth French Army in the south. Then, as the British troops got on his rear, he leaped across the Marne, above La Ferté, and madly assailed the Sixth French Army along the Ourcq. Here, however, he no longer dreamt of snatching victory out of the jaws of defeat. His final outburst of fierceness was a well-planned operation to thrust back the Sixth French Army, and thus enable him to get his guns away to the Aisne valley before the British army took him full on the rear.

On the whole, this operation by Kluck was a success. He managed to retreat in good order. Some of his light field artillery, however, had to be sacrificed in the continual rearguard actions against our troops. The 1st Lincolnshires captured one of the batteries on a ridge between the Marne and the Aisne. The German battery of six guns was holding up the British advance. Two companies of the Lincolnshires made a rapid roundabout march down a valley and through a wood. There, screened by the trees, they crept up to the German gunners. At last they were only two hundred yards from the battery, and the Germans were still busy firing at the force in front of them. The Lincolnshires extended along their flank; each man aimed carefully, and at the first round every gunner dropped—some two hundred men and officers. The English marksmen only fired once.

They could not take the six guns, however, because our distant artillery, in turn, got the exact range of the German battery and began to drop shells on it. Four of the guns were smashed before the eyes of the disappointed Lincolnshires, who in the end only obtained two sound, uninjured examples of Krupp's specialities. The incident is highly significant. Between the extraordinary marksmanship of our infantry and the deadly skill of our gunners there was not much chance for a German army that was only equal in numbers to ours.

For nearly two generations German military authorities, headed by the elder Moltke, had cried down our regular troops and cried up their conscript soldiers. Bismarck had the impudence to remark that if our Army invaded Germany he would merely ring for the police and have our troops locked up. It would not, in his opinion, be worth the trouble of getting soldiers to deal with them. On the part of men like Moltke this view of the matter was mainly one of policy.

A PARTY OF FRENCH SCOUTS AT WORK.
Unique photograph of a party of French scouts advancing in face of the enemy across a piece of ground thickly covered with gorse.

He knew that men who volunteered for a soldier's career and trained for war for many years, and often fought in the frontier conflict of a great Empire, were much superior to amateurish, half-trained, pressed troops who had been only one or two years in barracks. But, as his country relied on the strength of millions of pressed men of the latter kind, Moltke, having the command of them, endeavoured to excite their self-confidence by deprecating the British soldiers. Moltke's successors, however, seem to have taken their great general's artful attempt to put the best complexion on his own bad case as a considered judgment by the highest authority of the value of the British regular soldier.

So there grew up the extraordinary German superstition, which may, perhaps, have still influenced Kluck when he learnt that the little army that had held him at Le Cateau was again advancing from the Forest of Crecy to attack his flank. While our men were chasing the best of the Kaiser's armies from the Marne to the Aisne, the comic papers of Berlin and Munich were publishing caricatures of long-legged men in the kilts and bonnets of Highlanders. The figures were labelled "Englishmen," and it was explained that Nature kindly provided these "Englishmen" with usually long legs, in order to enable them to run away from a fight quicker than the soldiers of any

PREPARING FOR SIEGE WARFARE IN THE OPEN.
French sergeant measuring the width of a new trench with a rifle.

INSTANTANEOUS CAMERA-RECORD OF THE EFFECT OF HEAVY SHELL FIRE.
Bombardment of a hillside in France on the slopes of which and on the flat ground adjoining shells were bursting. The roofs of workshops can be discerned amidst the smoke behind the rows of trees lining the large field in the foreground.

BATTLEFIELD HONOURS FOR FRENCH SOLDIERS.
Every brave deed of the French soldiers was at once recognised and the men decorated on the next possible occasion within sound of the contending forces. The above photograph shows a general of division calling out the men and handing them their coveted decorations.

WHERE EAST AND WEST HAVE MET.
Two of the swarthy sons of Africa who fought so gallantly for France.

other nation. In the decisive event, however, it was the first-line troops of Germany that excelled in speed of flight. It was, however, good tactics the way that Kluck kept them on the run for forty miles. His army certainly saved itself from destruction or surrender by the agility of its retreat.

We only took a few thousand prisoners and a few field guns and Maxims amid the thick woods that dappled the country north of the Marne. But in the rearguard fighting the enemy continued to suffer heavily. On Thursday, September 10th, an infantry column of Sir Horace Smith-Dorrien's corps was marching towards the Aisne, and the scouts observed another infantry column tramping along in the same direction by a parallel road a little distance away. At first it was thought this was another part of the British army. Then it was seen that the distant troops were dressed in grey uniforms. They were headed off and trapped in a sunken road, and there captured or shot.

It was wet weather; both armies were drenched, and the roads were muddy and heavy-going. All the way

FRENCH SUPPLY COLUMN ON ITS WAY TO THE FRONT.
The pack mules are laden with ammunition for the machine-guns, which the French Army used with such deadly effect against the Germans and brought up so quickly at decisive points in many an action that without their aid might have ended differently.

GROUP OF WOUNDED GERMAN PRISONERS AT A TEMPORARY RED CROSS HOSPITAL IN FRANCE.

there was a considerable amount of fighting, and the German troops, worn out, unfed, and broken spirited, were very roughly handled by our men. Seeing that our troops were battling victoriously and continually advancing for seven days—from dawn on Sunday, September 6th to nightfall on Saturday, September 12th—when the enemy made a stand, the losses they inflicted on their retreating foes in the week must have been terrible.

Strong German rearguards of all arms—infantry, cavalry, and artillery—tried to stay our progress on the northern upper course of the Ourcq on Thursday, September 10th. Sir John French deployed most of his forces for the attack. On the right, towards the pretty village of La Ferté-Milon, where Racine, the greatest of French dramatists, was born, Sir Douglas Haig's and Sir Horace Smith-Dorrien's army corps swept forward under the cover of a fierce fire from their guns. On the left, beyond Neuilly, two cavalry brigades rode out on a flanking swoop. The action was a splendid success. Thirteen guns, seven machine-guns, large quantities of transport, and some two thousand prisoners fell into our hands

On September 12th the pursuit was at a complete end, and a new phase of the vast campaign opened.

GERMAN PRISONERS CAPTURED BY THE BRITISH AT LA FERTÉ-MILON.

A SANCTUARY FOR FRIEND AND FOE.

Interior of church in the vicinity of Meaux used by the French military authorities as a hospital where the wounded, friend and foe alike, were tended with kindly care.

THE GREAT RETREAT OF THE GERMAN ARMY FROM THE BANKS OF THE RIVER MARNE.

As a whole, the retirement from the Marne of the invading armies of the Kaiser was conducted in as good an order as marked the retirement of the allied armies from the Belgian frontier towards Paris. On the other hand, the Germans, caught successively on flank and rear, and forced to battle for life in every section of the battlefield, suffered very heavy losses. In many cases the troops, by the confession of their own officers, were demoralised. In the region of Nancy alone—at Amance and Lunéville—there were by September 10th, 1914, some 31,000 dead Germans, mostly first-line troops. The Prussian Guards left on the field one man out of three of their original numbers, and one out of two of their actual fighting force. Between Paris and the Vosges the mainspring of German aggressiveness was broken.

HISTORIC CHATEAU OF MONDEMENT.

THE "HOUGOMONT" OF THE MARNE.

CHAPTER XXXV.

THE LINKED BATTLES OF EASTERN FRANCE.

The Retreat of Kluck Exposes the Flank of Second German Army—The Battle of Montmirail—The Battle of St. Prix and Sezanne Plateau—Prussian Guards Caught in Marshes of Saint Gond—Rout of the Saxon Army—The Duke of Würtemberg's Forces Attacked on Two Sides—Crown Prince's Attempt to Force a Path between Verdun and Toul—Heroic Defence of Fort Troyon—Its Importance to the Advancing Battle-line of the Allies—Defeat of Crown Prince—Attempt to take Allies in the Reverse from Nancy—Defeat of the Bavarian Army—Kaiser Sends His White Cuirassiers to Destruction—The French Iron Division Takes the Offensive—General Decisive Victory of the Franco-British Armies.

WHILE the British Expeditionary Force was operating to the south-east of Paris in the second week of September, a general battle was raging between all the first-line armies of France and Germany. It was the greatest conflict known to man. The lines stretched from a point below the Forest of Compiègne to a point just above Verdun; they curved downward from Verdun towards Toul, and then bent south-eastward to Nancy. The twisting firing-line was more than two hundred and fifty miles long, and more than four millions of Frenchmen and Germans were ranged along it.

Running from left to right were the First German Army, under General von Kluck; the Second German Army, under General von Bülow; the remains of the Third German Army, formerly under General von Hausen; the Fourth German Army, under the Duke of Würtemberg; the Fifth German Army, under the Crown Prince; the Sixth German Army, from Metz and Saarbrücken, under General von Heeringen; and the Seventh German Army, under the Crown Prince of Bavaria.

Opposed to them were the Sixth French Army, under General Maunoury; the British Expeditionary Force, under Sir John French; and the Fifth French Army, under General Franchet d'Espérey—all these three gathered against the First German Army—Kluck's. Then there were the Ninth French Army, under General Foch; the Fourth French Army, under General de Langle Cary; the Third French Army, from Verdun, under General Sarrail; and the Second French Army, under General Castelnau, operating round Nancy.

General d'Espérey faced Kluck; General Foch faced Bülow and part of Hausen's force; General de Langle Cary faced the Duke of Würtemberg and the rest of Hausen's force; General Sarrail faced the Crown Prince's army and Von Heeringen's forces; and General Castelnau, with the Second French Army round Nancy, faced the Kaiser himself with a force of Bavarian troops, nominally under the command of the Crown Prince of Bavaria. Between these opposing armies fighting had been going on for more than a week, and in some sections contact had been continuous since the opening clash on the Belgian and Lorraine borders. Day by day the French had been pushed further south, the pressure at last being apparently equal against both their western and eastern wings.

As we know now, it was only the eastern French wing—General Sarrail's army of Verdun and General Castelnau's Toul-Nancy army—that was in any extreme danger. But to the advancing German armies it appeared at the time as though the entire French line continued to give before their attack. By September 5th the invading armies, from Paris to Verdun, had crossed the Marne and the Marne Canal, and some of their outposts were moving, far below the capital, towards Central France.

On this Saturday—September 5th—there was an especially fierce action between the Fifth French Army, under D'Espérey and Kluck's advancing force.

GENERAL JOSIAS VON HEERINGEN.
He commanded the Sixth German Army from Metz and Saarbrücken. Born in 1850, he fought in the Franco-Prussian War, being wounded at Wörth. Between 1909 and 1912 he was Prussian Minister of War.

D'Espérey's army was apparently hurled across the Marne toward the Upper Seine by the driving sweep suddenly made by the German commander. In the night the French entrenched on the hills south of the Grand Morin stream —their left wing near the village of Courtécon, their right near the town of Esternay, on the river. Some fifteen miles behind them, at Provins and Nogent-sur-Seine, were some mounted German reconnoitring bodies. These, however, were suddenly cut off by a strong force of French cavalry, under General Conneau, that closed the gap between Courtécon village and the hidden British army, extending from the Forest of Crecy. The gap had been left open only to encourage Kluck to retreat farther into the ambush prepared for him. But he wisely refused to get right out of touch with Bülow's army, and swerved still more eastward, and struck at D'Espérey's position. Conneau's cavalry then moved up to support the Fifth French Army.

The hidden British army

At the same time as Kluck attacked, Bülow, the Duke of Würtemberg, the Crown Prince, General von Heeringen, and the commander of the Second German Army swept forward. But all the French line stood firm. A happy rumour had spread through the French forces, and the next day—Sunday, September 6th—the rumour was confirmed. To all the troops General Joffre then issued his famous order:

"At the moment when a battle is about to begin, on which the welfare of the country depends, I feel it incumbent on me to remind you that this is no longer the time to look behind. All our efforts must be directed towards attacking the enemy and driving him back. An army which can advance no farther must at all costs hold the ground it wins, and allow itself to be killed on the spot rather than give way. No faltering in the present circumstances can be tolerated."

Every son of France knew what this meant. For years the French doctrine of "the offensive return" had been discussed in the barracks, till the most backward of peasant recruits got to understand the broad outline of it. The French armies would have at first to withdraw from the sudden, overwhelming German onset. The German lines of communication would lengthen out and absorb troops, the invaders would grow tired with incessant marching and fighting, and then the French armies, after their long recoil, would spring out on the grand attack.

Nobody expected that the offensive return would have been so long delayed. But the temporary French loss of a considerable stretch of territory was more than balanced by the German loss of a large proportion of military strength. The main German lines of communication ran for more than two hundred miles through hostile country, and the railways, along which supplies came, were open to attack by all the old means, and by the still more destructive new method of bomb-throwing from aeroplanes. The Third German Army, under General von Hausen, had been so worn out by the advance that it had disappeared on the decisive day, its remnants being absorbed by General von Bülow's forces and the Duke of Würtemberg's army. Altogether the German losses were far heavier than the French, and the French had had about five weeks to increase their war material. All that the remarkable striking power that the Germans had won at the start by their aggressiveness and efficiency of organisation had now been recovered by the French. In fact, in the chief matter—ammunition supplies—the defenders now had a marked advantage over the invaders.

GENERAL JOFFRE AND STAFF PASSING THROUGH A FRENCH VILLAGE.

The French Generalissimo, one of the world's "silent organisers of victory," was the idol of the whole French Army. Constantly on the move, he left nothing to chance, and his ever-vigilant control was felt along the entire French lines.

General Joffre's main armies rested on the railway running along the Upper Seine, with branch feeding lines running northward towards Esternay, Sezanne, Vitry-le-François, and Bar-le-Duc, but not always emptying into these towns, as some were held by the enemy.

But close to these towns the five main armies rested, with practically all the locomotives, trucks, and railway carriages of France at their service. For the general rolling-stock of the northern French lines had retreated with the armies, and the French Military Staff handled the railways in an admirable manner. Never had the field armies of France been so well supplied with food and ammunition as in their great battle for national existence.

Some, at least, of the German armies, on the other hand, were running short of ammunition and general supplies. Many troops were worn out by excessive marching, and rainy weather and lack of food further contributed to weaken them. In the Champagne district there was a wild outburst of drinking among the German soldiers, which dulled their feelings of fatigue, but scarcely increased their fighting ability. The drunken, armed brutes ravaged many of the hamlets and small towns in a frightful, uncivilised manner, but many of them paid on the spot for their savage destructiveness. This was especially the case with some of the spoilers under the command of the Crown Prince of Germany—himself a robber of the treasures of a Frenchwoman's chateau. They perished in thousands round the scenes of their ravaging.

An Imperial pilferer

The only thing that sustained the German troops amid their weariness, hunger, and discomfort was the general thought that their triumphal entry into Paris, and their feasting on the spoils of the conquered capital, were as certain as the sunrise, and almost as near. There was

FRENCH PICKET LEAVING A FARMHOUSE IN THE EARLY MORNING TO RELIEVE THEIR COMRADES IN THE TRENCHES.

A graphic picture of what life on active service is like. These men, after a brief period of repose in a farmhouse—repose often broken by a visitation of the enemy's shells—are seen sallying forth soon after dawn to the slow but deadly work of the trenches, to which the French temperament found it so difficult to accommodate itself in the early stages of the Great War, but in which our gallant Allies afterwards proved themselves more than a match for the enemy. Our picture affords a striking contrast to that of the farmstead in normal times.

only one more battle to fight—an easy affair against a fleeing enemy—and then the richest land in the world was theirs to batten on. The following order of the day, signed by Lieutenant-General Tülff von Tschepe und Weidenbach, and addressed to the Eighth German Army Corps, is typical of the frame of mind of the commanders of the invading forces:

"Vitry-le-François, September 7th, (10.30 p.m.).

"The object of our long and arduous marches has been accomplished. The principal French troops, after having been continually pressed back, have been forced to accept battle. The great decision is undoubtedly at hand. To-morrow the whole strength of the German Army, as well as the entire force of our army corps, is bound to be engaged all along the line from Paris to Verdun. I expect every officer and man to do his duty unswervingly, to his last breath, to save the welfare and honour of Germany, despite the hard and heroic fights of the last few days. Everything depends on the result of to-morrow's battle."

French and German orders contrasted

This historic document, picked up by a Frenchman after the German retreat from Vitry, lacks the confident spirit of General Joffre's similar order, as well as the heroism of his Spartan command to his army to perish rather than fall back. The difference in the dates—the French commander wrote some thirty-six hours before the German general—is equally significant. The captain of France was striking a full day before his blow was expected to fall. This was probably due to the fact that Kluck, on the western German wing, by failing to notice the British force on his flank, pushed on with his attack against the Fifth French Army without dreaming of being attacked himself by an overwhelming combination of forces. Naturally, while Kluck remained ignorant of his own fate, no suspicion of it was entertained by the commanders of the other German armies. Thus, the idea of a general French offensive movement was slow in spreading along the German lines.

Advantage of surprise with the French

All this was excellent from the French commander's point of view. He had the advantage of surprise as well as the advantage of attack, and his plan of action was one of the most simple and the most perfect in military history. It was practically impossible for it to fail. In spite of the fact that the numbers of the opposing armies were about equal, General Joffre was bringing two Frenchmen against each German, and two French light field-guns against each German light field-gun.

"Only numbers can annihilate," said Nelson. He usually managed, when an enemy had more ships, still to bring two British ships against every hostile ship. He accomplished this apparent impossibility by a simple trick first devised by a Scotsman, and communicated by him to Admiral Rodney. Two hostile fleets usually went into action with their battleships arranged in a long line. The Scotsman—Clerk, of Edinburgh—suggested that instead of each British warship attacking the hostile vessel in front of it in the old-fashioned way, the British fleet should sail in a straight path through the enemy's line of battle, then bend round half the line, so that each

THE ENEMY IN THE ARGONNE.

German artillery in the hilly and thickly - wooded district of North-Eastern France.

WITH THE FRENCH DEFENDERS OF THE ARGONNE.

Wounded soldiers being removed from the trenches.

of the enemy vessels there had a British warship in front of it, and another behind it. Having destroyed half the enemy's forces in this way, the successful fleet pursued the other half.

Napoleon achieved a similar result by similar means. By a frontal attack with a concentrated mass of troops he pierced the enemy's line, then surrounded half of it, destroyed that half, and proceeded to defeat the remaining half. He always tried to have, at the decisive spot, double the number of troops that his opponent had, in spite of the fact that he often was, on the whole, barely equal, or even inferior, to the enemy in numbers.

Napoleon's successor to leadership in warfare—Moltke the elder—thought that the Clerk-Rodney-Nelson-Napoleon method of breaking the enemy's line had been antiquated by the great increase in defensive power produced by modern artillery and long-range rifles. He was of the opinion that a sound frontal attack would fail against a sound defence. He inclined to remain on the defensive in his centre, with massed gun fire there to beat back the enemy, and throw out his wings and cut the hostile lines of communication in an enveloping movement. This was a return to the primitive method of attack, and as Moltke usually had a larger force on the battlefield than his opponents, he was able to arrange for his wing columns to deploy in an encircling movement.

General Joffre's plan was more subtle than Moltke's, and less audacious than Nelson's or Napoleon's. He quietly attacked the Germans on their western wing, where Kluck was advancing against the Fifth French Army, while the British force was advancing in turn against him.

Kluck had to give way. Sir John French drove fiercely on his flank, and threatened to surround him, while General d'Espérey held him in front. Kluck retired with all speed, with both the British force and the Fifth French Army pursuing him. As he crossed the Marne to escape destruction he left unguarded the flank of the connecting German army—Bülow's. The British force took over the pursuit of Kluck's troops, with the help of the Sixth French Army. Meanwhile, General d'Espérey, with the Fifth French Army, curved westwards, and drove against the flank of Bülow's troops. They already had the Ninth French Army, under General Foch, attacking them in front. Being taken in the flank by D'Espérey at the same time, they, like Kluck's force, had to retreat with all speed. General d'Espérey and the Fifth French Army helped to pursue them.

In the meantime, General Foch in turn directed his tired but victorious men against the flank of the Prussian Guards

FRENCH BATTERY OF ARTILLERY SHELLING THE GERMAN LINES NEAR THE ARGONNE FOREST.

From quite an early period in the war fierce battles raged in the district of North-Eastern France known as the Argonne, and stretching from the plateau of Langres and the Monts Faucilles on opposite sides of the River Meuse. Of the two chains of hills forming the Argonne the west forms a continuous ridge, which constitutes a kind of natural defence, and is intersected by narrow defiles.

and the flank of the Duke of Würtemberg's army. This army also had an opponent in front—General de Langle Cary. The Duke of Würtemberg had to retreat, and Foch pursued him. As Würtemberg retired he exposed the flank of the Crown Prince's forces. These were attacked sideways by General de Langle Cary's men, while in front and to the east they were held from Bar-le-Duc to Verdun by the Verdun garrison army under General Sarrail. The Metz army tried to intervene, but failed to get quickly enough to the help of the Crown Prince and turn the tide of battle. So the Crown Prince had to retire, and with his retirement the main battle was won all along the line by the French.

It will thus be seen that although the scheme of combined actions was lengthy in operation it was simple in principle. Two French or allied armies acted against one German army. Each French soldier under D'Espérey, Foch, and Langle Cary fought two battles. He first held one German force in front and helped to drive it back. Then he swerved and attacked the flank of another German force and, when it retreated, pursued it. He had to do double work. The result was that he doubled the fighting strength of France in the most critical period of her history. General Joffre's plan required that his troops, wearied most of them by long marches and severe conflicts, should suddenly show a power of continual endurance and attacking ability equal to that of two German soldiers. The French Commander-in-Chief knew his men. He knew what an extraordinary access of spirited strength would flow in upon the Frenchman when he was given, after a long ordeal of mere resistance, the opportunity for a sudden, victorious leap forward. Joffre trusted, in the great week, to the élan of his race.

FRENCH CYCLIST SCOUTS.
These men are taking advantage of a natural trench in a patch of open country in North-Eastern France.

CONSTANT VIGILANCE THE PRICE OF VICTORY.
French infantry scouts making their way through brushwood, which afforded excellent cover, on the outskirts of a wood in the Argonne district.

When you shoot a tiger, and the blood is choking its lungs, you must leap aside for your life, for even in its death agony the tiger will die charging. There is much of this fury of the charge in the Frenchman's way of fighting. He defends himself best by attacking, and the tradition of the unexpected victories he won, by a tiger charge in the hour of defeat, is the chief reason why the modern German commanders always order an attack by way of defence. This way of fighting, however, is an acquired thing among the North Germans. They do it methodically, mechanically, because Clausewitz showed that it was Napoleon's way of winning. Napoleon, however, was only putting to good use the fundamental fighting instinct of the French race.

Joffre used the same instinct of his race in a different way. He took into consideration the disadvantages of

FRENCH SOLDIERS IN A FOREST BIVOUAC IN THE FIGHTING AREA.
Another view of the Argonne country, showing a detachment of our Allies snatching a brief interval for rest and refreshment after an arduous and exhausting march.

continually displaying the élan of attack in the era of Maxims, quick-firing guns, and magazine rifles. He taught the French soldier to be patient and wary and stubbornly defensive. Then, in the great decisive battle, when he had completely outmanœuvred the younger Moltke, he used the old, wild, furious, triumphant élan of France, and by means of it doubled the actual fighting powers of his three main armies—D'Espérey's, Foch's, and Langle Cary's. In the special conditions of battle which he had designed the racial quality he elicited from his troops was almost equal in value to a reinforcement of another half a million men.

The old, triumphant elan of France

As Lord Kitchener put it, General Joffre showed he was not only a great military leader, but a great man. With a moulding power not wholly dissimilar from that of Oliver Cromwell, he uncovered, in the period of France's extreme peril, the deepest springs of the national character. He brought fully into play, almost for the first time in modern history, the tenacity and patience that characterise the French peasant. Then, having thus tempered the spirit of France, he suddenly allowed the widest scope for the strange, leaping ardour of attack that carries the Frenchman through all fatigue and danger to death or victory.

How they fought, the three main French armies, the Fifth, the Ninth, the Fourth! For days they stonewalled the last, desperate onsets of the German forces; then for days they attacked and wheeled and attacked and pursued. From the 5th to the 14th of September the great battle raged, and it was only on the last day that the decision was obtained. While the victorious troops of General Maunoury and Field-Marshal Sir John French were assailing General von Kluck's men in their new fortress on the plateau of Soissons by the Aisne River, the movement they had set going still swung undecisively. Until Monday, September 14th, it was quite possible that the British Expeditionary Force and the garrison army of Paris would have again to retire on the French capital. Their sectional victory near Meaux depended entirely upon the speed with which the continual flanking operation against each German army was carried out. For at Fort Troyon, by the heights of the Meuse between Verdun and Toul, a great German force from Metz was waiting to get through. The small garrison at Troyon was falling; the fort was being shattered. It was most vital that the Crown Prince's army should be forced to retreat before it could complete the destruction of Fort Troyon and join across the Meuse with the Metz force. Hence the tremendous importance of the chain of events between the Fifth French Army and the Third French Army.

FOR LOVE OF HIS COUNTRY.
A French "Territorial" on guard. The Territorial force in France is the counterpart of the German Landsturm. The man in our picture was in private life a prosperous farmer. With thousands in like case, he left his farm and his home ties without affectation or sadness, and changed his plough for a rifle to save the soil of his beloved country from the proud foot of the would-be conqueror.

The Fifth French Army, composed of men that had fought at Charleroi and had since been reinforced, was commanded by General d'Espérey. These troops had at first suffered from the able manner in which the Germans used their machine-guns. Machine-guns were employed in larger numbers by the enemy than by the Allies. Each French or British battalion had usually only two machine-guns; a German battalion often had six. They were concealed very skilfully in woods and sheltered places, and the French troops were then lured to an attack, and shot down at short range in close formations. But by the time the Allies arrived at the Marne the French had grown wary, and taken to advancing in extended order in the British fashion. When Kluck in turn attacked them with the best first-line regiments of Prussia—an army corps from Old Prussia and contingents from Brandenburg, Westphalia, and Hanover—the Frenchmen kept their fire until the Germans were at close range. Then they volleyed at them. Kluck kept to his old tactics of trying to get round the flank of his opponent. He was, however, soon brought up by the cavalry division under General Conneau, assisted by its horse artillery. Then he tried to break the French front, but his grey masses of troops were scattered by the French 3 in. guns and the rifle fire of the infantry. Finding his losses too heavy on one side, the German commander swerved round to the other, and brought up from Coulommiers and Montmirail new columns, that deployed in lines five men deep and advanced over a brook and up the hills, only to be again repulsed.

All through Saturday and Sunday, September 5th and 6th, Kluck vainly tried to justify his swerve from Paris by making his new opponents bend or break. By Sunday evening the effect of the British surprise attack on the German flank made itself felt on the German front. First came the culminating onset of the Prussians. The German commander massed every available man against the Fifth French Army, and endeavoured, in a frenzy of despair, to hack a path to victory through the valley of defeat. Kluck was a man of the stamp of Hindenburg, the leader against the Russian forces. A sort of human bull, tricky when he thought he could play with his foe, and uncommonly agile for his size, but given to blind, fierce, battering rushes when he felt himself outplayed.

Kluck's frenzied bid for success

He was certainly courageous. That is to say, he sacrificed his men in a terrible manner in a desperate attempt to save the situation and his own fame. But all his efforts were hopeless. He was trapped; his heavy artillery was far away on the Ourcq; his cavalry was held by the British advance, and an army corps had also to be thrown out towards his flank to prevent sudden, overwhelming disaster. On Sunday night he knew he was a beaten man, and

GENERAL DE LANGLE CARY.
Commanded the Fourth French Army facing the Duke of Würtemberg's and part of General von Hausen's forces.

GENERAL FRANCHET D'ESPEREY.
He led one of the two French armies which, with the British force, were opposed to the First German Army under General von Kluck.

GENERAL SARRAIL.
In command of the Third French Army from Verdun, opposed to the armies of the German Crown Prince and General von Heeringen.

to ask his neighbour, General von Bülow, to help him.

On Monday part of the Second German Army co-operated with Kluck's forces in attacking D'Espérey's men. Bülow assailed the eastern wing of the Fifth French Army at Esternay, and Kluck desperately renewed his attack on the centre and western wing. But Bülow soon had all he could do to resist his immediate enemy, General Foch, with the Ninth French Army operating along the ridge of high country by Sezanne. At the same time Kluck was now severely pressed by the swiftly advancing British force, that was trying to wedge between him and his rearguard on the Ourcq.

The battle on the first section of the field was over. Kluck could only fight a delaying action. He threw out some 60,000 men to hinder the British forward movement to his rear, and withdrew with his main force to the north-east towards Bülow's army.

He had at last grasped the situation. Bülow could not help him. It was Bülow's flank that was menaced. So he retired towards Montmirail, eastward of his own line of retreat, in order to reinforce the flank of Bülow's army. But at the first sign of his weakening offensive the spirit of attack awoke in the Frenchmen he had been assailing. They carried village after village at the point of the bayonet, threw the Germans across the Grand Morin on Monday, September 7th, and then stormed over the hills to Montmirail on the Petit Morin.

Tuesday, September 8th, was the critical day in the action of the Fifth French Army. Kluck had then completely lost the battle against the British; his rearguard on the Ourcq, as well as his rearguard on the Marne, was in danger. But with fine courage he stuck to Bülow's flank at Montmirail, and with part of Bülow's army tried to beat off D'Espérey's troops. Naturally, all the German forces were linked closely together by a system of field telephones, and Kluck was well aware that he now had to fight for time for the stroke against Fort Troyon fully to succeed. All that had been lost by him in the west would be more than recovered if a path between Verdun and Toul could be opened in the east, bringing the Metz army through the shattered, divided lines of General Sarrail's forces. Also, further south at Nancy an immense movement against the rear of the French battle-line was still proceeding.

So Kluck and Bülow fought with fierce tenacity to maintain their position. But the British Army had got into a non-stop swing that carried it by Monday night to the bank of the Marne. The Fifth French Army, with larger numbers to fight against, was equally irresistible. The gunners with their terrible quick-firers knocked the heart out of the entrenched German infantry, and the French bayonet came into play round Montmirail in a manner that Napoleon, who had fought the Prussians in the same town, would have admired. At night, lighted on their way to victory by their flaming villages, the French troops battled onward, slaughtering the invader at last in the hand-to-hand fighting and the house-to-house actions, in which the Frenchmen's initiative and dash tell against any sort of war machinery.

Initiative and dash tell against machinery

It was just on a hundred and eight years since Auerstadt and Jena—a hundred and eight years since Frenchmen had seen the backs of Prussians in a decisive national battle. At Montmirail in 1814 Napoleon could not win again, for all his skill, against his old foes. But at Montmirail in 1914 General Joffre prevailed once more over the Prussians. The numbers of the enemy slain by the bayonet

HOW THE EVER-READY MEN OF THE BRITISH ARMY SERVICE CORPS LOOKED AFTER THE WANTS OF OUR BRAVE SOLDIERS IN THE FIRING-LINE.

Bully beef and other rations being distributed by men of the Army Service Corps to British infantry fighting the advancing Germans during the retreat to the Marne. As they fell back before the Teuton invader our soldiers, hungry, but defying fatigue, were well cared for by the Army Service Corps, whose motor-lorry drivers had a herculean task in reaching the constantly shifting lines at the front. With unfailing courage the Army Service Corps men ran to and fro along the trenches with armsful of bully-beef tins and bread for the combatants, regardless of the hail of shrapnel bullets flying around them.

PLACE STANISLAS AND RUE HERE, NANCY.
The Place Stanislas is the principal square in Nancy, and is named after Stanislas Leszcinski, who, after abdicating the crown of Poland in 1735, resided here as Duke of Lorraine till his death in 1766. On the right is a view of the cathedral, built in 1742.

were unusual on a modern battlefield. It was the Frenchman's way of punishing the ravagers, spoilers, and cruel hordes of the new Attila. He thought of the women of Northern France and Belgium, of the thousands of unarmed villagers, country-folk, and townspeople who had been murdered, and, where he could, he used the steel instead of lead bullets. From Montmirail to Chateau Thierry on the Marne, where the left wing of the Fifth French Army pursued Kluck's main force, the heights and hollows and woods were strewn with dead and wounded Germans. It was heavy fighting all the way, but the French soldier had a stern sense of exhilaration in it. The heavier the fighting, the heavier the losses. And he was so terrible and quick in his work of retribution that his was not the heavier loss. By September 9th he had thrown Kluck over the river, and driven in the flank of Bülow.

PLACE DE LA CARRIERE, NANCY.
Another view of this lovely French city. On the left is shown the Porte de la Craffe.

The Ninth French Army under General Foch, one of the most expert of French strategists, then came fully into play as an offensive force. General Foch rested on the high land round Sezanne, with a very dangerous tract of country in front of him. It consisted of the marshes of Saint Gond, running east to west for some ten miles, and extending north and south for one to two miles. The marshes were the source of the Petit Morin River, that formed a canalised ditch into which the marsh dykes drained. The marsh and morass was being reclaimed, and four sound country roads ran over it.

Happily for France the process of reclamation had not been completed. For the German commander launched the Prussian Guard, with its guns, on the right wing of General Foch's Ninth Army, across the marsh of Saint Gond. Some 30,000 men, with 75 guns, 200 Maxims, and a long train of ammunition vehicles, mostly motor drawn, cannot advance very quickly over four narrow country ways. These had to be given up to the heavy motor vehicles, and most of the guns were drawn over the fairly firm reclaimed marshland.

The marsh is a longish pocket of clay in a large hollow in the calcareous plateau of Sezanne. The clay had partly dried in the hot summer weather, and, though still wet at bottom, it was so thickly caked over on the surface that, with its covering of marsh grass, it supported the Prussian guns.

It is the boast of the Prussian Guard that it never retires. It is an army corps of men picked for their uncommon strength of body and high stature. It is the spearhead of the German Empire, and when it strikes it is designed to penetrate the enemy's line or perish valiantly in the attempt. In the war of 1870 it had won glory at St. Privat by charging up a long slope against a terrific French fire, and holding its ground when other German troops were giving way. Now it was sent against the left of the French centre to break up General Joffre's plan of bringing two French armies on the front and flank of each German force. If General Foch could only be driven back the intricate sectional French turning movement would be stopped at the point of real danger. The bending back of Kluck's wing would not then be the beginning of a general defeat.

The Prussian Guard remained true to its old traditions. It did not retire. But this was not due to its courage. On the afternoon of Wednesday, September 9th, when Kluck had been thrown over the Marne, the Guards

PALAIS DU GOUVERNEMENT, NANCY.
So certain were the German General Staff of capturing Nancy, one of the most beautiful towns in France and the capital of the old Duchy of Lorraine, that the Kaiser came to watch the victory from a hill close by. He had to leave rather hurriedly. This was in September, 1914.

FRENCH DRAGOON MACHINE-GUN SECTION GALLOPING INTO ACTION UNDER A HEAVY FIRE.
The French Army adopted the Hotchkiss as its machine-gun, a weapon of ·315 calibre, identical with that of the Lebel rifle, with which both cavalry and infantry were armed. The pieces were mounted on a wheeled carriage.

entered the marshes. They concealed their batteries and trenches among the rushes, and spent the night in the hollow, with the intention of making a surprise attack next morning on General Foch's army, which was now advancing northward along the plateau towards St. Prix and Epernay. It suddenly came on to rain in the night, a heavy rain that soaked the caked clay. All the surface water from the Sezanne plateau streamed into the hollow, and by dawn many of the men were waist high in water, and their guns and limbers were embedded to the axles.

Then from the surrounding heights the terrible 3 in. French quick-firers entered on their deadly work. The French gunners, working on their own familiar countryside, got the range of the enemy at once. A general salvo drove the spike of the French guns into the earth. There was no further need to get the range. By a special device the batteries then became semi-automatic range-finding instruments of destruction. Loaded and fired with extreme quickness by the detachments, they mechanically swept every acre of the marshes.

This section of the battlefield became a chess-board ruled by invisible lines by the French fire-control officer.

Terrible work of the French "75's"

On every front square he pitched a shell or shrapnel that destroyed everything in the square. Then, without re-aiming, the guns, each dropped a shell along the second line of squares, and so on, till the last line of squares at the end of the marsh was covered by the salvo of the massed quick-firers.

The Prussian Guard did not retire; in spite of its efforts at retreat, it perished. Men as well as guns were bogged in the watery clay, and when next the Prussian Guard appeared on the battlefield at Ypres it was formed of the rest of the reserve troops of the famous corps, largely filled out with hastily-trained recruits. Frederick the Great's famous regiment, enlarged with the increase of Prussia's military power to an army corps, was buried in the marshes of St. Gond. Ten thousand dead men were found there, and the carts, artillery, and dead horses of the corps.

There were two highways running on the plateau between the marsh. One ran by St. Prix to Epernay, the other ran by Morains with the railway towards Rheims. General Foch divided his forces and advanced along the heights by both roads. A hurricane of shrapnel from his guns, directed by aeroplanes at the German columns, heralded his progress and cleared his path.

German morale "absolutely broken"

On the night of September 9th Bülow ordered his western wing to retire down the St. Prix road. Most of his heavy artillery, it appears from a letter by an officer of his Tenth Army Corps, was being used at Maubeuge. The French had 6 in. howitzers as well as 3 in. quick-firers, and they beat down every attempt by the Germans to delay the march of the French infantry. "Our morale was absolutely broken," a German officer of the Tenth Corps admits. "Our first battalion was reduced from 1,200 to 194 men. These numbers speak for themselves. It was like hell, only a thousand times worse. In spite of unheard-of sacrifices we have achieved nothing."

This was not altogether correct. Bülow's western wing suffered thus terribly because it had to fight a dreadful rearguard action to Epernay, and then through the Forest of Rheims to the cathedral town and the Aisne valley. In the meantime Bülow was swerving eastward with his main force, as Kluck had done, in order to protect in turn his neighbour, Duke Albrecht of Würtemberg, from the inevitable flank attack by General Foch.

The Duke of Würtemberg had penetrated in force farther south than any other German commander. He held the town of Vitry-le-François and the villages along the road to Paris. His army made the chief attempt to pierce the French front, with Bülow's eastern wing assisting in the operation. Three of General von Hausen's army corps also took part in the attack. These three corps were very badly handled. They stood between General Foch and his main objective, the Würtemberg flank, and, happily for the French, instead of standing on the defensive they attacked furiously. From the woods around the flaming hamlet of Lenharée the French batteries sent a murderous fire, and the entrenched and hidden French artilleryman used his rifle with shattering effect on the compact masses of Saxon soldiers. The 178th Regiment, of two battalions, lost all its officers and 1,700 men.

Field telephones and fire control

The French gunners, in the forest fighting, had telephone wires running from every good point of observation, and fire-control officers were hidden in the foliage with the talking mechanism in their hands. Both the French machine-guns and the quick-firers were under distant fire control, and the enemy was usually lured on in large numbers by a pretended French retirement and then practically annihilated. The Saxons, under General von Hausen, were the first to give way.

They apparently began to retire after their defeat on September 8th, when Kluck was still holding out on the extreme western wing. On the critical day, September 9th, when the Prussian Guards were marching into the swamp of St. Gond, a large number of the Saxons had withdrawn far to the rear at Chalons. Their feet were bleeding and deeply cut by excessive marching. The men were too worn out to fight, and hopelessly demoralised by their tremendous losses. They can scarcely be said to have counted in the decisive conflict, though Bülow and the Duke of Würtemberg gathered any fighting remnants that were available.

This extraordinary rout of Hausen and his Saxons—originally some 150,000 men, with the cavalry of the Guards in addition—was a great and decisive achievement. It left a gap in the German line that neither Bülow nor the Duke of Würtemberg was able to fill in time. Foch was irresistible, with his terrible way of clearing his advancing front with shell and shrapnel, drawing on a vast store of artillery ammunition, and "watering" the ground for a mile in front of his advance guards. On September 10th he curved westward and shook the flank of the powerful Würtemberg forces.

The Duke of Würtemberg had been in turn attacking and beating off the Fourth French Army, under General de Langle Cary, for five days or more. The duke had an especially strong and numerous body of troops, as befitted a Royal commander. His victories were intended, like those of the Crown Prince, to increase the prestige of the ruling families of Germany. He had an excellent chief of staff, who arranged the operations, but allowed the duke to take all the credit for them. This is the way in which German princes strive to maintain that family fame for personal genius in warfare which they presume they inherit from some remote ancestor. If Nature will not supply them with this hereditary trait, the German Military Staff does.

The German claim to genius in warfare

However this may be, the Fourth German Army, under the Duke of Würtemberg, certainly fought well. By Sunday, September 6th, it had taken the little historic

A CHARGE "A LA BAIONNETTE"—WHERE THE FRENCH SOLDIER IS ALWAYS AT HIS BEST.
It is part of the belief of many students of war that every battle is won by the bayonet in the last issue. The belief found effective support on many occasions when the French had opportunities of meeting the foe with cold steel, to which the German soldiers as a whole displayed a very decided aversion.

town of Vitry across the canal of the Marne. But the French army held the heights by the town, and the French guns were trained on the canal bridge and on the German trenches in the valley. So intense was the fire from them that the enemy had to abandon many of his trenches, and the slaughter by the bridge was demoralising. The action lasted late into the night, and ended in a German withdrawal. In the morning the French attacked on the right, with a view to relieving the pressure against General Sarrail's sorely pressed Third Army.

The attack was repulsed; but the Duke of Würtemberg was firmly held by a most violent assault, in which both sides suffered heavily. The general decisive battle all along the line had now opened, and the French were animated by the spirit of the offensive. Their artillery continued to dominate the field of action round Vitry, and at the canal bridge more than half the German troops were destroyed. The men in the trenches were without food, and at midnight they crept into the fields and ate raw potatoes.

For four days the German troops at Vitry continued to deepen and extend their trenches, and on Thursday, September 10th, the private soldiers thought that the battle was drawing to a close, as the French gun fire slackened. Suddenly it broke out furiously on the western wing of the Fourth German Army, towards La Fère Champenoise. Foch had struck the flank, and the turning movement was beginning. A German report ran that two French army corps also managed to pierce the enemy's lines. Savage hand-to-hand fighting began. The Germans fought with the butt, so did the Turcos; but the French kept to the bayonet. Brigades clashed and struggled till they fell or tramped on their foes. In one place 3,500 German corpses were found mingled with 1,500 French bodies. This seems to have been the general proportion of the heavy losses on this section of the battlefield, though where the French guns had been working in the daylight there were only heaps of German dead.

Savage hand-to-hand fighting

At two o'clock on the morning of Friday, September 11th, the Germans retreated in the darkness from their trenches, and marched for six hours northward. "We were told," wrote a German soldier entrenched at Vitry, "that we were only executing a turning movement, and that it was not a retreat. But it had all the appearances of a flight. We suffered in a terrible way, and were utterly worn out. At Souain we met a Saxon army corps, and could not understand what it was doing there. We dug trenches in the pouring rain. Suddenly a shower of French shells and shrapnel arrived, and we were compelled to draw back, as our trenches were not finished. All the army corps fled."

'Only executing a turning movement"

This was on Saturday, September 12th. The village of Souain is several miles north of the town of St. Menehould, in the Argonne Forest. St. Menehould was the headquarters of the Crown Prince in the attack he was making on the Verdun army. The German front was close to Bar-le-Duc, two days' march south from St. Menehould, three days' march south from Souain. That is to say, General de Langle Cary's advance guards, with guns, were not merely on the flank, but almost in the rear of the original position of the Crown Prince. There was a rumour that the Kaiser's heir only escaped by a quarter of an hour. He moved from St. Menehould to Montfaucon, some ten miles above Verdun. Here he was able to draw help from the Army of Metz, that was making a feint attack on Verdun, but acting more strongly against the chain of forts between Verdun and Toul. As a matter of fact, the Crown Prince's army was in no immediate danger. It had retreated from the neighbourhood of Bar-le-Duc on Thursday, September 10th, when the German line began to give way. So rapid was its retreat, that the German wounded were left on the field of battle.

Most of the high, wooded, difficult country of the Argonne Forest, however, was still tenaciously held by the Crown Prince. Here it was he needed all the help General von Heeringen and the Metz garrison could give him. For between the two German armies the passage of the heights of the Meuse had almost been forced at Fort Troyon.

The Crown Prince had only feinted at the great fortress of Verdun. The French garrison held him off by extending their trenches outwards for some miles, and bringing out hidden, mobile batteries to prevent German howitzers from coming within range of the armoured and concrete forts. The Crown Prince, acting on the instructions of General von Moltke, swerved round Verdun to the west, struck at the trench running along the road to Toul, reached the heights of the Meuse and thus cut General Sarrail's garrison army into two separate parts. One held Verdun; the other operated round Bar-le-Duc.

On the opposite side of the Meuse, however, the communication between Verdun and Toul seems to have been maintained. A chain of hill forts connected the two fortress towns. The hill forts were well designed to repel an attack coming eastward from Metz, but on the western bank of the Meuse, where the Crown Prince's troops were established, there was a height overtopping by some sixty feet the hill on which Fort Troyon had been built.

Some heavy German siege-guns—11 in. Krupp howitzers with pneumatic recoil mechanism—were dragged up the

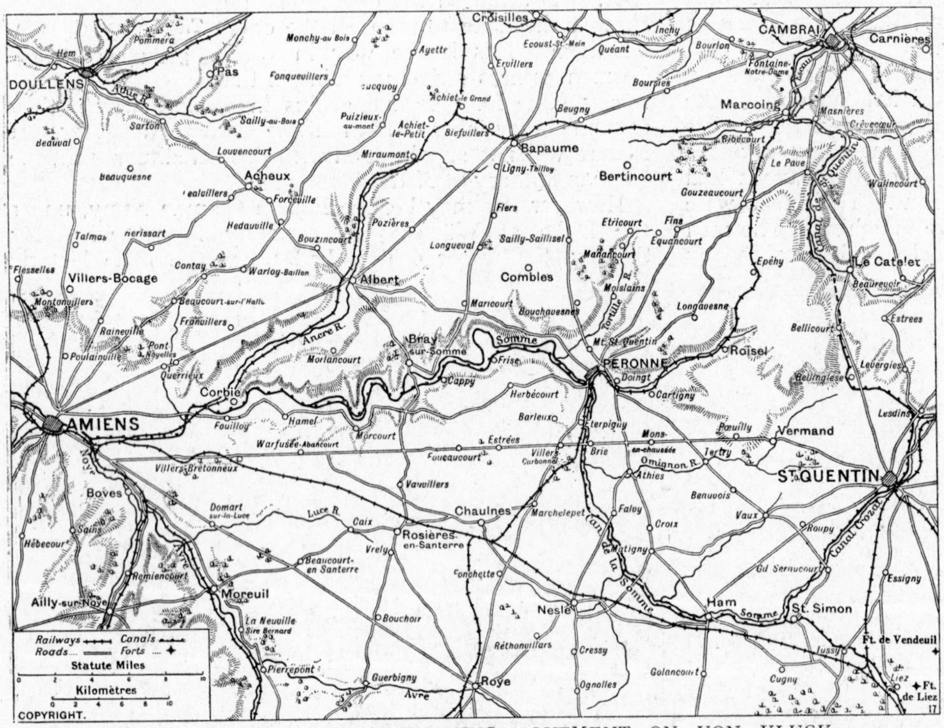

SCENE OF THE ALLIES' TURNING MOVEMENT ON VON KLUCK.

The country to the east of Amiens towards the Upper Oise, the scene of the turning movement against the German right in September, 1914, is open and eminently fitted for the operations of large armies. The ground is gently undulating, the fields are large, and for the most part unfenced, dotted with many strongly-built farmsteads. The roads often run in a perfectly straight line for many miles.

MAN TO MAN AT LAST! FRENCH INFANTRY PURSUING A FLYING GERMAN BATTERY IN A RAIN-SWEPT VALLEY OF THE ARGONNE.

For long, weary hours had the French lain in their rain-sodden trenches. Then, as darkness was approaching and the tempest at its height, news came that the army of the German Crown Prince was in retreat. The order was given "Charge!" At last it was man and man, and the bayonet had its chance. Our artist has supplied a vivid picture of one incident—the pursuit by French infantry of a flying German battery in the valley of Bellefontaine. The valley is in the Argonne district, to the west of the great fortress of Verdun. The ground was sodden with the rain and water was pouring down to the bottom of the valley in swift torrents. Over this drenched ground the heavy German guns had to be hauled, but they became more firmly fixed in the mud as they proceeded.

CONTRASTS IN THE GREAT WAR—THE A'FUL THUNDER OF

British artillerymen working their guns unconcernedly amid a hail of German projectiles. Apart from the devastating effects of the "Jack Johnsons"—the big siege-guns of the Germans—their ordinary field artillery, though deafening in concussion, appears to have caused comparatively little damage, and our men soon got used to it, especially when they found that the shells burst up One of our artillery officers counted one hundred and sixty shells fired battery between dawn and sunset without causing injury to man or horse. shells," he said, "on striking the ground immediately shoot upward, and

Men of the Royal Army Medical Corps searching for wounded in a wood at night-time by the aid of acetylene motor-car lamps and electric hand torches. There had been heavy fighting all day. Two British battalions had advanced through the wood, partly along the grass roads and partly through the thickly-tangled undergrowth, and all the time under fire from German shrapnel, which ca heavy losses. All around the trunks and branches of the trees were shatte After penetrating the wood and repulsing several German charges, the Br retired at dark, having forced the enemy back. The wood was full of woun

AND THE BENEFICI NT WORK OF THE ARMY MEDICAL CORPS.

no lateral spreading of the débris. Unless a man, or horse, or gun is hit there no damage done. In fact, after the first few shells were fired by the enemy gunners served their guns with absolute indifference to the strenuous deavours of the Germans to dislodge them." During the opening months of the Great War the enemy tried by all the means in their power to create "a moral effect" disadvantageous to the Allies. The terrific explosiveness of their shells was part of this policy. So was the savage display of "frightfulness" against unarmed civilians. But the policy failed all along the line.

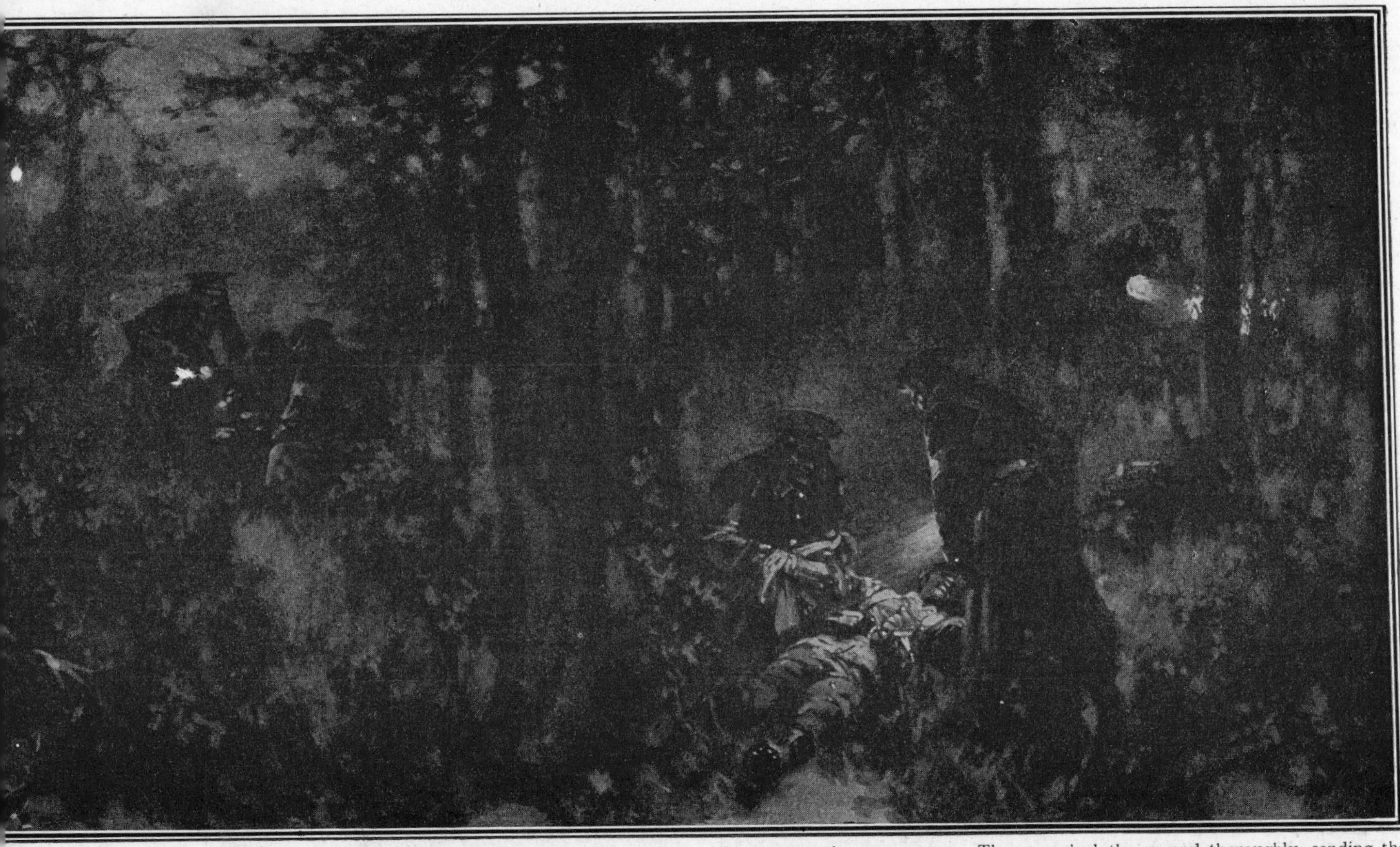

en, British and German, and owing to the darkness and the thickness of the rushwood the task of locating and attending to them was one of the utmost fficulty. But, as our picture shows so vividly, the men of the Royal Army edical Corps displayed all their traditional energy, devotion, and resourcefulness in meeting the emergency. They searched the ground thoroughly, sending the rays of light from side to side as they went, and at once moving towards any point whence came answering cries for help. The German wounded received the same care and attention as the British.

FRENCH AND GERMANS AT CLOSE QUARTERS IN THE FOREST OF ARGONNE.

A German artist's idea of the frenzied fighting that took place in September, 1914, in the Forest of Argonne, between the French and the forces under the command of the German Crown Prince. The struggle in the Argonne went on without definite result into 1915.

hill, and the fort was subjected to a terrible bombardment. A few miles to the east, at Thiaucourt, were the headquarters of the commander of the Metz field army, waiting to pour his troops through the gap made in the eastern fortifications of France.

In the meantime he helped the Crown Prince to retain a complete hold on the Forest of Argonne, and marched troops round Verdun to reinforce him.

The fateful thread at Troyon

Even with General de Langle Cary operating on his flank, and General Sarrail fiercely assailing him, the Crown Prince was able to make a desperate struggle for victory. Amid the dense brushwood and tall trees and tumbled rocks of the Argonne ridge numerous small bodies rocked in hand-to-hand conflicts. But at last the Germans were driven to the northern part of the forest, and General Sarrail recovered full possession of the western heights of the Meuse and relieved Fort Troyon. This was done on September 14th, barely in time. The Fort of Troyon was a heap of ruins, only four serviceable guns remained, and the heroic garrison—bravest of men—were reduced to forty-four men. On so fine a thread hung the destiny of France.

Had the Crown Prince succeeded at Troyon, he could have cut Verdun from Toul, and brought its end very near. Still more important, he could have opened short new lines of communication with the depots of Western Germany, and thus greatly eased and strengthened the invading armies. Finally, the French battle-front from the Argonne to Soissons could have been taken in flank by the Sixth German Army from Lorraine. Forty-four Frenchmen with four guns, in a heap of ruins that was being bombarded by 11 in. howitzers, held out just long enough to prevent this. It was one of the supreme achievements of the war.

General von Moltke—though his plan did not work out at the last moment, owing to the slow and unskilful advance of the Crown Prince's army—showed himself on the whole a very able strategist. In him General Joffre met no mean antagonist. Moltke planned as solidly as the French Commander-in-Chief. As we have seen in the previous chapter, General Joffre was not content to mass two armies, the Sixth and Fifth, against Kluck. He prepared for accidents by bringing the British force also against Kluck.

In somewhat the same way Moltke, having placed the means of a great success in the hands of the Crown Prince, did not rely wholly upon the unexpected side-stroke through the Verdun-Toul fortress line. He also struck lower down at Nancy, where another German army was ready to take in reverse the Franco-British advancing line in the north. Apparently, the drive in force through the Gap of Nancy, between Toul and Epinal, was accounted more promising even than the attack on Fort Troyon. In the first days of September, when the main allied armies were still desperately fighting to maintain their position to the east of Paris, the southern stroke at Nancy, full on their flank, may have seemed the most important of all operations. The Kaiser came in person to watch it being carried out.

On August 20th the army of Toul and Nancy, while advancing across the frontier towards Saarburg, had been confronted at Mortagne by two German armies and severely defeated. General Castelnau, the French commander, threw out artillery supports and got the troops over the border in some sort of order, and concentrated on the ring of wooded heights round the beautiful capital of French Lorraine, known as the Grande Couronné of Nancy. Here he was attacked by the two victorious Bavarian forces on August 22nd, and part of the field army of Metz struck southward to co-operate in the assault. After a week of give-and-take fighting the German Commander-in-Chief appears to have fixed on Nancy as the spot at which he would reply to the French concentration of forces against General von Kluck round Paris. At the time, Fort Troyon had not been placed in peril by the progress of the Crown Prince's army. Nancy was an open gate through which all the strong forces in German Lorraine and Alsace could pour into Central France, far in the rear of General Joffre's main armies. The weakness already shown by the French at Mortagne was seductive, and part of the field army of Metz and two Bavarian forces, with the famous White Cuirassiers of the Guard and other cavalry, first under the command of the Crown Prince of Bavaria and then of the Kaiser in person, massed for the grand attack on Friday, September 4th.

The famous Iron Division of France

The main French defensive position was on the plateau of Amance, rising a thousand feet, six miles north-east of Nancy, with the Forests of Champenoux and Saint Paul beneath it. The French frontier force had been seriously depleted in order to strengthen the northern French armies, to which General Pau had hastily gone with all the troops that could possibly be spared. Only the garrisons of Toul and Nancy remained. But with them was the greatest of French infantry bodies, the Iron

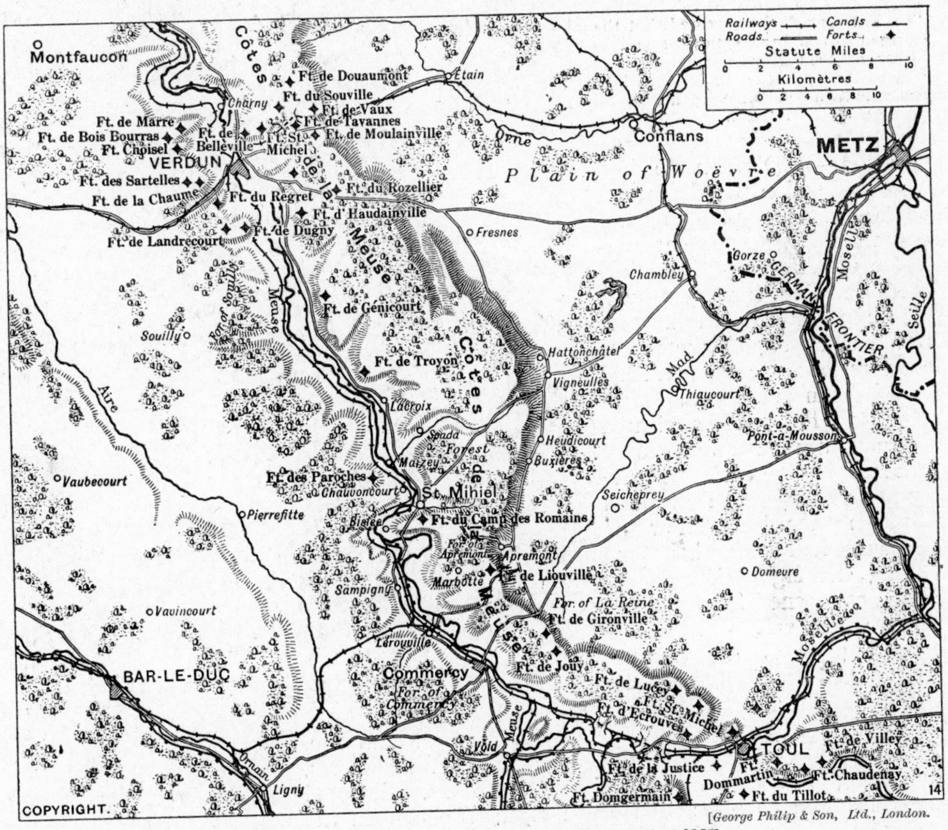

[George Philip & Son, Ltd., London.

MAP OF THE VERDUN-TOUL FORTRESS LINE.

When the eastern frontier defences of France were recognised after the war of 1870-71, Verdun and Toul were made into great fortresses, and the Cotes de la Meuse—the "Heights of the Meuse"—between these places were fortified by the placing of strong forts on their summits so as to command the passes from the plain of Woevre and the approaches to the Meuse bridges. After heavy fighting in September, 1914, the Germans crossed the Meuse at St. Mihiel.

PILLAGED BY THE GERMAN CROWN PRINCE.

The Baroness Debaye stated that the German Crown Prince stayed two days in her chateau near Champaubert and himself pillaged the museum, which contained a valuable archæological collection.

Division—le Division de Fer. To this division the defence of the Amance plateau was entrusted. An excellent provision of artillery—3 in. quick-firers and 6 in. howitzers—was set in position on the height; but a thick fog blanketed the country for some days and hid the German operations.

When the weather cleared German airmen swept over Amance to reconnoitre the French position, and the Iron Division then learnt how the Germans had spent their time during the fog. Four heavy batteries opened fire upon the French. By salvos of twenty-four big shells the German guns tried to pulverise the defence. The French infantry and gunners had to retire to the village of Amance. But here, also, the German reconnaissance officers, in flying machines and captive balloons, detected the defending troops, and a storm of shells shattered the village and sent the peasants flying. The troops went back to their first position, and found that their guns, which had been skilfully hidden, had not been struck.

It was warm work in the trenches—the men could not raise their heads without getting wounded. They had to bring their injured comrades into the deep ditches they had dug to save them from more wounds or instant death. Night and day the racket went on. The French gunners made a pretence of bravely maintaining the artillery duel. But they gradually slackened the fire, gave out ragged volleys, and then ceased.

Kaiser's vision of conquered Nancy

By September 8th the plateau was silent, and the Kaiser, standing on a neighbouring height and surveying through his field-glasses the summer scene, with Nancy in the distance, ordered the grand infantry attack. The Bavarian battalions came out of the Forest of Champenoux with bands playing at their head, as in Kaiser manœuvres. They climbed up the plateau in close formation. When they were half-way to the top, and only two hundred yards from the trenches, the Iron Division rose with a yell and charged down on them with the bayonet.

The Bavarians, taken at a disadvantage, broke and fled. The men of the Iron Division returned to their trenches. But their enemies did not escape. Close above the trenches were the hidden batteries of 3 in. quick-firers. There were marks for getting the range all down the hill. The gunners took the nearest mark and then mowed the Bavarians down, rank by rank, with horrible quickness, by their mechanical gun-pointing device. Only a few Bavarians got to the woods. But there were plenty more of them—for there were three Bavarian army corps against one French infantry division. Six times the Bavarians charged up the plateau. Six times they were massacred. Then the Kaiser ordered the White Cuirassiers of the Guard to storm the French trenches. Up came the famous cavalrymen in their shining breastplates. But the 3 in. guns raked them. At the foot of the hill the bodies in places were piled six feet high, and when the survivors tried to shelter behind this awful barrier, the terrible French guns on the height smote through the dead to the living.

Bavarians and Cuirassiers mowed down

The Kaiser departed, leaving the Crown Prince of Bavaria the sorry task of carrying on the decisive attack on Nancy. Wilhelm had seen himself riding through the capital of Lorraine, the most beautiful Renaissance city in Northern Europe, at the head of his White Cuirassiers. But most of the White Cuirassiers were dead—they formed part of the dreadful mass of 20,000 men cumbering the foot and lower slopes of the plateau. The German commander begged an armistice to bury his dead on the evening of September 9th. It was reported that his gunners used the truce to

THE IMPERIAL PILLAGER'S "DUG-OUT" BETWEEN RHEIMS AND VERDUN.

Photograph of the "dug-out" or bomb-proof shelter occupied by the German Crown Prince during his stay behind the German lines in North-Eastern France before the retreat of the Germans beyond the Marne. It was afterwards occupied by French Red Cross nurses. Inset: The German Crown Prince and two officers of his staff.

PRACTISING FOR THE PROMISED PARADE THROUGH PARIS.

German soldiers "goose-stepping" before their Crown Prince prior to their unexpected and sudden retreat to the Aisne. Inset: Prince Wilhelm Friedrich of Prussia in the uniform of the Death's Head Hussars, of which he was Colonel for about two years.

drag into position the heavy guns with which they angrily bombarded Nancy. But this bombardment did not alter the course of events. On Thursday, September 10th, the French Iron Division and its artillerymen took the offensive. The 6 in. howitzers were suddenly brought into action, and, with the 3 in. quick-firers, they swept the Forest of Champenoux, where the Bavarians had vainly gone for shelter. Acre by acre the woodland was searched with deadly melinite shells, until no foeman remained among the shattered trees except the dead and the badly wounded. The slaughter of the invisible enemy was over by eleven o'clock in the morning, owing to the mechanical means of fixing progressive ranges for the guns after the first shot. Nancy was saved on the day that the western wing of the main German armies was retreating beyond the Marne and the outskirts of Paris. Four days later, as we have seen, Fort Troyon was relieved, and the Crown Prince of Germany was in difficulties.

Kluck's skill in retreat

The victory of France was not so decisive as perhaps General Joffre expected. Only General von Hausen's Saxon army suffered anything like a rout. The skilful disposition of heavy artillery with which Kluck strengthened his flank guard against the Sixth French Army prevented the Allies from getting successively on the lines of communication of the retreating German forces. As a whole, the retirement of the invading armies was conducted in as good an order as marked the retirement of the allied armies from the Belgian frontier. On the other hand, the Germans, caught successively on flank and rear, and forced to struggle for life in every section of the battlefield, suffered very heavy losses. In many cases the troops, by the confession of their own officers, were demoralised.

In the neighbourhood of Nancy alone, at Amance and Lunéville, there were by September 10th some 31,000 dead Germans, mostly first-line troops. The Prussian Guards left on the field one man out of three of their original numbers, and one out of two of their actual fighting force. Their White Cuirassiers, dying under the eyes of their Emperor, were practically all destroyed. The Saxon army also must have been very badly cut up, for it appears not to have been worth while to re-establish its three corps under a new commander when Hausen was dismissed from his generalship-in-chief. Literal decimation—one dead man in ten—for the entire invading forces actually in the fighting-line would probably be an underestimate. For both the shelling and shrapnelling were peculiarly deadly, and the bayonet was used with murderous effect all along the line. The proportion of killed to wounded in the first grand Franco-British victory must have been unusually high. Telling mainly on the best class of German troops and their finest commissioned and non-commissioned officers, the general defeat sapped much of the fighting power of the most aggressive people in the modern world. Their new levies afterwards came on bravely enough, with a show of the old fierce spirit of the offensive peculiar to a nation inflated with military pride. But these new troops lacked the warlike skill of the first-line men. Between Paris and the Vosges the mainspring of German aggressiveness was broken.

THE LAST TRENCH: THE HIGH-WATER MARK OF THE TIDE OF GERMAN INVASION IN FRANCE.

Directly south of Chalons, in the direction of Arcis-sur-Aube, lies the village of Mailly; and just south of it was the trench marking the high-water mark of the tide of the German invasion in France. This trench was never taken. Here the French held their ground until the enemy had been driven beyond the Marne. "When," writes our special war artist, Mr. Sydney Adamson, "I last saw the trench, after the battle, a simple wooden cross marked the grave of those who died there. Near by another grave was indicated by a stick with a soldier's cap on it. I have seen several graves so marked, and they always remind me of the custom in Turkey, where a man's red fez is placed upon his coffin, and afterwards a carved and painted fez crowns the marble pillar which shows in Arabic who lies there."

BIRD'S-EYE VIEW OF TOWN OF SOISSONS DURING THE FIGHTING ALONG THE AISNE.

CHAPTER XXXVI.

THE COURSE OF EVENTS FROM THE MARNE TO THE AISNE.

The King's Messages to the Dominions Overseas and to the Princes and Peoples of India—Thrilling Episode in the Imperial Parliament—Moslem Opinion—The Press Bureau Reorganised—Act against Trading with the Enemy—Parliament and the New Army—Britain's Hospitality to Victims of the War—Incidents and Accidents at Sea—The Wreck of the Oceanic—Exploits of the German China Squadron—Policing the North Sea—Precedents for the New Naval Brigades—M. Millerand and Lord Kitchener—Cardinal Mercier's Terrible Story—Hélène Vacaresco's Address to France—M. Verhaeren on Belgian Courage and Ideals—German Calumnies—The Rally of South Africa—General Botha's Great Speech—Japan and Peace—Operations in Nyasaland—Great Meeting in the London Opera House—Mr. Churchill on the Work of the Navy.

PARLIAMENT reassembled at Westminster on September 9th for a short session necessitated by the discharge of Imperial business. In both the Commons and the Lords scenes of unexampled enthusiasm were witnessed. Never before in these historic chambers was patriotic emotion more profoundly and unreservedly manifested. First of all came the reading of the King's Message to "the Governments and Peoples of my Self-Governing Dominions," and to the "Princes and Peoples of my Indian Empire." Then followed the epoch-making recital by Mr. Charles Roberts, Under-Secretary for India, in the Commons, and by the Marquis of Crewe in the Lords, of the telegraphic despatch from Lord Hardinge, Governor-General, announcing that the rulers of Native States in India, who numbered nearly seven hundred, had with one accord rallied to the defence of the Empire, and offered their personal services and the resources of their States for the war.

His Majesty's Message to the Governments and Peoples of his Self-governing Dominions was as follows:

"During the past few weeks the peoples of my whole Empire at home and overseas have moved with one mind and purpose to confront and overthrow an unparalleled assault upon the continuity of civilisation and the peace of mankind.

"The calamitous conflict is not of my seeking. My voice has been cast throughout on the side of peace. My Ministers earnestly strove to allay the causes of strife and to appease differences with which my Empire was not concerned. Had I stood aside when, in defiance of pledges to which my kingdom was a party, the soil of Belgium was violated, and her cities laid desolate, when the very life of the French nation was threatened with extinction, I should have sacrificed my honour and given to destruction the liberties of my Empire and of mankind. I rejoice that every part of the Empire is with me in this decision.

HIS HIGHNESS THE AGHA KHAN.

In addition to directing the community of sixty million Moslems—of which he was the spiritual head—to place their personal services and resources unreservedly at the disposal of the Government, he volunteered to serve as a private in any infantry regiment of the Indian Expeditionary Force.

"Paramount regard for treaty faith and the pledged word of rulers and peoples is the common heritage of Great Britain and of the Empire.

"My peoples in the Self-governing Dominions have shown beyond all doubt that they whole-heartedly endorse the grave decision which it was necessary to take.

"My personal knowledge of the loyalty and devotion of my Oversea Dominions had led me to expect that they would cheerfully make the great efforts and bear the great sacrifices which the present conflict entails. The full measure in which they have placed their services and resources at my disposal fills me with gratitude, and I am proud to be able to show to the world that my peoples oversea are as determined as the people of the United Kingdom to prosecute a just cause to a successful end.

"The Dominion of Canada, the Commonwealth of

Australia, and the Dominion of New Zealand have placed at my disposal their naval forces, which have already rendered good service for the Empire. Strong expeditionary forces are being prepared in Canada, in Australia, and in New Zealand for service at the front, and the Union of South Africa has released all British troops, and has undertaken important military responsibilities, the discharge of which will be of the utmost value to the Empire. Newfoundland has doubled the numbers of its branch of the Royal Naval Reserve, and is sending a body of men to take part in the operations at the front. From the Dominion and Provincial Governments of Canada large and welcome gifts of supplies are on their way for the use both of my naval and military forces, and for the relief of the distress in the United Kingdom which must inevitably follow in the wake of war. All parts of my Oversea Dominions have thus demonstrated in the most unmistakable manner the fundamental unity of the Empire amidst all its diversity of situation and circumstance."

THE PRUSSIAN WAR LORD IN HIS ELEMENT.
Newspaper reports credited the Kaiser with exceedingly rapid journeys between the "fronts" in both the eastern and western theatres of war. Our photograph shows him with members of the Great General Staff of the German field army, conversing with an officer who had just been decorated with the Iron Cross.

GENERAL ALEXANDER VON KLUCK IN THE FIELD.
"Old One O'clock," as he was termed by the British soldier, is seen seated at the foot of the steps shown in the photograph. But for his masterly conduct of the German retirement to the Aisne the Allies might have turned the retreat into a rout.

The first part of the King-Emperor's Message to the Princes and Peoples of India was in the same terms as that to the Self-governing Dominions, and it concluded as follows:

"Among the many incidents that have marked the unanimous uprising of the populations of my Empire in defence of its unity and integrity, nothing has moved me more than the passionate devotion to my Throne expressed both by my Indian subjects and by the Feudatory Princes and the Ruling Chiefs of India, and their prodigal offers of their lives and their resources in the cause of the Realm. Their one-voiced demand to be foremost in the conflict has touched my heart, and has inspired to the highest issues the love and devotion which, as I well know, have ever linked my Indian subjects and myself. I recall to mind India's gracious message to the British nation of good-will and fellowship which greeted my return in February, 1912, after the solemn ceremony of my Coronation Durbar at Delhi, and I find in this hour of trial a full harvest and a noble fulfilment of the assurance given by you that the destinies of Great Britain and India are indissolubly linked."

When his Majesty's message was read in the Parliaments of the Dominion of Canada and the Commonwealth of Australia it was received with great cheering and the singing of "God Save the King." In the New Zealand Legislature Mr. Massey, the Premier, said that the Dominion, like the rest of the Empire, was prepared to see the war through, whatever it might cost in life. Every male citizen and the property of every citizen in New Zealand were at the disposal of the Empire.

India's great tribute to Imperial ideals

The story which Mr. Roberts unfolded in the Commons from the Viceroy's telegraphic communication was unlike anything which had ever been heard in the Imperial Parliament. It was a real romance from the East, with all its variety, movement, and colour, and accepted as one of the finest tributes ever paid to Imperial ideals. With the Commander-in-Chief's approval, the Viceroy had selected for active service with the Indian contingents in France and Belgium the Chiefs of Bikaner (with his camel corps), Kishangarh, Ratlam, Sachin, Patiala, the Heir Apparent of Bhopal, a brother of the Maharajah of Cooch Behar, with cadets of other noble families. The veteran Sir Pertab Singh, Regent of Jodhpur, would not be denied his right to serve his King-Emperor, in spite of his seventy years; and his nephew, the Maharajah of Jodhpur, who was but sixteen years old, insisted on going with him. The Maharajahs of Gwalior, Rewa, Kashmir, Mysore, the Maharajah and the Maharani Maji Sahiba of Bharatpur, the Rajah of Akalkot, the Rajah of Pudukota, the Gaekwar of Baroda, Mir Ghulam, Ali Khan of Khairpur, offered troops, camels, horses, money contributions, and even their personal jewellery. Several of the chiefs combined, in addition, to provide a hospital ship. Most remarkable of all was the offer of troops and contributions from beyond the borders of India, such as from the ruler of Nepal, and from the Dalai Lama of Tibet, which latter stated in making his offer that Lamas innumerable throughout the length and breadth of Tibet were offering prayers for the success of the British Army, and for the happiness of the souls of all victims of war. Many hundreds of telegrams and letters had also been received by the Viceroy expressing loyalty and desire to serve the Imperial Government, either in the field or by co-operation in India, from communities and associations, religious, political, and social of all classes and creeds, the most notable of which were from a vast variety of Moslem leagues, Hindus, Orthodox Sikhs, and Parsees. The Delhi Medical Association offered a field hospital, and Bengalee students and many others offered services for an ambulance corps and other medical aid.

The Committee of the London All-India Moslem League passed on September 8th, at an emergency meeting, the following resolutions: (1) "That the Committee of the London All-India Moslem League desire to convey, through the favour of the Right Hon. the Secretary of State for India, to his Majesty's Indian troops their good wishes for success in the opportunity accorded to them to share with their British comrades-in-arms in the defence of the Empire on the battlefields of Europe. (2) That the Committee further desire to place on record their conviction that the Moslem States will in the titanic struggle in which the nations of Europe have become involved do all in their power to avoid being drawn into the vortex; and that the Turkish Government will unswervingly maintain the neutrality which it has hitherto faithfully observed, and not allow the Ottoman people to be goaded by malign attempts into any deviation from strict fidelity to its pledges."

In the House of Commons complaints were made as to the reticence of the Press Bureau and the inadequacy of the news furnished to the public by it, and the Prime Minister announced that the Bureau had been reorganised, and that, at the request of the Cabinet, the Home Secretary, Mr. McKenna, had accepted responsibility for it. Among the Emergency Bills introduced was one authorising the appropriation of charities—which under deed could not possibly be applied in existing circumstances—to the Prince of Wales's Fund while the war lasted.

More important still was the measure, which ran through all its stages, relating to trading with the enemy. Under this Act a Supplement to the "London Gazette" of September 9th contained a revised Proclamation revoking by Clause 1 previous Proclamations on this important subject, and substituting therefor the present one, which proceeds as follows:

Trading with the enemy

"(2) The expression 'enemy country' means the territories of the German Empire and of the Dual Monarchy of Austria-Hungary, together with all the Colonies and Dependencies thereof. (3) The expression 'enemy' means any person or body of persons of whatever nationality resident or carrying on business in the enemy country, but does not include persons of enemy nationality who are neither resident nor carrying on business in the enemy country. In the case of incorporated bodies, enemy character attaches only to those incorporated in an enemy country.

"The following prohibitions now have effect (save so far as licences may be issued): (1) Not to pay any sum of money to or for the benefit of an enemy. (2) Not to compromise or give security for the payment of any debt or other sum of money with or for the benefit of an enemy. (3) Not to act on behalf of an enemy in drawing, accepting, paying, presenting for acceptance or payment, negotiating, or otherwise dealing with any negotiable instrument. (4) Not to accept, pay, or otherwise deal with any negotiable instrument which is held by or on behalf of an

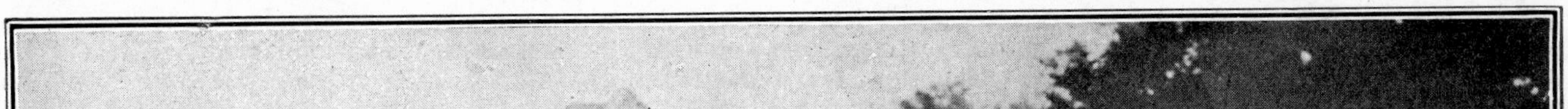

HOW THE WAR LORD WENT TO WAR—THE EXTENSIVE PLANS FOR THE KAISER'S COMFORT.

German papers gave extended accounts of the plans at the Great Headquarters in the east and west of the war area for the comfort of the Kaiser. Wherever this was possible, the most luxuriously-appointed residence was set apart for the Emperor. Where no permanent building was suitable the Kaiser had his specially-designed motor-vehicle. Above is given the first photograph taken of the Emperor's kitchen, with preparations for a meal being made by members of the Imperial suite. The most elaborate precautions were taken to safeguard the food from being tampered with, the military chefs carrying on their duties under the immediate supervision of members of the Kaiser's suite.

GERMAN INFANTRY ADVANCING TO THE ATTACK—FROM A DRAWING BY A GERMAN ARTIST.

enemy, provided that this prohibition shall not be deemed to be infringed by any person who has no reasonable ground for believing that the instrument is held by or on behalf of an enemy. (5) Not to enter into any new transaction, or complete any transaction already entered into with an enemy in any stocks, shares, or other securities. (6) Not to make or enter into any new marine, life, fire, or other policy or contract of insurance with or for the benefit of an enemy; nor to accept or give effect to any insurance of, any risk arising, under any policy or contract of insurance (including re-insurance) made or entered into with or for the benefit of an enemy before the outbreak of war. (7) Not directly or indirectly to supply to or for the use or benefit of, or obtain from, an enemy country, or an enemy, any goods, wares, or merchandise, nor directly or indirectly to supply to or for the use or benefit of, or obtain from any person any goods, wares, or merchandise, for or by way of transmission to or from an enemy country or an enemy, nor directly or indirectly to trade in or carry any goods, wares, or merchandise destined for or coming from an enemy country or an enemy. (8) Not to permit any British ship to leave for, enter, or communicate with, any port or place in an enemy country. (9) Not to enter into any commercial, financial, or other contract or obligation with or for the benefit of an enemy. (10) Not to enter into any transactions with an enemy if and when they are prohibited by an Order-in-Council made and published on the recommendation of a Secretary of State, even though they would otherwise be permitted by law or by this or any other Proclamation."

Insurance for an enemy's benefit

The Proclamation went on to warn all persons who, in contravention of the law therein set forth, should commit, aid, or abet, any of the aforesaid acts would be guilty of a crime, and would be liable to punishment and penalties. There was, however, a provision that where an enemy had a branch locally situated in British, allied, or neutral territory, not being neutral territory in Europe, transactions by or with such branch should not be treated as transactions by or with an enemy. There was, further, a provision that nothing in the Proclamation should be deemed to prohibit payments by or on account of enemies to persons resident carrying on business or being in British Dominions, if such payments arose out of transactions entered into before the outbreak of the war, or otherwise permitted. A final proviso was that nothing in the Proclamation should affect anything expressly permitted by Imperial licence or a licence granted by a Secretary of State or the Board of Trade, whether especially granted to individuals or as applying to classes of persons.

In connection with this campaign against trading with the enemy, the Commercial Intelligence Department of the Board of Trade initiated a movement for assisting British manufacturers and traders to capture trade formerly in German, Austrian, and Hungarian hands. In the first place, they formed on their premises in Whitehall a permanent exhibition of samples and goods formerly purchased from enemy sources; and in the next place, with the view of making that exhibition of the greatest value to British manufacturers and traders, the department arranged a series of "exchange meetings" between buyers desirous of obtaining such goods and British manufacturers who might already be producing or be likely to produce similar goods in this country. These meetings took place at Wakefield House, Cheapside, London, E.C., and afterwards at Basinghall Street.

Import, wholesale, and shipping houses which had formerly purchased goods from the enemy countries were asked to bring samples of these goods for inspection by manufacturers and suppliers; and the Board of Trade gave an assurance to the firms forwarding samples that every care would be taken to ensure that the ordinary channels of trade now existing as between the original manufacturers and the final consumer would not be interfered with. The seasonal demand for toys and games for the approaching Christmas made it desirable to deal with that trade first, the exports of which from Germany in 1912 amounted to two and three-quarter millions sterling. The result was that the British manufacture of such toys and games was immediately expanded or started of new by individual enterprise and by patriotic organisations.

REMARKABLE CAMERA PICTURE OF THE EXPLOSION OF A PROJECTILE FROM A GERMAN 12·5 IN. GUN.

GERMAN "KULTUR" IN EXCELSIS: ROYAL IRISH RIFLES TO THE RESCUE.

"You see some very sad sights in villages where the Germans have been," wrote a non-commissioned officer of the Royal Irish Rifles. "They plunder and destroy everything they can. Some of them are simply beasts. One night I was in charge of a scouting party of eight men. On entering a village we saw a light in one of the houses. On looking through the window we saw thirteen Germans in the room. They were all half drunk, and empty wine bottles were scattered all over the place. An officer was sitting on the mantelshelf, and in the middle of the soldiers were an old woman and two girls. We rushed into the house. Every man in the room was killed. I had the satisfaction of shooting the officer, who fell off his perch like a log. We then captured their horses, and rode them back to our own lines."

CRUISERS OF THE ROAD IN ACTION—BRITISH ARMOURED MOTOR-CARS DISLODGING GERMAN SNIPERS.
In France as well as in Belgium the armoured motor-car did valuable work against the snipers and raiders of the enemy. They were fitted with Maxims and light quick-firing guns. The quick-firers were directed against snipers lurking in villages and isolated buildings, and the Maxims scattered them when they were driven into the open.

These efforts afforded employment to scores of thousands of young people and old who, from the dislocation of business in certain trades, had been thrown out of work—with, of course, the additional effect of establishing permanently a native industry of interesting and economic importance. The same course was pursued with the German trade in earthenware, china, and enamelled hollow-ware, which amounted to four and a quarter millions, and cheap cutlery to the amount of one and a quarter millions. But the most satisfactory capture was that of electrical apparatus and appliances, the value of which in 1912 imported from Germany to Great Britain reached no less a sum than just over eight millions. Probably quite as much of these goods of German manufacture were imported into British Dominions, Colonies, and Possessions overseas. Although this is a slight anticipation of chronological facts, it may here be stated with satisfaction that the system devised by the Intelligence Department of the Board of Trade practically resulted in the transfer of the manufacture and distribution of all these products from German, Austrian, and Hungarian hands to home and colonial manufacturers, merchants, and agents.

Board of Trade and British industries

On September 10th the Prime Minister moved in the House of Commons a Vote providing for a further 500,000 men for the Army. In commending the Vote to the House, Mr. Asquith said that the number of recruits enlisted since the declaration of war, exclusive of those who had joined the Territorials, was 439,000 up to the evening of September 9th. The time had not come when recruiting activity should be in any way relaxed. We should want more rather than less "Let us get the men. That is the first necessity of the State. With the addition of another 500,000 men, we shall be in a position to put something like 1,200,000 men into the field. This is the provision made by the Mother Country, and is exclusive of the Territorials, the National Reserve, and the magnificent contributions promised from India and the Dominions." The Vote was instantly agreed to.

FRENCH COLOURED TROOPS CHARGING GERMAN TRENCHES.
One of the most noteworthy phases of the Great War has been the eagerness and devotion of the coloured troops in the French Army and the Indian troops in the British Army in the fight for the freedom of Europe from the domination of the "mailed fist" of Germany. This illustration has a particular interest, having been drawn by one of the best-known German war artists at the front.

While this clear-eyed and determined policy was being thus resolutely prosecuted by the Government, with the support of the vast majority of the nation and of the Empire, a note came on this September 9th which almost seemed to indicate that there was the tiniest of a rift in the lute. Perhaps it would be more correct to say, changing the metaphor, that a small faction made an attempt to bring disharmony by the shrill piping of a falsetto whistle. This unmusical coterie secretly issued to many people a circular letter—which, however, had been composed some weeks previously—in which it was stated that: "There are very many thousands of people in the country who are profoundly dissatisfied with the general course of policy which preceded the war. They are feeling that a dividing point has come in national history, that the old traditions of secret and class diplomacy, the old control of foreign policy by a narrow clique, and the power of the armament organisations have got henceforth to be combated by a great and conscious and directed effort of the democracy. We are anxious to take measures which may focus this feeling and help to direct public policy on broad lines, which may build up on a more secure and permanent foundation the hopes which have been shattered for our generation in the last month. The objects we have in view are:

"(1) To secure real Parliamentary control over foreign policy, and to prevent it being again shaped in secret and forced upon the country as an accomplished fact.

"(2) When peace returns, to open direct and deliberate negotiations with democratic parties and influences on the Continent, so as to form an international understanding, depending on popular parties rather than on Governments.

"(3) To aim at securing such terms as this war will not, either through the humiliation of the defeated nation, or an artificial rearrangement of frontiers, merely become the starting-point for new national antagonisms and future wars."

The circular went on to say that there was an immediate need of a propaganda of the

A French "75" which had taken up a position in a beet-field in an attack on the German lines in Northern France.

Another view of one of the wonderful "75's" (3 in. quick-firers) of the French artillery in action.

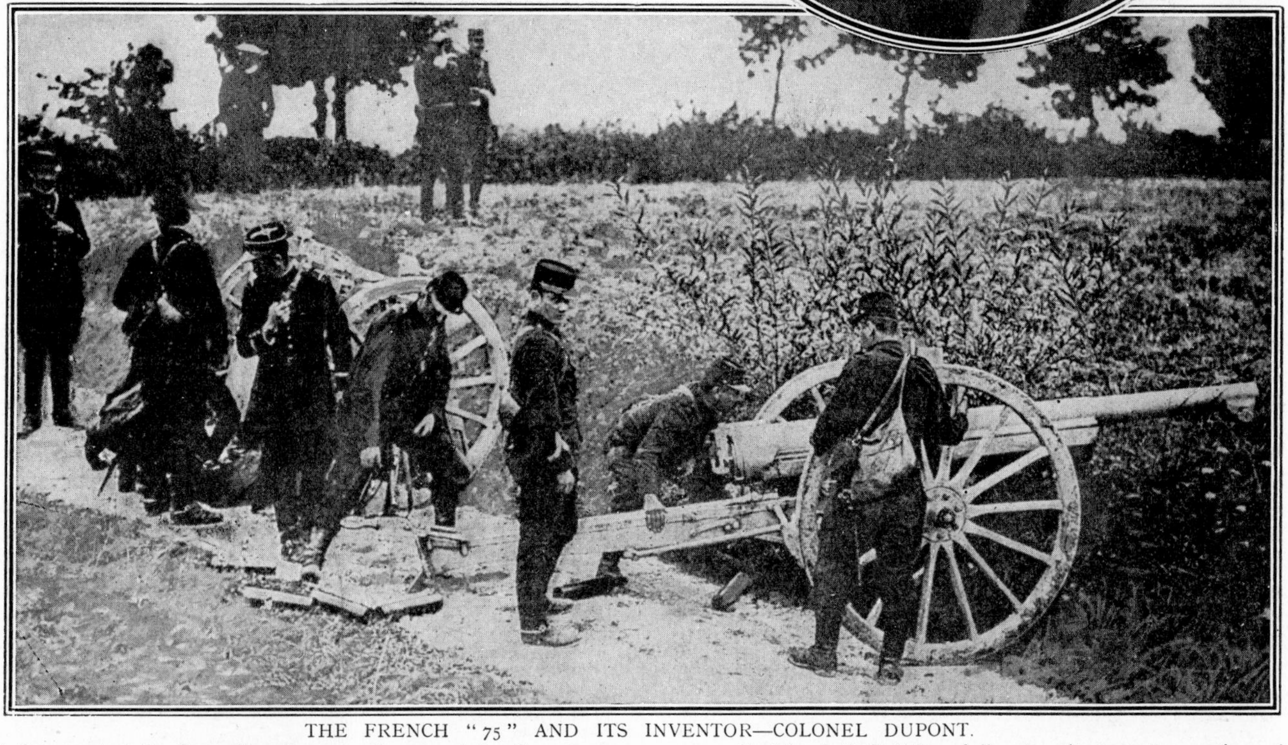

THE FRENCH "75" AND ITS INVENTOR—COLONEL DUPONT.

At the outset of the Great War the preponderance of the German gun-power gave the enemy a great advantage in attacking fortified positions, particularly at Liège and Namur. But it was not long before the balance was equalised by both British and French. Particularly was the early French discrepancy in artillery made up by the wonderful "75's" of the French. Inset: Portrait of Colonel Dupont, inventor of this gun.

above opinions by the issue of books, pamphlets, leaflets, which could be scattered broadcast, and asked for subscriptions towards the cost thereof. This precious document was signed by J. Ramsay Macdonald, formerly chairman of the Labour Party in the House of Commons, Charles Trevelyan, who had resigned an under-secretaryship in the Government on the declaration of war, Norman Angell, and E. D. Morel. The circular fell as flat as a sodden damper, which effectually silenced its own authors.

London a cosmopolitan hostel

When the eyes of our people were not cast oversea to the theatre of war, in which our own soldiers were creating a new renown for British arms, worthily supported by the heroic efforts and sacrifices of our Belgian, French, and Russian allies, their hearts were stirred with compassion for the woes and the sufferings of the victims of German barbarism in Northern France, Flanders, and Brabant. For six weeks after the outbreak of the war citizens of other nations poured into England, till London became a vast cosmopolitan hostel. Belgians whose homes had become smoking ruins; Frenchmen on whose lands and fruitful vineyards the soldiers of three nations were fighting; Russians whom the outbreak of hostilities surprised in some alien country—all sought these shores. Here, too, were many of our enemy subjects—Germans and Austrians who were in England when the war broke out, and chose to prolong their sojourn. These were added to by Teutons for whom the attractions of war had no delight, and who rushed hither from Paris and elsewhere. This invasion turned London into a city where foreign tongues were heard on every hand. In fact, in some quarters it was hard to find good, honest English speech.

It is a characteristic of the British nature in times of distress that a Divine compassion falls towards the afflicted multitude, from West End to East End, like the gentle rain from Heaven. In the presence of all-too-apparent misery and helplessness among the scores of thousands of refugees, charitable organisations sprang up as mushrooms in the night for their relief and comfort. In every quarter, too, a generous hospitality was privately offered to family parties of refugees from one up to six persons, according to the accommodation, in the homes of thousands of well-to-do citizens. But this was felt to be not enough, and on September 9th Mr. Herbert Samuel announced in the House of Commons that the British Government had offered the hospitality of the British nation to Belgian victims of the war. A committee, of which Lord Gladstone was chairman, opened a central office in Aldwych, with a large reception-hall attached, and there provision was made for the immediate transfer of the homeless wanderers, not otherwise accommodated, to homes—not only in London, but in towns and villages all over Great Britain and Ireland. Of course, not all the refugees were without means. Some were well provided with money, others had British investments, and many of these settled in central boarding-houses, or in attractive London suburbs.

Nor was our practical sympathy confined to those who had reached our shores. In response to an appeal by the Belgian Minister in London for the relief of distress among those who either could not leave their native land, or who clung to their devastated hearths, an immediate response was given, and immense quantities of foodstuffs were despatched to Belgium for distribution.

" FOR WOMEN MUST WEEP."

Scene near the village of Barcy, after the fighting along the Marne. Two French women were seen laying a tribute of flowers on the graves of some of the men who had fallen from the ranks of the army of civilisation.

The September Navy List included, in addition to the names of over a hundred trawlers, the following merchant vessels commissioned as H.M.'s ships—in other words, as auxiliary cruisers: Alsatian, Anglia, Aquitania, Armadale Castle, Cambria, Carmania, Caronia, Empress of Asia, Empress of Britain, Empress of Japan, Empress of Russia, Engadine, Himalaya, Kinfauns Castle, Macedonia, Maori, Mantua, Marmora, Oceanic, Osiris, Otranto, Riviera, Scotia, Tara, Venetia, and Victorian. From the above list had later to be deducted the White Star twin-screw Oceanic, of 17,274 tons, 28,000 horse-power engines, with a speed of 20 knots. Her captain was William F. Slayter, the commander, H. Smith (R.N.R.), and the crew numbered 400. During a cruise off the North of Scotland on September 8th she became enveloped in a fog and ran on the rocks. The Aberdeen steam-trawler Glenogil observed the accident, and made several efforts, with other trawlers which came to the rescue, to drag the Oceanic off the rocks, but without avail, and the big cruiser became a total wreck. The officers and crew were rescued, and afterwards taken to Aberdeen.

It may be well here to recount various incidents of sea warfare or adventure in the second week of September. On arrival at his base port the master of the Grimsby steam-trawler Agatha reported a diabolic German ruse for sinking trawlers and neutral ships of commerce. While fishing in the North Sea on September 9th he sighted a ship's boat afloat, and, concluding that some disaster had occurred, steered towards it. A boat was put out, and the derelict was found to be a ship's lifeboat equipped with sails, masts, and oars. A line was secured to it and passed to the trawler, which intended to tow the prize home. As soon as the towing began an explosion occurred, luckily too far distant from the trawler to do damage. A careful examination was then made, and it was found that a mine had been attached to the lifeboat by ropes and wires in such a manner as to explode and blow up any ship which steamed alongside the lifeboat to pick it up. On the same day the master of the Grimsby trawler Howe reported that he had seen a steamship strike a mine in the North Sea and founder. Though he made all speed to the scene, nothing to identify the vessel could be found.

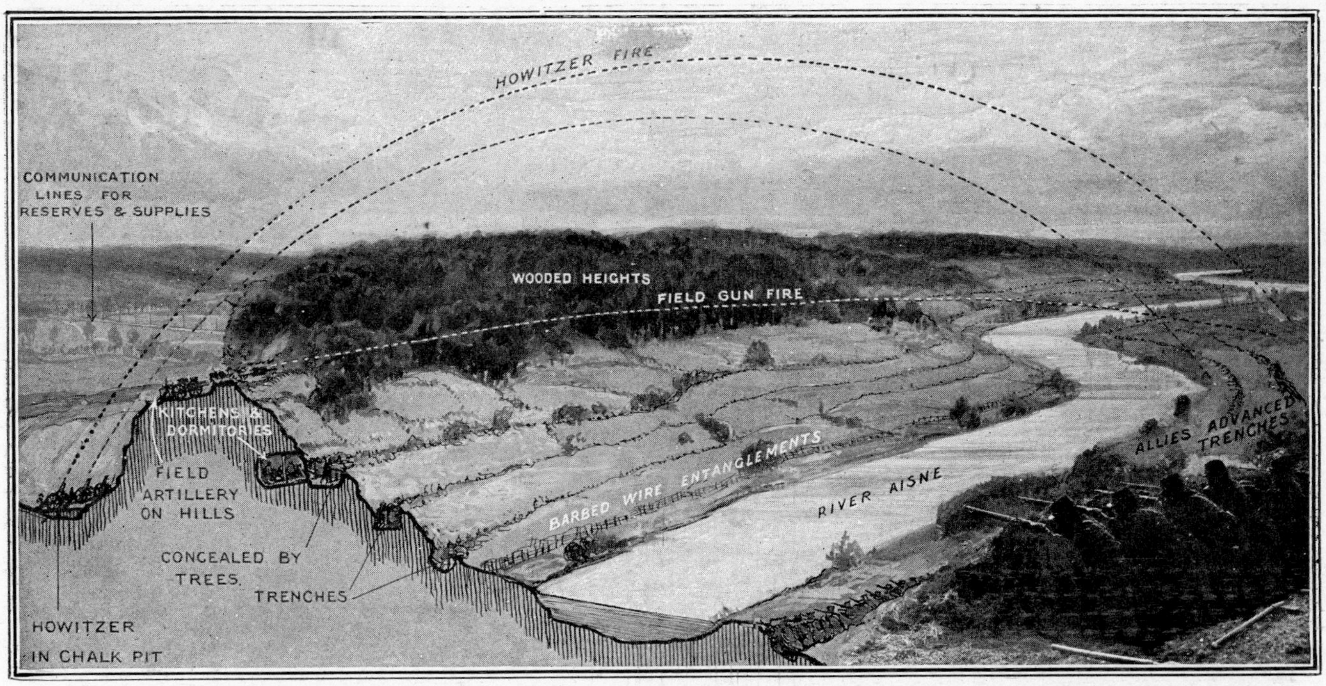

DIAGRAMMATIC VIEW OF THE AISNE VALLEY, SHOWING HOW THE GERMAN TRENCHES WERE DISPOSED.

The above sectional view cuts across the River Aisne from north to south. On the north bank were the trenches and covered ways of the Germans, with their heavy artillery in the rear disposed in quarries. The field artillery threw shells with a flat trajectory, while their howitzer shells, one type of which became familiar as "Jack Johnsons" to our troops, sailed in great semicircular sweeps over the river. In the foreground may be seen the French troops in an advanced trench. The German stand, between Noyon and Berry-au-Bac, had railways parallel to and behind it.

The master of the Howe also reported that previous to this his trawl-net had picked up a mine, which however did not explode. The same day another trawler brought to Grimsby wreckage comprising the wheelhouse, part of the deck casing, and the ship's bell of the steam-trawler Nelson, of Grimsby, which it was therefore feared had been mined. A German cruiser also on the 9th captured the trawler Capricornus, sank it, and took the crew to Wilhelmshaven as prisoners. The Leith trawler Pollux was overhauled by a German cruiser about the same date and sunk, her crew being also taken as prisoners to Wilhelmshaven.

The Holland-Amerika steamer Noordan, bound from New York to Rotterdam with one hundred and sixty German reservists on board, was brought into Queenstown by a British cruiser as prize on September 9th. The German reservists were interned in Ireland. A German collier with 5,000 tons of Welsh coal on board was captured by H.M.S. Vindictive in the Atlantic on September 10th, and on the same day two large German ships—the Orlanda, with a cargo of nitrate valued at £40,000, and the Goldbeck with a cargo of timber—were captured and brought into Falmouth. The German four-masted barque Urania, with a cargo of nitrate for Hamburg worth £35,000, was captured in the Channel by a British warship and brought to Plymouth. The French auxiliary cruiser La Savoie captured in the Channel the Holland-Amerika liner Nieuw Amsterdam, with four hundred German and two hundred and fifty Austrian subjects on their way to join the colours in their respective countries. These were interned in France and the ship made a prize. The Dutch steamers Fortuna and Atlas were likewise on the same day captured with contraband of war on board by the French cruisers Friant and Lavoisier, and taken as prizes to Brest. During the same period British and French torpedo-boats in the Adriatic discovered and exploded lines of mines which the Austrians had laid at Antivari and Dulcigno, and also near Cape Volovitza.

Further afield it became known at the beginning of September that the German China Squadron had, on the declaration of war against Germany by Japan, as the Treaty associate of Great Britain, left the Far Eastern seas and scattered—the Emden (to become famous in the Indian Ocean), and the Scharnhorst, Gneisenau, Nürnberg, and Stettin in the Pacific. On the 7th a four-funnelled cruiser displaying the French flag appeared off Fanning Island, a coral atoll in the Pacific, and first landing-place of the All-British cable which runs from Bamfield, British Columbia, to Southport, Moreton Bay, Queensland, Eastern Australia, touching, after leaving Fanning Island, Fiji, and Norfolk Island. Shortly after it was discovered that the cable had been cut, and later the deed was traced to the Nürnberg, which in addition to flying false colours had rigged an additional false funnel, and so disguised had eluded two Australian gunboats waiting for her outside Honolulu on September 1st.

VANDALISM AT SOISSONS.

The abbey of St. Jean des Vignes, at Soissons, with one of its beautiful spires shattered by German shell fire.

About the same date the Gulf liner Messina, on a round voyage of the Polynesian Islands from and to Sydney, New South Wales, put in at Nauru, one of the Gilbert Islands, included in the German Western Pacific Colonies. The German resident magistrate and party came off in a boat, hailed the Messina, and demanded to be taken on board. "By whose orders?" shrewdly asked the mate. "By orders of his Majesty the German Emperor," replied the magistrate. The mate laughed, ordered full steam ahead, and the Messina, of which the wily Teuton had hoped to make an easy

HUMAN MOLES IN THE AISNE BATTLEFIELD.
One of the British trenches in the hard-fought Battle of the Aisne. In the foreground is shown a heap of accoutrements of soldiers who were asleep in the straw at the bottom. Inset: A view within a British trench in a wooded part of the country.

prey, gained the open sea and safely arrived at Sydney. The Secretary to the Admiralty made it known through the Press Bureau that on September 9th and 10th strong and numerous squadrons and flotillas had made a complete sweep of the North Sea up and into the Heligoland Bight. The German Fleet, however, made no attempt to interfere with these movements, and no German ships of any kind were seen at sea. The naval correspondent of the "Times," writing on this, made a comment worth reproduction here. "Every now and again during the previous month," said he, "an operation of this description approached in its swoop the enemy's coasts, and offered an opportunity to his fleet to accept the challenge if he thought fit to give battle. This aspect, however, was merely of secondary importance to the fact that the British Fleet's patrol was well maintained, that their means of getting intelligence were entirely satisfactory, and that while the Germans by their mining operations had interfered more or less with their own free movements, they had not in the slightest degree affected ours."

The independent observation may here be made that Admiral Jellicoe's Fleet, intact and unseen, was at the period under review not only assisting our gallant troops in France and helping our Allies in both the land theatres of war, but without its continued existence all our efforts to augment and increase the forces of the Empire at the actual seat of war would have been hampered if not brought to naught.

The efficient methods involving unceasing vigilance, mostly under cover of darkness, by which the policing of the North Sea is effected was described naïvely by two trawler skippers to a newspaper correspondent. The first said he had just come from Iceland, and between that island and the Faroes, and the sentinel Shetlands and Orkneys, he encountered a solid wall of warships, which made it impossible for any craft to break through undetected. Of course, his trawler was subjected to the utmost scrutiny by the officers of a cruiser; but after being released, he was followed by two torpedo-boat destroyers until he reached his home port, so as to ensure that he was really, as he had declared, a British trawler. The other skipper who was interviewed was in charge of a North Sea boat which, after fishing, came under the lee of the land each night and anchored. "On one occasion at two o'clock in the morning a cruiser suddenly appeared alongside us," exclaimed he. "All his lights were extinguished, and the quiet way in which that big cruiser came up and the clever tactics the commander showed in getting alongside us without doing any damage was astonishing. Talk about cats seeing in the dark, these naval officers are wonderful. When the cruiser reached us, all we could see was a huge black object hemming us in. A voice shouted out: 'Who are you?' I replied, 'The——.' 'When did you leave?' 'On——,' I answered. 'What were your orders when you left?' I told him, and in a flash the commander of the cruiser shouted back 'All right.' Directly the commander had finished talking to me, another voice from the stern of our vessel sung out: 'The name is quite correct, sir.' A submarine had crept up behind to verify our name and number, and although all the crew had come on deck to see what was happening, not one of the men aft had caught sight of the submarine. I have seen the British Navy in times of peace, but to see it in war-time makes you feel proud of it. No swank; simply good old Nelson's motto all the time."

Our sentinel warships in the North Sea

Mention was made in Chapter XXXIII. of the decree of the Admiralty, made with the sanction of the King, for the creation of special Naval and Marine brigades for employment either on sea or land. Lord Fisher, in the stirring address to the men of the First Naval Brigade, of

SHELTERS FROM THE WEATHER MADE BY OUR MEN IN THE INTERVALS OF FIGHTING IN THE TRENCHES DURING THE BATTLE OF THE AISNE.

AN OFFICER'S SHELTER ON THE AISNE.

ANOTHER "SNUGGERY" BEHIND THE FIRING-LINE.

HOLE MADE BY THE BURSTING OF A "BLACK MARIA."

SIDELIGHTS ON THE LIFE OF OUR MEN DURING THE FIGHTING ON THE AISNE.

Cavalry as well as infantry took part in the work in the trenches on the Aisne. A system of regular reliefs was organised, and the men relieved constructed shelters where they could rest and recuperate in comparative safety from the shells of the enemy and the inclemency of the weather. Some of the shelters were beautifully made. The two lower photographs are of the trenches themselves.

IN THE FIRE ZONE OF THE BIG GERMAN GUNS.

View of the village of Augy. The German position was on the hills in the distance, on which their big guns were placed. Our troops had to pass over the country here seen under deadly shell fire. The road was only partially safe by night. Inset: Farmhouse destroyed by German guns during the fighting on the Aisne.

which he was appointed commander, emphasised the fact that even where the Fleet did not lend a hand visibly, operations on shore could only be carried on under its protecting arms. The brilliant naval correspondent of the "Times" pointed out that, as a matter of history, in all our wars for many centuries past the Navy directly and materially helped the Army. "Seamen and Marines," he said, "have acted side by side with their soldier comrades, and in many instances miles and miles inland, and far from their natural element. Men who joined to fight by sea, whose instincts were permeated by salt water, who had been carefully trained to handle and work the ship's guns, threw everything nautical aside except their experience and discipline, and landed to act as artillery and infantry.

"In any consideration of the use to be made of naval brigades on shore it is essential to remember that the ships of the Fleet must never be so weakened by withdrawals from their crews as to leave them unable to fight at sea. The needs of the Fleet must be the first consideration. There have been occasions, both in our own history and that of other nations, when this vital principle has been forgotten. On this occasion, however, no such mistake will be made. We have it in Mr. Churchill's words that only 'If at any time the naval situation becomes sufficiently favourable to enable this force to be definitely released by the Admiralty for military duty, it will be handed over to the Army.'

Conditions of naval co-operation on land

"There is ample precedent for the movement which is now going forward so well. As early as Elizabethan times sailors were frequently employed on shore to assist the soldiers in attacks upon fortified towns, and it is related

BRITISH BATTERY IN ACTION AGAINST THE GERMANS ON THE AISNE.

The British guns were placed against a background of trees, and so were partially screened from the enemy's fire, and also from observation by German aircraft.

VIEW OF THE BATTLE AREA NEAR BRAISNE.

The outskirts of Braisne are to be seen on the right. In the distance is the village of Chassemy, over which the enemy's high-explosive shells were bursting. Over the road shown in the picture and through Chassemy British supply columns passed nightly to the foot of the distant hills. Inset: French dragoons and British infantry moving forward to attack the German right flank on the Aisne.

how on more than one occasion the experienced and careful sea commanders divided their men into companies and drilled them in land formations before using them for this purpose. Although the joint expedition sent to the West Indies by Oliver Cromwell was not a success, the sailors from Admiral Goodson's fleet proved themselves, as seamen have frequently since, the handy men who could be relied on to be handy, not only in a battle, but in those other qualities required when a proper corps of sappers or the regular commissariat and transport arrangements of an army were wanting. It will be remembered that Collingwood, when employed with a naval brigade in America, described his work as 'supplying the Army with what was necessary for them.'

Past services of marines on land

"In Stuart times the Marines were established, and there can be no question that they were designed, at least in part, to provide small-arm men which could be landed in case of necessity, and would have some knowledge of warfare on shore. In later times the Marines have over and over again been called upon to assist their comrades of the land service. A naval brigade of which Marines formed a large proportion was mainly instrumental in taking Gibraltar, although the seamen also played a part in this affair. Our Indian Empire, moreover, is the gift of sea-power, not only because if we had been beaten at sea the victories on shore would have been useless, but because associated with the soldiers there were naval brigades. Often during the varying fortunes of our arms

GUNS OF A HOWITZER BATTERY OF THE R.F.A. IN ACTION DURING THE BATTLE OF THE AISNE.

To counteract the effects of the heavy guns brought down to the Aisne from Maubeuge by the Germans, the British artillery was reinforced by four 6-inch howitzer batteries, specially sent out for the purpose at the request of Sir John French.

FRENCH DEFEAT THE GERMAN IMPERIAL GUARD IN A VILLAGE WHICH CHANGED HANDS FOUR TIMES.

The village of Sommesous, shown in Mr. Sydney Adamson's spirited drawing, is on the railway between Troyes and Chalons, about eighteen miles south of the latter town, and about ten miles east of Fère Champenoise. In the fighting between the German Imperial Guard, under the Crown Prince, and the 36th and 236th Regiments of French infantry, the village changed hands four times. The church and the adjacent houses were reduced to ruins before the place was finally taken by the French. The above drawing was examined by a French general and a number of Staff officers, and received the official approval of the French Etat-Major. Some of the German soldiers seen on the left of the picture are without the cloth coverings to their helmets, having lost them during the fighting.

in the East, the Army was supplied with its artillery and siege-guns from the ships. When the Navy placed guns of position at the Army's disposal for use before Ladysmith it was by no means a novelty in our sea annals.

"Everyone will remember in this connection Nelson's assistance to the land forces at the sieges of Bastia and Calvi. There, as elsewhere, the seamen showed themselves capable of doing the work required of them with whatever was handy. Their sea training enabled them to make shift when the requisite means were unavailable. Of course, behind the capabilities and adaptability of the seamen were the energy and determination of the commander. And all this work went forward under the sure shield of Hood's fleet. In later times, Captain Peel's men in the Mutiny, Rawson's Benin Expedition, Seymour's dash for Peking, and many other occasions when our sailors have formed naval brigades, and have performed duties on land with credit to themselves and country, will occur to everyone. Nor should it be forgotten that in the war of 1870 it was the French sailors who manned the guns of Paris, and that Admiral Jaureguiberry formed a brigade of seamen which did excellent service in the Army of the Loire.

"As we have looked to naval brigades in past times, so we must again avail ourselves of their assistance in our hour of stress."

A GERMAN BATTERY TRYING TO ESCAPE THE SEARCHLIGHT.
In the Aisne district the country is devoid of hedges, and is intersected by roads that dip into hollows here and there, and then run across open, exposed tracts of land. The German battery in our picture was endeavouring to move under cover of the darkness when it was detected by searchlight of the Allies, and made the most frantic efforts to escape from the ghostly beam

At the conclusion of the operations on the Marne, M. Millerand, the French Minister for War, sent from Bordeaux the following cordial message to Lord Kitchener:

"I have much pleasure in sending you, by the desire of General Joffre, the following telegram:

"'The Commander-in-Chief of the French Armies expresses to Lord Kitchener his warm thanks for the constant support given by the British force to our Army throughout the whole of the operations.

"'At the present moment this support is particuliarly valuable, and it is being manifested in a most energetic manner in the battle actually in progress against the German right wing.

General Joffre's thanks to Lord Kitchener

"'I express my deep gratitude to Field-Marshal French, who has constantly given to our armies the most effective co-operation.'

"Allow me, in the name of my Government, to add to General Joffre's thanks the expression of my gratitude."

Lord Kitchener replied as follows:

"Kindly accept and transmit to General Joffre my warmest thanks for the telegram which you have been so kind as to forward to me.

"I wish to assure you and, through you, General Joffre, with what satisfaction the British Army finds itself co-operating with the French Army, and how proud we are of being able to render that assistance of which you speak in such generous terms, and upon which you can always rely with full confidence."

The French Legislature did not prolong its session after the transfer of the Government from Paris to Bordeaux. But parliamentarians refused to disband, and Bordeaux came to be known as Paris by the Sea. In Paris itself there was on September 10th a great patriotic demonstration, when the flag of the 94th German Infantry, captured two days before near Senlis by Captain de Sannois, of the hussars, was carried in procession to and deposited in the Hôtel des Invalides.

The Paris "Temps" on September 9th printed an account of an interview given to a French journalist by Cardinal Mercier, Archbishop of Malines, in which his Eminence presented a terrible picture of the misery suffered by his unhappy country as the result of the German invasion. "As I travelled through Belgium," said the Cardinal, "the spectacle of its unhappiness seemed to tear me back to my devastated Malines, to the side of my King, and of my Suffragan of Liège—to-day hostage, to-morrow perhaps martyr. All along the roads I could see unburied bodies mingled with the carcases of horses. I could recognise some of the faces; here lay one of my fellow-students, and there was a fine young fellow whom I had confirmed. What has taken place in Belgium is not war, but the outcome of hate; the Germans are taking their revenge for the stigma that has been attached to them as violaters of neutral territory. Terrified by their orgy of blood, they imagine that History will forget their shameless infraction of a treaty. These savages, who dare at every step to invoke the name of God, not only attack harmless creatures made in the image of the Deity, but wage war even against the Divinity. In undefended towns, after having bombarded houses, they have given churches to the flames, and they have used the wooden statues on the altars as torches to light them to their deeds of blood. In Malines, a peaceable, undefended town, they made a target of the Church of St. Rombolt; and Louvain, the university town, pride of the Netherlands—the town where, as student and then professor, I knew so many young Italians—Louvain has been burned by the Germans, under the pretext that the inhabitants had fired on the soldiers!

"These bomb-carrying Germans wanted to strike at the head of Belgium. They wished to raze to the ground Belgium's intellectual capital, throwing into the flames alike the contents of the laboratories and libraries. Ought not the word 'Droit'—standing out in letters of gold on the old buildings—to have made them shudder? German deeds in Belgium have nothing to do with war, either of the old days of chivalry or the modern and scientific form. It is an eruption of barbarians into a prosperous, honest, and industrious country. It is a blind ebullition of rage against God, against His temples, against art, sacred or secular and still more against God in the massacre of helpless women and children. When the lake of blood left by the Germans in Belgium has dried up, it will be necessary to look for a slab of stone large enough to be a record of these crimes against the rights alike of Heaven and of humanity. But I will not lose hope. Belgium is brave, and she will rise from her bed of ashes. I shall see that resurrection from the tomb where I shall soon be laid."

IN A GERMAN TRENCH ON THE AISNE.
Many of the German trenches on the Aisne were most elaborately constructed, especially with a view to enabling some of the occupants to rest and smoke while their comrades kept watch and ward.

GERMAN OFFICERS' HUT IN THE AISNE REGION.
The structure looks rather more picturesque than comfortable. It was adorned with a horse-shoe; but if this was meant to bring the occupants good luck, they forgot how it should have been placed, and put it the wrong way up. Inset: A German trench captured after a stiff fight at Villers-Cotterets, showing mangel-wurzel left behind. There was no trace of any other foodstuff.

Was it any wonder that, after such an impassioned outbreak, Hélène Vacaresco, the great Rumanian poetess, should have sent the following sympathetic address to France:

"My thoughts are with you, nameless and distant craftsmen, whose fine churches in France have been destroyed by nameless hordes.

"Nameless, say I! Nay, for they are known as Havoc, Blind Brutality, and Fury; and we picture their devastating numbers as the maddened goddess of Envy, holding a sword in one hand and a lighted torch in the other. She sweeps through the land, and leaves nought but ruin in her wake; even the noblest buildings crumble before her.

"Dear far-off workers of stone and gold, whose souls seem mingled in the walls of the cathedrals, you breathe on us as we pass down the naves, and we are filled with peace and holiness. What must you think of that dishevelled figure and her furies?

Rumanian sympathy with France

"You bequeathed to the world immortal splendours, and had no wish for glory for yourselves. Your work was for God alone; that through it the peoples of the ages to come might see Him as they did, and feel Him in their souls as you felt those brilliant colours of the rainbow, clouds, and sea so well depicted in your stained-glass windows.

"You were quite certain that once that miracle, which needed all your powers and strength, was accomplished, no one on earth could possibly disturb the harmonies of your exalted dreams.

HEADQUARTERS AT BRAISNE OF THE G.O.C. 3rd DIVISION, SECOND CORPS.

On the right is a view of Braisne, where heavy fighting took place between the British and the Germans who had taken shelter in the houses and fired through the shuttered windows. Bertram Stewart, the Scottish Yeomanry officer, who was imprisoned in Germany in 1910 on an espionage charge, was killed in Braisne.

"Till the end of the world the beauties of your marble flowers would be unshaken. The dust of kings would crumble at their feet. Rumours of victories and defeats would hover round them like the murmuring of bees; and still your glorious and Divine work would remain for ever ascending to the heavens with your immortal ideals.

"There are many places now where your souls return from the heavens, where their love has bound them; and I hear them weeping piteously for the glories and the grace that are no more. At Louvain, at Rheims, at Senlis, and even at Arras your indignant souls float over sad and woeful ruins.

"It seems as if civilisation has been destroyed, for amidst the devastated remains loud rise the lamentations of those who even yesterday were numbered amongst the blessed and the happy. But their sanctuaries have been violated and destroyed, they lift up their hands to God and cry their sorrow at His feet; and on all sides appear those who will avenge them."

Another distinguished poet—Belgium's own—Emil Verhaeren, contributed a striking article on the courage and ideals of his fellow-countrymen to "Les Annales," from which may be quoted the following paragraphs:

Emil Verhaeren on Belgian ideals

"However unhappy their fate, the Belgians do not possess the right to lower themselves to complain, nor to dwell on their wretchedness. They owe it to themselves to be worthy of their soldiers, who all of them were heroes.

"That women hunted from their villages, with a troop of children hanging to their skirts, should go lamenting along the high road of hunger, flight, and exile, is a thing one can understand. But men, above all those who think and are capable of will and action, must not echo those cries of pain which have already been heard all too long.

"Formerly, those who in our country dreamt of a greater Belgium did not think of an increase of territory in Europe, nor of the development of an Empire in Africa. They had in view only a Belgian renaissance, which should be both economic and intellectual. They wanted a more and more perfect and active industry, they wanted more and more modern and living thought. They sought for influence, and not for conquest.

"And never since Belgium has existed has this influence been higher. True it is that for the moment our factories are silent, and appear no more to have their panting respiration or flaming breath. Yet no one believes them dead. As soon as the war is ended they will come to life again, like wondrous monsters. Whatever the weight of ash covering them it will seem light to their thousand tentacles, all of which will spread out and find points of support in the restored light.

"We shall be young and ready as we never have been. Up to now danger had not visited our nation. We were too sure of the morrow. We lived like rich people who know not what distress means. War, to our eyes, was an affair for others.

"It has come to us, formidable and ferocious, at a moment when we had no thought of it. Like a mountain, the sides of which fall away to crush us, the compact Empire of William descended upon us. We were alone, few in number. We were attacked treacherously and unfairly. We massed hastily at Liège in old forts. We were compelled to improvise our courage, to invent our resistance, to awaken a new soul in ourselves. All this was done in one day, in one hour, in one instant, and we were the astonishment of the world.

TYPICAL SHELTER IN A VILLAGE NEAR THE AISNE.

The inhabitants of the Aisne villages sought refuge in their cellars from shell fire during the fighting on the Aisne.

"Oh, those never-to-be-forgotten improvisations of valour and glory! Some among us, on seeing our little troopers starting out for the frontier, could not refrain from prophecy.

"They will only be food for cannon. Our Army does not exist, nor our fortresses.

"Four days later, a name unknown the evening before

POSITIONS OF THE RIVAL ARMIES DURING THE CLOSING DAYS OF SEPTEMBER, 1914, LOOKING NORTHWARD FROM THE CITY OF RHEIMS.

Rheims was a city of Gothic towers and modern factory shafts. The cathedral was remorselessly shelled, and the houses all round it were burnt out, but at this time other portions of the city do not appear to have suffered so severely. The River Vesle is seen flowing from the city on the left towards Condé, Missy, and Soissons. Beyond are the heights above the Aisne, averaging some four hundred feet. The British were fighting on the north bank of the Aisne.

was in everybody's mouth. Little boys disguised themselves as General Leman, girls sold his photograph in the streets—a remarkable tactician had compelled the respect of all. Nay, more. Those little troopers were both timid and happy. They doubted still the admirable part they had played ; women kissed them, and we carried them in triumph.

"If we have by our obstinate and manifold resistance enabled France and Great Britain to arm themselves, to organise and save themselves, it is not for us to say it too loudly. But in doing this we have done a still more important thing.

"Our little Belgian soldiers at Liège and Haelen represented an entire past of culture and civilisation. If France incarnates both Greece and Rome, we can affirm that they defended and maintained them at the point where their existence was most threatened. It is owing to this that their act, so simple, suddenly became so great. We need not fear to evoke in comparison with them the memory of Thermopylæ. The fate of the Spartans was similar to that of the people of Liège. A handful of men, just as in olden times, saved the world.

"If we only consider this immense and supreme service rendered to the West, nothing but pride should remain in our hearts. Tears would dishonour us. Let us say to ourselves that Belgium, among all peoples, was chosen in order that one of the highest of human prodigies should be accomplished by her, that she should have the honour of being the first and the most necessary of the ramparts which modern civilisation erected against the ferocity and savagery of a thousand years, and that its history will join that of the rare little nations who will be immortal. Let us say to ourselves again that during these tragic hours we have lived with such intensity that all our past national existence is not worth this sudden and superb minute beneath the lightning stroke. It seems to me as though, before it, we were not even a people. We wore ourselves out in petty quarrels, we disputed about words and not realities, we delighted in schism, we reproached ourselves with our origin, either Flemish or Walloon. We tried to be advocates, merchants, civil servants, without troubling ourselves to be proud and free citizens. The danger has been more wholesome to us than safety. We have discovered ourselves. We have closed up our ranks in such unity of force and courage, we have formed such a square of resistance and tenacity that, in the eyes of some, Belgium dates only from yesterday, and never has she felt herself more rich than at the moment when, deprived of territory, she has nothing but her King by which to know herself and to which to rally."

A superb minute beneath the lightning

By way of confounding contrast may be placed the monstrous views which the Kaiser and his Chancellor attempted vainly to impose on the American people as the truth. Dr. von Bethmann-Hollweg on September 9th addressed a long disquisition to the United States Press against British policy, in which he sought to justify Germany's attitude. He declared that "Great Britain, jealous of Germany's development, and desirous of crushing the Germans by force, would have to accept responsibility for the present war. Britain began an unscrupulous war against Germany, and opened a campaign of lies and calumny. If the German troops had set fire to Belgian villages it was because Belgian women and girls had put

DELIBERATE BOMBARDMENT OF RHEIMS CATHEDRAL BY THE GERMANS.

Rheims Cathedral, over which the Red Cross was flying, was repeatedly shelled by the German gunners in September, 1914. The roof was fired, as was the scaffolding round the north tower. The stone sculptures decorating the interior of the western wall were irretrievably damaged, while the greater part of the facade, the north tower, and the clerestory were calcinated beyond repair. Half the stalls were destroyed. All the wonderful glass in one nave is no more, and that of the apse was greatly damaged. Our photograph was taken during the fire.

out the eyes and cut the throats of German troops billeted on them." In conclusion, the Chancellor said that "the German Emperor had authorised him to make this statement, and to declare that he had full confidence in the American sense of justice."

This tirade was followed up by a telegram sent by the Kaiser to President Wilson of the United States, in which he protested against the alleged employment of dum-dum bullets by the British and French troops. His Majesty, justifying the burning of Louvain, said: "My heart bleeds that such measures should have been unavoidable, and at the thought of the innumerable innocent persons who had lost their homes and their property as the result of the criminal and barbarous actions of the Belgians."

Correspondents of newspapers published in neutral States were invited to attend at the Foreign Office in Berlin on September 8th, and a general there gave an exhibition of dum-dum bullets alleged to have been found on the battlefields where the British and French met the Germans. He intimated that this violation of the Geneva Convention would, in the end, compel Germany to answer the barbarous methods of warfare adopted by her enemies by herself adopting similar measures!

These statements were sent by wireless telegram to Copenhagen and issued there, upon which the British and French Ministers in the Danish capital protested in the strongest language against the German accusation. They declared that dum-dum bullets had no existence so far as the French and British armies were concerned.

A special session of the Parliament of the Union of South Africa was opened on September 9th by Viscount Buxton, the new Governor-General, who had happily arrived the day before at Cape Town. Lord Buxton's first act was to read a personal message from King George acknowledging the many proofs of loyalty displayed by South Africa in common with the rest of the Empire, and of its determination to play a part in the great conflict forced upon Great Britain. The message further stated that his Majesty relied with confidence upon the people of South Africa to maintain and to add fresh lustre to the splendid traditions of courage, determination, and endurance which they had inherited.

General Botha, at the evening session, moved the following resolution: "That this House, fully recognising the obligations of the Union as a portion of the British Empire, respectfully requests the Governor-General to convey a humble address to his Majesty, assuring him of its loyal support in bringing to a successful issue the momentous conflict which has been forced upon him in defence of the principles of liberty and international honour, and of its whole-hearted determination to take all measures necessary for defending the interests of the Union, and co-operating with his Majesty's Imperial Government to maintain the security and integrity of the Empire, and further humbly requesting his Majesty to convey to his Majesty the King of the Belgians its admiration for and its sincere sympathy with the Belgian people in their heroic stand for the protection of their country against the unprincipled invasion of their rights."

South Africa's part in the Great War

The General spoke with the deepest feeling, which commanded the earnest attention of a thronged House. The Imperial Government had, he said, at this most critical time, informed the Union Government that certain war operations in German South-West Africa were considered to be of strategic importance; and that if the Union Government could undertake these operations they would be regarded as of great service to the Empire to which South Africa belonged, and was now involved in one of the greatest and cruellest wars which had ever befallen humanity. To forget, said General Botha, their loyalty to the Empire in this hour of trial would be scandalous and shameful, and would blacken South Africa in the eyes of the whole world. Of this South Africans were incapable. They had endured some of the greatest sacrifices that could be demanded of a people, but they had always kept before them ideals founded on Christianity, and never, in their darkest days, had they sought to gain their ends by treasonable means. The path of treason was an unknown path to Dutch and British alike. In conclusion, the General said he felt it was the duty of South Africa to assist in relieving the sufferings and privations inflicted by the war, and the Government therefore proposed to offer South African products—as mealies, and tobacco for the soldiers, and brandy for medical purposes.

General Botha and the path of treason

Sir Thomas Smartt, Leader of the Opposition, in an impassioned speech seconded the resolution, stating that, in every sense, in the interests not only of the Empire at large, but of South Africa especially, the war should be brought to a successful issue. He was sure that the Prime Minister's speech would send a thrill of pride through the home countries and the whole Empire, at knowing that in the day of danger South Africa had been true to her trust, and had remembered her obligations as well as her privileges of free citizenship.

BRITISH ARTILLERY IN THE AISNE DISTRICT—WAITING TO GO INTO ACTION.
"On former occasions," wrote Sir John French, in his despatch to the Secretary of State for War on October 8th, 1914, "I have brought to your lordship's notice the valuable services performed during this campaign by the Royal Artillery. Throughout the Battle of the Aisne they have displayed the same skill, endurance, and tenacity, and I deeply appreciate the work they have done."

When the House resumed the following day General Smuts delivered an address in Dutch, which was repeatedly punctuated with cheers, in support of the loyal address to the King, and the resolution which had been proposed by the Premier. He reminded the House, in thrilling phrase, that the sufferers from German brutality and ruthlessness were their own kinsmen, the offspring of their common ancestry in Belgium, which was being laid waste, and in France. The people of Belgium and France, with Great Britain, were engaged in a gigantic struggle for the freedom which was so dear to South Africans, and which South Africans had secured through blood and tears. With forceful eloquence General Smuts recalled the Peace of Vereeniging, by which South Africans had secured the fullest liberty, which, thanks to Great Britain, they to-day enjoyed. The Government had ample information in its possession, which for obvious reasons could not be published, that the German Government for years past had had designs on British South Africa, and had contemplated its acquisition. It was against that Government and the German military caste, not against the German people, that South Africa in common with the rest of the Empire was at war.

General Smuts afterwards introduced measures for an additional Loan Appropriation Bill of two millions; for guaranteeing war risks on the importation of foodstuffs; the control of the exportation of foodstuffs; the institution of an advisory banking committee, and the disposal of the output of the gold mines. He added that the Government intended to re-establish the Mint, which would issue gold coins for purely local circulation, while the Currency Bill empowered an increase in the issue of bank-notes. The General, concluding his review of the shrinkage of revenue on account of the war, said that the country would require £7,000,000 for the year 1913-14 on capital account. The Imperial Government had agreed to advance this amount, and the thanks of the country were due to the British Treasury for the way in which they had come to the assistance of South Africa, without which the position would have been serious.

The debate on the Royal address and on the measures introduced by the Government was continued on September 11th, and then both address and the Bills mentioned were passed.

The nine Labour strike leaders who had been deported some months previously were by decision of the Government allowed to return to South Africa; and an amnesty was granted to the men in prison for offences committed during the railway strike in January, 1914.

At Johannesburg on September 10th a number of sticks of gelignite were found on the tracks of different levels of the Luipaardsvlei gold mine, and all German and Austrian miners employed on the property were discharged. A German was also apprehended for being in possession of the component parts of a wireless installation.

With the sanction of Lord Kitchener three hundred Scandinavians and four hundred other foreigners resident in the Transvaal were on September 11th enrolled as a corps for oversea service on the lines of a Foreign Legion, under the command of a Dane named Fredericks.

At this date among the gifts announced from beyond the seas were 1,500 horses from the Government of the Province of Saskatchewan for the use of the Army; from the farmers of New Zealand all the chaff required by the Dominion's Expeditionary Force, while a surplus of 250 tons was sold for the benefit of the war fund. From Melbourne, Australia, 550 cases of goods were despatched to the Red Cross Society, while £1,400 realised by a concert given by Madame Melba was remitted to the same society. The Legislative Council of the Falkland Islands voted £2,250—a sum equivalent to a contribution of £1 per head from every inhabitant—towards the Prince of Wales's National Relief Fund, with an additional sum of £750 privately contributed. The Combined Court of the Colony of British Guiana passed unanimously a resolution asking

Generous gifts from overseas

CROSSING A TEMPORARY FOOTBRIDGE UNDER WITHERING SHELL FIRE AT VAILLY.

Ordered to cross the Aisne at Vailly, in order to secure the high ground north of the river, the 8th British Brigade found that, although the bridge had been blown up by the Germans, they had left in their hasty retreat a small temporary footbridge, with ropes attached all ready for the supports to be pulled away at the last moment. The brigade crossed this fragile structure under a withering shell fire, but, happily, with few casualties.

NORTHAMPTONS TREACHEROUSLY CUT DOWN BY AN AMBUSHED ENEMY.

Some men of the A Company of the Northamptons were engaged with a slightly larger force of the enemy, when the latter held up a white flag in token
Germans had been firing from behind a slight ridge. As our men advanced towards them, one or two laid down their rifles, and then all fell flat on the gr
a second line of Germans rose from behind the ridge and fired over them. The small British line, taken by surprise, were cut down on every side by the do
rifles before British help could arrive.

BRITISH TROOPS RESTING IN A DISUSED QUARRY ON THE AISNE.

As a result of the extensive quarrying in the Aisne district for generations past, the hillsides are honeycombed with caves, which afforded resting-places for our troops between the fighting, store-houses for supplies of all kinds, and occasionally mess-rooms for officers. The floors were strewn with straw to give warmth, and, except for draughts, these caves were found to be fairly comfortable. The caves were also used as shelters by the people of the Aisne villages.

SHORT SHRIFT FOR

Attracted by the moveme
uniform motoring near t
stopped the pair, when
were shot. The sup

THE BRAIN OF THE ARMY PROTECTED FROM GERMAN SHELLS.

On at least one occasion the British Headquarters was established in a subterranean apartment, which was not merely bomb-proof, but, with its ample fireplaces, also provided a most comfortable retreat from the inclemencies of the weather. Here, by lamplight, plans were worked out; the various scraps of information supplied by civilian volunteers and Intelligence Department agents pieced together with the aid of maps, and all the routine work of a Staff performed in comparative security.

ıe
ly
ın

:E BATTLE–FRONT.

d woman in Red Cross
some British soldiers
t they were spies, and
oved to be a man.

BRITISH BURROWS IN THE BATTLE OF THE AISNE.

The above drawing, finished from sketches made in the trench it represents, makes clear the wonderful British defences at the Battle of the Aisne. The surface sheds and roofs of straw made for concealment, and the loopholes at which the defenders were posted gave a clear view of the approaches and the barbed-wire fences erected to prevent a sudden rush attack. The straw covering the floors of the trenches rendered them more or less comfortable for those who were temporarily resting.

WAR LIFE IN A SANDPIT BEHIND THE BRITISH LINES IN THE CHAMPAGNE COUNTRY.

Lance-corporal Jarvis, V.C., R.E., placed it on record that his company spent three weeks on the edge of a deep sandpit, where there were three tiers of "dug-outs," in which the men lived. The place was about fifty yards in the rear of the British lines and trenches. "I myself," he said, "spent eleven days there; and, although we were exposed day and night to showers of shell, we had only one man wounded."

his Majesty's Government to accept from the colony a gift of a thousand tons of sugar produced there. The gift was accepted by the Secretary for the Colonies, Mr. Harcourt, on behalf of the Government, with warm appreciation of the loyal and patriotic action of the colony.

Baron Kato, the Japanese Foreign Minister, authorised on September 9th the following statement to be made regarding the treatment given to Japanese subjects imprisoned or otherwise detained in Germany and Austria: "I am painfully shocked at the news of the most unkind and outrageous treatment accorded to peaceful Japanese residents by the German Government, and the unpardonable discourteous acts of the Austrian people against our Ambassador. These are in striking contrast to the carefully-courteous and magnanimous treatment and the absolute protection of rights which ambassadors and resident Germans and Austrians here (in Tokyo) have been accorded and now continue to receive at the hands of the Government and people of Japan. It is difficult for us to understand how the Governments and people of countries boasting high culture and civilisation should permit the disgrace of their good name by such shamelessly wanton outrages."

On the same date Baron Kato declared to the Russian and French Ambassadors in Tokyo that Japan would not make peace with Germany until the end of the war in Europe. It was explained that it was not necessary for Japan to make any declaration to Great Britain of her adhesion to the declaration in London, inasmuch as the Treaty of Alliance between Japan and Great Britain provides, inter alia, "that the High Contracting Parties will conduct the war in common and make peace in mutual agreement." In the case of France and Russia no such understanding existed, and explanations of Japan's views were consequently made to the French and Russian representatives in Tokyo.

The German Emperor and the General Staff took up their quarters on September 10th at the German Legation in Luxemburg. A large force of Uhlans were encamped round the Legation, and at night it was guarded by aeroplanes which employed searchlights to prevent any hostile airship approaching the town.

The steamer Bethania, which had been acting as a collier to German cruisers in the South Atlantic, especially the Dresden and Karlsruhe, for which she had six hundred tons of coal and six months' provisions, was on September 10th captured and brought to Kingston, Jamaica. There were four hundred prisoners on board, most of whom, according to the Admiralty announcement, formed the crew of the Kaiser Wilhelm der Grosse, who escaped in a collier when she was captured and sunk by H.M.S. Highflyer off the Oro River on the West Coast of Africa at the end of August. Between September 10th and 14th the German auxiliary cruiser Emden captured six British ships in the Bay of Bengal. Five of the vessels were sunk. The other, with all the crews on board, was released and ordered to make for the nearest Indian port.

Sinking of the Kaiser Wilhelm der Grosse

The Nyasaland Protectorate, which for fourteen years—between 1893 and 1907—was known as the British Central African Protectorate, was invaded on September 8th by a force four hundred strong from German East Africa. This force at sunrise on September 9th attacked Karonga, which is the chief station in the northern end of the British Protectorate and the starting point of the Stevenson Road which runs to Lake Tanganyika. The Germans had come from Songwe, their frontier station eighteen miles from Karonga, which was defended by one officer, fifty African rifles and police, and eight civilians. After three hours' resistance a column of the main British force operating in the Protectorate arrived at Karonga, and engaged the enemy, who fought with great determination, and were only finally driven towards Songwe after repeated bayonet charges. The enemy lost seven officers killed and two wounded, two field-guns, and two machine-guns. The number of rank and file of the enemy killed was not ascertained. The British losses included four whites killed and seven wounded. Nyasaland owed its existence to the missionary activity of Dr. Livingstone and the energy of a number of British officials, such as Captain Foote, Sir H. H. Johnston, and Sir A. Sharp in later years. The population is a million, of which less than eight hundred are Europeans. Our Protectorate extends along the whole of the western shore of Lake Nyasa, which lake was shared in common by the British, Portuguese, and Germans.

Fighting in the Nyasaland Protectorate

BEHIND THE SCENES OF THE FIGHTING ALONG THE AISNE.
A posse of German prisoners brought to the grounds of a French chateau under a British guard.

With the Battle of the Marne, described in Chapter XXXIII. as "the turning of the tide," an inspiring and memorable demonstration of British parties comprising every shade of political opinion took place in the London Opera House on the evening of September 11th.

The Marquis of Lincolnshire, President of the National Liberal Club, presided, and with him on his immediate right was Mr. J. F. Remnant, M.P., Chairman of the Constitutional Club, while on the platform were the most conspicuous representatives of the Government and Opposition, and of the Irish National and Ulster parties, members of the House of Commons, bishops of the Church of England and of the Church Catholic, leading Free Church clergymen, the mayors of the metropolitan boroughs, and the members of the Joint Committee of the National and Constitutional Clubs. Quite ten thousand people were eager to hear the call to arms, and overflow meetings were held in the Kingsway Hall and in the open air near by.

At the principal meeting in the Opera House there was an impressive opening ceremony. The band of the Coldstream Guards played in turn the National Anthems of Belgium, Serbia, Russia, Japan, and France, while the

GERMAN ORGY STOPPED BY FRENCH SHELLS OUTSIDE A PLUNDERED INN AT FERE CHAMPENOISE.

Before evacuating Fère Champenoise, some German troops looted the Hotel de Paris. They then tugged a piano-organ into the street and danced to its music, swilling what remained of the beer; for their Headquarters' Staff, after occupying the place for several days, had taken away with them 6,000 francs' worth of champagne. The revelry was rudely shattered by the French, who shelled the Germans out of the position.

whole audience, led by their chairman, stood in their places. His lordship then said that that mighty gathering had assembled to express their admiration of our gallant troops and their brave Allies, and to pledge themselves to reinforce them again, again, and again. A few short weeks ago Germany claimed to lead in culture and enlightenment. That day her name was received everywhere with hatred and execration. Germany's butchery, devastation, and brigandage in Belgium and France, and her cowardly practices at sea, had horrified the whole civilised world. It was the purpose of the meeting to make certain that those barbarities would never be repeated. The Kaiser, called the arbiter of peace in days gone by, would go down to history as a savage incendiary and the dynamiter of Louvain.

The First Lord of the Admiralty, Mr. Churchill, who had a great reception, moved the following resolution: "That this meeting of the citizens of London, profoundly believing that we are fighting in a just cause for the vindication of the rights of small States and the public law of Europe, pledges itself unswervingly to support the Prime Minister's appeal to the nation, and all measures necessary for the prosecution of the war to a victorious conclusion, whereby alone the lasting peace of Europe can be secured." The First Lord began with the dignified assurance that though these were serious times he came there that night in good heart and with full confidence for the future. It was quite clear that what was happening in France and Belgium was not what the Germans had planned. But if the battle had been as disastrous as, thank God! it appeared to be triumphant, he should have come before his vast audience with unabated confidence and with the certainty that we had only to continue in our efforts to bring the war to the conclusion wished and intended, although he admitted it would not be a very easy victory. We had entered on the war reluctantly after having made every effort compatible with honour to avoid being drawn into it. It would be a long and a sombre war, with many reverses of fortune and hopes falsified, but we must derive from our cause, from the strength which is in us, from the traditions and history of our race, and from the support and aid of our Empire all over the world the means to make this country overcome obstacles of all kinds and continue to the end of the furrow, whatever the toil and suffering might be.

Referring to the Navy, the right hon. gentleman said that the war had then been in progress only five or six weeks, and that in that time we had swept German commerce from the seas, had either blocked into neutral harbours, or blockaded in their own harbours, or hunted down the commerce destroyers of which we used to hear so much, and from which the enemy anticipated such serious loss and damage to us. All our ships, with inconsiderable exceptions, were arriving safely and punctually at their destinations. We were transporting easily, not without an element of danger, but safely and successfully, great numbers of soldiers across the seas from all quarters of the world to be directed upon the decisive theatre of the land struggle. We had searched the so-called German Ocean without discovering the German flag; and there was no reason why we should not keep the same process of naval control and have the same exercises of sea-power on which we had lived and are living. By one of those dispensations of Providence, which appeals so strongly to the German Emperor, the nose of the bull-dog had been slanted backwards so that it would breathe with comfort without letting go. In the next twelve months the number of great ships that would be completed for this country would be more than double the number completed for Germany, and the number of cruisers three or four times as great.

Why the nose of the bull-dog was slanted

Having been supported by Mr. F. E. Smith, K.C., M.P., and Mr. Will Crooks, M.P., the resolution was adopted by acclamation at all three meetings.

BRITISH SOLDIERS ON GUARD IN A VILLAGE ON THE AISNE.

CHAPTER XXXVII.

HOW THE BRITISH ARMY CROSSED THE AISNE.

Zwehl Hastens from Maubeuge to Stop the Gap in the German Lines—Field-Marshal von Heeringen comes from Lorraine to Help Kluck and Bülow—German Position on the Plateau of Soissons—British Cavalry Clear the Hills by the Aisne—Our Army Crosses the River under a Terrific Bombardment—Bridges Blown Up as Soon as Pontoons are Floated—Battalions Cross on Rafts and Rowing Boats—Checks at Venizel, Missy, Vailly, and Chavonne—Sir Douglas Haig Discovers Gap in Enemy's Defences—Our First Division Storms the Heights of the Aisne—The Great Fight Round the Sugar Factory—Dominating Artillery Positions Won—British Army Reinforced—Tremendous German Counter-Attacks—Wonderful Charge by the Northamptons—Our Troops Cling on the Slopes and Save the Situation—Deeds of Heroism in the Darkness—A Highlander Routs a German Column and Holds a Bridge.

WHILE the main French armies, with the British force, were breaking the German advance along the Marne River, the frontier fortress of Maubeuge was engaging the attention of General von Zwehl and the Seventh Reserve German Army Corps. No one knew it at the time, but the fate of all the armies of invasion depended on what was happening at Maubeuge. If the Maubeuge garrison could have but held out a couple of days longer than they did, the German retreat to the Aisne valley would have been changed into a disastrous and overwhelming rout.

Unhappily for the Allies, the heavy Krupp siege-howitzers shortened in a surprising manner the period of resistance of Maubeuge. The mighty German siege train, with its mobile howitzers sending down 11 in. shells from concealed positions on the Belgian border, completely battered in the circle of armour-plated concrete forts. For the French at that time seem to have relied too much on the delusive lesson of Port Arthur, and in spite of the teaching of their famous commander, General Langlois, they had not protected Maubeuge by open-air earthworks, with moving guns, as they had protected Verdun. By September 6th the forts were smashed, and in places only a hole in the ground showed where they had existed. The next day Maubeuge was taken.

This was the very day when Kluck, in his new position to the south-east of Paris, recognised that he was imperilled. Both Kluck and Bülow seem to have lent some of their heavy artillery to Zwehl to help him reduce Maubeuge. As Zwehl also had the great siege train prepared for the reduction of Paris, he became, in spite of the comparative small number of his available troops, the only possible saviour of the defeated armies. Could he get the big guns up in time to prevent the German retirement from becoming a rout?

Zwehl was a veteran of the 1870 war—a white-haired, heavy-jawed fighting man, with an iron will. It was on September 8th that he learned the main German armies were breaking. He collected 9,000 reserve troops, which were soon strengthened by 9,000 more. So, with about a division, he marched for four days and three nights southward to the help of the threatened German western wing. He had to bring his siege-guns to the cathedral city of Laon, overlooking the Aisne valley and the plateau to which Kluck and Bülow were retiring.

Zwehl worked his men and horses in a tremendous way. In the last twenty-four hours of marching, his eighteen thousand troops are said to have covered forty miles. They arrived at Laon at six o'clock in the morning of Sunday, September 13th, and within an hour they were in action. By holding their ground until some twenty-two thousand reinforcements arrived they saved the German lines from being completely broken. They lost over 8,000 men, but, for the time, saved Germany. Over Zwehl, directing all the operations, was Field-Marshal von Heeringen, commander of

BRITISH BIPLANE IN FLIGHT GUARDING A SUPPLY CONVOY.

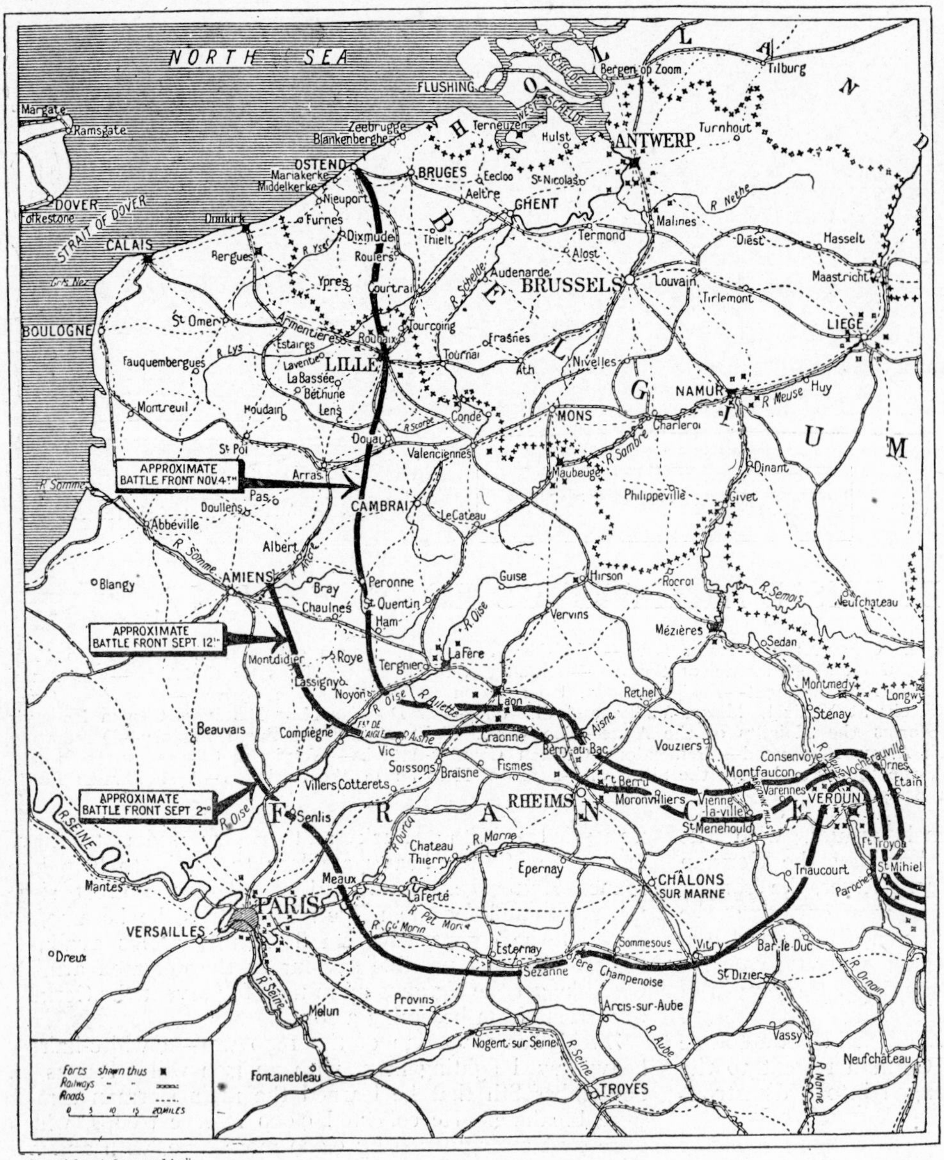

Copyright: "Geographia."

MAP INDICATING THE APPROXIMATE POSITIONS OF THE WESTERN BATTLE-LINE BETWEEN SEPTEMBER 2ND AND NOVEMBER 4TH, 1914.

the Seventh German Army from Metz. Kluck was reduced to a very subordinate position, though the Allies did not know it at the time. They had completely beaten his men in their terrible pursuit from the Marne to the Aisne heights. Bülow's troops were in no better condition for fighting. Hausen's army was smashed and panic-stricken, and the Duke of Würtemberg's troops were worn out and demoralised. Their rearguards were fleeing without a fight. It was Heeringen, with something like a quarter of a million of fairly fresh troops coming from the north of Verdun, and Zwehl, arriving from Maubeuge with the great siege train designed for the reduction of the Paris fortifications, that held together the fatigued, drenched, and dispirited host of beaten invaders.

Kluck had done his utmost by Friday, September 11th. By this time he had got most of his artillery over the Aisne River, at Soissons, and dragged most of his men up the heights north of the stream. At all important points south of the Aisne he posted strong rearguards to delay the advance of the allied forces, while he prepared to make a stand on the plateau above Soissons. But though by the most arduous exertions he had kept his retreating troops intact, the condition of his infantry was prophetic of complete disaster. The men were utterly worn out. Only their artillerymen with the heavy German guns were able to retard the flanking movement of the Sixth French Army under General Maunoury. Even the heavy German field-guns could not keep back the British force. For our men also had heavy guns and howitzer batteries, and in the two rearguard actions against the British advance on September 10th and 12th the Germans lost about forty-eight guns as well as some 4,000 men.

If the French armies had been as well provided with heavy artillery as was the British force, the retreating German western wing might have been driven from its main line of communication. This consisted of the trunk railway running from Cologne to Liège and Namur, to Maubeuge, St. Quentin, and Noyon. Unhappily for the cause of the Allies, the position which the Germans occupied in the defence of the railway was very strong. They fixed their headquarters at the old cathedral town of Laon, lying on a great hill that fell away in wooded slopes sinking southward into broad valleys that rose again in a long, forested plateau along the Aisne.

This plateau was the supreme barrier to any further advance by the victorious Franco-British armies. It was the strongest natural fortress in Northern Europe, and it had been studied by the Germans with particular care for a century. For there the Prussian army, under Blücher, had beaten off the French army, under Napoleon, in the campaign of 1814. Napoleon, like Joffre, had won a great series of battles on the Marne against the Prussians, but, by retreating to the plateau of Soissons, Blücher managed to turn the tables on the famous French commander.

This was the achievement that Heeringen hoped to repeat in similar circumstances in 1914. Many of the finest Prussian troops were under his command; he had a lively knowledge of Blücher's tactics, and the German Military Staff had done everything possible to facilitate the defence of the heights. Some of the chief quarries near Soissons had been especially worked by German firms in peace time, with the result that positions had been prepared and every yard of the plateau carefully mapped out for artillery fire. Germans engaged for years in businesses at Soissons and Rheims were at hand to advise about details of the ground, and help in laying out the entrenchments and gun-sites. Employees in these German businesses—some of them Frenchmen of a scoundrelly sort ready to betray their country—were scattered about the country south of the Aisne River, and provided with secret underground telephone communications, by means of which news of the movements of the French and British troops could be sent to the German Staff. Near Rheims, for instance, were two spies—man and wife—who lived in a detached house, fitted with a telephone that communicated with the German lines. The man was a Frenchman who had got into trouble with the police, and had then been

Prepared German gun-sites at Soissons

VIVID CAMERA RECORD OF A DRAMATIC MOMENT DURING THE BATTLE OF THE AISNE.

The above vividly interesting photograph was taken by a British officer at a moment when a shell was passing over a high road during the Battle of the Aisne. The alarm of men and horses is very clearly depicted in their attitudes, and the whole scene conveys to us a remarkable impression of the reality of modern warfare. Inset: Loading up supplies for the troops in the firing-line. The supply waggons went out nightly from the rear to the trenches, which were on the distant hills just over the Aisne.

engaged as a casual messenger by a German wine firm at Rheims. He had a store of red and blue rockets, which he let off in a neighbouring wood—the red to indicate that an ammunition convoy was arriving in the lines of the Fifth French Army, the blue to show that the French troops were moving. The villain also spied on two French batteries near his house, and telephoned to the Germans the various ranges, elevations, and general working of the guns. He thus rendered the fire of the batteries quite ineffective. He was often visited by a German officer who had also worked as a foreman in the German wine firm at Rheims, and came in the disguise of a French sergeant to obtain fuller reports.

Such was the system of espionage organised throughout the country occupied by the allied armies when they faced the Germans entrenched on the plateau of Soissons. The plateau lies about midway between Paris and the French frontier. It extends for some thirty-seven miles, from the Forest of the Eagle, near the cathedral city of Noyon in the west, to the hill town of Craonne, above Rheims, in the east. It is a flat, high tableland, cut into a wide, deep valley by the River Aisne, and further eroded by the brooks that have worn a series of steep ravines and valleys in its southern slopes.

Organised German espionage

The ravines divide the high land by the river into a number of natural bastions that all join on to the main long wooded ridge that towers some four hundred and fifty feet in places above the broad, low stream. The entire plateau thus formed a great, flattish embankment on which guns and howitzers could be placed, safe from aerial observation, in the trees, so as to dominate the Aisne River. Then, protecting the gun positions from infantry attack, were the outlying spurs, steep and wooded and hard to climb, where brigades of riflemen, with machine-guns and light artillery, swept the river crossings and defended the approaches.

All the natural difficulties that Napoleon had vainly contended against in his disastrous attack on Blücher were enormously enhanced by the highly increased power of modern artillery and long-range small firearms. Our troops were faced with the most tremendous and perilous task that men have ever been called on to carry out. They had to storm, by a direct frontal attack, the high, fortified positions of the First and Second German Armies. They had no heavy siege-artillery, such as General von Zwehl was hurrying to the assistance of Von Kluck and

BRITISH GUNS BEING FIRED FROM A CONCEALED POSITION ON THE FOE IN HIDDEN TRENCHES ON THE AISNE.

This picture brings home to us the vast difference between modern war conditions and those of only comparatively recent times. Quite a number of our wounded returned from the Battle of the Aisne without seeing a single German combatant. The struggle on the Aisne developed very quickly into a big-gun duel between concealed artillery. As the trenches on both sides were also hidden, the only visible signs of fighting, apart from the dead and wounded, were the puffs of smoke in the air. The guns shown in our picture were placed advantageously on high ground.

Von Bülow. They were also outnumbered in machine-guns. In order to get within rifle range of the hidden masses of foes entrenched on every wooded scarp and ravine cliff they had to cross a river valley, broadening from half a mile to two miles, and next bridge the Aisne River, a hundred and seventy feet wide. All this had to be done under a terrific, incessant fire of shell and shrapnel. When the river was at last bridged with pontoons, they had to climb the spurs, with Maxims and innumerable rifles blazing at them at short range, while howitzers on the plateau raked them with a cross fire.

It was not a battle of man against man. It was a one-sided contest between eighty thousand young British athletes and a gigantic, systematised, and long-prepared machine of war, forged by Krupp and other Teutonic armament firms, with a hundred and forty thousand riflemen, gunners, and cavalrymen behind it. It would have been no disparagement of the courage of our soldiers had they failed to force the passage of the Aisne against such an array of machinery of death. Just on the British right the Turcos, who are among the most fearless souls with mortal breath, were driven back to the ford of Berry-au-Bac. And further westward, in the more level land around Rheims, the German guns blew the Fifth French Army from a very important hill position, and prevented the French for months from retaking it. On the British left the Sixth French Army was, for a time, held up south of Soissons, until our artillery cleared the way for them, and it was hurled back to the river, after almost reaching the plateau.

BRITISH INFANTRY FORCING THEIR WAY THROUGH GERMAN WIRE ENTANGLEMENTS.

Incidents of this kind were numerous during the great siege-battle of the Aisne. The entanglements were laid like snares in the woods and in the open, and carefully aligned so that they could be swept by guns which were invisible from our side of the valley, while the enemy's fire was aided by their searchlights.

But, despite the terrible disadvantages under which they attacked, the British troops not only crossed the valley of death, but seized and held a commanding position on the plateau of Soissons. The British advance began on Sunday, September 12th, with a magnificent piece of work by the Queen's Bays and other cavalrymen of General Allenby's division. Running south-east of the Aisne River was its tributary, the Vesle, which had cut a deep valley in the southern tableland. The Germans held this southern line of heights as well as the northern plateau. They occupied, in fact, all the hilly region of the Aisne, and before our army could attempt to cross the river it had to clear the southern hills. This was done by the cavalry under General Allenby. By one of those swift and sweeping "hussar strokes" that the Germans talk about but seldom achieve, our cavalrymen swept from the town of Braisne, on the Vesle, the strong German detachments that Bülow had thrown out as advance guards. Over the difficult high wooded ridge between the Vesle and the Aisne the beaten German forces were driven by the British horsemen, with the assistance of the infantry and gunners of the 3rd Division under General Hamilton. By the evening of Saturday, General Hamilton's men were able to bivouac below the hill of Brenelle, after getting their guns on that height, from which they could reply to the German batteries hidden in the ridge across the Aisne.

Brilliant British cavalry work

The 5th Division, under Sir Charles Fergusson, dragged its guns to the neighbouring height of Ciry, and marched down the western bank of the Vesle to the main river. The valley of the Aisne was some two miles broad round the front where the valley of the Vesle opened into it, and here it was that the British force first got into difficulties. For the waters of the two rivers had worn away the tableland only on the northern side, leaving a great stretch of flat-bottomed land over which our guns had to fire. On the northern side, held by the Germans, the steep spurs came close to the water's edge, so that the enemy's light artillery and machine-guns could fire at short range at our troops, while the German heavy guns also caught our men on both flanks when they crossed the river.

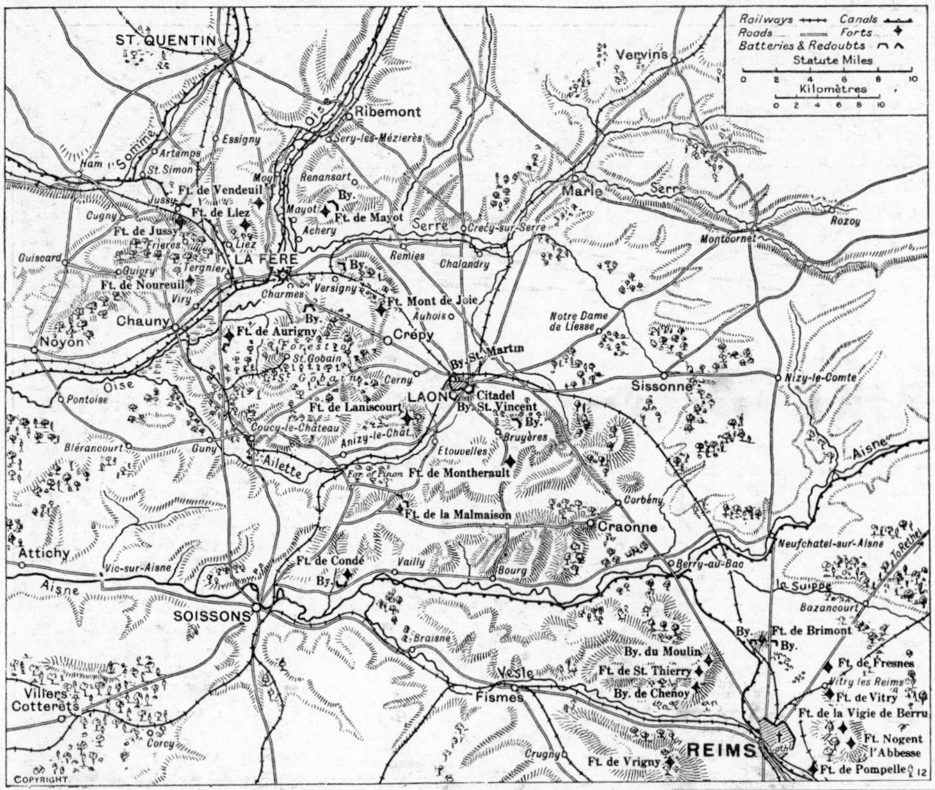

George Philip and Son.

MAP OF WESTERN AREA OF THE AISNE BATTLE-GROUND.

The map shows the plateau held by the German right in the Aisne fighting. The plateau slopes upwards in a north-east direction to the crest of the line of heights that looks down on the plains stretching to the Argonne, and known as the Falaises de Champagne.

where the Crown Prince's army was operating.

In the new disposition of the army of invaders there was one weak spot. Moreover, practically all the troops were dead tired and approaching complete demoralisation. In the open country between Rheims and the Argonne Forest, where their entrenchments were hastily made, they showed, under French artillery fire, something like panic. On the other hand, the allied troops, though victorious, were at least equally fatigued. The French had been fighting with extraordinary exertions, doing double work in many cases, assailing one German army in front, then taking another on the flank, and finally pursuing the retreaters. The British Expeditionary Force had not had a single day's rest since the opening of the Battle of Mons. For three weeks the men had marched and fought, till their feet were bleeding and

So confident were the Germans of repulsing a British attack at this point that they left a bridge at Condé, near the meeting of the waters of the Vesle and the Aisne. Nearly every other bridge they destroyed, but they preserved the bridge at Condé, partly as a lure to induce Sir Charles Fergusson to attack them at the spot where their means of defence was strongest, and partly as a sallying path along which they intended to sweep down on our troops when our men had been compelled to retreat. Even on Saturday the fierce opposition which all the Second Army Corps, under Sir Horace Smith-Dorrien, encountered on either side of the Condé bridge showed that the Germans were prepared again to offer battle. For both Fergusson's 5th Division and Hamilton's 3rd Division, composing together the Second Army Corps, met with a strong resistance on the afternoon of September 12th.

Field-Marshal von Heeringen's achievement

The fact was that the armies of Kluck and Bülow had been united for the defence of the plateau of Soissons, under Field-Marshal von Heeringen, hastily sent from the country round Verdun, where he had been assisting the Crown Prince with the Seventh German Army from Metz. The situation round Verdun was too ticklish for any considerable part of the Seventh Army to be detached and sent to reinforce Kluck and Bülow's troops. But Heeringen, reputed to be one of the most stubborn and brilliant of German fighters, appears to have justified his reputation. He lined out Kluck and Bülow's men on the heights from Noyon to Craonne, called in the forces occupying the country far to the west round Amiens, and placed them on his flank at Peronne and Saint Quentin. He brought down by rail troops from Belgium. He reorganised the broken Saxon army, and retiring the Duke of Würtemberg's beaten and weary troops from Rheims, settled them on the low swell of land running from the eastern end of the Soissons plateau, along the River Suippes to the middle of the Forest of Argonne.

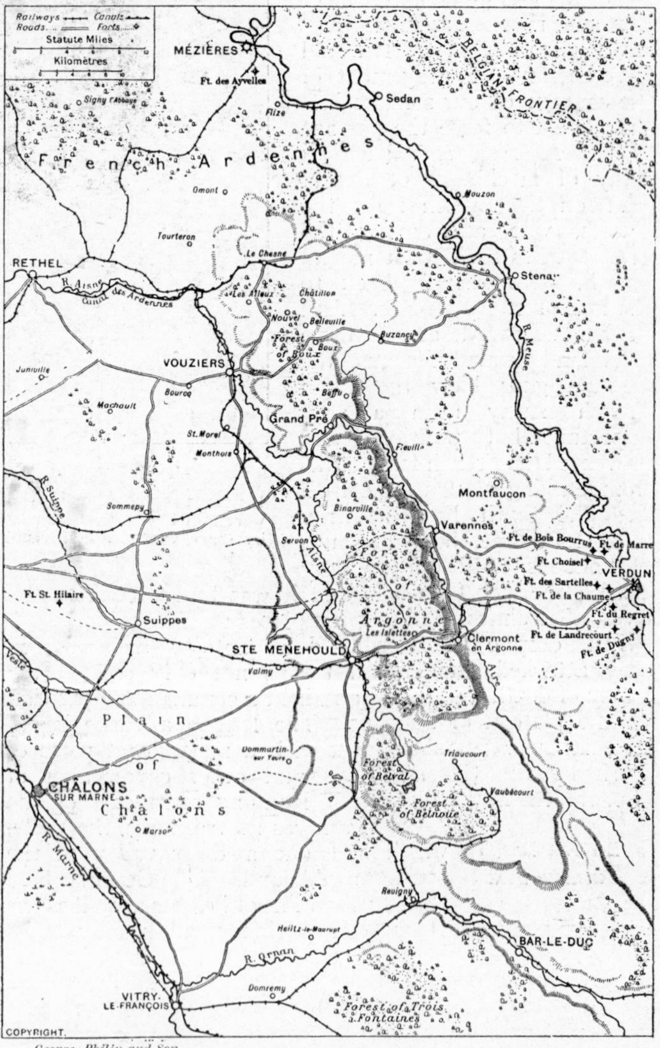

George Philip and Son.

MAP OF EASTERN AREA OF THE AISNE BATTLE-GROUND.

The Argonne is famous in French history as the natural barrier behind which French armies have resisted invasions from the eastward. It faces the gap between Verdun and the Belgian frontier. Possession of the plateau by the French threatened the line of German retreat.

"SEARCHLIGHT" FIRED FROM A GUN: A PARACHUTE LIGHT-BALL SHELL.

The above picture illustrates an ingenious Krupp device for warfare in the dark—the firing of shells enclosing a powerful illuminant, with parachute attachment. Within the shell was a folded-up parachute, which dropped when the shell burst, while clockwork mechanism suspended below lighted the illuminant. This illuminant remained in the air for several minutes.

BRITISH LOG-ARTILLERY DRAWS THE GERMAN FIRE.

Whenever German airmen saw a masked battery of allied artillery they dropped smoke bombs on it to indicate its position to their own gunners. In this picture an enemy aeroplane is seen flying away after dropping some of these bombs, the smoke from which is seen rising in two streaks. However, instead of being a real battery, it was a dummy one constructed of logs and wheels, screened among bushes. The enemy thus wasted their shells on it. Meanwhile the genuine battery was concealed in a wood and making ready to reply. Immediately in the foreground is one of the Aisne quarries, from which our men were watching the effect of their ruse.

their faces haggard for want of sleep. A sense of victorious power kept them going, and man for man they were still ascendant over the German soldiers they had driven half-way back to the French frontier. But so skilfully did Heeringen place the overpowering force of artillery belonging to the First and Second German Armies, that, save for one defect, the plateau of Soissons was almost as impregnable as Gibraltar.

The German field-marshal did not rely on Kluck and Bülow's infantry. They almost tumbled with fatigue into the trenches they made on the wooded heights above the Aisne. While they rested and snatched sleep in turns, the German gunners protected them and saved the situation. By the time the German infantrymen were badly needed as a guard to the dominating guns they had fairly recovered from their exertions. Meanwhile, their artillerymen held the field, and, owing to their remarkably advantageous position, they at first turned the Battle of the Aisne into the terrible kind of machine-made warfare which had for years been the ideal of the German Military Staff. Each battery of light field-guns operated, under a fire-control officer, in conjunction with well-placed pieces of heavy artillery. Together, they poured from the forested ridge a direct fire into the river valley.

Situation saved by the German gunners

Then at some distance behind the ridge, on the slopes falling towards Laon, were the batteries of howitzers that could shower their shells and shrapnel over the plateau by high-angle fire. Field-telephones linked these howitzers with the fire control of the direct-shooting guns on the ridge, so that a double hurricane of high-explosive shells could be directed against each assailing column that tried to cross the Aisne. Close to the river, on the spurs mirrored in the water, observation officers were perched in the trees, from which telephone wires, strung from trunk to trunk, connected them with the fire-control centres. Some of the observation officers were also in secret communication with spies in the British lines, and could direct the long-range German guns against distant and apparently invisible masses of our troops.

Heeringen's plan was identical with that which Blücher had adopted against Napoleon. He intended to let the Sixth French Army, operating west of Soissons, the British Expeditionary Force, advancing between Soissons and Bourg, and the Fifth French Army, driving on towards Craonne and Berry-au-Bac, shatter themselves against the defence of the famous plateau. Then, with the German guns playing on the dispirited and retreating Allies, Heeringen designed to cross the river again in another great march towards Paris, in which the Franco-British forces would be completely routed, if not enveloped. In the meantime the German infantry was getting some rest in the trenches, and large reinforcements were on the way to strengthen them for the grand counter-attack.

Second march on Paris planned

Sir John French, however, was not the man to allow an enemy to win any advantage from his hesitation. While doing all he possibly could in the circumstances to give the British troops enough rest to carry them farther, Sir John acted with swift and decisive vigour. Saturday night was a night of labour for his engineers and many of

HUGE SHELLS BURSTING HARMLESSLY IN A BRITISH TRENCH.

In the British trenches along the Aisne huge 200 lb. German howitzer shells came crashing down in some places at the rate of one every two minutes. They made great craters where they fell, but the soft, claylike soil absorbed their energy, and our men soon got accustomed to them, and christened their effect "the mud bath." In the trench shown above, no one was seriously injured after three hours' furious shelling, even the soldier seen on the right, knocked over by an explosion, was only half-smothered with Mother Earth.

his gunners, and some of the troops had to do entrenching work. All the guns were got into position in accordance with the commander's plan for the coming battle, and the ground was dug in the widest part of the valley as cover against the German fire. Sections of the bridge trains belonging to the First and Second Army Corps pushed on towards the river in the darkness, and at daybreak the great attempt to force the passage of the Aisne was begun.

Sir John French had no means of ascertaining in what strength the enemy held the opposite plateau, nor in what manner the enemy's forces were arrayed. But he concluded, from the resistance met with on Saturday afternoon, that there were at least three German army corps opposed to him. That is to say, the enemy had the advantage of numbers as well as the advantage of an extraordinarily strong defensive position. For though there were nominally three British army corps, the Third Corps was incomplete—it lacked two brigades of infantry, and had little more, apparently, than half the artillery of a full army corps.

British reconnaissance in force

There was only one sound way of discovering the enemy's disposition—to attack him vehemently. This reconnaissance in force was made at dawn on Sunday, September 13th. Down to the empty river valley, one of the most beautiful and picturesque scenes in France, where the autumn sunlight was playing on the misty orchards and white villages by the water edge, and the green, quiet ramparts above, the British army advanced in brigades. It had entered the death-trap so carefully prepared for it.

DEATH IN THE BARN: AN INCIDENT IN THE BATTLE OF THE AISNE.

Private G. Drury, of the Northamptonshire Regiment, described a night spent with several other wounded men in a barn which was shelled by the Germans during the fighting along the Aisne. "When the bullet found me it was growing dusk, and as there was little chance of being picked up that night, I started to crawl away." He managed to reach a barn where he found seven other wounded men. Weak from loss of blood, he lay there half-dazed, "until there was a terrific crash, and the whole place seemed to fall in on us. A shell had struck the barn near the door. In the morning the whole place was a wreck, and only two others and myself were alive."

HEROISM OF THE "MUDLARKS"—MURDEROUS WORK ON THE AISNE.

One of the most striking incidents of the long-drawn-out Battle of the Aisne was related by Private J. Green, of the Loyal North Lancashire Regiment. Finding all the bridges had been blown up when the Aisne was reached, the engineers immediately set to work with their pontoons; but the Germans, from a sheltered position, had the range beautifully. "As soon as one raft was got into position the poor fellows were knocked over like ninepins by the murderous fire. When one man fell over into the water another took his place, and the river was full of wounded." Six times was the bridge destroyed before our men were able to get across. "The bravery of the chaps was magnificent."

All along the river for twenty miles, from Soissons to Bourg, our troops went forward. For a while the morning haze veiled the general movement of attack, but by nine o'clock many of our men had come under an incessant gun fire, which they were to endure for a month.

Round Soissons the Third Army Corps, consisting of General Snow's division and the 19th Infantry Brigade, acted for a time with the right wing of General Maunoury's Fifth French Army. The day before, their heavy guns had shelled the Germans from the Mont de Paris, south of Soissons, and thus enabled the Zouaves and Turcos to drive the common foe back on Soissons. Then, when the bridging train of our Third Army Corps arrived, the commander, General Pulteney, sent the engineers to build a pontoon bridge at Soissons for the French troops. It was built under a heavy fire, but destroyed by the terrible heavy German howitzers. The Turcos crossed the river in rowing-boats, and had a fierce struggle in the ancient cathedral city.

Pontoon bridging under heavy fire

Meanwhile the four British infantry brigades, forming General Pulteney's force, struck north-eastward of Soissons, and the leading brigade crossed the river at Venizel. The road bridge there had been blown up by the Germans, but they had not completely wrecked it.

Our sappers quickly repaired it sufficiently to enable the 1st Somerset Light Infantry, the 1st East Lancashires, the 1st Hampshires, and the 1st Rifle Brigade to get over, and some artillery was man-handled over the water. Picking plums as they went along, with shells falling on them, these troops of the 11th Infantry Brigade assembled at Bucy-le-Long at one o'clock on Sunday.

Directly above them was the great hill of Vregny, one of the chief German artillery positions, and along the wooded edge of it were hidden machine-guns. But, in spite of bullets and shrapnel, the 11th Brigade clambered up the slopes, fighting forward for three hours and a half, until the German Maxim fire grew so terrible that they could not make any further headway against it. But the brigade held on to the ground it won. And as by this time a pontoon bridge had been constructed at Venizel, the 10th Brigade—1st Worcesters, 2nd Seaforth Highlanders, 1st Irish Fusiliers, and 2nd Dublin Fusiliers—also got across to Bucy-le-Long, with most of the light field-guns. There was practically no protection at the foot of the plateau against the shells, shrapnel, and bullets poured down on our men; but the 12th Brigade worked over the slopes to the ravine of Chivres, and when night fell some of the troops of the Second Army Corps came up and helped to retain some of the ground won.

Assault of the great hill of Vregny

The Second Army Corps had also had a severe task to gain a footing over the Aisne. Finding that the bridge at Condé was too strongly held to be carried by assault, Sir Horace Smith-Dorrien divided his forces, and with them made two attacks. One was directed at the village of Missy, some two and a half miles west of Condé; the other was launched against the town of Vailly, three miles east of Condé. The 13th Brigade, composed of the 2nd Scottish Borderers, the 2nd West Ridings, the 1st West Kents, and the 2nd Yorkshire Light Infantry, headed Sir Charles Fergusson's 5th Division, in the advance on Missy. The bridge had been blown up by the Germans, who left small bodies of troops at the water's edge to hinder the British advance, while the entrenchments on the spurs and the plateau were being completed. According to a peasant living at Missy, the Germans had already been working sixteen days on fortifying the heights.

A murderous fire was directed on our scouts, and when our engineers tried to throw a bridge across the stream their pontoons and rafts were shelled and wrecked. Our artillery, however, then came fiercely into action, and searched the woods by the river in a terrible manner, so that both the German machine-gun sections and riflemen fell or retreated. In the night some troops were rafted over, three men at a time. They entrenched near Missy, but were subjected to such an overpowering, unceasing gun fire that they had to bide in their dug-outs for the next sixteen days. The West Kents were among the battalions that struggled valiantly into the Missy mouse-traps. In the daytime it was death to show one's head above the trench, for German observation officers were in the trees overhead, directing the guns, and snipers occupied the wooded heights. When our artillery opened fire they retreated, but came back again, and our men were directly under such a heavy cross-fire from the concealed German batteries that they could not advance. It was checkmate for the British at Missy.

Checkmate for the British at Missy

So most of the 5th Division swerved still more westward, and crossed between Missy and Venizel, and helped the men of General Pulteney's advanced columns to hold the ravine of Chivres against a heavy counter-attack. In the meantime the other half of Smith-Dorrien's Second Army Corps had also got into difficulties at Vailly. The 8th Brigade that led the attack was formed of the 2nd Royal Scots, the 2nd Royal Irish, the 4th Middlesex, and the 1st Gordon Highlanders. Roused at three in the morning, in a torrent of rain, the brigade traversed a plank over the canal running by the Aisne, and their engineers threw a pontoon over the river, by which they reached the hostile bank.

AT THE JUNCTION OF THE OISE AND THE AISNE—FRENCH INFANTRY ON THEIR WAY TO ATTACK THE GERMAN RIGHT.

The Oise is flowing towards the right in a south-westerly direction, and the Aisne is on the right, at a point where the two streams join. The confluence is just above Compiègne. In the foreground of our picture French infantry are seen marching along the towing-path of the Oise, making their way in the direction of Ribecourt and Noyon. Shells in the air over the woods and hills beyond the placid streams also indicate the presence of war in a region where, normally, Nature wears her most peaceful aspect.

HOW THE GERMANS DUG THEMSELVES IN ON THE NORTH BANK OF THE AISNE.

The above illustration shows very graphically how the Germans "dug themselves in." They constructed the most elaborate shelters and trenches, deep enough to cover themselves up to their armpits, and to enable them to fire on a level with the ground, with emergency protection against enfilading fire. To conceal the trenches they placed leafy branches in front of them, as shown on the right of the picture, to give the appearance of ordinary clumps of bushes, between the stems of which they fired, the smokeless powder used materially aiding the concealment.

There, however, they were held up by an extraordinary shell fire. The Germans had previously measured all the ranges exactly, and their batteries continued the bombardment for three weeks, just as at Missy. Our troops dug trenches in the north bank, but found themselves, when they settled down, in a terrible position. For by ill-luck some of their trenches were so badly situated that the German guns and Maxims enfiladed them. There was nothing to do but retire as speedily as possible. So it was checkmate for the British also at Vailly.

And at first it seemed as though Sir Douglas Haig, operating still higher up the river with the 1st and 2nd Divisions of the First British Army Corps, would not be more fortunate than General Pulteney and Sir Horace Smith-Dorrien. The Guards Brigade and the 5th Infantry Brigade advanced in forking lines. The Guards—the 2nd Grenadiers, the 2nd and 3rd Coldstreams, and the Irish Guards—went across the valley of death in quick rushes and, crossing the canal at Presles, attacked the German position at the village of Chavonne. But the enemy's machine-guns swept the approaches, and here also the German batteries on the heights had the exact ranges of every object, with observers near the river to telephone each movement of the British troops. Pontoon bridging was impossible, but late on Sunday afternoon one battalion of the Guards rowed over the river in boats, and then beat back the enemy from the bank.

Four miles higher up the Aisne, at Pont Arcy, was a break in the plateau, where a wide ravine ran to a narrow neck of high land. A canal went northward along the ravine and through a tunnel in the neck of the plateau. This was the scene of action of the 5th Brigade—composed of the 2nd Worcesters, the 2nd Oxford and Bucks, the 2nd Highland Light Infantry, and the 2nd Connaught Rangers. The bridge at Pont Arcy had been blown up by the Germans, but one of its broken girders still rose partly from the water. Along the broken girder the men crossed in single file, while the enemy's guns sent shells bursting round them, and the sappers by the afternoon flung a pontoon over, in spite of the bombardment. Towards the evening all the brigade crossed the river and dug themselves in.

So from Soissons to Pont Arcy the British Expeditionary Force, after a terribly trying day, only managed to win a few perilous footholds on the lowest slopes of the great plateau. As the Germans, to the number of 140,000, held the great towering ridge above our men, and held it with heavier artillery and more numerous machine-guns than our army possessed, our position at the foot of their vast, open-air fortress was very chancy and dangerous. For this reason, most of our divisional generals only kept a battalion or two on the northern bank of the Aisne on Sunday night. The battalions formed bridge-heads to secure the crossings that had been gained and prevent the German troops from coming down to the water's edge again. The rest of the troops remained on the southern side of the valley of

BRITISH MOTOR SCOUTS IN NORTHERN FRANCE.

As the war lengthened the corps of motor-cyclists on service in the field strengthened. In the capacity of despatch-riders and scouts our motor-cyclists rendered splendid help, their dash and mobility alike enabling them to supplement cavalry work in many important directions.

slaughter. This was a triumph for the German gunners. They had defeated all our attempts between Soissons and Pont Arcy to carry any outlying part of the ridge by storm.

Yet the pressure our men exerted with such stubborn bravery made a deep impression on the German commander. His troops, though concealed on the wooded slopes, had apparently suffered as heavily as ours. For our artillerymen had been working all day long searching the green scarps and forested hills with a furious fire. So Field-Marshal von Heeringen withdrew at night his main infantry force to the topmost ridge, where a road known as the Chemin des Dames, or Lady's Walk, ran at a height of six hundred and fifty feet on the top of the plateau, two miles north of the Aisne River. Strongly entrenched detachments of German riflemen however, were still left in commanding positions on the lower jutting slopes, with powerful artillery to support them. There they could have held back any British advance in force until the heavy German guns and howitzers on the ridge massed their fire and slaughtered our troops in thousands. The guns indeed did in the end bring down some ten thousand of our men, but the expected British retreat from an untenable position, which Heeringen designed to convert into a rout, did not take place.

GENERAL VON ZWEHL.
He brought up the big German guns from Maubeuge to the Aisne

FRENCH TRENCHES ON THE FLANK OF A HILL NEAR SOISSONS.
At certain points along the line of battle in Northern France the French constructed alignments, which were dug into the hillside in the manner shown above. These dug-outs served as resting-places for the soldiers. They were for the most part constructed in superimposed rows, with steps leading down to the valley below.

For though most of the British army failed to win a secure position on the plateau of Soissons, there was one weak spot in the German line of defence, and by ordering a general reconnaissance in force, Sir John French discovered this weak spot by Sunday evening. While Sir Douglas Haig's 2nd Division was battling against superior forces at Pont Arcy and lower down the river, his 1st Division, under Major-General Lomax, had an amazing success. Less than two miles east of Pont Arcy the canal from the north was carried over the River Aisne on an aqueduct near the village of Bourg. The 1st Division was supported by the Cavalry Division, under General Allenby, thus forming some 20,000 men, which was the strongest fighting force that Sir John French concentrated on one point of attack along the valley. The British commander had, of course, good reasons for massing men in this manner on his extreme right wing. His scouts had found the position at Bourg was weakly held by the Germans. So where the enemy was weakest Sir John French struck hardest. All his other operations served the purpose of fully engaging Heeringen's forces as far as Soissons, and eastward of that city the furious attack of the Sixth French Army compelled the German commander to put out all his strength to resist it. And on our right the Fifth French Army was engaging the enemy strongly.

There was a gap in the German defences round Bourg, and General von Zwehl's men, marching to fill it, were still a day away. The result was that Sir Douglas Haig, who personally directed the advance of his 1st Division and General Allenby's cavalry, made remarkable progress. At first things went as badly as elsewhere on the river. By means of a small pontoon bridge, some of the infantry crossed east of the canal bridge. A brigade of cavalry started to follow them. When, however part had got across, the enemy opened fire on three sides—rifles, Maxims, field-guns and howitzers. The cavalrymen reached the town across the river, and tried to ascend the spur held by the Germans. But they could not advance against the bombardment, which set on fire the town behind them. They asked the infantry entrenched by the town for the needed help. No, the infantrymen could look after themselves. So, by the pontoon swept by the German guns and howitzers and rifles, the cavalry retired. By a marvellous chance they had no man killed and only a few wounded, yet they had been operating for three hours on the hostile side of the Aisne.

The main forces of the 1st Division were still more fortunate. Meeting with scarcely any opposition, they crossed towards Bourg over the canal aqueduct and, with the cavalry on its outer flank, drove the enemy back towards the main ridge. By Sunday evening the 2nd Infantry Brigade—composed of the 2nd Sussex, the 1st North Lancashires, the 1st Northamptons, and the 2nd King's Rifles—which were the spearhead of the British army on the Aisne, had climbed more than three-quarters of the way up the ridge, and threw their outposts far in front of the hamlet of Moulins, where they rested. Their commander, General Bulfin, had with him all the light field-guns of the 25th Artillery Brigade, and at daybreak on Monday, September 14th, he roused his troops and again sent them forward.

GENERAL BELIN.
The "right-hand man" of General Joffre.

Some of his officers had scouted ahead at night, in spite of the fatigue of the labours on Sunday, and had discovered that a considerable force of Germans held a beet sugar factory at Troyon, close to the top of the plateau and the Chemin des Dames. So at three o'clock in the morning the Sussex Regiment, the North Lancashires, and the King's Royal Rifles crept up the height and attacked the factory, which had become, like the farm of Hougomont at Waterloo, the key to the position of both armies.

THE DEADLY GAME OF HIDE-AND-SEEK ALONG THE VALLEY OF THE AISNE.
French dragoons with a machine-gun in a field in the vicinity of Soissons. When photographed they were hiding behind some straw on the look-out for a party of German scouts reported to be scouring the neighbourhood.

Had the wet heavy mist that veiled the hills cleared away, our aerial scouts would have seen a long column, with a huge artillery train, hastening from Laon towards the road above the factory. These were General von Zwehl's 18,000 infantrymen, with guns from Maubeuge, coming as fast as their general could drive them up the northern slopes of the plateau to the aid of Bülow's dispirited army on the ridge. Bülow was being attacked eastward at Craonne by the Turcos and French infantry of General Franchet d'Espérey's Fifth Army. Our leading brigades were on the slope of the hill of Craonne, as well as advancing on the height in front of them. Neither Bülow on the east of the tableland nor Kluck on the west could spare men to strengthen the weak German lines round the sugar factory at Troyon. Field-Marshal von Heeringen, directing the defence by field telephones from Laon, had nothing with which to stop the gap when Sir Douglas Haig was striking with all his force.

For when, on Monday morning, Sir Douglas found that General Bulfin's three brigades were not strong enough to storm the sugar factory, he brought up the 1st Brigade round Troyon. The 1st Coldstream Guards joined in the frontal attack upon the former position, while the rest of the 1st Brigade—the 1st Scots Guards, the 1st Royal Highlanders, and the Munster Fusiliers—acted on the left of General Bulfin's force. This was the bold, decisive movement on the part of Sir Douglas that won the day and enabled the British Army to add one more resounding victory to its glorious annals.

During the severe pressure thus brought to bear on the German lines, a party of the North Lancashires captured the sugar factory before Zwehl's men arrived to strengthen the enemy's position at Cerny, on the Chemin des Dames road. By noon on Monday the two advanced British brigades held a straight line near the top of the ridge between the factory and the Chemin des Dames. But as Zwehl's men were arriving north and east of the factory, and using shell fire and Maxim fire against any British attacking force, no further headway could be made. In fact, all the 1st Division was at once hard put to it to maintain the ground they had won. For Zwehl was a fierce, hard, straight hitter of the old Prussian school.

Capture of the factory at Troyon

He sent out reconnoitring patrols to the south-west of Sir Douglas Haig's position on the heights, and discovered

SCENE DURING THE SHELLING OF SOISSONS.
Shell bursting over Soissons, during the bombardment of that place by the Germans. Inset: Entrance to the famous quarries at Soissons, where the Germans entrenched themselves, but were "dug out" by the French.

"HOME FROM HOME" ON THE AISNE.
Comfortable huts of wood, with rush-thatched roofs, were built by the French as rest houses in the intervals of trench work on the Aisne.

UNDER AND ABOVE GROUND ALONG THE AISNE.
Above are two graphic views within and without the French entrenchments along the Aisne. The lower view shows alterations and repairs in progress. Inset is seen a soldier at one of the observation points, from which the enemy's movements could be detected.

in the morning there was a gap between the 1st and 2nd Divisions. Practically all the available men of the 1st Division occupied the ground east of the road running from Bourg to Cerny. The leading brigades of the 2nd Division—the Guards Brigade and the 6th Infantry Brigade—were working up the ravine at Ostel and the valley of Braye, separated from each other by a high hill held by the Germans, and with some seven miles of difficult country between Ostel and the sugar factory. Both of these separated brigades were held up by German gun and Maxim fire. The Guards had to pass through dense woods, under a terrible storm of shrapnel and bullets, and it was not until some of their gallant gunners brought a section of the field artillery right into the firing-line and blew away all opposition that the Guards fought a path to the foot of Ostel ridge.

In the meantime the 6th Brigade—made up of the 1st Liverpools, the 2nd South Staffordshires, the 1st Berkshires, and the 1st King's Royal Rifles—passed over the ground won by the 5th Brigade the day before, and moved along the valley of Braye towards the narrow neck of the plateau. But here also the German artillery fire was so skilfully and massively directed as to make any infantry advance impossible. Both from the ridge in front and from the hills on either side the German guns thundered. Sir Douglas Haig determined to clear the hills that flanked the valley. This was indeed necessary in order to ensure the advance made round the sugar factory on the neighbouring heights. So a superb force of guns—the 34th Brigade of the Field Artillery, the 44th Howitzer Brigade, and batteries of sixty-pounders—came to the help of the infantry. This Thor-like thunderstroke broke down the German war machinery in the Braye valley, and the brave 6th Brigade was able to press onward. A footing was won on the heights round La Cour de Soupir, and farther to the north-east, at Chivy, near the Chemin des Dames.

A Thor-like thunderstroke

By this time, however, General von Zwehl had got full control of the situation. Collecting the troops that held the ridge, and re-forming them with his 18,000 men—soon increased by reinforcements to 40,000—he was able to assume the offensive. For both in gun power and rifle power he had at least double the strength of the British general, and the magnificent advantage of position increased the fighting force at his disposal. Before the gap between the hills and valleys, where Haig's separated 1st and 2nd Divisions were struggling, could be closed by the successful advance of the 6th Brigade and the Guards, Zwehl struck through it. He sent a strong infantry column over the road from Cerny to Bourg. But when it reached the heights north of Pont Arcy, the last brigade of the 1st Division, which was trying to connect with the troops of the 2nd Division, came upon it. It was the Queen's, the South Wales Borderers, the 1st Gloucester Regiment, and the 2nd Welsh Regiment that stood in the way of the German movement which aimed at cutting Sir Douglas Haig's army corps into two fragments and surrounding the Guards Brigade and the 6th Brigade.

BRITISH MILITARY BRIDGE OVER THE AISNE.
The Royal Engineers, having completed their work, are resting, while various sections of their comrades in the combatant ranks are passing over, some of them with improvised rain cloaks over their shoulders.

Only two of the British battalions went forward to stop the German column. But by giving the Teutons, who were mainly reserve troops, the mad minute of rapid rifle fire, mingled with a stream of bullets from four Maxim guns, the compact grey mass was shattered and thrown back. This for a time relieved the pressure on the Guards and the 6th Brigade, but the connecting force from the 1st Division was again attacked in the afternoon before it had joined across the hill of Chivy. For about one o'clock on Monday General von Zwehl ordered all his troops to advance, and every man in the First British Army Corps was tested to the limit of his endurance and fighting ability.

Four miles of debatable land

The space between the British lines near Troyon and the German lines near Cerny was carpeted with the bodies of dead and wounded men. In one violent sweep the British, according to General von Zwehl, got into his lines and forced his troops back, but he recovered the ground by a counter-attack. The debatable land between the two forces was four miles long and half a mile wide, and such was the fury of battle that all who attempted to reach the wounded were themselves killed. For two days and nights the men in the trenches heard the heartrending cries of the injured, helpless men, and the sounds almost drove the troops mad. The Germans acquired an insane ferocity, and took a diabolical delight in shelling the buildings from which the British Red Cross flag was flying. Their snipers brought down our stretcher-bearers and Red Cross men, and turned war into murder. But the intensity of hatred that brought out the baseness of the Germans did not increase their fighting ability.

Our men were cool and steady at their deadly work, in spite of the anger burning in their bodies. They tempted their enemies to attack, and mowed them down with a rifle fire that was almost as overpowering as a machine-gun stream of bullets. By no force that Zwehl could bring against them could he shift the men of the 1st and 2nd Infantry Brigades from the commanding height they had won. For three weeks the number of dead men continued to increase as the terrible slaughter took place between the hostile lines. The smell of the decaying corpses became so fearful that the soldiers on both sides smoked tobacco for three weeks without a break to keep themselves from sickening. The available tobacco in the German Army was commandeered for use by the troops at Cerny to induce them to stick to their dreadful position. According to General von Zwehl, he lost some 9,000 men in vain endeavours to hurl the British from their position.

The only occasion when he was near success was on the Monday afternoon when he just arrived from Maubeuge.

A REGIMENTAL KITCHEN ON THE AISNE.
A shell fell here, killing a number of the men seen in the group shortly after this photograph was taken.

He could not break the British line near the Chemin des Dames at Cerny, but a second attempt he made to cut the connection between Sir Douglas Haig's 1st and 2nd Divisions was with extreme difficulty countered, for he succeeded in driving a wedge between the two British forces, and even got on the lines of communication of the Guards Brigade and the 6th Brigade. The Guards, who were the farthest off from their directing general, put up a magnificent fight.

Germans' enormous artillery advantage

The 6th Brigade, meeting with a shattering rifle fire from a height, stormed the hill and took it with the bayonet. Then, as the Germans were flying in all directions, a double hail of machine-gun bullets struck the victors. Some of the King's Royal Rifles saw two German machine-guns on the top of a hayrick; they set the hay alight and the machine-gun men were burnt. The fighting was hard and terrific, and the fire of the German guns and howitzers was calculated to demoralise any ordinary troops. For when the guns from Maubeuge were added to the unusually powerful ordnance of the German western wing, the German superiority in artillery was enormous.

By a massed cross gun fire at the critical spot, followed by a rushing infantry attack, Zwehl at last cut Sir Douglas Haig's forces into two. And, though all the British troops of the First Army Corps fought on heroically, they could do no more than hold their ground. What was needed was more men to occupy the position against which the Germans were progressing in their enveloping movement. Sir Douglas had used his last man, and he called for aid on his Commander-in-Chief. Sir John French placed the Cavalry Division of some 9,000 men at the disposal of his brilliant general, and, with the horsemen fighting in infantry fashion, Haig lengthened out the left flank of the Guards Brigade and secured it from being turned.

When the Germans closed for the great attack the position of the Guards had altered since their scouting patrols had studied it. Our crack regiments fought with the remarkable skill and bodily strength, which, joined to their steadiness of nerve, make them among the most splendid infantrymen in the world. In the end the enemy were driven back after losing a great number of men and twelve guns, and the main movement against the First Army Corps ended in a British success.

At the same time the 6th Brigade, menaced by the same German movement, was working through the next valley eastward past the hamlet of Beaulne-et-Chivy. About one o'clock on Monday the Germans attacked them as they moved up the hillside, where the shells fell on them all the way. Some battalions sheltered in the thick woods between the open spaces, but these were also searched by the hostile gunners. On the crest of the main hill two lines of German infantry were entrenched, with machine-guns at intervals, but as the British brigade had an unusual number of light and heavy guns as a support, their infantry attack was covered by such a terrible shrapnel fire as no German could stand. The foes were driven out of the trenches, and as they retreated in huge masses over the opposite hillside, our guns caught them and mowed them down like fields of wheat. Our men entrenched on the position they won at Chivy, within a thousand yards of the main German lines on the top of the plateau.

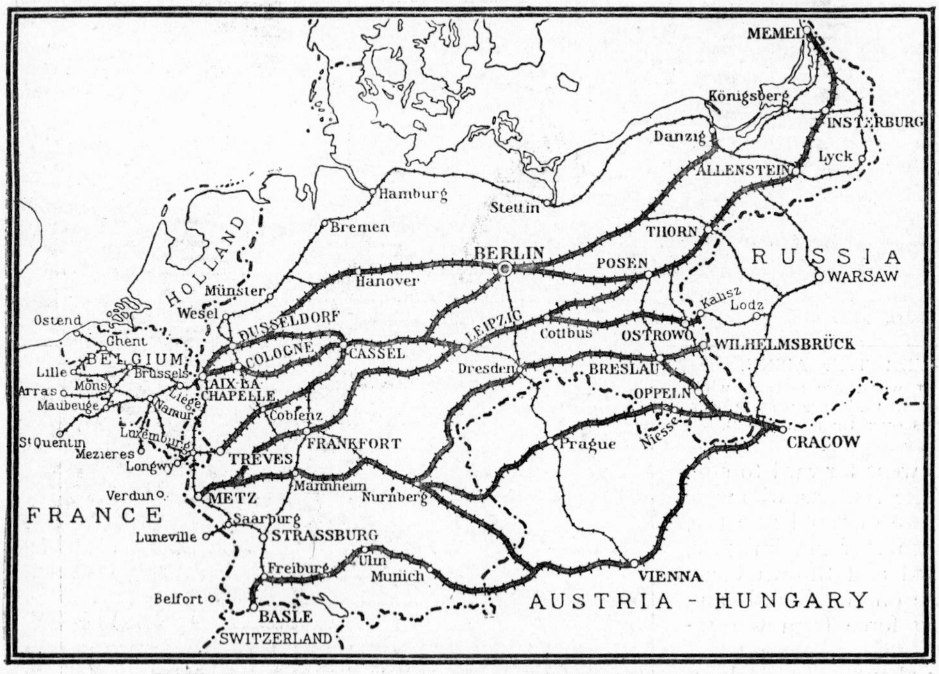

HOW THE GERMAN ARMY CORPS SWUNG TO AND FRO.

The above map of the main German railways and their connections will enable the reader to understand how the Germans were able to transfer their troops east or west, in response to the pressure exerted by the Allies or according to the requirements of the German Headquarters Staff.

On Monday night the British trenches stretched from a point north of the sugar factory at Troyon to Chivy, then across the valley of Braye to La Cour de Soupir and Chavonne. Eastwards of the British force were the Moroccan troops entrenched in steps on the right rear. Westward the 3rd Division, forming the right wing of Sir Horace Smith-Dorrien's Second Army Corps, was entrenched a mile north of Vailly. It had advanced towards the heights of Aizy till it was checked by a fierce artillery fire, under cover of which a German infantry column delivered a counter-attack. This compelled General Hamilton to withdraw towards Vailly. The 4th and 5th Divisions, near Missy and Bucy-le-Long, were still subjected to a terrific bombardment, and could do no more than maintain their ground at the foot of the hills of Vregny and Chivres.

The peculiar formation of the ground between Soissons and Missy, as Sir John French afterwards remarked in his despatch, made the high German positions, defended with modern artillery firing 8 in. shells a distance of 10,000 yards, practically impregnable.

The 5th Division could not remain alive on the southern edge of that flat-topped Chivres hill, as the German batteries on the Vregny hill were able to direct a flank fire on the British trenches. The troops, therefore, had at last to retire towards the villages of Marguérite and Missy, which their commander, Sir Charles Fergusson, retained throughout the long siege battle, though his trenches were on much lower ground than the enemy occupied only four hundred yards away.

British force the passage of the Aisne

All that had been accomplished between Soissons and Vailly by Tuesday, September 15th, was to maintain a strong number of bridge-heads along the Aisne, at the foot of the great buttressed tableland. But between Vailly and Bourg the First British Army Corps and the Cavalry Division held a series of commanding heights which enabled the entire force and part of the Fifth French Army to cope on fairly equal terms with the German armies.

FRENCH ALPINE CHASSEURS, WHO GAVE A GOOD ACCOUNT OF THEMSELVES IN THE VOSGES.

Specially trained and equipped for mountaineering work, the "Chasseurs Alpins" displayed their excellent fighting qualities in the Vosges. In the above picture we see a group of these intrepid mountaineers resting for a meal outside a village churchyard. Inset: A detachment of "Chasseurs Alpins" in action with one of the guns, which were specially made so as to be readily taken to pieces for transport by mules.

IN THE GERMAN TRENCHES ON THE AISNE DURING A NIGHT ENGAGEMENT.
From a drawing made on the spot by a German artist.

The passage of the Aisne had been forced, in spite of the tremendous siege-artillery and the extraordinary number of field-guns with which the plateau of Soissons had been defended. Far from breaking against the vast natural fortress as Napoleon's troops had broken against Blücher's in 1814, the Allies of 1914 had won such a footing on the heights that Heeringen's armies were besieged, and they continued to remain in the inferior position of an attacked garrison force for many months.

Heeringen at first did not tamely submit to this condition of things. When the effect of General von Zwehl's reinforcement of men and guns was exhausted—which quickly happened on Tuesday, September 15th—there was a day's interval of relaxed effort. During this the 3rd Division under General Hamilton, at Vailly, advanced again up the ravine of Vailly and recovered the ground it had lost near Aizy hill. It was done by massing our artillery fire on the German trenches on the heights, where the enemy suffered so severely from shell and shrapnel that he evacuated his position. This was then seized by our troops and made another important point of power against the main hostile fortified lines on the topmost ridge. The next day, however, Heeringen received large new forces. His own Lorraine army, whose operations had become insignificant after the Crown Prince was compelled to retire from the gap he had blown in the Verdun-Toul line, was drawn on for reinforcements. All the men that could be spared in Belgium were railed down, through Maubeuge, to the distributing centre at Laon, and great masses of soldiers of the reserve and militia classes were obtained from Germany. Moreover, the men of Kluck's, Bülow's, Hausen's, and Würtemberg's armies were recovering from the wear and fatigue of the retreat from the Marne. Though strangely reduced in number by death, injury, and sickness, the troops of the four beaten forces were young men of the first line, composing the supreme striking force of their Empire. They were now supported by siege-howitzers as well as by thousands of their own powerful field-pieces.

Heeringen strongly reinforced

The German machine of war was really stronger than it had been on former battlefields, and, though the human element was weakened by defeat, the reinforcements brought the number of the troops up to something like two millions and a half. Deducting the men retained in Belgium and Lorraine and Alsace, there were probably nearly two millions of German soldiers entrenched from Peronne to the north of Verdun and round Nancy, or within call as reserves on the nearer lines of communication. This was a considerably larger force than General Joffre was using for attack in his great lines, for the French Commander-in-Chief still held to the Napoleonic doctrine of maintaining away from the fighting-line a large reserve army. On these considerations the German Military Staff, of which Helmuth von Moltke was still chief, determined to attempt to recover the offensive.

On Thursday, September 17th, the Battle of the Aisne thus entered on a new phase. From Compiègne to the hills of the Suippes and the Argonne Forest the Franco-British forces were no longer the attackers. The positions they had won on the slopes of the plateau of Soissons, on the hills round Rheims, and on the low ridges of the plain of Champagne were all violently assailed by hostile infantry, advancing by day and night after their guns had bombarded the allied lines.

German attempt to recover the offensive

It was, however, the First Army Corps that had to bear the brunt of the great German counter-attack on Thursday, September 17th. As the Fifth French Army had not been able to get a high footing on the hill of Craonne on our right, our right flank could be continually threatened from the heights eastward of those won by our 1st Division. The French Moroccan troops, ranged down our flank, were an excellent support, but the enemy's artillery round Craonne rendered any advance we made towards Cerny only a temporary affair. Sir John French reckoned that he could have carried the ridges in front of our lines by means of the new 6th Division, but the position at Craonne would have left our right flank open to attack.

Even as it was, our flank was fiercely assailed on Thursday

FIGHTING IN THE WOODED REGION OF THE ARGONNE.

German infantry in their trenches. Part of the force under the Crown Prince, whose tactics in the Argonne were regarded generally as a failure.

afternoon by General von Zwehl's reinforced troops. By way of diversion, the 2nd Northamptons, occupying the most advanced position on the allied front, with their trenches on the Chemin des Dames on the plateau, attacked the German lines at Cerny. The affair began in a very remarkable way. A company of one hundred and sixty Northamptons, with a captain and two lieutenants, had dug themselves in along the road on Monday. In front of them was a turnip-field, across which, at a distance of two hundred and fifty yards, was the foremost trench of General von Zwehl's troops. Directly opposed to the one hundred and sixty Northamptons were some five hundred Germans, and the Englishmen were kept under a continual bombardment, night and day, with infantry attacks at intervals, so that they could get scarcely any sleep.

It rained heavily, and the roadside trench filled with water, that rose to the knees of the defenders. German snipers shot any man who showed above the earth. The captain had been shot though the head, and one of the lieutenants had been fatally wounded. Food and water could only be provided by men crawling up on their stomachs in the darkness. But the Germans did not have it all their own way. The marksman of the Northampton company, his head wreathed in turnip-leaves, was stretched out at length in the middle of the turnip-field, under the torrents of rain. Any head showing against the northern sky-line received a bullet from the English sniper.

The sniper in the turnip-field

Some seventy wounded Germans, rescued from the battlefield on Monday, rested behind the British trench under cover of a haystack, but on Wednesday a German shell set the hay on fire and burnt most of the Germans, who were too badly wounded to crawl away. On Thursday the five hundred Germans across the turnip-field apparently sickened of the terrible, wearing struggle. They made some attempts at a rush, and were broken up by our rifle fire. Then they put up their arms or held out their rifles as a signal of surrender. The remaining officer of the Northamptons—a sub-lieutenant of less than a year's service—was cautious. He motioned to the Germans to quit their trenches and come over the turnip-field and give up their arms. They came over in a mass.

GERMAN "SPLINTER-PROOF" IN THE AISNE AREA.

The German trenches were wonderful examples of Teutonic thoroughness. They were usually three feet in depth and constructed on scientific principles in parallel lines, flanked by others in which machine-guns were concealed. They had, at intervals, "splinter-proof" shelters such as that above illustrated.

The lieutenant went to meet them. A German private tried to parley. The British officer shouted for the German officer to step forward. Meanwhile the Germans were coming forward and were close to the trench. Then a German officer with a sergeant and private advanced. "You surrender, for you are my prisoner!" said the young lieutenant. "No! You are mine!" yelled the German. Either he was beside himself with anger at seeing how small was the force to which he was surrendering with his men—or, more likely, the affair was a carefully premeditated act of treachery.

The lieutenant of the Northamptons at once shot the German officer and non-commissioned officer, but the German private with them put a bullet through him in turn. The small company of Northamptons at the time were standing in front of their trenches, taking rifles from the nearest Germans and shaking their hands. But the greater number of the enemy retained their weapons, and

A CAVE WHICH ACCOMMODATED A WHOLE BRITISH CAVALRY SQUADRON.

Around the Aisne plateau the cliffs are riddled with caves, in which the villagers kept their firewood, hens, pigs, etc. In one of them an officer recorded that he found a whole squadron of British cavalry, and room for a regiment beside. He found there also any number of women and children, and teams of oxen and horses; also a donkey with a German bullet in him. This cave had only one small entrance.

began to fire point-blank at the Englishmen. So a wild tussle began on the edge of the British trench, with the outnumbered defenders in a hopeless position.

Fortunately, at a range of four hundred yards from the roadside trench, the Queen's Regiment—the West Surreys—held their line. One of their machine-guns flanked the position of the Northamptons so as to assist in repelling any hostile charge. The machine-gun section of the Queen's had been disabled, but the commanding officer, Colonel Warren, with the help of Captain Watson, served the gun. They poured a devastating fire into the mean-spirited tricksters, until a shrapnel shell from a German gun burst by the Maxim and shattered it and killed both officers.

In the meantime some of the Coldstream Guards, who had also seen the disaster to the heroic Northamptons, came up at the double, as the German curs were fleeing from the Maxim fire. The Guards got among the wretches with the bayonet, and scarcely a hundred out of five hundred, of them got away. Three hundred were shot or bayoneted and a hundred surrendered to the Coldstreams. It is a pity their surrender was accepted, for out of the hundred and sixty Northamptons who had been deceived by their first offer only twelve men were left standing, and four of these were wounded.

BUSY SCENE AT A FRENCH AVIATION BASE.

Repairing landing wheels for aircraft at an aviation base in Northern France.

It was a terrible afternoon for all the Northamptons. Scarcely had the rest of the battalion steadied their raging anger at the foul trick played on their heroic leading company, when some 3,000 Germans of the 53rd Regiment, expecting no doubt that the affair had at least weakened the British defence, advanced over the turnips. From the furious "Cobblers" and the Queen's the new assailers got so lively a welcome that those of them who retained the use of their legs turned and ran.

But this was not sufficient revenge for the Northamptons for their betrayed comrades. They wanted to get among the Germans with the bayonet. They soon got their chance. Under cover of a mist that came over the plateau, some of Zwehl's troops, finding the British front trenches impregnable, began to press severely on the right flank. As a counter-stroke, the Northamptons and Queen's, reinforced by the King's Royal Rifles, were ordered by Sir Douglas Haig to drive up against the German lines round Cerny.

Naturally, the Northamptons led. Veiled by the mist, they crawled over the turnip-field without being discovered. Close to the German trenches they rose and charged with the bayonet, stabbed the surprised line of enemy troops, then went on to the crest of the plateau, where Zwehl had dug in a second line of men to protect his guns. Again the Northamptons reached the German trenches, through a hail of bullets and machine-gun fire. But the enemy were in such force that many Northamptons died as they were using their bayonets furiously. Their terrible charge, however, held the enemy, and the Queen's quickly worked up to a point from which they enfiladed the German lines from the left, while the King's Royal Rifles wheeled on their right. At the same time a squadron of our cavalry joined in the attack, and the Germans were driven over the ridge with heavy loss. This magnificent advance on September 17th lifted the wing of the British army right on to the plateau. It was our high-water mark on the Aisne. It was, moreover, carried out at a time when Heeringen had strongly reinforced his armies and launched them on that general offensive against the allied front which was intended to knock the British and French armies out of their positions and result in a great disaster to them.

The advance on the height was so successful that Sir John French thought of taking the bridge at Condé, lower down the river, and consolidating the positions of the two divisions of the Second Army Corps. But Sir Horace Smith-Dorrien was satisfied with the situation of his men. He had his guns so disposed that a German force trying to sally over the bridge would be annihilated. Any British advance would automatically force the enemy out of Condé. So the German was allowed to remain in possession of it.

PRESIDENT POINCARE'S BOMBARDED VILLA AT SAMPIGNY.
When at Triancourt, in the Meuse district, the Germans pillaged and wrecked the house of M. Lucien Poincaré. At Aubecourt they destroyed the chateau of his parents. They then bombarded the village of Sampigny, where the French President had his own villa and was the owner of most of the property.

In fact, Sir John French resolved not to push the Germans back anywhere, but to wait for them to attack and then punish them. For on Thursday, General Joffre informed the British commander that he had been compelled to make a new plan. All the allied armies in action had now to hold the Germans in the present position. A new French force was being sent north to assail and, if possible, turn the western flank of the enemy at Peronne.

With this new movement the Battle of the Aisne entered on a third phase. First there was the allied offensive; then the German counter-offensive; now it had become a containing operation, with the decisive action happening elsewhere. As it would take some time for the effect of General Joffre's new plan to make itself felt by seriously weakening the German power of offensive, our troops

CAPTURED GERMAN OFFICER BEING EXAMINED BY MEMBERS OF A FRENCH GENERAL STAFF.
As the official British "Eye-Witness" pointed out, since the composition of the larger formations of all armies was known, it was possible to extract vital information from the connection of even a single soldier killed or captured at a certain point with a certain battalion. It was part of the duties of a General Staff to piece together the information gained from prisoners, as well as from their own agents.

had to deepen and improve their trenches, and arrange for a regular sort of open-air siege warfare. But the Gloucesters, holding a foremost position on the height near Chivy, west of the lines above the sugar factory at Troyon, found on Friday night, September 18th, that attack was still the best means of defence. They took the enemy's trenches in the darkness, and captured two machine-guns.

Enemy's trenches taken in the darkness

All the front positions of the First Army Corps were furiously attacked by the Germans that night. In many cases the Germans were not content with one repulse, but brought up their reserves, and after bombarding our trenches, came on again in close compact masses, lit by our searchlights and pierced by our field-guns. Where the shrapnel failed to scatter them, the rapid fire of our infantry broke up the German formations. On Saturday evening, September 19th, and throughout Sunday the First Army Corps was subjected to fierce attacks by daylight and in the darkness. Zwehl, no doubt, was now fully reinforced to 40,000 men, and he had in addition portions of Bülow's and Kluck's armies which had been placed under his command. Having, unlike Kluck, no full experience of the stopping power of the British magazine rifle in the hands of British marksmen, both Heeringen and Zwehl tried continually by mass infantry attacks to hurl our men down from the heights they had won. But what 8 in. siege-artillery shells could not effect, no sacrifice of cannon fodder could accomplish. None of our dominating gun positions was lost, and on September 23rd these gun positions became more formidable. For four 6 in. howitzer batteries arrived from England, and enabled Sir Douglas Haig and Sir Horace Smith-Dorrien to play the German game, and get cross-fire and high-angle effects at longer distances than the enemy had arranged for when he completed his entrenchments.

With these additional weapons of siege warfare, the British positions became absolutely secure. Both Sir John French and his men began to tire of their inactivity, and the British commander worked out a scheme of new operations before Calais, that led, early in October, to the shifting of the British Expeditionary Force to the new battlefield around Ypres. So, from the British point of view, the operations on the Aisne came to a close.

But never will the Aisne be forgotten by either Frenchmen or men of the British Empire. The part our troops played in the assault upon the greatest natural fortress in Northern Europe ranks among the finest military achievements in our history. The river flats, the forested slopes, the winding ravines, the upper heights were scenes of many acts of British heroism that will never be told.

One of the most romantic of these exploits was carried out by some privates of the 1st Coldstream Guards. With their Colonel Ponsonby, a party of the Coldstreams went out at night to the German lines to discover the positions of the enemy's machine-guns. This they did, but while stumbling among the German troops, they were also discovered, and a fierce rifle fire was directed at them. Colonel Ponsonby was shot, and fell in the open ground under the German fire, and two of his men—Private Jones and Private Vennicombe—dashed through the stream of bullets towards their officer's body.

He had been shot in the leg, and was unable to walk. They carried him back to the main body of reconnoitres—forty in all—and it was seen that the only thing to be done was to retire. Under the leadership of an officer of the Black Watch, the men got into the shelter of a wood, carrying the wounded colonel with them. Then they found they were in the German lines, with two hostile outposts before them. One of the enemy's convoys passed close to them, but they were not strong enough to attack. After a tramp of some six miles the party got through the German position at Cerny, four men carrying the colonel in turn, and rejoined their battalion in the morning.

A WAR PHOTOGRAPHER'S NERVE: REMARKABLE INCIDENT IN THE VOSGES.
A French despatch-rider having had his horse shot by the enemy, dismounted and dashed into a house on the roadside, where a party of his compatriots were resting. A few seconds later the Germans were accounted for. The photographer who had the temerity to halt and take the picture escaped injury.

In a lower part of the battlefield, during the fierce German attack all along the allied front, a daring feat was performed by a Highlander. He was one of a small detachment of one hundred and fifty Scotsmen who were guarding a bridge-head by the Aisne towards Soissons. No attack was expected, and the detachment was merely placed by the bridge as an ordinary precaution. But suddenly the Germans, on the scarp overlooking the river, opened fire, and under cover of the guns a strong hostile force, far outnumbering the British detachment, sprang from the wooded slopes and came on at a run towards the bridge. At first the Highlanders kept the attackers back by steady, rapid fire; but the Germans, though dropping and slackening their pace as they sought for cover, drew nearer and nearer. At the same time a larger hostile force, in a compact column, also came into view on the road leading from the plateau to the bridge.

One of the Highlanders leaped from the ground, where he had been firing from cover. He had seen that the Maxim gun at the other end of the bridge had ceased working, as all its section had been killed. Running forward under a hail of bullets he reached the Maxim, swung it with its tripod on his back, and carried it at a run across the bridge. The belt was at once charged, and the soldier sat down and opened fire on the nearing German column, while his companions held back the other Germans.

How a Highlander kept the bridge

So well did the solitary Highlander direct the machine-gun that he emptied the cartridges in the belt right on the head of the column. The German troops broke and fled for shelter on either side of the road, leaving a heap of dead and wounded. Soon after the Highlander tumbled down by his gun, with thirty bullets in his body. But he had saved his comrades and kept the bridge; and the enemy afterwards retreated to the heights.

WOUNDED SOLDIERS CHARGE THE GERMANS—GALLANT DEED OF YORKSHIRE LIGHT INFANTRY.

"About twenty of us," stated Private Crossland, of the Yorkshire Light Infantry, "were lying wounded in an underground cellar beneath a small chapel, adjoining a roofless farmhouse blackened with shell fire. We thought we were safe, when suddenly we were attacked by a score of Germans. Only nine of us were capable of resistance, and with rifles and revolvers and anything we could lay hands on we went for the enemy, and after a fierce tussle accounted for all but two. Four of our men were recommended for the D.C.M., and one—a sergeant—for the V.C."

WITH THE MEN OF THE FIRST C

Staff-Captain C. H. Vandersluys, of the 4th Infantry Brigade, part of the Canadian Contingent which arrived in England on October 15th, 1914.

Men of the First Canadian Contingent constructing barbed-wire and live-wire entang during their training on Salisbury Plain.

Part of a hut kitchen in the camp of the First Canadian Contingent on Salisbury Plain. The commissariat department had to arrange for the feeding of nearly 30,000 men.

Band of the 12th Battalion of the First Canadian Contingent. They were pho outside one of the specially constructed huts.

An early morning shave under difficulties. The carpenter's wooden trestle afforded a somewhat rough-and-ready substitute for the barber's chair.

Officers of the 12th Battalion (left to right): Lieutenants S. Ryder, Sanson, and Adams; C Fraser, McAvity, Van Wart, Ogilvie, and Sutherland; Lieutenants Stirling and McNalle

CONTINGENT ON SALISBURY PLAIN.

exceptionally rainy autumn and winter, training on Salisbury Plain rendered road-making a necessary part of the operations.

Captain H. H. Van Wart and Signalling Section of the 12th Battalion of the First Canadian Contingent at work with the heliograph.

men of the First Canadian Contingent getting their hands in at entrenching work on the outskirts of their encampment on Salisbury Plain.

Another view of the Canadians in training on Salisbury Plain. The beginning of a trench near a pine plantation. The men look very fit.

e 12th Battalion (back): Lt. Morgan, Lt. Adams, Capt. Sutherland, Lt. McDonald, Lt. Brosseau, Avity, Lt. Bowen; (front): Lt. Cramford, Capt. Van Wart, Maj. Guthrie, Capt. Dove.

Two men of the First Canadian Contingent returning from leave. They are meeting their old friend the mud, which, despite the road-making, proved invincible.

GERMANS FORCING A FRENCH FARMER TO THRESH HIS CORN FOR THEIR BENEFIT.

The Germans have never tired of repeating Napoleon's jibe at the British as "a nation of shopkeepers." But the conduct of the Germans in the Great War would seem to have shown a desire on their part to qualify as a nation of shoplifters. From Crown Prince to private they plundered wherever they penetrated, in the chateau of a baroness or the simple home of a peasant. They even collected crops and forwarded them to the Fatherland; and the above picture shows a French farmer being compelled to thresh his corn for the benefit of the ruthless invader.

SENEGALESE AND FRENCH TROOPS ON THE ROAD TO RHEIMS.

CHAPTER XXXVIII.

BATTLES AND BOMBARDMENTS OF THE AISNE AND SUIPPES.

Sixth French Army Forces Passage of Aisne—Wild Struggles in Ravines and on Heights—Bombardment of Soissons—Fifth French Army Swings Up the Headland of Craonne—Reinforced German Armies Counter-Attack—Attempts to Pierce French Centre Fail—The Maddened, Baffled Enemy Destroys Rheims Cathedral—Raid on French Railway Communication—Death's Head Hussars Mowed Down by Gun Fire—Prussian Guard Trapped Amid Vineyards—Forest Fighting in the Argonne—Metz Army Captures Fort Between Verdun and Toul—French Stop the Gap on the Heights of the Meuse.

IT was no fatigue on the part of the Allies that prevented the French armies, in the Battles of the Aisne and Suippes Rivers, from driving into the German fortified positions and winning a series of points of vantage there. The French were less successful than the British mainly because they lacked a weapon with the range and weight of shell of our heavy field batteries. When the Germans turned to make a stand, on the plateau of Soissons and the swell of low heights running from Rheims to the Argonne Forest, they brought their siege-artillery on the scene. The big German howitzers, beginning with 6 in. shells and increasing to 11 in. shells as the Maubeuge train arrived, dominated the battlefield. The French 3 in. field-gun and small field-howitzer, though admirable in a struggle in the open field, were not long-ranged enough for the new kind of siege warfare that began on the Aisne.

The result was that the French soldiers suddenly found themselves at a disadvantage. Yet they redressed the balance in armament by the vigour and steady persistence of their infantry attack. At need, they charged the German guns with the bayonet, and at the loss of half a battalion won the hostile battery. Even when the German armies were so strongly reinforced that they outnumbered the French by three to two in men, and had behind them an overpowering superiority in heavy artillery, the French continued to hold them back. The French never lost the position of being the besiegers; the Germans never recovered from the position of being the besieged. In other words, General Joffre retained the power of initiative that he won by the victory of the Marne. He was always acting on the offensive, and compelling the German Commander-in-Chief—Moltke or Falkenhayn or Kaiser Wilhelm—to answer his moves. At no time was the enemy able to recover from his first great defeat.

THE WRECKED ROOF OF RHEIMS CATHEDRAL.
Photograph showing the destruction by fire of Rheims Cathedral, the "Westminster Abbey of France," in September, 1914.

Fierce and continual, however, were the efforts that the German armies made to resume the power of initiative and act on the offensive. At an early stage in the new campaign they won the tactical power of attack. They attacked with surprising fury. They threw the Franco-British armies all along the front on the defensive; they won various points of advantage between Noyon and Soissons, and between Craonne and Rheims and the Argonne ridge. But they never recovered the initiative. General Joffre was their master. He decided what plan of attack they should adopt, and forced them to follow that plan. Such is the power of initiative in the hands of a man with a genius for generalship.

At first General Joffre's subordinate commanders had matters in their own hands. They merely had to pursue the retreating German armies, and attack them when they threw out rearguards or made a general stand. General Maunoury, with the Sixth French Army, attacked General von Kluck, with the First German Army, from Noyon to Soissons. Then, as we have seen, the British Expeditionary Force attacked part of Kluck's army, and Zwehl's new army, and part of

Bülow's army, between Soissons and Bourg. From a point a few miles below Bourg to Rheims, General Franchet d'Espérey, with the Fifth French Army, attacked Bülow's main force that held the bold headland of Craonne. South of the Suippes River, General Foch and General de Langle Cary attacked the armies of the Duke of Würtemberg and the Crown Prince. Round Verdun, General Sarrail, with the Second French Army, was menaced by the Bavarians and a remnant of the Metz garrison, who were using 12 in. howitzers.

The main force concentrated round Metz, under the command of Field-Marshal von Heeringen, was withdrawn westward to reinforce Kluck, Zwehl and Bülow. At the same time the German troops in Belgium, under General von Böhn, were railed southwards to Laon to strengthen further the four armies under Heeringen. All this was done, towards the end of the second week in September, with a view to bringing a preponderating force of men and guns to bear against the Sixth French Army, the British force, and the Fifth French Army. It was designed to force back or break the western wing of the allied front, so that the Germans could recover the initiative and resume their march on Paris.

MAJOR-GENERAL S. H. LOMAX.

While Sir Douglas Haig's 2nd Division was battling against sûperior forces at Pont Arcy and lower down the Aisne, his 1st Division, under Major-General Lomax, had an amazing success against the enemy near Bourg.

Some days elapsed, however, before the effect of this new German concentration made itself felt. In the meantime all the Allies made progress. To General Maunoury and his Sixth Army fell the first honours of the Battle of the Aisne and Suippes. Marching from the Ourcq in pursuit of Kluck's troops, General Maunoury spread his forces out on a wide front from the Forest of Compiègne to a point below Soissons. He cleared Compiègne of Germans, and then at the point where the Aisne flows into the Oise he crossed the first-named river and advanced towards the cathedral city of Noyon, through the Forest of the Eagle—le Foret de l'Aigle.

First honours of the Battle of the Aisne

But this second tract of woodland was dominated by the eastern scarp of the plateau of Soissons. On this high, flat forested tableland, scarred with quarries, tunnelled with caves, and hollowed and seamed on its southern face by valleys and ravines, Kluck had placed his heavy artillery. It formed, on its northern edge round Nampscel, a lofty, level embankment which connected all the outlying southern spurs with each other, so that guns and men could be shifted about the high lands, without crossing the ravines through which brooks fell into the Aisne. The worn, narrow tableland resembled a gigantic fortress wall, and jutting out at intervals were bastions from which the river valley of the Aisne could be dominated by artillery fire, and any attacking party caught on the flank as it attempted to storm the main rampart.

On Sunday and Monday, September 13th and 14th, the passage of the river was forced. The French engineers threw pontoon bridges over the Aisne at Vic and Fontenoy, with the German guns shelling them from the outlying spurs of the plateau. Under the unceasing bombardment the French infantry crossed the wide stream and began to penetrate into the ravines. Fighting magnificently, they pushed the Germans from the slopes above the river, the handy little French field-gun clearing the ground in front of them by shrapnel fire. They occupied the ravine of Nouvron, a few miles east of Soissons, and entered the valley of Morsain above Vic.

Crux of the Battle of the Lower Aisne

This valley of Morsain was the crux of the Battle of the Lower Aisne, in which the Sixth French Army was engaged. It began near the river, in a ravine with a narrow, winding neck dominated by two rugged prolongations of the main ridge of the plateau. The narrow neck afterwards widened into a broad hollow, extending for some miles at the base of the chief natural embankment. On the east side Nampscel could be attacked from it; on the west side the heights round Nauvron might be carried from it. On the other hand, this inner valley in the tableland was practically encircled by the main rampart and its southern spurs. An army could be trapped in it, and then annihilated by the ring of guns on the heights.

BRIGADIER-GENERAL E. S. BULFIN, C.V.O., C.B.

He was repeatedly mentioned in despatches by Sir John French. Up to the evening of November 2nd, 1914, when he was somewhat severely wounded, " his services continued to be of great value."

General Maunoury boldly risked annihilation. He sent one of his army corps through the narrow neck above Vic. Disregarding the strong hostile force of artillery and infantry men on the slopes of the narrow passage, the French soldiers advanced rapidly under a heavy fire. They struck out towards the central ridge, and then veered and tried to get in the rear of the German advance guard, and cut them off from the principal German position. But the attempt failed. The Germans had by this time been strengthened. Heeringen, with the Seventh German Army, had taken charge of the entire defence of the plateau from Nampscel to Craonne.

French holding on by the river flats

He massed guns and troops against Maunoury's men, and by Wednesday, September 16th, the French were back to the Aisne at Vic, desperately fighting to keep their footing on the northern bank. It was just like the position of the Second British Army Corps on the same day at Missy. The Germans had the advantage of a high position, heavy howitzers, and superior numbers of troops. All the French could do was to hold on by the river flats, under a terrible bombardment, and dig themselves into some sort of shelter.

There was a similar course of events in the valley of Nouvron westward, above Fontenoy. While Kluck, with his own tired, dispirited troops, was alone trying to hold all the high lands against his pursuers, the French Zouaves, weary with marching and fighting, but still full of dash, swept through the narrow neck and took the village of Nouvron. Then Heeringen arrived with reinforcements, collected from Belgium, Maubeuge, and the lines of communication, and flung the French back towards the river.

On Wednesday night, September 16th, it looked as though the extreme left wing of the Franco-British forces was about to be shattered. From the spurs above the Aisne the German searchlights swept the darkness with their beams, moving slowly over the river valley till, in the lane of white radiance, the French trenches could be perceived by German fire-control officers. Then the guns on the heights roared in a horrible chorus, and flung their shells in concentrated fury on the hastily-made earthworks near the stream. It was then that the French soldier learnt to dig as he had never dug before. Under the 8 in. shells from the siege-howitzers, all the French traditions of military science inherited from the Napoleonic period became for the time valueless. The French had to go further back to the almost-forgotten system of the old-fashioned trench battles of the days of Vauban and Turenne.

The same thing happened a little higher up the river at the beautiful historic cathedral city of Soissons. Here the British force co-operated with the right army corps of General Maunoury in both the advance on the city and the crossing of the river. On Saturday, September 12th, the Germans still held the Mont de Paris, a hill south of Soissons, against the attack of the right of the Sixth French Army. But, with the help of the heavy guns of our Third Corps, the Zouaves and Turcos got the German rearguard troops on the run, and pursued them to Soissons, where they destroyed the bridges as they retired. When the section of bridging train allotted to our Third Corps arrived near Soissons, our engineers tried to throw a large pontoon bridge across the stream there. But the powerful German howitzer batteries on the height above the city were masters of the situation. Our bridge was shelled and shattered before it was completed, and the French had to get over the river in boats and rafts.

German rearguard pursued to Soissons

Even then the town could not be held by the Allies. For the enemy's guns were placed in the quarries of Pasly, two miles to the north, in positions prepared in peace time by German quarry-owners, working, no doubt, under the direction of the Great Military Staff at Berlin. From these howitzer platforms there began a terrific bombardment, which destroyed half the town, smote the beautiful abbey church of St. Jean des Vignes, struck the exquisite cathedral, gutted the hospital and seminary, and annihilated entire streets of dwelling-places.

Such was the return that the enterprising German merchants of Soissons made for the courteous, hospitable friendship which the simple, kindly townspeople had for years given them. They planned the destruction of the historic cathedral city of the Aisne—a quiet, unfortified, open town, mirrored in the waters of the loveliest river

BRITISH OFFICERS AT THE FRONT.

The circular photograph shows, in the order named, Colonel Greenly, General Gough, and Major Seligman engaged in a consultation on a railway line in Northern France. In the lower photograph are to be seen Major Seligman and General Gough (first and second figures from the left), and General Allenby (the left figure at the door of the motor-car).

KEEPING UP THE LINES OF COMMUNICATION.
French telegraph section re-establishing broken telegraph and telephone wires in the village of Foyon.

valley in France. No progress could be made by the French troops at Soissons, who were mainly turbaned Turcos from Algeria and Morocco. These coloured soldiers of France cleared the streets by splendid impetuous charges, backed by machine-gun sections and covered by field artillery that kept down the enemy's gun fire. But when the last German was forced out of Soissons, and the German rearguard was turned in the south-east at the village of Chauny, nothing more could be done. On a semicircle of heights beyond the River Aisne the German batteries were posted, with infantry entrenched in front of them at a distance of 1,300 yards from the centre of the town. From three points—Pasly, Braye, and Crouy—the Germans looked down on Soissons and observed every movement of the French troops and every arrival of supplies. At any sign of activity, a devastating, concentrated gun and howitzer fire was directed on the French.

Germans impregnable on the heights

It was absolutely impossible to storm the heights. Any attempt, by day or by night, when the searchlights played from the hills, provoked a tempest of shrapnel shells that annihilated everything living on the slopes. As the French had only their light field batteries, they could make no effective reply to the howitzers hidden in the distant quarries. For months the bombardment of Soissons went on, without any marked success on either side. The German position was impregnable; the French position was too stubbornly held to be taken.

South of the city, on the hills where the French guns were placed, the soldiers could see, in the rain-washed air of September, the prospect of that unhappy part of their land that the barbarian was trampling. In the west was the foliage of Compiègne, far in the north-west the town of St. Quentin—a panorama of wooded hills, grey villages set in yellow fields of grain, files of poplars marking the roads; and below, the flashing waters of the Aisne and the canal, with the steeples of the cathedral and the gate of the abbey, where Thomas à Becket had lived.

Across the steeples sang the German shells, and along the valley on the right an observer could mark the flash of the British guns, and trace the rings of smoke as their shrapnel burst over the German lines. The jar and roar of cannon in front, around, and on either side were stunning to the ear. Most of the people of Soissons fled, but a remnant of some two thousand lived on till the end of the year in cellars, clinging to their shattered homes, and starving when the German artillery fire prevented the revictualling trains reaching them and the advanced French troops.

When matters were at their worst

Matters were at their worst on Wednesday night, September 16th, all along the front of the Sixth French Army from Soissons to Compiègne. The French troops had not only to hold the enemy back on the Aisne, but to advance northward along

IN THE WAKE OF THE "FUROR TEUTONICUS."
Ruins of a small French village as it was left by the German invaders.

the eastern bank of the Oise River, and try to get behind his tremendously strong position on the plateau. General Maunoury had not sufficient men to do these two things. In fact he was very hard put to it on Wednesday to retain his footing in the Aisne valley against the reinforced armies that Heeringen was hurling at him.

But General Joffre still continued to control the situation. He was using his Sixth Army to test the full strength of the forces that Heeringen had collected. The French Commander-in-Chief had a large reserve formed up on the flank of General Maunoury's front. He was waiting on events so as to put this reserve to the best use. But the pressure on the Sixth Army became so severe that a considerable force of the reserve was detached on Wednesday and sent towards the Aisne. General Joffre had correctly concluded that the great struggle by the plateau of Soissons was not a mere delaying rearguard action on a large scale. It was a battle, in which the Germans were vehemently using all their available forces to obtain a decision.

French reserves brought to the Aisne

The methods adopted by the French commander in this new critical position of affairs were characteristic of him. They were both bold and subtle, vigorous and cautious. Sir John French's army had won an important position on the plateau on the eastern side, and General Joffre did not want to forgo, if possible, this gain of a direct vantage point. On the other hand, he did not intend to follow Napoleon's plan of attack on

HOW THE SURRENDER OF RHEIMS WAS DEMANDED.
Immediately before the bombardment of Rheims in September, 1914, German parlementaires entered the town, under a flag of truce, to demand its surrender and the payment of a war indemnity. They were blindfolded and, accompanied by French officers, made the entry in motor-cars.

"BUSINESS AS USUAL" IN SHELL-SHATTERED RHEIMS.
A baker's shop in stricken Rheims having been completely destroyed by the daily bombardment of the German batteries, the proprietor moved next door, and coolly continued his "business as usual."

Blücher in the same place, and risk everything on a storming advance against a strong enemy in a magnificently defensive position. So he divided his reserve. Part went to reinforce the Sixth Army for a sweeping movement up the heights, part went to the rapid formation of a new Seventh Army, under General Castelnau, which was ordered to make a flank attack from the west against the German lines of communication.

Heeringen could not have it both ways. He could not reinforce his front strongly all along the plateau, occupying with men and guns all the spurs as well as the main ridge, and at the same time retain a large army in reserve for a turning movement round Compiègne. It was necessary to induce him to counter-attack along the entire river valley, in order to judge what force of infantry he was using on the plateau with his guns. When this was done on Wednesday night, the disposition of his troops was far more clearly revealed than it had been during the first Franco-British attack on the heights. There was no subtle gift of strategy in Field-Marshal von Heeringen's make of mind. He was simply a heavy hammerer, who aimed directly at his opponent's front with full force.

Inducing Herringen to counter-attack

To make quite sure about this very important point, General Joffre, when sending a reinforcement to his Sixth Army, ordered it to attack at dawn with the utmost vigour. The attack would not only test Heeringen's right wing, from which any possible turning movement would develop, but, in conjunction with the strong action of the British force on his centre and the Fifth French Army on his left wing at Craonne, it would engage the attention of the German commander until General Castelnau arrived against his flank.

So on Thursday, September 17th, the men of the Sixth French Army advanced. At Soissons they were content merely to hold the Germans back. Their two main assaults were delivered lower down the Aisne, at Fontenoy and at Vic. Through the two narrow-necked valleys of Nouvron and Morsain poured the Frenchmen, with their picturesque kinsmen the Zouaves, and their brown-faced and black-faced fellow-subjects from the African colonies. They brought no heavy guns across the river, but with their 3 in. field-piece—the "soixante-quinze"—throwing twenty-five small shells a minute, and their machine-gun, they searched the wooded spurs above the Aisne, and by the afternoon checked the German counter-attack.

A BRIDGE BUILT BY SIX H NDRED GERMANS IN FIVE DAYS.
This remarkable structure, five hundred and forty-six yards in extent, was built of materials found in the neighbourhood, across a wide tract of marshy land in Northern France. The work took five days to complete, and was done by working parties numbering in all six hu..dred men.

Then the French infantryman, in swift, continual rushes, climbed up the buttresses of the great plateau, took the German machine-guns in a series of heroic storming movements, and at last drove the enemy back to Nampscel and even beyond that hill village. The German lines were pushed right on to the main ridge of the tableland, towards their headquarters at Laon, on the next height. But despite the splendid gallantry of the Frenchmen, they could not get a firm lodging on the highest points above the river valley. All that bayonet and bullet and 3 in. shells could do, they did.

Heroic French storming movements

But the German heavy machinery of war was too powerful for them to entrench by the ridge. They had arrived some three days too late on the heights. General von Zwehl had preceded them with the siege-artillery from Maubeuge for distribution along the plateau. Large forces of fresh troops had been added to Kluck's defeated forces, and vast new supplies of ammunition had been parcelled out from Laon.

Another thing that seems also to have told against the French in the swaying struggle on the central slopes towards Nampscel was the superior proportion in which machine-guns were used by the German battalions. In many cases a German battalion had six machine-guns, while a French battalion had only two. In the fighting in rough, wooded, difficult country, where surprise ambushes could easily be arranged by Maxim sections against large bodies of infantry, this special superiority in light armament was as useful to the Germans as their superiority in heavy artillery.

In the end the Sixth French Army had to withdraw once more towards the Aisne, and two months passed before it again began to advance, more slowly, but more surely. Furnished with more machine guns, with heavier field-guns throwing a 37 lb. shell a distance of eight miles, and with mobile siege-artillery, General Maunoury's force in November crept eastward round the plateau along the Oise at Tracy le Val, and won several important positions on the heights above the Aisne. Meanwhile, the unyielding resistance of the Sixth French Army along the Lower Aisne, like the stronghold of their British neighbours along the higher reaches of the river, contained the enemy and reduced him to the position of a besieged garrison. The plateau of Soissons became the largest entrenched camp in the world, with the Allies sapping and mining their way into it and keeping three or more German armies immobile in front of them for many critical months in the general campaign. In these vast siege operations the Fifth French Army, under General Franchet d'Espérey, took as important a part as the British Expeditionary Force and General Maunoury's troops. General d'Espérey, wheeling up on the British right, had probably the most difficult bit of the plateau in front of him. Between his left wing, near Bourg on the Aisne, and his right wing at Rheims, the great headland of Craonne rose above the plain of Champagne. The height forms the western edge of the tableland of Soissons. It is the culmination of the north river ridge, and its steep sides and flat top make it easy to defend with modern artillery and difficult, in any circumstances, to attack. It is indeed the crowning impregnable height of the natural fortress of France.

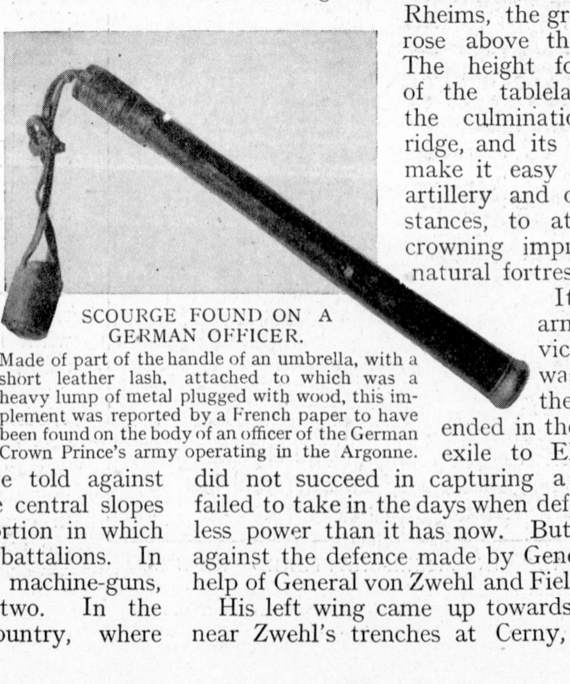

SCOURGE FOUND ON A GERMAN OFFICER.
Made of part of the handle of an umbrella, with a short leather lash, attached to which was a heavy lump of metal plugged with wood, this implement was reported by a French paper to have been found on the body of an officer of the German Crown Prince's army operating in the Argonne.

It was here that Napoleon's army broke down after its victory on the Marne, and was shattered by Blucher in the 1814 campaign that ended in the French Emperor's first exile to Elba. General d'Espérey did not succeed in capturing a position that Napoleon failed to take in the days when defending artillery had much less power than it has now. But he avoided being broken against the defence made by General von Bülow, with the help of General von Zwehl and Field-Marshal von Heeringen.

His left wing came up towards the Chemin des Dames, near Zwehl's trenches at Cerny, to protect the flank of

GERMAN SHARPSHOOTERS IN TREES LOCATED AND BROUGHT DOWN BY A BRITISH MACHINE-GUN.

A number of our men having been sniped by an invisible enemy while passing to and from the firing-line, it occurred to a bright young officer to turn a machine-gun on some trees in the distance. The result was "a fine bag of German sharpshooters." It was officially stated that non-commissioned officers in the German Army were offered Iron Crosses if they could penetrate the British lines at night. These men sometimes succeeded in getting right behind our lines to favourable spots, from which they were able to use their rifles with deadly effect.

the 1st Division of the British force, after the great success on the plateau. But, as we have seen in the previous chapter, Sir John French found it would be dangerous to advance his men any farther on the ridge, so long as the Germans had the headland of Craonne on our right. In these circumstances, General d'Espérey endeavoured to improve the allied front by a magnificent reconnaissance in force against the Craonne heights. With the entire weight of the Fifth Army he swung up against the abrupt headland on Thursday, September 17th.

French attack on the Craonne heights

A most desperate and stubborn battle ensued. The French lacked long-range artillery, and could not cover their advance by gun fire from the other side of the Aisne River valley. The most they could do was to hold the enemy by the river spurs, but they swarmed up the slopes on the eastern side of the plateau, and simply by the swiftness and vigour of their infantry rushes got as far as Craonne village, which is not quite at the top of the main height. Some of the leading troops appear to have fought their way to the main height by Friday, September 18th. But they could not lodge there against the terrible cross-fires that were directed on to them from the German batteries. After taking prisoners from the 11th and 12th German Army Corps, the French had to withdraw towards the river and act on the defensive.

They had crossed the Aisne at the old ford of Berry-au-Bac, on the road running from Rheims to Laon, past the headland of Craonne. Unfortunately for them, the German commander, Heeringen, had massed men and materials along this road for an attack on Rheims. All the guns that Zwehl and Bülow could spare from the plateau were combined with the artillery of the broken Saxon army, and got into position on the Rheims-Laon road. On Thursday night, September 17th, the heavy

GERMAN SAVAGERY AT SENLIS.
Ruined residence of the Mayor of Senlis. He was shot by the Germans, who razed this beautiful old-world town to the ground.

FUGITIVES ON THE RUINED RAILWAY-STATION AT SENLIS.
On their retreat to the Aisne, part of the German army passed through Senlis, which, on their departure, they bombarded on the ground that some of their men had been fired at. The above photograph shows a crowd of would-be travellers waiting at the wrecked railway-station in the hope of getting by train to Paris. Inset: "Business as usual" at Senlis railway-station in spite of the bombardment. Notice the smashed roof.

COURTYARD OF THE RUINED HOTEL DE VILLE, SENLIS.

siege-howitzers also arrived there from Maubeuge, according to a diary by a German officer picked up some days afterwards during the German counter-attack. Though this remarkable mass of ordnance was no doubt of use in assisting the guns on the plateau to repel the French attack on Craonne, this was not the principal object for which it had been collected.

The German Commander-in-Chief had selected the level tract of country between the Aisne at Berry-au-Bac and Rheims and Chalons for the supreme effort of his strengthened forces. A considerable number of his reinforcements, including all the first-line troops that could be spared from the Lorraine army, were coming from an eastern direction. There was no cross-country railway linking the eastern German wing to the western German wing. The French Military Staff had left the large region between Verdun, Rethel, and Rheims without direct railway communication, with a view to impeding such a transfer of invading troops. The consequence was that no German turning movement in the west, round Compiègne, was immediately practical.

Railways and German strategy

On the other hand, there was a direct main line of railway communication running from Rheims northward through Rethel, Mézières, Luxemburg, to the great German war depot at Coblenz, on the Rhine. A branch line from Metz to Luxemburg also connected the garrison force at Metz with the German lines round Berry-au-Bac and the Craonne headland. Everything thus conspired to induce the German Commander-in-Chief to concentrate in front of Rheims, by Berry-au-Bac.

All the operations on the plateau of Soissons, by Field-Marshal von Heeringen and Generals von Kluck, von Bülow, and von Zwehl, became of secondary importance. Owing to the failure of the Sixth French Army, the British Expeditionary Force, and the Fifth French Army to drive Heeringen's forces from the tableland, their actions also became of secondary importance. The chief scene of engagement

CAMERA PICTURES OF THE DESOLATION WROUGHT BY THE GERMANS IN SENLIS.

The invaders laid a heavy hand on the beautiful old town of Senlis. The view in the centre of the page shows a party of French people walking through the ruins. The left-hand picture is of the entrance to the town, and its companion view shows another part of the ruined city.

DISASTROUS EFFECTS OF A GERMAN SHELL ON A PARTY OF BRITISH WOUNDED.

During the fighting on the Aisne a party of British wounded were being attended by a Red Cross doctor in a room in a country house, when a shell from the German lines, coming through the window, burst in their midst. The doctor and nearly all the soldiers were killed on the spot. The incident was described by a private of the Black Watch who was in the room a few minutes before the explosion, and who went into it again shortly after the disaster. The victims were about a dozen in number, and belonged to the Cameron Highlanders.

between the Germans and the Allies in the third week of September was the country around Rheims. Here the German commander delivered the blow by which he hoped to recover the grand power of the initiative that he had won at Charleroi and lost at the Marne.

He intended, by a violent frontal attack, backed by heavy artillery fire, with howitzer bombardments, to pierce the French front between Rheims and Suippes. Even if the first attack failed, he hoped to push back the French lines sufficiently to win possession of all the valuable railway running across the plain of Champagne from Verdun and St. Menehould to Rheims. With this railway just behind him, he could manœuvre his troops for the final frontal assault.

It was on Friday, September 18th, when the Fifth French Army was repulsed from Craonne, that the German counter-attack on the French centre was made. Here, from Rheims to the little town of Souain, the Ninth French Army, under General Foch, had a hard task to beat back the host of invaders. For, in retiring from Rheims about six days before, the Germans had kept possession of the chief French forts of the district. The French had dismantled these old-fashioned forts so as to make Rheims, with its glorious cathedral, an open town, safe from bombardment. The chief fort was on the wooded heights of Nogent l'Abbesse, only seven thousand yards from the cathedral city. The Germans placed their heavy artillery on this position, and entrenched their infantry around it, and along the River Suippes, that runs into the Aisne near Berry-au-Bac.

German advantages at Rheims

During the first days of the pursuit the French took a lower spur of the Nogent heights, and, what was more important, captured the hill of Brimont, some nine thousand yards north-west of Rheims. Brimont, however, was again lost by a fierce German attack by the reinforced armies. The enemy then possessed the two points of vantage. He brought his troops from the wooded ridge north of the Suippes, and entrenched them some five or six miles closer to Rheims. He dominated the city with gun fire from Brimont and Nogent; he ruled the Suippes valley with artillery lined out on the Suippes ridge, and across the Aisne at Craonne his howitzers stopped any forward movement by the French.

Our Allies held two heights to the east—one at Pouillon, between the Aisne and the Vesle, and one, known as the Mountain of Rheims, near Verzenay, south of the Vesle. But the light French field-guns, placed on these edges of the southern river plateau, could not reach the German positions. By a series of night infantry attacks, supported by a terrific gun fire directed by searchlights, the Germans tried to break the French lines on the plain. But each time the compact masses of grey figures approached the French trenches they were shattered by the 3 in. French guns. The fact was that from their two lines of heights on the west of Rheims the soldiers of France were as strongly posted for a defensive battle as were the Germans on the east and south-east.

All the men the Allies had lost in their attempts to storm the plateau of Soissons were avenged by the dreadful losses the Germans suffered in trying to break the French centre. In places south of the Marne the German ranks had fallen in swathes, like lines of mown hay. But south of the Aisne, where the plain of Champagne began, they fell as they had fallen round Nancy—one line on the top of another, till their dead and wounded built up a ghastly rampart of agony in front of the French positions. This was mainly the work of the terrible semi-automatic light French gun, working with its automatically correct time-fuse setter for the shrapnel and melinite shells.

In German guns the fuse is set by hand by one of the artillerymen. He does his work more or less skilfully, and the shell explodes with more or less uncertainty, either in front or behind the mark found by the range-finder. The French gunners, however, have an instrument called a "debouchoir," which, when the range is given, prepares the fuse with mechanical exactitude, so that the shrapnel or high-explosive shell bursts at the right fraction of a moment over the mark at which the gun is pointed. By a mechanical device on the gun the mark can be altered in a little more than two moments to another given position, and the automatically regulated fuse again explodes the shell over the new mark. By this fearful machinery of war the French field batteries again and again piled up the attacking German infantry, that was still employed in the old-fashioned, unscientific mass formations. The heavy German batteries at Brimont and Nogent could not seriously interfere with the light French guns on the western heights. The distance over the plain of Rheims was too great. It was eight miles from Brimont to the French position just south of Berry-au-Bac, and some seven miles from Nogent to the Mountain of Rheims, near Verzenay. The artillerymen on both sides had any hostile advancing troops at their mercy, but they could not damage each other's guns on the opposite heights. As the Germans were the attackers, they suffered, and the slaughter went on, by night and day, until they withdrew out of range towards the low ridge by the Suippes, and towards the higher hills of Nogent l'Abbesse.

Terrible work of French batteries

It was then that the Prussian commander of the heavy artillery at Nogent began to bombard Rheims Cathedral. He afterwards pretended that the cathedral was shelled as a military necessity, because French observation officers were seen to be using the towers to direct their guns. The Kaiser and General von Moltke and the Great Military Staff supported this stupid attempt to palliate the act of vandalism when they learnt, to their surprise, that the entire civilised world was shocked by the deeds of their gunners. But it was pointed out that the French soldiers already held heights some six hundred feet above the plain at Pouillon and some five hundred feet above it at the Mountain of Rheims, and therefore had no need to endanger their finest cathedral by showing themselves on the towers.

There was also the statement of the venerable Archbishop Landreux that no officers had been permitted to use the church for military purposes. Five nights before the bombardment began, a searchlight, placed on the tower to protect the non-combatants of the city from bomb-dropping airships, had been removed. This removal was carried out especially to save the cathedral from any attack on any grounds. Far from the sacred building being employed for warlike purpose, it had been turned into an hospital for wounded German soldiers. There were sixty grey-clad officers and men lying in knee-deep straw in the nave. Above, from the two towers, Red Cross flags were flying.

When these facts were published, the German military authorities shifted the grounds of their excuse. They alleged that there was a French battery near the cathedral, and that it was so placed as to bring the sacred building in the line of fire from the opposing German battery. As a matter of fact, there were some French guns a mile to the north of the cathedral, and some other French guns two miles to the south of it. It was the latter battery which the Germans, in their last gross lie, said that they were aiming at when they smote the cathedral. As was said by the American author, Mr. Richard Harding Davis, who was in Rheims when the bombardment began, "to accept the German claim we must believe that, continuously for four days, they aimed at a battery, and, two miles from it, hit the Cathedral of Rheims."

German lies about Rheims

Even in the hour of their defeat the Prussians were not so blind with rage as that. Their marksmanship was, in fact, exceedingly good. They were firing 6 in. shells at a distance of some 7,000 yards—from Nogent l'Abbesse hill. Adjoining the cathedral is a well-known hotel with a German proprietor. The gunners pitched their shells so exactly for four days—from Saturday, September 19th, to Tuesday, September 22nd—that each fell on the cathedral and the archbishop's palace and robing-room of the Kings of France, without a splinter injuring the German hotel hard by.

There is no creature on earth so diabolically spiteful as a bully who has been badly beaten but not yet thrashed into whimpering, grovelling cowardice.

GERMAN INFANTRY MARCHING OFF IN THE HALF-LIGHT OF EARLY MORNING FROM BURNING SENLIS.

When the Germans passed through Senlis on their way to the Aisne, it is said that some of the populace, infuriated at the conduct of the invaders, fired at them in the streets. In revenge, the Germans shot the mayor and other leading citizens, and put the fine old cathedral town to the flames. In the remarkable camera picture which is reproduced above, the enemy are seen moving off in the half-light of early morning, silhouetted against the lurid sky over the burning city.

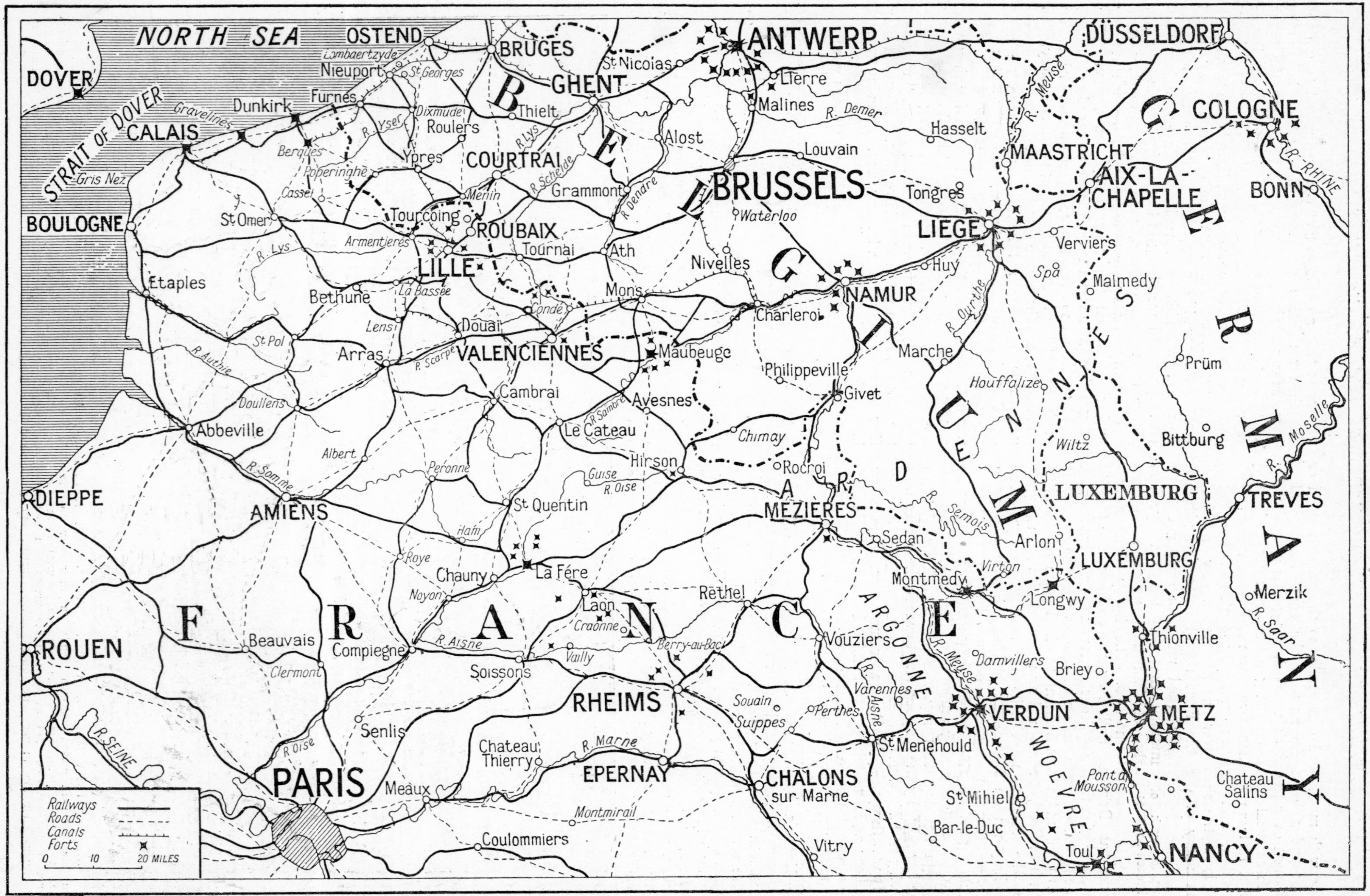

MAP OF THE RAILWAYS, RIVERS, AND PRINCIPAL CANALS IN NORTHERN FRANCE AND BELGIUM FROM THE GERMAN FRONTIER TO THE SEA.

BRITISH NERVE TELLS IN A SURPRISE ENCOUNTER.

A British officer, with a small company of men, was passing through a wood in the North of France when, on coming to a clearing, the little force almost ran into three German officers accompanied by about forty men and two machine-guns. The surprise was mutual. But the British officer at once demanded the surrender of the German party, and the latter, thinking that their opponents were only the advance guard of a large body of cavalry, immediately complied. One of the German machine-guns was captured by the British and the other destroyed.

The Prussian Guards, stationed round Nogent l'Abbesse, were badly beaten bullies. They had left something like half their number in the marshes of St. Gond, and when they tried in the night attacks round Rheims, on Thursday and Friday, to avenge their losses they had met again the terrible fire of the light French gun. In front of their gunners, at dawn on Saturday morning, rose like a fortress of paradise the most glorious cathedral in the world. It was the most perfect of all monuments of the French genius, a mighty yet delicate mass of sculptured stone, adorned with thousands of the finest statues of the flowering period of Gothic art—the beginning of the thirteenth century. The great jewel-like windows of ancient stained-glass were miracles of deep, full, glowing, harmonious colours. All that was fine and noble and splendid in German architecture and sculpture of the Gothic period—the structure of Cologne Cathedral in the Rhineland, the sculptures of Bamberg Cathedral in Bavaria—was derived from the French work of Rheims.

The loveliest possession of the French race

Rheims had been the school of art from which the civilised part of Germany in the thirteenth century learnt to model and build. Our own Westminster Abbey is a work in the French style. All Gothic works of the supreme period throughout Europe are in the French style. Of this style Rheims, the cathedral in which all French kings were crowned and anointed, was the consummate flower. It was the loveliest possession of the French race, even as the Parthenon was the loveliest possession of the Athenians. For this reason—and for this reason alone—the beaten, exasperated, spiteful Germans, impotently raging from a series of defeats, destroyed it. Hurled back from the Marne in a long, disastrous retreat, then gripped and held between the Aisne and the Suippes, where they endeavoured to recover from their greatest defeat since Jena and Auerstadt, the Prussians and Prussianised Teutons were reduced to the condition of homicidal maniacs, lacking the power to slaughter their opponents.

For more than a generation they had boasted that at the next opportunity they would bleed the French people white. But in less than six weeks after the opening of hostilities it was they who were bleeding to death. They had invaded France with over a million first-line troops, and already they had close upon a million casualties; they were using up their second line of reserves, and calling out their boys and untrained men. Desperately concentrating all available troops and guns for a final attempt to pierce the French lines and win the victory they needed before they swung across Europe to meet the Russians, they swept out in the fiercest of their frontal attacks, only to be driven back to their trenches, leaving another hundred thousand of their dead and wounded between the Oise and the Meuse.

A deed of cowardice and brutality

In one of these attacks the Germans collected the French soldiers who had surrendered in a previous fight, and arranged them in a compact line before their front ranks, and then drove them forward at the point of the bayonet to act as a shield against the fire from the French trenches they were trying to rush. This deed of extreme cowardice and brutality is mentioned officially in one of the descriptions by the "Eye-Witness" attached to the British army on the Aisne. While he was relating it, the Germans at Nogent, having perhaps no prisoners of war to torture and murder in this Teutonic manner, wreaked their baffled, insane wrath upon the sculptured stones and pictured windows of Rheims Cathedral.

They began by bombarding the dwelling-places of non-combatants in the city with 6 in. howitzer shells. On Friday, September 18th, the shrapnel shattered the cathedral windows and killed two wounded German soldiers lying on the thick straw in the nave. Then the shells

GENERAL VIEW OF THE TOWN OF METZ.
Metz, the fortified capital of German Lorraine, has in normal times a garrison of 25,000 men. During the early part of the war the army of Metz poured into the Woevre country by way of Mars-la-Tour, Chambley, Vignuelles, and Chaillon, just north of St. Mihiel.

began to dig great holes in the streets of the open town, and batter the houses of peaceful citizens and deposit the heaps of rubbish in the cellars. Women and children ran and stumbled amid the fallen masonry, seeking for shelter in the caves of the champagne bottlers, or streaming toward the city gate into the open country. At first the people were calm under the bombardment, but as evening drew on the women became at times panic-stricken. They fled down the streets weeping, praying, crossing themselves, and screaming in terror when the shells fell.

At eight o'clock on Friday night the howitzers ceased firing. The Germans were afraid that the position of their concealed batteries on the neighbouring hill would be disclosed by the flames showing in the darkness where the howitzers were fired. But at dawn on Saturday the bombardment was resumed. Night had brought counsel, and the gunners now aimed directly at the cathedral. One of the shells struck the scaffolding erected round the left tower for the purpose of restoration work. The wood flamed, and the fire quickly spread to the old arched roof of oak above the lower roof of stone. The molten lead dropped on the straw in the nave, on which the wounded Germans were lying. In the meantime the entire scaffolding about the cathedral was burning and calcining the stones, and shells were still falling.

Archbishop Landreux and his brave assistant, Abbé Chinot, a young, athletic, manly priest entrusted with the care of the cathedral, called for volunteers to save the injured enemies of their country. Helped by nurses and doctors, the archbishop and abbé carried or dragged the wounded men out of the flaming straw and through the north portal.

GERMAN TRANSPORT PASSING THROUGH A RUINED VILLAGE IN NORTHERN FRANCE.
The upper photograph, on the right hand, shows the quaint little town-hall of a small place near Rheims where the invader set up his headquarters for the time being.

There then occurred one of the most dramatic and memorable scenes in the history of France. A wild mob of townspeople surrounded the cathedral porch and blocked the way. They were men maddened by the vision of their great historic church in flames, by the bombardment of their homes, by the murder by shell fire of five hundred of their kinsmen and neighbours. The sight of the grey figures of the Germans drove them to frenzy. They shouted for the barbarians to be left to the fate their own countrymen had wrought for them. They refused to allow their hated wounded foes to be helped out of the burning cathedral.

THE BRITISH IN FRANCE.
Queen's Own Oxfordshire Hussars, one of the first of our Yeomanry regiments to go to the front, passing through a French village. Inset: Temporary headquarters of General Gough.

Grey-haired Archbishop Landreux and Abbé Chinot came forward and stood between the raging crowd and the helpless, suffering Germans. Some of the townsmen had raised their rifles. "You must first kill us," said the aged archbishop, "before you kill them."

The rifles were lowered, the shouting died to a murmur, the murmur to silence. The mob opened, and the Red Cross doctors and nurses, with the archbishop and abbé leading, carried the wounded men to a place of safety. In the distance the comrades of the men thus rescued from an agonising death continued to shatter and deface with their howitzer shells the nave where Joan of Arc stood at the coronation of the King of France, after she had saved her country from the invader. The heat of the fire, started by the shells, had turned the statues they failed to batter into images of dust that crumbled into powder when pressed by a man's hands.

No photograph of the ruins of the cathedral reveals its condition. In a year, when frost and rain have worked upon the calcined carvings and masonry, much of the detail that still shows to the eye will have peeled and crumbled off. By the winter of 1915 at latest Rheims Cathedral will only be a great, desolate ruin. The fairest thing existing on earth, since the Venetians destroyed the Parthenon at Athens, has vanished.

Only by combining, in imagination, what is best in Chartres Cathedral with what is best in Amiens Cathedral will future generations be able to form an idea of the original glory of Rheims. Even then the idea will be below the vanished reality. For the statues of the façade of the coronation cathedral of France were the flower of the last high creative period in monumental art since the period of Phidias. Those at Amiens cannot compare with them, as the Amiens front was not completed. What a joy for an Empire of but forty-four years of existence to have destroyed the loveliest work in Christendom! It may be that Belgians and Frenchmen will make no attempt to restore the ancient glorious buildings in Louvain, Malines, Termonde, Ypres, Rheims, and Arras. They may let the ruins stand to remind the world what German culture was at the height of its power.

When the German is half-drunk, he is either very gross and brutal, or extremely sentimental. If German commercial travellers are still welcomed in Belgium and Northern France after the great peace, we shall see at evening in the cafés of Louvain, Rheims, Arras, and Ypres the maudlin sons of the Fatherland declaiming, with tears in their eyes, over the sins of their nation. For bullies are curs at heart with some means of mastery to their hand. When the German is absolutely beaten and disarmed he will weep like a neurotic woman, partly in order to relieve his feelings, but partly to excite the pity of the men who have beaten him. Some standing examples of his achievements in the days of his hegemony in Europe will help to keep him penitent for several generations, and recall to other people what is concealed beneath his facile sentimentality and adaptiveness of temperament.

The German force at the height of Nogent l'Abbesse, from which the cathedral was bombarded, did not escape without punishment. At dawn on September 26th, after failing in a night attack on the French lines, some 15,000 Germans, including all that remained of the Prussian Guards corps, advanced down the old Roman road towards the Camp of Attila. Their object was to destroy the railway line between

TRAINLOAD OF CAPTURED GERMAN GUNS.
The guns are being taken through a French village on their way to England. On September 10th, 1914, thirteen guns, seven machine-guns, about two thousand prisoners and quantities of transport fell into our hands.

INFANTRY ADVANCE UNDER SHELL FIRE AGAINST GERMAN TRENCHES IN THE NEIGHBOURHOOD OF ARRAS.

For this attack over three hundred guns were brought up to assist the advancing Allies, and a deadly shell fire was poured into the German position, with the result that our men were able to gain the enemy's trenches with very little loss. In this way the Germans were slowly but surely pushed back in their efforts to break through to the west. Hardly any entrenched troops can withstand the effects of concentrated shell fire, and when the guns had prepared the way the attacking troops advanced with fixed bayonets to complete the work. Near Arras fighting of this kind went on day by day.

Rheims and Verdun, by which the French were manœuvring their troops and transporting ammunition and food supplies.

General Foch, however, learnt the enemy's movements, and prepared to counter them. A regiment of French cavalry was ordered to ride forward at full speed, occupy the village of Auberive, on the Suippes, and there fight a delaying action against the hostile columns. This was done to give time for a large body of French infantrymen at Jouchery, some five miles away, to march out and catch the main German force.

At six o'clock in the morning Auberive was occupied by the French cavalry. The High Street and byways were barricaded, and machine-guns were hoisted on house-tops and other points affording a wide sweep of fire. By this time the French artillery was some three miles away, on the road from Jouchery to Auberive. The German commander got to know of it, no doubt from his aerial scouts. He sent two thousand of the Death's Head Hussars, forming the cavalry arm of the raiding movement, to cut off the French guns.

The artillerymen were at St. Hilaire, on the Suippes, still between Jouchery and Auberive. On their left flank was a stretch of vineyards and freshly-ploughed fields. Through the vines and across the furrows the hussars charged. The surprise attack was well launched. It looked as though the horsemen would be amid the guns before the Frenchmen could bring their pieces into action.

In two minutes the artillery teams were unharnessed and the horses placed in the rear. The yelling lines of hussars drew nearer—the commands of their leaders could be heard round the guns. With lowered lances they galloped within three hundred yards of the artillery. Another eighty yards they were allowed to travel. "Fire!" rang out the French command. Through the blue smoke the gunners could see the horses rear up beneath the bursting shrapnel and fall. The front squadrons broke, but the supports galloped up and rallied to the charge. Again the guns thundered. Amid the vines and furrows were things that looked in the distance like rags trailing there. Sometimes one of the larger objects moved; it was a wounded horse trying to rise. Otherwise nothing could be seen. It was level, open country, and the French 75 millimetre gun has a range of some miles. No hussar escaped.

Death ride of the German Hussars

Meanwhile, the French cavalry at Auberive had delayed the main forces of the enemy as long as possible, and were retreating towards St. Hilaire. The victorious guns, rattling again as the horses dragged them along, advanced to meet their retiring dragoons. Just as the juncture was effected at St. Hilaire, in the Suippes valley, the Prussian Guard with its field-guns arrived.

The French gunners were not so successful this time. The German infantrymen held back, while their field batteries, posted on a favourable site, opened a bombardment on the French guns. Then the guardsmen crept forward through the vineyards to snipe the artillerymen. But, instead of attempting to defend their guns, the French dragoons moved forward to outflank the Prussians. At the same time, bayonets could be seen over the farther low hedges of grape-vines. The French infantry was arriving; one battalion of Zouaves was creeping round the rear of the attacking columns.

By the time the German commander became fully aware of what was happening his forces were almost surrounded. Only on his right, in the direction of Rheims, was there a gap, and that was quickly closing. Through it the German columns with their guns streamed, and to cover their retreat some 3,000 men of the Guards Corps sacrificed themselves. They charged five times at the closing lines

FRANCO-GERMAN ARTILLERY DUEL IN THE ARGONNE.
The German objective in the Argonne district was to obtain control of the road connecting their positions on the western outskirts of the forest with Varennes on its eastern edge, where the right wing of the German forces was trying to invest Verdun from the north. But it is difficult country for artillery movements, and the French took full advantage of the opportunities it afforded for cleverly concealed batteries, against which the Germans directed a searching shrapnel fire.

GETTING A HEAVY GERMAN HOWITZER INTO POSITION.
A German 21 centimetre (8·27) howitzer, which fired a 248 lb. shell, the dense black smoke arising from the explosion of which won for it the names of "Black Maria," "Jack Johnson," and "Coal-Box." The range was 8,900 yards. The wheels were surrounded with linked steel plates faced with wood, and when the howitzer was fired the wheels rested on mats of cane with steel plates between them.

of French troops. Each time they were terribly repulsed. After the fifth assault barely a hundred men were left standing, and they were all wounded. So they turned their rifles down—a sign of surrender. Naturally, the Frenchmen treated them well, for they were brave men—the only Prussian Guardsmen in the Great War who exemplified the heroic traditions of their old corps. They saved the entire German force from destruction.

The well-known Irish novelist who writes under the nom de guerre of George A. Birmingham has published an article expressing doubts as to the remarkable series of defeats suffered by the Prussian Guards Corps. He said it had been first severely cut up at bayonet point by the Turcos at Charleroi, then bogged and slain in tens of thousands in the marsh of St. Gond. Then, as we now see, it lost three thousand more men at St. Hilaire, and afterwards it was almost entirely destroyed by British troops round Ypres. It does seem a superhuman accumulation of disasters for a single body of soldiers.

Blunted spear-point of the German Army

But, in matter of fact, the modern Prussian Guards consisted originally of an army corps of first-line troops, with a large reserve. After the Battle of St. Hilaire the original army corps of 40,000 men was practically destroyed. It was the reserve units, with perhaps freshly-trained recruits to fill out the battalions, that emerged afterwards at Ypres, only to fall, and break completely the traditions of the Guards by giving ground.

The Prussian Guard was intended for use only in the most vital operations. It had to go on till it dropped; then take cover, and hold on till it was killed or reinforced. This, however, it failed to do on almost every important occasion in the Great War. The spear-point of the vast German Army, it was soon blunted and then broken, repaired, and broken again. There were rumours that some thousand Guardsmen were at last marched out, unarmed and helpless, and offered as a target to the Allies, in order to teach the corps to die. Even a German general is unlikely to have murdered his men in this fashion. But the mere fact that such a legend should have spread to Holland, shows to what state the morale of the crack Berlin corps had at last been, in current opinion, reduced.

In defensive tactics German leadership was certainly good. Along the valley of the Suippes, only a day after the retreat of the German centre was concluded above Souain, the enemy was admirably entrenched. He made at once deep ditches, protected from shrapnel fire by cover, and began to hollow out underground roomy caves in which to rest and sleep. Protected by his artillery on the low swell of ground in the rear, the German soldier displayed in defensive trench warfare a laborious application that quickly made all his lines impregnable. Had General Foch and General de Langle de Cary, operating between Rheims and the Argonne Forest, continued to attack, they would have seen the Ninth and Fourth French Armies melt away like snow in spring-time.

Defensive trench warfare

Both generals, however, had been fighting the Germans, now on the attack, now on the defence, since the first retirement from Northern France. They knew exactly the weak point in Teutonic tactics. In attacking operations German leadership was brutally bad; the troops were handled without any economy of force. The lines were denser than was properly required with good soldiers armed with long-range magazine rifles. The supports were closer to the firing-line than was necessary with stubborn and well-trained leading troops.

Bullets and shells that missed the Germans in the firing-line struck the reserve companies that were feeding the

BRITISH MILITARY CAR TRAPPED NEAR SOISSONS.
At night time German cavalry took up positions on roads between the opposing lines, and after distributing broken wine bottles over the ground, retired to a spot convenient for sniping. Mr. W. F. Bradley was caught in one of these traps near Soissons, and while he was putting on a spare wheel his companions took cover, their fire making the Germans withdraw.

front ranks and filling the gaps left by the men put out of action. All this costly close formation of the German infantry was a mark of a lack of science and intelligence in the officers responsible for the training and leading of the men. In spite of the new machines that Krupp had made in large numbers for them, the German squirearchy that officered the Army had learnt nothing of the practical handling of men in war since 1870.

They had reduced their forces to the same condition as that into which the Prussian Army fell only six years after the death of Frederick the Great. The Franco-British lines on the Aisne and Suippes Rivers ran near the Argonne Forest through the town of Valmy. Here, six years after Frederick the Great died, a French revolutionary general in 1792 had defeated the Prussians and Austrians under the Duke of Brunswick. Now the Germans under the Duke of Württemberg were undergoing a similar experience of unexpected defeat, after a similar period of military hegemony in Europe.

Brutal leadership of German officers

Goethe, who witnessed the first Battle of Valmy, in September, 1792, prophesied, against his own countrymen, that the victory of the new French democracy had opened a new era in the history of mankind. He saw in it the downfall of the system of princely privilege and peasant serfdom that fettered the development of the peoples of the European continent. He hailed France as the redeemer of nations, and the French cannonade at Valmy as the salute of guns at the birth of a new movement of liberty.

But for a hundred years afterwards this movement had been prevented from spreading into Germany. The old system of feudalism had transformed itself, in the course of aggressive wars abroad and strong-handed subjection of the working population at home, into a scientific bureaucracy. The ancient tyranny of the noble classes was exerted in a new form with a firmer grip and a larger scope. But again the French guns at Valmy, in September, 1914, echoed over the wild Forest of Argonne, bearing the same message as that which had first disturbed and then inspired the courtly, egotistic German poet of genius attached to the train of the Duke of Weimar. Again the democracy of France, once more attacked unawares in the midst of its religious, social, and political difficulties, was proving, from the cannon's mouth, that the spirit born of freedom was stronger than all the cunning and force born of military despotism.

FINE WORK OF THE LINCOLNS ON THE AISNE.

During the Battle of the Aisne, two companies of the Lincolns were ordered to attack a German battery which, situated on a hill, was trying to silence some British guns on another hill about a mile away. Making a wide detour, our men managed to enter the wood right in the rear of the enemy, and got within two hundred yards of them before they were discovered. They took seven guns, and not one of the German gunners escaped.

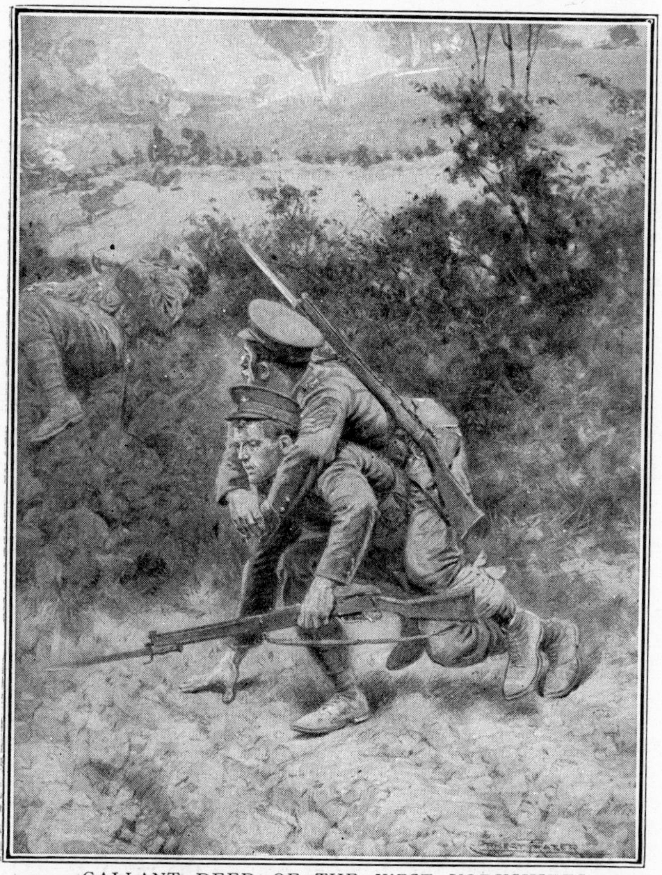

GALLANT DEED OF THE WEST YORKSHIRES.

In a gallant charge on the German trenches during the conflict on the Aisne, a company of the 1st West Yorkshire Regiment (The Prince of Wales's Own) was almost wiped out. Private Charles Bell, seeing his sergeant drop, bandaged him as well as he could, and then, to quote his own words, "started for home," crawling along the ground with the sergeant on his back. After about two hours they reached safety and the field transport.

For months the battle continued to rage round Valmy. At first the Fourth French Army, under General de Langle de Cary, carried the towns of Vienne and Varennes on either side of the northern part of the Argonne ridge. Then, on September 24th, when the Germans were reinforced, the French were driven back on St. Menehould and the Verdun-Rheims railway line. The enemy next tried to take the railway, and almost succeeded on Sunday, September 27th. But the ground he won in the morning was recovered by the French in the evening. Round St. Menehould General Gérard, with a single French army corps, not merely held out against two German army corps, one of which, the Sixteenth, had come from Metz, but he steadily pushed the invaders back by a continuous action amid the rocks and woods of the Argonne that lasted for months.

French efficiency in the Argonne

Operating in concert with this little army was a force under the famous General Dubail, whose high and brilliant genius for war has been one of the superb revelations of the campaign. He was called from the hills around Nancy to help General Sarrail, the commander of the field army and garrison of Verdun, in the fighting on the east of the Argonne ridge and along the heights of the Meuse between Verdun and Toul.

To the French people the incessant combats in the wild, beautiful, rocky, upland Forest of Argonne have the same interest as the struggles of our men at Le Cateau, the Aisne, and Ypres have for us. There in a region of narrow defiles, shaded by sombre trees, of swells and hollows girdled by impassable thickets, every woodland way is marked by graves, every clearing is known by the slaughter that occurred there.

GENERAL VON FALKENHAYN.

He succeeded Moltke as Chief of Staff. Inset: General Wernher von Voights-Retz, who tried to succeed Moltke, but became Quartermaster-General of the German armies.

In this broken maze of country, offering at every step opportunities for ambushes and surprise attacks and feint retreats over mined ground, the French troops withstood the most violent of all the enemy's attacks. They countered him in his double advance from east to west, from Metz to Verdun, and from north to south, from the frontier to the Marne. The men holding the Argonne were the pivot on which General Joffre swung his men in the retreats of August and the advances of September.

If General Helmuth von Moltke had had his way, when he was still Chief of Staff, the defeat on the Marne, the counter-checks on the Aisne and the Suippes, and the baffled attempts at a turning movement in the west, would have been concluded by the massing of three-quarters of a million men for the recapture of the Argonne Forest. It was because the Kaiser decided against this plan, and, with the help of General von Falkenhayn, developed a scheme of his own for using the men at Ypres and La Bassée, that Moltke retired from the practical commandership-in-chief.

It must be said of Moltke that he at least knew best where to strike, though, after his first successes in August, he usually failed to strike swift and hard enough. The Argonne was the danger-point for France. That was why Joffre had three of his best generals there, and many of his keenest, trickiest, and most skilful troops. The first of the new heavy artillery was sent to them, with some of the more mobile siege-guns of Verdun. They formed the pivot. If the pivot became unsteady, all the armies reposing on it would falter.

German effort to turn the French flank

There was a day in September when it seemed as if the pivot was shaken and the entire northern line of Franco-British forces put into danger. On September 15th the army of the Crown Prince, which had been trying to break a new gap of invasion at Fort Troyon, below Verdun and Toul, was compelled to retreat. By a terrible bombardment it had just reduced to a heap of ruin the fort that kept the German forces round Metz from turning the French flank. But the Crown Prince had to retire before he opened the new gateway into France.

Then General von Heeringen, who had been commanding the Metz army, took over the control of the western positions on the plateau of Soissons. But the man he left at Metz in his place did not lack initiative and driving power. Thrown back towards Metz in the third week in September, when many of his first-line troops went to reinforce the fatigued and dispirited northern German armies, the new commander at Metz gathered from over the Rhine a fresh host of second-line soldiers, and some Skoda howitzers, capable of throwing 12 in. shells an unusual distance.

Prussian advance across the Woevre

Clearing a broad path for his troops, in the last week of September, by watering with shell and shrapnel the ground ahead of his march, the German commander advanced from his battle quarters at Thiaucourt across the flattish land known as the Woevre country. It lies between Verdun and Toul, and as it approaches the upper course of the Meuse, the Woevre plain rises into a line of bare hills known as the Heights of the Meuse. A chain of French forts on these hills, including Fort Troyon and the Camp des Romains, connected the defensive works of Toul and Verdun and kept out the invaders.

The German commander seized one of the lower hills, at a distance of some miles from the Camp des Romains and the Meuse River. There did not seem much danger in this. The guns of the fort could not reach him, and he would have to come nearer to attack the fort. But he did not. He had a surprise packet for the French garrison. It consisted of the new 12 in. Austrian howitzer, divided into three parts, each drawn by a motor.

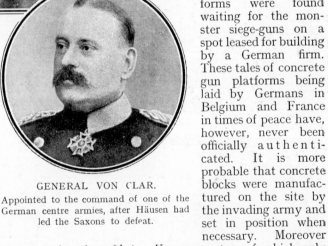

GENERAL VON CLAR.

Appointed to the command of one of the German centre armies, after Häusen had led the Saxons to defeat.

It was afterwards reported in a French newspaper that concrete platforms were found waiting for the monster siege-guns on a spot leased for building by a German firm. These tales of concrete gun platforms being laid by Germans in Belgium and France in times of peace have, however, never been officially authenticated. It is more probable that concrete blocks were manufactured on the site by the invading army and set in position when necessary. Moreover—except for the 16½ in. Krupp mortar, of which only eight existed when war broke out—the large howitzers, with their pedal wheels, are understood to have special pneumatic and hydraulic recoil chambers to cushion the shock and obviate the delay of bolting the many-tonned pieces to fixed platforms.

It is true that Krupp's were bad at designing recoil chambers for very heavy artillery. Our battleships and battle-cruisers have had 13½ in. guns for several years, while the completed capital ships of the German Navy were only

A GERMAN COIGN OF VANTAGE UNDER THE RED CROSS.

The Germans sought to justify the bombardment of Rheims Cathedral by pretending that the French used the towers for observation purposes. But they themselves committed this very offence at Vitry-le-Francois. Here, after they had hoisted three Red Cross flags on the cathedral, their officers, as testified by the mayor and a score of reputable citizens, reported from one of the towers the movements of the French troops and batteries.

HUNTING THE LURKING FOE IN A FRENCH VILLAGE.
After the seizure of the village by the British, the latter had to scour the streets for German stragglers. In our picture a trooper is seen trying a door behind which a German might have been hidden, a comrade is following, while close by is an officer with his revolver ready for emergencies.

armed with 12 in. guns. This tremendous superiority in British naval gun fire was partly obtained through a mistake made by the firm of Krupp. They undertook to arm the more recent German battleship with a 14 in. gun that would pulverise any British vessel. The great gun was made and mounted in ships designed to carry it, but at the firing trials it was found that the recoil chamber and mounting were inadequate to stand the strain. The German Navy had to fall back on the outclassed 12 in. guns.

But we may take it that the design of recoil chambers and mounting for a mobile 11 in. howitzer was not beyond the inventive—or initiative—faculty of the professors that Krupp's employed. As for the 12 in. howitzer manufactured by Baron von Skoda in Austria, the invention of which has been attributed to an American, this can also be fitted with a mounting that makes the bolting down of the piece unnecessary. It would be so large a loss in mobility—the one thing needful—if an attacking howitzer, requiring to be moved whenever its position was searched by a defending gun of equal range, had always to be bolted to a slab of artificial rock before it could be used.

ARRIVAL OF X-RAY APPARATUS AT A FRENCH BASE.
Arrival at a French base, in close touch with the fighting-line, of X-ray apparatus, indispensable in dealing with complicated wounds and locating bullets.

However this may be, the Skoda howitzers were a terrible surprise for the garrison of the Camp des Romains on the Heights of the Meuse by the town of St. Mihiel. They had no guns capable of replying to the mighty 12 in. high-explosive shells that dropped on their hill fort from a distant position they could not discern. The German infantry, entrenched with light field-guns and Maxims, prevented the small body of defenders from making a reconnaissance in force. General Sarrail moved many troops down from Verdun, and the commanding general at Toul moved up many troops from the south. But with heavy artillery brought by railway to Thiaucourt, close to

German surprise for the French

A CAPTURED SUSPECT.
Suspected spy in charge of a mounted escort being taken for inquiry before the French general at Baccarat, a town to the south-east of Lunéville.

the scene of the action, the German commander kept off both the Second and Third French Armies, and continued to blow another gateway of invasion through the Camp des Romains.

Under the continual shower of devastating 12 in. shells the fort quickly crumbled. When the guns were put out of action, the Metz army advanced under cover of a general bombardment of all its guns and the fort was captured. Great was the joy in Germany. At last a breach had been made in the famous fortressed line, which had seemed so strong to the Great Military Staff at Berlin that it brought Great Britain into the conflict by the invasion of Belgium rather than lose a hundred thousand men in getting between Verdun and Toul.

French surprise for the Germans

Glorious were the prospective results of the advance through the gap of a large powerful German Army, composed of the new Lorraine forces, and every soldier that could be spared from the Russian fields of war. If half a million men could be poured over the Meuse by St. Mihiel, they would arrive far behind all the main Franco-British armies from the Argonne Forest, the Suippes and Aisne River valleys, and the heights west of Noyon and St. Quentin, in Northern France. Joffre would have to retire hastily all his forces below Paris, and leave Verdun to its fate, and pivot his troops on Toul for the grand decisive battle.

INHABITANTS OF RHEIMS SLEEPING IN ONE OF THE WINE-VAULTS DURING THE GERMAN BOMBARDMENT.

All this had been foreseen by the commander of the Metz army and Helmuth von Moltke. It was the reason why they had planned and carried out the attack on the fort of the Camp des Romains. But it had also been foreseen by General Joffre. After the previous nearly successful attempt on Fort Troyon, the French Commander-in-Chief had been quite prepared to see the Verdun-Toul line breached somewhere in the middle. He was well aware of his weak point; he strengthened it before it gave way.

When the Germans advanced from the fallen fort towards the Meuse their commander was suddenly brought up. On the hills above the sunken stream the French had concealed more powerful batteries than those used in the lost fort. Marksmen were entrenched under shrapnel shelters on the nearer heights, and General Dubail, the most terrible fighter in France, directed the operations. All his guns and men were hidden. There were light "seventy-fives," buried in pits, and served by cave men who had nothing to do, unless the enemy succeeded in crossing the river and tried to storm the heights. Then the "seventy-fives" would work as they worked when the Kaiser shattered the First Bavarian Army and the White Cuirassiers of the Guards Corps in an attempt to storm the Grand Couronné de Nancy.

In front of the "seventy-fives" were the rapid-fire field-howitzers, also sunk in turf-roof pits, with their painted muzzles indistinguishable by aerial scouts from the hill pass. Farther behind were the heavy field-guns and siege-artillery from Toul. They all formed a semicircle round the position on the Heights of the Meuse, from which the Germans might try to cross. Then across the stream, flanking the German army on either side, were the French field forces from Toul and Verdun.

The price of German advance too high

Directly in front of the Germans was prepared a terrific cross-fire of bullets, shells, and shrapnel from three points of the compass. Behind them, as they advanced, shells would fall from the river heights held by the Toul and Verdun garrisons, which were also pressing them on both sides. The French were asking the Germans a toll of a good deal more than the proverbial hundred thousand men for the passage across the Upper Meuse. Moltke thought that the price was too high. Falkenhayn, when he succeeded as Chief of Staff, came to the same conclusion.

So from Aisne to Upper Meuse the Germans were held.

WORKING PARTY OF RHEIMS LADIES KNITTING IN ONE OF THE DIMLY-LIT WINE-VAULTS OF THE CITY.

CONVALESCENT WAR HORSES AT AN ARMY VETERINARY CAMP.

CHAPTER XXXIX.

THE RAILWAY BATTLES OF NORTHERN FRANCE.

General Joffre Brings Up His Reserve—How He Handled the French Railway System—German Method of Fighting with Railways—Menace of New French Army Alters German Plans—Castelnau Strikes at German Railway Communications—Fierce Struggle Round Noyon and Peronne—General Joffre Forms Another General Reserve—Franco-British Lines Extend to the Sea—German Commander Reinforced—Pushes French Back from St. Quentin—French Stand at Roye and Quesnoy—New German Plan of Campaign—Falkenhayn Succeeds Moltke—Attack Round the Coast by Way of Lille Intended.

FROM the point of view of General Joffre, the Battle of the Aisne came to an end on September 20th, 1914. For after the general reconnaissance in force made by the Sixth French Army, the British Expeditionary Force, and the Fifth French Army, the French Commander-in-Chief decided that the line of river heights held by the strengthened German forces was too strong to be carried by a frontal attack. So he directed that the enemy should be retained along the front, and thus opened the new phase of siege warfare along the Aisne. His plan was to sap the strength of the Germans by reversing the apparent positions of the two opposing hosts, and compelling the foe to leave his rifle pits on the plateau and then to attack the trenches of the Allies.

He carried out this scheme by suddenly bringing sharp and severe pressure to bear upon the western flank of the German lines. The leading factor in modern French strategy is an apparent waste of fighting force. The commander usually keeps one large army unemployed in the rear, round some railway centre, from which it can be railed to any point on the front. It constitutes his general reserve. No matter how fierce and bitter the struggle may be in the firing-line, the general reserve does not come into action unless a disaster or victory is imminent. It is a reservoir of force kept for great decisive moments.

Napoleon handled the general reserve in a masterly way in his small, old-fashioned contests, in which horse traction and the marching power of the soldier limited the battle-front to about two miles. But with the invention and development of steam traction and telegraphic communication, the manœuvring of troops in civilised countries, over a gridiron of railways, became a vast and complicated business. Moltke simplified it by abolishing the method of the general reserve. He put all his available soldiers into the fighting-line, timing their advance and attack so that they should be simultaneous along the great battle-front. From the railways he asked only that sweep, speed, and punctuality of transport which would enable him to bring every man and gun on to the battlefield in accordance with the time-table of the fight.

GENERAL DE MAUD'HUY, G.C.M.G.
He commanded a fine body of French troops between Arras and Lille.

Field-Marshal von Hindenburg, Moltke's most famous pupil in railway warfare, recently employed the same method. At Tannenberg he allowed the Russian General Samsonoff to advance between two lines of East Prussian railways. He first flung out a heavily-gunned force to hold up the Russian front, then by the two railways he brought up two large bodies of troops on the flanks of the Russian army, and almost encircled it. As we shall see, the new German Commander-in-Chief, General von Falkenhayn, adopted an identical method in his attack upon the French army in and around Lille. Using two converging lines of railways, one running towards the north and the other to the east of the French position, he put every available man into the trains, in an attempt at a rapid and overwhelming concentration of force.

The method is easy, quick, and simple. It has, however, the disadvantage of being obvious. When the available forces of an enemy are known, and he has long lines of railway communications running through hostile countries—such as Belgium and Northern France—his few possible moves can be studied on the map. And both by aerial observation and by the ordinary system of espionage, the rolling-stock by which his concentrations and manœuvres are affected can be kept under surveillance.

This is one of the reasons why the German invading armies never succeeded in surprising the French Military Staff after the first frontier battles at Mons and Charleroi. Only by little combinations of forces, within marching distance of each other, could the enemy make any unexpected concentration. What he won by this old-fashioned, limited method was usually lost through a subtler use of railways by the French.

LIEUTENANT-GENERAL SIR WILLIAM ROBERTSON, K.C.V.O., C.B., D.S.O., QUARTERMASTER-GENERAL WITH THE BRITISH EXPEDITIONARY FORCE.

"In such operations as I have described," wrote Sir John French, in his despatch of September 7th, 1914, descriptive of the Battle of Mons and the retreat to the Marne, "the work of the Quartermaster-General is of an extremely onerous nature. Lieutenant-General Sir William Robertson has met what appeared to be almost insuperable difficulties with his characteristic energy, skill, and determination; and it is largely owing to his exertions that the hardships and sufferings of the troops, inseparable from such operations, were not much greater." Born in 1860, Sir William served with distinction in India and South Africa. Our illustration is from the fine portrait in oils by Mr. John St. Helier Lander.

CHARGE OF THE FRENCH LIGHT CAVALRY AFTER TH

The incident so vividly depicted in the above spirited drawing took place at Lassigny, a village on the high road between Montvidier and Noyon, in the heart of the cider country. Here, when General Joffre began his great effort to turn the enemy's right flank above the Aisne, the Germans strongly entrenched themselves; but when the French guns had silenced the G batteries, the enemy were surprised by a dashing charge on the part French Light Cavalry. The details of the above picture are vouched fo correspondent who supplied the artist with the facts from which he w

MAN ARTILLERY HAD BEEN DESTROYED AT LASSIGNY.

al Joffre's new plan was communicated to Sir John French on September 1914, and in accordance with it the troops under General Castelnau ed the enemy's flank-guards from the Oise to Arras. The Germans ted that their forces round Noyon were soon demoralised; and the French, advancing from Lassigny, specially distinguished themselves. A German officer writing home at this time, testified that "only the fine flower of our troops is still alive. The others cannot resist so many misfortunes, and fall to earth, killed by the efforts and sufferings that duty imposes on us."

GALLANTRY OF THE 1ST WEST YORKSHIRES IN THE BATTLE OF THE AISNE.

During the Battle of the Aisne the 1st West Yorkshires were sent to relieve the Guards Brigade on the British right on the night of September 19th, 1914. Next morning they were ordered to reinforce the first line, which was being heavily attacked. For a quarter of a mile they advanced under a hail of shrapnel and machine-gun fire. Out of 1,150 only 206 afterwards answered the roll-call. Among the killed was Lieut. E. W. Wilson, the officer who is seen falling. The picture is from a sketch and description furnished by Sergeant J. F. Woodcock.

For the French, who have for centuries been remarkable for their power of originality, have revived Napoleon's use of a general reserve, and worked out a brilliant system of employing it on the immensely long modern battle-front. The reserve consisted of [illegible] rolling-stock, and auxiliary motor-vehicles, collected at various transport centres, with men, guns, horses, and supplies ready for railway movement to any point along the front of two hundred or more miles. No study of railway maps could disclose the point at which this reservoir of force would be employed. In fact, part of it was sometimes kept in movement on the rails to distract the enemy's spies and disturb the German Military Staff with feints of attack, that might develop in a single night into a violent onset hundreds of miles distant from the transporting centres.

WRECKED HOTEL DE VILLE AND BELFRY AT ARRAS.
Between October 5th and 30th, 1914, the Germans bombarded Arras three times, wrecking the sixteenth-century Hotel de Ville and the beautiful belfry. Arras was destroyed by the Vandals in 407, and by the Normans in 880; was besieged in 1414 and 1479; taken by the Prince of Orange in 1578; and again besieged in 1640 and 1654 by Condé, and rescued by Turenne.

All that the German commander could do in answer to this continual secret menace was to press continually against the French front, and prepare on his own exposed flank for any eventuality. By pressing on in front he tried to compel General Joffre to use his general reserve for a defensive purpose. But, naturally, the German commander was never able to feel quite sure that he had succeeded in this design. He certainly did not succeed in it by the counter-attacks he made against the Franco-British positions on the Aisne and Suippes in the third week of September. General Joffre, as we have seen, sent some reinforcements to General Maunoury's Sixth Army between Noyon and Soissons, but at the same time he continued to build up his general reserve.

The mere threat of it saved the whole of North-Eastern France. All that the Germans soon afterwards violently and vainly struggled for—the entire occupation of Belgium, the seaports of Dunkirk and Calais and the heights of Gris Nez, opposite Dover—were theirs for the taking at the beginning of the Battle of the Aisne. They occupied the important city of Amiens, far to the south of the places they afterwards desired to reach. They retained the Belgian Army in Antwerp, and had brought up the siege-artillery for the rapid reduction of the last Belgian stronghold. What is still more important, they also had in Germany large masses of troops of inferior quality, but well provided with artillery, and with these they might well have been able to strengthen and extend their lines eastward to Amiens and the sea coast.

The factor that saved North-Eastern France

Instead, they suddenly abandoned Amiens in the second week of September, and withdrew all their eastern forces towards their main lines of communication round St. Quentin and Cambrai. Such was the effect of the menace of General Joffre's reserve army, held far in the rear. The Germans could not divine at what point he would strike with it. They feared alike a terrible, reinforced assault on their front, where the British soldiers had already nearly wedged through, or a French advance up the Oise River, cutting off their western detachments and assailing their main railway communications with distant Cologne.

As a matter of fact, General Joffre had arranged to strike at the German communications from Amiens. He placed his new army under General Castelnau, one of the heroes of the battles round Nancy, and launched it across Northern France on September 20th. By way of keeping the enemy still further occupied, another French force—composed of Territorial divisions, oldish men of the militia class—operated under General Brugère to the north of Castelnau's army.

This remarkable effort did not exhaust the reservoir of force at the disposal of the French Commander-in-Chief. As soon as General Castelnau had engaged the enemy's flank-guards from Noyon to Arras, another French army of young, first-rate troops was formed and railed, under the command of General Maud'huy, to the region of Arras and Lens. Territorial divisions on September 30th

VIEW OF THE TOWN OF ALBERT.
Albert, a town on the River Ancre, was wrecked by the Germans in the autumn of 1914.

extended the French lines to Lille, and from Lille to Dunkirk a thinner stretch of British and French Marines and British sailors, with armoured motor-cars, carried the Franco-British front to the sea. Large detachments of the allied cavalry—French dragoons and hussars, British heavy and light horsemen, and the chivalry of India, brought up with their mounts from Marseilles—strengthened the line from Lille to the Channel.

Such were the complete dispositions of the allied forces barely a fortnight after the enemy turned to make a stand by the Aisne and the Suippes Rivers. German military authorities themselves admit that the way in which General Joffre handled his railways was a revelation. He had clean surpassed them in the kind of modern strategy in which they thought they excelled everybody. They had thoroughly studied the military capacity of the railways of North-Eastern France. General von Kluck and other German Army commanders had visited the country some years before the war, and examined the ground from Rheims to Noyon, and from Arras, Amiens, to Calais. While they were busy at this work of personal reconnaissance, the French commander of the army corps at Amiens—his name was Joffre—was also riding about the region, and carefully studying it, as one of the great battlefields of the future. And now that the obscure and neglected major-general once stationed at Amiens had become the captain of France in the year of her great destiny, the work he had done, after his return from the conquest of Timbuctoo, was bearing good fruit.

Joffre's earlier study of the battlefield

IN THE TOWN OF ROYE (SOMME).
An old street of quaint shops in the once prosperous town of Roye, now little more than a name.

On September 17th the German troops round Noyon were placed under the command of Field-Marshal von Heeringen. They consisted of men drawn from Hamburg, Bremen, and Schleswig-Holstein province. Some hundreds of motor-vehicles were employed in transporting battalions of infantry to the fighting-line, as many of the men were too fatigued to march. They had tramped a hundred and fifty miles in five days, with insufficient food, and were still badly fed. When the flank battle opened on September 20th they immediately fell to pieces.

Motor transport of the invader's battalions

Both the rifle fire and the gun fire of the new French army were murderous. Violent in attack and tenacious in defence, General Castelnau's men fought down all opposition. Only the heavy German artillerymen of the Government gunnery school could make any impression on the French soldiers. The Germans admit that their forces round Noyon were soon demoralised. "The time came," writes one of their officers, "when a man mocks at all feelings of humanity and civilisation. When a party of our soldiers came on a house, you can be sure that they left nothing. All their terrible instincts awakened into power. Our 17th Division is no longer a division, but a little company at the end of its strength and ammunition. I must say that our leaders have not acted as men of skill and foresight. Their attitude strikes one as that of bewildered, troubled souls who are no longer masters of themselves."

On September 21st Heeringen sent a Bavarian reinforcement to the beaten and distracted force guarding his western flank. There was another fierce fight round the woods of Ribecourt, with the French advancing from Lassigny along the Oise. Again the French won, and the German officer, writing home to his family, draws a significant picture of the way in which men of his nation strangely wilt under defeat.

"What will happen to us? I do not know and I dare not forecast. Many of our men are dying from fatigue and privation. Our officers especially are in a state of nervous exhaustion. They cannot do anything more. Our horses, that for weeks have fed, watered, and slept

FIFTEENTH-CENTURY TREATY HOUSE AT NOYON.
The ancient town of Noyon, in the Department of the Oise, was the scene of the Coronation of Charlemagne in 768. Calvin was born there in 1509. The fighting-line crept up from Compiègne, through Noyon, St. Quentin, Peronne, and Arras to Armentières.

VIEW OF THE CITADEL OF ARRAS.
Arras, the capital of the Pas-de-Calais, was bombarded by the Germans on October 5th-8th, 21st-24th, and 30th. Those who saw it afterwards described it as "a modern Pompeii." At Arras was signed the treaty of peace after Agincourt.

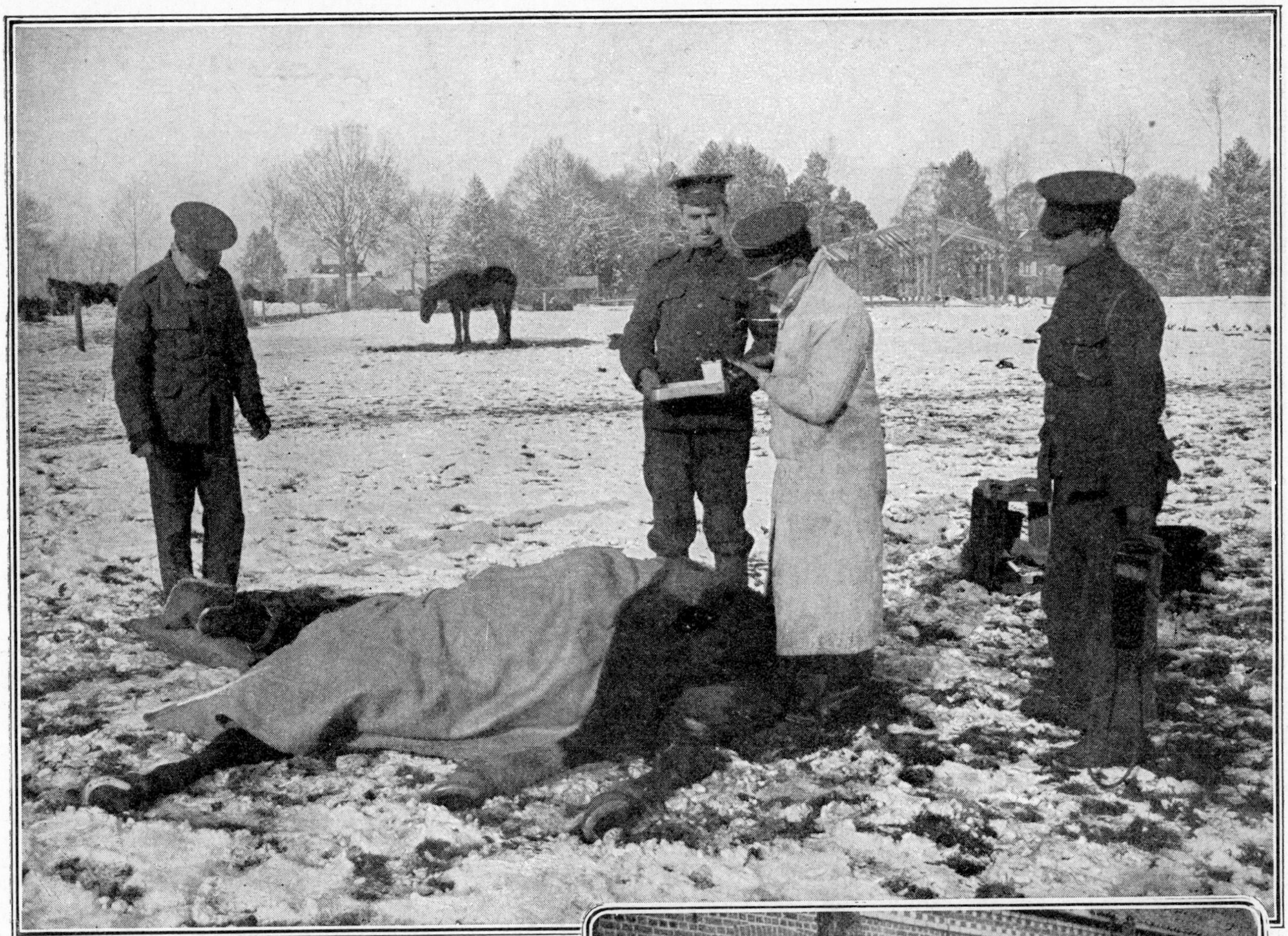

TENDING A WOUNDED HORSE: AN OPERATION IN THE FIELD.

The operation was performed under chloroform for the removal of a shell splinter. The above photograph is the property of the R.S.P.C.A. Fund for Sick and Wounded Horses.

SHELL HAVOC AMONG ARTILLERY HORSES.

The destruction of horses in the Great War was only less appalling than the human slaughter. Our photograph is of a team killed by a German shell, which also killed the two drivers.

with their saddles on, suddenly fall on the ground and lie stone-still. The same thing is happening to the mass of our soldiers. Only the fine flower of our troops is still alive. The others cannot resist so many misfortunes, and fall to earth, killed by the efforts and sufferings that duty imposes on us."

Seldom has the extraordinary way in which sickness and exhaustion rapidly tell on a dispirited army been so vividly described. Though Heeringen was making at the time a tremendous effort on his front, along the Aisne heights, his flank was growing weaker and weaker. General Castelnau drove fiercely in, on a line stretching some sixty miles, from Arras in the north to Ribecourt near the Aisne. East of Arras the French Territorial troops penetrated to the historic city of Cambrai, close to the edge of the former battlefield where the Second British Army Corps, in the retreat from Mons, made its heroic stand against the forces of Kluck. Peronne was taken on the road to the important railway centre of St. Quentin; and Tergnier, another knot of German lines of communication, was menaced.

German communications menaced

The impetuosity and skill of the French troops were magnificent. In the valley of the Oise, for example, Lieutenant Verlin, with fifty men, held up six thousand hostile troops. The small party was engaged in a reconnaissance on the right bank of the river, where Uhlans were vaguely reported to have been seen. The officer sighted the enemy in large numbers, and ordered his men to rejoin their regiment without showing themselves. But the Germans discovered the little force, and fired on it as it took shelter in a wood. But when Lieutenant Verlin got his men safely amid the trees, he spread them out on a very long front, and there, by good marksmanship and quick dodging from tree to tree, they made the enemy think the wood was held by at least a regiment. The Germans brought up guns and searched the forested tract with shrapnel, but the Frenchmen were so few that they did not suffer much from the gun fire. Had the Germans at any time charged, they would have won without a struggle. But they were over-cautious, and after holding the ground till midnight, and losing thirty-seven out of fifty men, the French retired and joined their regiment.

Advancing between the Oise and Somme Rivers, General Castlenau pressed forward towards the railway junction of Tergnier, from which the German batteries and troops on the heights of the Aisne were supplied with ammunition and supplies. The heavy German siege-artillery could only be withdrawn with any speed along the railway from Laon to Tergnier, and Tergnier to Maubeuge. So the holding of the line was absolutely vital to Field-Marshal von Heeringen. He brought the Bavarian army by rail from Alsace, and placed it on the canal running from the Somme to the Oise, in front of the railway line. The

NIGHT ATTACK ON THE GERMAN TRENCHES DURING THE BATTLE OF THE AISNE.

Attack and counter-attack by night as well as by day followed in quick succession during the fighting along the Aisne, in the efforts of the enemy to establish ascendancy. The desperate nature of the fighting may be estimated by the fact that between September 12th and October 8th, 1914 the British losses, as given in Sir John French's despatch, in killed wounded, and missing, totalled 561 officers and 12,980 men.

proximity of the railway also enabled him quickly to move heavy artillery towards the canal. The result was that the French were beaten back at last to Roye.

But the attack on Tergnier had only been undertaken with a view to keeping the enemy engaged all along the line, from Compiègne to Arras. The principal attempt to cut the German lines of communication was made from Peronne on St. Quentin, far to the north. Toward St. Quentin Heeringen had withdrawn all the western German forces; but they were quite insufficient to make any sort of stand against the army of General Castelnau. German army corps had to be hurried towards the critical railway junction, at the highest possible speed, to save the entire German host from a retreat and a rout.

For more than a week the battle swayed furiously between French forces coming from Amiens through Peronne and German forces coming from Belgium and Lorraine and the Vosges Mountains through St. Quentin. Hand-to-hand fighting went on for days. The French charged the enemy almost continuously with infantry and cavalry, and when they gave ground under gun fire, the Germans in turn charged them. They fought over and over the same ground, until there were ten miles of dead bodies. They went on fighting across the corpses of comrades and foes, until the road became blocked, and still they went on fighting. The artillery on both sides was driven now forward and now backward, above the dead lying on the rain-sodden ways, until there was no need to bury the bodies. They had been ground into the muddy earth and covered. In between the two advancing and retiring lines of field-guns were two armies of foot soldiers, struggling in desperate fury with both bullet and steel.

Furious hand-to-hand fighting

Terribly eager to use the bayonet was the French infantryman. He was, at times, too eager. For the enemy was remarkably effective in defence. The Germans had, as Heeringen afterwards admitted to a neutral visitor, learnt something from the British soldier. They entrenched most vigorously, and then, with concealed machine-guns and hidden field-artillery, waited for the French attack. The Germans, however, could not rely on their rifle fire to stop a bayonet charge, as our troops did all the way from Mons to Ypres. German marksmanship was not equal to that, but their artillery fire, from defensive positions over ranges they had taken, was undoubtedly good.

The French suffered at first from the dash and passionate courage of their infantry. But, with their quick intelligence, they soon adapted themselves to the new tactics, and took, in turn, to retreating at the least opportunity. This brought the Germans out of their trenches into the open, and beyond the cover of their heavy artillery fire. So then the light French field-gun came fully into play, and properly prepared the way for an infantry attack in rushes ending in a bayonet charge.

How Frenchmen sacrificed their homes

Every village was the scene of fierce, protracted struggles. In house-to-house warfare the Frenchman was a scientific fighter—cold, lucid, passionless, and mercilessly effective. He surrendered his villages to the enemy, and then battered them to shapeless ruins with his own guns. The German took long to find good cover in any hamlet from which he was driving his opponents, while the French, as their foes admitted afterwards, were very skilful in using any kind of wall as a creeping shelter. But what surprised the Germans was the way the Frenchmen sacrificed the homes of their own people.

FRENCH CARRYING A VILLAGE IN A NIGHT ATTACK.

There was fierce fighting at close quarters in the battles west of the Aisne, and many villages were carried by our gallant allies at the point of the bayonet. The Germans had dug trenches at the entrance to each hamlet, and had placed their machine-guns in the houses, but they were powerless to withstand the furious charges of the indomitable French infantry, eager to get to work on the enemy with the bayonet.

Each village was held until the Germans brought up guns that overpowered the French field-artillery. The French then retired, sending their country-people ahead of them along the road to Amiens. A rearguard was left to amuse the enemy, but it was also withdrawn without a serious struggle. The Germans then moved up to take possession of their new point of vantage. Their infantry cautiously advanced, entered the street, and then threw out patrols to keep in touch with the retiring enemy.

When the infantry and cavalry were well enough established to make any attempt on the new artillery position disastrous, the guns moved forward towards their new site. But before they arrived the village was a flaming waste, strewn with the bodies of German soldiers. The French gunners had only withdrawn a mile or two, and trained each battery carefully and exactly, so as to bring a fire over every house. As soon as the Germans collected in triumph, a hurricane of shrapnel and shell burst above them. Each distant gun sent a shell dead over its mark every three seconds or so. There was no time to escape. The victorious infantry was blown or riddled to death, and the French soldiers came forward in extended order and recovered the ground. One more quiet, lovely French village had disappeared, but what did it matter? Some thousands of Germans had been buried in or around it, and it was easier for France to replace bricks and mortar than it was for Germany to breed and train more fighting men.

Infantry blown or riddled to death

The charming old village churches were shelled alike by friend and foe. As a British artillery officer complained, when the struggle was extending to the sea and he was taking part in it, some of our uninformed war correspondents were rather inclined to cant about the vandalism of the Germans. Grievous crimes against the ancient lovely monuments of civilisation they undoubtedly committed at Louvain, Senlis, Rheims, Termonde, Malines, Ypres, and Soissons. But, on the other hand, the modern system of fire control of long-ranged guns practically makes any tower or steeple on the battle-front a mark for shells. The French and Belgians were hard put to it when the enemy was entrenched around one of their churches.

For then, without a doubt, German fire-control officers, with telescopes and range-finding instruments, were watching from the church tower, and directing by telephone the fire of their batteries on to their opponents' guns and troops. By wrecking the tower with shell fire, our allies could save the lives of hundreds of their men, perhaps thousands of them, and turn a check into an advance. Were they to forgo all this to save one of their beautiful old churches? They did not forgo it. The church tower fell. Naturally, the enemy was much less hesitant. He shelled and wrecked any high object from which his opponents might be able to survey his lines and watch his movements.

Watch-towers indiscriminately shelled

This is one of the unfortunate results of the terrible progress in modern artillery science. Heavy guns now have a range of seven miles; some of our great pieces of ordnance can send a shell more than ten miles. By observing, from a high position, the distant target with the range-finding instrument invented by a British man of science, a mark at a distance of six or seven miles can be struck with remarkable accuracy, after a shot or two by way of trial. Captive observation balloons and flying machines with wireless telegraphic apparatus are more or less useful; but there is nothing so good as the steady outlook from a church tower.

Advancing brigades cannot take balloons with them, and aeroplanes are not yet numerous enough to be employed with every field battery. But in Europe there

A GALLANT IRISHMAN'S SPLENDID STAND.
After a shell fire lasting from dusk till the afternoon of the following day the Germans rushed a certain position held by the British. In one section of the deep shelter trenches, when help arrived, only one out of fifteen British soldiers was still defying the enemy. He was an Irishman, and fell unconscious from the effects of his wounds.

are village churches rising over every mile or two of country. All armies used them in turn, and in turn destroyed them when occupied by the enemy. Never was there so horribly destructive a war as the Great War. It transformed the temples of the Prince of Peace into the watch places where Thor and Mars, the old gods of war of the Teutonic and Latin races, exulted above the slaughter and bitter fumes of the battlefield.

In their first sweeping movement the French troops got within reach of the railway near St. Quentin, and one of their adventurous scouts tapped a telephone wire connecting two stations held by the Germans. He overheard an operator send instructions for two armoured German trains to be despatched. Jumping on his bicycle, the scout rode back to his field headquarters, and returned with a detachment of soldiers with machine-guns and sappers with dynamite. The line was dynamited, and the two trains came thundering along into the terrible ambush. The first was wrecked and thrown off the track, and the second collided with the wreckage, just where the machine-guns were trained on the line. Two trainloads of troops were killed or taken prisoners, and a good deal of ammunition was also captured.

Railway holocaust near St. Quentin

St. Quentin, however, could not be captured. The German commander, apprised by his aerial scouts of the French advance, worked his railway system in turn to its complete capacity. From Belgium, through Maubeuge, from Germany, through Liège and Namur, from Alsace and Lorraine, through Rethel, troops and artillery and ammunition were conveyed to the threatened junction. By means of their heavy guns the German reinforcements pushed the French back on the road to Peronne, and by September 25th they had won the town, and their advance guards were on the way to Amiens.

The light French artillery had to abandon position after position, owing to the fearful concentrated fire poured on it. Early in the afternoon the shells began to fall round the cross-roads where the general and his staff were. The general was urged by his officers to retire. "No," he said. "As long as I stay here the troops cannot retreat. We have got to hold on." He stayed till three farms close by were set on fire by the German shells. After that he still remained by the cross-roads, and thus won the day. For at the end of two hours the enemy's fire somewhat slackened, and the French infantry went forward. By the evening the French batteries occupied the positions from which the German guns had been firing.

Grim tenacity of the French

In the night time the French used an extraordinary method of harassing their foes. Flying columns of heavy cavalry went out as quietly as possible, and got as close as they could to the enemy's lines without rousing them. Then, when some German sentry fired in alarm, the French dragoons put their horses at the gallop, and charged full speed across the German bivouacs. They burnt convoys and motor-cars, upset the petrol, did all the damage they could, and threw the camp in wild alarm. At last the dragoons were compelled to shelter in a wood, in the rear of the German lines, where neither they nor their horses had anything to eat for two days.

They hoped to be relieved by a successful advance of the French army, but this did not take place. So again, in the middle of the night, the horsemen charged straight through a German encampment, yelling, and slashing with their swords, and taking everything in their way—ditches, and hedges, and barriers. Strange,

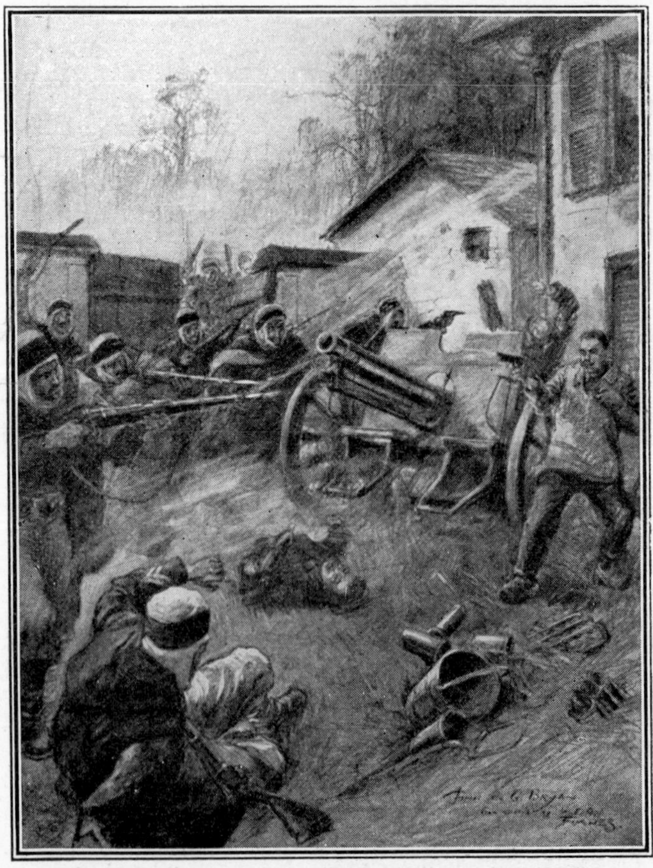

BRILLIANT EXPLOIT OF MOROCCAN CAVALRY.
Near Furnes the Germans had managed to conceal a gun on a farm, and dressed the gunners as peasants. The device was discovered by a party of Spahis, who, awaiting a favourable opportunity, surprised the enemy, captured the gun, killed the gunners, and dealt swift justice to those who had been bribed to allow the Germans to place the gun on the farm.

A HASTY WAYSIDE BREAKFAST WITH GENERAL JOFFRE, G.C.B., AT THE FRONT.

The French Commander-in-Chief, General Joseph Jacques Cesaire Joffre, is seen on the right of the picture, which represents an early morning breakfast during one of the long motor rides taken by General Joffre to various points of the great operations controlled by him. The meal referred to must have been quite a chance affair, and the camera suggests that the famous general was the first to finish. When King George was in France (December 1st-5th, 1914) he conferred on General Joffre the Grand Cross of the Order of the Bath.

FRENCH TROOPS RETAKE A VILLAGE DURING THE FIERCE STRUGGLE FOR VERDUN.

The above picture is from a photograph taken by a French officer during the recapture, in October, 1914, of Ville-en-Woevre, a village in the department of the Meuse, some twelve miles east of Verdun.

unexpected, ghostly, shrieking figures, they excited such alarm that most of them managed to escape from bullets and bayonets and get safely back to their own lines.

At the cost of dreadful carnage, the hastily gathered new German army succeeded in pushing General Castelnau's force back to the hills of Lassigny and the town of Roye.

It was again the lack of heavy field-artillery that prevented the French from driving home the advantage they first won, and breaking in on the enemy's line of communications at St. Quentin. Each French army corps took the field with one hundred and twenty 3 in. guns. This was all its ordnance. Each German army corps had one hundred and eight guns of similar calibre, together with thirty-six light howitzers with a range of over four miles. In addition, it had sixteen heavy field-howitzers throwing a 6 in. shell over five miles, and some heavy cannon throwing a forty-pound shrapnel, or shell, six and a half miles, and eight 8 in. howitzers with a range of five miles. Thus in all, each German army corps possessed some forty pieces of heavy artillery, throwing large, murderous shells from one mile to two and a half miles farther than any French field-gun could reach. The 6 in. field-howitzer of the Germans, especially, was a terrible weapon. Its 88 lb. shell, with 17½ lb. of high-explosive, burst into seven hundred splinters of steel, and no gun-shield could withstand it.

German advantage in field-artillery

For some years before the war the best French artillery experts, such as General Maitrot, had pointed out the heavy disadvantage under which their armies would have to fight against the more powerfully weaponed invaders. But the majority of French representatives in Parliament would not consent to spend the money required on national armament. They could not bring themselves to think there was any danger of war. So, as in 1870, the French Army went into the fight with guns that were outranged by the artillery of their enemy. And, as in 1870, the French gunners had in many cases to run their guns up at the gallop, shelled for a mile or more on the way, until they were within striking distance of the longer ranged batteries of heavy German field-artillery.

It was not brilliant tactics. But there was no choice. The only alternative was to retreat—and where would the retreat stop?—or heroically struggle on through extreme danger, and by superb courage and decision get close enough to the enemy to return his fire. The flat region about the middle course of the Somme River is a country of large farms, given over to the growing of sugar beets. Through this dry, level land the Germans had little difficulty in moving their heavy field-artillery with almost as much speed as their light guns were drawn. In a few days they had occupied a wide tract between their railway communications and the firing-line of General Castelnau's army. In front of Noyon they held the hills of Lassigny and the railway centre of Chaulnes, where the line from Amiens to Rheims and the line from Paris to Cambrai cross. The French held Lihons and Quesnoy en Santerre, Roye and Ribecourt on the Oise above Compiègne.

But though the French were driven back from the main railway track by which the German armies were fed, munitioned and reinforced, they were not defeated. No force of men and heavy guns that the German Commander-in-Chief sent against them at Roye, Quesnoy, and Lihons, could shift them from the positions they took up. Each point of vantage they held was furiously attacked. At Quesnoy the Germans lost in one day six thousand men. Then in revenge for the loss of Quesnoy, they advanced on Lihons, on the highway to Amiens. As usual, the enemy began with a heavy bombardment of the already battered and shattered village. The French gunners made only a feeble reply, and soon ceased completely to maintain the duel

Costly German advance on Lihons

Thinking the place was at last theirs to take, the Germans poured out on the road from Chaulnes, only a mile and a quarter distant. But when they reached the outskirts of the village, the French infantry, who had been hiding in the ruined houses, received the attackers with a rapid rifle fire, followed by a bayonet charge. The Germans retreated with all speed, but again the French caught them and punished them. For there were quick-firing guns, also concealed by the village, and they opened a murderous shrapnel bombardment upon the thronging fugitives and brought many of them down.

For months this k nd of warfare went on, each side entrenched in the beet-fields, behind the broken walls of sugar factories, and spirit distilleries and farms. Along a wide belt of land, over which the contending armies swayed, there was nothing but burnt ruins and the wreckage of hundreds of thousands of homes of a once happy race of cultivators living in a once fertile, pleasant, peaceful country. Prosperous towns like Roye and Albert became little more than names; their smoking streets were shelled into heaps of rubble before the bricks cooled; then the rubble was scattered by guns searching again for infantry using the last remnants of walls as cover. During the winter the batteries of heavy howitzers and long-range cannon, ordered in desperate urgency by the French Government, were ready for delivery in large numbers. All along the French front the effect of the new armament began to be felt. There was a resilience in the French lines around Roye and Lihon and Albert, now that General Castelnau had an artillery power equal to that of his opponent. The gallant French infantryman had lost none of his vehemence of attack, while digging for months making intricate, zigzag ditches and underground passages as protection against the enemy's gun fire. Having saved France by his spade, and continued the besieging operations begun in the Aisne valley, he was just as ready as ever to use the bayonet when his gunners had beaten down the hostile batteries.

Streets shelled into heaps of rubble

But after the check to the turning movement against the German flank, nearly four months passed before the French troops were fully provided with heavy field ordnance. In the meantime, the Germans tried, in a series of furious assaults at different points, to smash their way through the allied front and get in turn a flanking offensive in the west.

Towards the end of September the German Military Staff planned an ingenious answer to the attack made a week before on their flank by General Castelnau's army. The French commander had attempted an outflanking movement on Peronne, some twenty miles above the German western wing. The Germans replied by a similar movement on Lille, some sixty miles above the French western wing. This driving attack by the enemy through Lille was the turning-point in the entire campaign. The conception of it, which was strongly opposed by Helmuth von Moltke, altered every detail of the German conduct of war in the western theatre. Moltke intended to bring all available forces to bear on the eastern wing front round the Argonne Forest and attempt to cut the Franco-British front near Verdun. The Kaiser, however, backed by Admiral von Tirpitz, desired most urgently to win to the sea coast.

For political reasons, it was wished to expose Great Britain to the menace of invasion, and to gain a line of ports near Dover and the Thames estuary, from which submarines could operate and impede the transport of troops and munitions from England to France. As Chief of the Great General Staff, Moltke had to take a wider view than Tirpitz and Bethmann-Hollweg had impressed upon the Kaiser. The diversion of the main military forces of France and Belgium towards the sea coast appeared to him a political demi-semi-naval move that promised no large results. He kept to the purely military point of view, in which an operation of a decisive nature against the Franco-British armies was required to be carried out successfully without delay, in order to free the twenty

The Kaiser's desire to win the sea coast

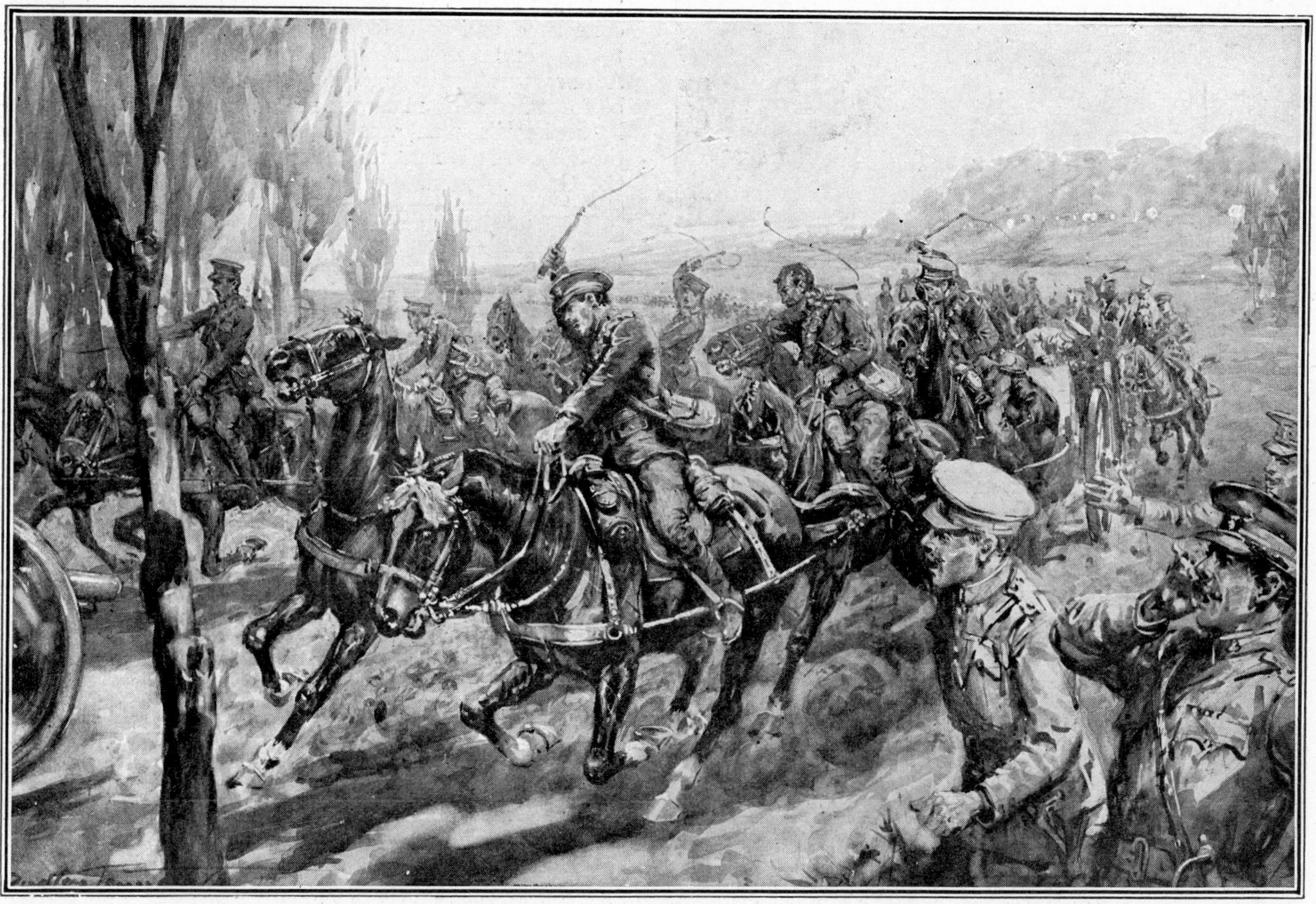

SAVING THE GUNS AT SOISSONS: AN INCIDENT OF THE FIGHTING ON THE AISNE.

Despite the heavy attacks of the enemy, about fifty British soldiers at Soissons stuck to their guns until their ammunition was exhausted. Happily, reinforcements came up in the nick of time, and the guns were saved.

BRITISH CAVALRY BIVOUAC IN NORTHERN FRANCE.

The scene reproduced for us by the camera is of one of the few occasions during the early part of the war when our cavalrymen were able to enjoy an interlude from their almost constant and strenuous work. And they were able to choose a very picturesque corner for their encampment.

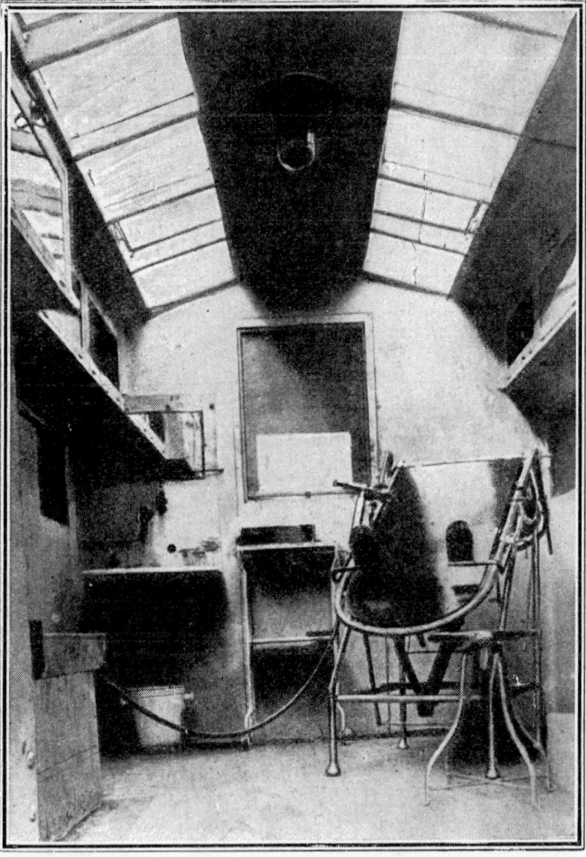

AN AUTO-'BUS OPERATING THEATRE.

When the history of the motor-'bus in war comes to be written the vehicle shown above should have mention. At one time plying between the Madeleine and the Place de la Bastille, in Paris, it was transformed into an operating-theatre, and taken to the front—a striking instance of the ingenuity of our French Allies.

army corps of the first-line troops for the conquest of Warsaw and Russian Poland.

For two months two and a half millions of German soldiers, including practically all the young, well-trained troops of the first line, had been struggling in the western field of war. This had allowed Russia to mobilise in such strength as to rout all Austria-Hungary's best troops, menace Budapest and Vienna, and win the oil-fields of Galicia. Now one of the chief industrial centres of Germany—Silesia—was also threatened. Half a million hastily-trained German recruits would soon be available. Though useless in operations where skilful, experienced, and marksmanlike infantry was needed, they could be employed in a mass attack to break the French lines near the Argonne, for there were fine artillery forces with superb equipment to back them.

Such seems to have been the view of Moltke. But his rival, General von Falkenhayn, acting as Minister of War, and eager for the practical fighting control of the armies in the field, sided with Tirpitz and the Kaiser. He drew up the plan of a brilliant new campaign. The result of it would please everybody. Belgium would be entirely conquered and occupied; the sea coast from the Scheldt to the Somme or Seine mouths would be at the disposal of Admiral von Tirpitz, and the wing of the Allies armies would be so turned as to make the march on Paris an easy matter. Falkenhayn's plan was adopted. Moltke retired under the colour of sickness, and the War Minister became Chief of the Great General Staff, a position equal to that which General Joffre occupied in France, with the exception that the French commander happily had no Kaiser to interfere with him.

First results of Falkenhayn's appointment

The immediate consequences of Falkenhayn's appointment were that the flank of the new German advance towards the sea coast had to be cleared by the reduction of the forts of Antwerp and the capture of the Belgian army. For with the intended movement at Lille, round the French western wing, the lines of German communication would be extended so much farther as to increase seriously the danger of hostile sallies from Antwerp. Moreover, the unoccupied Belgian coast, where British Marines were holding the seaport of Ostend, was even more dangerous than Antwerp. The German Staff could not tell what force of men Lord Kitchener might land there, either to co-operate with the Belgian Army, or to sweep down directly towards Lille and take the new German army in reverse.

While the former German Chief of Staff had kept in view only the true objective of his western forces, the comparatively small Belgian army operating around Antwerp had not mattered. Hemmed in by German garrison forces round Brussels, it was too far away to imperil the German railway communication that ran from Maubeuge to Namur and Liège. So long as the Belgians were contained well beyond this railway, their activities against the militia corps set to bar their sallies did not tell on the decisive struggles in France. In the more mobile pieces of their siege-artillery, the German retaining forces round Antwerp had mighty long-range weapons which quite redressed the balance between their oldish Landwehr infantry and the more vigorous and enduring young Belgian troops. For, like the French, the Belgians were lacking in heavy field-artillery.

Had Moltke so wished, the bombardment of Antwerp could have begun soon after the fall of the French frontier fortress of Maubeuge in the first week of September. Austrian gunners in charge of the 12 in. Skoda howitzers, and German gun sections with the 11 in. Krupp mortars, were then waiting at Brussels and elsewhere for work. Verdun was unapproachable, and Paris became still more remote. Only Antwerp was assailable. But Moltke regarded the attack on the Belgian stronghold as a distraction. He still held to the old programme of concentrating against France, with a view to so injuring her that troops of the second and third class could be used to retain her broken armies, while the troops of the first line were swung across Europe against Russia.

German strategy and field tactics

It is difficult to find fault with Moltke's strategy. It was as sound as it was obvious, and no doubt the older Moltke was the originator of it. The trouble was that the German soldier of the new generation was an inferior fighting man to the French soldier of the new era. The French also possessed in General Joffre a commander with more genius than any German leader in the western theatre of war. The superiority of certain sections of the German armament—their unusual number of machine-guns and their heavy artillery—was not sufficient in the end to compensate for their defects in human material. So the strategical plan of the two Moltkes, bettered in various details by the constant labours of the Great Military Staff, proved impossible of execution.

Nothing, however, was gained in adopting, in the middle of the campaign, the new and inferior plan of Falkenhayn. German strategy had not been at fault; but German field tactics, such as the overmarching of the men and the constant attacks in mass formations, had been defective, and the training of German troops had been bad. These defects, as we shall see in the course of this history, were only enhanced by the new leadership of the enemy.

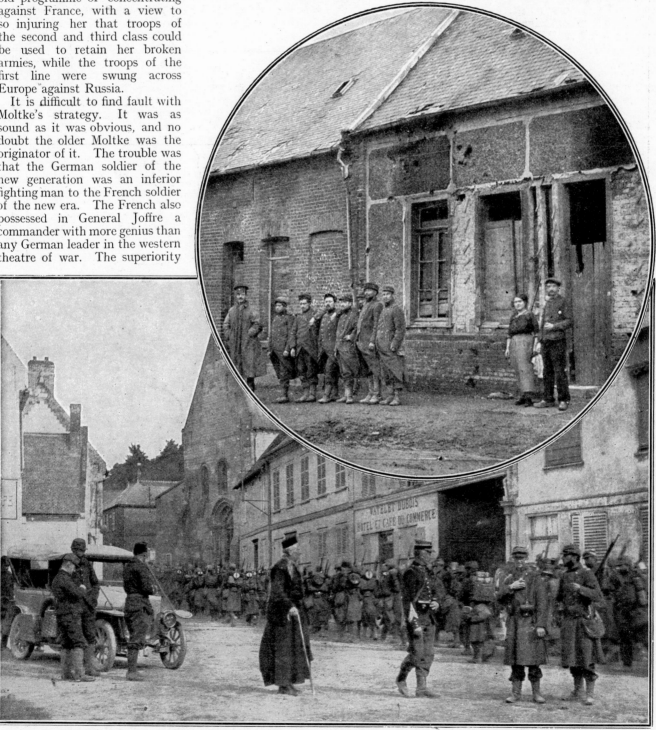

THE TRAMP OF ARMED MEN THROUGH THE DESERTED VILLAGES OF NORTHERN FRANCE.

Save for an occasional abbé or curé, and the fairly constant passage of troops or despatch-riders, the villages of Northern France were deserted in the autumn of 1914. The circular view was taken in the ruined town of Albert after its bombardment, the survivors shown including one British officer. A deep hole in front of the group was made by a shell, and there are shrapnel marks on the building behind them.

BRITISH 60-POUNDER BATTERY AT WORK IN THE VINEYARD DISTRICT OF FRANCE, OCTOBER, 1914.

The battery was helping to cover a flanking movement against the German position 7,500 yards away on the right. French shells are bursting over the German lines, the famous "75's" of our allies being placed on the left. In the middle distance British reserves are advancing, and more to the right German shells are sending up bursts of dark earth. The gun on the left of the British battery has just been fired; that on the right is being loaded. The British 60-pounders have a 5 in. calibre, and a range of 10,000 yards, and are furnished with a recoil attachment.

THE ALLIES SHOULDER TO SHOULDER: A MIXED PATROL OF FRENCH AND BRITISH TROOPS CUTTING THEIR WAY THROUGH A TOWN HELD BY THE ENEMY.

When details of all the operations on both sides can be fu ly studied in the voluminous publications of the French, German, British, and Belgian Military Staffs—which will appear years after the war is over—it will probably be found that General Joffre retained such initiative that he was able to make the Germans adopt their new plan of attack round the sea coast.

Ideas forced upon the Germans by General Joffre

We must remember that, some weeks before the Germans advanced towards Lille, the Franco-British lines already extended from Switzerland to Dunkirk, with a sort of naval bridge-head at Ostend, where a fresh British army could land and link on with both the Belgian force at Antwerp and the French force at Lille. By September 30th General Joffre, moreover, had another large army of first-rate troops, under General Maud'huy, which he was deploying between Arras and Lille.

Three of his best generals — Sarrail, De Langle de Cary, and Dubail—were operating round the Argonne Forest in anticipation of the move that Moltke had intended to make. So we may conclude that when General von Falkenhayn, assisted by the Kaiser and Admiral von Tirpitz, planned the new movement towards the sea, he only acted in accordance with the ideas which General Joffre had forced upon the Germans. Moltke, who might have won through in Hindenburg fashion, by sticking with Prussian stubbornness to his own view of the case, was, happily for the Allies, replaced by a more impressionable man. It was very likely the nervous, excitable temperament of the Kaiser himself that laid him open to the subtle influences which General Joffre was exerting, and so brought about the resignation of Moltke and the rise to power of a more pliable, incompetent, courtier Chief of Staff.

The heroic Belgian Army holding its last ditch

Only for the heroic, outnumbered, outgunned Belgians was there any great danger in the new plan of campaign formed by the new German commander. France had to lose Lille and Douai, and see the beautiful old buildings of Arras shattered by the enemy's guns; but the French temporary loss in territory and resources round Lille was more than redeemed by the advantage won in lengthening and weakening the enemy's front, and putting out of action some hundreds of thousands of German troops. When, however, the Belgians were threatened by a bombardment of Antwerp, their entire military force and even their national existence were endangered. It seemed at the time to be the last stand of the saviours of international law and morality against their mighty, brutal aggressors. The heroic Belgian army was holding its last ditch, apparently, with terrific odds against it. All the civilised world—of which Germany now formed no part—looked with deep, tragic interest towards the first event of Falkenhayn's new plan.

A GERMAN TRENCH IN THE ARGONNE.

THE RUSSIAN FLEET IN THE BALTIC.

CHAPTER XL.

EARLY GAINS AND LOSSES IN THE WAR BY SEA.

Our Submarines Blockade the Throat of the Elbe—First Success of our Underwater Craft—E9 Sinks a German Cruiser and Destroyer—Three British Armoured Cruisers Torpedoed off Holland—"It's a Long, Long Way to Tipperary, when you have to Swim There"—What we Gained in the Disaster to the Aboukir, Hogue, and Cressy—Triumphant Trick by Russian Admiral—German Cruiser Squadron Defeated in the Baltic—Teutonic Submarines sink the Russian Pallada—Combined French and British Fleets' Operations in the Adriatic—Historic Duel between Armed Merchant Liners—How the Cunarder Carmania sunk the Cap Trafalgar—The Dwarf and the Spar Torpedo—German Merchant Fleet Captured—Successes of the Elusive Emden—Pegasus Keeps the Flag Flying at Zanzibar—Capture of New Britain, German New Guinea and South-West African Town of Lüderitzbucht—The "Notorious Hymn of Hate"—British Sailors Bomb the Zeppelin Shed at Düsseldorf.

IN the first glorious fortnight of September, when the armies of the Allies, in both the western and eastern theatres of war, were throwing back the invaders, the quieter and even more effectual work of our fleets was being carried on with rigour. There was no turn in the tide of war at sea. From the beginning it had flowed in the direction controlled by our Admiralty, and though in the course of the month of September the Germans won some advantages in commerce-raiding and submarine operations, the silent and inevitable pressure of our Grand Fleet told heavily against the enemy on both land and sea.

As all the German warships not only avoided a conflict, but made no attempt to control their own North Sea coasts, our adventurous and far-ranging submarine commanders had little opportunity of displaying their daring skill. Our light and armoured cruisers, with destroyer flotillas, were spread over the North Sea and down the English Channel, reconnoitring and searching merchant-ships for contraband, and guarding both the British and Belgian coasts from a naval raid. Even our battle-cruisers in the second week of September swept the Bight of Heligoland, and found no enemy visible in German home waters.

There were thus many of our vessels exposed to torpedo attack by hostile underwater craft. Our fast new cruisers were, however, in little danger, as their speed enabled them to elude any submarine, and even at times fight it on equal terms by quick ramming manœuvres. But in order to police the seas, our Admiralty had been obliged to put into commission some old slow cruisers, manned by reserve crews, and these vessels were the natural prey of the German submarines when their destroyer flotillas were not spread round them.

The Germans had already got in the first blow ever delivered by a submarine, and had sunk the Pathfinder. For some time it was thought that this ship had been destroyed by a contact mine, but when the news of the real cause of the disaster spread, in the second week of September, to the outposts of our Grand Fleet, our submarine officers grew eager to find an opportunity for revenge. At the time our underwater craft were blockading the very throat of the Elbe. The German Admiralty, like our own, was waiting to see what the submarine could actually do. In the meantime Admiral von Tirpitz followed his usual practice of imitating British tactics, and exposed only his oldest and slowest cruisers to underwater attacks.

One of these boats, the Hela, was steaming between Heligoland and the Elbe on Sunday, September 13th. She was an obsolete light cruiser of 2,000 tons, manned by one hundred and eighty officers and men. The wind was freshening, and the sea was beginning to get up, and the tumbling, whitening water helped to conceal the periscopes of several British submarines that were stalking the cruiser. At half-past six in the morning one of our submarines got within torpedo range, when the Hela was about six miles off the German coast. It was Lieut.-Commander Max K. Horton, in E9, to whom the opportunity came of striking the first deadly blow from the British side in underwater warfare.

ADMIRAL VON ESSEN.
Commander of the Russian Baltic Fleet.

THE FIRST FIGHT BETWEEN ARMED MERCHANTMEN.
The British auxiliary cruiser Carmania (Captain Noel Grant) sunk the German armed merchant cruiser Cap Trafalgar off the east coast of South America on September 14th, 1914. The above photograph shows the shattered bridge of the Carmania after the battle.

He dived as soon as he sighted the enemy, and launched two torpedoes at her. There was an interval of only fifteen seconds between the two shots. The first struck the hostile cruiser in the bows, and the other exploded amidships. Probably the magazine was struck, for the Hela burst into flame, and sank in an hour. As there were other German vessels close at hand, Lieut.-Commander Horton again submerged his boat. When he rose for another cautious sight the Hela had disappeared. She was at the bottom of the sea, but most of her crew had been rescued. The British submarine was never seen by the enemy, and was therefore never shot at.

The next achievement by our submarines was also accomplished by Lieut.-Commander Horton. When his boat was relieved he stayed for a few days in Harwich, and then set out for a new station off Emden Harbour. This was the centre of German torpedo-craft activities, from which both submarines and destroyers issued to harry our fleet. Destroyers were reckoned to be a match for submarines. Indeed, in fleet operations, it was their work to scout for them, and injure them either by gun fire or by ramming. Their much superior speed and their very shallow draught, it was expected, would make them practically unassailable by torpedoes. A torpedo that would destroy a cruiser would pass harmlessly under the keel of a destroyer.

E 9's daring exploit off the Ems River

Lieut.-Commander Horton, who had been studying submarine operations for some years, was keen to tackle the craft reckoned the most dangerous to his kind of boat. Towards the end of the first week in October he submerged in the enemy's harbour, and kept his crew amused by a gramophone concert and bridge playing. It is said that when he took his first peep through the periscope he found a destroyer too near him to loose a torpedo at her.

THE BRITISH AUXILIARY CRUISER CARMANIA.
After the sinking of the Cap Trafalgar the Admiralty sent the following telegram to Captain Noel Grant: "Well done! You have fought a fine action to a successful finish."

The force of the explosion might have wrecked his own boat. He let the destroyer steam away for six hundred yards, and then fired his two forward tubes, with an interval of five seconds between the two shots. The first shot missed, but the second, travelling near the surface of the water, caught the destroyer amidships. The explosion lifted her in the air, and tore her in two. It was the S126, a vessel of four hundred and eighty tons and twenty-seven knots speed, launched at Dantzic in 1904. She had three four-pounders, three torpedo-tubes, and a crew of sixty. Again the invisible conqueror submerged, while a flotilla of German destroyers cruised above him, and found nothing to shoot at. By October 7th E9 and her skilful, daring crew were safely back once more at Harwich, where she was nicknamed the "double-toothed pirate."

The brilliant victor was a young man of thirty, already distinguished for his gallantry in saving life at the wreck of the P. and O. liner Delhi, off Morocco, in the winter of 1911. He was then a lieutenant in one of the battleships that helped in the rescue work, when the Princess Royal and her husband and daughters were saved. His submarine boat, E9, was one of the newest and most powerful submarines in the world. She was over eight hundred tons, with accommodation for a crew of twenty-eight men, and an air-supply enabling them to stay under the sea for twenty-four hours. Her Diesel engines and electric accumulators gave her a range of action of three thousand miles, and she was fitted with four 21 in. torpedo-tubes and a couple of twelve-pounder guns.

Success in submarine warfare, however, does not always depend upon the efficiency of the boat. One, at least, of the small, old-fashioned submarines in Emden Harbour soon proved to be as deadly as the fastest and most powerful of our craft at Harwich. It was commanded by Lieutenant Otto Weddigen, a brilliant German submarine officer. His U9 was an old type, but he and his crew were so accustomed to her that a new modern craft would have been less effective in their hands. For when a submarine fires, the whole vessel has to be handled like a gun, and steadied on the mark by delicate and skilful handling of her helm. The torpedo-tubes are usually fixed in the vessel's side, and cannot be aimed independently. Straightness of aim depends on the way the men handle the boat. So the longer they have lived in her and learned her individual ways in responding to her helm, under all sorts of conditions, the better their marksmanship is.

THE GERMAN EAST AFRICAN PORT OF DAR-ES-SALAAM.
From her base at Zanzibar, in the early days of the Great War, H.M.S. Pegasus (inset) made a successful expedition to the German East African port and railway head of Dar-es-Salaam. Here she sank a German gunboat, the Moewe, and a floating dock, and destroyed the wireless station.

After landing for a hasty wedding, Weddigen embarked at Borkum in his old small boat, bent on some striking achievement that would make his strange honeymoon trip famous.

His orders were to cruise round the coast of Holland and Belgium and attack the vessels that the British Admiralty were sending to defend the Belgian seaports. For the German system of espionage in the British Isles was working with remarkable efficiency. Weddigen travelled on the surface, except when he sighted vessels. Then he submerged, and did not even show his periscope, unless it was absolutely necessary to take bearings. After voyaging more than two hundred miles from his base, he arrived at dawn on Tuesday, September 22nd, some sixteen knots north-west of the Hook of Holland. Here he spied, about six o'clock in the morning, the three old British armoured cruisers, the Aboukir, Hogue, and Cressy, cruising in a single line twenty miles from the Dutch coast, without any destroyers to scout for them. For some weeks they had been patrolling the lower area of the North Sea, between the mouth of the Thames and the island of Texel. It was work for which they were not suited. They were large vessels of 12,000 tons each, and fourteen to fifteen years old. They needed each a complement of 800 officers and men, and were slow, both in speed and in manœuvring power, and made huge targets for attack, alike above and below water. They formed no part of the Grand Fleet under the command of Sir John Jellicoe, but were apparently despatched and controlled by the Admiralty, with a view to watching over the approaches to Belgium.

Loss of the Aboukir, Hogue, and Coessy

It was a mistake to employ such slow old ships with large crews, consisting mainly of Fleet reserve ratings, who had not had time to settle down to their common work. It was also an error of judgment to allow their destroyer flotilla to become separated from them. On the other hand, the Admiralty felt it would be unwise to weaken the Grand Fleet by detaching for general patrol work many of the fast light new cruisers, which would be urgently needed in front of the Fleet in case of a Fleet action. There was a risk that Germany would suddenly attack on the sea, now that her great land campaign had failed on both fronts. Nothing could be allowed to diminish the fighting efficiency of our Grand Fleet. Yet the lower area of the North Sea needed to be patrolled in sufficient force to guard Belgium against a cruiser raid, and defend our transport of troops and war material across the Channel from interruption and disaster.

British sacrifice to neutral commerce

The most scientific method of doing this was to mine the Thames estuary and the northern entrance to the English Channel. But our Admiralty was averse from impeding neutral commerce in the lower North Sea, though the vast German mine-field in the upper stretch of these waters had already caused serious losses to Danish, Norwegian, and Swedish merchant ships. Probably from political considerations with regard to Holland and Scandinavian countries, our Admiralty hesitated to close the North Sea in any way. Had we set out vigorously to starve Germany into surrender, at no matter what distress to neighbouring neutral countries, we could have ended the war by Christmas. But this stern Nelsonic method was deemed inadvisable. So nothing remained but to put matters to the test, and try if the old armoured cruisers of the Cressy class could escape from the fate of the Pathfinder. It must be remembered that neither the capabilities nor the limitations of the submarine had been entirely discovered by actual warfare. One of our modern cruisers of the town class had sunk a German submarine

H.M.S. CUMBERLAND'S PICKET-BOAT IN THE CAMEROON RIVER.

This operation of our naval forces on the West Coast of Africa resulted in the unconditinal surrender of Duala, the capital of the Cameroons, to a Franco-British force commanded by Brigadier-General C. M. Dobell, D.S.O., following a bombardment by H.M.S. Cumberland and Dwarf. An attempt to blow up and then to ram the Dwarf failed, and several hundred prisoners fell into our hands, while the Cumberland captured eight German merchant steamers and a gunboat off the mouth of the river. Our picture is from a sketch by an officer who took part in the expedition.

ASTROLAVE BAY, GERMAN NEW GUINEA.
The Australian Expeditionary Force seized the town and harbour of Kaiser Wilhelm's Land, German New Guinea, on September 24th, 1914.

by the unexpected manœuvre of ramming her. It was hoped that the old armoured cruisers might be able to carry out the same kind of attack, if hostile underwater craft menaced them.

But Lieutenant Weddigen gave our sailors no opportunity for smashing into his frail boat. When he first sighted the three cruisers on the misty morning they were within the range of his torpedoes, but too far off for anything more than a chance shot. So he went down again, and drove closer in towards the middle ship, the Aboukir. He then shot up his periscope again, and got another flash of the position before he went into action. Then, reaching a good firing point, he loosened a torpedo at the middle ship. He was about twelve feet under water at the time, and as his men handled the boat as if she had been a skiff, he got the shot off true on the mark. Climbing towards the surface, he obtained a sight through his periscope. Round the Aboukir rose a fountain of water, a burst of smoke, a flash of fire, and part of the stricken cruiser rose in the air. The victor heard the roar, and felt the surges of water sent through the sea by the explosion. Through his periscope he could see the brave crew, with their broken ship sinking beneath them, standing, faithful to death, at their posts, ready to handle their guns if an enemy were visible. But none was, for Weddigen submerged his periscope, and waited by the sinking ship.

He had seen the Hogue and Cressy coming to her aid. As in the former case of the Pathfinder, our sailors thought that their ship had struck a mine. The periscope of the

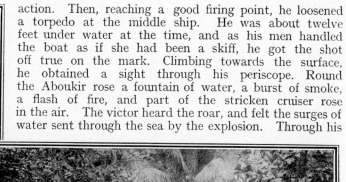

GERMAN GOVERNOR'S BUNGALOW AT HERBERTSHÖHE.
An Australian naval landing-party, under Commander A. H. Beresford, overcame a superior force and captured Herbertshöhe, in the Bismarck Archipelago, on September 11th-12th, 1914.

PANORAMIC VIEW OF LISSA.
The famous Island of Lissa, in the Adriatic, after its occupation by a Franco-British garrison on September 19th, 1914, became a naval base for the Allies.

DUALA, THE PRINCIPAL PORT ON THE CAMEROONS.
Duala, from which Germany was fed with important tropical commodities, surrendered to the Allies on September 27th, 1914.

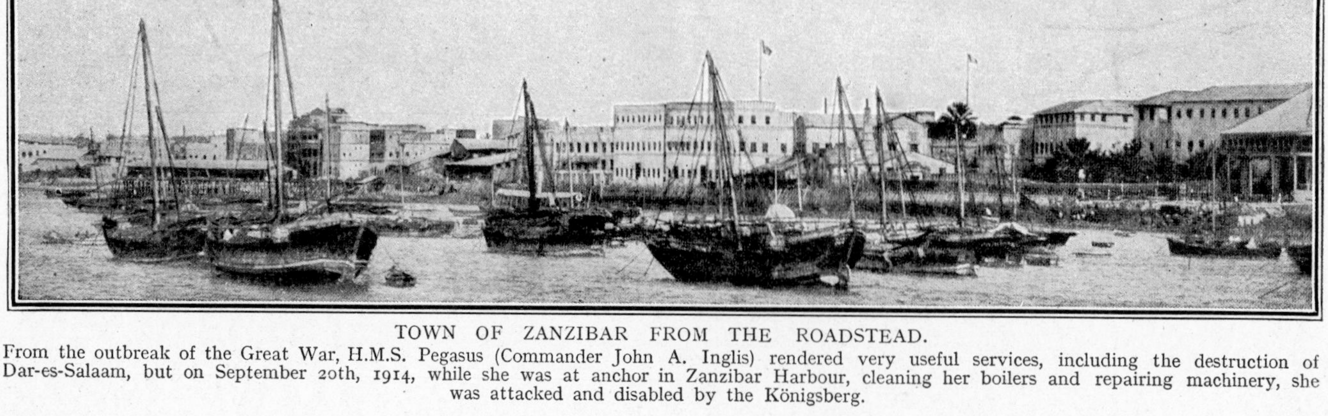

TOWN OF ZANZIBAR FROM THE ROADSTEAD.
From the outbreak of the Great War, H.M.S. Pegasus (Commander John A. Inglis) rendered very useful services, including the destruction of Dar-es-Salaam, but on September 20th, 1914, while she was at anchor in Zanzibar Harbour, cleaning her boilers and repairing machinery, she was attacked and disabled by the Königsberg.

AT SEA ON A GERMAN SUBMARINE.
A nightcap before turning in. From a drawing by the well-known German war artist Professor Hans Bohrtt.

hostile underwater craft was not visible, and the force of the terrific explosion was much greater than that of an ordinary torpedo charged with gun-cotton. The fact was the Germans were using in the war-heads of their torpedoes the new chemical trinitrotoluene, which produces a greater explosive effect than gun-cotton, but is less safe to the users than the ordinary nitro-carbon compounds. The result was that the comparatively small amount of chemical contained in the German war-head blew as wide a hole in the Aboukir as the explosion of a large gun-cotton contact mine would have done.

This misconception of the cause of the disaster led to further loss. For, thinking they were in no danger from an active enemy, the Hogue and the Cressy steamed up to rescue the men of the Aboukir. Weddigen had scarcely to move out of his position in order to get his torpedo depth and train his boat against the nearer of the approaching vessels. This was the Hogue. The torpedo got home on the second armoured cruiser, but the shot was not so successful as the first, as it did not strike under the magazine. For twenty minutes the ship lay wounded and helpless on the surface. Then there was a second explosion, caused probably by another torpedo hitting near the magazine, and the great vessel heaved and half turned over, and sank.

Fatal misconception of the cause of disaster

By this time the commander and men of the Cressy knew that the enemy was upon them. In fact, as the Aboukir sank, the men on the Cressy saw the track of the torpedo aimed at the Hogue. The captain of the Cressy at once began to steam a zigzag course by the scene of the double disaster, in the hope of being able to rescue the sailors struggling in the water, and at the same time to get an opportunity of sighting and attacking the enemy. All the light guns were trained on the surface of the sea in various directions, and any flashing foam-break on the tumbling waves that looked like an emerging periscope was fired at. One of the gunners who was afterwards rescued stated that he distinctly saw a conning-tower ascend, and got a shell on it that sank the submarine. Weddigen, however, says that the British guns had nothing to shoot at. The next German torpedo missed the target, but at half-past seven the enemy got home so deadly a stroke that, in five minutes after being struck, the Cressy turned completely upside down. After remaining in this extraordinary position for twenty minutes, she sank at five minutes to eight.

In all, 62 officers and 1,400 men were lost with the three British cruisers. The Aboukir lost 25 officers and 502 men; the Cressy, 25 officers and 536 men; and the Hogue, 12 officers and 362 men. The saved numbered only 59 officers and 858 men—917 in all. The loss of the three obsolescent cruisers was of no importance. Our Navy had started the war with a preponderance in ships—much more like two to one than sixteen to ten. Moreover, our construction programme was so advanced that in the next twelve months we should have twice as many battleships completing as Germany, and about four times as many cruisers. So great was our superiority in material that we could have afforded to lose one battleship a month, and yet have retained our advantage over our rival for sea-power. The German losses in swift, modern light cruisers, in Heligoland Bight and the Baltic, outbalanced our wastage of naval material.

Our loss in men greater than at Trafalgar

But our heavy loss of good men was an irretrievable blow. The submarine attack had cost us a thousand more lives than the winning of the Battle of Trafalgar had done. But though our men went down to their death with no chance of showing their skill and courage in a fight, they did not die in vain. They gave their country one more memorable inspiring example of absolute and perfect heroism. In some respects, indeed, they even eclipsed the grand tradition of the Birkenhead. But something had

BRITISH DESTROYER ESCAPING FROM A TORPEDO FIRED BY A HUNTED ENEMY SUBMARINE.

Deadly as the submarine proved in circumstances favourable to its particular form of warfare, our swift cruisers and destroyers moved far too rapidly for the "unterseeboote" to be certain of getting its torpedoes home. The above picture gives a vivid impression of the value of expert seamanship, which, next to good gunnery, gained for us so many material advantages in the trying operations in the North Sea.

altered in the British character since the disaster to the Birkenhead. The men were just as steady and cool, as they waited for the boat to slip from under them. They stood to their posts, waiting for instructions, until the officer in command gave the order for each man to do his best to save his own life. The Cressy continued firing when the ship had a list of forty degrees. Weddigen, peeping at them through his periscope, bore witness to their steadiness and fearlessness. "All the while," he said, "the men stayed by their guns, looking for their invisible foe. They were brave, true to their country's sea traditions."

All this showed that the fibre of our race had not relaxed since the days when the Birkenhead went down. But when the end came, and the men were fighting for life in the water, struggling to escape from the suction of the great sinking masses of rent and flaming steel, a wonderful new quality of character was manifested. In one of the most sudden, overwhelming, awful catastrophes that our fighting sailors have ever known, the men, swimming and treading water for their lives, burst light-heartedly into song. "It's a long, long way to Tipperary," said some men as they struggled in the sea. "It is, if you have to swim there," replied a brilliant Cressy gunner. Immortal is the jest, and immortal are the circumstances that inspired it. It was like a granite rock breaking into flower. For beneath all, at the base of all, subsisted the old, stern, dogged Roman courage of our forefathers, and growing out of it was a new cheery smiling gaiety of the Hellenic sort. Thus surely did the heroes of Salamis and Marathon, triumphing in the power and righteousness of their cause, go down to death with a song on their lips.

TAKING A DISABLED SUBMARINE IN TOW.
Disabled submarine in the act of hailing her parent ship. The drawing gives a good idea of what work in the Navy is like in winter time.

Dutch and British vessels in the neighbourhood tended the survivors, many of whom were conveyed in some of the cruisers' boats to the rescue ships. There are many fine, thrilling tales of quiet or happy heroism. Captain Johnson, of the Cressy, spent his last moments directing his sailors to take hold of anything floatable that would enable them to keep their heads above water until the destroyers came up. He was last seen gripping a handrail on the bridge, as the ship went over. Captain Drummond, of the Aboukir, directed his men how to save themselves when the ship was sinking, and then, when his crew were in the water, he and his men swam about, helping the poor swimmers among them. Captain Nicholson, of the Hogue, was also the last man to leave his ship. He was seen on the bridge, waving his cap in cheerful defiance of death. But as the ship went down, he was carried free, and his men, who were swimming or floating about, gave him three cheers when they saw him swimming clear of the lost cruiser. Great as was the loss of life, it would have been still greater but for the promptness and gallantry of the four vessels that hastened to the scene of the disaster. Two of them, the Coriander and J.G.C., were Lowestoft trawlers; the other two, the Titan and Flora, were Dutch vessels. While the cruiser Lowestoft and a flotilla of British destroyers were racing to the spot, in answer to a wireless call, the fishermen managed to save many sailors, who would probably have been exhausted before naval assistance arrived. One trawler, flying the Dutch flag, however, is said to have departed immediately after the disaster, as though eager not to help in the work of rescue. It was suspected that she was a German vessel, under false colours, that had been sent to the scene of the expected submarine operations, in order to screen the underwater boats from observation, and enable them to take the British cruisers entirely by surprise.

Thrilling tales of quiet or happy heroism

The three sunken cruisers, though large and powerful

GERMAN CRUISER EMDEN'S EXPLOIT AT MADRAS.
During its raiding cruise in the Bay of Bengal the German cruiser Emden shelled the oil-tanks at Madras, doing considerable damage; but it is on record to the credit of the captain that he confined his attention to property, where he might have given a display of that "frightfulness" which later distinguished his colleagues' raids on undefended holiday towns on the East Coast of England.

ships, belonged to an old-fashioned class, that was surpassed in speed by many of the enemy's heavier-gunned battleships. Before the war broke out, our Admiralty had decided that no more money should be spent in repairing them, and that they should go into the sale list as soon as they showed serious defects. Thus, apart from the toll of life, their loss was of small naval significance. They were the price our country had to pay while learning all the possibilities of submarine attack in the new and strange conditions of naval warfare. When, some months afterwards, our battleship Formidable, steaming in line with other powerful units, was struck by what appeared at first to be a mine, the captain warned the other ships to attempt no rescue, but manœuvre to avoid submarine attack. The other important battleships, with their large crews, that were thus saved from the enemy's torpedoes, must be reckoned against the heavy cost in brave trained men of our first important lesson in submarine warfare. Had the attack on the squadron, of which the Formidable was part, been the first of its kind, we might have then lost other ships more important than the Hogue and Cressy.

New and strange conditions of naval warfare

The disaster off the Hook of Holland has also a curious technical interest. Both the German Admiralty and Lieutenant Weddigen claimed that only one German submarine was engaged in the attack on the three cruisers. Our sailors, however, aver that there was a flotilla of hostile underwater craft engaging in the attack. Besides the evidence of their eyes, we have theoretic support of the probable correctness of their observations, U9 was a small 250-ton boat, with only three torpedo-tubes. Two of the tubes were carried forward, and one aft, the after tube being a reserve one that would not in a general way be used. The boat was not big enough to do much in the way of carrying spare torpedoes; and, in any case, a 250-ton submarine capable of reloading her tubes when in a submerged condition did not exist. Modern torpedoes are from fourteen to nineteen feet long, weigh up to over a ton and a quarter, and carry from 250 to 350 pounds of high explosive.

We know that at least six torpedoes were fired, one missing, and five hitting. Such was the actual number of torpedoes seen by our men. It is the lowest possible figure, in which no allowance is made for unnoticed torpedoes which missed. It may be that U9 did most of the work, and that the German Admiralty thought it worth while to sacrifice the whole truth, and create the impression that one old-type German submarine was more than a match for three old British armoured cruisers. Things were not going well with the German armies on either front, and as the German Military Staff had taken to concealing the true facts from the public, the German Admiralty may also have indulged its imagination, in order to increase the amount of soothing syrup it was able to offer to the Teutonic public. From Russia we learnt that the German Admiralty also needed much soothing mixture itself.

For another naval mystery of far more than technical importance was discussed in the early part of September. First came a statement by our Press Bureau that trustworthy information had been received on September 4th that seven German destroyers and torpedo-boats had arrived at Kiel in a sinking condition, while other vessels had sunk in the neighbourhood of the canal. About a fortnight later it was rumoured from the Baltic that two German cruiser squadrons, with destroyer flotilla, had been hunting down passenger steamers in separate directions, and converging at last, mistook their own for enemy ships and engaged in a lively battle. This was offered as the explanation of the arrival of crippled warcraft at Kiel Harbour.

But some months later a Russian authority at Petrograd allowed the astonishing facts of the matter to be published. It appears that towards the end of August the German Baltic cruiser squadrons were becoming inconvenient to our Russian allies. The German ships began to cruise in the waters that Admiral von Essen, the commander of the Russian Baltic Fleet, had resolved firmly to hold. Moreover, the Germans were using their ships for the purpose of putting severe pressure upon Sweden.

Russian admiral's simple but telling trick

The new Russian battleships had not been completed, and the Russian Navy in the meantime was much inferior in force to the German. So Germany was trying to blockade Russia in the Baltic, as we were blockading Germany in the North Sea. German light cruisers began to appear round Libau, the only ice-free naval port of Northern Russia. Admiral von Essen boldly determined to risk a large part of his fleet rather than allow the enemy to carry out his plans. Being unable to fight an open battle with any chance of success against the great naval force that the German commander could bring up, Admiral von Essen used a simple but telling trick.

He altered the appearance of several of his cruisers and destroyers by means of temporary additions, and made them closely resemble in outline certain German units. He had the disguised vessels painted in German colours, and then in foggy weather, about August 27th, he slipped out and contrived to join, in the Gulf of Finland, the German squadron which was threatening Russian waters and ports. Probably the Russian Intelligence Department had been able to provide the commanders of Russian vessels with German signal books. However this may be, the disguised Russian squadron got close up to the enemy without rousing any suspicions. Suddenly they opened fire, and wrecked the Magdeburg, one of the newest of German light cruisers, with twelve 4.1 in. guns, an armour belt of $3\frac{1}{2}$ in., and an actual speed of twenty-seven knots. To escape sinking she ran on the rocks, and was there blown up by the Russian guns. Another German cruiser, possibly the Augsburg, whose turbines were afterwards reported to be damaged, was severely handled, and, as we have seen from our Press Bureau announcement, half a score of German destroyers were shelled and either sunk or badly crippled.

The surprise engagement was quickly finished, and the Russians, having got their blow in, withdrew before the enemy touched them. From the German point of view, the disaster was discreditable to their Navy, and the serious loss of their prestige which would have occurred in Scandinavia made them keep a dead silence about the affair.

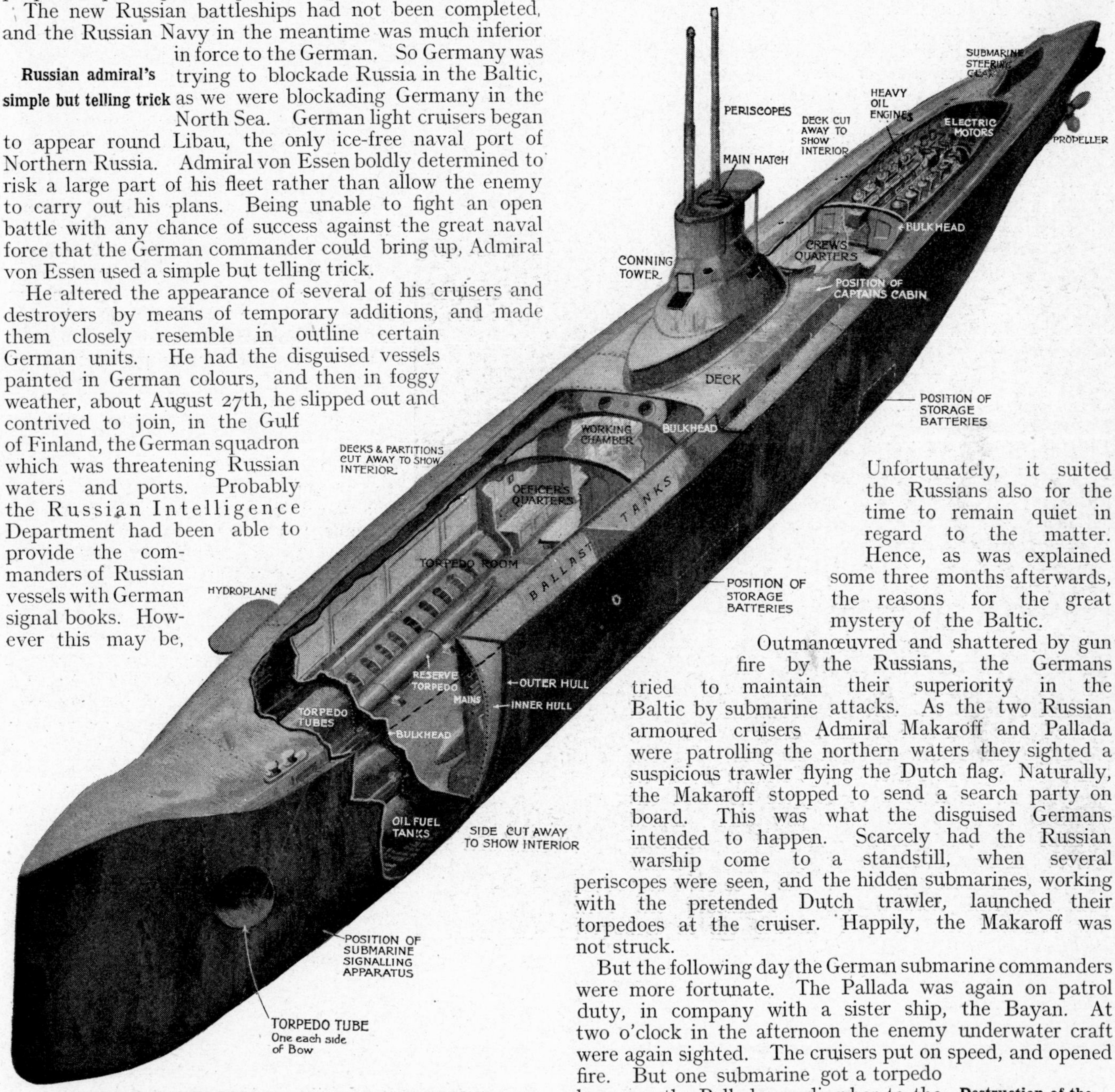

SECTIONAL VIEW OF A GERMAN SUBMARINE ("UNTERSEEBOOTE").

Our illustration shows some of the distinctive features of the modern type of German submarine, notably its flatter deck and boat-shaped contour.

Unfortunately, it suited the Russians also for the time to remain quiet in regard to the matter. Hence, as was explained some three months afterwards, the reasons for the great mystery of the Baltic.

Outmanœuvred and shattered by gun fire by the Russians, the Germans tried to maintain their superiority in the Baltic by submarine attacks. As the two Russian armoured cruisers Admiral Makaroff and Pallada were patrolling the northern waters they sighted a suspicious trawler flying the Dutch flag. Naturally, the Makaroff stopped to send a search party on board. This was what the disguised Germans intended to happen. Scarcely had the Russian warship come to a standstill, when several periscopes were seen, and the hidden submarines, working with the pretended Dutch trawler, launched their torpedoes at the cruiser. Happily, the Makaroff was not struck.

Destruction of the Russian cruiser Pallada

But the following day the German submarine commanders were more fortunate. The Pallada was again on patrol duty, in company with a sister ship, the Bayan. At two o'clock in the afternoon the enemy underwater craft were again sighted. The cruisers put on speed, and opened fire. But one submarine got a torpedo home on the Pallada, sending her to the bottom so quickly that few of her five hundred and sixty-eight officers and men escaped. Her loss was a blow to the incomplete Russian Navy, for she was a modern warship, launched in 1906, with two 8 in. guns and eight 6 in. rapid-firers.

Of all the allied fleets the French was for long the most fortunate in escaping from serious loss. The main French naval force, combined with our Mediterranean Fleet, under the command of the brilliant French commander, Admiral Boué de Lapeyrère, held all the Austrian warships in the blind alley of the Adriatic. To assist the land operations of the Montenegrins, the Austrian fortress of Cattaro, on the edge of their frontier, was bombarded by the allied fleets on September 10th. Then the forty warships steamed to the famous island of Lissa, where the Austrian Navy had won in bygone days a great victory over the Italian Fleet.

The signal station was shelled on this island, and on Pelegosa and Lesina. All the coast of Southern Dalmatia was searched, and mines, lighthouses, signal stations, and wireless stations were destroyed. This was done with a view to impeding the Austrian Fleet in any sortie from its base at Pola. Then on September 19th a garrison was landed at Lissa, and British and French flags were hoisted over the conquered island, which was made the base of the Franco-British naval operations against the southern Teutons. The occupation of Lissa was not only good naval strategy, but excellent political tactics.

It told on public opinion in Italy. For all Italians remembered Lissa, where, in 1866, the first general engagement between ironclads was fought, ending in the victory of the Austrian Admiral von Tegetthoff. Many Italians were growing eager for a chance to avenge their old defeat off the island, and recovering the territories they had lost. The action of the Franco-British fleet helped to quicken this movement in Italy. One Italian naval officer tried to anticipate events, and stole off in a submarine to take part in the operations of the allied forces. Though he was stopped on the way, his too premature action did not tend to make his countrymen any more inclined to passive neutrality. The adventurous submarine stealer was a human straw, showing in what way the wind of Italian thought and feeling was then blowing.

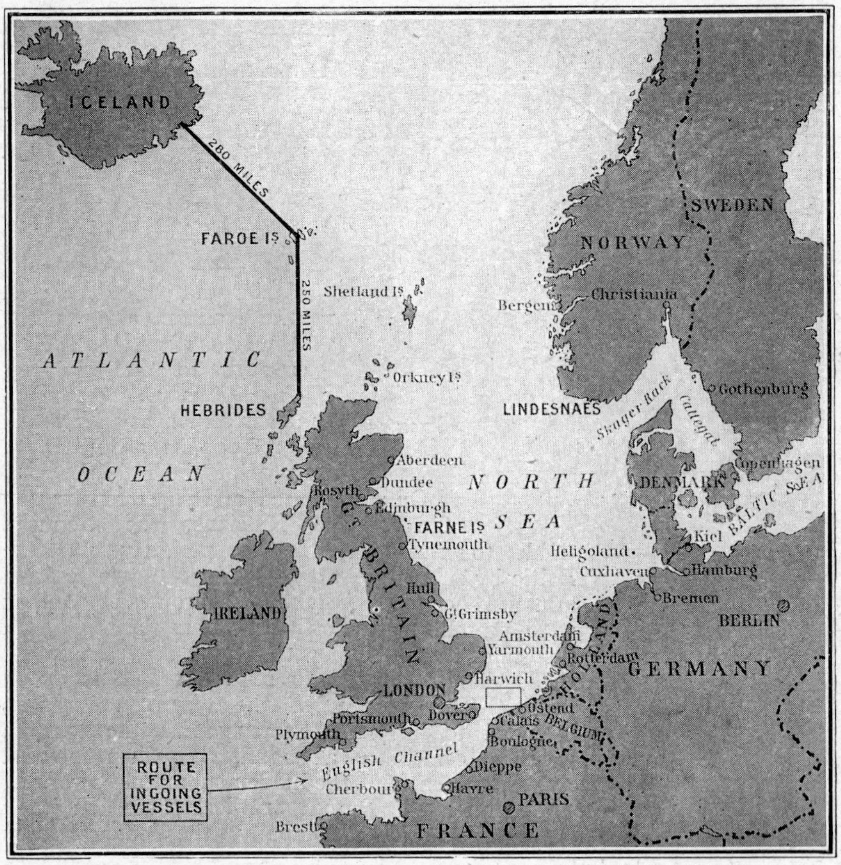

WHERE THE NORTH SEA WAS CLOSED TO INCOMING VESSELS.

The above map indicates the limits beyond which, after a certain date in November, 1914, vessels entering the North Sea sailed at their own risk. The northern entrance was closed from the Hebrides to Iceland through the Faroe Islands. The only entrance was by way of the English Channel. The British mine-field, laid on October 2nd, was between the Goodwins and Ostend, and between Foulness and the opposite coast.

By the beginning of October the British blockade of the North Sea became even more scientifically effective than the Franco-British blockade of the Austrian shores of the Adriatic. For on October 2nd, moved by the disaster to the Aboukir, Hogue, and Cressy, and by the increasing activities of the enemy's submarines, our Admiralty closed the lower area of the North Sea. A system of minefields was laid between the Goodwins and Ostend, and between Foulness and the opposite coast. The result was that the mouth of the Thames and the northern entrance to the Channel were sealed to any raiding hostile warships. German submarines could, perhaps, creep underneath the mines at considerable peril, but some time passed before they had a conveniently near base at the Bruges seaport for such operations. In the meantime our Grand Fleet kept on guard in the north.

Lower area of North Sea closed by mines

While this great blockade of German commerce and naval power was proceeding, with a few submarine incidents that scarcely revealed anything of the tremendous pressure our naval superiority was exerting on the enemy, there was more of the old romance of sea warfare in outpost affairs on distant oceans. Here also the main naval force of the British Empire was being used with such quiet strength that the happy peoples who benefited from it paid but little attention to its unostentatious efficiency. Along all the great trade routes, food and stores, raw material and manufactures, were being transported with little or no interruption.

Armies of a size that would have settled the fate of empires a hundred years ago were moving in vast fleets of troopships from India and the Oversea Dominions, without the enemy being able to impede them. Naturally, however, some of the enemy's cruisers and commerce-raiders were able to do a little damage in waters from which our warships were temporarily absent. The policing of the main trade routes, the convoy of great numbers of troopships, and the maintenance of the blockade of the North Sea and Adriatic, allowed a few scattered armed cruisers and German merchantmen to capture and sink a very small proportion of our mercantile marine.

But even when our naval forces were most busily employed in the main work of the Great War, the German corsairs did not have things all their own way. One of the most romantic and interesting of sea fights occurred in the South Atlantic between a Cunard liner, the Carmania, and the splendid new German liner, the Cap Trafalgar. They met on the morning of September 14th, off Trinidad Island—not the West Indian island of that name, but a rock, about four miles by two, lying in the South Atlantic some seven hundred miles east of Brazil. The Carmania had been equipped as an auxiliary cruiser, and sent to reconnoitre the little island. Her look-out spied three steamers westward of the lofty, lonely rock. They all fled when the British ship came into sight. But when it was seen that the Carmania was alone, the largest of the three German ships evidently changed her mind, turned round, and steamed up to attack. Then Captain Noel Grant, commanding the Cunarder, saw that the curious liner, which suddenly hoisted the German ensign, was a foe worthy of his guns. For the Cap Trafalgar was the pride of the Hamburg-South American line. She was built in 1913, eight years after the Cunarder, for the express purpose of ousting the Royal Mail steamers from passenger and carrying traffic in the South Atlantic. She was now painted to resemble a Castle liner, and had come fully armed and equipped to the usurped German base at Trinidad Island to destroy our shipping.

In size, speed, and fighting power, the two armed liners were about equal, and they were both manned mainly

AN ALGERIAN SHARPSHOOTER AT WORK IN THE SHELTER OF A WOOD.

Among the most resourceful of the coloured troops fighting with the Allies were the Algerians or Spahis. They served with distinction during the Aisne battles, and in the subsequent advance to the North of France. When fighting in wooded districts the Spahis fastened themselves to trees with a camel-hair thong to prevent them from falling in the event of being wounded, and again and again held back the enemy by their fire.

French artillerymen serving one of the famous "75" guns and shelling a German position in a village street in the North of France, while the infantry, sheltered behind some buildings, waited to attack with the bayonet. The infantry had attacked the village in the first place, but could not make progress beyond the first house. Then a young artillery officer brougl a "75" into the main street. With a few shots he destroyed the shelters o

ENCH VILLAGE WITH THE AID OF A "75" GUN.

emy, who were only a few yards off. The French infantry waiting, as shown, hind broken walls, to see the result of the duel, cheered their colleagues, and n proceeded to clear the village, which, in a few minutes, was once more in French hands. Our picture shows the scene during the bombardment. The efficiency of the French gunner was recognised very early in the war, and the mobility of the famous "75" was quickly appreciated by both friend and foe.

THE GUERILLA ELEMENT IN THE GREAT WAR—WHERE THE TURCO WAS AT HIS BEST.

Frequent mention has appeared in official communiqués of house-to-house fighting in Flanders and Northern France. Our drawing supplies a vivid idea of the ferocity of such warfare when the Turcos were taking part in it. The scene of the struggle above illustrated was the east bank of the Ypres Canal, between Elverdinghe and Pilkum. Here the Prussian infantry were surprised and annihilated by the redoubtable Turcos, whose active and sanguine temperament made them more than a match for their more phlegmatic and less alert adversaries.

by naval reservists. They had no armour, and their triple tier of decks offered such colossal targets as made a miss by a trained gun-layer at fighting range an impossibility. Each had a speed of eighteen knots. The Carmania had a tonnage of 19,524 tons, and mounted eight 4·7 in. guns. The Cap Trafalgar had a tonnage of 18,710 tons, and mounted eight 4·1 in. guns. In spite of their somewhat smaller calibre, the German guns, being of more modern make, had a low trajectory and were more effective at long distances. The opponents were thus well-matched, and the historic importance of this even fight between British and German sailors, under absolutely equal conditions, was enhanced by another circumstance. It was the first naval engagement of its kind in history between two unarmoured ocean liners. The action raged hotly for an hour, but out of a British crew of four hundred and twenty-one men there were only

H.M.S. BERWICK.
Sister ship of the Cumberland. She ran down and captured the Hamburg-Amerika liner Spreewald on September 12th, 1914.

nine killed and twenty-six wounded. From the sunken Cap Trafalgar some three hundred and ten survivors, picked up by a collier, were afterwards landed at Buenos Ayres. The officers and men of the Carmania won their brilliant, historic little action by superb seamanship and superior rapidity and concentration of fire. "Well done!" telegraphed the First Lord of the Admiralty to Captain Grant when the news reached London. "You have fought a fine action to a successful finish."

On the day that the Carmania was breaking up the plans of German commerce-raiders on the American side of the South Atlantic, the enemy was vainly trying to interfere with our naval forces on the African coast of the great ocean. In the Cameroon River, leading up to Duala, the principal port of the important German colony of the Cameroons, our gunboat, the Dwarf, with Commander Frederick E. K. Strong in charge of it, was attacked by a German steamboat. In the darkness of night, on September 14th, the hostile boat tried to blow up our vessel by running on it with an infernal machine (technically, a spar-torpedo) in the bows. The sharp look-out kept on the Dwarf gave the alarm in time, and the steamboat was captured.

German tactics in the Cameroons

Two nights afterwards the Germans tried another desperate manœuvre to sink the British gunboat. A German merchant-ship, the Nachtigall, got up full steam in the river, and swung up in the darkness against the small British craft. The design was to ram the gunboat. But again the British sailors were on the alert, and it was the big steamer that was wrecked, with a loss of fourteen men killed, and twenty-two missing, who were probably drowned in the darkness. The old British cruiser of the county class, H.M.S. Cumberland, under Captain Cyril Fuller, came up the Cameroon River to assist the gunboat. The Germans apparently then turned their attention to the more important ship. Two more steam-launches were prepared for a spar torpedo attack. One carried the explosive machines and the other assisted in the operation. Both were destroyed, one German being killed, and three more, with two natives, taken prisoners.

Captain Fuller soon won full compensation for these wild and ineffectual attempts on our ships. And the reason for the desperate manœuvres of the Germans was made plain. Behind our warships was a Franco-British expedition, organised at Freetown and Dakar, and composed of a landing force of infantry and guns. The fine German port of Duala, from which Germany was fed with important tropical commodities, was swiftly attacked, and it surrendered without conditions on September 27th.

Surrender of the fine German port of Duala

Then it was that the captain of the Cumberland was fully repaid. Without a struggle, he captured one-quarter of the entire fleet of the Woermann Line, the largest shipping company operating between Germany and the West Coast of Africa. The Woermann Company had a capital of one million pounds sterling, and thirty-nine vessels of the gross tonnage of 112,616. The

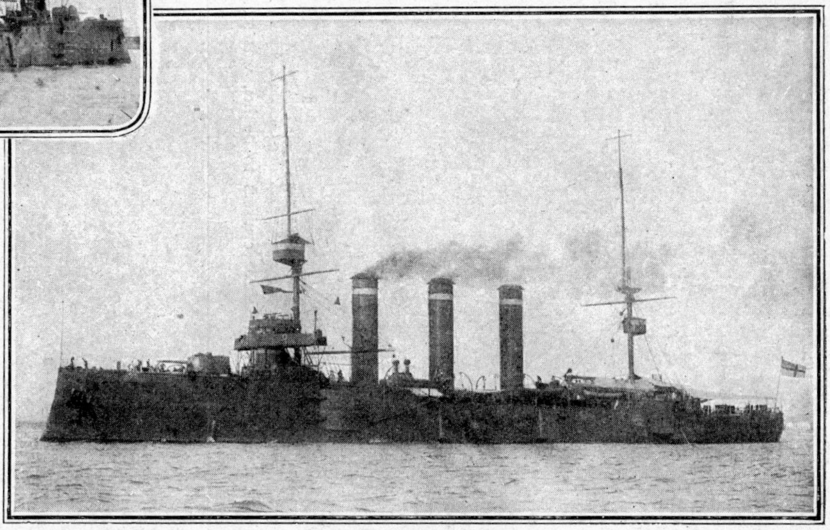

H.M.S. CUMBERLAND.
British cruiser of the "County" class (Captain Cyril Fuller), which assisted in the operations in the Cameroons, and captured one quarter of the fleet of the Woermann Line.

Cumberland captured eight Woermann ships, whose tonnage amounted to 28,016, and a vessel of the Hamburg-Amerika Line was also taken. All the vessels were in good order, and most of them contained cargoes and considerable quantities of coal. The German gunboat Soden, was likewise captured, and turned at once to good use, by being commissioned for service under the British flag.

The sister ship of the Cumberland, the Berwick, commanded by Captain Lewis Baker, was also successful in a fight against the commerce-raiders. On September 12th she ran down and captured the Hamburg-Amerika liner the Spreewald, a vessel of 3,900 tons, which had been fitted out as an armed merchant-cruiser. At the same time two colliers were taken, loaded with six thousand tons of coal, and a hundred tons of provisions for the supply of German cruisers operating in Atlantic waters.

Of all the ships that the German Admiralty skilfully scattered about the sea for the destruction of our commerce, one only had anything like a fairly successful career. None of the others did as much damage as a well-handled warship should have done. Only the light cruiser the

The Aboukir, the first of the three cruisers to be hit, was struck by a torpedo.

The Hogue, in an attempt to help the Aboukir, was also struck and sank shortly after.

THE BRITISH NAVAL LOSSES IN THE NORTH SEA ON SEPTEMBER 22nd, 1914, WHEN THE ABOUKIR, HOGUE, AND CRESSY WERE TORPEDOED BY GERMAN SUBMARINES.

THE BRITISH NAVAL LOSSES IN THE NORTH SEA ON SEPTEMBER 22ND, 1914: HOW THE CRESSY, THE LAST OF THE THREE CRUISERS TO BE HIT, WENT DOWN.

Although struck amidships, the Cressy continued to fire violently before she sank to the bottom.

Emden, with Captain Karl von Müller in command, gave a full display of the possibilities of commerce-raiding. Müller was a gallant sailor, well known to many of our naval officers. Some time before the war he stayed in one of our village inns with some of our naval officers, and played with them a game at pretended commerce-raiding, at which he proved the winner. The game consisted in throwing rings round hooks passing through a board on the wall of the inn—an old-fashioned rural pastime in our country. Every time Müller ringed a hook he claimed that he had captured a ship.

How thoroughly Germany prepared

When war broke out he was nominally at Tsing-tau, with the German China Squadron, under Admiral von Spee. At our China station we then had a sufficient force to master all Spee's ships. But the latter outmanœuvred us by slipping out secretly before war was declared. This is another instance of the thoroughness with which Germany prepared for aggression, at a time when even her ally Austria-Hungary was ready to arrive at a peaceful settlement. So the Emden got away. But our forces guarding the Pacific were so strong that nothing was heard of her for six weeks. However, she was in touch with the world-wide system of German espionage, and, hearing that the Indian Ocean was partly unguarded, through our warships there being engaged in convoying the Indian troopships, she suddenly appeared in the Bay of Bengal in the second week of September.

Accompanied by the Hamburg-Amerika liner Markomannia, acting as collier, the cruiser came up the Bay. By intercepting wireless messages, she learned the position of all vessels in the waters. At nine a.m. on the morning of September 10th she made her first victim of the Indus. Müller transferred the crew to his own ship, and then sank the British vessel by ten shells from the 4 in. guns. In the afternoon of the next day the Lovat was sighted and sunk. The day after the Kabinga was taken, and used as a prison-ship for the captured crews. On the same day the Killin was sunk, and the Diplomat—quite a good day's work in all. On September 14th the Trabbock was captured and sunk by a mine. When all the prisoners were placed in the Kabinga, which was ordered to proceed to Calcutta, Captain Müller with his collier accompanied the vessel to within seventy-five miles of the sandheads at the mouth of the Hooghley.

If all the Germans had made war in the sportsmanlike and civilised manner of Captain Müller, his country would have remained on terms of friendship with her rivals when the great struggle was over. Müller waged war in a very skilful and effective manner, and in the hour of victory he acted like a gentleman. His officers treated their prisoners generously, giving up their cabins to them, and supplying them with the best food they had. In parting they bade them the most cordial farewell. They said at the time that they had little hope of getting out of the Bay of Bengal.

Exploit of the Emden at Madras

But this was only a strategical statement, intended to put their opponents off their guard. Captain Müller designed more than a raid on our commerce in those waters. He sank another ship, and sent her crew to Rangoon. Then, on the evening of September 22nd, he steamed up to Madras Harbour and began to shell the oil-tanks of a Burma oil company. An empty tank was riddled, and another, containing a million and a half gallons of liquid fuel, was set on fire. A ship in the harbour was struck, and the telegraph office and some goods trucks on the harbour wall, but only two men and one boy in the harbour were killed. If the Indian peoples had been adverse from their British administrators, as most men in authority in Berlin vainly imagined was the case, the bazaar rumours of the Emden's exploit might have been troublesome. As it was, the affair, though admirably executed, only intensified the loyal feelings of the Indian peoples.

Getting out into the Indian Ocean, Captain Müller continued his commerce-raiding exploits, and in a few

FOUNDERING OF THE ABOUKIR. THE CAPTAIN'S LAST COMMAND.
"As the Aboukir was sinking," said Stoker J. Mills, "the captain gave out an order, just like on any ordinary occasion. 'If,' he said, 'any man wishes to leave the side of the ship he can do so. Every man for himself.' Then," added Stoker Mills, "we gave a cheer and in we went."

days captured and sank the British steamships Tumeric, King Lud, Liberia, and Foyle, and took the collier Buresk. The crews were transferred to the steamer Gryfedale, which was also captured, but released in order to take the British sailors to Colombo. By this time a considerable number of British, French, Russian, and Japanese warships—including several cruisers of high speed—were trying to round up the brilliant and adventurous raider. But many weeks had still to pass before Captain Müller was run to earth.

In the meantime the Australian Fleet, which had also sent some ships in pursuit of the daring corsair, lost one of its submarines. This was AE1, a fine new powerful boat of the latest type. Early in the year, under Lieutenant - Commander Besant, son of the famous novelist, she had made the voyage from Portsmouth to Sydney without a mishap, and showed fine seaworthy qualities. Built by Vickers, at Barrow, in 1913, she was an 800-ton boat, fitted with 21 in. torpedo-tubes. In the third week of September she was cruising in fine weather in deep water, and by some unexplained accident suddenly sank. She was manned by Australian naval ratings, who had undergone a course of training in submarine work, and these were joined by several Portsmouth naval reserve men, who volunteered for service in the first Australian submarine. The water where she sank was so deep that there was no hope of locating the wreck.

The end of H.M.S. Pegasus was a glorious disaster in the stirring month of September. She was a light cruiser, a little over 2,000 tons, and was built in 1897, carrying eight 4 in. guns of an old pattern, which made her suitable for the scrap-heap rather than for active service. As a matter of fact, she had been sent to the lumber-room some ten years before the war broke out. But as there were not enough modern cruisers to replace all the old types of these ships on foreign stations, the Pegasus was retained, under Commander Inglis, at Zanzibar. From this base she made a successful expedition to the German East African port and railway-head of Dar-es-Salaam. There she sank a German gunboat and a floating dock, and badly crippled the enemy commerce-raiders by destroying the wireless station.

It is only a short distance from Zanzibar to Dar-es-Salaam. But even this brief voyage was more than the old machinery of the cruiser could stand. After striking her blow for the Empire she went into Zanzibar Harbour, and defects in her engine-room made a complete overhaul necessary. On Sunday, September 20th, she was resting, sadly and helplessly, on the water, while her boilers were being cleaned and her machinery repaired. At five o'clock in the morning the German cruiser Königsberg approached at full speed, disabled a British patrol-boat with three shots, and then opened fire on the broken-down Pegasus. The German warship was built in 1905, and was armed with 4 in. modern guns, with a longer range and a greater energy than the obsolete weapons of the British vessel.

She began shooting at 9,000 yards' distance, and though all the broadside of the Pegasus stubbornly tried to reply, her old guns were put out of action in fifteen minutes. Even if her guns had been able to reach the enemy, however, she would still have been unable to move and bring them to bear on him. He was able to choose his own position, far beyond the range of the gunners of the Pegasus, and, firing from a distance of five miles, he pounded away at the helpless target.

Glorious end of the old Pegasus

Shell after shell struck the British cruiser, tearing down the upper works, smashing the guns, around which most of the slaughter of the crew occurred. When the decks were strewn with dead and dying men, the Germans ceased

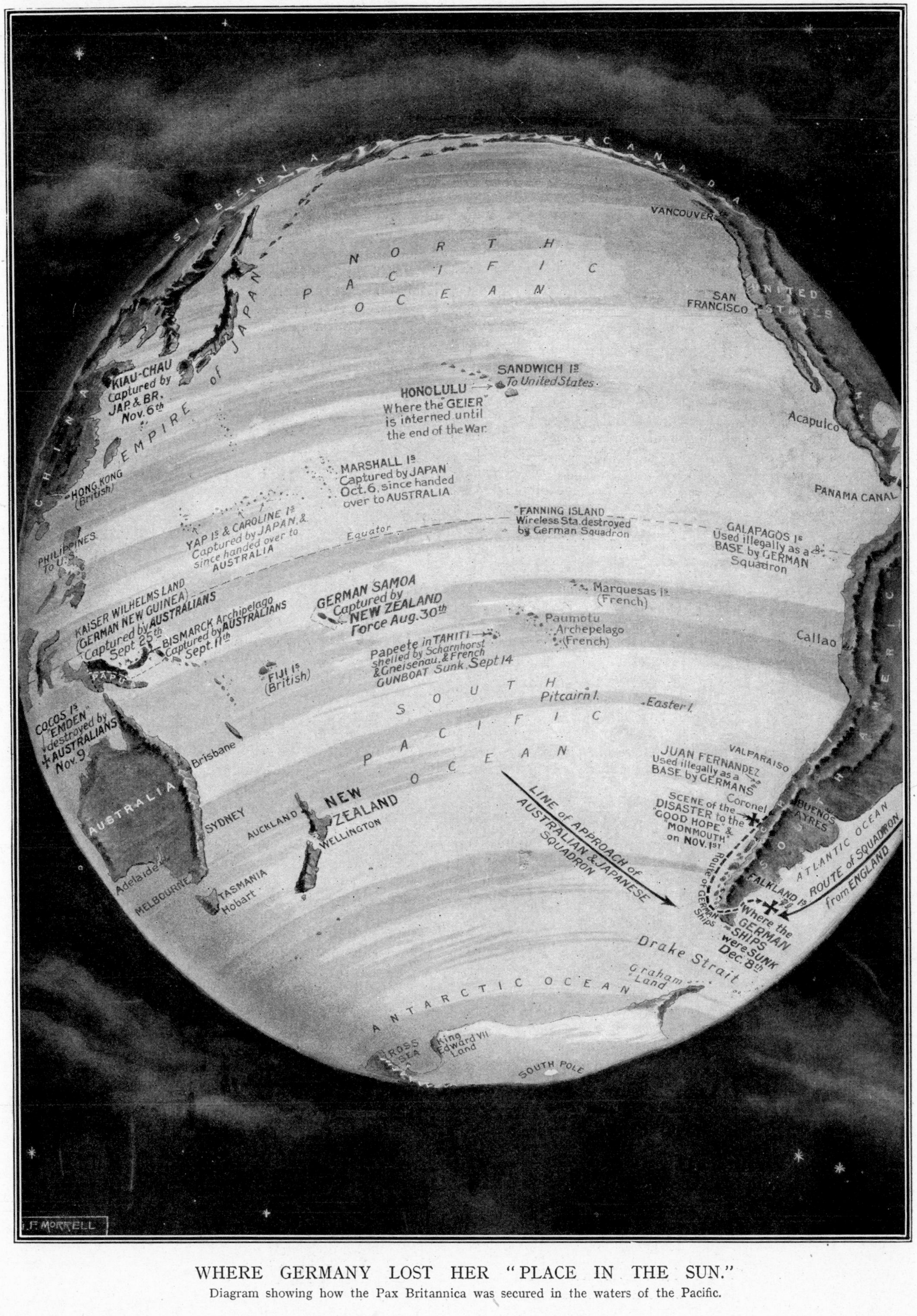

WHERE GERMANY LOST HER "PLACE IN THE SUN."

Diagram showing how the Pax Britannica was secured in the waters of the Pacific.

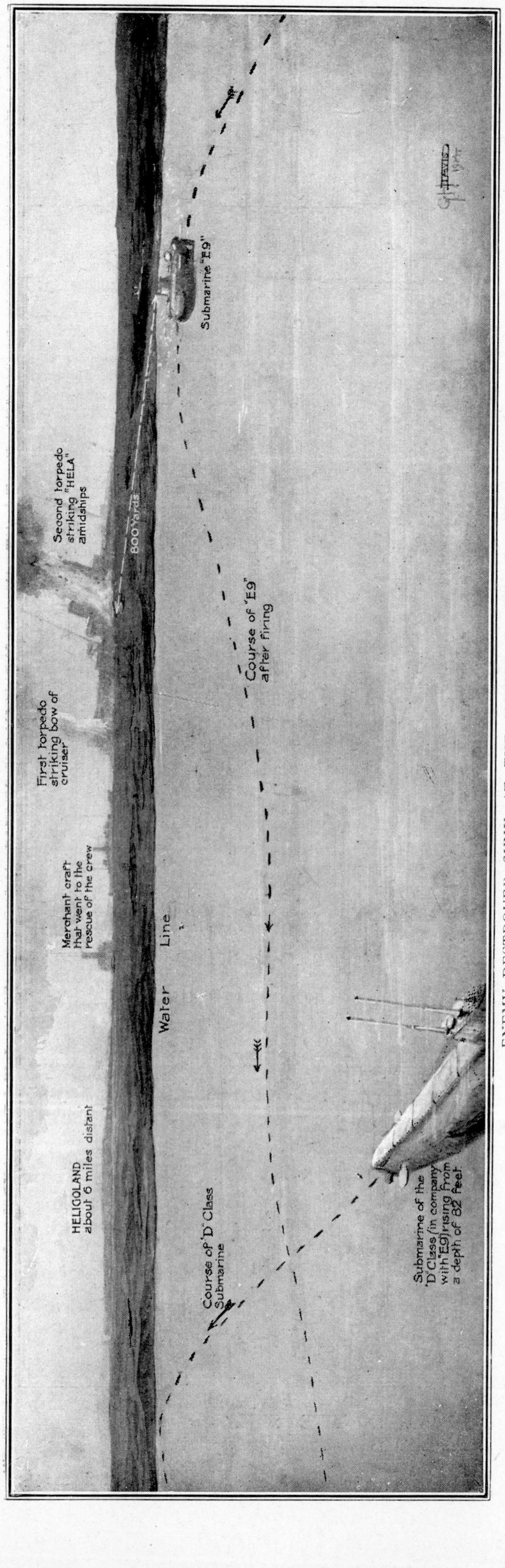

ENEMY DESTROYER SUNK AT THE MOUTH OF THE EMS RIVER.

Shortly after Submarine E9 had sunk the German cruiser Hela, six miles south of Heligoland, her gallant commander (Lieutenant-Commander Max K. Horton) returned safely, after having torpedoed and sunk the German torpedo-boat destroyer S126 off the mouth of the Ems River. The Hela was sunk on September 13th, and the S126 on October 7th, 1914.

firing for five minutes. Thinking that the action was over, all the men who had been able to find shelter came on deck to succour their wounded comrades. But this was the moment chosen by the Königsberg for another terrible bombardment. She battered the Pegasus almost beyond recognition, and holed her on the water-line till she listed heavily. Out of the crew of 234 men there were 34 killed and 61 wounded.

Dreadful was the scene in the shattered, helpless, immovable old vessel. But amid the continual bursts of high-explosive shells the British sailor rose to the full height of heroism. Under the enemy's fire the British flag was shot from the mast, and fell on the deck. At once it was seized, and held aloft by two Marines, who dauntlessly stood in the most exposed position in their ship, in order clearly to show the enemy that the flag was still flying. It drooped for a moment when one of the gallant fellows had been killed by a shell. Immediately another Marine took the place of the dead man, and the flag continued to show bravely amid the hurricane of high-explosive projectiles spreading death and destruction all around. And the hand-held flag was still flying from the smashed and silent Pegasus when the German cruiser fired a last shot and steamed away from her work of slaughter.

How British Marines kept the old flag flying

It was no German victory. The Pegasus had finished her work, and the damage done to her was not worth the cost in German ammunition. The death or disablement of ninety-five British sailors had no effect whatever on the course of the war. But the way they kept the flag flying was an inspiration to all the fighting men of our Empire.

As our naval forces were usually arranged about the seas of the world, in effective concentrations, the German sailors and colonial troops had quite as many opportunities for displaying a courageous spirit, transcending the material circumstances in which they fought. But though the German was usually a good fighter, he did not show much grim or flamboyant dauntlessness. The German soldier, especially, bred up to rely on the great Prussian war-machine, took rather too scientific a view of man-to-man fighting. In favourable conditions he fought well, but anything like an heroic stand against odds seems to have offended his sense of caution and calculation.

He had an excellent opportunity for making the world ring with his fame when the Australian squadron, under Vice-Admiral Sir George Patey, approached the tropical island of New Britain. This was one of the old British possessions, discovered by Captain Cook, but weakly handed over to Germany in 1884, at the expense of the interests of Australia and New Zealand. The large island, three hundred miles long and sixty miles broad, inhabited by head-hunting cannibals, was renamed New Pomerania, and the German settlement on it, Herbertshöhe, became the seat of German government for German New Guinea, the Marshall and Caroline Islands, and the German half of the Solomon Islands.

Ever since Bismarck, working through an unscrupulous, Hamburg firm of South Sea traders, had seized these territories, the people of Australia had objected to their new, dangerous, and intriguing neighbours. So when the Great War broke out, the German Government of Herbertshöhe vigorously prepared to defend itself against the fate that their people had earned by thirty years of treachery in trading, and the murderous persecution of British and Australian rivals.

Capture of Herbertshöhe by the Australians

The roads through the bush round Herbertshöhe were mined. Miles of trenches were dug, and multitudes of the cannibal natives were armed to assist the German forces. At dawn on September 11th a naval landing-party, under Commander J. A. H. Beresford, of the Australian Navy, established themselves on shore without the enemy's knowledge. There were six miles of thick bush between them and the town of Herbertshöhe, and the enemy's scouts soon discovered their presence.

In all the circumstances, the Australians, composed of naval reserve forces, might have expected defeat. Many of the Germans had rifles, and they had marked all the ranges, and there were miles of tropical undergrowth to hack through, with head-hunting sharpshooters firing from the trees, and sniping in the thick, tangled jungle. But the tall, lean, wiry Australian is one of the most resourceful and original fighters in the world. He has all the doggedness of the old British stock, with a peculiar resilience of mind and character, the combination of which makes him a supreme guerilla fighter. He stuck to his job for eighteen hours, in the course of which he taught the Germans some surprising lessons in bush fighting. There were thousands of miles of bush in his own country, and he was quite at home among the head-hunters and the missionaries of German "Kultur."

Yard by yard he fought on, winning about six hundred yards in an hour. Towards noon on September 12th he was within attacking distance of a long trench in front of Herbertshöhe. But by this time he had put such fear into the heart of every German that the battle abruptly ended with the unconditional surrender of the enemy. After eighteen hours' fighting in the most difficult country in the world the Australians had only lost six lives. The enemy's losses were much larger, but the numbers are not known. The German forces were more numerous, as the governor had concentrated all his armed men from New Guinea and elsewhere to defend the wireless station and the chief settlement. On September 24th the Australian Expeditionary Force gathered the full fruit of its victory by occupying German New Guinea and seizing the town and harbour of Kaiser Wilhelm's Land. So, without a struggle, 70,000 square miles of territory, containing valuable unexploited resources, was lost to Germany.

BIRD'S-EYE VIEW OF A BRITISH DESTROYER. TAKEN FROM A SEAPLANE FLYING ALOFT

The seaplane from which the above photograph was taken was flying at a height of some two hundred and fifty feet above the sea.

While this swift and resounding work of reconquest was proceeding, the warships of the British Empire were operating with another of our self-governing Dominions in the general disruption of Germany's "world-power." Of all the vanishing colonial empire, on which the Teutons had spent so much treasure and labour, there was no part they more highly prized than their diamond town of Lüderitzbucht, in German South-West Africa. Lying on a natural harbour, at the terminus of a railway line 1,300 miles in length, Lüderitzbucht was the captain jewel in the carcanet of German possessions round the world. For close to it were the newly-discovered German diamond-fields, worked by a Government syndicate, that was obtaining yearly about £1,000,000 worth of stones. But on September 27th an expeditionary force, despatched by the South African Union, came into the harbour and summoned the town to surrender. The demand was at once complied with, for the main German garrison had apparently retreated the day before, in order to avoid a fight.

The choking, impotent fury with which the Germans in Europe witnessed these striking exhibitions of the range and vigour of action of the British Navy was ineffable. No German could express it. But a Jew, Ernst Lissauer, managed, with the chameleon-like versatility of his race, to find words for them in his notorious "Hymn of Hate."

French and Russian they matter not,
A blow for a blow and a shot for a shot;
We love them not, we hate them not,
We hold the Vistula and Vosges-gate,
We have but one and only hate,
We love as one, we hate as one,
We have one foe and one alone.

He is known to you all, he is known to you all,
He crouches behind the dark grey flood,
Full of envy, of rage, of craft, of gall,
Cut off by waves that are thicker than blood.
Come, let us stand at the Judgment place,
An oath to swear to, face to face,
An oath of bronze no wind can shake,
An oath for our sons and their sons to take,
Come, hear the word, repeat the word,
Throughout the Fatherland make it heard.
We will never forgo our hate,
We have all but a single hate,
We love as one, we hate as one,
We have one foe, and one alone—
ENGLAND !

In the captain's mess, in the banquet-hall,
Sat feasting the officers, one and all,
Like a sabre blow, like the swing of a sail,
One seized his glass held high to hail;
Sharp-snapped like the stroke of a rudder's play,
Spoke three words only: "To the Day!"

Whose glass this fate?
They had all but a single hate.
Who was thus known?
They had one foe and one alone—
ENGLAND !

Take you the folk of the earth in pay,
With bars of gold your ramparts lay,
Bedeck the ocean with bow on bow,
Ye reckon well, but not well enough now.
French and Russian they matter not,
A blow for a blow, a shot for a shot;
We fight the battle with bronze and steel,
And the time that is coming Peace will seal.
You will we hate with a lasting hate,
We will never forgo our hate,
Hate by water and hate by land,
Hate of the head and hate of the hand.
Hate of the hammer and hate of the crown,
Hate of seventy millions, choking down.
We love as one, we hate as one,
We have one foe and one alone—
ENGLAND !

But the effect of this outburst was mitigated by a German professor, who explained to his countrymen that hatred was the only psychological defence against the emotion of fear. It was because our country was most feared by the new barbarians that it was the most hated.

Deep, personal, wild fear, amounting to a panic, was indeed aroused in the Rhineland cities of Germany towards the end of September by an unexpected feat by British sailors. The Naval Wing of the Royal Flying Corps had watched over the transport of the British Expeditionary Force across the Channel, and patrolled the British, French, and Belgian coasts on the watch for enemy ships. Then, under Wing-Commander Samson, the naval airmen had worked with a strong squadron of aeroplanes, first from Ostend, and next from advanced bases round Dunkirk. The airmen searched for bands of Uhlans, and by wireless messages directed our seamen, using armoured motor-cars, in several successful skirmishes against the German cavalrymen.

British raid on the Zeppelin shed at Dusseldorf

All this, however, was but a prelude to the main work on which Commander Samson and his men were bent. What they had in view was the Zeppelins and Zeppelin sheds of the Rhineland. And, on September 23rd, Squadron-Commander Gerrard set out with a detachment of airmen towards Cologne and Düsseldorf. There was a slight fog that enabled the flying men to travel at a height of nine hundred feet, without being seen from the earth. On nearing the Rhine they broke up into two divisions. One went to Cologne, but found the fog so thick there that the Zeppelin shed could not be seen. So they returned without attempting to kill or injure non-combatants in the great fortified city. Flight-Lieutenant Collet, in the division directed against Düsseldorf, was more fortunate. He found the shed visible, and landed three bombs on the sheds. All the airmen returned safely to their base.

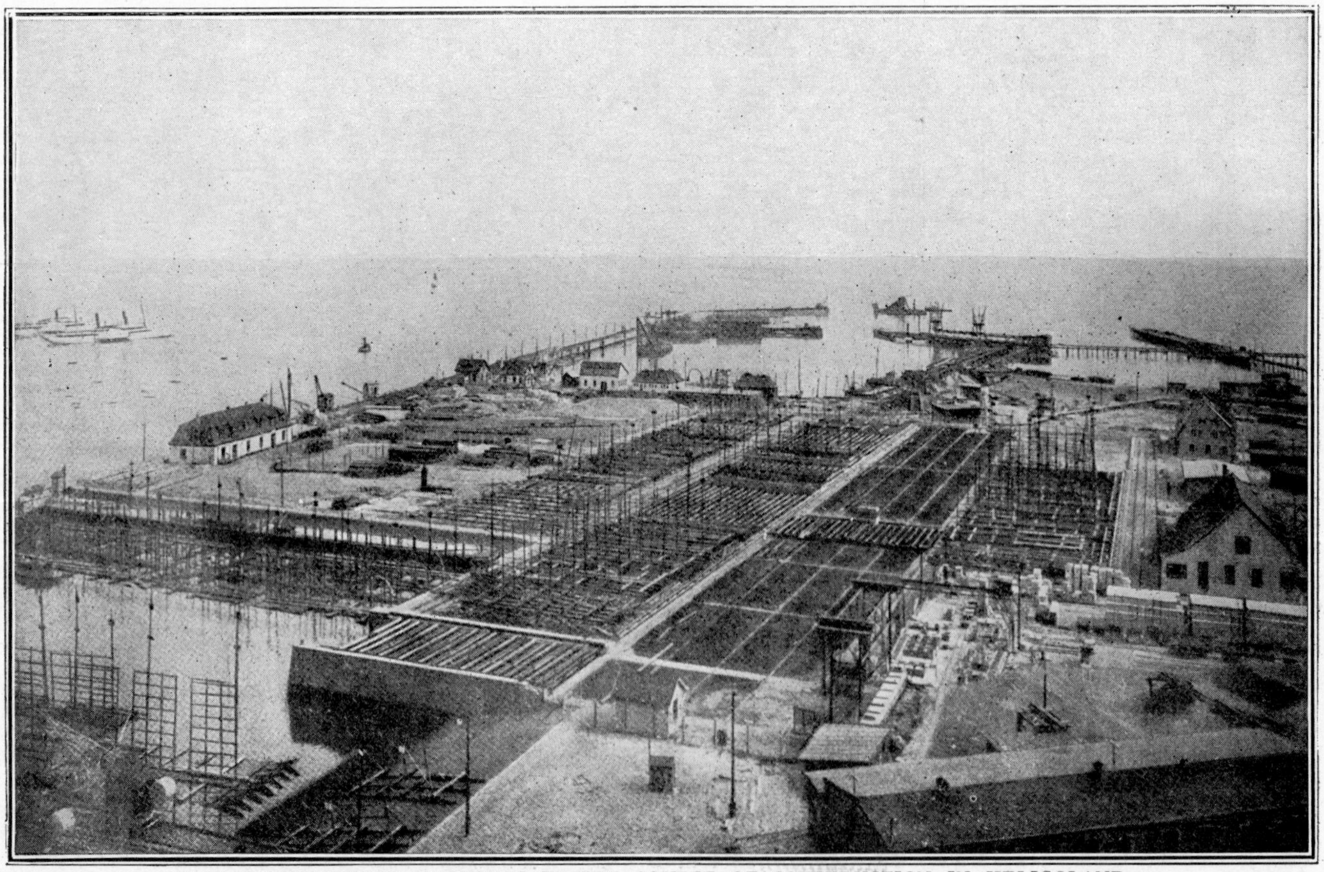

NEW TORPEDO-BOAT HARBOURS IN THE COURSE OF CONSTRUCTION IN HELIGOLAND.

From 1807 to 1890 Heligoland was a British possession. It was then ceded to Germany by Lord Salisbury in return for certain concessions in East Africa. From the beginning of their occupation the Germans set to work to convert the island into a strongly fortified naval base. In addition to their expenditure on armaments they made heroic attempts to preserve their new possession from sea erosion. Our photograph was taken in 1912, when it was expected that the new harbours would be ready in 1914.

GENERAL VIEW OF BUCHAREST, RUMANIA'S HANDSOME CAPITAL.

CHAPTER XLI.

PLOT AND COUNTERPLOT AMONG THE ARMING NEUTRALS.

Effect of the Allies' Victories on Neutral Powers—Turkey Preparing to Strike—Bulgaria Willing to Wound but Afraid of Being Hurt—Struggle between King and People of Rumania—Decision to Attack Austria when Armament Completed—Why the Rumanians Held Back—Difficult Position of Italians: Suspicious of France, Grateful to Prussia, and Friendly to Britain—Italy in "Sacred Egoism" Decides to Recover Her Lost Provinces—Austrian and German Intrigues at the Vatican—Cardinal Mercier, of Belgium, Intervenes—Pope Benedict Desirous of Peace—Initial Attitude of the Swiss—Swiss Military Censorship Works for Germany—Switzerland Partly Recovers Her Senses when Allies are Victorious—Splendid Beneficence of the Dutch—Position of the Scandinavian Nations—Professor Oswalt Undoes the Work of Sven Hedin and Björnson—Dernburg's Audacious Intrigues in the United States—German-American Forces Organised to Provoke War with Triple Entente Powers and Japan—The Right to Search—Americans Reject the Laws they Laid Down.

By the middle of September the series of definite and important victories won by the Allies in both theatres of war began to affect the position of many neutral Powers of the world. Some of these were neutral from either inclination or disinterestedness. Others were so from fear of the consequences of siding with either of the tremendous leagues of warring nations. Some were decided for action, but irresolute about the date when they would begin hostilities.

Turkey had practically been won over by the Teutons, and was only manœuvring to draw all the sympathies of Mohammedans with her. The so-called Party of Union and Progress in the Ottoman Empire had degenerated into a strong-handed clique of military adventurers, headed by the murderous charlatan Enver. He was surrounded by Jews and Germans who reduced him, by the skilful use of flattery and money, to the position of vassal to Kaiser Wilhelm.

Apparently one of the chief designs of Enver was to obtain a fighting alliance with the Bulgarians, who had beaten him in the Balkan War, and to induce the still more powerful Rumanians to remain at least neutral while Bulgaria attacked Serbia in flank, and Turkey used her European army to defeat and destroy the Greeks. This plan of action had been sketched out by the Austrians, who had already shown in the Second Balkan War their weak grasp of realities by egging on and backing Bulgaria in a vain struggle for dominion against the Serbians and the Greeks.

Bulgaria, defeated and dispossessed of territory by the combined action of Serbia, Greece, and Rumania, in the Second Balkan War, still remained sore and sullen and somewhat vindictive. But her ruler, Tsar Ferdinand, was resolved not to make another grave mistake. Had he but acted fairly in the division of spoil between the Balkan allies after the successful war against Turkey, there would probably have been no Great War in 1914. For, supported by her Balkan allies, and less directly by Russia, France, and Britain, Serbia would not have tempted the Austrians and Hungarians to settle the Balkan problem by a punitive expedition.

ENVER BEY.
Commander-in-Chief of the Ottoman Army.

During the first month of the war the Tsar of Bulgaria and his ministers showed as much favour to the Teutonic cause as they dared. They prevented Russia towards the middle of September from sending ammunition supplies to the pressed but victorious Serbians. At times they publicly expressed the desire to see the triumph of German and Austrian arms. By the end of the month, however, the attitude of the Bulgarian governing class had changed. For the extraordinary and tremendous series of victories won by Russian generals over all the first-line troops of Austria-Hungary made the Bulgarian Government rather anxious about its own position in regard to Russia. Bulgaria, broken by two recent wars, would lie at the mercy of the great victorious Power that it had begun to offend seriously. The arrival at Sofia of Mr. Noel Buxton and his brother, who had come to discuss with all the Balkan peoples a just and fair proposal for the settlement of all their differences, renewed in the Bulgarians their faith in the disinterestedness of the British Government. Then there was the fact that Bulgaria owed her very existence to Russia, and most of the Bulgarian peasants still regarded the Russian Tsar as the protector of their race. Their German ruler, Ferdinand, had led them astray by listening to Austria and Germany. A popular revolution was quite possible if he again tried to lead them away from their fighting brother Slavs into the camp of the Teutons. In all these circumstances the Bulgarian Government became more disposed to remain quite neutral.

Not so their old opponents the Rumanians. The vivacious and passionate Latin people of Rumania did not wait for French and Russian victories in order to proclaim their sympathies and outline their future course of action. The miraculous early success of the small and almost exhausted Serbian nation against the forces of Austria-Hungary was sufficient inspiration to the Rumanian people. Just across their western frontier, in the Hungarian province of Transylvania, four million Rumanians were held in bondage by the Hungarian magnates. All the machinery of politics, social conventions, and administration had been employed for half a century by the Hungarians to oppress, debase, and denationalise their Rumanian fellow-subjects. For many years every decent free Rumanian had dreamed of the possibility of a war of liberation, and it was the deep, silent, heart-buried hope of the possibility of waging such a war some day in favourable circumstances that made the Rumanian Army of five hundred thousand men a real force in European politics. For the Rumanian had drilled with passionate earnestness to make himself a soldier of the first class. No tax intended to finance an improvement in the Rumanian Army met with any opposition from the Rumanian peasantry. Such was the respect they inspired that in the Second Balkan War the Bulgarians had readily yielded territory rather than fight them. The attempts of both Austria and Germany to get better terms for their defeated catspaw had failed.

Rumanians in bondage to Hungarian magnates

Now, when the great day had come for the war of liberation, the Rumanian soldier was eager for the fray. Unfortunately, a prince of the House of Hohenzollern reigned over Rumania. He was King Carol, who had proved himself a wise, enterprising man of constructive genius. Much did the Rumanian people owe to him, and by reason of his claim to gratitude upon them they were placed in a tragically awkward position. For he would not fight against the Imperial leader of his house. It was said that he had pledged his word to the German Emperor not to take part in the struggle.

Towards the latter part of September it looked as though the intense contest between popular aspiration and dynastic allegiance would end in a revolution. With a magnificent strength of character that compelled admiration, King Carol stood out against the pressure of his people's wishes, until the strain completely undermined his health towards the end of September, and brought him quickly to the grave. His death was most fortunate for the Rumanian people. It was the greatest of all the great services he had done to them. For in the presence of his corpse the popular clamour for an immediate war died down. The new king and his ministers assured the people that nothing but the interests of the nation would guide their policy. The ministers studied the end and measured their means, and concluded that the time was not yet ripe for action.

King Carol's great service to Rumania

We cannot blame them; least of all can any Russian blame them. The statesmen of Rumania remembered the consequences of their generous action in the Russo-Turkish War of 1878. It was a Rumanian army that mainly helped in the decisive attack upon Plevna, and the Rumanians were rewarded by the annexation of their fertile province of Bessarabia by the men who had come to them for help. The memory of this extraordinary event did not weigh upon the younger generation of Rumanian soldiers; but their old statesmen could not easily forget it. This time they wanted

THE SINKING OF A GERMAN DESTROYER IN THE NORTH SEA.

The new light cruiser Undaunted (Captain Cecil H. Fox), accompanied by the destroyers Lance, Lennox, Legion, and Loyal, engaged four German destroyers (115, 117, 118, and 119) off the Dutch coast on October 17th, 1914, and "sunk the lot." Thirty-one men of the enemy ships were rescued. Our illustration is of the sinking of one of the destroyers, as seen from a vessel going to the rescue of the German sailors.

guarantees from the Russian Government, and pledges from France and Britain. Not only Transylvania was claimed by them, but Bessarabia also. Diplomatic discussions dragged on for months.

In the meantime Rumania entered into an understanding with Italy. Popular aspirations in Italy were identical with those in Rumania. For Austria held two important parts of Italian territory under her rule. The Italians distrusted the French almost as much as the Rumanians did the Russians. Ever since the French occupation of Tunis some Italian statesmen had thought that the two leading Latin nations would have to fight one day for the mastery of the Mediterranean. Even as late as 1912 certain small incidents during the Italian campaign in Tripoli had led the Italians to think that President Poincaré was, in spite of his marriage to an Italian lady, hostile to the expansion of Italian power. There had also been bitter tariff battles between France and Italy, and partly as a result of this economic strife German finance and German industrial leadership had won very considerable power in the manufacturing districts around Milan. Not a little of this ill-feeling between France and Italy had been astutely provoked by Bismarck in the old days. It was part of his general scheme for keeping France isolated.

With regard to Britain, Italy's situation was clearer and yet difficult. It was very largely owing to the fact that Britain entered into the Great War against the Teutons that the Italians nobly manœuvred for a position of neutrality. As soon as the Italian Foreign Minister saw, in 1913, that Germany was bent upon an aggressive war, in which Britain would probably be engaged, he withdrew from the Triple Alliance. He did not do so formally, but practically, by refusing to act in any case in which Germany or Austria had not been first attacked. On the other hand, every Italian statesman in a position of responsibility was distinguished by a lively sense of honour. Ever since Prussia and Italy had made war together upon Austria, in 1866, the Prussian and the Italian had worked together. German finance and German technical science had helped to develop Northern Italy into one of the most brilliant and important centres of industry in Europe. Many Italian men of science owed their genius to an alliance between their own southern vivacity of intellect and the methods of patient and thorough research learned from German universities. The old, strong traditional affection for Britain was the poetry of the international relations of Italy; the feeling of respect for German organisation in science and industry was the prose of their international politics. This was one of the reasons why Italy hesitated to weaken Germany by an attack on Austria.

SPREADING THE TRUTH FROM THE SKIES.

To their duties of scouting and fighting French airmen added the task of dropping leaflets with the following inscription: "To the German soldiers: It is not true that we Frenchmen shoot or ill-treat German prisoners. On the contrary our prisoners of war are well treated and obtain plenty to eat and to drink. Those of you who are disgusted with your miserable condition may, without fear, unarmed, inform the French outposts. You will be well received. After the war everyone will be allowed to return home. These leaflets contain a plain statement of the true state of affairs concerning the treatment of German prisoners."

Italy's traditional affection for Britain

Italy's hesitation in this respect was increased by another strong current of thought and feeling in Italian life. Modern Italy is not only a nation; she is also a spiritual empire. Ever since the noble Italian families of the Renaissance period succeeded in winning a practically absolute control over the College of Cardinals, the Papacy has remained an appanage of the Italian nobility. All the fields for exercising their undoubted genius for diplomacy—fields lost by French, Spanish, and Austrian conquests in Italy, and scarcely recovered by the democratic movement of national insurrection—were more than replaced by the spiritual dominion they exercised through

SINKING OF THE RUSSIAN CRUISER PALLADA IN THE BALTIC.
When on patrol duty with a sister ship, the Bayan, in the Baltic, the Pallada was struck by a torpedo from a German submarine and sent to the bottom so quickly that few of her crew of five hundred and sixty-eight officers and men escaped.

the Papacy. So long as France remained a professed Catholic Power her political weight on the Papacy was a balance to that of Austria. But when the French Republic in recent years became a fierce and active anti-Catholic force in the world, and the centre of much of the atheistical or anti-clerical movement that disturbed all the Latin countries, the Papacy was naturally compelled to act in self-defence.

The result was that the great power of the Roman Catholic Church inclined to Austria-Hungary and Southern Germany and the Rhineland, and the clerical element in Italy worked strongly to prevent that country from going to war with the Teutonic Empire. A desire to see the freethinkers of France overthrown tended at times to prevail over all other considerations. As Russia represented the old, schismatical Church of Constantinople, the directors of the policy of the Papacy did not look with much favour on Russian interests. Great Britain also was mainly a schismatical or heretical Power, and her triumph promised to help the old faith but little. With the Protestant part of Germany, on the other hand, the Papacy had come to an arrangement, after beating Bismarck himself in the height of his power. The Catholic party in Germany practically held the balance between the Protestant-Conservative party and the free-thinking Socialistic party.

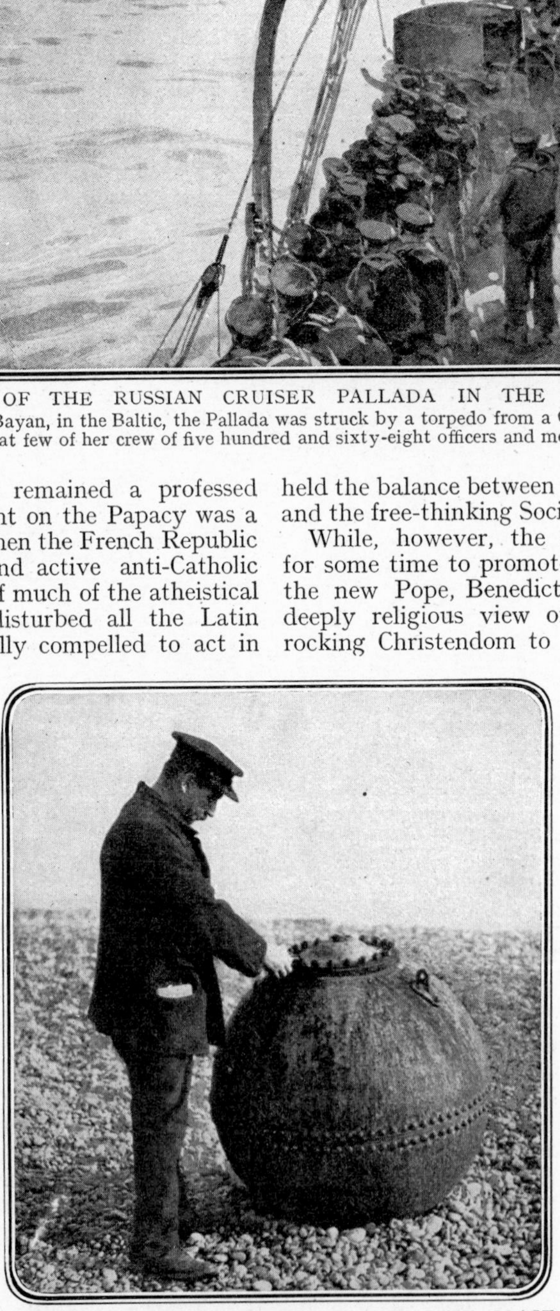

SEA-MINE WASHED ASHORE ON THE EAST COAST.
The bomb shown in our photograph was washed ashore on our East Coast in October, 1914. When in position in the sea it was designed to float the other way up, the anchor chains being attached to the eye-holes seen above.

While, however, the organ of the Vatican continued for some time to promote the cause of the Teutonic allies, the new Pope, Benedict XIV., took a larger and more deeply religious view of the terrible struggle that was rocking Christendom to its foundations. He was a wise, feeling, statesmanlike man, who seemed to reveal a gift for constructive diplomacy equal to that of Pope Leo XIII. Close to his side was Cardinal Mercier, of Malines, one of those heroic princes of the old Church, who force even disbelievers, and nonconformists to the ancient historic creed of Western Europe, to admire the miraculous vigour with which the Church of Rome returns to her noblest traditions. High above the subtle politicians of the College of Cardinals towered the modern apostle from the Belgians, stamped in the character of those early bishops of Western Europe who faced Hun and Goth and other barbaric Teutons, and subdued the savagery in them by a sublime manifestation of the personal forces of civilisation and Christianity. There were German and Austrian Cardinals at Rome, and German and Austrian Jesuits, who degraded their creed for political ends.

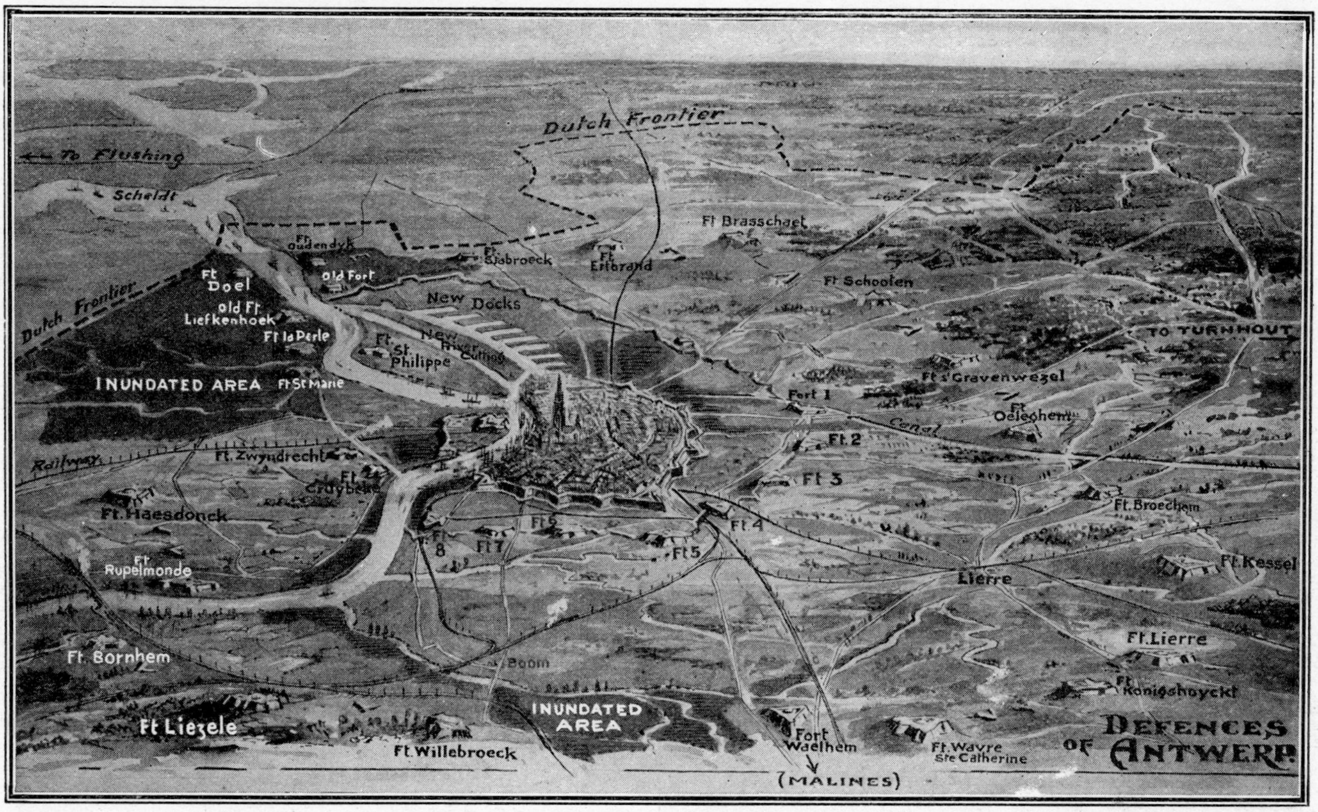

PICTORIAL MAP INDICATING THE AREAS INUNDATED BY THE BELGIANS IN THEIR DEFENCE OF ANTWERP.

But the great Belgian, by his sincerity and veracity, and the genius inspired by the sight of the sufferings of his innocent country, triumphed over all the politicians. By a direct personal appeal he won the newly-elected Pope over to his side. Then the Catholics of France were able to state that many of the French soldiers, hitherto indifferent, or even incredulous, in the matter of religion, had begun to ponder the mysteries of life, while facing death continually on the battlefield. The wild, bright, eager French mind was being tempered and hardened in the furnace of war. Even many French politicians of the anti-clerical school were beginning to modify their feelings of antagonism—some through policy, some through genuine sympathy with the growing religious current in their national life.

It looked as though all would be regained that had been lost when Cardinal Rampolla—the friend of France—had been thrust from the chair of St. Peter after his election by the veto of Austria. There were grounds for a new compromise between the Papacy and the French Republic. Such a compromise had ever been the aim of Pope Leo XIII. and his adviser and true successor, Cardinal Rampolla. Pope Benedict appeared to incline to revert to the statesmanship of the greatest of modern Popes, and, with a view, perhaps, to assisting her ally and to promoting the interests of the large number of Catholics in her dominion, Great Britain took the unusual step of sending a representative to the Church of Rome. This historic renewal of diplomatic relations with the Church to which our country once paid Peter's Pence, in memory of the debt we owed Rome for converting the pagan Anglo-Saxons of England to Christianity, excited considerable distress in certain Protestant circles.

They protested. But the power that brought Protestant Bismarck to his knees was too strong for us to resist. We had Belgian interests to protect as well as our own, the interests of millions of Irishmen, and the interests of old British families that did not change their faith at the Reformation. From a purely political point of view, the action of the British Government was sound and statesmanlike. Even Japan, that had not yet officially adopted the Christian faith, followed the example of Britain and sent a representative to the Vatican.

COUNT JOHANN VON BERNSTORFF.
German Ambassador at Washington. Devoted great energy to pro-German Press campaign in the United States.

In so far as Pope Benedict followed his natural feelings and used all his influence for peace, he helped the Teutons, and lengthened the period of suffering of the Catholics of Belgium. In the meantime, however, the Italian Government was deciding the problem of intervention in its own way. As her Prime Minister, Signor Salandra, put it, "a sacred egoism" became her guiding principle. In plain words, she was bent on recovering her lost provinces from Austria by any available means. The Teutonic Powers could make sure of her remaining neutral by yielding to her, without a struggle, the Trentino and Trieste. Austria, however, was disinclined to the bargain. Italy therefore turned to the Powers of the Triple Entente. To them she made in effect, if not in actual words, a larger demand. She required not only the two Italian-peopled districts of Southern Austria, but also a considerable part of the coast-line of the ancient Venetian territory of Dalmatia.

PROFESSOR WILHELM OSTWALD.
Famous German chemist. He tried to win over the Scandinavian nations to the idea of incorporation with "the Greater Germany which was to be organised after the war."

This province was peopled mainly by the Serbian race, but Venice had conquered it in the old days, and had built many of the towns on the coast. About half the coast could be given to Serbia, thus allowing her an outlet to the Adriatic Sea, and the rest was required by Italy.

All considered, the proposal was a fair one. If Italy put an army of a million men into the field, the cost in blood and treasure to her people would be great. She could not send her men out to die simply for love of the fair blue eyes of Britannia and the poetry of Lord Byron. All that we had done to promote the national independence of Italy in the old days was partly balanced by what the Germans had done in helping Italy to maintain herself as a great Mediterranean Power against France. Italy therefore waited until either of the two contending leagues of nations should accept her terms. In the meantime she armed for the fight. Both her exchequer and her war stores were depleted by the long war against the Turks and Arabs in Tripoli. Months were required in order to bring her large Army up to a position of strength in which it could venture to engage the forces of a great European military Power with a good chance of success. Guns were needed, and shells for the guns. For, though Italy had the finest light field-artillery in the world, she had not a sufficient number of batteries. Moreover, the war had shown that a large number of heavy mobile howitzers were absolutely necessary. With the Teutons standing in their last ditch, all their great guns behind them, heavy artillery and, perhaps, vast stores of shell and shrapnel would be required. Italy was also assisting Rumania in the manufacture of ammunition. In this way months passed without either of the two important neutral Powers coming to an active decision.

Italy's debt to Britain and Germany

The position of Greece in the Great War was more clearly defined. Like most of the Balkan States, she was seriously weakened in treasure and war material by the struggle with Turkey, and the subsequent fight with Bulgaria. Many of the Turks were still anxious for another war with the Greeks, with a view to recovering the Ægean Islands. Both Powers had been making a supreme effort to obtain a naval preponderance. Turkey had ordered two battleships from Britain, and Greece had purchased two battleships from the United States. The action of our country in taking over, at the outbreak of the war, the two ships building in our yards for Turkey was both a stroke of diplomacy in the Orient and a naval measure in the North Sea. It prevented Turkey from going to war with Greece with any chance of success at sea. The arrival in the Dardanelles of the Goeben and the Breslau did not alter this condition of things. For any action by the German battle-cruiser and her light consort would bring into the field of war the Russian Black Sea Fleet and the Franco-British Mediterranean Fleets. Greece was thus made strong at sea and bound to the Triple Entente by ties of gratitude and interest. The removal of the Turkish menace left her hands free for her principal work of maintaining peace in the Balkans. As the Greek Premier, M. Venezelos, explained to the Chamber of Deputies at Athens on September 13th, Greece was in a position of conditional neutrality. In the general interests of the Balkan people, she had contracted an alliance with Serbia. If either Bulgaria or Turkey tried to take advantage of the difficulties of the Serbians, and assist the defeated Austrians by attempting to stab Serbia in the back, Greece would intervene. As both Turkey and Bulgaria were well aware that the Rumanians would act in such a case in operation with the Greeks, the peace of the Balkans was maintained. The Turko-Bulgarian menace, however, had a considerable

Position of Greece in the War

DR. WOODROW WILSON.
President of the United States. In the first week of the war he offered his services for mediation between the belligerent Powers.

effect upon the course of the Great War. For it was one of the main factors that induced the Rumanian statesmen to hold back from joining in the attack against Hungary.

In Switzerland also the Teutons gained a success, owing to the thoroughness with which they prepared for war. The Swiss Army was almost entirely officered by men of the German type, in the closest sympathy with the Teutonic powers. The Swiss democracy had no voice in the matter; their Prussianised war Staff had both their minds and their bodies in its tyrannous grip. Immediately on the outbreak of the war it established a military censorship solely with a view to Germanising Swiss thought and feeling.

Efforts to Germanise Swiss thought and feeling

Only the French-speaking Swiss, who obtained their information through France, remained truly and stubbornly neutral. For this reason they were often dominated by Germans, who managed the best hotels and controlled some of the important industries in their districts. It is easy to see why the Germans took so much trouble to ensure the active sympathies of the Swiss. Not only was Switzerland one of the two gates into France, but she was also an important back door for evading some of the most vital consequences of the British and French blockades of the North Sea and the Adriatic.

By the end of September, however, the German Swiss began to count the cost of their actions. The victories of the Serbians, Russians, French, and British could no longer be concealed from the Swiss people. The Germanised censorship relaxed, and the French Swiss—always the most brilliant journalists of their conglomerate nation—began to make their power over public opinion felt. For months a verbal duel waged between German Berne and French Geneva, while Swiss Italians veered round towards the Allies, in sympathy with popular Italian feeling. The German Swiss, however, retained the bent of mind with which they began, together with the practical control of the Army. President Hoffmann was a figurehead. It was simply downright fear of the consequences of their actions that made the members of the ruling party in Switzerland modify their action. France had a considerable control over the wheat supply of the Swiss, and she naturally used this instrument to modify the outrageous conduct of the Swiss military censors. By the end of the month Switzerland was more or less effectively neutral.

THE LATE KING CAROL OF RUMANIA.

King Carol I., who died on October 10th, 1914, was a prince of the House of Hohenzollern. A wise, enterprising man of constructive genius, but German sympathies, his death was the greatest of all the great services he rendered to Rumania, for it was likely that the intense contest between popular aspiration and dynastic allegiance would have ended in revolution.

KING FERDINAND OF RUMANIA.

King Ferdinand I., nephew of the late King Carol. Aged forty-nine. He married, in 1892, Princess Marie of Edinburgh, a daughter of the late Duke of Saxe-Coburg-Gotha, and has six children, the eldest, Prince Carol, being twenty-one years old.

As a side door for evading the blockade, Switzerland, however, was less important to Germany than Holland. Rotterdam, with its large colony of Germans and German Jews, was a Rhine port controlling the main artery of German commerce. The Germans naturally desired the Dutch to remain nominally neutral, but practically favourable to the German cause, and help them to mitigate the effects of the naval blockade by transforming Rotterdam into a new Hamburg. This placed the Dutch Government in an extremely awkward position. From an economical point of view, Holland had become to a large extent one of the chief transporting centres for Westphalia. Rotterdam was a seaport of the vast German industrial district stretching from Düsseldorf to Essen. The modern prosperity of Holland was largely based upon the German hinterland behind it.

Awkward position of the Dutch Government

If the Dutch had been a spiritless people, to whom money was everything, they might have thrown in their lot with the powerful and industrially progressive modern German Empire. They stood to lose by everything that hindered or diminished German trade, and they stood to gain by everything that favoured and increased it.

FLIGHT FROM ANTWERP DURING THE BOMBARDMENT.
Thousands of the citizens awaiting their opportunity to cross the Scheldt.

In addition to these economical considerations, there was the memory of the Boer War that told against Great Britain. The Boers were Dutchmen—Dutchmen of the heroic age of Tromp and De Ruyter. In their distant settlement by the half-way house on the old route to India, they had preserved the spirit of the brave old fighting days, when Holland was able to dispute with Britain the mastery of the seas and the command of all the outlands of the earth. Towards the nation which abruptly brought to an end the independence of the Transvaal and the Orange Free State, the Dutch people were not favourably inclined. German politicians were well aware of this condition of things, and exploited it to the utmost of their power. Even the unparalleled magnanimity with which the Liberal Government of Great Britain handled the situation in South Africa after the war did not entirely remove the grudge against our country felt by the Dutch.

Spirited independence of the Dutchman

Holland, however, never fell to the position that Switzerland occupied in the first two months of the war. There was that in the soul of the ordinary Dutchman which rebelled against any pressure from any foreign country. Neither the naval power of Britain nor the military and economical power of Germany daunted his spirit. Placed between the upper and the nether millstones, between the power of Britain to cut off supplies and starve him, and the power of Germany to deal with him as she had dealt with the Belgians, the Dutchman underwent a transformation. Dutch Jews and German Jews, and German importing houses, continued to dodge or dare the contraband laws. The real Dutchman, however, suffered a change similar to that which happened to the British soldier in the retreat from Mons. It was the streams of anguished, hopeless fugitives crossing the Dutch border from the Walloon districts of Belgium that influenced the Dutchman and determined his attitude. It made him willing, if need arose, to face the embattled power of Germany with the same grim and desperate courage with which his ancestors had faced Spain and France in the days of Philip II. and Louis XIV. During the Siege of Liège the German Staff had almost been tempted to turn through Holland for an easier path. The Dutchman remembered this. For the rest, the Dutch nation generally kept strictly to the letter and the spirit of international law, and tried to deal fairly between the contending leagues of nations.

Political and economic factors in Denmark

The position of the Scandinavian countries somewhat resembled that of Holland. Their economic ties to the German Empire were less close. For example, in regard to the agricultural products, Britain had been, and remained, a better market for Denmark than was Germany. In the case of the Danes, moreover, many men still living remembered the war with Prussia and Austria over Schleswig-Holstein, and their memories had been continually refreshed by the treatment meted out to Danes in the conquered territories. On the other hand, there were older memories of the way in which Britain had conducted the great Continental naval blockade in the days of Nelson. For we had then attacked and captured the Danish Navy merely to forestall a possible move against Sweden, another neutral nation, by Napoleon. The Danes believed we were quite capable of again acting with the utmost rigour, if our

GERMAN SHELL PLOUGHS UP THE PAVEMENT.
All the windows were shuttered and many places along the Antwerp streets were littered with débris of shell-fire.

national life appeared to be in desperate danger. From a pure theoretical, democratic point of view the Danish nation wished for the triumph of the Triple Entente, and the recovery of the Danish-peopled district of Schleswig-Holstein. In the meantime they hoped that the blockade of the North Sea would proceed without any rigorous treatment of neighbouring neutral countries, and many of their farmers tried to balance the increasing cost of fodder by selling horses to the German Army.

The Norwegians, practically the same race as the Danes, were in a rather more fortunate position. In spite of the comparative smallness of their population, their old genius for seafaring had enabled them to create in modern times an important mercantile marine. Their country was rich in timber and animal produce, much of which was supplied to our land and to Germany. The Norwegian sailors were endangered by German mines in the North Sea; but the shipowners, at least, reaped a full harvest from the extraordinary rise in the cost of ocean transport produced by the stoppage of German shipping, and the employment of British merchant vessels as troopships and military supply-ships. Being one of the most intensely democratic people on earth, the Norwegians favoured the Allies—and imported a somewhat remarkable amount of copper!

Bjornson's son and the German reptile Press

Germany wanted this metal, and perhaps the type of Norwegian whom Ibsen used to depict with bitter scorn was not averse to making money by providing the means of slaughtering other democratic and God-fearing nations of Western Europe. The son of Ibsen's old friend, Björnson, went publicly over to the side of the Germans, and became one of the chief apostles of Prussianism to Denmark and Norway. He tried to palliate the German atrocities in Belgium and Northern France, and spread every gross falsehood about the policy of Britain, France, and Belgium that the reptile German Press invented. Yet his father had been the prophet of democracy in Norway, and had probably done more than any other man to restore the independence of the Norwegian nation, after centuries of subjection to Denmark and Sweden.

In the neighbouring country of Sweden, the famous explorer of Central Asia, Sven Hedin, degraded himself to the position of a gramophone in the service of the German Press Bureau. Beginning with the misrepresentation of the aims of Russia, Hedin ended by adopting the perverse ideas about Britain which the Germans, in a frenzy of fear and hatred, invented. In the early period of the war most of the Swedes seemed to

ANTWERP DURING BOMBARDMENT: THE RUSH TO THE QUAY VANDYKE.

Every conceivable species of conveyance was utilised for the Belgian exodus from Antwerp. Our photograph shows the beginning of the congestion on the Quay Vandyke. Castle Steen, with its memories of the Spanish Inquisition, is seen in the background on the right. Inset: Refugees drifting down the River Scheldt.

SUPLEMENTO

Cien dirijibles alemanes bombardean los campamentos de los aliados

Horrible confusion i fuga de ingleses i franceses

TERROR EN PARIS

Los primeros derrotados llegan a esta capital con las terribles noticias i los habitantes aterrados huyen hacia el Sur-Oeste. El Zar de Rusia, el Rei de Inglaterra i M. Poncairé telegrafian al Kaiser.

THE FATHERLAND

Fair Play for Germany and Austria-Hungary

Vol. I.—No. 6 Edited by George Sylvester Viereck, Frederick F. Schrader September 14th, 1914 Price, 5 Cents

THE UNHOLY ALLIANCE

England has summoned the Mongol; France calls upon the Moor; Russia sends her Cossacks to attack our German Kinsmen. WHERE ARE THE SYMPATHIES OF THE AMERICAN PEOPLE?

THE KAISER'S OFFICIAL LIARS AND THEIR WORK.

The amazing campaign of lies and calumnies which the Kaiser officially instituted early in the war was something unconceived by merely civilised peoples, and the peculiar product of "Kultur." Herr Dernburg, seen above (left), went to New York to pollute the United States with German lies, one of his innumerable agencies being a weekly paper "The Fatherland," from which we reproduce a page in miniature; while Dr. Hamann, the chief of the Germany Press Bureau at Berlin (seen on the right), deluged the whole world with false news and infamous inventions, his machinations extending as far as little towns in Chili, where lying "supplements," written and paid for by German agents, were issued by the venal and powerless local Press. We give an example above. The "news" headings read: "One hundred German airships bombard Allies' camps. Horrible confusion and flight of English and French. Terror in Paris. The first fugitives arrive at that capital with the terrible news and the terror-stricken inhabitants flee towards the south-west. The Tsar of Russia, King of England, and M. Poincaré telegraph the Kaiser." Naturally, the text assured us that the allied rulers were suing for peace!

have had a decided bias towards Germany. This was largely due to the preparations that Germany had made for the control of the Swedish Press, and other instruments for influencing public opinion. The Germans worked upon the old Swedish grudge against Russia for obtaining, during the reconstruction of Europe in the days of Napoleon, the Duchy of Finland. For though Sweden received in compensation the kingdom of Norway, she had since lost this owing to her lack of tact in handling the Norwegians. She still bore ill-will against the Russians, and feared they would end by absorbing the whole of Scandinavia. Groundless as the fear was, it was sufficient for the Germans to work upon. They had the chief share in supplying Sweden with goods, while our country had the chief share of Swedish imports. The result was that the German commercial traveller was a greater force in Sweden than was the British commercial traveller. By combining patriotism and business, in modern Teutonic fashion, he greatly helped to influence the Swedes against the Allies.

Exploiting Sweden's fear of Russia

Germany, moreover, exercised considerable pressure on Sweden by means of her Baltic Fleet. It was to diminish this pressure that the Russian Admiral von Essen made a surprise attack on a German cruiser squadron towards the end of August, and sank the Magdeburg and several German destroyers. The happy consequence was that the Swedes took to using their minds in a more free and independent manner, and in spite of the contorted efforts of Sven Hedin's intellect, popular opinion in the country by the end of September became a little more friendly to the Allies. For all that Hedin did was undone by the famous German chemist Ostwald.

This man was a supreme incarnation of the scientific virtues and practical vices of the modern German professor. In his own special field of knowledge he had done much good work. But the universal fame and honour, which he had won by his labours in chemistry and physics, turned his mind. Like Haeckel, of Jena, and Lasson, of Berlin, he wanted to imitate the heroic German professors of the age of Napoleon. They had been content to excite the courage of the Prussians in the years of gloom that followed the disasters of Jena and Auerstadt. This work was not necessary at the present time, so Ostwald launched out into the wider field of warlike politics, and tried to win over the Scandinavian nations.

Ostwald proposed to them that they should, without a struggle, become incorporated in the Greater Germany which was to be organised after the war. The Teuton, he proclaimed, was the only man with a veritable genius for organisation, and the Swedes, Norwegians, and Danes should be struck with anticipatory gratitude for the work Germany intended to do for them after she had won the empire of the world. This amazingly tactless and disconcerting statement, made by one of the greatest leaders of German science, did more for the cause of the Triple Entente than the most eloquent of French or British orators could have achieved.

By the end of the historic month of September the only neutral white race that caused any anxiety to the Allies was the Americans. To the task of influencing public opinion in the United States, the German Government had bent the larger part of the energies that it could spare from the actual conduct of the war. There were nearly eleven million persons of German, Austrian, and Hungarian stock in the States, including some powerful financiers and trust magnates of German-Jewish or German origin. For some years previous to the outbreak of the war the German Government had endeavoured to preserve and intensify a feeling of German patriotism in America, by a ramifying system of local German associations.

RESCUE OF THE CREW OF A SINKING GERMAN SEA-RAIDER.

A German submarine, U18, was rammed off the Scottish coast on November 23rd, 1914. It was shortly afterwards seen on the surface, with its crew on deck and the white flag flying. The British destroyer Garry came up just as the submarine was sinking, and rescued Lieutenant von Hennig, two other officers, and twenty-three men, one only being drowned.

SYMPATHETIC HOLLAND AND THE DISTRESSED BELGIANS.

Dutch Army service waggon at a frontier town affording temporary aid to the fugitives from Antwerp. The view immediately below is of Belgian refugees on the road to Holland with household goods hurriedly packed on a donkey-cart.

The organisation of the Teutonic forces in the United States appeared to offer a grand opportunity for action directed from Berlin. First of all Count Bernstorff, the new German Ambassador, was appointed local director of this large and favourable factor in American politics. Hermann Ridder, the editor of the German-American paper, the "Staats Zeitung," was made leader of the local German reptile Press. Then, as Count Bernstorff displayed, in the interviews that American journalists had with him, an inability to appreciate and work upon the American mind, the main part of his task was entrusted to Bernard Dernburg.

Dernburg scarcely deserved his position. He was one of the few men of genius produced in modern Germany, and like most of his countrymen with high ability in practical affairs, he came of Jewish stock. He was the son of the editor of the "Berliner Tageblatt," and after learning banking business in New York with Thalmann & Co., in early manhood, he had returned to Berlin, where he won a high position in German finance, and became at last Colonial Secretary in the Imperial Government. His admirers proclaimed him the Joseph Chamberlain of Germany. But though the Kaiser shared their admiration, the old prejudices of the Prussian nobility against their brilliant Jewish fellow-subjects led to Dernburg's overthrow. But for this prejudice he might have become the Disraeli of the leading Teutonic Empire.

The degradation of Dernburg

It was somewhat of a degradation to a man of this calibre to dispatch him to the United States on a mission directly opposed to the position of neutrality taken up by the American Government. For Dernburg had to plot and scheme in an underhanded way against the proclaimed policy of President Woodrow Wilson. But, by a mixture of audacity and subtlety, amounting almost to impudence, the German Jew carried on his work. He professed to come to America to collect for a Red Cross fund. But this was only a very transparent cover for a bold and pertinacious attempt to raise a great German war loan, mainly through German-Jewish-American bankers.

American interests in the Teutonic Empires

The scheme failed. Many of the bankers already had large personal or family interests in the affairs of the Teutonic Empires. And, looking at the matter as hard-headed business men, they were disinclined to risk much more money just for the sake of Bernard's dark and eloquent eyes. They were more concerned about means of saving their German and Austrian investments from the threatening wreckage of German power than about helping the Kaiser in his overwhelming difficulties.

So Dernburg, with the co-operation of Count Bernstorff, tried to work towards another end. Towards the middle of September both the German Government and the German Military Staff came to the conclusion that they had started a war which they were unlikely to bring to a successful conclusion. They recognised that they had made a mistake in singling out France and Russia for attack. Britain was their most formidable opponent. For the British plan of campaign, which they had once despised, was already proving to be comprehensive in scope, and deliberate and deadly in execution. By reason of their great naval power, the British people were bankrupting and starving out the German Empire,

THE EXODUS FROM ANTWERP INTO HOLLAND.

The great majority of the refugees from Antwerp found their way into Holland, and nothing could exceed the kindness shown to them by the Dutch people. The above photographs were taken during the flight along the roads leading to Dutch territory.

HOW THE RUSSIAN BALTIC FLEET PUTS TO SEA IN WINTER.

During the winter months, when most of Russia's Baltic ports are ice-bound, the Russian Fleet is enabled to put to sea by the aid of the ice-breaker Ermack, shown in the above picture. The vessel was built in England by the firm of Sir W. G. Armstrong, Whitworth & Co., to designs by Admiral Makaroff, and is able to clear a passage through ice over twenty feet thick.

while they were growing tremendously in military strength by building up a volunteer army of two million young men. At the same time, London still ruled the money markets of the world, and as Dr. Solf, the new German Secretary for the Colonies, confessed, she had invisible weapons of industrial warfare, which were more terrible in their effect on German national life than were the new gigantic Krupp howitzers.

In short, the Kaiser and his Ministers and generals and admirals were ready to make peace. Naturally, they wanted peace on their own terms—no war indemnities, no cession of territory, and no disarmament. Apparently Mr. Oscar Straus, a former American Ambassador to Turkey, was entrusted with the delicate and ticklish task of opening negotiations, through his own Government, with all the contending Powers. It was a pretty move to induce the American Government to approach Germany as well as Britain, France, and Russia, when the entire movement for peace was a German intrigue—at least in its origin.

Naturally, nothing came of it. It may be that at the inception of the scheme the Germans thought that the pacific influence of Pope Benedict on the one side and, on the other side of the world, the equally disinterested desire of President Wilson to see the war end speedily, might have some power to sway the minds of their enemies. When it was patent that nothing of this sort could shake the determination of the Powers of the Triple Entente, the German-American movement for peace was pursued with a different end in view.

Germany's bid for American sympathy

It was calculated that the general sympathy of the American people would be stirred by the spectacle of millions of peace-desiring Teutons being bled white by hordes of savage, vindictive Russians, Frenchmen, Britons, Belgians, Serbians, Montenegrins, and Japanese. The American, like the Briton, cannot help feeling for the under-dog. While Field-Marshal von Hindenburg was preparing to trample Russian Poland into mud, and to starve, cripple, and terrorise the Poles, by the mightiest movement of invasion in modern times, the appeal for sympathy with the kind, pacific, hard-pressed Teuton was carried on.

It might well have succeeded, but for one thing. Well-known and well-trusted American war correspondents

CHEERING A BRITISH TRANSPORT ARRIVING AT ANTWERP WITH PART OF THE NAVAL CONTINGENT ON BOARD

The Royal Naval Division, under the command of Major-General A. Paris, C.B., reached Antwerp in the early part of October, 1914, and included men of the First and Second Naval Brigades and Royal Marine Brigade. The force, declared Sir John French, after "a comprehensive review of all the circumstances," was "handled by General Paris with great skill and boldness." Inset: The inundations, intended by their elders to prevent the horrors of a German invasion of Antwerp, afforded Belgian children opportunities of playing new games.

had travelled through Belgium, and faithfully set down the things they saw. The native-born American accepted their evidence, especially after it was generally known that an American girl living in Belgium had fallen into the hands of German soldiers, with most dreadful results. Moreover, the American public had read all the diplomatic correspondence concerning the outbreak of the war that had appeared in print. The majority of them had made up their minds that Belgium, France, and Britain were fighting, not only for their own lives, but for the general principles of international law and democratic civilisation.

But though all the native-born American peoples were averse from the intrigues of the Germans, there was one small but powerful group of American men who were inclined to make trouble with the Powers of the Triple Entente. These men were connected with various trusts, that had large controls over the production of various materials urgently needed in Germany and Austria for carrying on the war or maintaining the general national strength. Copper, cotton, petrol, and india-rubber, for example, were selling in Germany at prices which would rapidly make the fortunes of large wholesale exporters.

American Trusts and the Allies

In 1812, towards the close of the Napoleonic wars, the United States had resumed hostilities with Britain over the question of the right of the British Navy to stop and search neutral ships. Bearing this in mind, some of the American trust magnates seem to have thought that they could conduct a very profitable commerce with the Germanic Empires by getting their ships exempt from contraband. Simple was the means—mere bluff of another war over right of search, according to the traditions of 1812. But what international laws there were with regard to the searching of neutral vessels had been changed in the course of a hundred and two years. By the irony of Fate it was the Americans themselves who had succeeded in making the rights of search more rigorous. During the American Civil War our shippers supplying the Confederates had tried to evade the confiscation of their cargoes by sending them to a neutral port, usually Mexican. To stop this practice the Americans had established the doctrine of continuous voyage. According to this doctrine, goods of a contraband sort, sent to neutral countries, but destined for the enemy, were liable to seizure.

But this did not still the agitation against the naval methods adopted by the Allies; and there were times when it seemed that the genius for intrigue of one brilliant German Jew might prevail over the silent and reserved policy of neutrality of President Woodrow Wilson.

MEN OF THE BRITISH NAVAL BRIGADE DRAWN UP ON THE OUTSKIRTS OF ANTWERP.

It was in response to an appeal by the Belgian Government that a British naval contingent, with some heavy naval guns, was sent to participate in the defence of Antwerp during the last week of the German attack. Inset: French Marines passing through Ghent on their way to take part in the defence of Antwerp.

VIEW OF ANTWERP FROM THE SCHELDT.

CHAPTER XLII.

THE BOMBARDMENT AND FALL OF ANTWERP.

The Cruel Shelling of Malines Cathedral on the Sabbath—Beaten by Soldiers, Germans Slaughter Women Coming from Prayers—Battles for the Path to the Sea—Decisive Belgian Victories Round Termonde—German General Makes a Mistake that Saves the French Coast—Desperate Position of Belgian Army in Antwerp—No Guns with the Range of the Austrian and German Howitzers—Fall of Antwerp Forts Certain—Belgians Undertake an Impossible Task to Help their Allies—Terrible End of the Garrison of Fort Waelhem—Ten Blackened, Burnt, Groping Figures Emerge from the Ruins—Fort after Fort Falling under a Rain of 12 in. Shells—The Raging, Murderous Struggle for the Nethe—Mr. Winston Churchill Arrives with the Naval Division—Scheme of Large Operations for the Relief of Antwerp—Sir Henry Rawlinson and the 7th Division Forced Back—The Bridge of Death at the Nethe—Shells begin to Fall in the City—The Dreadful, Tragic Flight of Half a Million Townspeople—Defending Forces Withdrawn—How the German Commander was Tricked—Empty and Costly Triumph of the Outplayed Teutons—Only the Husk of a City Won by Them.

THE fall of Antwerp was the most tragic episode in the greatest of wars. For months the heroic little Belgian Army had stood against the mightiest military power in the world, and towards the close of September it was expected that Antwerp would be relieved by the far-reaching operations of the Franco-British armies gathering about Lille. But the enemy was too quick in his double attack against the Allies. By a supreme effort, General von Falkenhayn collected every available soldier, and flung his last reserves against the extending French line. Then, with some 125,000 young, fresh troops of the first-line armies, and the siege-artillery collected for Paris, he began the attack on Antwerp.

Characteristically cruel was the manner in which the Germans opened their campaign against the Belgian Army in its last stronghold. At 9.30 o'clock on the morning of Sunday, September 27th, the townspeople of Malines came out of their beautiful old cathedral of St. Rombold, and stood talking in groups in the large, ancient market-place, surrounded by picturesque gabled houses of the sixteenth century. In front of them rose the old Cloth Hall, built in the days when Mechlin, as the Flemings call their town, was the Manchester of Northern Europe. Many of the older women who came out of the cathedral— faced, black-clad, working-class women—were th mous Mechlin lace-makers, esteemed throughout the world for the delicacy and beauty of their work. As they gathered together for a gossip, there was a distant roar, a loud shriek, and overhead a dreadful explosion, as the first shell struck the cathedral.

The gentle German, with the assistance of the gentle Austrian, was resuming his work of terrorising the harmless and peaceful non-combatant population of Belgium. All day the great shells rained on the stricken town, some fifty falling every hour. The glorious thirteenth-century cathedral, with its richly-carved choir and its magnificent tower, with the finest chimes in the world, was most completely destroyed. The railway-station and barracks were set on fire, and the magnificent old buildings, erected in the days when Mechlin was the capital of both Holland and Belgium, were wrecked and burnt. Ten of the townspeople were killed, and very many more wounded. Most of them fled northward to Antwerp, the two outermost Antwerp forts, Wavre and Waelhem, being only two miles north of Malines.

No military purpose was served by this sudden destruction of an open town. The Germans, moreover, offended against the laws of civilised warfare by giving no notice of the intended

LIEUT.-GENERAL SIR HENRY RAWLINSON.
He commanded the British forces operating in the neighbourhood of Ghent and Antwerp.

THE FALL OF BELGIUM'S LAST STRONGHOLD.

FUGITIVES FROM ANTWERP CROSSING THE PONTOON BRIDGE OVER THE SCHELDT.

The siege of Antwerp commenced on September 28th, 1914. The bombardment of the city began on the night of October 7th, and the enemy entered the deserted streets on the 9th. Between October 7th and 9th nearly 500,000 people left Antwerp for Holland, Ghent, Bruges, and Ostend. Soon after the authorities had warned all who could to leave, every avenue of approach to the pontoon bridge across the Scheldt leading to St. Nicolas and Ghent was rendered impassable by the press of vehicular traffic. On the afternoon of the 7th and the morning of the 8th the Civic Guard went from house to house telling the inhabitants to flee. During those two days the scenes on the roads to Holland, declared the "Times" correspondent, could hardly have been equalled by any migration in the history of the Israelites, Kalmucks, or Tartars. In addition to the exodus to Holland, the correspondent saw a crowd estimated at 150,000 blocking the ferry and the pontoons.

THE ARMOURED TRAIN AND THE ARMOURED MOTOI

Detachment of the British Naval Brigades going to take up thei in the trenches outside Antwerp. Inset (left): Belgian shar firing on the enemy from an armoured train. While the big being trained on the German trenches, picked shots were on

An armoured train in action at Antwerp. So that it might be able to fire at the big German siege-guns, which eventually won the day for the enemy, an armoured train, manned by Belgians and British, sallied out from the beleaguered city and contrived to give a good many checks to the besiegers.

Armoured trains played a conspicuous part, not only in the defenc Antwerp, but also during the later battle for the coast-line. They solidly built, but the discharge of their guns caused a recoil which made whole train rock on the metals.

CAR IN ACTION DURING THE DEFENCE OF ANTWERP.

rtunities of volley or individual firing. Some of the armoured re armed with anti-aircraft guns. Right: Armoured motor-car by men of the Royal Marine Light Infantry at Lokeren, north place part of our First Naval Brigade was cut off by the Germans.

moured motor-car scouring the roads around Antwerp. Just ahead from one of the attacking army's big guns is seen to have burst, ng off a terrific cloud of thick, black smoke. The Belgian officer rge of the car is looking through his glasses to see what damage has been done. A Belgian officer, Lieutenant Henkart, was, perhaps, the first to draw attention to the advantages of the armoured motor-car. He placed himself and two of his cars, manned by his own servants, at the disposal of the Belgian Government.

THE REIGN OF TERROR: ON THE QUAYSIDE OF THE RIVER SCHELDT.

During the German bombardment of Antwerp, when bombs dropped from Zeppelins and shells from the German siege-guns caused a conflagration visible from the Dutch border, barges and small steamers along the Scheldt quays took on human freight as rapidly as they could—their owners, it is said, charging the terror-stricken fugitives twenty francs a head for the brief trip into Dutch territory.

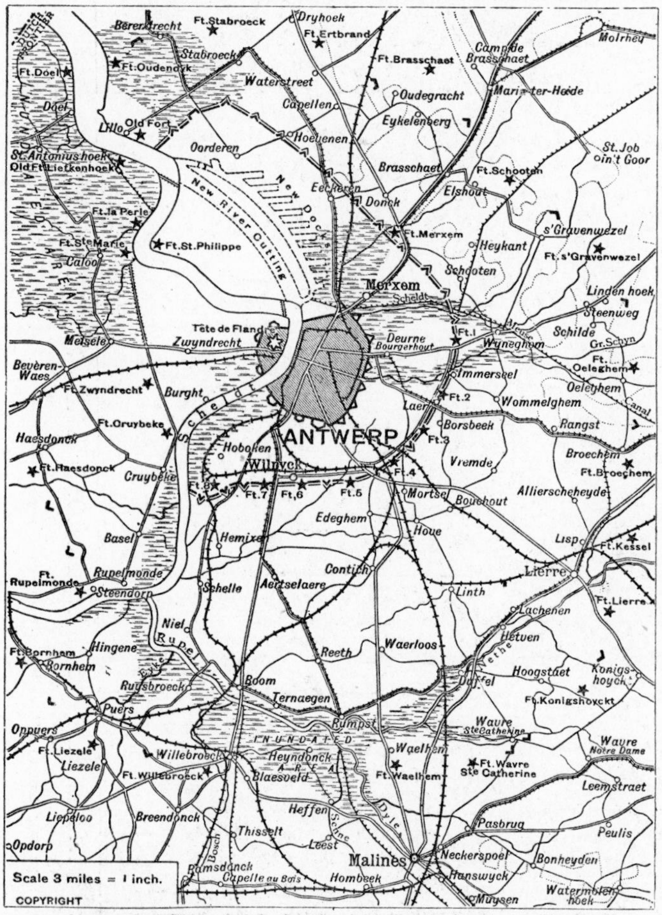

MAP SHOWING THE FORTIFICATIONS OF ANTWERP.

Eight years before the Great War General Brialmont's advanced forts were linked together by a new line of defence to replace the old ramparts.

bombardment. The fact was that the wrecking of Malines and its cathedral, like the wrecking of Rheims Cathedral, was a deed of devilish spite. On the previous day, Saturday, the German commander of the attacking forces, General von Beseler, had attempted to cut the communications of the Belgian Army in Antwerp by a movement westward on Termonde. There was then a gap of only forty miles between the left wing of the German forces and the Dutch frontier. If Beseler could have closed this gap by a further advance northward to the town of St. Nicolaes, on the railway line from Antwerp to Ghent and Ostend, he would have completely encircled the Belgian Army. He would also have made it impossible for any reinforcement to reach Antwerp.

His attempt at an enveloping movement was, however, defeated by a sortie of the defenders. The front of the Germans stretched for twenty miles, almost to Ghent, with only a small Belgian advance force holding the bridge of Termonde across the Scheldt against them.

The enemy brought his field-howitzers along the Flemish plain, and pressed the Belgians very hard. At two important points, the village of Audegem, about two miles south-west of Termonde, and the village of Lebbeke, a little distance south-west of the same town, two parties of seven hundred Belgian troops held the Germans off all the morning. When a third of the little Belgian forces had fallen, they were reinforced, and, driving at the enemy, they forced him back down the roads towards Alost and Brussels.

Terribly did the Germans suffer. For the Belgians gave them no rest, but continued the pursuit on Saturday night and Sunday morning, and drove them out of Alost, which town they had occupied for three weeks. Some thousands of Germans were killed and wounded. It was out of revenge for this great and disastrous defeat—a defeat with extraordinary consequences for Germany—that the decivilised neo-barbarians bombarded the cathedral city of Malines on Sunday morning.

Fateful error of General von Beseler

It is scarcely too much to say that, after the Battle of Termonde, General von Beseler lost his head. It would be rating his mistake too highly to say that it deprived the Germans of all chance of victory in the western theatre of war. For even if the mistake had not been committed, it is doubtful whether the German flanking movement between Lille and Calais would have succeeded. But Beseler's lack of initiative, tenacity, and genius for war, certainly resulted at Termonde in an apparently local disaster with extraordinarily wide-spread effects. No study of strategy is necessary to judge his error. Anybody with ordinary common-sense can see that he should have concentrated all available forces against the Belgians at Termonde—a hundred thousand men, if necessary—in order to cut their communications with the coast, and to drive them back into Antwerp. This should have been done before siege operations were started, and the larger part of the more mobile artillery should have been employed in this absolutely vital operation.

But little things have large effects on little minds. It was quite a little thing that upset the balance of the German general's intellect—a mere rumour. Somebody on the Belgian Military Staff was artful enough to spread the report that a large British force was momentarily expected to land at Ostend, and speed up by railway against the western wing of the German forces. On Sunday morning the perturbed German commander sent out Uhlan patrols, who spent all their time questioning the Flemish peasants as to the whereabouts of the new British army. Perhaps our Marine force at Ostend had moved about the country a little; perhaps the Belgian villagers thought that even an imaginary British column would rid them for a time of the presence of the hated invader. However this may be, some of the reconnoitring Uhlans returned to headquarters with

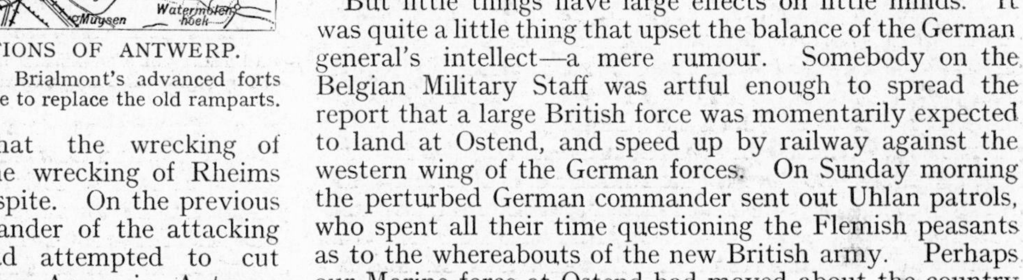

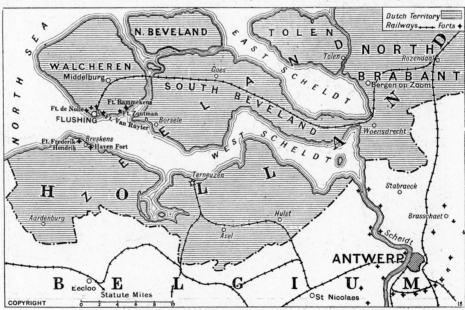

THE COURSE OF THE SCHELDT FROM ANTWERP TO THE SEA.

DEVELOPMENT OF THE ATTACK ON ANTWERP: ARTILLERY ACTION ACROSS THE RIVER DYLE.

The attack on Antwerp developed seriously when Malines was finally occupied by the Germans. Our picture illustrates the artillery duel across the River Dyle. German shells are seen coming over Malines from artillery posted beyond it, to the right. On the left is a battery of Belgian howitzers in action. A big German shell is bursting near them, and not very far from an ambulance where Red Cross nurses are tending the wounded. Belgian infantry were posted along the line of the river. In the air, to the left, may be seen two German observation balloons, which have been struck and are being brought down by Belgian shell fire. Similar balloons were used by the Germans at Antwerp to direct their artillery fire against the besieged city.

sufficient vague information at second-hand to determine their commander to retire eastward and concentrate between Brussels and Louvain.

By this means the Belgian Army was saved, even when Antwerp fell some eight days afterwards. For all through the bombardment the Belgian line of communication with the seacoast was kept open. On some days the Germans massed thirty thousand men against it, but these strokes came too late. General de Guise, commanding at Antwerp, always managed to bring up sufficient troops to hold the railway to the coast, while his opponent, General von Beseler, was stupidly concentrating mainly against the weak and indefensible rings of Antwerp forts.

Right from the beginning there was no hope for Antwerp. The Belgian Army's desperate defence of their last stronghold was but a gesture of heroism by a little nation dying in immortal fame and in the hope of a glorious resurrection.

BRITISH NAVAL MEN IN THE ANTWERP TRENCHES.
The top photograph shows men of our Naval Brigades carrying ammunition into the trenches that formed part of Antwerp's inner line of defence. The middle view is of British and Belgians fraternising in the trenches; and the lower view gives a good idea of the way in which the British sailors improved the trenches that had been dug for them, with timber and sandbags.

The old semicircles of armoured forts had become worse than useless. With the surprising development in power of modern siege-artillery, Antwerp had ceased to exist as a fortress. Its great structures of armoured concrete, with their cupolas of thick, hardened steel, were merely death-traps. A line of earthworks in an open field would have formed a far safer defensive position.

The proper method of strategy would have been for the weary and outworn Belgian Army to have retreated by rail towards Dunkirk. In so doing, however, it would have released 125,000 young athletic German soldiers for the attack upon the French line between Lille and Calais. That line would then have been broken. It would have been broken at least a week before the British army moved up from the Aisne valley to strengthen it. Thus the Belgians had once more to stand in the breach, and protect France against an overwhelming surprise attack. They had to hold at least three, and possibly four, first-rate German army corps round Antwerp for as long a time as was humanly possible, in order to prevent this force from being thrown against the feeble Northern French line, and sweeping down towards Havre and Paris again.

Every Belgian officer knew the hopelessness of the task.

THE HEROIC DEFENCE OF LIERRE.
A barricade hastily constructed by British Marines with sandbags and carts.

BLOCKING THE ROAD AT VIEUX DIEU.
From this place the British and their Belgian colleagues were compelled to retreat.

A BARRICADE OUTSIDE ANTWERP.
Men of the British Naval Brigades building a barricade of sandbags outside Antwerp.

German siege-artillery was a terrific power. Manonvilliers, a very strong, isolated French fort, had been shattered in a week. The last of the Liège forts had fallen after a bombardment of seven days, while those of Namur barely held out fifty hours. Even the strong modern defences of Maubeuge, with a large garrison, had been completely battered into shapeless ruin in eight days. The forts of Antwerp, designed by General Brialmont thirty years before, and gunned with artillery of small calibre and short range, were doomed. Their fall was not a question of days, but a matter of hours. They had only 6 in. guns.

The flaming, passionate courage of the Belgians

Yet, knowing all this, the heroes of Belgium stuck to their job. Their courage was of that flaming, passionate sort that puts things again, and yet again, to mortal hazard. Antwerp, their beloved Antwerp, with its picturesque streets, its historic and romantic memories, its treasures of native art, its multitudes of free and independent townsmen—Antwerp, with its far-stretched lines of forts, built in the old days to shelter the entire Army—could not be tamely surrendered. Belgium would not play for safety. Her forces were worn out by countless battles and skirmishes, and sadly diminished by a fighting resistance of two months against an overpowering host of invaders. But the Belgian had ceased to calculate his chances of life. Cost what it might—even the destruction of the entire military forces of the nation—Antwerp should not be surrendered without a struggle.

It was the most sublime spectacle in the annals of warfare. Antwerp, with its old and useless forts, looked like being the burial-place of the Belgian troops. Yet, standing by the grave of their power as an independent people, the Belgians jumped in, rifle in hand, and used the grave as a fighting-trench. It was six weeks since they had withdrawn from the field into their last stronghold. Had they at once, on August 17th, the date of their retirement, devoted themselves entirely to reorganising the defences of the fortress, they could have made it impregnable. They could have taken the guns out of the forts and used them as mobile batteries, and have obtained 12 in. weapons from England, for use on moving platforms running on a railway track. By this means they could have made Antwerp as difficult to reduce as

WITHDRAWAL OF THE GARRISON FROM ANTWERP.
The Belgian Army and the British Naval Brigades passing through the outskirts of the doomed city.

REMARKABLE INSTANCE OF TEUTON GENEROSITY.
German Marines carrying the belongings of Belgian refugees who had been persuaded to return to Antwerp.

Przemysl or Verdun. This, however, was not done. For the Belgian troops were occupied in making continual sallies against the enemy's forces, and threatening his lines of communication, in order to relieve the pressure on the French and British troops in the south. Never in history has there been such self-sacrificing conduct towards allies as the Belgians continually displayed. Their Christian courage far surpasses that of the Spartans and Athenians. Not till the Belgian showed what was in him did man know what the spirit of international fraternity could achieve. The Belgians saved the modern world, the modern spirit of humanity, the modern faith in the plighted word of States. Strange as it may sound, the deaths and wounds of Belgian soldiers, the sufferings of Belgian people, redeemed the crimes of the Germans. For they erased the effect of German international treachery from the mind of the world. So long as countries put faith in treaties between nation and nation, so long will the example of Belgium have a Christlike power upon man.

International fraternity *v* international treachery

The attack on the Belgians' last lines of defence began on Monday, September 28th. The Austrian artillery detachment at Brussels brought forward their 12 in. siege-howitzers to concealed positions behind the Malines-Louvain railway embankment, far beyond the reach of the old 6 in. Krupp guns in the Antwerp forts. Having manufactured them, the Germans knew that these guns had an effective range of only about five miles. The Austrian siege-howitzers, on the other hand, threw their terrible shells with mathematical exactitude to a distance of seven and a half miles, and with fair marksmanship to a distance of nine miles, They opened fire on Fort Waelhem and Fort Wavre Ste Catherine. All the day and all the night the shells continued to fall on and around the forts. With anything like equal artillery on both sides, this nocturnal bombardment would have been more disastrous to the Germans than to the defenders. For the flames of the attacking howitzers could clearly be seen in the darkness from the captive observation balloon employed by the Belgians. It would have been easy to have planted shell after shell among the besieging batteries, if only the Belgians had had ordnance of a proper range fixed on movable trucks

PREPARED FOR A SKIRMISH WITH THE FOE.
Bluejackets forming the crew of an armoured train, with their rifles, ready for an encounter with the Germans.

ANTWERP'S CALVARY: FUGITIVES PAUSE TO PRAY BEFORE AN IMAGE OF THE CRUCIFIXION.

Near the crypt of Antwerp Cathedral is a shrine, representing the scene of the Crucifixion. The figures are Our Saviour on the Cross and Joseph and Mary on either side. The group of sculpture is protected from the elements by a plain wooden roof. The sacred spot is enclosed by a balustrade of carved stone, on which are scroll-shaped tablets recording the tragedy of Calvary. Hurried as was the flight of the citizens of Antwerp, many found time to turn aside to the shrine and prostrate themselves in prayer before the Virgin, asking her aid in their terrible plight. The cathedral was not injured by the bombardment, but it is recorded that many buildings near were destroyed, a fact which suggests that it did not owe its escape to the German gunners, though it is understood that King Albert sent a plan with its site marked upon it to the German commander, begging that this historic building might be spared.

RUTHLESS ADVANCE OF THE GERMAN INVADERS.

Our view is of the village of Contich, seven miles from the Central Station of Antwerp, on the Turnhout Railway. When the great Krupp guns had fired the buildings seen above, the few remaining inhabitants fled in panic towards the city, in the vain hope of finding some protection there.

BRIDGE BLOWN UP BY BRITISH MARINES.

A bridge in Antwerp which was blown up by British Marines as the Germans advanced. The German artillery had started a conflagration in the buildings near by.

behind their lines. As it was, the defenders were impotent to reply to the long-distance fire from the Skoda 12 in. batteries and the Krupp 11 in. batteries.

The time-fuse of one of the shells that were thrown in the Belgian lines, where it failed to explode is understood to have been set for 15,200 metres. This is about nine and a half miles, a larger distance than the Skoda howitzer is reckoned to cover. So it is possible that the Germans had even more powerful siege-artillery before Antwerp than is generally supposed. Something between a 12 in. howitzer and a 16 in. howitzer may in places have been employed. For the enemy was so anxious to reduce Antwerp with the utmost speed, and to release his army corps for operations between Lille and Dunkirk, that he massed every available machine of destruction against the Belgians.

Germans pay for despising their enemies

The attackers, however, were so confident in their overpowering weight of metal that they were caught by a very simple trick. Early in the bombardment, one of the forts in the outer ring of defences quickly exploded and burst into flame. A brigade of German infantry, entrenched just beyond the range of the Belgian guns, rose and charged across the fields to capture the ruined stronghold, and hold the gap in the fortressed line against the defending troops. But when they reached the fort, guns, machine-guns, rifles, and live electric-wire entanglements caught them in a trap. The flame had been produced by pouring petrol on some lighted straw brought into the fort for the purpose. One-third of a German brigade fell around the slopes; the rest fled, with shrapnel and Maxim fire sweeping them as they ran. Scarcely a fortnight before, the commander of the French fort at Troyon had lured on and half-annihilated a large body of German infantry by the same device of apparently setting his fort on fire. If the Germans had not so despised their enemies, they would not have been caught twice within a fortnight by the same easy trick.

The Belgians also succeeded in bringing off the most primitive of all artillery manœuvres—the dead-dog dodge. They slackened their fire and encouraged the Germans to grow venturesome, and to push forward their howitzer batteries belonging to the field-artillery. Between the Belgian forts were lines of trenches held by the Belgian Army, with light field-artillery operating behind the troops. For some time the German gunners seemed to have certain of these trenches at their mercy. They pushed forward three batteries to complete the work of annihilation. But a semicircle of thunder and flame suddenly opened before them. Every dead Belgian gun came to life again. Two of the German batteries were destroyed, and the other managed to harness up its guns and to get away.

These were the only successes of the outranged and

THE BURDEN OF SORROW ON THE BROAD BOSOM OF THE SCHELDT.
Barges, fishing-boats, steam lighters, and a variety of other small craft were utilised to carry the fugitives from Antwerp to the hospitable borders of Holland. The unvarying kindness of the Dutch people and the beautiful weather were the two redeeming features of the day that witnessed the fall of the city which was once the commercial capital of the world.

overpowered forts. The five hundred men garrisoning Fort Waelhem were the first to suffer, as their comrades at Liège and Namur had suffered. They took part in the sortie on Malines, and then retreated to the fort. On Monday the first German shells fell short, and the garrison began to hope they would be able to resist. But soon one of the 12 in. Austrian howitzers landed a shell on a cupola and smashed it. All Monday night, shell and shrapnel rained down on the buildings of the fort, giving the garrison neither rest nor respite. The Belgian guns salvoed in reply, but could not reach the enemy.

Terrible end of garrison at Fort Waelhem

By Tuesday morning the situation was critical. The shells were still falling with an infernal tumult on the armour of the cupolas, and just at noon another of the curved, shielding roofs of hardened steel was put out of action. At twenty minutes past twelve the bombardment increased in fury. Three large projectiles struck the garrison building and completely destroyed it, twisting the iron stairs, smashing the vault, blowing up the walls to the foundation, and setting the wreckage on fire. The troops then sheltered in the underground passage, waiting for the hurricane of high-explosive shells to slacken and enable them to return to their guns.

It was in the crowded subterranean shelter that the great catastrophe occurred. A shell dropped in the ammunition magazine, to the left of the underground gallery, and the flame and fume of the terrible explosion of the magazine swept through the thronged passage. Out of more than a hundred men only ten escaped—ten blackened, burnt, blinded, tortured figures, crawling in the darkness over the charred bodies of their comrades. And while they crept out into the daylight towards the postern, the shrapnel continued to fall around them, and shell after shell ground the shattered concrete to powder, gave the battered armour-plate another wrench, and the overturned guns another useless hammering.

It was a vision of hell such as the imagination of Dante never attained. And it was not a vision, but the work of Christians fighting against Christians—the work of a great empire organised for scientific research and for the advancement of human control over the forces of Nature. Practically everything on the scene was German. The guns and the armour-plate of the fort had been constructed by Krupp, and it was he and his associate in the commerce of warfare—Skoda, of Pilsen—who manufactured the howitzers and shells by which the fort was destroyed. Frau Krupp and her father had made hundreds of thousands of pounds out of the Belgians, and then obtained another large fortune out of the German people for newer and larger machinery of destruction to wreck the earlier examples of Krupp manufacture. It is said, moreover, that the Krupp guns built for use in Antwerp were specially constructed to wear badly when put to lengthy use. Oh, deep and far-seeing were the plans which Germany made for the war that was yet vainly designed to end in her conquering the world!

Behind Fort Waelhem were the principal waterworks of Antwerp, and by bombarding the reservoir with 12 in. shells the Germans burst the banks on Wednesday, September 30th. The flood of water drowned some of the Belgian trenches, and certain of the defenders' field-guns were submerged, and only rescued with great labour. The inundation also hampered the defence by interfering with the carrying of supplies and ammunition to the neighbouring section of the Belgian lines. In Antwerp itself the destruction of the water supply naturally had distressing results, and it terribly increased the danger of a conflagration, and of the rise and spread of an epidemic. In the meantime, all the chief forts in the southern sector of the defences went the way of Fort Waelhem. Wavre Ste. Catherine was the first to fall; then, after three days of continuous bombardment, Lierre and Koningshoyckt were silenced. The village of Lierre was set on fire, and the dense column of smoke that poured up from it in the windless autumn air was visible from a great distance.

The raging, murderous struggle for the Nethe.

With the fall of the south-eastern outer forts on Thursday, October 1st, the defence of Antwerp became impossible. For there was a gap of over ten miles in the circuit of fortifications, through which the enemy could pour his troops, while watering the path in front of them with shell and shrapnel. Moreover, the destruction of the principal Belgian forts allowed the Germans to move their heavy siege artillery northward for another two miles, and thus to get within bombarding range of the city. The small tidal river, the Nethe, flowing behind the southern ruined forts into the Scheldt, was the only remaining defence of the Belgians. For the picturesque ancient ramparts of the city were, of course, useless against modern siege-howitzers, and the line of inner forts, placed about two miles outside the city of Antwerp, were half a century old, and equipped only with 4 in. guns. They were still useful against infantry attacks, but the ordinary field-artillery of the modern army could have demolished them in a few hours. It was the outer recent forts, designed by General Brialmont in 1879, and completed in November, 1913, that guarded Antwerp. When a large sector of these defences was destroyed, only the River Nethe and the entrenched infantry behind the river offered any real obstacle to the onset of the German forces.

And this last obstacle, in the circumstances, was an exceedingly slight one. For by massing the fire of both their siege-artillery and their field-artillery on the shallow, hastily-made, and open earthworks by the river, the Germans subjected the Belgian troops to such a tempest of vast, high-explosive shells and heavy, wide-spreading shrapnel shots as mortal men had never known. What our troops suffered by the Aisne flats was nothing to what the Belgians suffered in the flooded expanses by Nethe River. All the machinery intended for the destruction of Paris was concentrated on some eight to ten miles of their trenches, with the light field-artillery of several army corps joining in the screaming, roaring, nerve-racking work. Even with this the Germans did not think they had sufficient advantages over the small Belgian Army. They desired to use their overpowering long-ranged ordnance with scientific exactitude.

So several German men and women who had lived for years in Antwerp, and had enjoyed the friendship of the heroic Flemings, and had, therefore, been exempted from banishment from the beleaguered city, now came forward to direct the fire of the German batteries. Sometimes as nurses or Red Cross helpers, sometimes as interested and friendly spectators of the struggle, they approached the trenches, studied the positions, and communicated the knowledge thus obtained to the attacking gunners. When the great peace comes, other peoples may be moved by the craven and hysterical signs of repentance that the ordinary German will show in order to renew intercourse with civilised countries. But it is doubtful if the Belgian will be moved. He knows the German now, and has paid a very heavy price for his knowledge. He will not forget. For generation after generation he will not forget.

WOUNDED BELGIANS AT AN ENGLISH COUNTRY HOUSE.

Large numbers of wounded Belgian soldiers as well as civilians found rest and shelter in England after the German occupation of Antwerp. Our artist in the above picture represents a scene which he witnessed at a mansion in Kent on one of those rare November days when the sun came out and the soldiers were able to take a turn in the garden.

How the Germans crossed the River Nethe

The Germans succeeded in crossing the Nethe. A dozen times their engineers advanced under cover of artillery fire, and tried to fling pontoons across the stream. The Belgians at first shot the engineers. Then, as they themselves were suffering heavily from the terrific bombardment, they adopted a more subtle means of defence. They let the pontoon bridges be erected, and waited until some battalions had partly crossed the river and were crowding the floating bridges from the farther bank. Then they opened fire with their light field-guns and machine-guns and rifles, sweeping the packed pontoons and banks. This went on night and day, till the Germans gradually built up a strange kind of bridge. Their bodies choked the river, and, mingling with the wreck of their pontoons, the corpses dammed and bridged the stream. But before this occurred, the Belgian Government had decided to leave Antwerp. Two steamers were chartered to sail for Ostend on Saturday, October 3rd, with the members of the Government and the staffs of the French and British Legations. But on Saturday morning the plan was suddenly changed. The Belgian Government resolved to stay on. Great Britain at last was sending help to the breached and overpowered stronghold of the Belgian Army. At one o'clock on Saturday afternoon a long grey motor-car, filled with British naval officers, entered the city. In it was a youngish, sandy-haired man in the undress uniform of a Lord of the Admiralty. It was Mr. Winston Churchill, and with him came General Paris, commanding a Marine brigade and two naval brigades, with a detachment of naval gunners with two 9·2 in. weapons and a number of 6 in. guns.

Mr. Winston Churchill's arrival in Antwerp

"We're going to save the city," said the most bustling member of the British Cabinet. But he had come a week too late to do so, and the forces he had brought with him, consisting mainly of untrained naval reservists, were inadequate to retrieve the situation.

Many of our men went into the trenches as soon as they

ENTRENCHED INFANTRY AND SCREENED ARTILLERY ASSISTING IN THE DEFENCE OF FORT DE BORNEM.

Fort de Bornem was, like the other forts encircling Antwerp, supplied with revolving turrets, and regarded, as all were, of exceeding strength till the great German siege-guns were brought up. These guns had a range nearly double that of the Belgian guns. The Belgian infantry were entrenched between the forts, with their field-artillery behind them, carefully concealed from enemy aircraft by covering branches. The Belgian shrapnel fire was powerful enough to prevent the enemy from charging across the open space which was cleared before the forts, but the German siege-guns proved far more powerful than they. The above drawing was made when the firing around Fort de Bornem was at its height.

arrived on Saturday evening. For the Belgian troops were utterly worn out by their long and severe exertions, and badly needed a rest. Some of our men were raw recruits who did not know how to handle a rifle, but they at least showed their native pluck by sticking in the trenches under the heavy bombardment. In all, they did not amount to more than eight thousand men, with two guns mounted on an armoured train, and four 6 in. weapons that operated in the inner ring of forts, behind Lierre. It was intended that they should only act as a defending advance guard, and the 7th Division and 3rd Cavalry Division of the British Expeditionary Force, numbering some 18,000 bayonets and sabres, under General Sir Henry Rawlinson, was marching up to Ostend to reinforce them. At the same time, large French, British, and Indian cavalry bodies were operating eastward of Lille, with a view to clearing the way for a northward extension of the Franco-British front. It was the effect of all these combined operations which Mr. Churchill had in mind when he said that Antwerp would be saved.

The scheme for the relief of Antwerp

But General von Beseler had made one mistake, and did not mean to make another. The tremendous advantage he had won on the southern sector was plain even to his mind, and he drove home the attack with sufficient determination to cover the lack of real generalship. All through the night of October 3rd he launched his infantry in massed formation across the Nethe by the shapeless ruins of Waelhem fort. The slaughter was terrible, but the German non-commissioned officers held their men together, even when there were only half-companies left to attempt to storm the Belgian trenches. When Sunday morning broke, the attacks still continued, until the Germans got their bellyful of fighting, and drew away to the river back to cover, leaving thousands of dead and wounded on the bank, and hundreds drowned in the water.

On Sunday night our Marines bore the brunt of the attack. They held some of the foremost trenches along the Nethe, between Lierre and Waelhem. The trenches were shallow and roughly made, and being open gave little protection against shell fire. The long-ranged guns of the enemy swept them from distant positions in the south, which the feeble defending artillery could not reach. Our casualties from shrapnel fire were very heavy; even veteran troops might have been pardoned had they abandoned the attempt to defend so indefensible a line. But our boys, untrained lads, some of whom had scarcely worn their uniform for a fortnight, went into the fight as they arrived, and bided their fate as steadily as the bearded, skilled men who fought beside them. Mr. Winston Churchill asked no one to undergo anything he was not eager to face himself. He took a rifle and stayed in one of the trenches near Fort Waelhem, and shot with the best of them. One of Mr. Asquith's sons was among the young recruits who proved their manhood and the mettle of the youth of their nation, under most desperate circumstances, and gave the Germans a foretaste of what the fighting qualities of the new British army would be when, with proper training, they took the field a million strong.

Mr. Asquith's son among the young British recruits

The massed attacks of the Germans on October 4th were first beaten off by our Marines. Then on October 5th the volunteer naval reservists arrived from the coast, and went straight into action north of Lierre. As they tramped down the cobbled and tree-shaded highway, they sang the new light-hearted British fighting-song, "It's a long, long way to Tipperary," while London motor-'buses from Piccadilly and Leicester Square rumbled behind them with supplies and ammunition. The townspeople were wild with joy at the sight of these thousands of bright-faced, strong-limbed sons of Britain. Their city, they felt sure, was to be saved at the last moment. But there were military men who noticed that many of these raw young troops were so badly equipped that they did not even carry pouches for the regulation 150 rounds of fire.

Some of their officers seemed to be as lacking in field experience as the men. Yet these raw troops, rushed into Antwerp on a hopeless task, placed in open trenches unsupported by effective artillery, and raked by a terrific shrapnel fire, held the enemy back for some days, and then retired in perfect order. Seldom, if ever, have we put worse troops into the field, and seldom, if ever, has our cause been upheld by braver men. On the Nethe they beat the compact multitudes of first-line German soldiers back from the river, and when dawn broke, with a rain of shrapnel lead, the British trenches were still held. At four a.m. on October 6th, however, the Germans made their terrible bridge of dead on the right of the British forces, and the Belgian troops there were compelled to retire. Consequently our right flank was exposed, and our men had also to withdraw quickly to prevent the enemy from taking them in the reverse.

The bridge of dead over the River Nethe

With this, the defence of Antwerp practically came to an end. For, as we have seen, the old inner line of forts was incapable of resisting modern siege-artillery. Our few 6 in. naval guns were almost as useless as the old-fashioned 4 in. guns of the fort. They could do absolutely nothing against the 11 and 12 in. howitzers possessed by the Germans and Austrians. Our 9·2 in. guns could not be mounted and got into position in time. Even in the German field-artillery there were heavy howitzers, with a longer range and a larger shell than the half a dozen guns that Mr. Winston Churchill sent to Antwerp.

Mr. Churchill had served as a cavalry subaltern. But he seemed to have lacked at Antwerp the large organising ability necessary in a commander of modern armies. He ran his head against the wide and well-laid plan of the German Military Staff, possessing vast resources for siege operations. Nothing less than a score of mobile 9·2 in. naval guns, with a squadron of aeroplanes searching for the enemy's positions, together with a large number of field-mortars for raking advancing columns of hostile infantry, could have turned the Nethe defence into a tenable position. All that the Belgians wanted was heavy artillery support. Even then their city might have been very severely bombarded. For as the outer forts had fallen in the south, the Skoda howitzers could have been brought much nearer the Nethe.

But it must have been said in Mr. Churchill's defence that the call for help from Antwerp probably came too late for any large measures of assistance to be undertaken. The situation round Lille was also critical, so that our War Office could not immediately spare any regular troops for fortress duties. The naval reservists were the nearest force to the point of embarkation, and could thus be carried most quickly to the spot where the need for them was urgent and bitter. The danger of the enemy winning to the coast and establishing submarine centres of operations at the new seaport of Bruges, or even at Ostend Harbour or Calais, was an Admiralty problem. Mr. Churchill tried to solve it.

Defeat of the enemy's main objective

Heavily as our naval reservists suffered in dead, wounded, and missing, they did not suffer in vain. By helping to prolong for nearly a week the resistance of Antwerp, they did much to defeat the main objective of the enemy. For the capture of Antwerp was only a secondary aim of General von Beseler. The principal objective of the German commander was the destruction or capture of the Belgian Army. In failing to achieve this, he was defeated in his chief purpose. Towards this defeat, our volunteer reservists, with their comrades of the Marine brigade, contributed in no small measure. What they actually did, in staving off the German infantry attack, was of local importance. What they potentially did, by their mere presence, by their sunny, cheerful faces, when the spirit of the heroic Belgian Army was clouded by the fall of the outer forts, was of European importance. They were messengers of hope, heralds of a sure though distant day of Belgian triumph. Before they came it seemed

BELGIAN REFUGEES' FIRST RESTING-PLACE IN LONDON.

On their arrival in London the Belgian refugees who sought shelter in this country were taken to a temporary haven in Aldwych, where they were entertained before being drafted to more commodious accommodation at the Alexandra Palace, Muswell Hill, and elsewhere. It was estimated in December, 1914, that about 1,000,000 refugees had abandoned Belgian soil. Of these some 500,000 or more found sanctuary in Holland, about 110,000 came to England, while a large number fled to France. Arrangements were made later for the accommodation of further refugees in England.

to the beleaguered saviours of civilisation that they were forgotten of the world. But when the little British force arrived, they knew they were not forgotten, and the springs of energy in their soul were renewed. From Antwerp to Ostend, from Ostend to Nieuport, along the Yser to Dixmude, the Belgian Army was to march in a glory of heroic resistance, exceeding anything in ancient or modern history. To have supported and encouraged men of this stamp in the darkest days of their campaign, is a great honour for a few thousand raw recruits to have won.

Belgian Army's heroic resistance

When the Germans had forced the passage of the Nethe, on the morning of Tuesday, October 6th, the defence of Antwerp was at an end. For General de Guise decided that the surrender of the city was inevitable. It could have been delayed for a week or a fortnight, but only at the cost of the destruction of all the historic buildings of Antwerp, and the death or injury of thousands of the townspeople. Moreover, any prolonged resistance would endanger the Belgian Army and the British forces, as the Germans were now making strenuous attempts to close the path of retreat between Ghent and the Dutch frontier. In this region a hostile German army corps was operating, and another army corps was moving to support it. Beseler was at last doing the right thing, from the point of view of the attacking side.

He was relying on his siege train for the reduction of Antwerp, and allocating to the heavy guns and howitzers only sufficient infantry to protect the batteries from assault. He was swinging his main forces against the western flank of the Belgian-British lines, where a series of fierce struggles were proceeding. In these circumstances General de Guise arranged to hold the remaining forts and the inner line of defences only so long as was necessary to cover the retreat of the allied troops. On Tuesday evening, therefore, the Belgian Army began to withdraw from Antwerp. Cavalrymen and cycling carbineers, with armoured motor-cars, crossed the Scheldt by the bridge of boats on the road to Ostend. Thirty large German steamers in the harbour were crippled by exploding dynamite in their cylinders and boilers. At daybreak on Wednesday morning the Belgian Government, with the Legations, left by steamer, transferring the capital of Belgium from Antwerp to Ostend. Mr. Winston Churchill also appears to have left that morning by motor-car, running under the protection of one of the armoured cars with machine-guns which had proved so effective against German cavalry.

"God Punish England!"

As remarkable as Herr Ernst Lissauer's "Hymn of Hate" was the form of greeting adopted in Germany. "God punish England!" (Gott strafe England!) was the form of address, to which the reply was: "May God punish her!" (Gott mög'es strafen!) This formula, which was used all over Germany, was celebrated in a set of verses by Herr Hochstetter. These appeared in the well-known German weekly "Lustige Blätter." We give Mr. G. Valentine Williams's translation:

This is the German greeting
When men their fellows meet,
The merchants in the market-place,
The beggars in the street,
A pledge of bitter enmity
Thus runs the winged word:
"God punish England, brother!—
Yea! Punish her, O Lord!"

With raucous voice, brass-throated,
Our German shells shall bear
This curse that is our greeting
To the "cousin" in his lair.
This be our German battle-cry,
The motto on our sword:
"God punish England, brother!—
Yea! Punish her, O Lord!"

By shell from sea, by bomb from air,
Our greeting shall be sped,
Making each English homestead
A mansion of the dead.
And even Grey will tremble
As falls each iron word:
"God punish England, brother!—
Yea! Punish her, O Lord!"

This is the German greeting
When men their fellows meet,
The merchants in the market-place,
The beggars in the street,
A pledge of bitter enmity
Thus runs the winged word:
"God punish England, brother!—
Yea! Punish her, O Lord!"

General von Beseler had given notice the evening before that he intended to bombard the city. The unhappy townspeople had gone to sleep on Tuesday night feeling confident that in a few days the Germans would raise the siege, as it was known that a new British force, under Sir Henry Rawlinson, was operating on their flank. But when the citizens went about their work the next morning they saw, with dread astonishment, on every wall and hoarding, a proclamation announcing the imminent bombardment. In the proclamation General de Guise recommended those who were able to depart to do so at once, while those who remained were advised to take shelter in their cellars behind sandbags.

It was the suddenness of the catastrophe, breaking in upon a period of renewed hope, that took the heart out of many of the peaceful people of Antwerp. The population at the time was well over half a million; for the city had become the refuge of some hundreds of thousands of fugitives from the shattered villages and bombarded towns of Belgium. In the famous stronghold of their nation they had thought they were at last safe from further attack by the host of murderers and torturers from Germany. Their nerves were already unstrung and their minds filled with terrible memories. So it is no wonder that some of them gave way to panic when they read the proclamation of doom.

Then began the immense, tragic flight of the inhabitants of Antwerp. Only three avenues of escape remained open — westward by road, to Ghent, Bruges, and Ostend; north-eastward by road into Holland, and down the Scheldt by water to Flushing Probably a quarter of a million escaped by river. Anything that could float was crowded with the fugitives—merchant-steamers, dredgers, barges, and canal-boats, ferry-boats, tugs, fishing-smacks, yachts, rowing-boats, scows, and even hastily-made rafts. There was no opportunity of maintaining order and discipline. The terrorised people at times crowded aboard until there was not even standing room on the decks. Very few of them had brought food and warm clothing with them, or had space in which to lie down. For two nights and two days they huddled together, chilled and famishing, on the open deck, while the German guns bombarded the great, beautiful old city from which they had fled.

Tragic flight of terrorised populace

On the roads leading towards Ghent and the Dutch frontier the scenes of anguish and misery, hunger and fatigue, were even more appalling. In many places civilians and soldiers were mingled in inextricable confusion.

THE RETREAT OF THE BELGIAN ARMY BEFORE THE GERMANS.
Section of Belgian Artillery passing through a country lane during the retreat of the Belgian Army from the Antwerp defences.

In the afternoon of October 7th the highway from Antwerp to Ghent was jammed from ditch to ditch. Every footpath and lane leading away from the invading army was so closely packed with fugitives that they impeded each other's movement. Young men could be seen carrying their frail old mothers in their arms, or helping their worn-out fathers by a pickaback ride. Wheelbarrows were sometimes used for this purpose, but more often they were packed with children too young to walk. There were monks in long, woollen robes, carrying wounded men on stretchers, and white-faced nuns shepherding along groups of war-orphaned infants.

Women still weak from childbed tottered along with their newly-born babes pressed to their breasts, their imaginations working almost to madness as they remembered the tales of what German soldiers had done to Belgian mothers and Belgian babes. Grey-haired men and women helped themselves along by grasping the stirrup-leathers of troopers, who were so exhausted from days of fighting that they slept in the saddle as they rode. Here a society woman, who had dressed at noon for a visit of fashion, stumbled along, carrying in a sheet on her shoulders her jewels and rich and heavy articles of precious metal. By her side was a frail, old lace-maker from Mechlin, whose bundle contained the simple, homely treasures of a cottage that no longer existed. The noise and the confusion were beyond mere imagination. The clamour was made up of the cries and shouts and moans of a nation in its agony. Men cursed their neighbours just to save themselves from weeping like women, and, amid their cursing, turned to help the poor creatures pressing against them. The heavy, quiet, slow-thinking, slow-moving Fleming, closely akin in origin to the Englishman, had been stampeded into terror. It was not the fear of death that moved him, but the fear of what the Germans might do to him and his women and children while life yet remained in their bodies. It was no rumours that shook him. He had already spoken in Antwerp to fugitives from the blackened and gutted scenes of atrocities.

RETURNING FROM THE TRENCHES.
A British Marine, wounded while helping to man the Antwerp trenches, being assisted back to the city by a comrade.

What especially added to the bitterness of the educated and directing class of townspeople was the memory of the part their city had played in crippling the national defence. It was from Antwerp that had come the strongest opposition to increasing the Army in the days when the German menace became apparent. Strategical railway lines had been constructed on the frontier, and every man in a responsible position in Belgium could see what was intended. But when the King and his Government proposed to reply to this threat against their neutrality by an increase in troops and guns, Antwerp had been one of the principal opponents of the scheme. This was probably due to the fact that so many Germans had settled in the port that by various means they won a large control over the

IN THE GERMAN TRENCHES AT LIERRE.
German soldiers writing home: A photograph taken after the fall of Antwerp.

trend of public opinion. They had preached the gospel of pacificism, like true descendants of a former Prussian preacher against war—Frederick the Great, who wrote his "Anti-Machiavelli" in order to still the suspicions of Europe until his army was ready to ravage Silesia. The similar movement of pacificism in our own country was no doubt headed by honest but deluded men, yet behind them a strong German influence could also be detected. If the Sea Lords of our Admiralty had not threatened to resign in a body in 1909, and thereby compelled the Liberal Cabinet to come to its senses and defeat the German attempt to outbuild us in new battleships, that which happened in Antwerp might well have happened in London. Our politicians failed us as completely as the Antwerp politicians failed their people. We owe our present position, under God, to the firmness of character and keenness of vision of our Sea Lords of the year 1909. Thus, as a nation, we cannot in any way blame the people of Antwerp for failing, in the days of peace, to prepare for warlike defence. We were deluded, and almost betrayed, by the same subtle intrigues as ended in the disaster that overtook them.

German "pacificism" in Antwerp and London

It will never be known how many people perished from hunger, exposure, and exhaustion in the flight from Antwerp. The fields and ditches along the westward road were strewn with the prostrate bodies of outworn women, children, and old men. For miles around, the countryside was as bare of food as a sand desert is of flowers. There was not a scarcity of provisions—there was absolutely nothing to eat. The fugitives stopped at farmhouses and offered all they possessed for a loaf, but the farmers' wives, weeping at the misery of their own people, could only shake their heads. It was on raw turnips that the richest and the poorest stayed their hunger; and many who did not profit by the opportunity, when passing the turnip-fields, had nothing. Near one small town on the Dutch frontier twenty children were born on Wednesday night in the open fields. The mothers were without beds, without shelter, and without medical aid. This occurred at a spot where an American observer chanced to be. At hundreds of other places along the lines of flight there were similar strangely piteous scenes, with no one even to record them.

As the fugitives were sleeping in the open air, on the night of Wednesday, October 7th, the bombardment of their city began. The first shell fell at ten o'clock, striking a house in the southern Berchem district, killing a boy and wounding his mother and his little sister. A street-sweeper lost his head as he ran for shelter; it was blown off by the next shell. All through the night the shells fell at the rate of five a minute. Most of them were shrapnel shells, which shrieked over the house-tops and exploded with a rending crash in the streets. The object of the Germans was to kill and frighten the people rather than to destroy the buildings. So, though a few high-explosive shells were pitched into Antwerp, the bombardment was mainly carried out with shrapnel. The idea, of course, was to terrorise the non-combatants so as to induce them to bring pressure upon the Belgian Government to surrender the Army and the city. But the persons who willingly remained to undergo the bombardment were not made of the stuff from which cowards are fashioned. Withdrawing into their cellars with food and candles, they protected the entrances with mattresses and pillows, and watched the night out with quiet fortitude.

ANTWERP UNDER GERMAN OCCUPATION.
A regiment departing for the firing-line from the German headquarters in Antwerp. Inset: Scene near the Steen Museum on the riverside, where uniforms, boots, transport, and all sorts of war material were discarded by the Belgians who were forced to seek safety in Holland.

In the meantime a large and gallant rearguard was holding the inner line of forts, and misleading the enemy by the stubbornness of its defence. For, with the British force, they still held some of the advanced trenches behind Fort Waelhem and Lierre, and though swept by a terrible shell fire, causing heavy losses, they kept off the German infantry. Supported by the small old guns of the inner forts, and by the skilfully-handled field-artillery of the Belgian Army, the heroic rearguard simply bluffed General von Beseler. Two days had passed since the German commander had forced the passage of the Nethe. He had an absolutely overpowering number of guns and howitzers, and a much larger force of infantry than the Belgian commander had left behind. Had he only pressed forward, as any man with a backbone would have done in the circumstances, he would have captured the larger portion of the Belgian-British forces, together with hundreds of guns and large supplies of war material. But being a man with so highly-developed a sense of caution that it could not be distinguished from timidity, he wasted the two critical days in searching his path of advance with artillery fire.

GERMANS PREPARING FOR A COUNTER-ATTACK.

Artillerymen hauling a gun into position at Antwerp after the occupation. The gun had to be dragged by ropes on a specially-made road, which wound round a hill to the required height. Inset: Further evidence of the German fear of a counter-attack. Germans mount a concealed gun in a culvert on the outskirts of Antwerp while their outposts scour the neighbouring hills.

He was apparently so afraid of falling into a trap and losing his large guns that nearly forty-eight hours passed before he brought them over the Nethe to bombard the city. By the evening of October 8th four of the inner line of forts had been badly battered from the western side of Antwerp, but the Allies still held the trenches two miles in front of these forts. No rushing attack was made on the belt of barbed-wire entanglements behind which our men and the Belgians were lying. Many of our volunteer naval reservists never saw a German. All their wounds were caused by shrapnel fire or shell splinters. Somehow the wonderful system of German espionage seems to have got out of working order at the time when it would have been most serviceable. For, as we have seen, Beseler still had at least an army corps of men south of Antwerp, with a tremendous power of artillery to back them up. With all the guns sweeping the forts and the spaces in between, where the Belgian field batteries were working, the position might have been carried at a loss of five or six thousand men. Beseler's infantry, however, had already suffered so heavily from Belgian rifle fire and machine-gun fire that he hesitated to attack.

Defenders' final retirement at night

The fact was, he suspected some sort of ambush, with perhaps land mines in the fields along his path, and concealed guns held in reserve. No other well-known German commander has shown such a lack of courage in an important operation of the war, with perhaps the exception of General von Hausen when leading the Saxon army in the battles of the Marne. But if Beseler did not know when to move, the leaders of the Belgians and the British knew when to retire. In the evening of Thursday, October 8th, General Paris saw that if our Naval Division were to avoid disaster an immediate retirement under cover of darkness was necessary. He consulted with General de Guise, and the Belgian commander fully agreed with him. Thus the final retirement began. All the night the British and Belgian troops crossed from the south of the city through the empty streets, where the shells were falling thickly, and passed over the Scheldt by the bridge of boats to the Ostend road.

ON GUARD AT THE DUTCH FRONTIER.

On the left of the photograph are German troopers; on the right, two Dutch infantrymen beside a roughly-made sentry-box.

EXCITING MOONLIGHT ENCOUNTER BETWEEN A BELGIAN MOTOR-CYCLE DESPATCH-RIDER AND A PARTY OF UHLANS.

E. Van Isacker, attached to the General Staff of the 4th Belgian Brigade, was returning to headquarters from a journey to the front on a 7 h.-p. motor-cycle. The light had gone, and the moon was just up. After travelling a few miles he found he was on the wrong road. As he was scanning the lettering on a signpost two Uhlans came up in his direction. He shot one, and the other, after exchanging shots, rode away. After a few moments a party of forty Uhlans appeared, attracted by the firing. With a wild rush Isacker pushed off his machine. It "fired" at once, and he was going at a good speed when the first of the Uhlans came round the bend of the road and began firing. Bullets whistled all around him. His cloak was pierced in no fewer than seven places. He outdistanced his pursuers, but, unluckily, at a bad corner, temporarily lost control of his machine. There was a terrible crash. He was picked up, tended at a farmhouse, and sent on to Ghent, where, after a week, he was discharged as unfit for further service.

Only the garrisons of the forts remained, working their guns with the utmost speed to engage the attention of the enemy, and frighten him from advancing on the city. Three of our battalions of the 1st Brigade of the Royal Naval Division—the Hawke, Collingwood, and Benbow battalions—holding the trenches south of the town and one of the forts there, were left behind, as by some mistake or accident the order for retirement did not reach them. It was some time before they found they were deserted, and withdrew from the position which they had so gallantly held. Meanwhile, the other garrisons, while keeping up the pretence of resistance, were destroying their war material and putting their guns out of action one by one, so as not to excite the suspicion of the enemy. At dawn on Friday morning they also withdrew westward through Antwerp and towards Ghent and Ostend.

Incendiary bombs across the wild and smoky sky

Meanwhile the bombardment of the falling city was at its height. In the darkness before the dawn incendiary bombs rocketed across the wild and smoky sky and fell upon the houses. By this time the Germans had got some of their great howitzers within striking distance of the streets around the centre of Antwerp. As the great shells hurtled through the air, they sounded at first like an approaching express train; but their roar rapidly increased in volume till the atmosphere quivered as before a howling cyclone. Then came an explosion, that seemed to split the earth, and a tall geyser of dust and smoke shot high above the stricken port. When a large high-explosive shell struck a building, it did not tear away its upper storeys or blow a gap in the walls. The entire house collapsed in rubble and ruin, as though flattened by a monster's hand.

When the 11 in. shells exploded in the open streets, they made pits as large as the cellar of a good-sized house, and badly damaged any building within a radius of two hundred yards. The earlier shrapnel fire seemed harmless in comparison. It appeared as if in a few minutes the whole of the city would be wrecked as though by an earthquake. The thickest masonry crumpled up like cardboard; buildings of solid stone were levelled, as a child levels things he makes with playing-bricks when he has tired of them. By Thursday night there was scarcely a street in the southern part of the city which was not barricaded by the wreck of fallen houses. The only quarter which escaped destruction was that which contained the handsome mansions of wealthy German residents of Antwerp in the Berckem district. The pavements were slippery with fallen glass. The streets were littered with tangled telephone wires, shattered poles, twisted lamp-posts, and splintered trees. More than 2,000 houses were struck by shells, and more than three hundred of these were totally destroyed.

Homes of wealthy German residents escape destruction

Flames roared from many of the smitten dwellings. A hundred and fifty could be seen blazing away at the same time, and as the water supply was cut off there was no means of fighting these fires. Had there been a wind, everything in Antwerp would have been consumed, and nothing but the charred wreckage of one of the most beautiful and busiest centres of industry on earth would have remained in the hands of the conqueror. No military purpose was served by the bombardment of the city. Far more effectual results would have been obtained by concentrating all the artillery fire on the inner line of forts and the trenches and mobile batteries that barred the advance of the German infantry. Antwerp was partly destroyed with a view to terrorising the peaceful population and filling their souls with the dread of the race that had burned and sacked Louvain and a score of smaller towns and villages in Belgium.

By night the scene was one of infernal splendour. The oil-tanks by the river had been fired by the retreating Belgians to prevent the conqueror making use of the large stores of petrol. The glare of the blazing oil illumined the streets of this City of Dreadful Night. The lurid, wavering pillars of fire from the burning tanks, the flames of the bombarded houses, the flash and thunder of the exploding shells, turned lovely, romantic Antwerp into a spectacle of volcanic sublimity and terror. In the river the falling shells threw up columns of water a hundred feet towards the pall of smoke, which, rising from the tanks, overhung the city like a cloud of death, such as Vesuvius flung over Pompeii and Herculaneum. And all this scene of gigantic horror and woe and destruction was the work of men who pretended to the leadership of civilisation!

BELGIAN ARMY PASSING THROUGH THE FAMOUS GHENT GATE AT BRUGES.
The retreat of the British Naval Division and the Belgian Army from Ghent onwards was covered by strong British reinforcements. Ghent was occupied by the Germans on October 11th, and Bruges on October 14th, 1914. The above picture was taken as the Belgian Army was passing through the celebrated Ghent Gate at Bruges.

Shells continued to fall on Friday morning, when a tall young man, in the plain uniform of a Belgian officer, took the rifle from a dead man in the trenches, levelled it, and shot at a German helmet. It was King Albert, the heroic leader of a nation of heroes, firing his last shot from Antwerp. By seven o'clock the last of the defending troops were believed to have crossed the river, and the bridge of boats was destroyed to prevent the enemy following them. After waiting an hour or two, to give the soldiers a good start, the burgomaster went out under a flag of truce to meet the German general and arrange the terms of surrender. It was reported that Beseler stated at the conference that, if the outlying forts were immediately surrendered, no money indemnity would be demanded from the city. A brilliant American war correspondent, who remained in Antwerp through the bombardment and took over the keys of German houses in the city from the American Consul and delivered these to the German authorities, makes the statement in question. If it is well founded, it shows how completely Beseler was deceived up to the last moment concerning the situation at Antwerp. For the forts had been abandoned, and they might have been taken by simply sending some soldiers to occupy them.

Beseler deceived up to the last moment

But the Germans were excessively cautious. At first Beseler only sent a few score of cycling troops into the city. They advanced very carefully from street to street and from square to square, until they formed a network of scouts. Behind them came a brigade of infantry, and hard on the heels of the infantry clattered half a dozen horse batteries. They galloped to the riverside, unlimbered on the quays, and opened fire with shrapnel on the last of the retreating Belgians, who had already reached the opposite side of the Scheldt. In half an hour the pontoon bridge had been repaired, and on Friday night a large force of troops passed over in pursuit.

Some result might have been achieved if this belated operation had been continued with the utmost energy. But the German Staff was too much bent upon impressing the empty city to carry on the pursuit with vigour. The triumphal entry of the victors did not begin till Saturday afternoon, when 60,000 German soldiers marched into Antwerp. Westward towards the seacoast, from Lokeren to Ghent and from Ghent towards Ypres and Ostend, there was abundant work awaiting an army of 60,000 young, vigorous soldiers. The Belgians were fighting their way to the sea; part of the British Naval Division was being harried by the Dutch border; German forces were trying to cut the railway line on one side and to envelop the 7th Division of the British Expeditionary Force, under Sir Henry Rawlinson, on the other side.

Yet this was the time when 60,000 German troops were kept in Antwerp, to pass in review before the new military governor, Admiral von Schröder! Surrounded by his glittering staff, the admiral sat his horse in front of the Royal Palace, on which a Zeppelin had tried to drop bombs when the King and Queen of the Belgians were there. The spectacle of the great military pageant was strange and astonishing. Except for one American war correspondent and one American war photographer, standing at the windows of the deserted American Consulate, the city was empty.

A strange and astonishing military pageant

For five hours the mighty host poured through the ravines of brick and stone, company after company, regiment after regiment, brigade after brigade. There were ranks of gendarmes in uniforms of green and silver, Bavarians in dark-blue, Saxons in light-blue, and Austrians in silver-grey. The infantrymen, in solid columns of grey-clad figures, were neither Landsturm nor Landwehr, but young, red-cheeked athletes, singing as they marched. "Germany, Germany Over All!" was the song they sang, each regiment headed by its band and colours. When darkness fell and the lamps were lighted, the shrill music of fifes, the roll of drums, and the rhythmic tramp of feet still continued.

"DEUTSCHLAND, DEUTSCHLAND UEBER ALLES": GERMANS ADD INSULT TO INJURY.

The Germans, when they entered Antwerp, caused a military band to play daily in the principal squares of the conquered city. Apart from units of the army of occupation and those "without a country," the listeners seem to have included only the German residents who had prepared the way for the invaders. When the enemy entered the city they found it practically deserted.

BRITISH ARTILLERY CAMP IN NORTHERN FRANCE.

CHAPTER XLIII.

OPENING BATTLES OF THE GREAT STRUGGLE FOR CALAIS.

Germans Attempt Two Tasks at Once, at Antwerp and Lille—British Army Begins to Move Towards the Coast—Sir John French's Plan for a Turning Movement—Delay in Railing our Troops to their New Position—Germans Attack Lille to Get Base of Operations against Calais—Gallant Struggle of Frenchmen against Great Odds—Falkenhayn's Scheme of a Mighty Cavalry Raid to Calais—Clash of Tens of Thousands of Horsemen by the River Lys—German Cavalry Taken by Surprise and Routed—Reinforced, the German Troopers Press Back the French Cavalry Divisions—Aviators Bomb a Column of Hostile Horse and Defeat It—How Fourscore Chasseurs Alpins Killed Four Hundred Germans in Estaires—General Gough and the 3rd Cavalry Brigade Arrive—Clearing the Woods and Hills of Enemy—Sir Horace Smith-Dorrien's Corps Advance towards La Bassée—Why La Bassée Could Not be Taken—The Germans are Pushed Back on Lille—Terrible House-to-House Fighting in the Black Country of Northern France.

AT the beginning of October, 1914, someone in high command in Germany was consumed with impatience. It may have been the Kaiser Wilhelm, who had just promised his soldiers that they should win a grand decisive victory in the western field of war before the leaves fell from the trees. He had 600,000 recruits, whom he was bringing into action before they were half trained; he had 1,500,000 middle-aged men of the Landsturm class, many of whom might, if needed, be brought into the fighting-line. He wanted his refitted corps of first-line and reserve troops to clear a path of advance towards the French coast for the new armies. This could well have been done when Antwerp had fallen. But the anxious, restless, disappointed Emperor could not wait. He desired a swift attack on France to free his best troops for operations in Russia.

The result was that the assault on Antwerp and the effort to outflank and turn the Franco-British front by an advance on Calais were undertaken at the same time. Both of these German plans were well conceived, so far as they went; but instead of being executed in proper order, they were carried out simultaneously. The German forces had thus to be divided, instead of being swung in overwhelming numbers, first against the Belgians and then against the French.

At Antwerp the Germans won the race, but failed to gain the prize. They retained so many men in the other operations aimed at Calais that the Belgian Army escaped. So the capture of the Flemish stronghold only resulted in increasing the concentrated military strength of the Allies, by bringing several divisions out of Belgium to prolong the main allied front. This front then stretched for four hundred miles, from Nieuport on the North Sea to Delle on the Swiss border. At the same time as this strengthening of the Franco-British-Belgian line was taking place the movement of the Germans against it was weakened by their operations in Belgium. They fell between two stools.

GENERAL VON DEIMLING.
He is said to have made his officers register an oath to "take Ypres or die."

This was not, however, wholly their fault. Sir John French took some part in making the enemy waver between two objectives. As soon as the British commander learnt that the new German Chief of Staff had ordered an attack on Antwerp, he resolved to anticipate, if possible, the attack on Calais, which was bound to follow. With this view, he proposed to General Joffre that the British Expeditionary Force should move quickly from the Aisne valley towards Lille and the country round the seacoast. The Commander-in-Chief of the western allied forces agreed to the plan. There was nothing more to do in the Aisne valley, and the British troops had so fortified their positions there and improved their trench systems that troops of the garrison class could take over their defensive work, and free them for more active fighting.

Sir John French had already received a new division which he could put to no immediate use in the Aisne action. And in addition to his three army corps, a fourth army corps was being organised in England, under General Sir Henry Rawlinson, for service in France. This fresh force, composed of the 7th and 8th Divisions and the 3rd Cavalry Division, was partly ready. The 7th Division and the Cavalry Division were immediately available for embarkation. But instead of sending them into France, Lord Kitchener, on October 4th, ordered them to go to Flanders. The British Expeditionary Force would meet them there. In the meantime, as we have seen, Sir Henry Rawlinson operated with the Belgian Army, trying first to sweep

"HANDS UP!" CAMERON HIGHLANDERS CAPTURING A GERMAN FORCE IN THE YSER COUNTRY.

How a party of Germans were discomfited by a much smaller number of the Cameron men is vividly shown in the above vigorously drawn picture. The incident, so graphically illustrated, took place in the Yser country, on October 23rd, 1914. The Germans, in the first place, had been driven to take shelter in the small house shown above. Their new position was then made untenable by British artillery fire. Just as they were making their appearance in the open again the Camerons dashed forward, took the enemy by surprise, and succeeded in holding them until the arrival of reinforcements put an end to this striking scene.

BRITISH INFANTRY HIDDEN IN A WOOD—"SOMEWHERE IN FRANCE."

In view of the devastating effects of modern artillery fire the old device of hiding in woodland is fraught with special perils. But we have seen how Sir John French, by adopting this ruse, was able to arrange an ambush against General von Kluck which took that able but too confident commander entirely by surprise and led him into one of the most decisive blunders in military history.

up to Antwerp and turn the flank of the attackers before the second line of defence was carried, and then working to protect and cover the march of the Belgians to the seacoast.

Had it been possible to move the main British Expeditionary Force rapidly from the Aisne towards the Belgian frontier, the stroke intended by Sir John French would have broken the German offensive movement. His idea was to turn the northern German wing by an advance from St. Omer or Hazebrouck, both near Calais. This would have had the effect of compelling the invaders to retire from both Northern France and Belgium. Antwerp would have been relieved without a local struggle, as soon as the main German lines were outflanked around Lille. The huge German reinforcements of half-trained recruits would not have retrieved the situation when the extended flank of the chief German armies was retreating. Their arrival would have only added to the confusion on the German lines of communication. As a matter of fact, General Joffre also had half a million recruits in a similar condition of training. He did not employ them. He wanted them to develop into fully-trained men before he used them. He was careful of their lives and also of his war material and his railway system.

The railways of Northern France were already working at high pressure. So great was the strain which was being put upon them, that even the execution of Sir John French's new plan of action was delayed. It took sixteen days to move the British army to its new position. The removal began on October 3rd, and it was not until October 19th that the First Army Corps, under Sir Douglas Haig, completed its detrainment at St. Omer. Some hundreds of trains were needed to carry the troops and guns; they brought the new garrison to Soissons and Fismes in the Aisne valley, and then departed northward with the British troops.

French's new plan of action delayed

In all cases, the change in the men holding the trenches along the Aisne had to be made at night under cover of darkness. For if the enemy had seen what was going on, he would have shrapnelled both the new-comers and the retirers as they moved in and out. All this impeded the operation, but it was not the principal cause of delay. The great difficulty arose from the fact that two important French armies were fighting across the path of the British line of movement. As the trains ran northward, they cut through the lines of supply of General Castelnau's army round Roye and General Maud'huy's army round Arras. Both these forces were rocking in fierce, incessant conflict with the Germans, and needed immense and continual trainloads of ammunition, stores, and reinforcements.

How the British movement was hampered

At Roye some of our men stopped on their journey to assist in the fighting at a critical moment. Moreover, neither General Castelnau's men nor General Maud'huy's men were stationary. They also were moving northward as they battled, trying to outflank the enemy, or answering an outflanking essay by him. They needed trains to carry them, as well as the numerous motor-vehicles they possessed. It was thus a long, delicate, and difficult task to move the British Expeditionary Force about one hundred and fifty miles towards Calais.

In the meantime the Germans were skilfully using the railways under their control for an advance seawards through Lille. Against this rich, stately, historic centre of the chief industrial district in France the invaders had two lines of attack. One army could assail the city eastward, using the railway from Valenciennes; another army could descend upon it from the north by the railway from Tournai. By reason of the junction there of the Belgian and French lines of communication with Cologne, Lille was a base of chief importance for the intended operations seaward. It had to be captured, and it seemed easy to capture, as it was held only by 2,000 troops of the militia class, with a single battery of light field-guns.

General Joffre took no means to strengthen the small garrison. It was not his plan to save cities. He was

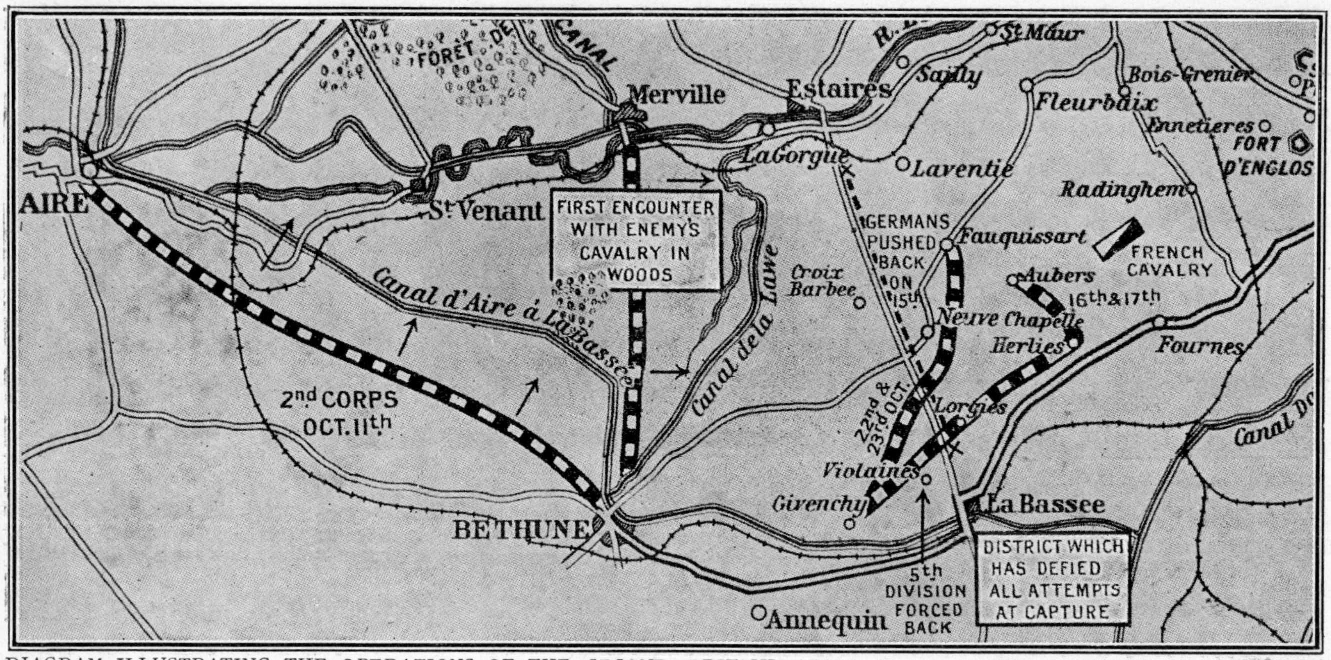

DIAGRAM ILLUSTRATING THE OPERATIONS OF THE SECOND BRITISH ARMY CORPS IN THE DISTRICT OF LA BASSEE IN OCTOBER, 1914.

saving France, and keeping his field armies strong against the enemy at the decisive points. It was not yet at all clear that the swing of the Germans westward was not a feint, and that the blow would not fall on the right spot—on the region between Rheims and Verdun. If the possession of Lille, with its coal-mines and woollen mills and famous manufactures, would encourage the enemy to take the wrong direction for the last great hammer-stroke on the Franco-British front—well, perhaps, the temporary loss of Lille was, from the military point of view, a national gain. Besides, it served to distract and scatter the German forces in Belgium, and so helped the Belgian Army in Antwerp, and also won time for the British movement to the north.

Temporary loss against national gain

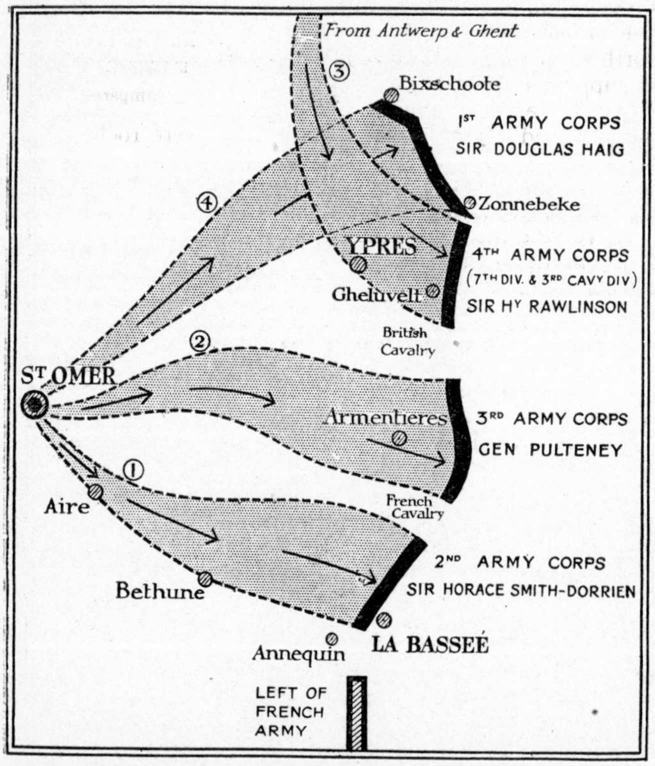

HOW THE BRITISH ADVANCED FROM ST. OMER TO THE YPRES-ARMENTIERES BATTLE LINE.

While three British Army corps moved eastward from St. Omer, in the directions indicated in the diagram, the fourth, which had been operating in the neighbourhood of Antwerp and Ghent, came south.

At first, General von Falkenhayn tried to sweep into Lille without a struggle. On Sunday, October 4th, a German armoured train, with a thousand infantrymen, ran into one of the Lille railway-stations. At the same time, some 3,000 German cavalrymen rode down from Roubaix in the north, and others came from the east. In all, there were some 8,000 German troops against 2,000 French soldiers. The battle opened about eleven o'clock in the morning round the railway-station. It spread through the boulevards and streets in the suburb of Fives. But, by fierce bayonet charges and the terrible fire from the four French quick-firing guns, the Germans were driven out by the evening, with the loss of many hundreds of their men and of two cannon.

This splendid stand made by the French troops against heavy odds had a happy effect. On Friday morning, October 9th, the German commander sent an army corps against the brave garrison—some 50,000 men against 2,000. It was the very day when the Belgian Army was retreating from Antwerp in considerable difficulties. The small garrison at Lille had drawn away an entire army corps from their brave allies, in the most critical hour in Belgian history!

At Lille, only the road to Bethune remained open. All the townsmen of military age left, under the guard of some of the soldiers, who had to fight to clear the way for them. For Lille was almost ringed round. The next day some Uhlans rode into the city; they were shot down. Then the bombardment began. But the Germans had not been able to remove their siege-artillery from Antwerp. Only a few small shells fell on Saturday night. It was on Sunday

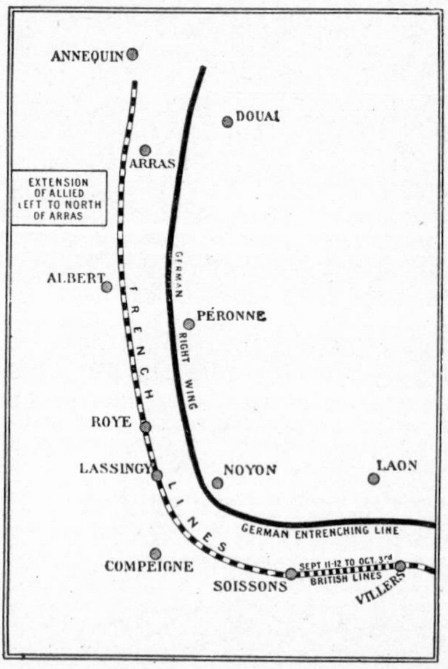

THE OPPOSING LINES BEFORE THE GREAT FLANKING MOVEMENT.

Early in October the position on the Aisne appeared to Sir John French to warrant a withdrawal of the British forces to support the northern flank of the Allies. Our men detrained at St. Omer.

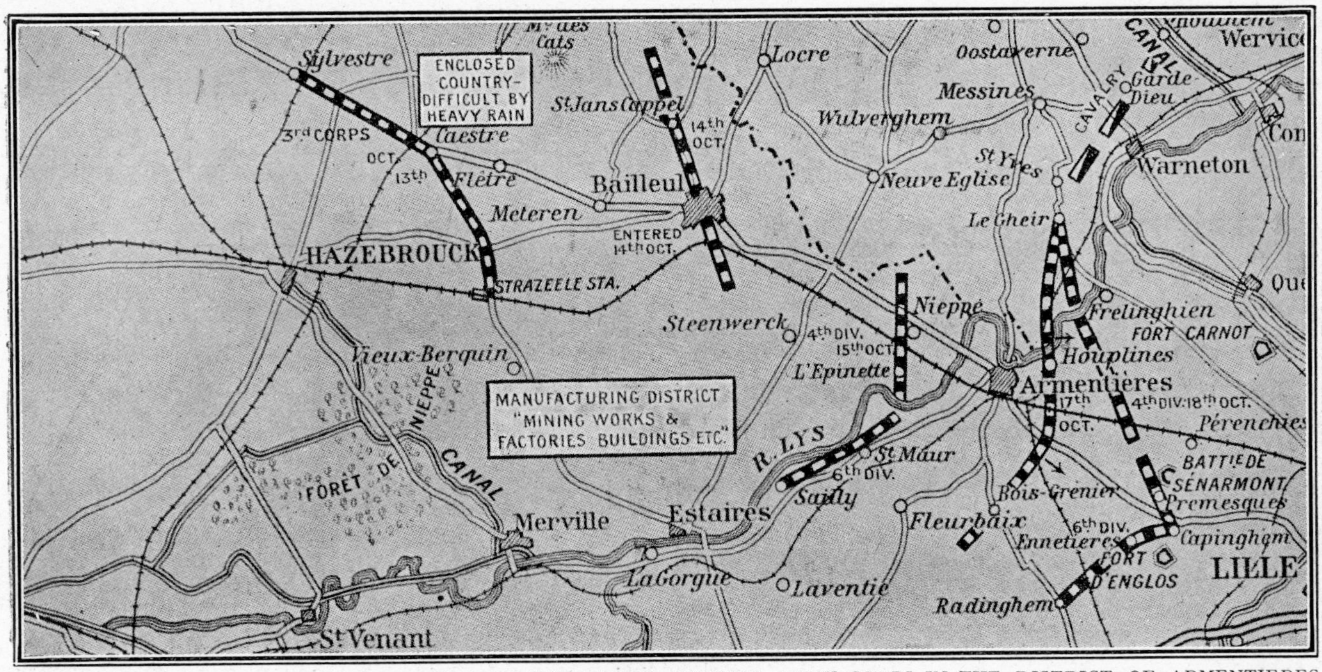

DIAGRAM ILLUSTRATING THE OPERATIONS OF THE THIRD BRITISH ARMY CORPS IN THE DISTRICT OF ARMENTIERES IN OCTOBER, 1914.

that the big howitzers were brought up on the railway, and placed in position. Then a rain of shells dropped on the centre of the city, and continued to drop until seven o'clock on Monday evening, October 12th. Some 1,200 houses were destroyed, and as all defence was impossible, the French soldiers escaped with their guns down the Bethune road, and Lille surrendered after a gallant and useful resistance.

Like the fall of Antwerp, the fall of Lille was a blow to the general peoples of the allied nations. It was an especial disaster to French industry, for it was the centre of a vast system of manufacturing towns and coal-mining hamlets, from which France obtained many of the chief necessities of civilised life. The huge stores of woollen goods and linen goods at Tourcoing, Roubaix, and Lille formed an important source of supplies to the German armies in the winter campaign. Even this did not exhaust the spoil of the nation, in regard to whom their allies, the Austrians, used to say: "Es gibt nur ein Raüber nest, und das ist Berlin." "There is only one robbers' den in the world; it is Berlin." For the Germans sold, in Italy and Switzerland, tens of thousands of pounds' worth of the manufactures they seized at Lille and the neighbourhood. They believed in making war pay its way, and the rights of private property in occupied countries were therefore abolished. It was reported, however, that some neutrals refused to purchase stolen goods even at bargain prices. Through their old-fashioned ignorance, they could not grasp the high, moral beauty of Deutsche Kultur.

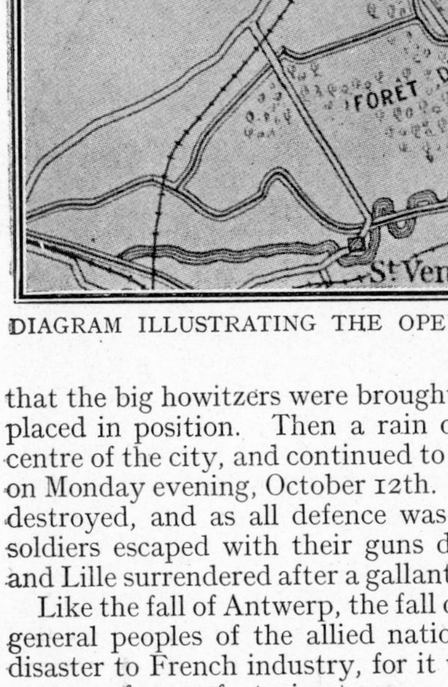

THE ENTRAINMENT FROM COMPIEGNE TO ST. OMER.

The withdrawal of the British forces from the Aisne began on October 3rd, when the 2nd Cavalry Division marched on Compiègne, and was completed on the 19th, when the First Corps detrained at St. Omer.

Before either Antwerp or Lille had fallen, some of the people of Calais began to fear that their town would also be taken by the enemy. Particularly on Thursday, October 8th, did the burghers of Calais look forward with apprehension to the prospect of standing another siege. For, in addition to the troops engaged at Antwerp and Lille and those operating against Belgian forces at Lokeren and part of the Fourth British Army Corps above Ghent, the German commander had thrown large masses of cavalry into the region between Lille and Calais. Some of the Uhlans were boldly venturing on reconnoitring expeditions to towns within a day's horse-ride to the North Sea.

Apprehension among the burghers of Calais

General von Falkenhayn had been inspired by the surprising raid of General Rennenkampf's Cossacks in East Prussia. By the swift onset of remarkably strong cavalry forces he intended to capture the northern coast-line of France, occupying all the country and holding the river

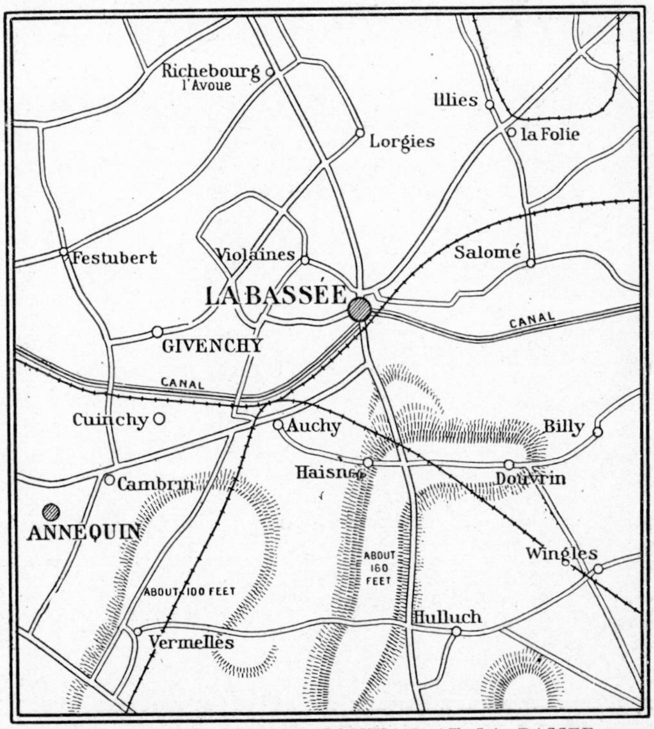

THE STRONG GERMAN POSITION AT LA BASSEE.
"On and after October 13th," wrote Sir John French, "the object of the General Officer commanding the Second Corps was to wheel to his right, pivoting on Givenchy . . . so as to threaten the right flank and rear of the enemy's positon on the high ground south of La Bassée."

bridges and heights with machine-guns and light field artillery. When the land had been won in this manner, and the defending troops driven into Calais, the new infantry formations would be railed down with an unusual amount of heavy artillery, and supported by a quarter of a million of first-line troops from Lorraine and Alsace. Then the march on Paris would be resumed, turning the Franco-British front, and forcing the evacuation of all the Allies' fortified positions from Arras to the Argonne.

German cavalry reconnaissance in force

The trouble was that this magnificent scheme of new operations largely depended for its success upon the results of the reconnaissance in force made by the cavalry. Every available horseman in the German lines was moved towards Lille, and several divisions of troopers were gathered for the raid by October 5th. Some of them advanced towards Lille from the east, while others swept down northward from Courtrai, with brigades of infantry with guns and machine-gun sections on motor-cycles, to support them.

All told, the raiding force outnumbered by two to one the French troops opposed to them. There were a division of French militia and some 9,000 Breton Marines around Dunkirk, and three brilliant French cavalry generals—General Conneau, General De Mitry, and General Moussy—were riding up in haste with their men. But at no time did the French forces approach in number those of the enemy.

WAYSIDE SCENE NEAR THE LITTLE TOWN OF NIEPPE.
On the morning of October 15th the Third Corps were ordered to make good the line of the Lys from Armentières to Sailly, which, in the face of considerable opposition and very foggy weather, they succeeded in doing, the 6th Division at Sailly-Bac St. Maur and the 4th Division at Nieppe.

On the other hand, our allies were favoured by the character of the country in which the struggle opened. For it was not suited to cavalry operations on a large scale. Near the coast was a tract of fenland, drained by innumerable dykes and canals. In some places the ground was low-lying, and could be flooded. High hedges and ditches cut up the agricultural district into small fields, and afforded excellent cover to the defending forces. Artillery power, on which the Germans greatly relied, worked at a disadvantage. There were no good gun sites. For the land was flat, and the views on every side impeded by belts of trees. The only line of heights of importance was that which began at the Mont des Cats between Hazebrouck and Ypres. East of this row of hills was a large system of industrial villages, linked together into a vast, unnamed mining and manufacturing city, forming miles on miles of streets, where a cavalry column could often be held up by a few determined men with a couple of machine-guns.

From a soldier's point of view it was a blind country, with opportunities for ambush at every hedge and every mining village; and to add to the difficulties, the immense plain was veiled in autumn mist. The German movement began with a night ride of three divisions of cavalry that came by Tournai and crossed the River Lys, moving towards Hazebrouck. It was at dawn on Tuesday morning, October 6th, that this body of nearly 20,000 horsemen came trotting along the right bank of the famous river where, four hundred years before, the chivalry of England and the chivalry of France had clashed together at the Battle of the Spurs.

Now another great cavalry battle was about to take place by the same river, in spite of the fact that most military experts held that cavalry was a wasted force in a modern battle. There were considerable grounds, indeed, for the new belief in the unimportance of the cavalryman. His scouting work was being carried out by airmen with a speed, an accuracy, and a range which he could not equal. His reconnaissance work was better performed by men in armoured motor-cars, and by motor-cyclists carrying a machine-gun. The modern parallel battle, with its lines of ditches, and its siege operations, had left cavalrymen nothing to do but to tether their horses and go into the trenches to perform infantry work there.

It was, in fact, this waste of an arm, which the Germans thought they had brought to a higher perfection than that of any other nation, that mainly led to the series of grand battles of horsemen between Lille and the sea. For years the Kaiser Wilhelm had practised immense cavalry charges at his grand manœuvres. He was proud of his mounted troops—more so than of any of his other soldiers. And, as the opportunity arose, he resolved that his favourite arm should distinguish itself in a great series of swaying, hand-to-hand conflicts that would mark the historic end of the employment on a large scale of cavalry forces.

By his long night ride the German commander hoped to take the French by surprise, and to advance at least half-way towards the sea without any strong opposition. But as the columns trotted along in the darkness, eyes in the hedge saw and numbered them, and messages ran along the telegraph wires to French headquarters. When the Germans began to see clearly through the morning mist, their leading squadrons perceived on the skyline a light cloud of dust. At first it seemed only a long thin line of floating gossamer stuff, such as the winds of autumn lift and carry over the wide level fields of beetroots. But the cloud drifted forward and increased in size. Silhouettes stood out against the Flemish plain; helmets could be seen, and horses' heads, and the glitter of lances.

The hostile horsemen surged first to the right and then to the left, forming a great semicircle, still sweeping against the Germans. Suddenly, at a distance of twelve hundred yards, the bugles rang out, and the trotting horses changed step, and began to gallop. To prevent themselves from being taken at a disadvantage by the charge, the Germans also spurred their mounts forward. But the Allies were not to be withstood. Onward they rode, with sword and lance ready to strike. With a terrific shock the opposing hosts met, amid bugle calls, neighing of the horses, and the yelling of tens of thousands of blood-mad men. And all around was such a thick haze of dust that a cavalryman could scarcely see ten steps before him the Saxon hussar whose sword stroke he had to parry, or the Prussian Uhlan who was using a pistol.

Clash of tens of thousands of horsemen

THE FIGHT FOR CALAIS: SANGUINARY ENCOUNTER BETWEEN FRENCH AND GERMANS AT LENS.

The mining town of Lens is situated on the River Deule, some ten miles north-north-east of Arras. Here, during one of the desperate attempts of the Germans to extend their line to Calais, amidst coal trucks, mine-heads, and iron and steel works, a sanguinary encounter took place between the French and German forces. Both sides barricaded themselves in the streets, and fought across the metals of the railway sidings. Eventually the Teutons were driven out with heavy losses, and to the moving strains of the famous Sidi-'Brahim bugle march of the French as they made their way triumphantly back through the town, the terrified inhabitants came up from their cellars once more to the light of day.

WORK AND PLAY BEHIND THE FIRING-LIN

In the above remarkablé picture, based upon a sketch made on the spot, many points of interest are focused. In a field seen on the right hand a number of British soldiers are finding brief relaxation in a game of football. On the roadway are to be seen British infantry on the march passing a regiment of French artillery going in the opposite direction. In the centre of the hig Staff motor-cars are passing to and fro. In the foreground are a few Ge prisoners in charge of French infantrymen. In the fields to the left m discerned a large number of horses tethered against hedges for shelter

EMARKABLE SCENE SKETCHED IN BELGIUM.

l observation. The same desire to escape the eye of reconnoitring airmen ticeable in the mixed colouring of the armoured train on the left. In the the rear of the armoured train is a captive observation balloon, and on the is a German Taube aeroplane. The road, typical of Belgium, is paved in the centre to a width sufficient to allow room for two motor-cars to pass; while the rest of it, after the passing of heavy traffic, is churned into a mud-track in which wheels sink to their axle-trees. In regard to the painting of the armoured train it may be noted that modern forts and gun-shields are similarly disguised.

TRAGEDY OF A MOVING FORTRESS: HOW FOUR HEROIC FRENCHMEN KEPT A GERMAN INFANTRY SQUAD AT BAY.

Few stories of the Great War are more moving than that told by the war artist M. Thiriat, and illustrated by him in the above picture. The scene was a desolate tract of Northern France. During a reconnaissance the party of which M. Thiriat was one came across a wrecked armoured motor-car, which appeared to be abandoned. Dead bodies of Germans were lying all round, and when the car was approached it was found to contain three dead French soldiers and one wounded. From the story told by the wounded man it appeared that he and his companions were trying to mend a burst tyre when they were suddenly attacked by a German squad. Entering the car they gave battle. The heroic struggle continued for an hour. His three comrades having fallen, the survivor fired at the remaining German and then fainted from loss of blood, to regret when help at length arrived that it came too late to save his gallant companions and left him alone to tell the tale.

Shouts of command went up in French, in English, and in thick-throated Flemish. The lancers drove home their long, terrible spears, the dragoons and cuirassiers, with their straight swords, feinted, and hacked, and thrust, some screaming as they fought, others working in deadly silence. The German cavalryman was never remarkable for his swordsmanship throughout the Great War. The French, with their trained gift of fence, got under his guard with ease, and though the Briton did not belong to a fencing nation, he had also been trained to use the sword with masterly force. One French horseman who took part in the action said afterwards that the work of slaughter became a mechanical job, in which he lifted and brought down his arm without thinking out his movements.

The chivalry of Prussia broke and fled

All the while the horses, seized with the same lust of battle as their masters, carried them deeper into the fight. The men's eyes were dimmed with the dust and sweat and blood—blood that spurted from those whom they struck, or blood that streamed from wounds on their own heads. Then, suddenly, as the allied horsemen were still lifting their red swords for another blow, they found nobody in front of them. Far away the broken chivalry of Prussia and Saxony and Bavaria showed their backs to the victors, and the bright cuirasses of the pursuers flashed dimly through the haze. When the dust settled on the plain, leaving a clear view, the tired men saw around them fallen bodies, horses who had lost their riders and riders who had lost their horses. Above the field of the dead the frightened, soaring larks began to call to their mates in the autumnal sky. The horsemen looked at each other, still astonished at the speed with which they had won the victory.

Driven back on the line running from Tourcoing to Armentières, the raiders took up positions in the mining and manufacturing districts. There they waited for reinforcements, and then, greatly increased in number, they sallied out again. Fighting went on continuously on Wednesday, October 7th, the Germans swinging more and more northward as General Conneau's cavalry corps worked against them from the west. By the next day the series of cavalry actions extended to the North Sea. The Kaiser certainly had his wish in regard to the magnificence of the conflict, for it was on a front of something like forty-five miles that the hostile horsemen met in continual actions.

Our sailors in armoured motor-cars, who had come to support our naval air division, had the time of their lives. For with the help of their airmen they could follow every German movement, and arrange an ambush at some cross-road, where an armoured car could sweep suddenly round upon a German squadron and shatter it with an abrupt and deadly gun fire. The French also used armoured cars. On one occasion there was trouble with the tyres, and the driver and his gunners alighted to repair the damage. They were seen by a large squad of German infantry, who crept up to an attack. The four Frenchmen clambered back into their immovable car, and used it as a fort against the Germans. After an hour's fighting three of them were killed, and the remaining man was wounded and dizzy. As he was fainting he saw a German helmet move, and shot at it. Some time after a French patrol passed by and saw the stranded car, and noticed the numerous bodies of enemies lying around. They found their wounded fellow-countryman, and brought him to his senses. The man had killed the last German just as he was swooning, and had then dropped unconscious on the little field of victory.

Thrilling story of French heroism

In the motor section of the cavalry forces, however, the Germans were not inferior in equipment to the Allies. In fact, they had the advantage. They did not rely much on armoured motor-cars, fitted with long-ranged guns, but sent out hundreds of motor-cyclists, armed with a small quick-firing gun. Even when painted with the strange, crude stripes of colour that so effectively hide an armoured train, the motor-car remained undesirably visible. It was, moreover, unwieldly in action, as it took some time to turn it round on the roads of Flanders.

The motor-cycle, on the other hand, was a weapon of greater possibilities, and the Germans certainly scored by employing it in an extensive manner. They have proved that it is more important than the horse in reconnoitring skirmishes. The machine is very small, and approaches as closely to invisibility as is possible. By taking advantage of the trees lining every road on the scene of the conflict, the riders were able to make long surprise rushes, and return in safety. They had not to depend upon the worn, broken highways, where perhaps shells had fallen and blown out great holes liable to wreck a heavy car; for their light machines ran at fifty miles an hour through the muddy side tracks.

THE MARKET-SQUARE OF LILLE.

Lille was held by only 2,000 French troops of the French Militia class. It was regarded by the Germans as a favourable base for their operations against Calais, and captured by them on October 13th, after a splendid defence covering nine days, a defence which served to draw an entire Germany army corps of 50,000 men from the force which was trying to cut off the retreat of the Belgian Army from Antwerp.

Brilliant motor-cyclists, who were also marksmen, were able to do an immense amount of damage in a few minutes. As soon as one of them reached his point of attack he dismounted, and tilted his machine slightly to the left, bringing the machine-gun into the proper position for manipulation. He was then able to sweep off a patrol or a transport convoy, and to remount and escape, almost before the attacked party were aware of his existence. His fleeing back, in any case, offered a very small and elusive mark, utterly different from the huge target presented by an armoured car in the throes of backing across a narrow road.

In the region some fifteen miles west of Lille, between the La Bassée Canal and the heights that begin with the Mont des Cats, the German motor-cyclists, backed by large forces of cavalry and infantry and artillery supports, managed at last to push back General Conneau's gallant horsemen, who had fought on our flank at the Battle of the

INDIANS GIVE THE LIE TO GERMAN CALUMNIES: A BRILLIANT BAYONET CHARGE.

The valour of our Indian troops came as a great surprise to the enemy. Landing at Marseilles on September 26th, 1914, they were in the firing-line in October. Our picture gives an eloquent illustration of their valour in one of their early engagements. A strong German force, advancing from cover in solid column formation, made a determined attack on a comparatively weak British entrenched position and carried it. Advancing farther, however, they came up against our reserves, which included a section of Indians. The latter, by their withering rifle fire, compelled the enemy to halt, and then charged with the bayonet. There ensued a fierce scrimmage. Then the Germans turned and fled, with the Indians slaying them right and left, and finally pursuing them back to the main German position.

Marne. Uhlan patrols began to appear in the towns leading towards Calais. The railway-station at Hazebrouck was stormed at the point of the bayonet by some Bavarian troops, and a garrison was placed at Estaires, a few miles east of Hazebrouck. The German position then jutted out north of General Maud'huy's army, and menaced him with a turning movement. So he moved his troops up towards La Bassée, and linked on with the French cavalry forces that were battling from Hazebrouck to the sea-coast.

The task set the French cavalry was to hold as much ground as possible, pending the arrival of the British army, and to keep the Germans so fully engaged that the Belgian and British troops in Flanders could not be overwhelmed or cut off. It was a desperately difficult job, but the difficulties of it only inspired the French to new efforts. When the position of affairs was extremely critical a fresh division of German cavalry was seen by an aerial scout, as it was engaging in a turning movement. No force was available to beat it back, but the French airman proposed a new way of meeting the hostile column of 5,000 horsemen. He loaded his machine with bombs, and departed, after giving two or three other aviators the direction of the enemy. They also loaded up with bombs. One after another the airmen flew over the long column, and rained down bombs that killed, wounded, and scattered squadron after squadron. As the roads were fenced in by high hedges, the column could not disperse into the fields when the airmen were sighted, and form up again when their sky foes had passed. All day long the aviators flew between the enemy and headquarters, loading up each time with bombs and swooping down through a shower of bullets to get near to their target. From dawn to dusk the extraordinary battle went on, and until darkness fell and covered them, the German horsemen were unable to escape from their aerial attackers. Their operation was completely stopped, and they were pursued and continually stricken all day long. Their horses in many cases became unmanageable with fright, and a considerable part of the column was put out of action before it withdrew at night towards its base on the Lys.

SURPRISE VISIT OF THE GURKHAS TO A GERMAN TRENCH.

In the night-fighting during the early part of the German attempt to break through to the coast the gallant Gurkhas gave a splendid account of themselves, and in the use of their traditional weapon the *kukri* (or "cooker," as the British soldier called it) carried terror into the hearts of the enemy.

Brilliant feat of four-score Chasseurs Alpins

In spite of the odds against them, the French cavalry, by Monday, October 12th, managed to hold the German raiders off Hazebrouck. But the Germans were able to advance towards Bethune in the south and Cassel in the north on the road to Calais. They still overhung the Tenth French Army under General Maud'huy. The French Staff, therefore, ordered that the enemy's advanced position at Estaires on the Lys should be driven in. Two thousand cavalrymen were detached and sent by night towards Estaires. Nearly every important movement was undertaken in the darkness, in order to escape the observation of hostile airmen. The cavalry by daylight lost all the advantage of the quickness of movement which their horses gave them. For as soon as they were spied by the aerial scouts, an ambush could be arranged in the direction they were taking. Like the first divisions of German mounted troops that tried to make a surprise raid, the horsemen on both sides trotted under cover of night from point to point, and made their attacks in the grey twilight of dawn.

While the two thousand French troopers were advancing in the darkness on Estaires, a young French lieutenant of the crack infantry corps of Chasseurs Alpins, with four-score of his men, was reconnoitring in the neighbourhood. The Germans had planted machine-guns controlling the bridge over the Lys, and a searchlight played on the river all night. Nevertheless, the Chasseurs got into the riverside village of La Gorgue, and at dawn went over the foot-bridge to Estaires. They were men accustomed to mountain warfare, and they had come from the Vosges, where they had brought to a high degree of perfection the art of taking cover. They crept from house to house, without causing an alarm, in spite of the fact that the little town was held by four hundred German troops. They found some of the Germans drunk, and the rest of them sleeping, and apparently even the sentries were either tipsy or drowsy. Going through the nearest houses, they discovered that every strong box and chest had been broken open and emptied by the burgling invaders. But this did not move them to wrath. Where the Crown Prince had led the way, it was only to be expected that the rank and file of the barbarian army would follow him. Even when the German colonel, more alert than his men, rushed out into one of the courtyards, pistol in hand, and shot at the lieutenant, the Chasseurs went on quietly. For the German commander missed his mark, and fell with a bullet through his forehead when the lieutenant quickly fired in reply. When, however, the Chasseurs reached the churchyard of Estaires they saw something that suddenly kindled them to the wildest fury. In the corner was a heap of bodies of peaceful townspeople, each bound and shot. A woman with child and an old feeble man were among the murdered non-combatants. The Chasseurs then began to kill. They went at it with the bayonet, and at the end of an hour all the four hundred ravagers and murderers were dead. It was just then that the two thousand French cavalrymen, having got across the river with great skill, cautiously advanced into the town. "We have already taken it, sir," said the lieutenant of the Chasseurs Alpins to the brigadier-general.

Ghastly discovery in a churchyard at Estaires

Estaires was the limit of the German advance from La Bassée. For the French pressure became so strong at this point that the raiding cavalry gave up for a while the idea of reaching Calais, and tried to extend more northward towards Dunkirk. They came within nineteen miles of this seaport in the second week in October. Had they been able to extend in force to the shore, they would have hemmed in the retreating Belgian Army by the sea road, and have surrounded the British force under Sir Henry Rawlinson at Ypres. The position became so threatening that the British general had to cut himself off from his line of communication, and send the troops holding the line back to England by steamer. The Germans, however, were trying to do more than they had power to accomplish. Breton Marines and French militia troops guarded the towns along the coast from Nieuport to Calais, and even along the German front from Lille to Cassel there were large gaps. Until they received more reinforcements from Courtrai, the German horsemen could not close the paths of the Belgian and British forces working down from the north.

Already, on Sunday, October 11th, their cavalry, holding some woods north of the canal running from Bethune to Aire, felt a new force of opposition working against them. They were engaged in surrounding Hazebrouck from the south, while another large German mounted force was creeping round the town from the north by the heights of Mont des Cats. The weather was misty, making aerial scouting almost useless, and some time passed before the Germans knew what was happening. They had entrenched outside many of the villages and had placed machine-guns, of which they had an extraordinary number, in the centre of the rooms of the cottagers, so that they commanded the streets from the windows. In the woods north of the canal they held their ground more lightly, with Jägers and riflemen collected round the paths that the French cavalry might take, while machine-guns were held ready to open fire. But not a glint of the bright French uniforms was seen.

Unexpected arrival of British cavalry

Half-invisible figures in khaki, carbine in hand, were moving between the trees. They were the 4th Hussars, and the 15th and 16th Lancers,

PICTURESQUE ALGERIAN CAVALRYMEN IN CHARGE OF A BATCH OF GERMAN PRISONERS.

Many of the prisoners were wounded and all were tired and in need of food. Their captors provided them with a good meal, for which they were very grateful. Inset: Germans collecting firewood for transport to the front.

GERMAN TROOPS CLEANING UP BEFORE LEAVING FOR THE FRONT.

German troops at their ablutions before leaving for the front. The railway-station arrangements seem to have been very methodical—witness the notice-board with its bold announcement of "Washing Water"—but no method could serve to eliminate the shame achieved in Belgium. Inset: An exceptional instance of German chivalry. Funeral of a French officer who had died a prisoner in German hands, but who was buried with military honours in the soil of his beloved France.

forming the 3rd Cavalry Brigade, under General Gough. As the Germans never expected to meet the British army so far north, they did not notice the green-brown moving forms. The British general was able to plant his guns and Maxims, with a view to getting a sweeping fire on the Teutons when they moved in the direction in which it was intended to force them. Then the surprise attack opened, and the Germans broke and fled eastward.

General Gough's surprise for the enemy

The 3rd Brigade swept the woods, and then joined hands with another body of British cavalry in the neighbourhood of Hazebrouck. In the night more British cavalrymen crossed the reconquered canal and moved in a north-easterly direction. They were scouting in advance of the Second Army Corps, under Sir Horace Smith-Dorrien, famous throughout the world for the stand it made at Le Cateau. It had been brought up to Aire on Sunday, October 11th, and it moved along the Lys in the darkness to link on to the left of the Tenth French Army, and then swing against the German flank at La Bassée.

The action opened on Monday, October 12th. The 5th Division, under Sir Charles Fergusson, advanced along the southern bank of the canal, while the 3rd Division crossed the waterway and battled towards Lille. The ground was very flat, which made it extremely difficult for the guns to drop their shells over the heads of our troops on to the enemy's position. Mining works, factories, and dwelling-places covered the land, and as the Germans held every building commanding the path of advance, and had machine-guns in the windows and on the roofs, it was costly and slow work for infantry to advance against such opposition. Each building that our scouts found to be strongly occupied had to be wrecked by shell fire, to enable our foot soldiers to go forward. It was house-to-house fighting almost from the beginning, and the Germans might have got off fairly easily if they had been as expert in street fighting as the French.

But instead of scattering when they lost the position, they tried to recover it by a counter-attack. It was then that our men made them suffer. Again and again they endeavoured to win back places they had lost, with the result that they were shot down in large numbers, and some of their machine-guns were shelled and destroyed. But by Tuesday, October 13th, our gallant 5th Division struck against a little German Gibraltar which was to prove a permanent obstacle in the path of the Allies. It consisted of the small industrial town of La Bassée, lying on a line of canals, some sixteen miles south-west of Lille. The canals formed a splendid system of moats in front of the German trenches, and to the south of the town there was some high ground on which the defending artillery was placed. The German guns swept all the flat country around for miles, and there was no site from which our artillery could effectually operate in reply.

La Bassee: A little German Gibraltar

The German commander, who chose that point of

vantage as a base for operations towards the coast, certainly knew his business. He could dispense with howitzers and use the long-ranged heavy field-gun with a plunging fire effect on any hostile position on the low-level plain. We could only reach him, after considerable delay, by hauling up our new 6 in. mortars. He replied by borrowing some of the lighter pieces from the great siege train that had been freed for general use by the fall of Antwerp. The consequence was that, with a commanding position on the only rising ground in the country, and with anything up to 12 in. mortars with a range of nine miles to draw upon, the commander at La Bassée was immovable. Beneath the fire of his guns our 5th Division was even more helpless than it had been on the Aisne flats with Kluck's guns and howitzers cross-firing on it. For in the Aisne valley our army at least had good gun sites on the southern plateaus, from which it could check some of the enemy's batteries. Sir Horace Smith-Dorrien at once recognised the position. He made no direct attack upon La Bassée, but pivoted the army corps at Givenchy out of reach of the hostile guns, and then wheeled his right wing northward between La Bassée and Lille. By this means he threatened to get on the right flank and rear of the hill on which the Germans had placed their artillery.

Commanding position of the German artillery

Up to this opening of the long series of terrific battles round Ypres and Lille the British soldier had no deep respect for the German infantryman. He thought the opposing artillerymen and the machine-gun officers were foes to be esteemed for their skill, but for the ordinary German foot soldier, led in mass formations, our men had little admiration after Mons and Le Cateau. Even on the Aisne, it was only the handling of the numerous German guns and the ability with which the German positions had been selected that made the British fighting man appreciate the professional talent for war of the principal militarist Power in the world.

Saxons and Bavarians show to advantage

But on the Lys and around Ypres the German infantrymen appeared to better advantage. Drawn largely from the Saxons of Saxony and the Celtic race of Bavaria, our new opponents showed more individuality and resilience than the Prussianised Northern Germans. Fighting with them were brigades of brilliant sharpshooters, who soon proved themselves expert in the art of sniping. Things did not go as well as was hoped by the Kaiser, who said he wished the Bavarians would meet the English—just once. They met the English, Scots, Irish, and Indians many times, and though they showed at first an eager courage to get to man-to-man conflict with the bayonet, they did not persist for very long in this attitude.

One lieutenant, who claimed to be the captor of Lille, and advanced against us with the 60,000 troops that had taken the city, wrote home after the first series of battles with our Second Army Corps: "People at home appear to have wrong ideas about the fighting spirit of our opponents. The British are the pluckiest and bravest enemies that we have. Every single man who has not been taken goes on shooting quietly, and these well-trained men shoot well. When we storm their trenches yelling, they stay steadily on in their trenches." That is a pretty good compliment from a bitter foe. In return we can fairly admit that the Bavarians, whom every Prussian contemned before the war for their lack of military exuberance, were the best German soldiers our men encountered. Except for their old, notorious,

PREPARED FOR DEATH, BUT SAVED BY A RED CROSS DOG.
In a corner of the Forest of Nieppe, not far from the River Lys, a British private and a French artillery sergeant, both sorely wounded, and passed by the tide of battle, sank down in a shaded hollow prepared to cross the River of Death together. Before they lost consciousness they clasped hands in token of friendship. Thus they were found by a Red Cross dog belonging to a French curé. They awoke in warm, comfortable beds in the good curé's house, under the care of ministering hands.

dreadful habit of killing their wounded foes in the frenzy of battle, the Bavarians proved themselves good fighters.

They certainly set our Second Army Corps a very hard task to win a few miles of country from them between La Bassée and Lille. They were in overpowering numbers; four army corps of the first-line, one reserve corps, one cavalry division, three cavalry corps, and a Landwehr infantry brigade were opposed to our Second Army Corps round La Bassée and our Third Army Corps round Armentières, with a French cavalry corps assisting them. At least three Germans to one Briton were standing on the defensive in prepared positions on difficult ground.

Great gallantry of the Dorsets

But such was the steady vigour of our onset that our Second Army Corps drove the enemy back continually for some days. The 1st Battalion of the Dorsets greatly distinguished themselves by the work they did from October 12th to 15th. On one day, October 13th, at Pont Fixe, in the neighbourhood of La Bassée, they held on to their position under a devastating fire. One hundred and thirty of them were killed, including their commanding officer, and two hundred and seventy wounded. But the enemy could not move them. On the other hand, no progress could be made by our forces neither on that day nor the next, when General Hubert Hamilton, the commander of the heroic 3rd Division, was killed.

Owing to a peculiarity in the British character, the death of the general was a heavy misfortune for the Germans. For the 3rd Division began to fight in a cold, steady fit of fury that nothing human could withstand. Working through the country between La Bassée and Estaires, they crossed the innumerable dykes on planks which they brought with them, and drove the enemy from village after village, though all the houses had been loopholed for defence. Bivouacking on Thursday night on the road from Estaires to La Bassée, they rose at dawn and continued their advance, and pushed the Germans farther eastward. Then at night the Lincolns and Royal Fusiliers carried the village of Herlies at the point of the bayonet, after taking Aubers in daylight with the rest of the 9th Infantry Brigade—the Northumberland Fusiliers and the Royal Scots Fusiliers.

The division was then north of La Bassée, and was in a position to wheel round on the flank and rear of the high ground where the enemy's heavy guns were planted. But our attack could not be driven home. Our troops got within a few miles of both Lille and La Bassée, fighting to the full pitch of heroism against an able and more numerous enemy. But nearly two more entire German army corps were moved up from the south, where they had been fighting against General Maud'huy's army. Our Second Army Corps was overwhelmed by four German cavalry divisions, two German army corps, and several battalions of Jägers, and other troops.

Heroic stand of Royal West Kents

Sir Charles Fergusson's 5th Division was driven out of the village of Violaines, two miles north of La Bassée, and though, by a terrible counter-attack made by the Worcesters and Manchesters, the multitude of Germans was held back, Sir Horace Smith-Dorrien had to retreat. It was on the night of October 22nd that he withdrew to Givenchy, just out of range of the La Bassée guns. Northward, his line stretched to the village of Neuve Chapelle, and here the first battalion of the Royal West Kents made a stand for ten days that ranks among the

Elliott & Fry.

LIEUT.-GENERAL SIR JAMES WOLFE-MURRAY, R.A., K.C.B.

He succeeded the late Sir Charles Douglas as Chief of the Imperial General Staff.

Lafayette.

THE LATE GENERAL SIR CHARLES W. H. DOUGLAS, G.C.B.

He was chief of the Imperial General Staff and First Military Member of the Army Council. He died on October 25th, 1914.

ARMOURED MOTOR-CAR IN ACTION: SURPRISING A PARTY OF UHLANS.

The Uhlans had the surprise of their lives, but the motorists escaped by sheer good luck from what might have been disaster. The encounter illustrated in the above picture took place not far from Arras. The car, manned by a party of Belgian scouts, was proceeding at a rapid pace in wooded country when a patrol of Uhlans emerged from cover. Shots rang out on both sides, but the swivelled machine-gun in the car was fired with such rapidity that the enemy were routed. The car, however, came within an ace of being wrecked by the body of a falling horse.

highest achievements of British troops. Their trenches were bombarded by massed batteries of 6 in. howitzers and numerous field-guns. The shells fell at the rate of a hundred an hour on October 26th. Everything was wrecked; the support trenches and communicating trenches were blocked, and to reach the firing-line the men had to run across a hundred and fifty yards of open ground swept by shrapnel, machine-gun fire, and by rifle fire. In the afternoon the big black-smoke shells began to burst right in the firing trench. When night fell, the German gunners changed from high-explosive shell to shrapnel. At one time ten shells burst every minute. When it was reckoned that all our men had been put out of action, the Germans charged. They came up in waves. Each wave was received by a mad minute of rapid fire, and when the last wave was breaking, the West Kents came out with the bayonet and broke it clean up. Afterwards the West Kents saved the line when it was broken on their left.

Wilts and Middlesex add to their laurels

When at last they retired from their trenches, led by Lieutenant Haydon, one of their few surviving officers, both divisions of the Second Army Corps hailed them as the heroes of the terrible fight. "There is not another battalion that has made such a name for itself as the Royal West Kent," said Sir Horace Smith-Dorrien. The Wiltshires also distinguished themselves in repulsing the attack against the 7th Brigade, and inflicted very severe loss on the enemy, while the Middlesex Regiment, by a splendid charge, recaptured the trenches out of which the Gordon Highlanders had been driven. Altogether, the battle around Neuve Chapelle was even a greater victory than the stand made by the same corps at Le Cateau. The fight at Le Cateau lasted for a day. At Neuve Chapelle the trenches were held for ten days against the same odds of four to one. The victory at Le Cateau was followed by a long retreat. The victory at Neuve Chapelle enabled the position to be held through the long campaign against all the tremendous attempts made by the Germans to break through and to occupy the north-eastern coast of France.

Terrible, however, were the losses of the Second Army Corps, owing to the length of line it had to defend, and the constant reinforcements which the enemy received. The German casualties were at least double those of ours; but as our losses fell on one army corps, while those of the enemy were distributed among four corps, our men were seriously weakened. Towards the end of October the Second Corps was partly drawn back into reserve, and the defence of their line was taken over by the Lahore and Meerut Divisions of the Indian Army Corps, assisted by two and a half brigades of British infantry and a large part of the artillery of the Second Corps. All things considered, Sir Horace Smith-Dorrien's troops could claim a tactical victory. For a great assault which fails is tactically a defeat. The assailing Germans withdrew, weakened both morally and materially, and in spite of their superior numbers they also had to be largely reinforced. Though all through the winter they continued to attack, they never prevailed, but their main position at La Bassée was gradually sapped and weakened.

Germans fought back village by village

To the north of the scene of operations of our Second Corps, a similar fortune befell our Third Corps under General Pulteney's command. The new corps was composed of the 4th Division—General Snow's—that had fought so well at Le Cateau, and the 6th Division, which had joined the Expeditionary Force on the Aisne heights after the first fierce fighting was over. They both detrained at St. Omer on October 11th, and moved the next day to Hazebrouck. From this town they swept out into action on Tuesday, October 13th, when the famous 19th Brigade stopped the German cavalry raid by seizing the villages eastward of the height of Mont des Cats. Having thus barred the road to the coast, the Third Corps fought the German cavalrymen and sharpshooters back, village by village, towards Armentières. The British troops were much superior in artillery power to the German raiders, but as the country was blanketed in fog, our guns were not of much use. By the time our gunners had a clear field, the Germans had their field-artillery behind them, and part of

Loading the lower deck.

At the trough.

Picking the draft.

On the road.

Corn.

Taking them up.

A new draft.

SKETCHES OF EQUINE LIFE: FROM AN OFFICER AT THE FRONT.

Great as have been the changes wrought by motor-power, the revolution has not done away with the need of the horse in war. He remains a most essential factor, and his help and his sufferings are deeply appreciated by officers and men. His health has been guarded and his wounds tended with greater solicitude than ever before. This series of charming pencil sketches illustrating, with sympathy and insight, phases of equine activity at the front, was sent to "The Great War" by a well-known animal artist on active service as an officer, and they are reproduced untouched.

FRENCH-AFRICAN TROOPS PREVENT VON MOLTKE'S DESPERATE ATTEMPT TO BREAK THROUGH THE ALLIED LINE ON THE MARNE.

A hand-to-hand encounter at Germigny l'Eveque, near Varreddes, where the Germans found themselves jammed into a dangerous angle on the River Marne. The line of the Sixth French Army rested on Varreddes, preventing any westward extension of the German forces. The French and British were pressing against the German lines to the eastward. In the course of the fierce struggle street-fighting occurred between a section of the French-African troops and German infantry. The colonial soldiers, armed with the long French bayonet, came round a bend of the road, as shown above, and the enemy, after a short resistance, were beaten back among the blazing houses and broken barricades. Here, as elsewhere, Eastern "barbarism" showed to advantage against Prussian "Kultur."

the siege train from Antwerp. The clerk of the weather was certainly unkind to the British army on this occasion.

A violent struggle took place at the village of Meteren, where the Fourth German Cavalry Corps and some thousands of Jägers had entrenched. Captain Montgomery, of the Warwicks, distinguished himself by leading a charge, in which his men captured the enemy's trenches at the point of the bayonet. The Seaforth Highlanders and 2nd Lancashire Fusiliers, the Royal Lancasters, and the Essex Regiment were also remarkable for their skill and rushing attacks. As night fell, General Pulteney's troops moved out to storm the town of Bailleul. But the Germans had taken the measure of our men, and hastily withdrew, leaving their wounded to our care. As the fog continued, our men went on in furious rushes, and captured the town of Armentières, and by Sunday got within a few miles of fallen Lille.

Meanwhile our cavalry divisions had been clearing the Mont des Cats and the westward hills of raiding horsemen and sharpshooters. They swept the country on the north of the advancing Third Corps, and a French cavalry corps, under General Conneau, which had acted with our army in the Battle of the Marne, cleared the region south of the Third Corps, and connected up with the Second British Army Corps still farther south. All the forces of French and British cavalry arrived victorious at the River Lys, about the time when General Pulteney's men crossed the stream on their way to Lille. The Germans kindly left most of the bridges intact, held some behind a barricade, and others were undefended. When the Allies arrived, the Germans were even repairing some of the bridges they had first blown up.

The reason for this was soon seen. The Germans had received huge reinforcements, and were eager to attack. The enemy were already superior in number, almost two to one, when they were being driven back. And our airmen found that the roads to Lille and beyond Lille were packed with grey columns marching to the fighting-line, that ran along the River Lys and extended over the stream towards Ypres.

ENTRANCE TO THE FRENCH FRONTIER VILLAGE OF BAILLEUL.
Bailleul was the scene of severe fighting, which eventually resulted in its occupation by the British on the morning of October 14th, 1914.

Sir John French could have strengthened all his thinly-held front against the coming attack. For on Monday, October 19th, the First British Army Corps, under Sir Douglas Haig, completed its detrainment and moved out towards Hazebrouck. He knew what a terrible strain he would put on his troops if he did not strengthen them, and enable them to place more men into the firing-line and more guns behind the trenches. Yet he left them as they were, each to face from three to four of the best fighting men in Germany. For he had decided to hold Ypres and the road northward to Calais. The Third Corps and the cavalry had to fight on unaided. Bringing up their heavy guns, the enemy took the offensive against the centre of our line held by the Third Corps. Our 12th Brigade was thrown back from the village of Le Gheir, after a terrific bombardment of their trenches. The retirement of the infantry endangered our cavalry forces holding a wood to the north by the hamlet of St. Ives. But Colonel Butler, of the Lancashire Fusiliers, led his battalion and the men of the King's Own Regiment in a counter-charge, and recaptured the trenches at Le Gheir. They were troops of a Saxon army corps that fought us in this fierce and decisive action. They came on in multitudes with great determination, only to be swept away by our men, who used their magazine rifles as though they had been machine-guns. A single Saxon battalion left four hundred dead right in our lines, and after taking a hundred and thirty prisoners, the Lancashire Fusiliers and the King's Own Regiment released forty of our men who had been surrounded and captured.

French's decision to hold Ypres

Tribute to Saxon chivalry

They had been exceptionally well treated by the Saxons, and had even been placed in cellars to protect them from the shells of our own guns. This little incident was remarkable as being the first occasion on which captured British troops were treated in a chivalrous manner by German soldiers. All through the campaign the Saxons fought with uncommon bravery, and yet in as civilised a manner as modern warfare allows. They were the only race of Germans who showed on land some of the gallantry in fighting which Captain Müller, of the Emden, had displayed at sea. It is said that our troops and the Saxons afterwards used to have a truce at early morning when our bathers took a dip in the River Lys, and the Saxons would warn us not to bathe when they were about to be relieved by Prussians, who would shoot our men in the river.

All through October 23rd, 24th, and 25th the massed attacks against the Third British Corps were continued. In some places our infantry were forced from their trenches by large, high-explosive shells that blew up the earthworks. Le Gheir and St. Ives still formed the storm-centre, with the wood of Ploegsteert stretching between them. Terrible was the slaughter done by the point-blank magazine fire of our men, as the Germans advanced in masses singing "The Watch on the Rhine." When the broken formations fell back they were caught by a storm of shrapnel from our guns. If they tried to shelter in villages and farm-buildings, our high-explosive shells shattered their places of retreat, and when they tore out into the open, again the shrapnel caught them.

Some German troops began to surrender voluntarily, but the German commander was resolute to succeed.

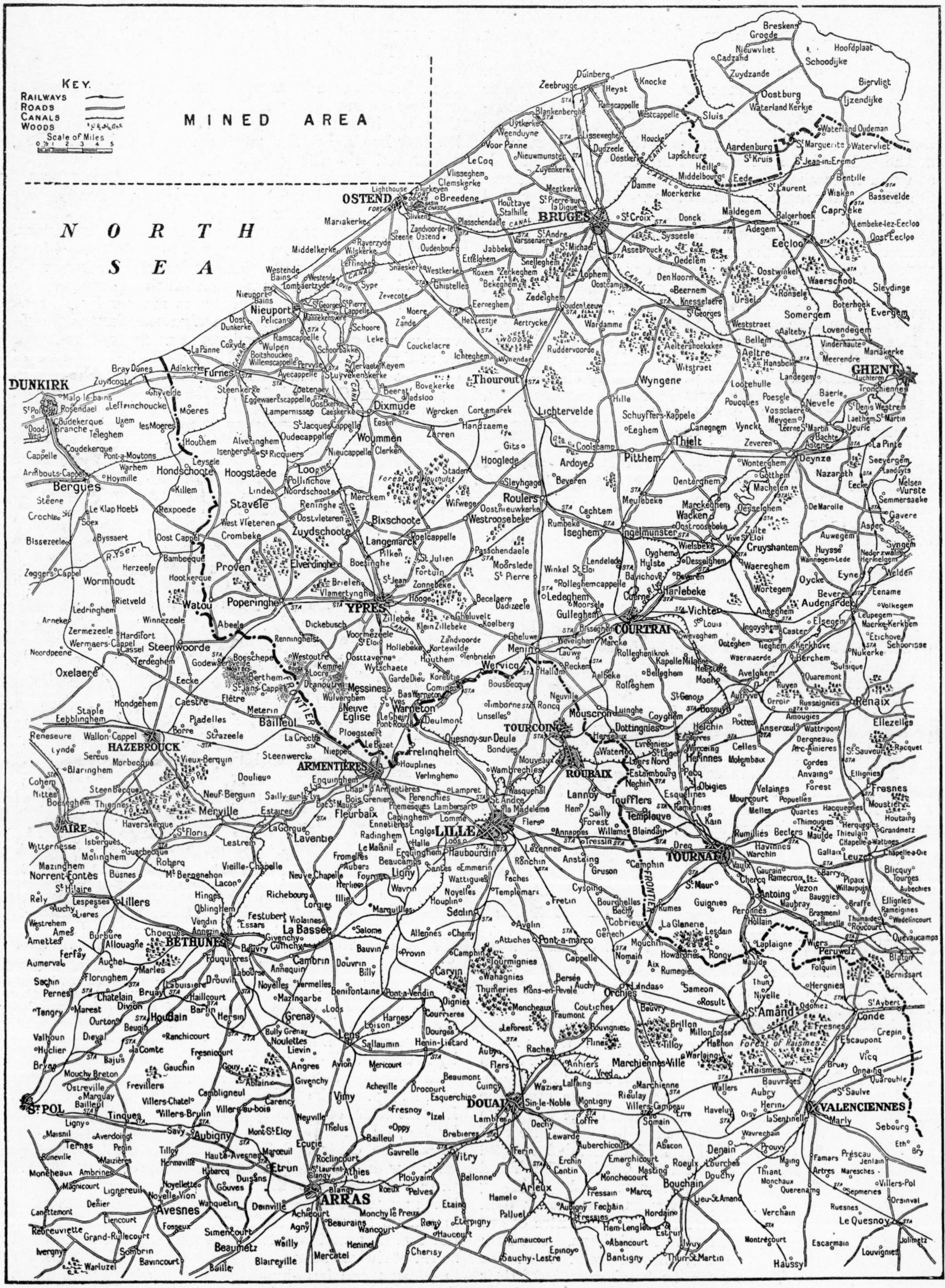

Courtesy of "The Daily Mail."

MAP OF THE YPRES-ARMENTIÈRES BATTLE AREA.

The above map illustrates the account of the fighting in the Ypres-Armentières battle area after the withdrawal of the British forces to the north from the Aisne in October, 1914. All the places mentioned in the despatch of Sir John French are indicated.

GERMAN INFANTRY RESERVES PASSING A FRENCH VILLAGE ON THEIR WAY TO THE TRENCHES.

He increased his artillery from the siege train which had been used round Antwerp, and brought an unparalleled power and speed of shell fire on to our trenches. At midnight on October 29th our 19th Brigade was attacked by twelve battalions of German infantry. They took some of the trenches of the Middlesex, but the Argyll and Sutherland Highlanders were hurled forward from our reserve, and with the old Gaelic fury of battle the Scotsmen drove in and either bayoneted or captured every enemy in the recovered trenches. The next day the line of the 11th Brigade was broken at the danger-point of St. Ives. Here the Somerset Light Infantry, magnificently handled by Major Prowse, counter-attacked, and won back the position in a wild, fierce, desperate struggle against far more numerous foes, who had been heartened by their victory. It was house-to-house fighting at St. Ives, against machine-guns firing from windows, loopholes, and doorways, with thousands of riflemen holding trench and barricade. Yet ten hundred Somerset men took the village from them and drove them back in disorder with our guns playing on them.

The old Gaelic fury of battle

General Pulteney's troops held the right centre of the British line, and the Germans only needed to bend them back a few miles in order to force our wings at La Bassée and Ypres to retire. The Third Corps was hammered from end to end and continually assailed at its weakest points. The attack went on night and day to the end of October. But in spite of the odds against him, General Pulteney was so sure of his men that, instead of asking for support from the general reserve, he extended his front on October 31st by taking over some of the trenches of the 1st Cavalry Division.

The 1st, 2nd, and 3rd Cavalry Divisions were doing infantry work on the north bank of the River Lys, from St. Ives to Messines, and then onward to Hollebeke, where they linked up with the defenders of Ypres. Their trenches had been hastily made on October 21st, after they were checked in trying to force the line of the Lys. For ten days the cavalry beat back continuous heavy infantry attacks made by Bavarian army corps, and in their shallow ditches they had to endure an unending rain of high-explosive shells and shrapnel bullets. Then, when they were weakened by the long and terrible bombardment and the succession of charges by massed infantry, two fresh Bavarian corps were brought up to assail them.

Our cavalrymen in the trenches

This was one of the most critical periods on the British front. The commander of the outworn, hard-pressed cavalry divisions turned for help to Sir John French. But the British Commander-in-Chief had used all his reserves on other points of the line. A French reinforcement would arrive in forty-eight hours. Could the cavalry hold out till then? There were some untried British Territorial troops at hand—a battalion of the London Scottish. No one could tell how these unprofessional soldiers would

RAIDING THE CORN-RICKS.
German cavalrymen threshing corn from raided ricks in the rear of their fighting-line in Northern France.

BRITISH MARINES IN KHAKI.
Royal Marine Light Infantry, for the first time wearing khaki, marching through a French coast town on their way to the front. Inset: French reservists removing their belongings to make room for British Marines on their arrival in France.

fight. The quality of the British regular was a known thing that his commander could build on. The Territorial, with less training and less experience, was a doubtful element. But there he was, if he could be used.

So the London Scottish moved up into the firing-line to support the 4th Brigade in the beet-fields round the village of Messines. It was on Saturday, October 31st, that the Territorials came under the fire of howitzers, cannon, and machine-guns as they advanced to their position. The London Scottish held on till twilight fell and then entrenched. At nine o'clock on Saturday night the Bavarians began to charge them, and the mass attacks continued until two o'clock on Sunday morning. The Territorials threw the enemy back time after time by rapid rifle fire; but in their last great effort the Bavarians, assaulting the front and left of the position in tremendous force, succeeded in getting round the flank of the regiment. Wild and terrible was the scene, illumined by a blazing house which the Germans had set on fire. Companies in support and reserve made a bayonet charge against the Bavarians, who had outflanked the firing-line and were attacking our front men from the rear.

Heroism of the London Scots

While fighting with bullet and bayonet was going on, and the Bavarians were working round both flanks with machine-guns and enveloping the regiment, the last reserve company came on with the bayonet. Again and again they charged, and kept the Bavarians from closing round, till at dawn the battalion retired under a cross-fire from machine-guns and rifles. They lost their position and suffered considerable punishment. But far more Bavarians perished round Messines than did Scotsmen. Thrown suddenly into a position of extreme difficulty, the London Scottish fought with splendid coolness and gallantry, and made memorable the historic event in the military annals of our Empire, when the first unit of our Territorial army went into action to assist the finest troops in the world—the professional soldiers of the British Isles.

This at least can be said of the London Scottish—they showed themselves, man for man, equal to the best conscript troops of Germany, who had been longer trained than they, and were equipped with more machine-guns. Sir John French was highly pleased with the result. Both the German and the British armies were exhausting their regular and first-line troops. The end of the Great War would depend on the quality of the new formations on both sides. We had found that the fresh German recruits were uncommonly brave and determined, but unskilful. The London Scottish, on the other hand, showed skill as well as courage. To them had fallen the high honour of showing the Germans what to expect from the millions of fresh volunteer troops that the British Empire would throw into the field at the proper time. They helped the hard-pressed cavalry divisions to hold the line during the critical period, and then a French army corps arrived, and the British dragoon guards, lancers, and hussars were able to retire and rest after twelve days' continual fighting in trench warfare against superior yet unsuccessful hordes of enemies.

Parade of the Landsturm before the Crown Prince of Bavaria during the German occupation of Lille.

Another view of the inspection by Prince Rupert of Bavaria of the German forces occupying Lille.

"MY BRAVE BAVARIANS": MEN THE KAISER HOPED WOULD "MEET THE ENGLISH JUST FOR ONCE."
The Kaiser's wish was gratified, but the result was hardly gratifying to him or to the Bavarians. The largest photograph shows a parade before the heir to the Bavarian throne (marked with a x), which took place at Comines, near Lille, on January 7th, 1915.

German traction-engines drawing heavy guns through a cornfield, and covered with foliage to screen them from the Allies' airmen.

CHAPTER XLIV.

THE INCOMPARABLE DEFENCE OF YPRES.

Unparalleled Fortitude and Endurance of the British Troops—Last and Greatest Achievement of the Last Professional Army in Europe—Three Infantry Divisions Against Five Army Corps—Tremendous German Superiority in Guns—The Immortal 7th Division Prepares Its Heroic Stand—Sir John French Foiled at Menin—Resolves to Hold Ypres at All Costs, to Save Calais, and Prevent German Turning Movement—Instead of Retreating, the Outnumbered British Force Advances Northward—Roads Thronged with Fugitives Hindering British Movement—Terrific Counter-Attack by Germans—Marvellous Feat by 7th Division—Slaughter of Half-Trained German Masses—The First British Corps Again Attacks—"Take Ypres by November 1st"—The Grand Assault on the British Trenches—The 1st Division Gives Way—Marvellous Recovery of Our Retiring Troops—The Worcesters Save the Day—Germans' Last Effort of Despair—Repulse of the Prussian Guard.

IN the way of war our race has done some great things in the past. We have not, like the ancient Romans, made a national trade of slaughter, and pushed on from conquest to conquest, for generation after generation. At least, we have not done so since Joan of Arc broke our power in France, and brought to an end the terrible Hundred Years' War, with happy results for both French and English. Since that time we have had no really national struggle for dominion. Taking us as a whole, we became manufacturers and merchants, and not Napoleon himself was able to force us to transform ourselves, even in self-defence, into a military people. Our campaigns have been carried out by a comparatively small force of volunteer sailors and volunteer soldiers, culled, by their own choice of the profession of arms, from the most adventurous spirits in our population. Many and important are the victories they have won for us, but none of them saw such a battle as our Expeditionary Force conducted round Ypres.

Ypres is the most glorious name in our military history. It stands for a display of heroic endurance and fighting skill with which we have nothing to compare. There have been battles with more decisive results and of more dramatic interest. Agincourt was such a battle, when our little army, under Harry of Monmouth, wasted by disease, was crawling to the coast to escape, but, being brought to bay, overthrew in a few hours all the chivalry of France, and conquered a kingdom. Agincourt was certainly a revelation of the bed-rock qualities of national character; but it was not so great a thing as Ypres. Ypres is the immortal heritage of our race. It is an honour and an inspiration to be contemporaries and fellow-countrymen of the men who held the road to Calais against the power of the mightiest military State that ever existed in the world. When Prussia developed into a nation in arms, and thus became, in spite of her small population, a great conquering power like ancient Rome, she compelled the chief Powers of Continental Europe to follow her terrible example. But owing to our insular position and to the might of our Fleet, we were still able to rely upon a small professional Army. For had we been the aggressors in a struggle with Germany, all would have gone well, except for unforeseen accidents. Our plan of attack was to blockade Germany with our Fleet, and so stop her seaborne commerce and cripple her industries for twelve months or more, while we built up a national army, trained by our regular soldiers. These would have become practically all non-commissioned officers, and formed a finer backbone than the German Army possessed. Then the land campaign would have begun, with France and Russia entering as our Allies, and Germany already in a condition of something like bankruptcy.

BRITISH CAVALRY LEADERS TAKING COUNSEL TOGETHER.

Generals Gough and Chetwode and Captain Howard-Vyse, photographed in the grounds of a chateau in France.

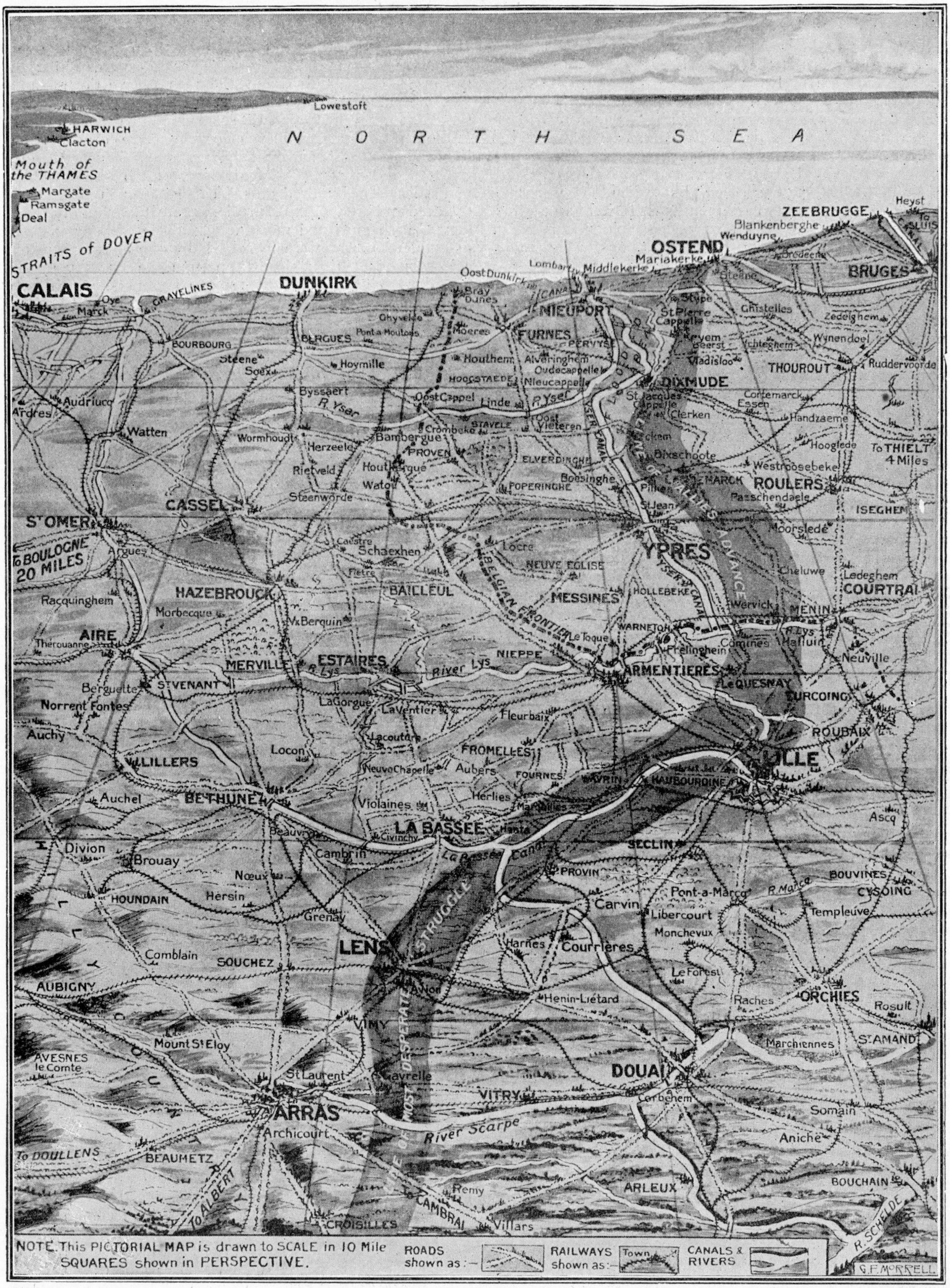

[*Drawn by G. F. Morrell.*

DIAGRAMMATIC MAP ILLUSTRATING THE DESPERATE AND REPEATED ATTEMPTS OF THE GERMANS TO BREAK THEIR WAY THROUGH TO THE FRENCH COAST.

The Germans know all this. It was one of the reasons why they engineered the war. They intended to cripple France and hem in Russia, and destroy, if possible, our small but brilliantly valuable professional Army before it could serve as a foundation to our national army. This was what inspired the German Emperor to issue his extraordinary command to his generals to exterminate our Expeditionary Force. In this he did not succeed, but when the war had lasted six months there were a hundred thousand casualties among our finest troops. Nearly all our first battalions were sadly depleted.

The finest soldier seen on earth

From these facts the defence of Ypres acquires its deep historical interest. For a short period between the glorious renaissance of the French spirit and the creation of our national army, the British regular soldier, the finest soldier seen on earth, stood in the gap. He was about to be absorbed in a larger organisation, in which the entire flower of British manhood was ranked. But before he was thus lost in a wider system, the opportunity occurred for him to show to the full what the old-fashioned soldier by profession could do. And he dimmed every military achievement in history.

Small were the forces that our Commander-in-Chief threw across the path of the Germans. They consisted of the 1st and 2nd Divisions—forming the First Army Corps under Sir Douglas Haig—and the 7th Division and 3rd Cavalry Division, which formed part of the Fourth Army Corps under Sir Henry Rawlinson. Had all the regiments been at full strength, the infantry could have put 36,000 bayonets into the fighting-line, and the cavalry some 5,000 sabres. The actual numbers of the British troops were less than these, as the divisions were war-worn. But as in the course of the struggle they were at last assisted by some men from the Second Army Corps, we can put their numbers at 40,000. Against them were brought up four German army corps—the 23rd, 25th, and 27th German Reserve Corps, and the 15th Active Corps—and finally some fifteen fresh battalions of the German Guard Corps. Landwehr troops were also employed against them in the early operations. Each German active corps had one hundred and forty-four light field-guns and howitzers, and twenty-five heavy pieces of artillery. Each reserve corps had at least one hundred guns. This gave them about four hundred and sixty pieces of artillery against two hundred and fifty British guns and mortars. But the odds against us in artillery power were increased by the Germans using a large part of their siege train from the country round Malines. They had about 120,000 bayonets, which was nearly four times the number in our trenches, and at the beginning of the struggle they seemed to have had even a greater preponderance in guns and howitzers. Their terrible superiority in artillery, however, was afterwards reduced by our getting naval guns and other pieces of ordnance from England, until we in turn had a marked advantage in shell and shrapnel fire.

Opening of an historic contest

The memorable contest opened on October 16th, when Lieutenant-General Sir Henry Rawlinson withdrew his men from Ghent to Ypres, fighting a desperate rearguard action all the way. The 7th Division and 3rd Cavalry Division had to retire before superior numbers of the enemy across a difficult country, without any lines of communication, and without any base. They held on to position after position, and made a stand at Thielt and another at Roulers before they entrenched in front of the beautiful old-world Flemish city of Ypres, which the Germans had occupied for some weeks. The arrival of the British troops, with a French Territorial division supporting them, caused deep joy among the townspeople of Ypres.

But the Germans were in overpowering numbers in the immediate vicinity, and with a view to beating them off, the weary 7th Division, that had marched thirty miles in a night, moved out against the hostile forces holding the neighbouring town of Menin. This movement was directed by Sir John French, as part of the general British operations against the western wing of the German front. The enemy was pouring strong reinforcements from Courtrai towards the fighting-line round Lille and La Bassée. The little town of Menin on the Lys cut through the German line of communications, and the British commander wanted to throw all the enemy's operations into disorder by the sudden occupation of Menin.

A force of German cavalry already held the Flemish town of Roulers, to the north of Menin. There was a French Territorial division, just north of Ypres, supporting Sir Henry Rawlinson's

FRANCE'S FAMOUS COLONIAL FORCES—FIRST-CLASS FIGHTING MEN.
Algerian troops drawn up in the square at Algiers in readiness for embarkation to France.
Inset: A group of typical Turcos photographed at Arras.

Wounded Turco returning to camp. Inset: Another swarthy son of Africa bathing his wound by a wayside farm.

Taking aim. The photograph shows very clearly the peculiar head-dress and uniform of the Algerian soldier.

ALGERIAN SHARPSHOOTERS ON THE MARCH THROUGH A VILLAGE IN NORTHERN FRANCE.

In action after action the Turcos, as the French Algerian troops of our French allies are popularly called, lived up to their reputation as terrible fighters and sons of a fighting race. This was especially the case during the heavy fighting between the Marne and the Aisne. All through they gave evidence of the pride they felt in being privileged to take the field side by side with white soldiers in defence of the Tricolour.

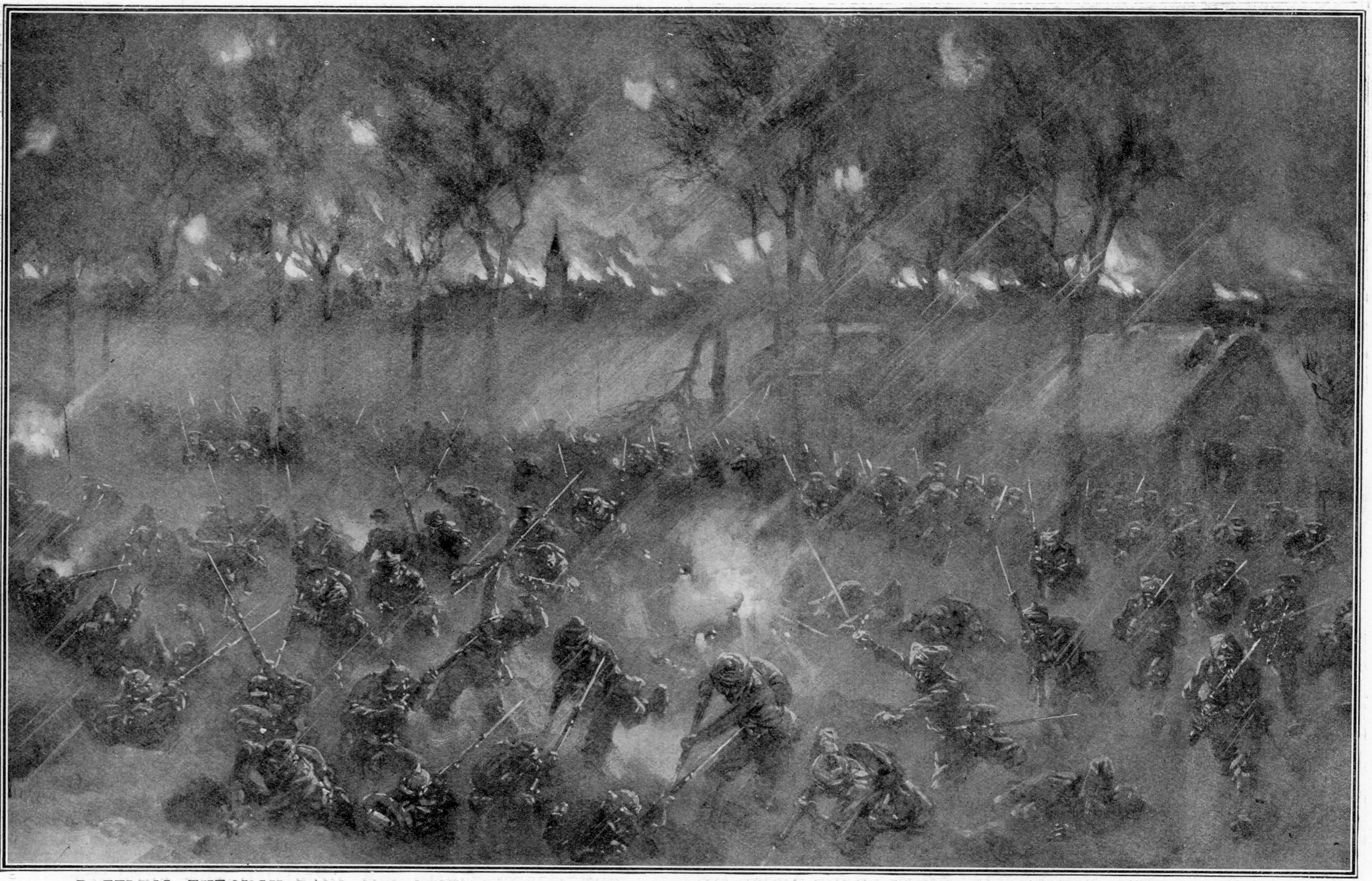

BATTLING THROUGH RAIN AND MIST: DRIVING THE GERMANS FROM THEIR TRENCHES OUTSIDE BURNING YPRES.

A realistic picture of a night attack by British and Indian troops on the enemy's trenches outside Ypres, from which flames are seen rising in the background. Ypres was regarded by the Germans as "the key to Calais," and it was at this once beautiful old-world Flemish city that the Kaiser is reported to have intended to announce the annexation of the whole of Belgium.

TURNING THE GERMANS OUT OF THEIR COVER IN THE WOODS TO THE EAST OF YPRES.

The fierce fighting, of which the above pictorial record gives a vivid impression, took place between Zonnebeke and Zillebeke at the end of October, 1914. The weather was bitterly cold and the ground heavy with snow. The gallant British infantry attack was preceded by a heavy artillery fire, and many of the enemy were found killed and wounded by falling trees.

troops, and Sir John French desired his subordinate officer to make a bold and even daring attack on the important point of passage at Menin. In fact, the entire scheme of British operations depended on the capture of this town without any delay. The advance of the rest of the British army was intended to be based upon it. Sir John designed to press back the whole western wing of the German front by outflanking it a little to the north-east of Lille. And the Germans were to be thrown into confusion round Lille, with the Allies driving with all their might on a line running south from Armentières to Arras and down to the Aisne.

British movement against Menin

But it could not be done. In his historic despatch, Sir John French half hints that he would almost have risked the destruction of the 7th Division in a vehement attempt to continue the British offensive movement. It is clear that he was much disappointed by the way things fell out. Sir Henry Rawlinson's infantry force of less than 12,000 bayonets was weakened by very severe marching, and large hostile columns of at least 40,000 bayonets were coming against them from the east and north-east. Some of them, indeed, were already threatening to turn the British flank. In spite of this, the movement against Menin was attempted on October 19th, but while the Infantry Division was advancing to the south-east, the cavalry was attacked from Roulers, and compelled to give some ground All along the road to Menin the enemy had a menacing, flanking position, from which they launched attacks against our small force. The entire British advance came therefore suddenly to an end only a week after the Second Army Corps under Sir Horace Smith-Dorrien had started the operations.

On the day on which the 7th Division drew back along the Ypres-Menin road, the First Army Corps, under Sir Douglas Haig, arrived from the Aisne valley and concentrated between St. Omer and Hazebrouck. Sir John French had then to decide upon his new defensive plan of campaign. Both his Second and his Third Army Corps round La Bassée and Armentières were in great difficulties. They were largely outnumbered and heavily pressed, and the Second Army Corps especially was in danger of being knocked to pieces.

The sound and obvious thing was for the British commander to fight on a shorter front. He would have to withdraw from Ypres, leave the whole of Belgium in the enemy's occupation, and expose Calais to attack in order to concentrate and save his army. According to all the rules of strategy the Germans had won the first part of the game. Westward of the British position there were only two or three French cavalry divisions, some French militia troops, and the fatigued and wasted Belgian Army to stand against the large reinforcements which the Germans were still bringing up. It would take some weeks for a first-line French army to be railed up to strengthen the allied front between Lille and the sea.

The position was one that tested and searched the character of the man who had to arrive quickly at a decision in regard to it. Sir John French showed an incomparable tenacity and heroic strength of will. He left his Second and Third Army Corps, without further support, to maintain against terrible odds their positions west and north of Lille, and he threw the First Army Corps into Ypres, to join on with the 7th Infantry Division and 3rd Cavalry Division.

Instead of retreating before the superior numbers of the enemy, the small, astonishing British army was to strike up north through Belgium towards Bruges and attack! This is surely one of the most daring strokes of war in our history. Sir John French designed to attract to his troops the full fury of all the German armies engaged in making the wide turning movement by the coast. He wished to give the brave Belgians a brief breathing-space, in which they might possibly be able to refit to some extent, and he also wished to take the full weight of the attack off the thin French line of Marines, cavalry, and militia troops which were co-operating with the Belgians along the Yser and in the country between Dixmude and Ypres.

Sir John French's daring design

The British Commander-in-Chief knew full well what he was doing. He was deliberately putting his men to the most tremendous ordeal in the annals of modern warfare. He was sacrificing them in tens of thousands, to prevent the Germans from reaching the Channel ports, and there establishing submarine bases for attacks upon our Fleet and our mercantile marine.

At the same time he was also protecting Paris from the swift, downward swoop of the invading armies that would immediately follow a successful turning of the far-stretched allied front. What told especially in the critical hour of the great decision was Sir John French's knowledge of his troops. He had spent years in training them, and in continually giving additional weight and edge to their fine fighting qualities. He had tested them severely in the retreat from Mons to the Marne. He still did not know what their breaking-point was. He took it that such a point did not exist, and sent his men forth to hold out against the enemy, until they dropped asleep or dead, or were succoured at the last desperate, extreme hour.

"If you can force your heart and nerve and sinew
To serve your turn, long after they are gone,
And still hold on, when there is nothing in you
Except the will which says to them 'Hold on!'"—

then, said Sir John French, in effect, you are the men for me, and I am the commander for you; together we must achieve the impossible. But not possessing Napoleon's gift of rhetoric, and being inapt to parade his emotions, the British Field-Marshal did not put it that way.

The scheme was for the heroic 7th Division to hold the country east of Ypres at Zonnebeke, and beat off the German forces coming from Roulers and Menin, while the First Army Corps advanced towards Thourout, far in the north, threatening Bruges and Ostend. The 3rd Cavalry Division, under General Byng, formed the right wing of the advancing force, and a body of French cavalry formed its left wing. The Belgian Army, though in the last stage of exhaustion after its long and difficult retreat, gallantly entrenched along the Yser, from Nieuport to Dixmude, to prevent the British striking force of 24,000 bayonets from being turned on the left flank. A force of Breton Marines held Dixmude.

Advantages of surprise attack lost

The advance began at dawn, on Tuesday, October 20th, while the enemy gathered in the Forest of Houthulst, some eight miles north of Ypres. It was most difficult for our troops to make their way towards the enemy, and all the advantages of a surprise attack were lost owing to the condition of the roads. They were blocked and packed by multitudes of peasants and townsfolk of Flanders, fleeing from the cruel invading Germans. Close behind the fugitives were two German army corps, which threw out detachments across the road to Thourout, and entrenched quite close to Ypres. Our men carried the villages of Poelcappelle and Passchendaele at the point of the bayonet, and then, still

LONDON SCOTTISH RESTING AT A WAYSIDE STATION A FEW DAYS BEFORE THEIR FAMOUS CHARGE.
A particularly happy camera-picture of the London Scots enjoying an impromptu meal and a smoke at a railway station in France. Inset: London Scots taking advantage of an opportunity for smartening up some of their belongings.

impeded by the incessant throng of fugitives on all the roads and paths, Sir Douglas Haig urged his army corps northward. And on it went, fighting at every farmhouse, opposed at every dyke and stream, but steadily pressing back the enemy all along the line of attack.

The Germans flung themselves on our thin, half-invisible firing-line, that went forward in rush after rush over the green, low-lying, fenlike plain. From the Forest of Houthulst on the left and Roulers town on the right large forces of the enemy tried to break and scatter or, at least, to hold up the British advance. But the khaki wave rippled onward, with another wave of the same colour far behind it, to allow German shells and bullets, that missed their first mark, a wide space in which to fall harmlessly. For our troops were so self-reliant and brought such a terrible power of fire against the enemy that their support and reserve companies could be kept at a remarkable distance from the leading line.

AFTER THEIR "BAPTISM OF FIRE!" A REMARKABLE SERIES OF CAMERA RECORDS.

The all-night battle in which the London Scottish took part on October 31st-November 1st, 1914, to the south of Ypres, was an event in which for the first time a complete unit of our Territorial Army fought alongside its sister units of the Regulars. Our photographs show groups of the hardy Scots after their "baptism of fire," which lasted from 9 p.m. till 2 a.m. They inflicted far more damage on the enemy than they received.

GENERAL GOUGH AT HIS HEADQUARTERS IN FRANCE.

This popular cavalry commander (in the centre of the photograph) is seen chatting with two members of his staff during a lull in the fighting along the Franco-Belgian frontier. General Gough was specially mentioned in Sir John French's despatches and promoted major-general for distinguished service.

The result was that they offered very little target, and a bullet that failed to hit a man in the firing-line did not land among the supports.

It was all a matter of marksmanship and strength of character. With the magazine rifle, taking ten cartridges in the magazine and one in the breech, men trained to rapid, steady, deadly fire, could form quite a thin line that was harder to break than the old-fashioned British square, by reason of its fire-power. If they took their job in a cool, easy, resolute way, the thin line could stop a charge of massed formations. For our well-trained regular infantryman could bring down at least a dozen enemies in one minute. His magazine held five more cartridges than did the German rifle, and—what is of more importance—the British soldier never fired wildly. His eye was on a mark every time he pressed a trigger, and the terrible swiftness with which he works the trigger, when giving a dense front of Germans rapid fire, was calculated to stagger and appal anything human.

Terrible swiftness of British fire

The British advance continued until about two o'clock in the afternoon. Then, however, the French cavalry had to give ground to the Germans, who were attacking them on our left, and withdraw over the Ypres Canal. This left the flank of our First Army Corps exposed, and our troops entrenched themselves on the ground they had won. Their line ran from the village of Bixschoote through Langemarck to Zonnebeke on the Roulers road. Here the 7th Division was being very heavily attacked. Its brave 22nd Infantry Brigade was hanging on to the outskirts of the village, with the German troops creeping round it. The 7th Cavalry Brigade was sent forward to help the infantry, and our men managed to cling on to the position.

All down the eastern line of defences protecting Ypres the struggle on the afternoon of October 21st was of a furious intensity. The French cavalry division was caught by a heavy shell fire at Poelcappelle, which caused it to withdraw, and the British line moved back with it. Farther down the front, by the wooded ridge of Zandvoorde, three miles from the Lys River, our 2nd Cavalry Division had a terrible time, and a gap was made on its left by an overwhelming German attack. But the 6th Cavalry Brigade swept out and filled this break in the line, and occupied the canal crossings to the north-west of Messines, linking on with the trenches of the Third British Army Corps.

All the while the heroic 7th Division was being shelled and charged, hammered by howitzers, and ripped by massed rifle fire. The front they held measured, from flank to flank, some eight miles. The normal garrison to such a front would not have been less than five thousand men to the mile, according to our own Staff teaching, and considerably over that number, according to foreign tactics of defence. Yet the Division, had it put every possible bayonet into the trenches, could only have mustered fifteen hundred to the mile. Day by day this number shrank, under the overpowering artillery of the enemy and the incessant charges of hostile infantry. The opposing troops numbered at the beginning over 75,000 men, and these are said to have swelled at last to five army corps of 200,000 troops.

The fight went on without ceasing, night and day, for nearly nineteen days. A captured German officer declared that his General Staff was firmly convinced that the stubbornly-held Britsh trenches were occupied by at least two army corps of 80,000 troops. In the end there was only the four-hundredth part of this supposed force fronting the enemy! For our twelve thousand infantrymen were blown to pieces by the great shells, worn out by want of sleep, and struck by shrapnel, until there were only forty-four officers and 2,336 men left. Yet until they were relieved and withdrew to rest and refit, they held out against the enemy.

Heroism of our 7th Division

In the 1870 campaign, no regiment of either French or German troops stood up victoriously under the loss of half its effectives. In the American Civil War only seven Confederate and two Federal battalions retained a fighting cohesion after five hundred men had fallen. Our 7th Division lost four-fifths of its men and yet held on. For days no one could approach them in sunlight, except by the communicating trenches. Then many of these trenches were wrecked by the German 6 in. shells, and the food and

INDIANS CARRYING A GERMAN POSITION: "IT WAS A GLORIOUS FIGHT."

Subadar Wasan Singh, of the 58th (Indian) Rifles, described to a Press representative how his regiment had their first encounter with the Germans early in November, 1914. "We had," he said, "been in the trenches all night, and at dawn we charged. Our men were delighted to get into the fighting at last." The position they were ordered to attack was on a farm, and the force of the enemy occupying it was a strong one. "It was a glorious fight while it lasted," declared the subadar; "but soon there were no Germans left, and some of our men won Paradise."

BRITISH ASSAULT ON FORTIFIED HOUSES IN A VILLAGE NEAR YPRES.

In the numerous and closely contiguous villages in the neighbourhood of Ypres, house-to-house and hand-to-hand fighting of the most desperate and deadly character was of almost daily occurrence during the early stages of the German effort to break through to the French coast. In addition to throwing up trenches outside the villages, the enemy occupied the houses and turned them in forts, placing machine-guns in the centre of rooms so that they co an approach through a window. As the barricades were capture turned to use by the captors; and the same thing occurred when hous

AN EVER-MEMORABLE HALLOWE'EN NIGHT: THE LONDON SCOTTISH CHARGE AT MESSINES.

Every October 31st Hallowe'en is observed with the customary ceremonies in the headquarters of the London Scottish. On the Hallowe'en of 1914, the 1st Battalion of the regiment passed so gallantly through an ordeal of fire as to win the special thanks of Sir John French. After advancing under heavy fire to the support of our cavalry in the trenches at Messines, they withstood a series of massed attacks by the Bavarians from 9 p.m. till 2 a.m. on morning, fighting with splendid coolness and great gallantry. As they their great charge the word was passed, "Remember you are Scottish."

FRENCH HEROISM IN THE ARGONNE: WHAT "A SLIGHT ADVANCE" IMPLIES.

nne forms an important section of the French frontier defences, and ely in the accounts of the fighting right from the beginning of the The village of Louppy-le-Chateau, the scene of the encounter illus- e, was alternately occupied by the Germans and the French, and the church tower and many of the houses were in ruins from bombardment and fire before the place was definitely held by our gallant allies. Our artist has supplied a vivid picture of what lies behind the laconic phrase, met with so often in the official French communiqués, "We have advanced slightly in the Argonne."

SETTLING AN OLD SCORE: BENGAL LANCERS' FIRST BRUSH WITH THE ENEMY.

e Boxer trouble of 1900 the Germans treated the Indian troops fighting de with undisguised contempt. In October, 1914, when our brave ps were brought into the fighting-line in the vicinity of Ypres, the as repaid with interest. The incident illustrated in the above stirring picture took place when the enemy were coming up in overwhelming force on what they thought was a weak part of the British line. The Bengal Lancers, who had arrived the day before, suddenly charged, and "swept into the Germans like a whirlwind." The Teutons broke and ran, being pursued for a mile.

BRITISH TRANSPORT TRAIN MAKING ITS WAY UNDER HEAVY SHELL FIRE ALONG THE SNOW-BOUND YPRES ROADS.

The above stirring picture illustrates what frequently happened behind the firing-line on one of those days which were officially described as "uneventful"—that is to say when no active operations of any special note stood out from the background of artillery bombardment. This bombardment, directed at the roads as well as the trenches, continued day and night with varying intensity.

ammunition supplies had to be carried across the fire-swept zone in the darkness of night. As the aim of the enemy was to wear down the physical strength of our men, they tried to prevent anybody in the 7th Division from getting any sleep. The scream and thunder of the high-explosive shells did not produce this result, unless they burst within the trenches. For our men became dead drowsy, and when their turn came for a rest they dropped into as deep a slumber in the holes they made beneath the parapets that the trump of doom could not awaken them. Nothing but the urgent need of every rifle to repel a massed infantry attack could bring them to their feet. So from dusk to dawn the German commander, General von Deimling, interrupted the eternal bombardment, and either tried to break through our lines, or made a sufficient feint to bring all our men to their feet.

This power of being able to wear down an enemy, until he is well-nigh crazy and helpless from sleeplessness and physical exhaustion, constitutes the chief advantage of an attacking force that largely outnumbers its opponents. The attackers can be divided into three or four sections. Each has a spell of hard work in the firing-line, in which it keeps the defenders at the utmost tension. Then it retires for sleep and refreshment, and returns again the next day with renewed vigour, while the defending force has been kept incessantly at work for twenty-four hours. Multiply twenty-four by nineteen, and add to the result the fatigues of fighting and long night marches which our Immortal Division had already undergone. The result is absolutely staggering. As a feat of endurance and resistance it is sublime. The defence was made in the open air, in rainy autumnal weather, with the narrow trenches draining the wet fields and giving a watery foothold to our men. Even Sir John French did not expect to expose his men to such an ordeal.

MUSIC AND MARS: AN INCIDENT NEAR YPRES.

Finding in a shell-battered house a grand piano and a store of classical music, a British officer imparted his discovery to a French Alpine Chasseur, and though the latter had to be back in the trenches within an hour, the two played a duet together. Meanwhile the Frenchman's comrades stole into the room quietly one by one, and furnished an appreciative audience. The incident took place near Ypres, and the piece played is stated to have been Schubert's " Unfinished Symphony."

Kaiser's colossal sacrifice of men

The German commander upset the plan of the Allies by bringing up army corps of half-trained troops, and launching them at the British trenches. Neither Sir John French, nor General Foch, who was directing the strategy on the northern front, had imagined that the new German formations would be thrown on to the field. The Great German Staff was eating its wheat green, instead of waiting for it to ripen. The new recruits were not yet fit to battle, especially under the terrible conditions of modern warfare, and many of the new officers also showed a lack of training and faults in leading. But they were all sacrificed in the desperate attempt made by the Kaiser Wilhelm in person to retrieve the defeat on the Marne by a victorious turning movement on the coast.

On October 23rd the first of the new German formations came on in masses, chanting patriotic songs, and marching to death with marvellous bravery. Our men reserved their fire till the close-packed multitudes were within a hundred—or even fifty—yards of the trench. Then they slaughtered them with point-blank rapid magazine shooting. Five times the unskilled but heroic recruits charged in overpowering numbers. But numbers did not matter. Each time our superbly-trained regular soldiers waited till the enemy advanced to very close range, and then gave them the mad minute of rapid fire, with British machine-guns rattling amid the fierce splutter of the rifles.

Each assault was easily beaten back. As the Germans broke, officers in our observation trenches telephoned to our batteries, and our artillerymen showered shrapnel upon the fleeing multitudes. A single British battery on this day of slaughter used, it is reckoned, eighteen hundred rounds of ammunition on the large, clear targets made by the masses of hostile troops.

British advance towards Pilkem

Earlier in the same day some of the regiments of the First British Army Corps, holding the villages north of Ypres, advanced towards Pilkem. Here the enemy had succeeded in penetrating some trenches held by the Cameron Highlanders; and to the 2nd Infantry Brigade, less the Royal Sussex Regiment, left in charge of another position, was set the task of recapturing the lost ground. Under General Bulfin, the 1st Loyal North Lancashire Regiment,

HEROISM OF THE 2ND WORCESTERS NEAR YPRES: RECAPTURE OF THE CHATEAU AND VILLAGE OF GHELUVELT.

Sir John French, who was at Hooge on the momentous October 31st, 1914, described the rally of our 1st Division and the recapture of the village of Gheluvelt as "fraught with momentous consequences. If," he added, "any one unit can be singled out for especial praise, it is the Worcesters." Gheluvelt commanded the approach to Ypres. The Worcesters lost three officers and one hundred and thirty men.

MESSINES (ABOUT MIDWAY BETWEEN YPRES AND ARMENTIERES): PHOTOGRAPH TAKEN DURING THE HEAVY FIGHTING IN OCTOBER, 1914.

with the Northamptonshire Regiment and the 2nd King's Royal Rifle Corps, swept out to attack. They were countered by a much larger force of Germans, but instead of giving ground, they pressed on all the day in a fierce, swaying, stubborn, terrible fight. Major Aubrey Carter led the North Lancashire battalion in the charge that won the day. Under a heavy shell bombardment and rifle volleys, the Lancashire lads steadily advanced close up to the enemy's trenches, beating down the hostile rifle fire by their own rapid and deadly marksmanship, with their machine-guns brought up into the firing-line to increase their fire effect. Major H. G. Powell, of the same Lancashire regiment, had retired from active service ten years before, and had rejoined his troops on the Aisne. Spraining his foot in the advance, he led his part of the battalion, with a chair in one hand and a stick in the other. Then he sat down before the enemy's trenches, in a storm of shells and bullets, and directed the operations from his chair until he was seriously wounded. Even then he would not leave, but some friends gave him no choice in the matter, and carried him off the field.

In the meantime the lads of the Red Rose fixed their bayonets, and, as evening fell, they carried the trenches by storm and captured over six hundred prisoners. The Northamptons and the King's Rifles at the same time followed them and helped to win the victory. The Third Infantry Brigade also distinguished itself at Langemarck, two miles to the north-west of Pilkem. When night fell there were fifteen hundred dead foes lying in front of their trenches. Forty thousand men had attacked them, and only ten thousand of these finished the day's fighting unhurt, according to a letter afterwards found upon a captured German officer.

The gallant 7th reinforced

Thus ended one of the most terrible periods in the long heroic defence of Ypres. For in the evening a division of the Ninth French Army Corps came into the town, and took over part of the line held by our 2nd Division. This division then moved eastward, and helped the sorely-pressed 7th Division. The next night our eastward trenches, against which the enemy was directing his fiercest, heaviest attacks, were further strengthened by the arrival of the 1st Division to reinforce the gallant 7th. The defence of the villages won to the north of Ypres was taken over by French Territorial troops, and our First, Second, and Third Infantry Brigades were concentrated in the woods around Zillebeke.

In spite of the tremendous forces gathering against him, Sir John French was not inclined to stand wholly upon the defence. He was especially anxious to draw the German attacks from the new French line north of Ypres, where French Territorials, oldish men of the militia class, with splendid courage, but less spring and experience than first-line troops, were filling the gap till the rest of the Ninth French Army Corps arrived. So having strengthened his lines by a concentration of troops, the British commander ordered the 2nd Division of Sir Douglas Haig's corps to advance against the enemy along the road to Roulers.

It was on Sunday, October 25th, that the Guards' Brigade, under Lord Cavan, with the other brigades of the 2nd Division, supported on their left by the Ninth French Corps and on their right by the battered but defiant 7th Division, made its sudden, amazing, and successful advance.

General Deimling taken unawares

General von Deimling was not prepared for a move of this sort, in which some 10,000 British infantrymen dared anything from two to three Bavarian army corps. Two of his field-guns fell into the hands of our troops, and the French, fighting with equal dash and mortal skill, captured six German machine-guns. With armoured motor-cars, equipped with quick-firers, the 2nd Division stormed through hamlets and farms, the defending detachments in the loopholed buildings being blown out and shattered by shell fire from the armoured cars and the light field batteries.

This astonishing leaping attack by the outnumbered, entrenched defenders of Ypres had the effect which Sir John French intended. The Duke of Würtemberg, conducting the German operations along the Yser against the Belgian and French forces, General von Deimling attacking Ypres, General von Fabeck co-operating with him, and Rupert, the Crown Prince of Bavaria, assailing the British troops round Lille, had a meeting. They decided that the three British divisions east of Ypres were a menace that must be met by an overpowering concentration of force.

As we have seen, our 7th Division was supposed to be four times the strength it was, and our other two divisions, with their assistant forces of entrenched cavalry, were similarly overestimated. The successful sortie towards Roulers, therefore, made Deimling anxious about his power even to retain our men. He asked for another army corps. The Fifteenth Corps of first-line troops was sent to him, and large bodies of the 150,000 Würtembergers and other corps which had been assailing the Belgian-French lines

BRITISH ENCAMPMENT IN NORTHERN FRANCE.

BRITISH LANCERS GOING INTO ACTION ACROSS AN OPEN STRETCH OF COUNTRY "SOMEWHERE IN NORTHERN FRANCE."

were moved eastward against Ypres. At the same time Sir John French motored to the headquarters of the First British Army Corps at Hooge, just east of Ypres, to examine into the conditions of the Immortal Division—the 7th.

Ever since its hasty embarkation at Ostend, and its march in aid of the Belgian Army at Antwerp, this incomplete half of the Fourth British Army Corps had fought greatly and suffered heavily. It was growing too weak to act as a separate army. So Sir John French arranged to merge it for a while in Sir Douglas Haig's corps, and place it under his command with the 3rd Cavalry Division, and Sir Henry Rawlinson returned to England to look after the mobilisation of his 8th Division.

Sir Douglas Haig then redistributed his forces. The 7th Division extended from the chateau near Zandvoorde to the Menin road; here it linked on with the 1st Division, whose trenches ran towards Reytel village, and the 2nd Division continued the British lines towards Zonnebeke. The Ninth French Corps, under General d'Urbal, held the line north of Ypres, and prolonged it towards Dixmude, where the Breton Marines were fighting. Southwards, from Ypres to the Lys, our cavalry fought and slept for weeks in ditches amid beetfields and along the canal, and by the river the Third British Army Corps stood against a host of Bavarians.

Weak spot in allied front

Ypres itself formed the weak spot in the allied front. It was one of the loveliest and most romantic cities on earth, fallen asleep in the Middle Ages in a forgotten nook in the flat, rich, marshy plain of Flanders. Its magnificent Cloth Hall, built by its proud warrior weavers in the days when the looms of Ypres were what the mills of Manchester now are, was a monument of noblest beauty and incomparable value. Its glorious thirteenth-century cathedral, its belfry, and thick cluster of picturesque, ancient houses made it one of the rare, exquisite, perfect cities of art in Europe. It was an enchanted place, with just a faint stir of life to give its beauty vividness and eternal significance.

The German Emperor had fixed upon Ypres as the historic scene of his proclamation of the complete conquest of Belgium. With Furnes, by the coast, it was the last Belgian town to escape the invaders, and as in its occupation by German troops the defeat of the British Expeditionary Force would be involved, the Kaiser Wilhelm was obsessed by the desire to conquer it. Violent, blinding passion and well-calculated policy were strangely mingled in the Imperial determination in regard to Ypres. From the strict, strategical point, of view, the breaking of the allied line at La Bassée or even farther south, was preferable, and the concentration of troops should have taken place there. For in the case of success a greater length of the northern Franco-British Belgian line would be cut and caught between the German point of advance and the seacoast.

"For the sake of Belgium"

On the other hand, the British position round Ypres was peculiarly inviting to the attackers. It formed a salient—that is to say, a wedge exposed to cross-fire from the surrounding German batteries on the north, the east, and south-east. Thus it was the weakest spot in the whole of the allied front. It was designed by the British commander to engage most of the attention of the German Chief of Staff. It jutted out perilously to both its defenders and attackers. It menaced an advance towards Bruges, shutting the Germans from the coast, and perhaps piercing their flank; it exposed the troops that held it to an assault from three sides.

By giving up Ypres, and strengthening and shortening his lines, Sir John French would have been in a stronger position of resistance. But he knew the mind of the man with whom he had chiefly to deal. He desired, as a matter of honour, to hold Ypres for the sake of Belgium, and as a matter of policy to prevent the intended proclamation of the conquest of the country of the heroic upholders of international treaties. But more than this, he flaunted Ypres in the face of the German Emperor as a bull-fighter flaunts a red flag in the face of the bull he is infuriating and distracting. Sir John French was of Irish origin. Ypres, so to speak, was the tail of his coat; he daringly trailed it close to his enemy. By leading the Germans to concentrate against him at this point he was, with subtle skill, easing the pressure against his weakened Second Army at La Bassée and against the sorely-pressed Belgian Army on the coast. Ypres, with its salient defences, was a study in the mastery of warfare. Its very weakness was so arranged as to sway the mind of the enemy, and compel him to act in a given direction.

And in this given direction the German commander acted. He selected the Menin road as his main path of assault,

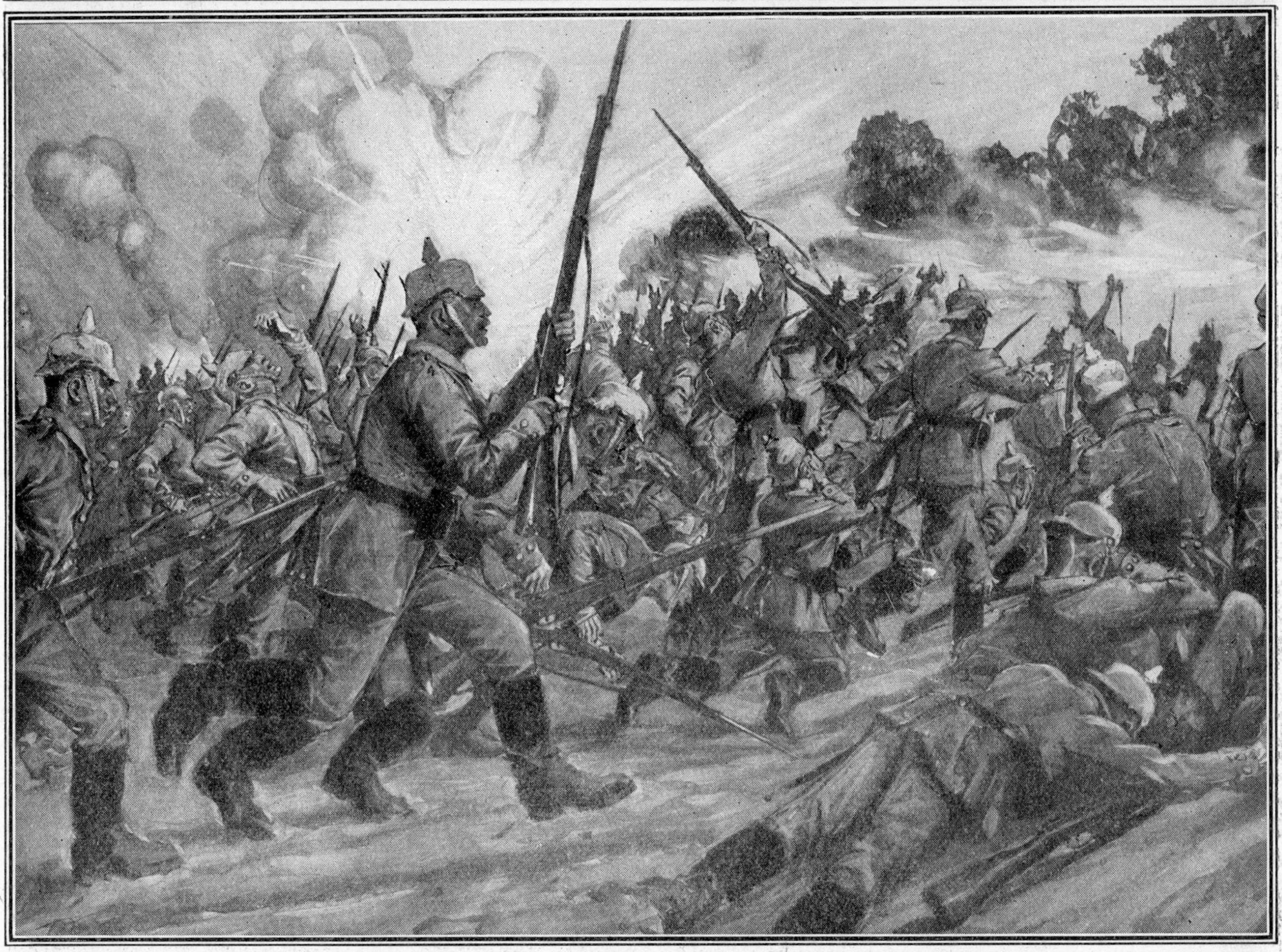

TWO ASPECTS OF THE ROUT OF THE PRUSSIAN GUARD BY THE BRITISH AT ZONNEBEKE.

The Prussian Guard were brought up in a supreme effort to break through Ypres. How the attack, prepared with great secrecy, was met is shown in the top picture. The Prussian advance, thrown into relief by an airship searchlight, was met with deadly musketry fire from the British, the first rank lying down, the next kneeling, and the men in the rear firing from a standing position. Then came a series of glorious British bayonet charges across the plain. The redoubtable Prussian Guard—to the number of about 15,000—were utterly routed, the confusion in their ranks before they broke and fled being graphically shown in our lower illustration.

and at dawn on Thursday, October 29th, the grand attack on Ypres opened. Naturally, Sir John French expected it. Even if he had not taken some part in arranging the affair, two German telegraphic messages, said to have been tapped by our operators, would have told him what was about to happen. The first ran: "Take Ypres by November 1st." The second was: "More men now, and we have them!" The second message, moreover, was well founded. It was touch-and-go at the time with the fate of Ypres and with the fortunes of the British Expeditionary Force. Happily, we touched and the Germans went—backwards!

The Twenty-fourth Army Corps from Lille, reinforced by the whole of the Fifteenth Active German Corps, swung against the British trenches east of Gheluvelt. The fighting was terrific, for instead of standing on the defensive, Sir Douglas Haig counter-attacked with all his forces. The 7th Division especially swept out of its trenches towards Kruiseik Hill, about three miles south-east of Gheluvelt. This hill had formed part of the British front, but the enemy had carried it the day before. Now the heroic 7th Division, supported by the 6th Cavalry Brigade, which was in turn assisted by covering fire from the trenches of the 7th Cavalry Brigade, came out suddenly against its host of foes.

A soldiers' battle

All the morning the battlefield was a melée of advancing and receding infantry forces, with the British field-guns pushing in as close as possible to shrapnel the charging masses of field-grey figures. For our outnumbered forces it was a soldiers' battle, in which the spirit, initiative, and skill of men and company officers chiefly counted. The slaughter they did was terrible, especially against the army corps which had come from Lille. By two o'clock that Thursday afternoon the Germans began to give ground; and when night fell Kruiseik Hill had been recaptured, with the help

ENCAMPMENT OF THE 12TH LANCERS AT KEMMEL CHATEAU.

The men of "the Supple 12th," a regimental sobriquet won by dash and resource at Salamanca, are seen above in a riverside meadow at Kemmel Chateau, south-west of Ypres. The colonel (Lieut-Colonel F. Wormald) and a number of his officers and men were specially mentioned in Sir John French's despatch of October 8th, 1914. Our smaller photograph shows an Indian hospital transport on the march.

Russell.
COLONEL GORDON WILSON,
Royal Horse Guards. (Killed.)

Lafayette.
CAPTAIN LORD RICHARD WELLESLEY,
Grenadier Guards. (Killed.)

Lafayette.
CAPTAIN CHARLES V. FOX,
2nd Scots Guards.

of the 1st Brigade who re-established most of the line north of the Menin road. It was a day of heroes, but the leader of them all was Captain Charles V. Fox, of the 2nd Scots Guards. By an extraordinary feat at Kruiseik Hill he captured two hundred German troops with five of their officers. A splendid sportsman, he was already famous as a sculler and boxer; he had won the Diamond Sculls at Henley, and had become one of the leading middle-weight boxers in the Army. He was afterwards wounded and taken prisoner in another fierce fight.

A day of heroes

The loss of Kruiseik Hill only made the German commander more desperately resolved to carry out the orders of his Emperor, and to enter Ypres by the end of the month. In the night he again concentrated his troops, selecting a new point of attack at Zandvoorde Ridge, a little to the south of Kruiseik. The ridge was held by the 7th Cavalry Brigade under a very brilliant officer, Brigadier-General Kavanagh. But the enemy got the range of the trenches exactly and massed their howitzer fire upon it at daybreak on Friday, October 30th, and the 6 in. shells completely blew in most of the earthworks. The cavalry withdrew to the next bridge towards Ypres-Klein Zillebeke. Their withdrawal exposed the right of the 7th Division, and this therefore had to bend back also towards the town. The situation then became critical, for the Germans had succeeded in making a deep dent in our lines and were able to bring their guns forward and to get wider cross-fire effects against the salient formed by our defences.

All day they continued to press the advantage they had won, but the Scots Greys and the 4th Hussars were moved up as a reserve force, and with their aid the 6th Cavalry Brigade made a grand defence and prevented the enemy from driving home his attack. In the night both sides prepared for the day of decision. The cavalry trenches on the southern flank were taken over by the Guards' Brigade, under Lord Cavan, and the 9th French Corps sent three battalions and a cavalry brigade to further strengthen the position. The Germans had almost reached the canal running from Ypres to the Lys, and forming the line of communications of our First Army Corps. The trenches at Gheluvelt, stretching towards the canal, were the very vitals of the British force, and the men there were ordered to hold the line at all costs.

Vitals of the British force

General von Deimling withdrew his battered Twenty-fourth Corps, and brought up the Fifteenth Corps, the 2nd Bavarians, and the Thirteenth Corps. To his troops he issued an order, stating that they had been entrusted with the task of breaking through the British lines to

Lafayette.
BRIG.-GENERAL KAVANAGH,
Commanding 7th Cavalry Brigade.

Elliott & Fry.
BRIG.-GENERAL EARL OF CAVAN,
Commanding the Guards' Brigade.

Elliott & Fry
BRIG.-GENERAL LANDON,
Temporary Commander 1st Division.

A GERMAN "CONSOLATION PICTURE": HEADLONG FLIGHT OF SERBS BEFORE VICTORIOUS AUSTRIANS.

The above picture, from a German paper, purports to represent the "flight" of the Serbs in November, 1914. As a matter of fact, they executed an orderly retirement into the interior before an enormously superior force of Austrians, who soon afterwards suffered an ignoble defeat.

Ypres, and that the Kaiser himself considered that on the success of their attempt depended the victorious issue of the war.

The contest began with several attacks and counter-attacks on Saturday morning along the road from Ypres to Menin. The village of Gheluvelt was situated on this road, at an almost equal distance from both towns. It was held by the 1st Division, whose trenches linked southward with the 7th Division. The Germans massed their guns and howitzers against our worn and shattered Immortal Division. Then they launched the larger part of their force of 72,000 bayonets against our 1st and 3rd Infantry Brigades, which had originally numbered only 8,000 bayonets, but were now desperately diminished by the wear of battle.

A chapter of disasters

Under the tremendous weight of the attack our line broke, and Gheluvelt was captured by the Germans. Then followed a chapter of disasters to our outworn and overpressed troops. The retreat of the 1st Division exposed the Royal Scots Fusiliers, who were holding some of the trenches of the 7th Division. The Scotsmen were cut off and surrounded, and at the same time the German commander massed one of his army corps againt the right wing of the weakened 7th Division. The German guns were brought rapidly closer to Ypres, bombarding the line of retreat of our broken and reeling forces. The headquarters of the 1st and 2nd Divisions were shelled; Major-General Lomax, directing the difficult movements of his 1st Division in its hour of peril, was wounded, and the force of the explosion rendered the General commanding the 2nd Division unconscious. Three Staff officers were killed and three wounded. The Germans had succeeded in striking down the directing minds of the troops they had defeated.

It was a complete catastrophe. Sir John French and Sir Douglas Haig watched the disaster from the village of Hooge, the next village on the Menin road after the lost position of Gheluvelt. They could see our men retiring just a mile in front of them. The British Field-Marshal had even more to think of than the scene of disaster before him. For just to the south of Ypres at Hollebeke, on the other side of the canal, General Allenby's Cavalry Corps was losing its trenches, and a heavy column of Bavarian infantry was pressing hard upon Messines. The Field-Marshal could give none of his generals any reinforcement.

General Landon, commanding the 3rd Infantry Brigade, took over the direction of the 1st Division. He moved it back, with the victorious enemy coming on against him in great strength. Then, at a wooded bend of the road, by one of those glorious resurgences of invincible spirit, the Division rallied, while an enfilading fire checked the enemy's advance along the road. The left of the 1st Division and the right of the 2nd combined and flung themselves against the right flank of the advancing German line. Admirably supported by the 42nd Brigade of Royal Field Artillery, the 2nd Worcestershire Regiment headed one of the grandest bayonet charges in our history and, in a raging hand-to-hand fight, recaptured the village of Gheluvelt. Profiting by this magnificent recovery, the left of the 7th Division also swung back almost to its original line. By half-past two on Saturday afternoon the connection between the 1st and 7th Divisions was re-established. This released the 6th Cavalry Brigade, which had been held in reserve for action on the Menin road. Two of its regiments were at once sent to clear the woods on the south-west, where strong parties of the enemy had penetrated between the 7th Division and the 2nd Brigade. The cavalrymen went to their job with a will, some of them mounted and some of them on foot. Taking the enemy by surprise, they slew large numbers of them by a movement as rapid as it was successful, and then, driving the rest of the Germans before them, they closed the last gap in our lines.

Our cavalry clear the woods

The great Battle of Gheluvelt thus ended in a general German defeat. Kaiser Wilhelm II. was unable to enter Ypres and proclaim the conquest of Belgium on the day he had appointed, and Calais receded as far into the distance as Paris had done after the Battle of the Marne. General von Deimling excused his defeat on the ground of the comparatively small number of his troops. The poor man had only three army corps against our wasted three divisions, reduced to less than 20,000 bayonets. On November 2nd he was given an additional army corps—the Twenty-seventh. So, including the Twenty-fourth Army Corps, shattered and drawn back to Lille, and the Fifteenth and Bavarian Thirteenth, and the Second, with other troops besides, General von Deimling was not so greatly outnumbered as he imagined. We have already learnt, from a captive German officer, that the trenches of our 7th Division were reckoned by the enemy to be held by two British army corps, and no doubt it was by extending this method of calculation that the German commander obtained a somewhat inaccurate idea of the troops opposed to him.

All this greatly helped our scanty, fatigued, and overladen men. The enemy began to fear them just when they were at their weakest. And for more than a week after the failure of the grand general attack on Gheluvelt the German infantry kept our forces busily employed, but without trying again to hack their way through our lines. On Monday, November 2nd, the pressure was still maintained on our trenches round Ypres, but on this day the Germans chiefly attempted to drive a wedge between that town and Armentières southward. The day before they had taken Messines and had also captured Wytschaete, some two miles farther north on the road to Ypres. Here, however, our cavalry and Territorials had been reinforced by French troops. As the Germans again advanced, the French counter-attacked on Wytschaete, which became a terrible No Man's Land, all its houses blazing to the sky, under the storm of shells from both the opposing armies.

"A terrible No Man's Land"

Even the semblance of pressure on our front at Ypres ceased from Tuesday, November 3rd. No hostile infantry were seen, the cannonade slackened, and many of our troops were able to take a much-needed rest. The heroic remnant of the 7th Division in this quieter week came out of their trenches to refit, while troops of the Second Army Corps took their place. All went well till the afternoon of November 6th, when the French force holding the line between Klein Zillebeke and the canal was driven in. The gap left our Guards' Brigade, under Lord Cavan, exposed, and the 7th Cavalry Brigade hurried up in support. General Kavanagh deployed the 1st and 2nd Life Guards north of the road, holding the Blues in reserve behind his centre. His gallant advance encouraged the French to resume the offensive, and the former movement continued until our cavalry halted by Klein Zillebeke, allowing their comrades in arms to reoccupy their trenches.

Kavanagh's gallant advance

Suddenly the French returned at the double, with the Germans pursuing them in great strength. General Kavanagh tried to stem the rush by throwing a couple of squadrons across the road, and considerable confusion occurred, ending in a melée of British, French, and Germans. To extricate itself, our Cavalry Brigade retired to the reserve trenches, and from these it protected the Guardsmen until Lord Cavan re-established his line with the assistance of the 22nd Infantry Brigade. The next day the Guards' Brigade and the Cavalry Brigade counter-attacked the Germans, and captured three machine-guns, but our men were unable to hold on to the forward line of trenches. The position they occupied, however, was strengthened by eight hundred rifles of the 3rd Cavalry Division taking

DESPERATE CHARGE BY ZOUAVES ON THE GERMAN RIGHT WING NEAR SOISSONS.
Another example of the war as seen through German eyes. The picture, representing an attack by Zouaves in the vicinity of Soissons, was drawn by Felix Schwormstadt from a sketch made on the spot by the German war artist Hugo L. Braune.

over the right section of the Guards' trenches, and providing them with a little local reserve force.

On the same day the attack was renewed along the Menin road, and at one point our line was forced back, only to be straightened out again in a few minutes. Meeting with an unkind reception in this quarter, the Germans massed in the afternoon on the south-east of Ypres, but no driving force was left in their multitudes, and the attack soon weakened. Farther to the south some four hundred of the new formations crept up under cover of a wood and advanced against the French. They came on with characteristic bravery and want of skill, to meet their usual fate—the bullet or a bayonet.

These futile attacks went on until many units in the armies of General von Deimling and General von Fabeck were shattered. All the fighting spirit was knocked out of them, and the new formations especially went to pieces. Against our men there had been brought up recruits who had only received two months' drill and who had practically no instruction in musketry, and no practice in entrenching. They knew how to die, and they died as bravely as any men could do. But they could not fight, and it was gathered from prisoners that the young men of the new corps were not withstanding the fatigue and privations of the campaign.

A GLIMPSE OF OLD-WORLD YPRES.
One of the water-gates of the city, guarding a canal entrance.
Inset: British convoy passing through one of the ruined streets.

The great German General Staff could not have had any illusion with regard to the qualities of their half-trained recruits, and it is difficult to see what sound reason they had for sacrificing them. With their astonishing bravery, the young men would have made fine and powerful troops after six months' training in trenchwork and instruction in musketry. When the bitter need for more first-rate men occurred in January and February, the new Chief of Staff and his Imperial master must have regretted they had gathered and consumed so much of the fine flower of the German youth before it was ripe for war. It is not only Belgium, Northern France, and Poland which has endured inhuman treatment at the hands of the Prussian War Staff. The whole of Germany has suffered in a more indirect but just as deadly a way.

Bravery of half-trained recruits

As a supreme effort against Ypres, General von Deimling sent to Arras for the greatest fighting force of the German Empire—the Prussian Guard. By Wednesday, November 11th, a division of the corps was railed up to Menin. It consisted of some 15,000 bayonets, many of them, no doubt, drawn from the reserves of the corps, which had been sadly broken up, first on the Marne, and then on the Suippes. The Prussian Guardsman is chosen for his great height and unusual strength, and, according to a German song, he dies but he never gives ground. The attack was prepared with great secrecy, but our men knew that something was in store for them from the furious bombardment that heralded the infantry charge. The artillery fire then directed on our trenches to the north and south of the Menin road was the fiercest and heaviest ever employed against us.

Prussian Guards' secret attack

Forewarned in this manner, Sir Douglas Haig and his divisional commanders set an ambush. As the attackers surged forward, they were not only met by our frontal fire, but were also taken in the flank by guns, Maxims, and magazine rifles, as they charged diagonally across part of our position. Terribly did they suffer; but, true to the traditions of the days of Frederick the Great, the survivors still swept onward. And such were the resolution and momentum of their mass that they broke through our front trenches in three places near the Menin road.

British lines, however, are constructed to meet just such an occasion as this. There were support trenches with enfilading fire to cross, and when the Prussian Guard went over these and penetrated into the woods behind our trenches, our Life Guards, armed with bayonets, came up against them. The Irish Guards, the London Scottish, and other regiments formed the last but one of the British lines. Through the gaps of the Irish Guards our Household Cavalry charged. Along they went, over the bodies of friend and foe, in the silent, terrible fury of battle with which the British soldier fights when he is desperate beyond thought. Having at last lost some seven hundred men in the wood, the Prussians forgot their glorious traditions and turned and fled. Again they came under the enfilading fire of our machine-guns, and

WORK OF THE GERMAN HUNS IN PICTURESQUE YPRES.

Our top left-hand picture shows the thirteenth-century cathedral of St. Martin in flames. To the right is a photograph of the famous "Halles des Drapiers" (or Cloth Hall), another thirteenth-century building, also set on fire by German shells. Inset is a small view of the Cloth Hall as it was; and below it, on the left, this once beautiful building as the flames were springing from tier to tier of its lovely facade. The two lower views show (left) the remains of the Market Hall, and (right) the interior of the cathedral after bombardment.

THE BURIAL OF THE HUN IN THE LAND HE HAD RAVAGED AND DESPOILED.
A chaplain of the Huns' army reading the burial service over a German soldier's grave in Belgium—perhaps one of the ravagers of women and children, and a torturer of civilians.

only a remnant of them succeeded in holding part of the line of captured trenches. At the same time another large body of German infantry made an attack to the south of the Menin road, as a concerted movement in the same scheme of operations. They failed entirely. For, as they massed in the woods close to our line, our guns opened upon them with such terrible effect that they clean lost heart before the action began, and did not push their assault home.

The repulse of the Prussian Guard brought to an end the first phase of General von Falkenhayn's plan of campaign in the western theatre of war. The entire occupation of Belgium, the turning movement by the coast, and the capture and conversion of Calais into a submarine base—all these designs became impossible of execution. With the Belgian Army strongly entrenched on the Yser and recruiting largely and gathering new strength; with the British force continually increasing in numbers and in artillery power; with nearly a million young Frenchmen in active training; with all these factors the Allied lines were impregnable. The Teutonic Empires, blockaded by sea, and hemmed in along a front of some fourteen hundred miles, were besieged. And as in all close siege operations a new force began to enter into the campaign—starvation.

SUNSET IN A BELGIAN CAMP.

BATTERED BUT UNBROKEN: BELGIANS EN ROUTE TO THE TRENCHES.

CHAPTER XLV.

THE BATTLES AND BOMBARDMENTS OF THE YSER.

The Fourfold Battle of Nieuport—Fighting on Land and in the Skies, on the Seas and under the Waves—General Foch Entices the Germans to Attack in Wrong Direction—Remnants of Belgian Army Turn at Bay Along the Yser—Germans Thrown Back by Unexpected Counter-Attack—The British Navy Comes to the Rescue of the Overpowered Belgian Artillery—Terrific Bombardment of German Coast Positions—Belgian Army Retires to Rest and Refit—42nd French Division and Breton Marines Keep Back Germans—How the Breton Sailors Defended Dixmude—Incessant Slaughter of the Enemy's New Formations—Germans Break Through the Belgian Centre—The Charge of the 42nd Division at Pervyse—Again at Ramscappelle the Algerians Save the Day—The Belgians Break the Sea-Dyke and Flood the Trenches—Disastrous End of the Würtemberg Brigade—The Marvellous Charge of the French Cooks at Zillebeke.

OF all the battles in the Great War the struggle for the Yser was one of the fiercest and singular in its strangeness. It was a land battle fought by destroyers against submarines, by seaplanes against batteries of siege-howitzers, by battleships against infantry. Hosts of men clashed on the land and in the skies, on the sea and under the waves. They dug themselves in the earth like moles; they wheeled and clanged in the heavens like eagles; they fought in the sea depths like the shark and the thresher-whale. And victory remained apparently doubtful until a Belgian engineer brought a new ally to the help of his heroic, outnumbered comrades-in-arms, and by opening the dykes let in the North Sea and, flooding the fields of Western Flanders, drowned the advancing Germans under the eyes of their Kaiser.

The most extraordinary thing about this series of extraordinary battles was its futility. Merely to undertake it was a catastrophe of the gravest kind. For the attempt signified that the German Military Staff had lost its balance, and was striking blindly. The correct road for a German advance on Calais was from Armentières and La Bassée. Such an advance, as we have seen, was essayed by the Germans a full week before they tried also the roundabout attack along the River Yser from Nieuport to Dixmude. But the two divergent aims entailed a disastrous division of all the available forces. Neither, therefore, was achieved, though the Germans were in overwhelming numbers. Never did General Joffre show such subtlety and deadly skill as in this affair. Perhaps, however, we should attribute the fine strategy of the Allies to General Foch, to whom his chief entrusted the task of co-ordinating all the movements of the Belgian, French, and British armies on the north-west section of the battle-front. At the beginning of the war General Foch commanded only an army corps on the Lorraine border. There he fought with such skill that the chief French army in the Battle of the Marne was put under his control. With this same army he afterwards broke the German counter-offensive east of Rheims, and became eminent as one of the greatest of French strategists of the neo-Napoleonic school. His way of fighting was terrible for his troops. For he asked them continually to do what Napoleon's veterans had done only after ten years of campaigning experience. He asked them always to be ready to hold, and even to force back, from three to four or even five times their number of enemies. Lannes' divisions had done this several times for Napoleon, after that great captain changed his manner of strategy in 1805. But Foch went further than Napoleon. For he required the modern conscript soldier, with barely more than two months' actual experience of war, to stand firmly and continually against overwhelming numbers.

GERMAN MARINES GUARDING THE APPROACH TO OSTEND.
Special preparations for the struggle for the mastery of the coast were secretly made by the Germans at Ostend; and the bridge on the road from Bruges was jealously guarded, so that no civilians should pass that way.

Yet the Belgians and the French did it. There were scarcely more than 40,000 effectives left of the original Belgian field army, when it gathered amid the fenland and dunes round the little town of Furnes, in the last nook of unconquered Belgian territory. For two months and a half the Belgians had been fighting against odds at Liège, Namur, Louvain, Haelen, Aerschot, Malines, Termonde, and Antwerp. In some of these heroic struggles they had faced the full might of the greatest military State on earth. So it was only the shattered remnant of the small army which drew up behind the Yser after the retreat from Antwerp. To add to their difficulties, the Belgian troops were short of munitions. Near at hand to help them were only 7,000 Breton Marines, under Admiral Ronarc'h, splendid fighters all, but without artillery. Then between Dixmude and Ypres were some French Territorial troops, who also lacked guns. Thus, while the British troops from Ypres to La Bassée were more than holding their own, and were, in fact, driving back the Germans twenty miles north, the flank of the allied position coastward was extremely weak.

And so General Foch allowed it to remain for some time. The only reinforcement he first sent up was the 24th French Division under General Grosetti. In all there may have been 59,000 Belgian and French troops, with deficient artillery power, left to fight against some 150,000 well-equipped German troops, under Duke Albrecht of Würtemberg. And General Foch was quite content that it should be so. He wanted to appear weak along the flat, dyked, difficult marshland through which the canalised Yser wound to the sea. It was a bait he held out to distract and

A BELOVED FIGURE.
King Albert leaving his headquarters in Flanders.

CAMERA-PICTURES OF BELGIUM'S HERO KING.
The King of the Belgians saluting the colours of the French 7th Regiment at Furnes, to the music of the German guns a few miles away. Inset: His Majesty chatting with an officer of the French General Staff.

divide the leaders of the German Army, who were bringing up some three-quarters of a million men with the intention of capturing Calais and turning the allied front. For the situation at Nieuport was fully under the control of General Foch, right from the beginning of the struggle on October 16th. He had only to order the dykes to be broken and the sluices raised, and the water in the low-lying fens round the Yser would form an impassable barrier to the enemy. But the general did not give such an order until the very last minute. For its execution would have released a mighty German force of men and guns for action in the right direction against the army of Sir John French or the army of General Maud'huy.

It was known that the Germans were convinced of the absolute impotence of the remains of the Belgian Army. The Belgians were supposed by the enemy to be broken in spirit, utterly demoralised, and reduced to a fleeing mob, lacking in munitions of war. It was on this idea that General Foch played. By a great exertion he could, perhaps, have thrown a large French force along the Yser. This, however, would only have frightened the enemy off; and if the allied line had been broken farther to the east, the troops along the Yser would have had to retire hastily, without a fight, to avoid being enveloped. To induce the Germans to expend their energies in the wrong place, the battered but unbroken little Belgian Army was placed in the trenches.

Everything conspired to the success of the French strategist's subtle and daring plan. The Germans were deeply disturbed over the escape of the Belgian Army from Antwerp. They urgently needed a victory in the field, not only to hearten their civil population, but to strike the imagination of certain arming neutral nations, such as Rumania. The complete and overwhelming destruction of the Belgian Army would, it was hoped, make the Rumanians pause, and facilitate the progress of the Teutonic cause in the Balkans when Turkey entered into the Great War. Then there was a domestic problem with a large bearing upon post-bellum German politics. The Kaiser had lost much of his popularity owing to his crude and unskilful foreign policy before the outbreak of hostilities. His people contrasted the condition of things in the days of Bismarck with the situation of affairs after the long reign of their brilliant but unstable Emperor.

The rift in the German lute

Even beneath the gag of the censorship murmurs could be heard from the working class, the middle class, and the commercial and industrial directing circles. The only justification for the privileges of the old aristocracy was continued success in the leadership of the war. And with a view to strengthening the claim to supremacy of the noble families and landed gentry who officered the Army, the scions of royal houses were made the nominal commanders of some of the principal hosts. Neither the Crown Prince of Germany nor the Crown Prince of Bavaria, however, had won much distinction in

STIRRING SCENES IN OLD-WORLD FURNES.

A fine camera record of a notable scene in the Market Square at Furnes, where King Albert reviewed the French troops and decorated the colours of the 7th Regiment with the Order of Leopold. Here, too, King Albert and General Joffre publicly thanked the Algerian troops who saved the day at Ramscappelle. **Inset:** A company of Belgian cavalry passing through Furnes on its way to meet the oncoming foe.

HOW THE GERMANS, PROVIDED WITH PLANKS, ADVANCED UNDER FIRE TO CROSS THE CANALS IN THE YSER DISTRICT.

German troops fighting in the Yser district were provided with planks, which served the double purpose of shields and bridges over the narrow waterways. When the front ranks of the invaders had succeeded in placing these temporary bridges in position, the ranks behind advanced in massed formation, to be met by a withering machine-gun and rifle fire which caused appalling slaughter.

France, though assisted by the most able Chiefs of Staff available. The plebeian General von Kluck and the obscure, retired General von Hindenburg had become, in turn, the popular favourites with both the people and the soldiers.

But by a stroke of luck the heir-presumptive to the Kingdom of Würtemberg, Duke Albrecht Maria Alexander, found himself at the head of five army corps in Western Flanders, with only the remnant of the Belgian Army barring his way for a sweep along the coast to Calais. He was offered a facile victory that would greatly help to restore the credit of the royal houses of Germany and their modernised feudal system of militaristic government. The German Emperor in person was close at hand to overlook the plan of operations of his new Chief of Staff. The upshot was that things worked out as General Foch desired them to do. In fact, the presence of the Duke of Würtemberg and the Kaiser caused a larger force to be abstracted from the main armies of attack and directed on the side issue along the coast. For, naturally, the royal prince had to be provided with a superabundance of men, to make absolutely sure of his much-desired success.

Duke Albrecht's hopeful outlook

CABBAGES AS COVER.
British trench dug just behind a row of cabbages. The German trenches were one hundred and eighty yards in front.

ON THE LOOK-OUT FOR A PRUSSIAN SNIPER.
Another view behind the shelter of the cabbage-patch. British sharpshooters on the look-out for a Prussian sniper who had been causing trouble. Some of the enemy snipers dressed themselves in khaki.

The operation opened on Friday, October 16th, when two German army corps advanced upon the Yser. It was a reconnaissance in force, undertaken with a view to ascertaining how the canalised river was defended. The Belgian Army was found to be holding not only the river but the villages north of it, such as Lombartzyde, Mannekensvere, and Keyem, while French Marines, with only machine-guns, occupied Dixmude. Thereupon, the Germans brought up their guns and bombarded all the allied line. The next day strong infantry forces were launched against all the outlying villages. Overwhelmed by numbers and lacking ammunition for their field-guns, the 1st Belgian Division was driven out of Mannekensvere, and the 4th Division was forced out of Keyem. They both retired across the Yser. But in the night the dauntless 4th Division returned over the river, and by a furious bayonet attack in the darkness recaptured all its positions at Keyem.

This was a sad surprise for the Duke of Würtemberg. Expecting only the task of keeping the Belgian Army moving before his guns and infantry columns, he had made no preparations against the counter-attack. But a considerable number of the men who had first fought the German army at Liège had survived to meet their foes on the last line of Belgian defence. Dirty, unshaven, tattered, beggarly figures they looked after ten weeks of campaigning and trenchwork. But the fire, skill, and stubbornness with which they battled disconcerted the plan of the German commander. He had to call for more troops in order to drive home his attack. He resumed his forward movement with increased vigour on Monday, October 19th, but unhappily he selected the coast village of Lombartzyde, a couple of miles north of Nieuport, as his objective. Only a single Belgian division—the 2nd—held the village, and the duke concentrated his troops against them with a view to hacking his way down the coast to Dunkirk, and so turning all the allied line. Backed by their light and heavy field-guns, the German infantry came on in dense masses. Three times the Belgians had to give ground under the terrible shell and shrapnel fire, but when the bombardment ceased they fought the German troops back with bullet and bayonet.

A bolt from the blue

Then suddenly the tables were turned. The undergunned Belgian Army, rapidly running short of artillery

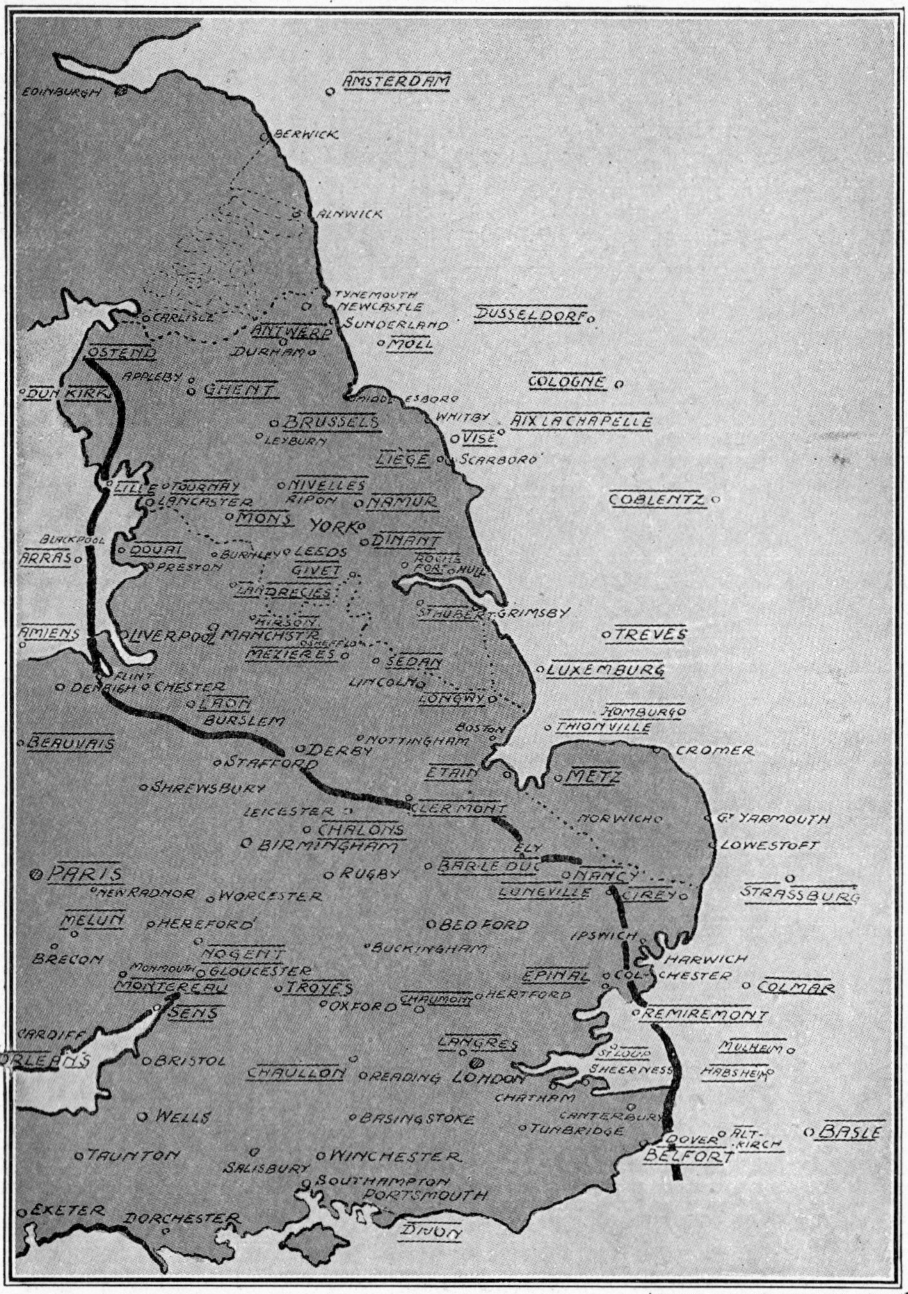

THE LONG-DRAWN BATTLE-LINE IN FRANCE.

The line from Ostend to Belfort coincided with the distance between Dover and Carlisle; and its extent will be the more easily understood by a study of the above drawing. The black line in the smaller map indicates approximately the German positions in Flanders in the closing days of October, 1914.

supplies, unexpectedly won a great advantage over their enemies. Three grey strange things drove in from the open sea towards the shore. An observation balloon went up with wireless apparatus, a protecting flotilla of destroyers spread out towards the river, and a squadron of aeroplanes swept high above the German gun sites. Then came six claps of thunder from the sea, and half a dozen

British Navy to the rescue

6 in. shells exploded with deadly marksmanship amid the German batteries. In a second, as the 4·7 in. stern guns came into play, there was another broken roar from the sea, and six 4·7 in. shells came screaming over Middelkerke, and crashed down among the German cannon.

The British Navy had come to the help of the Belgian Army with a strange type of warship. At the outbreak of the war, Messrs. Vickers had just completed three river warships for a foreign country through which a great river ran—Brazil. The ships were flat-bottomed, with a draught of only 4½ feet, but they carried armoured turrets, with two 6 in. guns forward, and two 4·7 in. howitzers aft. Our Admiralty saw at once how admirably designed these monitors were for service as off-shore batteries in land operations. As the battle-front extended nearer to the coast, the monitors—renamed Severn, Humber, and Mersey—anchored at Dover, under the command of Admiral Hood, stripped and ready for action. On Sunday, October 18th, came the call for help from the allied commanders in Flanders. On Sunday night the monitors were steaming, lights out, along the Belgian coast, and their young gunnery lieutenants were watching the Germans digging coast trenches by flare-light and measuring the ranges. Detachments of our sailors with machine-guns landed from the monitors to assist in the defence of Nieuport, but it was mainly the naval guns that saved the situation.

When first their great shells fell on the batteries and heavy guns of the Germans, and began to relieve the artillery pressure on the 2nd Belgian Division, the Germans tried to beat our monitors off by bringing up their 6 in. howitzers, and placing them in concealed positions among the dunes. Vickers, of Barrow, however, are very good gun-makers, and the products of Krupp's factory, though of equal calibre, lacked both the range and the penetrative power of the English gun. Our ships steamed

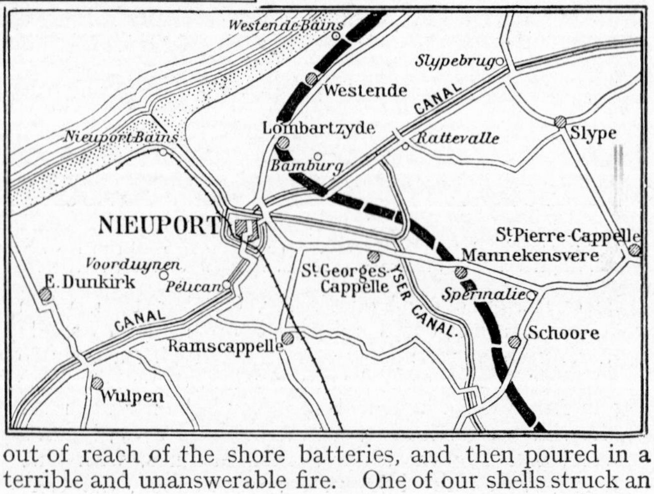

out of reach of the shore batteries, and then poured in a terrible and unanswerable fire. One of our shells struck an ammunition waggon, and caused an explosion which for the time sadly diminished the German rate of fire. On one day, it is said, six of their batteries were put out of action and 1,600 Germans killed.

At the urgent request of the Duke of Würtemberg,

the submarine flotilla at Emden speeded south, with a store of torpedoes, and attacked the monitors. Usually, however, a torpedo strikes at a depth of about twelve feet under the water. As the monitors had a draught of only 4½ feet, the great deadly missiles passed harmlessly beneath their flat bottoms.

Moreover, the presence of German submarines merely added to the difficulties of the enemy's coast army, by bringing a strong force of British destroyers to the scene of action. And when the destroyers were not engaged in chasing submarines, their 4 in. guns helped in the bombardment of the German batteries and trenches.

The whole naval operation was that deadliest kind of attack—a flank attack. The Germans had brought their guns up against the Belgian lines, and sited them with a view to getting a wide traverse of fire on the Belgian positions. In many cases the hard, firm, close coast road running from Ostend to Nieuport had been chosen for gun positions in preference to the dyked and marshy fenland. Then, on a sudden, the devastating and overwhelming bombardment

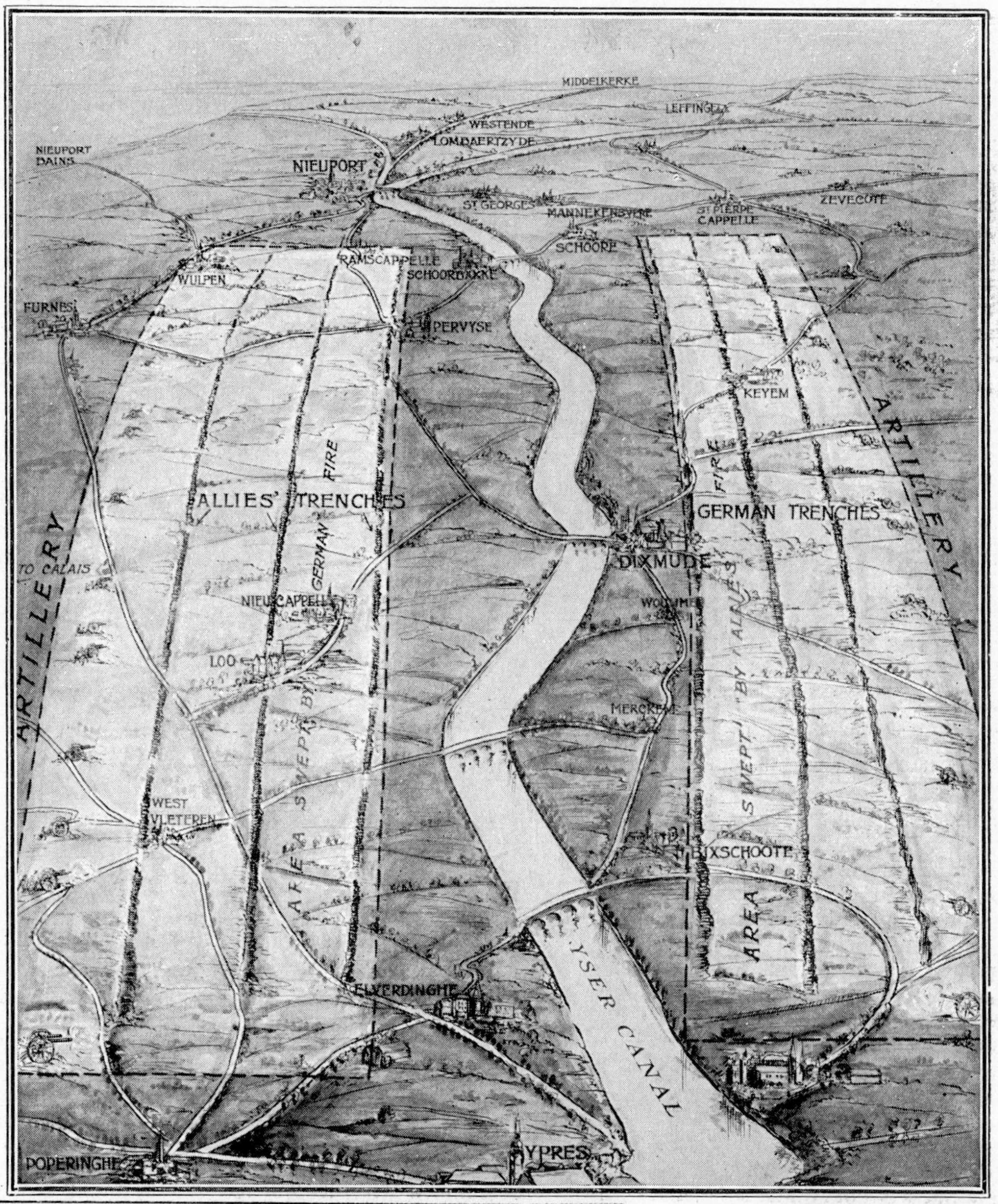

THE DEADLOCK ALONG THE YSER.

By the middle of November, 1914, the Germans and the Allies had dug themselves in and set up an artillery fire, the intensity of which precluded any advance on either side except at terrible cost.

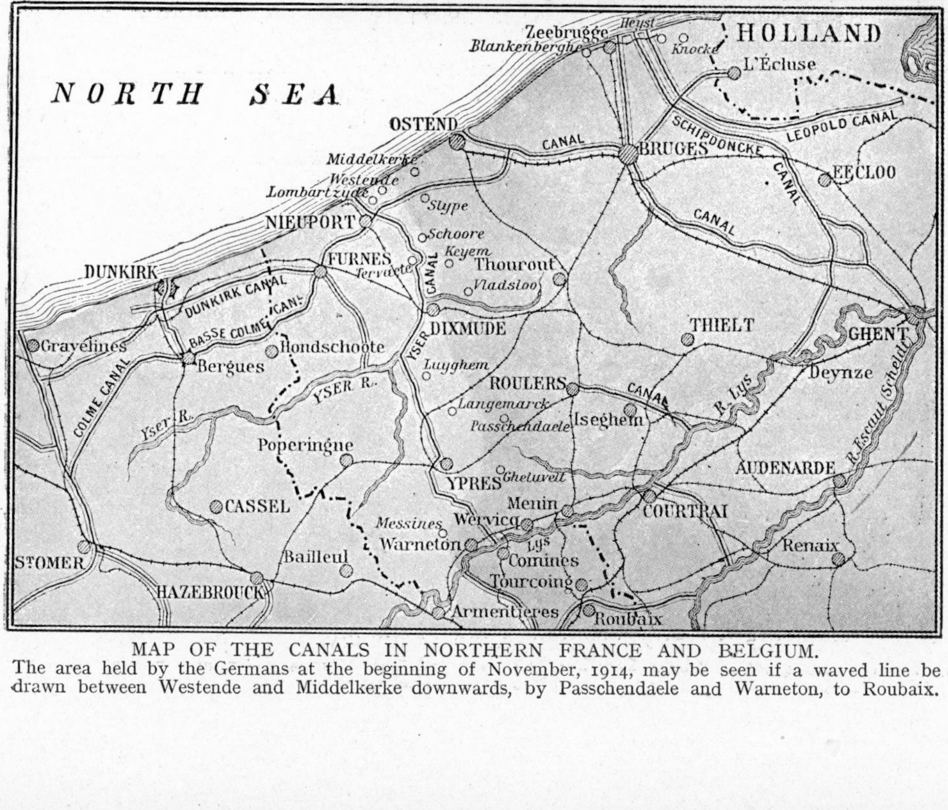

MAP OF THE CANALS IN NORTHERN FRANCE AND BELGIUM.

The area held by the Germans at the beginning of November, 1914, may be seen if a waved line be drawn between Westende and Middelkerke downwards, by Passchendaele and Warneton, to Roubaix.

of 6 in. and 4 in. British shells struck the German gunners when they thought they were at the point of winning a victory. It was the first time in German history that military operations had been interrupted by sea-power, and it took the German commander clean by surprise. He was jerked out of his orbit of action in somewhat the same way as Napoleon the First had suddenly been brought up at Acre by British sea-power, when he was marching through Syria intent upon the conquest of the Orient.

Not until the war is over shall we know what our first modern essay in amphibious warfare

WITH THE GERMAN GUNNERS IN FLANDERS.

German field-pieces being brought up through heavy country to fortify the enemy's right wing in Belgium. Inset: Lieutenant von Bismarck, as ordnance officer, reading a despatch in Flanders.

The only reply they could make was to haul up their new long-range cannon and their heaviest siege-howitzers, and to place them amid the dunes. By this means they managed to make matters, for a day or two, a little more exciting for our monitors and destroyers and for the French destroyers that joined in the coast battle. The position of affairs then was that the German howitzer batteries were in the same fix as the forts of Liège, Namur, Maubeuge, and Antwerp, over which they had so easily triumphed. They formed a fixed mark, discernible by our aerial scouts and by our observation officers in tethered balloons. Our ships, on the other hand, continually changed their position with the speed of an ordinary railway train. They zigzagged about the sea at high mobility, and only by the most extraordinary luck could a hostile battery straddle them with a salvo of shells. And all this was only the beginning of the naval element in the great land battle for Calais. For on October 27th, when the Germans had diminished their artillery power at other critical parts of the lines of trench warfare, in order to concentrate their heaviest ordnance along the shore, their 11 in. and 12 in. howitzers were mastered by a new naval unit. H.M.S. Venerable, with a broadside of four 12 in. guns, and an additional armament of twelve 6 in. quick-firers, came into action. The great naval guns reached farther inland, and places at which Germans had gathered to escape the fire of the monitors were blown up and wrecked by the terrible 850 lb. shells.

German batteries in a fix

cost Germany. The mere expense in war material involved in the subsequent fortification of the seaport of Bruges must have seriously diminished German artillery power on the actual battlefield. And the large number of men mobilised in trenches on the coast, as a protection against the possible landing of a British raiding force, was another item of loss. Our ships shelled Zeebrugge, attacked Ostend, drove the Germans out of Middelkerke, and with long-range fire swept the country for six miles inland. The only effective means of defence was to attack our monitors and destroyers with light and armoured cruisers. But if the Germans had sent a squadron down to the Belgian coast it would have been cut off by a part of our Grand Fleet.

The fleet dominated all the coast as far as the inland village of Slype. Ramscappelle, over four miles from the coast, remained at last the only point which the

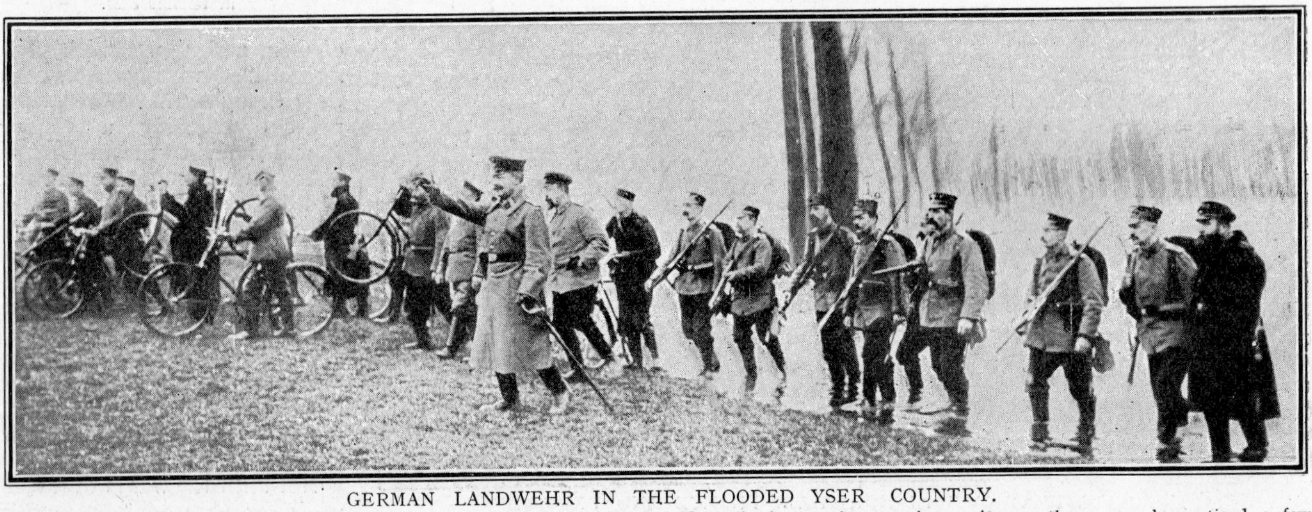

GERMAN LANDWEHR IN THE FLOODED YSER COUNTRY.

Company of a Landwehr regiment making its way through the flooded Yser district to the trenches. Among them may be noticed a few regulars, drafted doubtless to give the necessary stiffening to partly-trained men.

A STRIKING CONTRAST IN PARADES.

Above is a remarkable photograph of an unopposed crossing of one of the Belgian canals by the army of invasion. The lock-gates had been closed, and there was no apparent cause for Teuton anxiety, but the inhabitants looked less concerned than some of the soldiers. The men in the smaller photograph seem to have been purposely drawn up for the convenience of the photographer, who describes his picture: "Church Parade of German Troops in a Belgian Town."

Germans could attack without coming under the fire of our fleet. And, as a matter of fact, even this village was not secure. For the range of our big naval guns was somewhat over eight or ten miles, and at flood-tide even a battleship could get closer to the shore than usual.

On land, the artillery on both sides fought at a disadvantage. The gunners had many difficulties to contend with. There was no good siting in the flat fenland, and the banks of the dykes and the lines of willows and osiers intersecting the country made it as impenetrable to the eye as if it were close-wooded. It was generally impossible to see more than half a mile ahead, and thus very difficult to discover where the enemy was, and what effect was being produced upon him. Then the autumnal haze that spread over the marshes very frequently during the long battle rendered aerial observation very uncertain. The gunners, therefore, had to rely very largely on their infantry in the firing-line and to fight their guns at short ranges. On the whole, this diminution of the power of the artillery was a great benefit to the Belgians. For though, on their left flank, the friendly naval guns more than redressed the balance, yet on their centre and right wing tremendous pressure was exerted against them by the German army. On Monday, October 19th, the village of Beerst, just north of Dixmude, was shattered by a terrific bombardment of German shells, and the 4th Belgian Division, entrenched among the ruins, was driven out by a violent and steady massed attack of the hostile infantry.

Fighting in the flat fenland

The neighbouring village of Keyem, which the 4th Division had recovered by a splendid bayonet charge, was also assailed, and many of the Belgian troops were in danger of being cut off. But the Belgian bayonet again won all that the heavy German field-howitzers had partly conquered. When night fell, and the mist thickened, the brave Belgian Division crept northward out of Dixmude with some thousands of the tall, tanned Breton fishermen, forming the French Marine Division. There was not much shooting, but with the silent steel the Belgians and Frenchmen thrust their way into Vladsloo, and got again into

IN AMBUSH AMONGST THE TOMBS.
German artillery officers testing a machine-gun mounted in a concealed position in a burial-ground at Dixmude. The man at the gun is sitting on the slab of a tomb.

Beerst. But as it was discovered that fresh strong columns of the enemy were pouring out from Roulers and striking westward, the defending force retired on the Yser, evacuating all the villages up to Keyem.

It was on this day that Sir John French threw his First Army Corps north of Ypres, and began his astonishing advance against the German forces between Roulers and Thourout. It was a fine, friendly, self-sacrificing plan, undertaken with a view to distract the German attention from the Yser. The idea was to keep the Germans vacillating between the weak Belgian-French defences on the river and the feeble-looking British salient at Ypres. As a result of the British movement, the new German reinforcements did not come into action against the Belgian front on October 20th. The Germans merely kept up a furious cannonade upon the Belgian line which lasted all night and continued the next day. On the coast a farm was taken from the 2nd Division, then recovered by the Belgians, and again lost. But this only brought the fire of our naval guns on the captured farm, wrecking it completely, and killing and wounding most of the troops which held it. At night the misty plain had a strange and terrible picturesqueness. Far through the light sea-mist shone the glow of the burning villages; tongues of fire came from warships and land batteries, and the incessant and widespread rain of bursting shells, flowering out upon a nocturnal sky dimly lighted by the conflagrant villages, made the horrible scene of destruction look like an enormous display of fireworks.

French's self-sacrificing plan

In this strangely-lighted darkness the German infantry concentrated an attack upon Dixmude. They had been thrown back from the same place in the daytime, but, increased in numbers, they crept up again in the gloom, only to be again shattered by rifle and machine-gun fire, followed by the inevitable bayonet charge. Though routed, they re-formed

RUINED CHURCH OF ST. JEAN AT DIXMUDE.
In their bombardment of Dixmude the fine old Church of St. Jean was reduced to ruins by the German gunners.

MOTOR-'BUS TRANSPORT FOR THE ALLIED TROOPS IN FLANDERS.
Troops were conveyed to both Ypres and Dixmude by motor-'buses which used to be on service in the streets of Paris.

MEN WHO FACED THE FULL MIGHT OF THE GREATEST MILITARY STATE ON EARTH.

Glimpses of the heroic Belgian Army after the fall of Antwerp. The top photograph shows a trainload of the men who attempted against overwhelming odds to defend Antwerp from the ruthless invader on their way to another battle area in the west. The lower view is of the landing at Zeebrugge of soldiers who had been through the fierce fighting at Namur. Inset: The Belgian General Dossin in consultation at Nieuport.

with the reinforcements continually pouring in from Thourout, and in the grey misty dawn they made a third attack in massed enveloping multitudes. But the weary and half-shattered Belgian 4th Division and the Breton Marines beat them back yet again with terrible slaughter.

Intellectual elite of Germany

But after these three quick smashing blows the German force still held together. Its reinforcements were largely composed of young Berlin recruits, officered by the intellectual élite of Germany—pale, spectacled, earnest faces, glowing with high spiritual courage. Though little trained in war, these university men rose to a height of dauntlessness exceeding the great traditions of the fighting scholars of Prussia in the War of Liberation. They went on till they dropped, and until they were brought down they kept all their men going, too. In the afternoon of October 21st they advanced for the fourth time against the Belgian-Breton force entrenched around Dixmude. But all their heroic steadfastness in attack was vain. They knew how to die gloriously, the new scholar-soldiers of Germany, but contempt of death could not prevail against the deadly skill of the experienced and revengeful Walloons, Flemings, and Bretons. When a Belgian trench wavered, sick of the slaughter of the masses in front of it, a shout would ring out over the rattle of the machine-guns and the racket of the rifle fire: "Remember Louvain!" Then all down the Belgian line the battle-cry would be taken up: "Remember Louvain! Termonde and Louvain!"

With that, the flame of vengeance burnt up again fiercely in the hearts of the Belgians. Their feeling of pity for the men whom they had at their mercy fell from them. They remembered how the German had massacred peaceful townspeople and villagers in the day of his triumph and power. And they bent again to their work of slaughter. Each clip of cartridges went so swiftly into the magazine, and the bullets streamed out with such rapidity against the large targets, that it seemed at times to the Germans as though every Belgian was working a machine-gun against them. As a matter of fact, the Belgians seem to have owed a considerable part of their power to resist the German massed attacks to a new instrument of battle. It was a small, light, and very handy machine-gun of American invention, with a simple air-cooling device that did away with the use of the cumbersome water-jacket. It had been offered to the British Government, but refused by them; the German Government had also rejected it; and when the war broke out, the defenders of Liège, thanks to the enterprise of their military authorities, were the only troops possessing the new gun. In the artillery battles it lost some of its importance, as the German field-batteries in overpowering numbers dominated the field. But in the mists, marshes, and the low-lying polders round the Yser the new machine-gun, in the hands of men with six weeks' experience in its use, had as deadly an importance as it had at Liège.

After their fourth defeat at Dixmude the Germans left in peace for a while this beautiful old Flemish town which their guns had battered into ruin, and concentrated for a new effort on the centre of the Belgian line. Halfway between Nieuport and Dixmude the Yser bulges northward, forming a salient loop between the village of Schoorbakke and the village of Tervaete. The Belgian trenches, following the loop of the river, constituted a sort of bastion of earthworks that could be shelled from three sides by the hostile batteries. And while getting this cross-fire effect for their guns, the Germans could bring up on the outer radius of the loop a wider front of attacking infantry than the Belgians possessed in their narrower space. It was not a question simply of the density of the attacking force, but of their wider front, and of their consequent heavier fire-power. The Belgian position formed what is known as a salient, and the breadth of it was so small that all the German guns surrounding it on three sides could reach any section of it. It was thus the weak point in the Belgian line, and it does not say much for the generalship of the Duke of Würtemberg and his staff that they should only have discovered the natural and inevitable weakness of this point in the defending line after four days and nights of continual battle. Only when the Germans had been continually repulsed at the seashore and at Dixmude did they concentrate in full force against the indefensible Belgian centre.

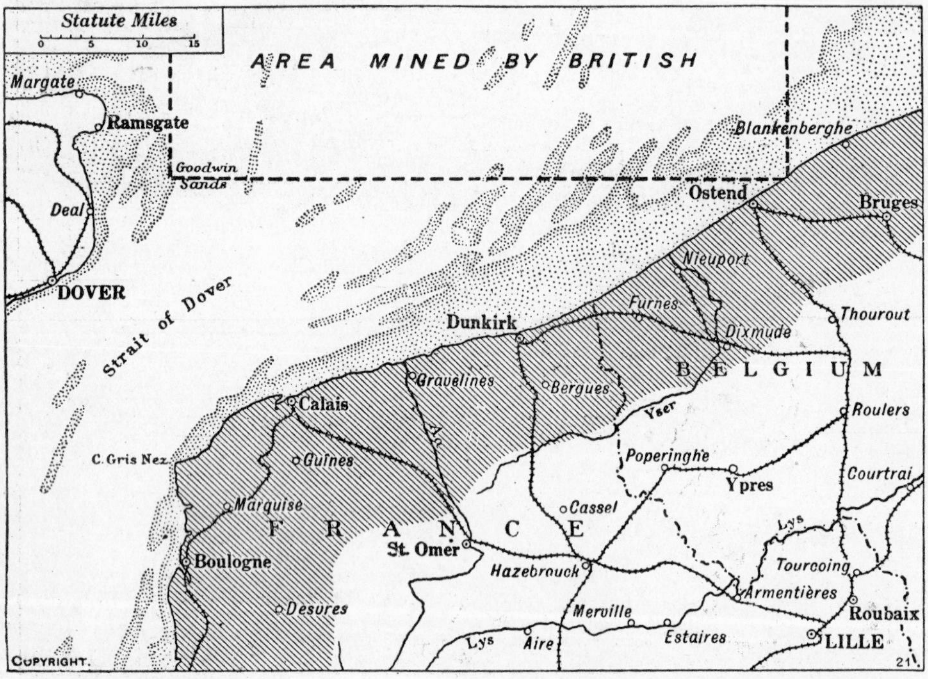

George Philip & Son.

MAP OF THE AREA COVERED BY THE BOMBARDMENT OF THE BELGIAN COAST.
The shallow waters and sandbanks preventing close access to the Belgian coast-line by vessels of heavy draught are shown by dots. The ruling on the land indicates approximately the zone within range of the biggest British naval guns from battleships lying outside the shallow water barrier.

Importance of Pervyse

From the beginning the Belgians knew they could not defend it, and prepared a new line. This lay some two miles in the rear, by the railway from Nieuport to Dixmude, and the cobbled, tree-lined highway running between the two towns, with the red roofs of Pervyse rising at the cross-roads. Pervyse was the centre of the Belgian operations, for through it a cross-road led to Furnes, the last town in Flanders. Furnes was only five miles from Pervyse, so the loss of this latter little town would involve the complete conquest of Belgian territory by the invaders. For even though the British held on to Ypres, which would have been doubtful if Furnes had fallen, the Germans would have been able to claim that they had driven the Belgian Army out of Belgium.

For this reason the Belgian troops held their weak salient on the river loop as long as possible. The Germans attacked them there in the afternoon of Wednesday, October 21st. They drove in on the left at Schoorbakke, where there was a bridge across the canalised stream.

SANGUINARY ENCOUNTER ON THE YSER BY THE VILLAGE OF RAMSCAPPELLE.

The Belgians had firmly entrenched themselves on one bank of the Yser. They had strengthened their position with doors and shutters from the houses in the adjacent village. The Germans had thrown up hasty field-works on the other side of the canal, which it was their object to cross. One bridge made by them was destroyed by the brave defenders. This was in the night time. In the small hours of the following morning the enemy succeeded in throwing another pontoon bridge over the water. It was then the fierce hand-to-hand encounter depicted above took place.

"ONE TOUCH OF NATURE": KING WINTER STRIKES BOTH FRIEND AND FOE.

Winter came suddenly in Flanders in November, 1914. Snow fell heavily and froze hard on the ground. The men in the firing-line no longer suffered the misery of living up to their necks in mud and slush. But the alternative was even more deadly, especially at night, in the open trenches. Many men became so stiff that they had to be lifted out on relief, and some had to be admitted to hospital with frost-bite. Our artist has chosen for illustration the conditions under which a number of German prisoners taken by the British were escorted to the base.

THE "HUMAN INTEREST" SIDE OF THE WAR: SIDELIG

A series of photographic impressions taken at

A SHELL THAT KNOCKED OUT SIX MEN.
The Zouave who is seen in the foreground of the above photograph is standing in a hole that had been made by a shell which knocked out six men who were by the wall against which another Zouave has taken up a position. The effects of the gun fire in the Great War were unprecedented.

THE MAKING OF A SPECIAL BOMB-PROOF.
The bomb-proof trench, the beginning of which is shown in this photograph, was made not far away from the guns, and intended for use during any specially severe bombardment by the enemy.

"A DAY OFF" WITH BRITISH GUNNERS IN BELGIUM.
Some men of the Royal Field Artillery taking advantage of a day "in reserve" on Zillebeke Lake. Though the incident illustrated took place in the middle of October, the weather was so beautiful that several of the men enjoyed the luxury of a bathe.

A GAME OF
Two of the officers in the above photog
home. Meanwhile, for a br

LONDON HO
Zouaves being instructed in the mechan
ment spoke English perfectly. He had
where he had been

TESTING TH
Ten seconds after the gun has been fire
with our observation scouts, calls out w
this case the messa

'HE EVERYDAY LIFE OF OUR SOLDIERS AT THE FRONT.

n officer with the British Expeditionary Force.

'IRING-LINE.
ne of chess. Another is writing a letter
e background is silent.

A GOOD BILLET FOR THE GUN TEAMS.
The scene is "somewhere in France." It represents a convenient farmyard at the foot of a rocky eminence, on which the battery had fixed up its guns. Pending a move to another vantage point, the horses were snugly billeted in the shelter afforded below.

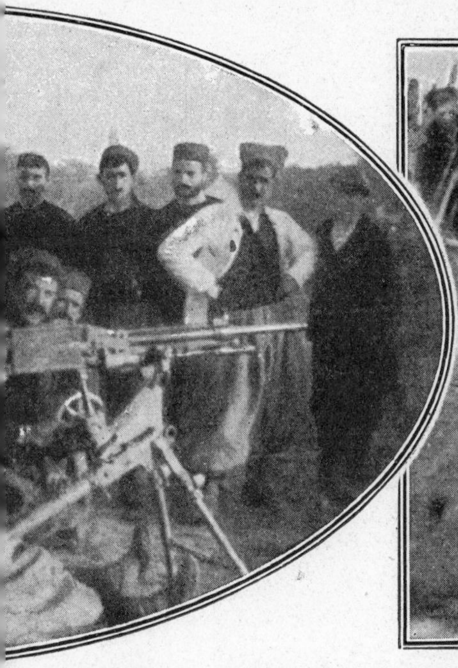

NERY EXPERT.
The sergeant in charge of this detach-
oin the colours from a hotel in London,
' a chef de cuisine.

ANOTHER VIEW OF THE BOMB-PROOF.
When the earth was taken out, roofing material was commandeered and placed over the dug-out, earth being replaced to the required depth. Dug-outs of this description afforded protection for about fifteen men.

IE GUN FIRE.
s ear to the wireless apparatus in touch
ort or over, to the left or the right. In
m our aerial scouts.

BEETROOTS AS A PROTECTIVE COVERING.
Though apparently a quite rough-and-ready affair, the "splinter-roof" shown above is complete. The seemingly rickety roof is covered with beetroots. The structure would keep out any splinters of shells, and afford safe protection from anything except a direct hit.

FRENCH TROOPS ADVANCING IN A SNOWSTORM THROUGH THE FLOODED DITCHES AND BARE WOODS OF SOUTHERN BELGIUM.

In this singularly moving and graphic picture, sent from the South Belgian battlefield in November, 1914, M. Paul Thiriat has portrayed with masterly pencil the severe conditions under which the French troops on the Allies' left wing were at that time operating. The country shown is an all but monotonous fenland, open to the horizon on the one hand and to purple or dull woods on the other, scarred with flooded dykes and gaunt, leafless willows and osiers, with here and there a brick-built village or farmhouse or a ruined mill. It was generally impossible to see half-a-mile ahead, and thus very difficult to discover where the enemy was. Altogether a picture to excite the deepest sympathy with the brave men who are playing so noble a part in the fight for freedom from German tyranny.

But the bridge was blown up, and no German who had crossed the Yser at this point returned alive. In the night many additional hostile batteries were hauled towards the loop, over which the enemy's guns of all calibres played with terrible rapidity for many hours. Had the Belgians possessed long-range, heavy guns, the continual spurts of flame from the German lines would have enabled them to mark down the enemy's gun positions, and then bring a concentrated fire in turn upon each German battery. Unhappily, the defenders had only a few light field-guns, and the limbers were nearly empty. For the ammunition had been needed in rearguard actions in the long retreat from Antwerp, and the five days' battle along the Yser had exhausted the remaining supply. The Belgian gunners, therefore, could not protect their infantry against the terrible 6 in. shells of the enemy's howitzers. All that the defending artillerymen could usefully do was to wait until the enemy's mass attack began, and then open upon the large, close, living target with the last shrapnel shells in the limber.

After battering and wrecking the Belgian trenches with high-explosive shell, the Duke of Würtemberg launched his infantry over the river at the village of Tervaete on Thursday, October 22nd. The attackers then got their first foothold on the left bank of the Yser. The 1st Belgian Division, worn out, hungry, and drowsy after sleepless nights of combat, counter-attacked. They failed, and their continually lessening numbers were still further decreased by the hail of bullets from German machine-guns in the lost village. Yet, with superb spirit, the Belgians rallied after their repulse, and again counter-attacked, and recovered Tervaete at the bayonet point.

THE SHATTERED SHRINE.
A pathetic but typical example of the sacrilegious work of the Prussian Huns on the Franco-Belgian frontier.

But this was the last success. For the Germans, still swelling with reinforcements and intent on driving through the weak Belgian centre, came on in the night with fresh forces and regained Tervaete and the passage of the Yser. Terribly exhausted were the Belgians. They had been continually marching and fighting since the opening of the attack on Antwerp, but still they held on in the loop of the river, entrenching between Tervaete and Schoorbakke. There the 1st Division, on Friday, October 23rd, strove to keep back the German advance on Furnes, while the 4th Division, with the Breton Marines, clung to the trenches round Dixmude. Between Friday night and Saturday morning the German commander swung his forces fourteen times against Dixmude, but every time they broke.

"Seven times we crossed the Yser," said a German officer afterwards, "and seven times we were beaten back. At last our dead formed bridges over which we again tried to pass, only to be repulsed once more." But this achievement was not gained at a slight cost. One-fourth of the remnant of the Belgian field army fell, and the rest were exhausted. For seven days along the Yser they held off four times their number of Germans, while the British Army was fighting for its life a little to the south at Ypres. Many Belgians stayed in the trenches all the time—fenland trenches, with the water oozing in continually and mingling with the rain puddles and rising over the men's feet. They had nothing to drink but the water of the ditches and canal they were guarding, and little time or opportunity for preparing a hot meal. Plastered with mud, wet and cheerless, they yet retained all their pluck and perseverance, and made some splendid bayonet charges.

Happily, many of them were able to go to Furnes to rest for a few days and refit, and their munition supplies were reorganised. Several batteries of heavy French howitzers arrived, and helped to make the artillery duel more equally balanced. For a week the Belgians had been hopelessly outranged and outweighted by the German ordnance. Frequently their batteries were obliged to cease fire and draw away to a fresh position, to avoid the tremendous shelling of guns and mortars massed upon them. Both the entrenched infantry and the convoys proceeding to the front were severely bombarded, and the German howitzers enjoyed complete immunity from attack while they pounded Dixmude, Pervyse, and Nieuport to ruin from a distance which prevented the Belgian batteries from replying.

But the new French howitzer batteries had quite as long a range as the German pieces, and with the batteries came a superb force of French infantry, the 42nd Division, under General Grosetti. It at once relieved the 2nd Belgian

THE HEROIC DEFENCE OF DIXMUDE BY BRETON MARINES UNDER ADMIRAL RONARC'H.

For weeks 7,000 Breton Marines under Admiral Ronarc'h, fighting in trenches up to their waists in water, kept two German army corps at bay. One night the enemy crept up to the French lines, driving some half-dozen of their prisoners before them. One of these prisoners shouted out a warning. The attack was repulsed. In the morning the dead body was found. The man had fallen, not from a bullet, but from an assassin's thrust through his back. Behind him, as "The Times" correspondent suggests, there had evidently been a German soldier instructed to kill him should he utter a word of warning to his compatriots.

FRENCH ZOUAVES IN CAMP BETWEEN THE DYKES.

Division in front of Nieuport, and then turned to help the 1st Belgian Division at Pervyse. At dawn on Monday, October 26th, the Germans made their grand effort to hew their way along the coast. Their troops, concentrated on the Mannekensvere road, advanced under cover of a storm of shell and shrapnel, and threw three pontoon bridges over the river and canal. The infantry poured across and made a resolute, violent attempt to carry Nieuport by storm. A French brigade operating beyond the town was in peril of being surrounded. But the men held, and Belgian supports—little rest they had, after all!—returned in haste from Furnes to support their allies.

A critical situation

In the meantime the allied artillery shelled the pontoons, and the French brigade retired on the trenches in front of Nieuport, and from there headed the Germans off. The enemy then turned and swept south on the villages of Ramscappelle and Pervyse. The gradual but steady progress he made could be marked by the way the bursting shells fell nearer and nearer to Furnes. Between ten and eleven o'clock in the morning the situation became critical. Orders were given for Furnes to be evacuated. The wounded were carried to the station, and a large number of the townspeople began to leave. Belgian soldiers, shelled out of their trenches, made their way to the rear, but fresh columns of their comrades, who had been resting in the villages between the lines, pushed along to the front, where King Albert, with cheerful, smiling, indomitable strength of soul, was holding his battered Army together.

Pervyse was the storm-centre, just midway between Furnes and the German concentration point, with a highway running through it from the two opposing camps. By the ruined church in the flaming, shell-swept village, General Grosetti, smiling, genial, and gigantic, sat in an armchair, with shrapnel bursting over him. There he encouraged his Division to press on through the bombardment and attack the advancing German infantry columns. His men—Arabs, negroes, French colonials, and Frenchmen of France—cheered him as they passed. The big man, sitting gay and confident in a rain of shell, inspired them with his own laughing heroism. On they swept, beyond the zone of the enemy's gun fire, into the safer belt of his rifle and Maxim fire. And there they held him.

The Germans had crossed the Yser merely to be brought up against the railway line. From the point of view of the defending troops, the railway, with the Nieuport and Dixmude road behind it, was a more comfortable position than the marshland. By the river and canal it had been impossible to dig a three-feet trench without getting eighteen inches of oozing water to stand in. All that the Germans had won was a series of drains calculated to cripple an army with rheumatic fever. They came, moreover, within the field of operations of the ingenious British sailor. Since Lord Fisher invented the first modern armoured train, in the campaign against Arabi Pasha, our naval men had specialised in this instrument of warfare. In Flanders they drove to the assistance of Belgian, French, and British troops wherever there was a track available for their queerly-coloured armoured locomotives and trucks. A British naval officer usually commanded, with expert British gunners and Belgian sharpshooters on the train.

SHARPSHOOTERS OF THE FRENCH COLONIAL ARMY IN ACTION ON THE SAND-DUNES NEAR NIEUPORT.

General Grosetti's heroism

A surprise effect was always designed. The train was held, manned and under steam, with loaded guns, a few miles from the scene of combat. When the struggle was at its fiercest, and all the enemy's batteries were disclosed and all his men deployed, then the armoured train would come in answer to a telephone call—almost invisible by reason of its wide stripes of crude colours, blending in the distance into a neutral tint, and almost unheard

BRITISH SOLDIERS PREPARING TO LEAVE OSTEND FOR A NEW BASE.

AN EVER-WELCOME GIFT TO A COMRADE ON SERVICE—A GOOD CIGAR

A BRITISH SOLDIER SEEKS EXPERT ADVICE ON A PROBLEM IN BELGIAN TOPOGRAPHY.

in the thunder and rattle of the fight. More than once its guns, opening unexpectedly at short range, silenced a hostile battery, and its shrapnel shells brought down five of the captive balloons used by the Germans for observation purposes. Worked with the dash and courage that distinguish the British seaman either on land or sea, these trains ran with impunity under the fire of hostile guns, as their great speed made them difficult to hit. At the end of a month's campaign merely one engine had been damaged, without being put out of action, and of the crew one Belgian rifleman only was wounded.

But great as our sailors were, they scarcely equalled the achievement of Admiral Ronarc'h's seven thousand Breton Marines. These men belonged to a class of French fighters with a glorious record in the former Franco-German War. But finely as the fathers had fought in 1870, the sons fought better in 1914. They were the talk of every bivouac in the northern armies. When General Joffre heard they were fighting waist-deep in water in the trenches at Dixmude, he said, with a slow, grave smile: "They are in their element." Chosen from the hardiest fishermen of Brittany, from the cod fishers of Iceland and Newfoundland, they endured the most terrible rigours without flinching. When the Germans tried to carry Dixmude by the mass and momentum of infantry column attacks, the Bretons, having only machine-guns, grouped them in fours, and then mowed down each column as it advanced. The head of each column never passed a certain point. It was like pushing strips of wood under a series of guillotine machines.

Admiral Ronarc'h's Breton Marines

One night, after days of fighting in the wet trenches, the Marines fell asleep. Even their officers, drowsy under the continual bombardment and unending infantry attacks, began to dream. There was a shout in the misty gloom. One of the officers awoke, and discerned a mass of enemies creeping up in the darkness. He roused the amphibians, and though dog-weary and muddle-minded, they recovered enough strength and alertness to repel the attack. In the morning, among the dead in front of their trenches, they found the body of one of their fellow-Marines. The Germans had driven some prisoners before them as a screen against the defenders' fire. Behind the dead Breton there had evidently been a German with a bayonet, ready to kill him if he made a sound. But the brave man, knowing how weary and drowsy his comrades would be,

A REST BY THE WAY—ON THE EDGE OF A SHELTERED COPPICE IN FLANDERS.

BRITISH COLONIAL TROOPS ATTACHED TO THE 3RD BELGIAN LANCERS.

had shouted a warning, and instead of being shot by mistake by his friends, he had been stabbed from behind by a cowardly assassin.

Nearer Ypres, at the bridge of the Three Grietchen, another Frenchman, belonging to a Zouave regiment, acted in the same way. The mass of advancing Germans was screened with captured French troops, and the defenders in the trenches hesitated to fire, thinking it might be a French force from the north retiring on their position. The captured Zouave understood it all, and he yelled: "For God's sake, fire on us!" Naturally, he fell with his comrades, but he brought about a French victory.

Dixmude itself was a scene of infernal desolation and terror. The German commander ordered that every house should be levelled to the ground. On the first days of the struggle the field-guns and howitzers of an army corps were massed against it. Then some of the 12 in. Austrian mortars were brought up by railway. The artillery general tried to obtain also two of the 16½ in. Krupp howitzers, but, much to his disappointment, they were needed on the coast to reply to the British warships. Even without these gigantic instruments of destruction, the little, beautiful, open Flemish town was quickly battered into mounds of rubble.

Dixmude pounded into rubble

There was not a yard of it unswept by shell fire, not a house in it that was not shattered. The square, where the venerable town-hall stood flaming, was a region of death and thunder. High-explosive shells and shrapnel continually burst over it, and a rain of German bullets, aimed at the Marines in the trenches near by, whistled across the square when they missed the nearer mark. Amid the crash of falling chimneys and the roar and clatter of shell-stricken houses, rising with the explosion and then tumbling and barricading the streets, the reserves of the little defending force sheltered behind the gapped and ragged walls while the wounded rested in the cellars. Sometimes the houses above the cellars would be set on fire, and the maimed or dying men beneath the flames had to be taken out hastily, under the fierce bombardment, and carried to some fresh retreat till the overworked motor-ambulances could convey them to Furnes. Then, as each Red Cross motor passed through the town, a cyclone of shells followed it beyond Oudecappelle.

The more desperate the Germans grew, the viler their conduct became. Behind the lines at Dixmude on October

BRITISH COLONIAL VOLUNTEERS WITH A DETACHMENT OF BELGIAN CAVALRY.

GERMAN HORDES CHECKED BY LAND AND SEA: THE GREAT STRUGGLE ACROSS THE SAND-DUNES AT NIEUPORT BAINS.

Supported by a preponderance of artillery and overwhelming numbers of infantry, the Duke of Würtemberg made a great attack on Lombartzyde on October 19th, 1914, with a view to "hacking his way" to Dunkirk. Lombartzyde was held by only a single Belgian division—the 2nd—and three times they had to give way under terrible shell and shrapnel fire. Then suddenly there came six claps of thunder from the sea, and half a dozen 6 in. shells exploded with deadly precision among the German batteries. The British Navy had come to the help of the hardly-pressed Belgians. This flank attack took the Germans completely by surprise. French destroyers took a hand, and the long-range naval gun-fire of the Allies swept the country fo six miles inland. Under cover of this fire from the sea the Belgians delivered a terrible onslaught on the invaders who ran helter-skelter from their entrenchments. For a time the German advance had to be abandoned. A private British-Belgian ambulance, run by British doctors, did heroic work in succouring the Belgian wounded.

THE KAISER'S GRAND OBJECTIVE.
This admirable picture map of the Channel coast-line from Dunkirk to Boulogne is the work of a German professor, and was published in Germany at the time when the Kaiser had ordered his impotent hordes to "take Calais or die." It shows at a glance how important to the German designs on England was the capture of Calais.

25th the American war photographer, Donald Thompson, saw a company hesitate to obey the order to advance into the firing-zone. And he saw the captain draw his revolver and shoot the man who hung back most. It was on this day that artillery practice on the allied motor-ambulances with a Red Cross, clearly seen from the German lines, was marked by an eye-witness of a neutral nation. The German soldiers were then deserting across the Dutch frontier by hundreds and even thousands. Yet with the 7,000 Marines at Dixmude, the 12,000 infantry of the 42nd Division at Pervyse and their Belgian supports, there were barely 40,000 men holding a front of some seventeen miles along the Yser. A quarter of the remnant of the Belgian field army was killed or wounded, and more than half the remainder had withdrawn to rest and refit, coming into action as reserves when danger pressed. The Breton Marines had also lost a quarter of their effectives. Dixmude was not taken by the Germans till November 11th, when it had lost its importance as a bridge-head over the Yser. The Bretons then merely retired across the canalised river, and, from the south bank, held the enemy back more easily than before, using boats armed with quick-firing guns against parties of Germans cut off by the inundation.

Great stand along the Yser

GERMAN NAVAL GUNNERS ON THE BELGIAN SAND-DUNES.
In the upper photograph we see Prussian cavalry entering Ostend.

In the meantime General Grosetti battled with the advancing invaders amid the dykes and marshes round Pervyse. After the Germans were thrown back between Tervaete and Schoorbakke, they turned their guns on Nieuport; and so overwhelming was the bombardment that ambulances could not get into the town to bring away the wounded. The Germans gathered at the village of St. Georges,

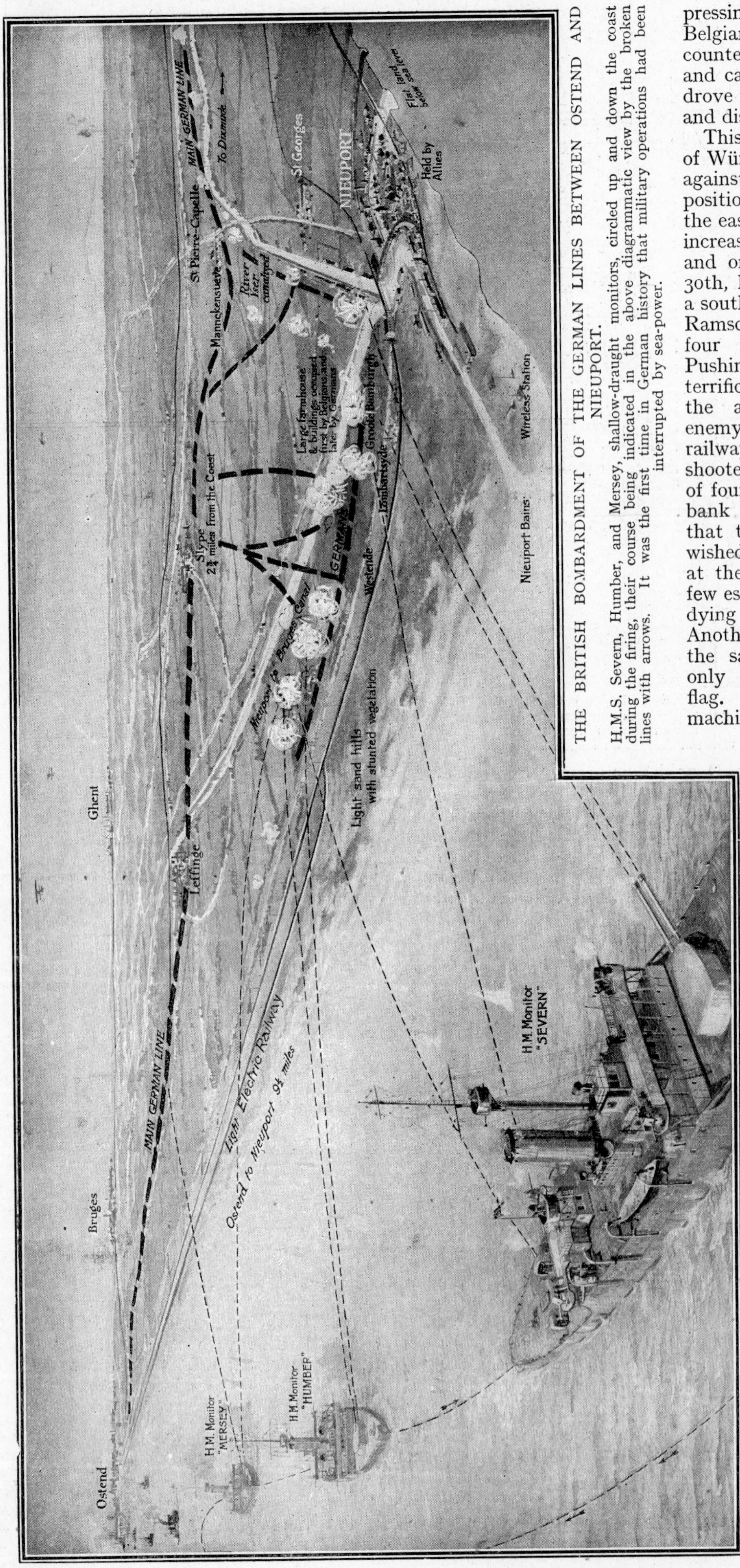

THE BRITISH BOMBARDMENT OF THE GERMAN LINES BETWEEN OSTEND AND NIEUPORT.

H.M.S. Severn, Humber, and Mersey, shallow-draught monitors, circled up and down the coast during the firing, their course being indicated in the above diagrammatic view by the broken lines with arrows. It was the first time in German history that military operations had been interrupted by sea-power.

pressing in great force on the trenches of the Belgian troops defending Nieuport. As a counter-stroke the Allies, with both infantry and cavalry, charged along the coast and drove the Germans there back in confusion and disorder on Westkerke.

Algerians save the day

This success in turn provoked the Duke of Würtemberg to put forth all his strength against the withdrawn centre of the allied position. Still feinting at Nieuport from the east, he still further increased his forces there, and on Friday, October 30th, he struck down in a south-westerly direction at the village of Ramscappelle. From there it was barely four miles across the fens to Furnes. Pushing back the allied troops with a terrific artillery fire, under cover of which the attacking infantry advanced, the enemy reached the eastern bank of the railway, held by some Algerian sharpshooters with Belgian supports. A body of four hundred Germans clambered up the bank and were shot at. They cried out that they were unarmed, and that they wished to surrender. Still the Arabs fired at them till they broke and fled. Only a few escaped. The rest were found dead or dying with their loaded rifles beside them. Another party tried the same game with the same result. Next, an officer, with only four men, advanced with a white flag. All were shot, and their hidden machine-gun captured. Then the Algerians charged and won the day. They were drawn up in the square at Furnes afterwards, and publicly thanked by King Albert and General Joffre.

On the northern bank of the Yser, on October 30th, was another potentate of Europe—a grey-haired man with a lined, careworn face, scarcely recognisable now that he had suddenly aged and clipped off the upturned ends of his famous Kaiser moustache. He looked like a beaten man, and in matter of fact his agents at the moment were trying to arrange a secret peace with France—offering her, by devious channels, the larger part of Alsace and Lorraine. All they asked in return was French help against Great Britain and the recognition of the German conquest of Belgium. If only he could threaten Calais, the German Emperor explained to the Duke of Würtemberg, the French nation would be anxious for peace.

Things were getting very troublesome for German troops on the Yser front. Since their first successful crossing over the river the polders had become very wet. Belgian engineers were raising the sluices here and there. They did not want wholly to discourage the invaders—that was not General Foch's plan. He wished to keep some 150,000 Germans hopefully employed along the Yser until the British force between Ypres and La Bassée was

HOW THE BRITISH MONITORS EVADED THE GERMAN FIRE OFF THE BELGIAN COAST.

The Germans tried to beat our monitors off by bringing up their 6 in. howitzers and placing them in concealed positions along the dunes. But our ships steamed out of the reach of the shore batteries, and replied with a terrible and devastating fire. With sides and guns protected, each monitor was armed with two 6 in. guns, two howitzers, four 3-pounders, and six rifle-calibre guns, and was capable of discharging a ton and a half of metal a minute. The monitors zigzagged about the sea at high mobility, their gunners directed by our aerial scouts and observation officers in tethered balloons. Later H.M.S. Venerable came up and bombarded the Germans further inland.

fully reinforced by the new French army under General D'Urbal. Yet, as the Germans began to press more strongly towards Furnes, the fens between the Yser and the last town in Belgium unoccupied by the enemy grew moister than even the rainy weather explained.

By the end of October there were several inches of water on the ground between the German and Belgian trenches. It was impeding the movements of the attacking infantry. In the historic Battle of Nieuport, in 1600, the Dutch had defeated the Spaniards by breaking the sea-dyke and drowning them. And German spies reported to the Duke of Würtemberg's headquarters that King Albert and his Staff were examining an ancient deed in which were shown the places in which the sea-wall had been designed to be broken when Vauban, the great French engineer of the days of Louis XIV., planned the new water defences of Nieuport. It was while the duke was hesitating at the sight of the rising water that Kaiser Wilhelm arrived. The Emperor was all for quick, vigorous action, especially as the date he had fixed for the proclamation of the entire conquest of Belgium was at hand. He made a personal appeal for volunteers. He needed a brigade to capture at any cost the Belgian trenches, and storm the sea-wall and hold it before the dyke could be broken, while the German army waded on to Furnes.

A brigade of Würtemberg infantry, famous for their courage, stepped forward. *"Ave, Cæsar, morituri te salutant!"* Bravely they volunteered for death, and the operation was executed under the eyes of the Kaiser, surveying the scene through his field-glasses. At mid-day, the brigade crossed the Yser on planks, under the protection of the fire of the massed German batteries. After the long, ghastly struggles for the river it was choked with broken boats, trees, floating fragments of planks, carcasses of horses, and human corpses. The Würtembergers massed on the left bank to attack, with the guns of their army shrapnelling their path of advance.

Some way in front of them was a hostile trench, with a line of caps just showing above the parapet. On these caps the German artillerymen especially directed their fire. But when the Würtembergers took the trench at the double they found there were no heads beneath the caps.

Russell.

LIEUT.-COMMANDER R. A. WILSON.
Commander of the monitor Mersey.

Lafayette.

REAR-ADMIRAL THE HON. H. HOOD.
Admiral in command of the Dover Patrol. He directed the operations off the Belgian coast.
(Photographed when a captain.)

Russell.

COMMANDER A. L. SNAGGE.
Commander of the monitor Humber.

THE BRITISH FLOATING FORTS WHICH SHELLED THE GERMAN TRENCHES NEAR THE BELGIAN COAST-LINE.
A striking photograph of the three British monitors—Severn, Humber, and Mersey—which opened the bombardment of the German positions along the Belgian coast-line between Ostend and Nieuport.

GERMAN PRISONERS AT FURNES.
The fenland and dunes round the little town of Furnes constituted the last nook of unconquered Belgian territory. It is noticeable that the prisoners in the above photograph included many mere boys.

SCENE IN BLANKENBERGHE DURING THE KAISER'S FRANTIC EFFORT TO COMMAND THE COAST.
German Uhlans and cyclist scouts receiving instructions in the main street of Blankenberghe. Inset: Forlorn and dishevelled German troops captured during the terrible battle along the Belgian coast. A battalion of them attempted to rush some of the Allies' field-guns, but all were annihilated with the exception of the unhappy men who figure in the photograph.

CAUGHT BETWEEN FIRE AND WATER: THE GERMAN ROUT BETWEEN DIXMUDE AND BIXSCHOOTE.

A brigade of Würtemberg infantry, responding to a personal appeal by the Kaiser, crossed the Yser on planks and advanced on the Belgian trenches, to be caught by the rising water let in from the dykes. After the long, ghastly struggles for the river, it was choked with broken boats, trees, carcasses of horses. and human corpses. The Würtembergers were engulfed with all their débris. Their guns stuck in the soft ground, and as they turned in flight the allied artillery poured salvos of shrapnel over them. An allied infantry force with an armoured car and a machine-gun added to the Würtembergers' discomfiture.